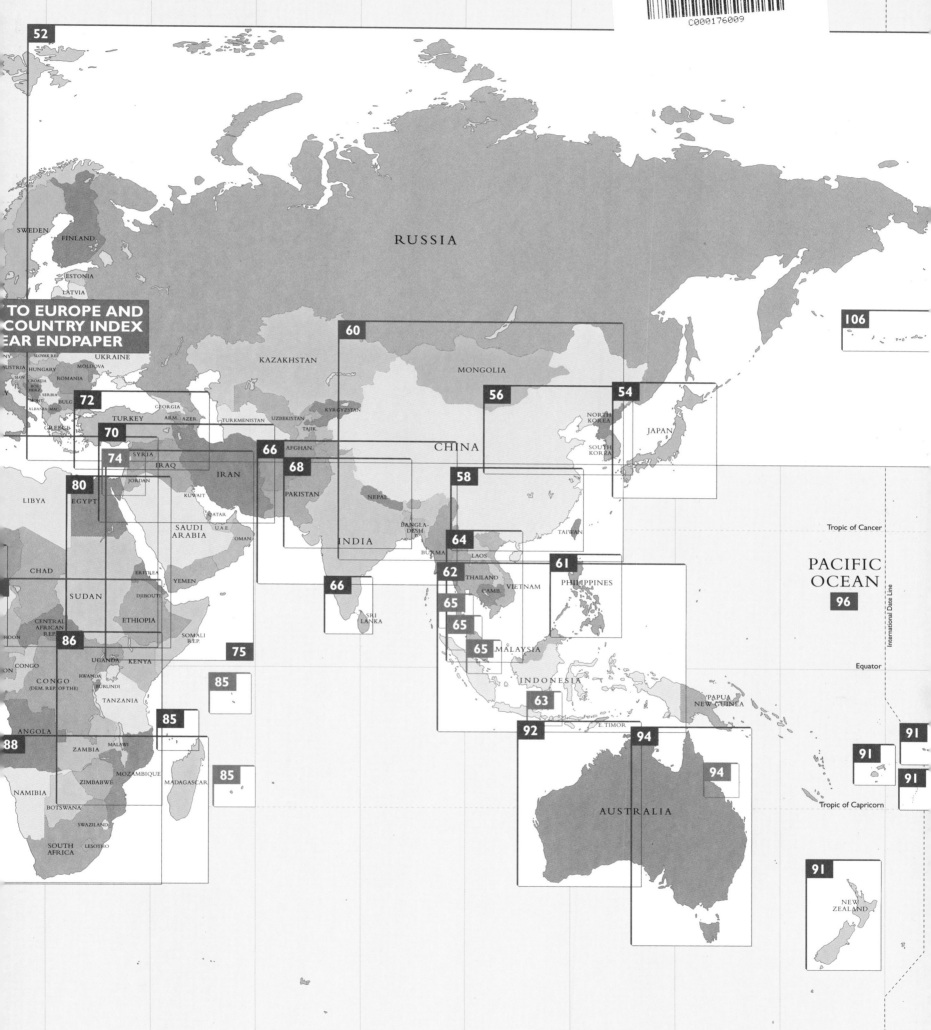

PHILIP'S

REFERENCE
WORLD
ATLAS

PHILIP'S

REFERENCE WORLD ATLAS

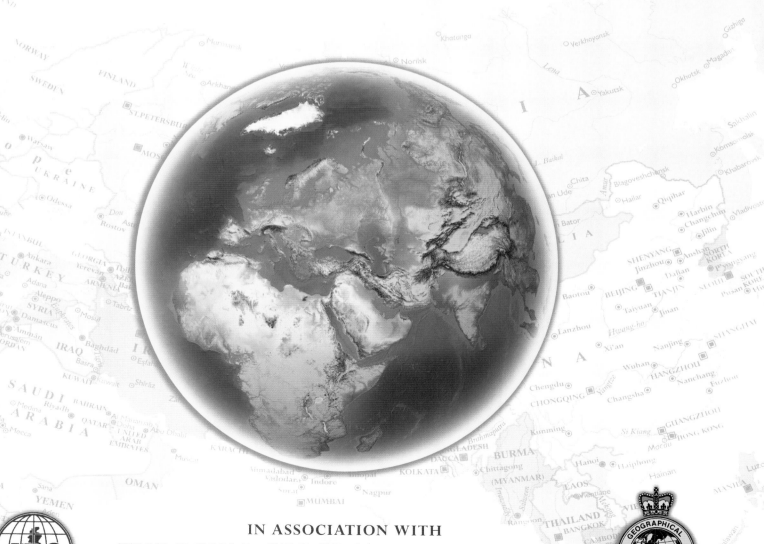

IN ASSOCIATION WITH
THE ROYAL GEOGRAPHICAL SOCIETY
WITH THE INSTITUTE OF BRITISH GEOGRAPHERS

NATIONS OF THE WORLD
Text
Keith Lye

IMAGES OF EARTH
All satellite images in this section supplied by NPA Ltd, Edenbridge, Kent, UK (www.satmaps.com)

© NPA Remote Sensing Department: Processing by Richard Chiles and Paul Karwinski: pages 65, 66 (bottom left), 67 (top), 67 (bottom), 68 (left), 68 (top right), 68 (bottom right), 69 (top left), 69 (bottom), 70 (top), 70 (bottom), 70–71, 72 (top), 72 (bottom left), 72 (bottom right), 73 (top left), 73 (bottom), 74 (top), 75 (bottom right), 76 (top), 76 (bottom), 76–77, 77 (top left), 77 (bottom right), 78 (bottom left), 78–79, 79 (top), 79 (bottom right)

Image courtesy Jacques Descloitres, MODIS Land Rapid Response Team at NASA GSFC: pages 66 (bottom right), 75 (bottom left)

Image courtesy Jeff Schmaltz, MODIS Land Rapid Response Team at NASA GSFC: page 66 (top)

Courtesy of the NOAA Coastal Services Center Hawai'i Land Cover Analysis project: page 77 (top right)

Satellite image courtesy of Space Imaging: pages 73 (top right), 74 (bottom), 75 (top)

Image provided by the USGS EROS Data Center Satellite Systems Branch: pages 69 (top right), 71 (top left), 78 (top)

Image by Jesse Allen, NASA Earth Observatory, based on expedited ASTER data provided by the NASA/GSFC/MITI/ERSDAC/JAROS, and US/Japan ASTER Science Team: page 71 (top right)

Image courtesy NASA/GSFC/MITI/ERSDAC/JAROS, and US/Japan ASTER Science Team: page 80

Published in Great Britain in 2007
by Philip's,
a division of Octopus Publishing Group Limited,
2–4 Heron Quays, London E14 4JP
An Hachette Livre UK Company

Copyright © 2007 Philip's

Cartography by Philip's

ISBN-13 978–0–540–09013–6
ISBN-10 0–540–09013–1

A CIP catalogue record for this book is available from the British Library.

Printed in Hong Kong

Details of other Philip's titles and services can be found on our website at:
www.philips-maps.co.uk

Philip's World Atlases are published in association with The Royal Geographical Society (with The Institute of British Geographers).

The Society was founded in 1830 and given a Royal Charter in 1859 for 'the advancement of geographical science'. It holds historical collections of national and international importance, many of which relate to the Society's association with and support for scientific exploration and research from the 19th century onwards. It was pivotal in establishing geography as a teaching and research discipline in British universities close to the turn of the century, and has played a key role in geographical and environmental education ever since.

Today the Society is a leading world centre for geographical learning – supporting education, teaching, research and expeditions, and promoting public understanding of the subject.

The Society welcomes those interested in geography as members. For further information, please visit the website at: www.rgs.org

User Guide

The reference maps which form the main body of this atlas have been prepared in accordance with the highest standards of international cartography to provide an accurate and detailed representation of the Earth. The scales and projections used have been carefully chosen to give balanced coverage of the world, while emphasizing the most densely populated and economically significant regions. A hallmark of Philip's mapping is the use of hill shading and relief colouring to create a graphic impression of landforms: this makes the maps exceptionally easy to read. However, knowledge of the key features employed in the construction and presentation of the maps will enable the reader to derive the fullest benefit from the atlas.

MAP SEQUENCE

The atlas covers the Earth continent by continent: first Europe, then its land neighbour Asia (mapped north before south, in a clockwise sequence), followed by Africa, Australia and Oceania, North America and South America. This is the classic arrangement adopted by most cartographers since the 16th century. For each continent, there are maps at a variety of scales. First, physical relief

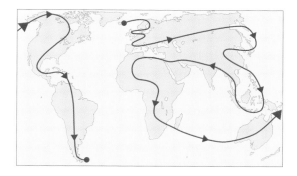

and political maps of the whole continent; then a series of larger-scale maps of the regions within the continent, each followed, where required, by still larger-scale maps of the most important or densely populated areas. The governing principle is that by turning the pages of the atlas, the reader moves steadily from north to south through each continent, with each map overlapping its neighbours.

MAP PRESENTATION

With very few exceptions (for example, for the Arctic and Antarctica), the maps are drawn with north at the top, regardless of whether they are presented upright or sideways on the page. In the borders will be found the map title; a locator diagram showing the area covered; continuation arrows showing the page numbers for maps of adjacent areas; the scale; the projection used; the degrees of latitude and longitude; and the letters and figures used in the index for locating place names and geographical features. Physical relief maps also have a height reference panel identifying the colours used for each layer of contouring.

MAP SYMBOLS

Each map contains a vast amount of detail which can only be conveyed clearly and accurately by the use of symbols. Points and circles of varying sizes locate and identify the relative importance of towns and cities; different styles of type are employed for administrative, geographical and regional place names to aid identification. A variety of pictorial symbols denote landforms such as glaciers, marshes and coral reefs, and man-made structures including roads, railways, airports and canals. International borders are shown by red lines. Where neighbouring countries are in dispute, for example in parts of the Middle East, the maps show the *de facto* boundary between nations, regardless of the legal or historical situation. The symbols are explained on the first page of the World Maps section of the atlas.

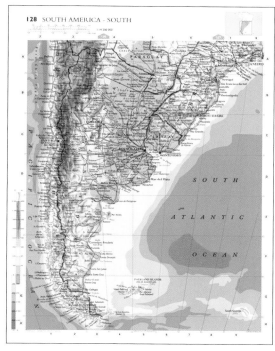

MAP SCALES

1:16 000 000
1 inch = 252 statute miles

The scale of each map is given in the numerical form known as the 'representative fraction'. The first figure is always one, signifying one unit of distance on the map; the second figure, usually in millions, is the number by which the map unit must be multiplied to give the equivalent distance on the Earth's surface. Calculations can easily be made in centimetres and kilometres, by dividing the Earth units figure by 100 000 (i.e. deleting the last five 0s). Thus 1:1 000 000 means 1 cm = 10 km. The calculation for inches and miles is more laborious, but 1 000 000 divided by 63 360 (the number of inches in a mile) shows that 1:1 000 000 means approximately 1 inch = 16 miles. The table below provides distance equivalents for scales down to 1:50 000 000.

LARGE SCALE		
1:1 000 000	1 cm = 10 km	1 inch = 16 miles
1:2 500 000	1 cm = 25 km	1 inch = 39.5 miles
1:5 000 000	1 cm = 50 km	1 inch = 79 miles
1:6 000 000	1 cm = 60 km	1 inch = 95 miles
1:8 000 000	1 cm = 80 km	1 inch = 126 miles
1:10 000 000	1 cm = 100 km	1 inch = 158 miles
1:15 000 000	1 cm = 150 km	1 inch = 237 miles
1:20 000 000	1 cm = 200 km	1 inch = 316 miles
1:50 000 000	1 cm = 500 km	1 inch = 790 miles
SMALL SCALE		

MEASURING DISTANCES

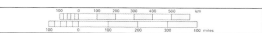

Although each map is accompanied by a scale bar, distances cannot always be measured with confidence because of the distortions involved in portraying the curved surface of the Earth on a flat page. As a general rule, the larger the map scale (that is, the lower the number of Earth units in the representative fraction), the more accurate and reliable will be the distance measured. On small-scale maps such as those of the world and of entire continents, measurement may only be accurate along the 'standard parallels',

or central axes, and should not be attempted without considering the map projection.

MAP PROJECTIONS

Unlike a globe, no flat map can give a true scale representation of the world in terms of area, shape and position of every region. Each of the numerous systems that have been devised for projecting the curved surface of the Earth on to a flat page involves the sacrifice of accuracy in one or more of these elements. The variations in shape and position of landmasses such as Alaska, Greenland and Australia, for example, can be quite dramatic when different projections are compared. For this atlas, the guiding principle has been to select projections that involve the least distortion of size and distance. The projection used for each map is noted in the border. Most fall into one of three categories – conic, azimuthal or cylindrical – whose basic concepts are shown above. Each involves plotting the forms of the Earth's surface on a grid of latitude and longitude lines, which may be shown as parallels, curves or radiating spokes.

LATITUDE AND LONGITUDE

Accurate positioning of individual points on the Earth's surface is made possible by reference to the geometrical system of latitude and longitude. Latitude *parallels* are drawn west–east around the Earth and numbered by degrees north and south of the Equator, which is designated 0° of latitude. Longitude *meridians* are drawn north–south and numbered by degrees east and west of the *prime meridian*, 0° of longitude, which passes through Greenwich in England. By referring to these co-ordinates and their subdivisions of minutes (1/60th of a degree) and seconds (1/60th of a minute), any place on Earth can be located to within a few hundred metres. Latitude and longitude are indicated by blue lines on the maps; they are straight or curved according to the projection employed. Reference to these lines is the easiest way of determining the relative positions of places on different maps, and for plotting compass directions.

NAME FORMS

For ease of reference, both English and local name forms appear in the atlas. Oceans, seas and countries are shown in English throughout the atlas; country names may be abbreviated to their commonly accepted form (for example, Germany, not The Federal Republic of Germany). Conventional English forms are also used for place names on the smaller-scale maps of the continents. However, local name forms are used on all large-scale and regional maps, with the English form given in brackets only for important cities – the large-scale map of Russia and Central Asia thus shows Moskva (Moscow). For countries that do not use a Roman script, place names have been transcribed according to the systems adopted by the British and US Geographic Names Authorities. For China, the Pin Yin system has been used, with some more widely known forms appearing in brackets, as with Beijing (Peking). Both English and local names appear in the index, the English form being cross-referenced to the local form.

Contents

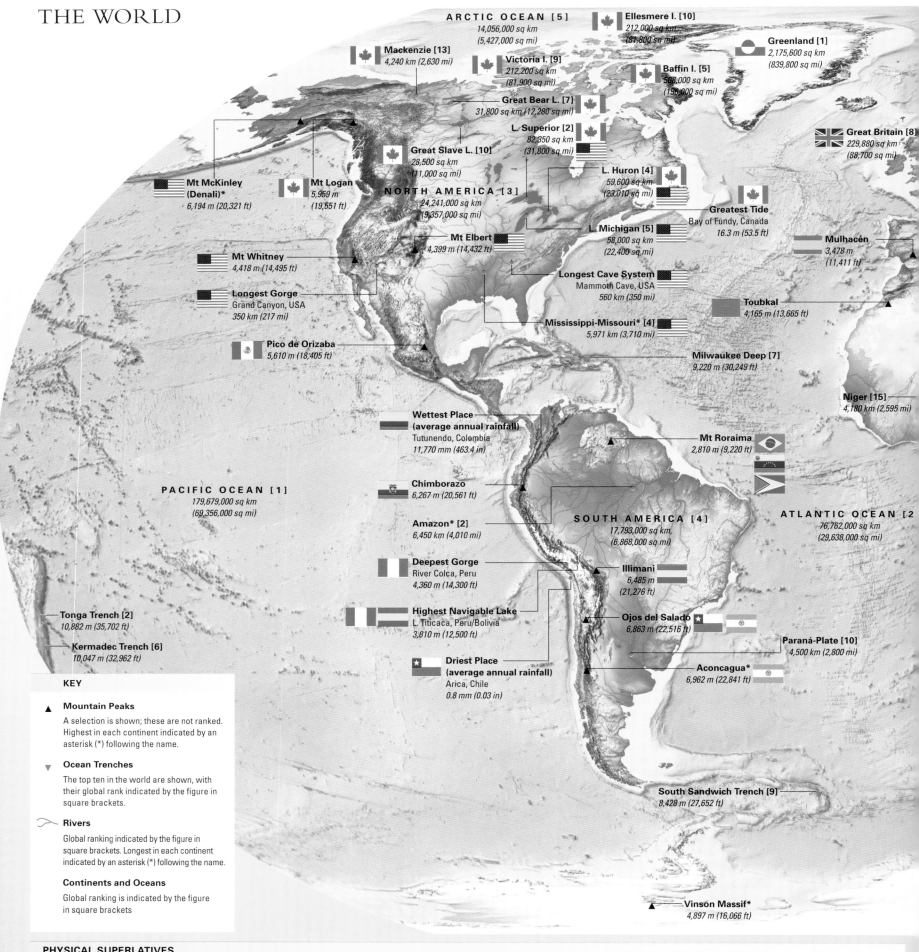

ARCTIC OCEAN [5]
14,056,000 sq km
(5,427,000 sq mi)

Ellesmere I. [10]
212,000 sq km
(81,800 sq mi)

Greenland [1]
2,175,600 sq km
(839,800 sq mi)

Mackenzie [13]
4,240 km (2,630 mi)

Victoria I. [9]
212,200 sq km
(81,900 sq mi)

Baffin I. [5]
508,000 sq km
(196,000 sq mi)

Great Bear L. [7]
31,800 sq km (12,280 sq mi)

L. Superior [2]
82,350 sq km
(31,800 sq mi)

Great Britain [8]
229,880 sq km
(88,700 sq mi)

Great Slave L. [10]
28,500 sq km
(11,000 sq mi)

L. Huron [4]
59,600 sq km
(23,010 sq mi)

Mt McKinley
(Denali)*
6,194 m (20,321 ft)

Mt Logan
5,959 m
(19,551 ft)

NORTH AMERICA [3]
24,241,000 sq km
(9,357,000 sq mi)

Greatest Tide
Bay of Fundy, Canada
16.3 m (53.5 ft)

L. Michigan [5]
58,000 sq km
(22,400 sq mi)

Mt Elbert
4,399 m (14,432 ft)

Mt Whitney
4,418 m (14,495 ft)

Mulhacén
3,478 m
(11,411 ft)

Longest Gorge
Grand Canyon, USA
350 km (217 mi)

Longest Cave System
Mammoth Cave, USA
560 km (350 mi)

Toubkal
4,165 m (13,665 ft)

Pico de Orizaba
5,610 m (18,405 ft)

Mississippi-Missouri* [4]
5,971 km (3,710 mi)

Milwaukee Deep [7]
9,220 m (30,249 ft)

Niger [15]
4,180 km (2,595 mi)

Wettest Place
(average annual rainfall)
Tutunendo, Colombia
11,770 mm (463.4 in)

Mt Roraima
2,810 m (9,220 ft)

PACIFIC OCEAN [1]
179,679,000 sq km
(69,356,000 sq mi)

Chimborazo
6,267 m (20,561 ft)

Amazon* [2]
6,450 km (4,010 mi)

SOUTH AMERICA [4]
17,793,000 sq km,
(6,868,000 sq mi)

ATLANTIC OCEAN [2
76,762,000 sq km
(29,638,000 sq mi)

Deepest Gorge
River Colca, Peru
4,360 m (14,300 ft)

Illimani
6,485 m
(21,276 ft)

Tonga Trench [2]
10,882 m (35,702 ft)

Highest Navigable Lake
L. Titicaca, Peru/Bolivia
3,810 m (12,500 ft)

Ojos del Salado
6,863 m (22,516 ft)

Paraná-Plate [10]
4,500 km (2,800 mi)

Kermadec Trench [6]
10,047 m (32,962 ft)

Driest Place
(average annual rainfall)
Arica, Chile
0.8 mm (0.03 in)

Aconcagua*
6,962 m (22,841 ft)

KEY

▲ **Mountain Peaks**
A selection is shown; these are not ranked. Highest in each continent indicated by an asterisk (*) following the name.

▼ **Ocean Trenches**
The top ten in the world are shown, with their global rank indicated by the figure in square brackets.

〜 **Rivers**
Global ranking indicated by the figure in square brackets. Longest in each continent indicated by an asterisk (*) following the name.

Continents and Oceans
Global ranking is indicated by the figure in square brackets

South Sandwich Trench [9]
8,428 m (27,652 ft)

Vinson Massif*
4,897 m (16,066 ft)

PHYSICAL SUPERLATIVES

Highest Mountains	Longest Rivers	Largest Lakes and Inland Seas	Largest Islands
1 Everest, Asia 8,850 m (29,035 ft)	1 Nile, Africa 6,695 km (4,180 mi)	1 Caspian Sea, Asia 371,000 sq km (143,000 sq mi)	1 Greenland, N. America 2,175,600 sq km (839,800 sq mi)
2 K2 (Godwin Austen), Asia 8,611 m (28,251 ft)	2 Amazon, S. America 6,450 km (4,010 mi)	2 Lake Superior, N. America 82,350 sq km (31,800 sq mi)	2 New Guinea, Oceania 821,030 sq km (317,000 sq mi)
3 Kanchenjunga, Asia 8,598 m (28,208 ft)	3 Yangtze, Asia 6,380 km (3,960 mi)	3 Lake Victoria, Africa 68,000 sq km (26,300 sq mi)	3 Borneo, Asia 744,360 sq km (287,400 sq mi)
4 Lhotse, Asia 8,516 m (27,939 ft)	4 Mississippi-Missouri, N. America 5,971 km (3,710 mi)	4 Lake Huron, N. America 59,600 sq km (23,010 sq mi)	4 Madagascar, Africa 587,040 sq km (226,660 sq mi)
5 Makalu, Asia 8,481 m (27,824 ft)	5 Yenisey-Angara, Asia 5,550 km (3,445 mi)	5 Lake Michigan, N. America 58,000 sq km (22,400 sq mi)	5 Baffin Island, N. America 508,000 sq km (196,100 sq mi)
6 Cho Oyu, Asia 8,201 m (26,906 ft)	6 Huang He, Asia 5,464 km (3,395 mi)	6 Lake Tanganyika, Africa 33,000 sq km (13,000 sq mi)	6 Sumatra, Asia 473,600 sq km (182,860 sq mi)
7 Dhaulagiri, Asia 8,167 m (26,795 ft)	7 Ob-Irtysh, Asia 5,410 km (3,360 mi)	7 Great Bear Lake, N. America 31,800 sq km (12,280 sq mi)	7 Honshu, Asia 230,500 sq km (88,980 sq mi)
8 Manaslu, Asia 8,156 m (26,758 ft)	8 Congo, Africa 4,670 km (2,900 mi)	8 Lake Baikal, Asia 30,500 sq km (11,780 sq mi)	8 Great Britain, Europe 229,880 sq km (88,700 sq mi)
9 Nanga Parbat, Asia 8,126 m (26,660 ft)	9 Mekong, Asia 4,500 km (2,795 mi)	9 Lake Malawi/Nyasa, Africa 29,600 sq km (11,430 sq mi)	9 Victoria Island, N. America 212,200 sq km (81,900 sq mi)
10 Annapurna, Asia 8,078 m (26,502 ft)	10 Paraná-Plate, S. America 4,500 km (2,800 mi)	10 Great Slave Lake, N. America 28,500 sq km (11,000 sq mi)	10 Ellesmere Island, N. America 212,000 sq km (81,800 sq mi)

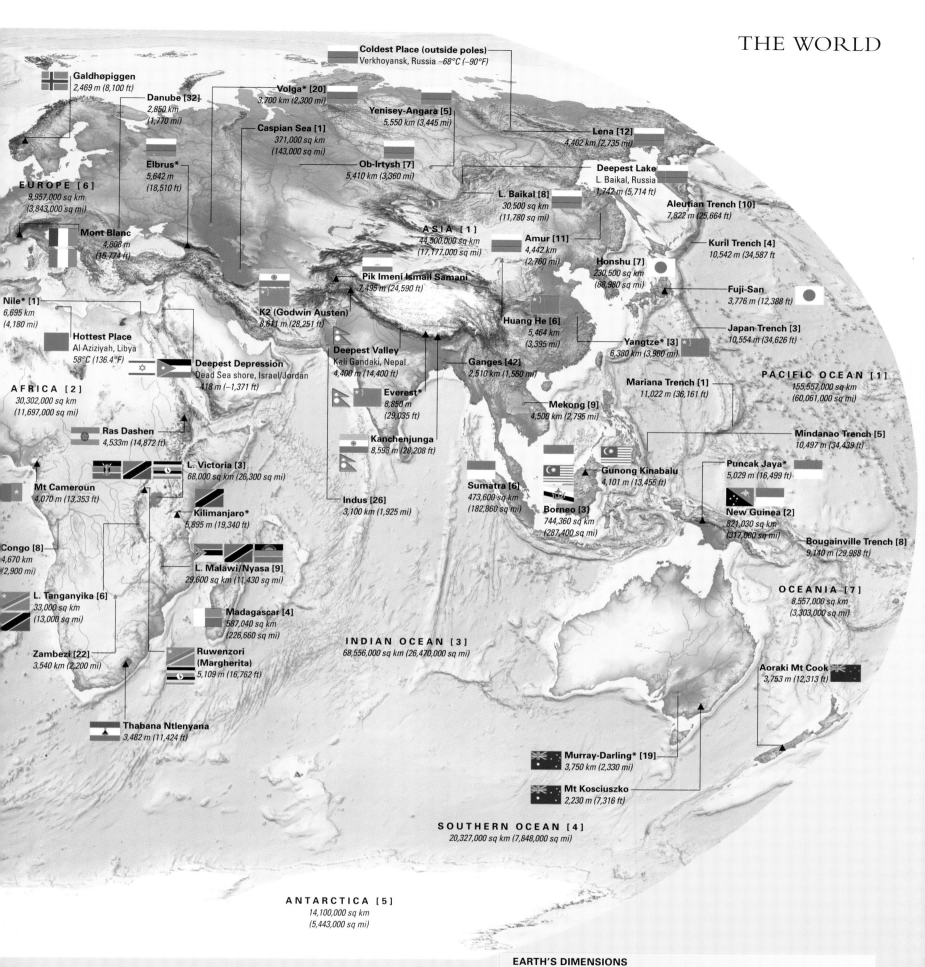

Galdhøpiggen
2,469 m (8,100 ft)

Danube [32]
2,850 km
(1,770 mi)

Coldest Place (outside poles)
Verkhoyansk, Russia −68°C (−90°F)

Volga* [20]
3,700 km (2,300 mi)

Yenisey-Angara [5]
5,550 km (3,445 mi)

Caspian Sea [1]
371,000 sq km
(143,000 sq mi)

Lena [12]
4,402 km (2,735 mi)

Elbrus*
5,642 m
(18,510 ft)

EUROPE [6]
9,957,000 sq km
(3,843,000 sq mi)

Ob-Irtysh [7]
5,410 km (3,360 mi)

Deepest Lake
L. Baikal, Russia
1,742 m (5,714 ft)

Aleutian Trench [10]
7,822 m (25,664 ft)

Mont Blanc
4,808 m
(15,774 ft)

L. Baikal [8]
30,500 sq km
(11,780 sq mi)

ASIA [1]
44,500,000 sq km
(17,177,000 sq mi)

Amur [11]
4,442 km
(2,760 mi)

Kuril Trench [4]
10,542 m (34,587 ft

Nile* [1]
6,695 km
(4,180 mi)

Pik Imeni Ismail Samani
7,495 m (24,590 ft)

Honshu [7]
230,500 sq km
(88,980 sq mi)

Fuji-San
3,776 m (12,388 ft)

K2 (Godwin Austen)
8,611 m (28,251 ft)

Hottest Place
Al-Aziziyah, Libya
58°C (136.4°F)

Huang He [6]
5,464 km
(3,395 mi)

Japan Trench [3]
10,554 m (34,626 ft)

Deepest Depression
Dead Sea shore, Israel/Jordan
−418 m (−1,371 ft)

Deepest Valley
Kali Gandaki, Nepal
4,400 m (14,400 ft)

Ganges [42]
2,510 km (1,560 mi)

Yangtze* [3]
6,380 km (3,960 mi)

PACIFIC OCEAN [1]
155,557,000 sq km
(60,061,000 sq mi)

AFRICA [2]
30,302,000 sq km
(11,697,000 sq mi)

Mariana Trench [1]
11,022 m (36,161 ft)

Ras Dashen
4,533m (14,872 ft)

Everest*
8,850 m
(29,035 ft)

Mekong [9]
4,500 km (2,795 mi)

Mt Cameroun
4,070 m (13,353 ft)

Kanchenjunga
8,598 m (28,208 ft)

Mindanao Trench [5]
10,497 m (34,439 ft)

L. Victoria [3]
68,000 sq km (26,300 sq mi)

Puncak Jaya*
5,029 m (16,499 ft)

Kilimanjaro*
5,895 m (19,340 ft)

Indus [26]
3,100 km (1,925 mi)

Gunong Kinabalu
4,101 m (13,455 ft)

Sumatra [6]
473,600 sq km
(182,860 sq mi)

New Guinea [2]
821,030 sq km
(317,000 sq mi)

Congo [8]
4,670 km
(2,900 mi)

L. Malawi/Nyasa [9]
29,600 sq km (11,430 sq mi)

Borneo [3]
744,360 sq km
(287,400 sq mi)

Bougainville Trench [8]
9,140 m (29,988 ft)

L. Tanganyika [6]
33,000 sq km
(13,000 sq mi)

OCEANIA [7]
8,557,000 sq km
(3,303,000 sq mi)

Madagascar [4]
587,040 sq km
(226,660 sq mi)

Zambezi [22]
3,540 km (2,200 mi)

Ruwenzori
(Margherita)
5,109 m (16,762 ft)

INDIAN OCEAN [3]
68,556,000 sq km (26,470,000 sq mi)

Aoraki Mt Cook
3,753 m (12,313 ft)

Thabana Ntlenyana
3,482 m (11,424 ft)

Murray-Darling* [19]
3,750 km (2,330 mi)

Mt Kosciuszko
2,230 m (7,316 ft)

SOUTHERN OCEAN [4]
20,327,000 sq km (7,848,000 sq mi)

ANTARCTICA [5]
14,100,000 sq km
(5,443,000 sq mi)

EARTH'S DIMENSIONS

Mean distance from the Sun	149.6 million km (93 million mi)
Average speed around the Sun	108,000 km/h (66,600 mph)
Age	4,600 million years
Mass	5.9×10^{21} tonnes
Density (water = 1)	5.52
Volume	$1,083,230 \times 10^6$ cu km ($260,000 \times 10^6$ cu mi)
Area	510 million sq km (197 million sq mi)
Land surface	149 million sq km (58 million sq mi) = 29.3% of total area
Water surface	361 million sq km (139 million sq mi) = 70.7% of total area
Equatorial circumference	40,074 km (24,901 mi)
Polar circumference	40,008 km (24,860 mi)
Equatorial diameter	12,756 km (7,926 mi)
Polar diameter	12,714 km (7,900 mi)

INSIDE THE EARTH

Layer	Density (water = 1)	Temperature		State	Thickness	
Crust (continental)	2.8	<500°C	(930°F)	Solid	c. 40 km	(c. 25 mi)
Crust (oceanic)	2.9	<1,100°C	(2,010°F)	Solid	c. 7 km	(c. 4 mi)
Upper mantle	4.3	<1,400°C	(2,550°F)	Molten	c. 900 km	(c. 560 mi)
Lower mantle	5.5	<1,700°C	(3,090°F)	Solid	c. 1,900 km	(c. 1,180 mi)
Outer core	10.0	<2,300°C	(7,170°F)	Molten	c. 2,200 km	(c. 1,370 mi)
Inner core	13.5	<5,500°C	(9,930°F)	Solid	c. 1,300 km	(c. 810 mi)

COUNTRIES: AREA

Country/Territory	Area sq km (thousands)	Area sq mi (thousands)
Largest		
1 Russia	17,075	6,593
2 Ukraine	604	233
3 France	552	213
4 Spain	498	192
5 Sweden	450	174
6 Germany	357	138
7 Finland	338	131
8 Norway	324	125
9 Poland	323	125
10 Italy	301	116
11 United Kingdom	242	93.4
12 Romania	238	92.0
13 Belarus	208	80.2
14 Greece	132	50.9
15 Bulgaria	111	42.8
16 Iceland	103	39.8
17 Hungary	93.0	35.9
18 Portugal	88.8	34.3
19 Serbia	88.3	34.1
20 Austria	83.9	32.4
Smallest		
1 Vatican City	0.0004	0.0002
2 Monaco	0.001	0.0004
3 Gibraltar (UK)	0.006	0.002
4 San Marino	0.06	0.02
5 Liechtenstein	0.16	0.06
6 Malta	0.32	0.12
7 Andorra	0.47	0.18
8 Færoe Is. (Denmark)	1.4	0.54
9 Luxembourg	2.6	1.0
10 Montenegro	13.7	5.4

Highest Waterfall
Utigård, Jostedal Glacier, Norway
800 m (2,625 ft)

Longest Road Tunnel
Lærdal, Norway
24.5 km (15.8 mi)

Largest Lake
Lake Ladoga

Longest Rail Tunnel
Channel Tunnel,
UK/France
50.5 km (31.4 mi)

Highest Dam
Grande Dixence, Switzerland
285 m (935 ft)

Largest Country
Russia

Most Populous Country

Country with Longest Land Border
19,990 km (12,414 mi)

Deadliest Volcanic Eruption
Laki, Iceland *(1783)*
9,350 deaths

Longest Suspension Bridge
Store Bælt, Denmark
1,624 m (5,328 ft)

Tallest Building
Triumph-Palace, Moscow
264 m (866 ft)

Largest Island
Great Britain

Largest Hydroelectric Plant
Sayano-Shushensk, Russia
6,721 MW

Largest Subway System
London
415 km (258 mi)

Busiest Airport
London (Heathrow)
67.9 million passengers per year

Longest River
Volga

Lowest Point
Caspian Sea
−28 m (−92 ft)

Oldest Country
San Marino *(301)*

Deadliest Earthquake
Messina, Italy *(1908)*
70,000–100,000 deaths

Newest Countries
Serbia
Montenegro
(June 2006)

Highest Mountain
Elbrus

COUNTRIES: POPULATION

Country/Territory	Population (thousands)
Most Populous	
1 Russia	142,894
2 Germany	82,422
3 France	60,876
4 United Kingdom	60,609
5 Italy	58,134
6 Ukraine	46,711
7 Spain	40,398
8 Poland	38,537
9 Romania	22,304
10 Netherlands	16,491
11 Greece	10,688
12 Portugal	10,606
13 Belgium	10,379
14 Belarus	10,293
15 Czech Republic	10,235
16 Hungary	9,981
17 Serbia	9,396
18 Sweden	9,017
19 Austria	8,193
20 Switzerland	7,524
Least Populous	
1 Vatican City	1
2 Gibraltar (UK)	28
3 San Marino	29
4 Monaco	33
5 Liechtenstein	34
6 Færoe Islands (Denmark)	47
7 Andorra	71
8 Iceland	299
9 Malta	400
10 Luxembourg	474

LARGEST CITIES

City	Population (thousands)
1 Moscow, Russia	10,672
2 Paris, France	9,630
3 London, UK	8,089
4 St Petersburg, Russia	5,315
5 Berlin, Germany	3,387
6 Athens, Greece	3,238
7 Madrid, Spain	3,017
8 Rome, Italy	2,649
9 Kiev, Ukraine	2,621
10 Birmingham, UK	2,373
11 Manchester, UK	2,353
12 Vienna, Austria	2,190
13 Lisbon, Portugal	1,977
14 Bucharest, Romania	1,764
15 Stockholm, Sweden	1,729
16 Minsk, Belarus	1,709
17 Hamburg, Germany	1,705
18 Budapest, Hungary	1,670
19 Warsaw, Poland	1,626
20 Barcelona, Spain	1,527
21 Kharkov, Ukraine	1,521
22 Novosibirsk, Russia	1,425
23 Tbilisi, Georgia	1,406
24 Lyons, France	1,353
25 Porto, Portugal	1,303
26 Marseilles, France	1,290
27 Nizhniy Novgorod, Russia	1,288
28 Yekaterinburg, Russia	1,281
29 Munich, Germany	1,195
30 Milan, Italy	1,183

COUNTRIES: WEALTH

Country/Territory	Annual Income (US$ per capita)
Richest	
1 Luxembourg	68,800
2 Norway	47,800
3 Ireland	43,600
4 Andorra	38,800
5 Iceland	38,100
6 Denmark	37,000
7 Austria	35,500
8 San Marino	34,100
9 Switzerland	33,600
10 Finland	32,800
Poorest	
1 Moldova	2,000
2 Georgia	3,800
= Montenegro	3,800
4 Serbia	4,400
5 Armenia	5,400
6 Bosnia-Herzegovina	5,500
7 Albania	5,600
8 Ukraine	7,600
9 Belarus	7,800
10 Macedonia (FYROM)	8,200

PHYSICAL SUPERLATIVES

Land Area
9,957,000 sq km (3,843,000 sq mi)

Highest Mountains
1 Elbrus, Russia *5,642 m (18,510 ft)*
2 Mont Blanc, France/Italy *4,808 m (15,774 ft)*
3 Monte Rosa, Italy/Switzerland *4,634 m (15,203 ft)*
4 Dom, Switzerland *4,545 m (14,911 ft)*
5 Liskamm, Switzerland *4,527 m (14,852 ft)*

Longest Rivers
1 Volga *3,700 km (2,300 mi)*
2 Danube *2,850 km (1,770 mi)*
3 Ural *2,535 km (1,575 mi)*
4 Dnepr *2,285 km (1,420 mi)*
5 Kama *2,030 km (1,260 mi)*

Largest Lakes and Inland Seas
1 Lake Ladoga, Russia *17,700 sq km (6,800 sq mi)*
2 Lake Onega, Russia *9,700 sq km (3,700 sq mi)*
3 Saimaa system, Finland *8,000 sq km (3,100 sq mi)*
4 Vänern, Sweden *5,500 sq km (2,100 sq mi)*
5 Rybinsk Reservoir, Russia *4,700 sq km (1,800 sq mi)*

Largest Islands
1 Great Britain, UK *229,880 sq km (88,700 sq mi)*
2 Iceland, Atlantic Ocean *103,000 sq km (39,800 sq mi)*
3 Ireland, Ireland/UK *84,400 sq km (32,600 sq mi)*
4 Novaya Zemlya (N.), Russia *48,200 sq km (18,600 sq mi)*
5 W. Spitzbergen, Norway *39,000 sq km (15,100 sq mi)*

Note: If a territory is not completely independent, the country it is associated with is also named (in brackets). The area figures give the total area of land, inland water and ice. The population figures are 2006 estimates where available. The annual income is the Gross Domestic Product per capita (measured using the purchasing-power parity method, enabling comparisons to be made between countries through their purchasing power) in US dollars; the figures are the latest available, usually 2006 estimates. The city population figures are taken from the most recent census or estimate available, and as far as possible are the population of the metropolitan area or urban agglomeration (for example, greater New York or Paris).

COUNTRIES: AREA

Country/Territory	Area sq km (thousands)	Area sq mi (thousands)
Largest		
1 China	9,597	3,705
2 India	3,287	1,269
3 Kazakhstan	2,725	1,052
4 Saudi Arabia	2,150	830
5 Indonesia	1,905	735
6 Iran	1,648	636
7 Mongolia	1,567	605
8 Pakistan	796	307
9 Turkey	775	299
10 Burma (= Myanmar)	677	261
11 Afghanistan	652	252
12 Yemen	528	204
13 Thailand	513	198
14 Turkmenistan	488	188
15 Uzbekistan	447	173
16 Iraq	438	169
17 Japan	378	146
18 Vietnam	332	128
19 Malaysia	330	127
20 Oman	310	119
Smallest		
1 Macau (China)	0.02	0.007
2 Maldives	0.30	0.12
3 Gaza Strip (OPT)	0.36	0.14
4 Singapore	0.68	0.26
5 Bahrain	0.69	0.27
6 Hong Kong (China)	1.1	0.42
7 Brunei	5.8	2.2
8 West Bank (OPT)	5.9	2.3
9 Cyprus	9.3	3.6
10 Lebanon	10.4	4.0

COUNTRIES: POPULATION

Country/Territory	Population (thousands)
Most Populous	
1 China	1,313,974
2 India	1,095,352
3 Indonesia	245,453
4 Pakistan	165,804
5 Bangladesh	147,365
6 Japan	127,464
7 Philippines	89,469
8 Vietnam	84,403
9 Turkey	70,414
10 Iran	68,688
11 Thailand	64,632
12 South Korea	48,847
13 Burma (= Myanmar)	47,383
14 Afghanistan	31,057
15 Nepal	28,287
16 Uzbekistan	27,307
17 Saudi Arabia	27,020
18 Iraq	26,783
19 Malaysia	24,386
20 North Korea	23,113
Least Populous	
1 Maldives	359
2 Brunei	379
3 Macau (China)	453
4 Bahrain	699
5 Cyprus	784
6 Qatar	885
7 East Timor	1,063
8 Gaza Strip (OPT)	1,429
9 Bhutan	2,280
10 Kuwait	2,418

LARGEST CITIES

City	Population (thousands)
1 Mumbai (Bombay), India	18,336
2 Delhi, India	15,334
3 Kolkata (Calcutta), India	14,299
4 Jakarta, Indonesia	13,194
5 Shanghai, China	12,665
6 Dhaka, Bangladesh	12,560
7 Tokyo, Japan	12,064
8 Karachi, Pakistan	11,819
9 Beijing, China	10,849
10 Manila, Philippines	10,677
11 Seoul, South Korea	9,888
12 Tianjin, China	9,346
13 Istanbul, Turkey	8,953
14 Tehran, Iran	7,352
15 Hong Kong, China	7,182
16 Chennai (Madras), India	6,915
17 Bangkok, Thailand	6,604
18 Bangalore, India	6,532
19 Yokohama, Japan	6,427
20 Lahore, Pakistan	6,373
21 Hyderabad, India	6,145
22 Wuhan, China	6,003
23 Baghdad, Iraq	5,910
24 Riyadh, Saudi Arabia	5,514
25 Ahmedabad, India	5,171
26 Ho Chi Minh City, Vietnam	5,030
27 Chongqing, China	4,975
28 Shenyang, China	4,916
29 Pune, India	4,485
30 Singapore City, Singapore	4,372

COUNTRIES: WEALTH

Country/Territory	Annual Income (US$ per capita)
Richest	
1 United Arab Emirates	49,700
2 Hong Kong (China)	36,500
3 Japan	33,100
4 Singapore	30,900
5 Qatar	29,400
6 Taiwan	29,000
7 Israel	26,200
8 Brunei	25,600
9 Bahrain	25,300
10 South Korea	24,200
Poorest	
1 Afghanistan	800
= East Timor	800
3 Yemen	900
4 Tajikistan	1,300
5 Bhutan	1,400
6 Gaza Strip (OPT)	1,500
= Nepal	1,500
= West Bank (OPT)	1,500
9 Burma (= Myanmar)	1,800
= North Korea	1,800

Largest Subway System
Tokyo
281 km (174.5 mi)

Busiest Airport
Tokyo (Haneda)
63.2 million passengers per year

Longest Rail Tunnel
Sei-kan, Japan
53.9 km (33.5 mi)

Longest Suspension Bridge
Akashi-kaikyo, Japan
1,991 m (6,533 ft)

Longest River
Yangtze

Largest Lake
Caspian Sea

Largest Country
China

Country with Longest Land Border
22,147 km (13,753 mi)

Oldest Country
(221 BC)

Most Populous Country

Lowest Point
Dead Sea
−418 m (−1,371 ft)

Largest Desert
Saudi Arabia
2,331,000 sq km (900,000 sq mi)

Tallest Building
Taipei 101, Taiwan
510 m (1,673 ft)

Longest Road Tunnel
Hsuehshan, Taiwan
12.9 km (8.0 mi)

Highest Dam
Rogun, Tajikistan
335 m (1,099 ft)

Largest Island
Borneo

Highest Mountain
Everest

Largest Hydroelectric Plant
Ertan, China
3,300 MW

Highest Waterfall
Dudhsagar,
Khandepar River,
India
600 m (1,964 ft)

Deadliest Earthquake
Shanxi, China (1556)
830,000 deaths

Deadliest Volcanic Eruption
Tambora, Indonesia (1815)
92,000 deaths

Newest Country
East Timor
(May 2002)

PHYSICAL SUPERLATIVES

Land Area
44,500,000 sq km (17,177,000 sq mi)

Highest Mountains
1 Everest, China/Nepal 8,850 m (29,035 ft)
2 K2 (Godwin Austen), China/Kashmir 8,611 m (28,251 ft)
3 Kanchenjunga, India/Nepal 8,598 m (28,208 ft)
4 Lhotse, China/Nepal 8,516 m (27,939 ft)
5 Makalu, China/Nepal 8,481 m (27,824 ft)

Longest Rivers
1 Yangtze 6,380 km (3,960 mi)
2 Yenisey–Angara 5,550 km (3,445 mi)
3 Huang He 5,464 km (3,395 mi)
4 Ob–Irtysh 5,410 km (3,360 mi)
5 Mekong 4,500 km (2,795 mi)

Largest Lakes and Inland Seas
1 Caspian Sea, W. Central Asia 371,000 sq km (143,000 sq mi)
2 Lake Baikal, Russia 30,500 sq km (11,780 sq mi)
3 Tonlé Sap, Cambodia 20,000 sq km (7,700 sq mi)
4 Lake Balkhash, Kazakhstan 18,500 sq km (7,100 sq mi)
5 Aral Sea, Kazakhstan/Uzbekistan 17,160 sq km (6,625 sq mi)

Largest Islands
1 Borneo, S. E. Asia 744,360 sq km (287,400 sq mi)
2 Sumatra, Indonesia 473,600 sq km (182,860 sq mi)
3 Honshu, Japan 230,500 sq km (88,980 sq mi)
4 Sulawesi (Celebes), Indonesia 189,000 sq km (73,000 sq mi)
5 Java, Indonesia 126,700 sq km (48,900 sq mi)

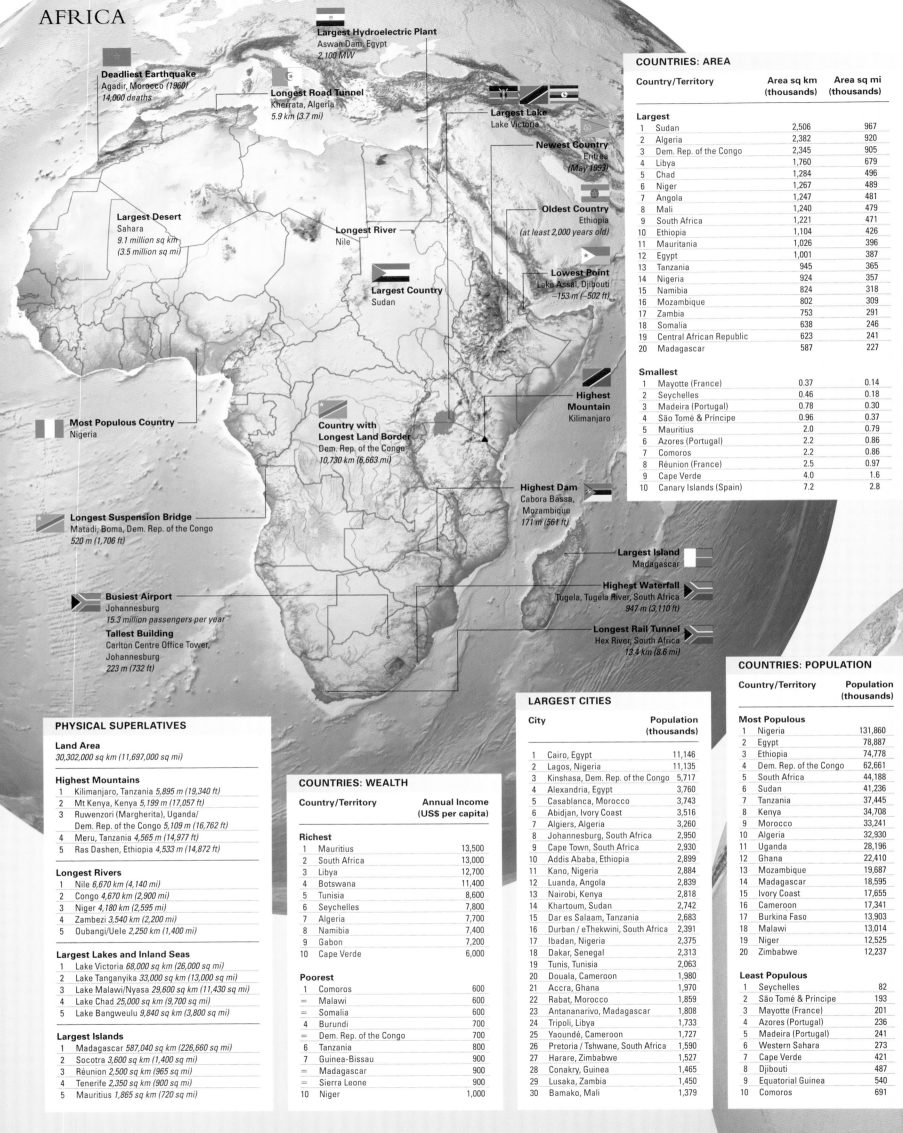

AFRICA

Largest Hydroelectric Plant
Aswan Dam, Egypt
2,100 MW

Deadliest Earthquake
Agadir, Morocco (1960)
14,000 deaths

Longest Road Tunnel
Kherrata, Algeria
5.9 km (3.7 mi)

Largest Lake
Lake Victoria

Newest Country
Eritrea
(May 1993)

Largest Desert
Sahara
9.1 million sq km
(3.5 million sq mi)

Longest River
Nile

Oldest Country
Ethiopia
(at least 2,000 years old)

Lowest Point
Lake Assal, Djibouti
−153 m (−502 ft)

Largest Country
Sudan

Most Populous Country
Nigeria

Country with Longest Land Border
Dem. Rep. of the Congo
10,730 km (6,663 mi)

Highest Mountain
Kilimanjaro

Highest Dam
Cabora Bassa,
Mozambique
171 m (561 ft)

Longest Suspension Bridge
Matadi, Boma, Dem. Rep. of the Congo
520 m (1,706 ft)

Largest Island
Madagascar

Highest Waterfall
Tugela, Tugela River, South Africa
947 m (3,110 ft)

Busiest Airport
Johannesburg
15.3 million passengers per year

Longest Rail Tunnel
Hex River, South Africa
13.4 km (8.6 mi)

Tallest Building
Carlton Centre Office Tower,
Johannesburg
223 m (732 ft)

COUNTRIES: AREA

Country/Territory	Area sq km (thousands)	Area sq mi (thousands)
Largest		
1 Sudan	2,506	967
2 Algeria	2,382	920
3 Dem. Rep. of the Congo	2,345	905
4 Libya	1,760	679
5 Chad	1,284	496
6 Niger	1,267	489
7 Angola	1,247	481
8 Mali	1,240	479
9 South Africa	1,221	471
10 Ethiopia	1,104	426
11 Mauritania	1,026	396
12 Egypt	1,001	387
13 Tanzania	945	365
14 Nigeria	924	357
15 Namibia	824	318
16 Mozambique	802	309
17 Zambia	753	291
18 Somalia	638	246
19 Central African Republic	623	241
20 Madagascar	587	227
Smallest		
1 Mayotte (France)	0.37	0.14
2 Seychelles	0.46	0.18
3 Madeira (Portugal)	0.78	0.30
4 São Tomé & Príncipe	0.96	0.37
5 Mauritius	2.0	0.79
6 Azores (Portugal)	2.2	0.86
7 Comoros	2.2	0.86
8 Réunion (France)	2.5	0.97
9 Cape Verde	4.0	1.6
10 Canary Islands (Spain)	7.2	2.8

PHYSICAL SUPERLATIVES

Land Area
30,302,000 sq km (11,697,000 sq mi)

Highest Mountains
1 Kilimanjaro, Tanzania 5,895 m (19,340 ft)
2 Mt Kenya, Kenya 5,199 m (17,057 ft)
3 Ruwenzori (Margherita), Uganda/
   Dem. Rep. of the Congo 5,109 m (16,762 ft)
4 Meru, Tanzania 4,565 m (14,977 ft)
5 Ras Dashen, Ethiopia 4,533 m (14,872 ft)

Longest Rivers
1 Nile 6,670 km (4,140 mi)
2 Congo 4,670 km (2,900 mi)
3 Niger 4,180 km (2,595 mi)
4 Zambezi 3,540 km (2,200 mi)
5 Oubangui/Uele 2,250 km (1,400 mi)

Largest Lakes and Inland Seas
1 Lake Victoria 68,000 sq km (26,000 sq mi)
2 Lake Tanganyika 33,000 sq km (13,000 sq mi)
3 Lake Malawi/Nyasa 29,600 sq km (11,430 sq mi)
4 Lake Chad 25,000 sq km (9,700 sq mi)
5 Lake Bangweulu 9,840 sq km (3,800 sq mi)

Largest Islands
1 Madagascar 587,040 sq km (226,660 sq mi)
2 Socotra 3,600 sq km (1,400 sq mi)
3 Réunion 2,500 sq km (965 sq mi)
4 Tenerife 2,350 sq km (900 sq mi)
5 Mauritius 1,865 sq km (720 sq mi)

COUNTRIES: WEALTH

Country/Territory	Annual Income (US$ per capita)
Richest	
1 Mauritius	13,500
2 South Africa	13,000
3 Libya	12,700
4 Botswana	11,400
5 Tunisia	8,600
6 Seychelles	7,800
7 Algeria	7,700
8 Namibia	7,400
9 Gabon	7,200
10 Cape Verde	6,000
Poorest	
1 Comoros	600
= Malawi	600
= Somalia	600
4 Burundi	700
= Dem. Rep. of the Congo	700
6 Tanzania	800
7 Guinea-Bissau	900
= Madagascar	900
= Sierra Leone	900
10 Niger	1,000

LARGEST CITIES

City	Population (thousands)
1 Cairo, Egypt	11,146
2 Lagos, Nigeria	11,135
3 Kinshasa, Dem. Rep. of the Congo	5,717
4 Alexandria, Egypt	3,760
5 Casablanca, Morocco	3,743
6 Abidjan, Ivory Coast	3,516
7 Algiers, Algeria	3,260
8 Johannesburg, South Africa	2,950
9 Cape Town, South Africa	2,930
10 Addis Ababa, Ethiopia	2,899
11 Kano, Nigeria	2,884
12 Luanda, Angola	2,839
13 Nairobi, Kenya	2,818
14 Khartoum, Sudan	2,742
15 Dar es Salaam, Tanzania	2,683
16 Durban / eThekwini, South Africa	2,391
17 Ibadan, Nigeria	2,375
18 Dakar, Senegal	2,313
19 Tunis, Tunisia	2,063
20 Douala, Cameroon	1,980
21 Accra, Ghana	1,970
22 Rabat, Morocco	1,859
23 Antananarivo, Madagascar	1,808
24 Tripoli, Libya	1,733
25 Yaoundé, Cameroon	1,727
26 Pretoria / Tshwane, South Africa	1,590
27 Harare, Zimbabwe	1,527
28 Conakry, Guinea	1,465
29 Lusaka, Zambia	1,450
30 Bamako, Mali	1,379

COUNTRIES: POPULATION

Country/Territory	Population (thousands)
Most Populous	
1 Nigeria	131,860
2 Egypt	78,887
3 Ethiopia	74,778
4 Dem. Rep. of the Congo	62,661
5 South Africa	44,188
6 Sudan	41,236
7 Tanzania	37,445
8 Kenya	34,708
9 Morocco	33,241
10 Algeria	32,930
11 Uganda	28,196
12 Ghana	22,410
13 Mozambique	19,687
14 Madagascar	18,595
15 Ivory Coast	17,655
16 Cameroon	17,341
17 Burkina Faso	13,903
18 Malawi	13,014
19 Niger	12,525
20 Zimbabwe	12,237
Least Populous	
1 Seychelles	82
2 São Tomé & Príncipe	193
3 Mayotte (France)	201
4 Azores (Portugal)	236
5 Madeira (Portugal)	241
6 Western Sahara	273
7 Cape Verde	421
8 Djibouti	487
9 Equatorial Guinea	540
10 Comoros	691

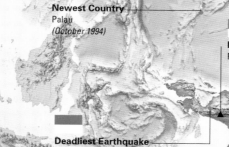

PHYSICAL SUPERLATIVES

Land Area
8,557,000 sq km (3,303,000 sq mi)

Highest Mountains
1. Puncak Jaya, Indonesia *5,029 m (16,499 ft)*
2. Puncak Trikora, Indonesia *4,730 m (15,518 ft)*
3. Puncak Mandala, Indonesia *4,702 m (15,427 ft)*
4. Mt Wilhelm, Papua New Guinea *4,508 m (14,790 ft)*
5. Mauna Kea, USA (Hawai'i) *4,205 m (13,796 ft)*

Longest Rivers
1. Murray–Darling *3,750 km (2,330 mi)*
2. Darling *3,070 km (1,905 mi)*
3. Murray *2,575 km (1,600 mi)*
4. Murrumbidgee *1,690 km (1,050 mi)*
5. Lachlan *1,370 km (850 mi)*

Largest Lakes and Inland Seas
1. Lake Eyre, Australia *8,900 sq km (3,400 sq mi)*
2. Lake Torrens, Australia *5,800 sq km (2,200 sq mi)*
3. Lake Gairdner, Australia *4,800 sq km (1,900 sq mi)*
4. Lake Mackay, Australia *3,490 sq km (1,380 sq mi)*
5. Lake Amadeus, Australia *1,032 sq km (400 sq mi)*

Largest Islands
1. New Guinea, Indon./Papua NG *821,030 sq km (317,000 sq mi)*
2. New Zealand (S.), Pacific Ocean *150,500 sq km (58,100 sq mi)*
3. New Zealand (N.), Pacific Ocean *114,700 sq km (44,300 sq mi)*
4. Tasmania, Australia *67,800 sq km (26,200 sq mi)*
5. New Britain, Papua NG *37,800 sq km (14,600 sq mi)*

Newest Country
Palau
(October 1994)

Highest Mountain
Puncak Jaya

Largest Island
New Guinea

Country with Longest Land Border
Papua New Guinea
820 km (509 mi)

Deadliest Earthquake
New Guinea *(1976)*
5,000–9,000 missing, presumed dead

Deadliest Volcanic Eruption
Mt Lamington,
Papua New Guinea *(1951)*
2,942 deaths

Longest Road Tunnel
M5 East, Australia
3.95 km (2.45 mi)

Busiest Airport
Sydney
26.4 million passengers per year

Oldest Country
Australia
(January 1901)

Most Populous Country

Largest Country

Longest River
Murray–Darling

Tallest Building
Q1 Tower,
Gold Coast
275 m (902 ft)

Largest Desert
Great Victoria, Australia
647,500 sq km (250,000 sq mi)

Highest Waterfall
Pieman, Pieman's Creek
715 m (2,346 ft)

Highest Dam
Dartmouth
180 m (591 ft)

Largest Hydroelectric Plant
Snowy Mountains
3,800 MW

Largest Lake
Lake Eyre

Lowest Point
Lake Eyre (North), Australia
−16 m (−52 ft)

Longest Rail Tunnel
Kaimai, New Zealand
8.9 km (5.5 mi)

COUNTRIES: AREA

	Country/Territory	Area sq km (thousands)	Area sq mi (thousands)
1	Australia	7,741	2,989
2	Papua New Guinea	463	179
3	New Zealand	271	104
4	Solomon Islands	28.9	11.2
5	New Caledonia (France)	18.6	7.2
6	Fiji Islands	18.3	7.1
7	Vanuatu	12.2	4.7
8	French Polynesia (France)	4.0	1.5
9	Samoa	2.8	1.1
10	Kiribati	0.73	0.28
11	Fed. States of Micronesia	0.70	0.27
12	Tonga	0.65	0.25
13	Guam (US)	0.55	0.21
14	Northern Mariana Islands (US)	0.46	0.18
15	Palau	0.46	0.18
16	Cook Is. (NZ)	0.24	0.09
17	American Samoa (US)	0.20	0.08
18	Wallis & Futuna Islands (France)	0.20	0.08
19	Marshall Islands	0.18	0.07
20	Tuvalu	0.03	0.01
21	Nauru	0.02	0.008

COUNTRIES: POPULATION

	Country/Territory	Population (thousands)
1	Australia	20,264
2	Papua New Guinea	5,671
3	New Zealand	4,076
4	Fiji Islands	906
5	Solomon Islands	552
6	French Polynesia (France)	275
7	New Caledonia (France)	219
8	Vanuatu	209
9	Samoa	177
10	Guam (US)	171
11	Tonga	115
12	Fed. States of Micronesia	108
13	Kiribati	105
14	Northern Mariana Is. (US)	82
15	Marshall Islands	60
16	American Samoa (US)	58
17	Cook Islands (NZ)	21
=	Palau	21
19	Wallis & Futuna Is. (France)	16
20	Nauru	13
21	Tuvalu	12

COUNTRIES: WEALTH

	Country/Territory	Annual Income (US$ per capita)
1	Australia	32,900
2	New Zealand	26,000
3	French Polynesia (France)	17,500
4	Guam (US)	15,000
=	New Caledonia (France)	15,000
6	Northern Mariana Is. (US)	12,500
7	Cook Islands (NZ)	9,100
8	Palau	7,600
9	Fiji Islands	6,100
10	American Samoa (US)	5,800
=	Niue (NZ)	5,800
12	Nauru	5,000
13	Wallis & Futuna Is. (France)	3,800
14	Marshall Islands	2,900
=	Vanuatu	2,900
16	Kiribati	2,700
=	Papua New Guinea	2,700
18	Fed. States of Micronesia	2,300
19	Tonga	2,200
20	Samoa	2,100
21	Tuvalu	1,600

LARGEST CITIES

	City	Population (thousands)
1	Sydney, Australia	4,388
2	Melbourne, Australia	3,663
3	Brisbane, Australia	1,769
4	Perth, Australia	1,484
5	Auckland, New Zealand	1,152
6	Adelaide, Australia	1,137

Largest Island
Berkner

Highest Mountain
Vinson Massif

Lowest Recorded Temperature
Vostok
−89.2°C (−111.5°F)

World's Largest Ice Cap
*30 million cubic km (7 million cubic mi),
representing 90% of the world's ice and
70% of the world's freshwater
Coverage = 13.7 million sq km
(5.3 million sq mi) or
97% of Antarctica's landmass
Mean thickness of ice = 2,300 m (7,546 ft)
Maximum thickness of ice =
4,776 m (15,669 ft)
(Dome Argus)*

Longest Glacier
Lambert-Fisher
Ice Passage
515 km (320 mi)

Largest Underground Lake
Lake Vostok
*14,300 sq km (5,649 sq mi),
at a depth of 4.0 km (2.5 mi)
below the ice surface*

PHYSICAL SUPERLATIVES

Land Area
14,100,000 sq km (5,443,000 sq mi)

Highest Mountains
1. Vinson Massif, W. Antarctica *4,897 m (16,066 ft)*
2. Mt Tyree, W. Antarctica *4,852 m (15,920 ft)*
3. Mt Kirkpatrick, Transantarctic Mountains *4,528 m (14,855 ft)*
4. Mt Markham, Transantarctic Mountains *4,349 m (14,268 ft)*
5. Mt Jackson, Antarctic Peninsula *4,191 m (13,751 ft)*

Largest Islands
1. Berkner, Ronne Ice Shelf *47,920 sq km (18,500 sq mi)*
2. Alexander, Bellingshausen Sea *43,200 sq km (16,630 sq mi)*
3. Thurston, Amundsen Sea *15,700 sq km (6,045 sq mi)*
4. Carney, Amundsen Sea *8,500 sq km (3,275 sq mi)*
5. Roosevelt, Ross Ice Shelf *7,500 sq km (2,890 sq mi)*

COUNTRIES: AREA

Country/Territory	Area sq km (thousands)	Area sq mi (thousands)
Largest		
1 Canada	9,971	3,850
2 United States of America	9,629	3,718
3 Greenland (Denmark)	2,176	840
4 Mexico	1,958	756
5 Nicaragua	130	50.2
6 Honduras	112	43.3
7 Cuba	111	42.8
8 Guatemala	109	42.0
9 Panama	75.5	29.2
10 Costa Rica	51.1	19.7
11 Dominican Republic	48.5	18.7
12 Haiti	27.8	10.7
13 Belize	23.0	8.9
14 El Salvador	21.0	8.1
15 Bahamas	13.9	5.4
16 Jamaica	11.0	4.2
17 Puerto Rico (US)	8.9	3.4
18 Trinidad & Tobago	5.1	2.0
19 Guadeloupe (France)	1.7	0.66
20 Martinique (France)	1.1	0.43
Smallest		
1 Bermuda (UK)	0.05	0.02
2 Anguilla (UK)	0.10	0.04
3 Montserrat (UK)	0.10	0.04
4 Virgin Islands (UK)	0.15	0.06
5 Aruba (Netherlands)	0.19	0.07
6 Cayman Islands (UK)	0.26	0.10
7 St Kitts & Nevis	0.26	0.10
8 Grenada	0.34	0.13
9 Virgin Islands (US)	0.35	0.13
10 St Vincent & the Grenadines	0.39	0.15

Highest Mountain
Mt McKinley (Denali)

Largest Island
Greenland

Largest Lake
Lake Superior

Tallest Building
Sears Tower, Chicago
442 m (1,450 ft)

Largest Country
Canada

Longest Road Tunnel
Ted Williams, Boston
4.2 km (2.6 mi)

Longest Rail Tunnel
Mount MacDonald, Canada
14.6 km (9.1 mi)

Largest Subway System
New York
370 km (230 mi)

Largest Hydroelectric Plant
Grand Coulee, United States
6,809 MW

Oldest Country
United States
(July 1776)

Most Populous Country

Country with Longest Land Border
12,034 km (7,473 mi)

Busiest Airport
Atlanta (Hartsfield)
85.9 million passengers per year

Highest Waterfall
Yosemite, Yosemite Creek,
United States
739 m (2,425 ft)

Newest Country
Antigua & Barbuda
(November 1981)

Lowest Point
Death Valley, United States
−86 m (−282 ft)

Largest Desert
Great Basin, United States
492,100 sq km (190,000 sq mi)

Deadliest Volcanic Eruption
Mt Pelée, Martinique *(1902)*
29,025 deaths

Longest River
Mississippi–Missouri

Highest Dam
Manuel M. Torres, Mexico
261 m (856 ft)

Deadliest Earthquake
Guatemala City, Guatemala *(1976)*
23,000 deaths

COUNTRIES: POPULATION

Country/Territory	Population (thousands)
Most Populous	
1 United States of America	301,139
2 Mexico	107,450
3 Canada	33,099
4 Guatemala	12,294
5 Cuba	11,383
6 Dominican Republic	9,184
7 Haiti	8,309
8 Honduras	7,326
9 El Salvador	6,822
10 Nicaragua	5,570
11 Costa Rica	4,075
12 Puerto Rico (US)	3,927
13 Panama	3,191
14 Jamaica	2,758
15 Trinidad & Tobago	1,066
16 Guadeloupe (France)	453
17 Martinique (France)	436
18 Bahamas	304
19 Belize	288
20 Barbados	280
Least Populous	
1 Montserrat (UK)	9
2 Anguilla (UK)	13
3 Turks & Caicos Is. (UK)	21
4 Virgin Islands (UK)	23
5 St Kitts & Nevis	39
6 Cayman Islands (UK)	44
7 Greenland (Denmark)	56
8 Bermuda (UK)	65
9 Dominica	69
10 Antigua & Barbuda	69

LARGEST CITIES

City	Population (thousands)
1 Mexico City, Mexico	19,013
2 New York, USA	17,800
3 Los Angeles, USA	11,789
4 Chicago, USA	8,308
5 Philadelphia, USA	5,149
6 Toronto, Canada	5,060
7 Miami, USA	4,919
8 Dallas-Fort Worth, USA	4,146
9 Boston, USA	4,032
10 Washington, USA	3,934
11 Guadalajara, Mexico	3,905
12 Detroit, USA	3,903
13 Houston, USA	3,823
14 Monterrey, Mexico	3,517
15 Montréal, Canada	3,511
16 Atlanta, USA	3,500
17 Guatemala City, Guatemala	3,242
18 San Francisco, USA	3,229
19 Phoenix, USA	2,907
20 Seattle, USA	2,712
21 San Diego, USA	2,674
22 Santo Domingo, Dom. Rep.	2,563
23 Minneapolis-St Paul, USA	2,389
24 San Juan, Puerto Rico	2,357
25 Havana, Cuba	2,192
26 Vancouver, Canada	2,125
27 Port-au-Prince, Haiti	2,090
28 St Louis, USA	2,078
29 Baltimore, USA	2,076
30 Tampa-St Petersburg, USA	2,062

PHYSICAL SUPERLATIVES

Land Area
24,241,000 sq km (9,357,000 sq mi)

Highest Mountains
1 Mt McKinley (Denali), USA (Alaska) *6,194 m (20,321 ft)*
2 Mt Logan, Canada *5,959 m (19,551 ft)*
3 Pico de Orizaba, Mexico *5,610 m (18,405 ft)*
4 Mt St Elias, Canada/USA *5,489 m (18,008 ft)*
5 Popocatépetl, Mexico *5,452 m (17,887 ft)*

Longest Rivers
1 Mississippi–Missouri *5,971 km (3,710 mi)*
2 Mackenzie *4,240 km (2,630 mi)*
3 Missouri *4,088 km (2,540 mi)*
4 Mississippi *3,782 km (2,350 mi)*
5 Yukon *3,185 km (1,980 mi)*

Largest Lakes and Inland Seas
1 Lake Superior, Canada/USA *82,350 sq km (31,800 sq mi)*
2 Lake Huron, Canada/USA *59,600 sq km (23,010 sq mi)*
3 Lake Michigan, USA *58,000 sq km (22,400 sq mi)*
4 Great Bear Lake, Canada *31,800 sq km (12,280 sq mi)*
5 Great Slave Lake, Canada *28,500 sq km (11,000 sq mi)*

Largest Islands
1 Greenland, Atlantic Ocean *2,175,600 sq km (839,800 sq mi)*
2 Baffin Island, Canada *508,000 sq km (196,100 sq mi)*
3 Victoria Island, Canada *212,200 sq km (81,900 sq mi)*
4 Ellesmere Island, Canada *212,000 sq km (81,800 sq mi)*
5 Cuba, Caribbean Sea *110,860 sq km (42,800 sq mi)*

COUNTRIES: WEALTH

Country/Territory	Annual Income (US$ per capita)
Richest	
1 Bermuda (UK)	69,900
2 Cayman Islands (UK)	43,800
3 United States of America	43,500
4 Virgin Islands (UK)	38,500
5 Canada	35,200
6 Aruba (Netherlands)	21,800
7 Bahamas	21,300
8 Greenland (Denmark)	20,000
9 Trinidad & Tobago	19,700
10 Puerto Rico (US)	19,100
Poorest	
1 Haiti	1,800
2 Honduras	3,000
= Nicaragua	3,000
4 Montserrat (UK)	3,400
5 St Vincent & the Grenadines	3,600
6 Dominica	3,800
7 Cuba	3,900
= Grenada	3,900
9 Jamaica	4,600
10 St Lucia	4,800

COUNTRIES: AREA

	Country/Territory	Area sq km (thousands)	Area sq mi (thousands)
1	Brazil	8,514	3,287
2	Argentina	2,780	1,074
3	Peru	1,285	496
4	Colombia	1,139	440
5	Bolivia	1,099	424
6	Venezuela	912	352
7	Chile	757	292
8	Paraguay	407	157
9	Ecuador	284	109
10	Guyana	215	83

COUNTRIES: POPULATION

	Country/Territory	Population (thousands)
1	Brazil	188,078
2	Colombia	43,593
3	Argentina	39,922
4	Peru	28,303
5	Venezuela	25,730
6	Chile	16,134
7	Ecuador	13,548
8	Bolivia	8,989
9	Paraguay	6,506
10	Uruguay	3,432

LARGEST CITIES

	City	Population (thousands)
1	São Paulo, Brazil	18,333
2	Buenos Aires, Argentina	13,349
3	Rio de Janeiro, Brazil	11,469
4	Lima, Peru	8,180
5	Bogotá, Colombia	7,594
6	Santiago, Chile	5,623
7	Belo Horizonte, Brazil	5,304
8	Pôrto Alegre, Brazil	3,795
9	Recife, Brazil	3,527
10	Brasília, Brazil	3,341
11	Salvador, Brazil	3,331
12	Caracas, Venezuela	3,276
13	Fortaleza, Brazil	3,261
14	Medellín, Colombia	3,236
15	Curitiba, Brazil	2,871
16	Campinas, Brazil	2,640
17	Cali, Colombia	2,583
18	Guayaquil, Ecuador	2,387
19	Valencia, Venezuela	2,330
20	Maracaibo, Venezuela	2,182
21	Belém, Brazil	2,097
22	Barranquilla, Colombia	1,918
23	Goiânia, Brazil	1,878
24	Asunción, Paraguay	1,750
25	Manaus, Brazil	1,673
26	Santos, Brazil	1,634
27	Córdoba, Argentina	1,592
28	La Paz, Bolivia	1,533
29	Quito, Ecuador	1,514
30	Montevideo, Uruguay	1,353

Tallest Building
Parque Central Torre Este, Caracas
221 m (725 ft)

Oldest Country
Colombia
(July 1810)

Longest Road Tunnel
Fernando Gómez Martínez,
Colombia
4.6 km (2.9 mi)

Deadliest Volcanic Eruption
Nev. del Ruiz, Colombia *(1985)*
25,000 deaths

Longest Suspension Bridge
Puente de Angostura, Venezuela
712 m (2,336 ft)

Highest Waterfall
Angel, Caroni River, Venezuela
980 m (3,212 ft)

Newest Country
Suriname
(November 1975)

Longest River
Amazon

Largest Country
Brazil

Most Populous Country
Country with Longest Land Border
14,691 km (9,123 mi)

Deadliest Earthquake
Western Peru *(1970)*
66,000 deaths

Largest Lake
Lake Titicaca

Longest Rail Tunnel
Tunelão, Brazil
8.7 km (5.4 mi)

Largest Hydroelectric Plant
Itaipu, Brazil/Paraguay
12,600 MW

Highest Mountain
Aconcagua

Largest Desert
Patagonian, Argentina
673,400 sq km (260,000 sq mi)

Largest Island
Tierra del Fuego

Lowest Point
Valdés Peninsula
−40 m (−131 ft)

PHYSICAL SUPERLATIVES

Land Area
17,793,000 sq km (6,868,000 sq mi)

Highest Mountains
1   Aconcagua, Argentina *6,962 m (22,841 ft)*
2   Bonete, Argentina *6,872 m (22,546 ft)*
3   Ojos del Salado, Argentina/Chile *6,863 m (22,516 ft)*
4   Pissis, Argentina *6,779 m (22,241 ft)*
5   Mercedario, Argentina/Chile *6,770 m (22,211 ft)*

Longest Rivers
1   Amazon *6,450 km (4,010 mi)*
2   Paraná–Plate *4,500 km (2,800 mi)*
3   Purus *3,350 km (2,080 mi)*
4   Madeira *3,200 km (1,990 mi)*
5   São Francisco *2,900 km (1,800 mi)*

Largest Lakes and Inland Seas
1   Lake Titicaca, Bolivia/Peru *8,300 sq km (3,200 sq mi)*
2   Lake Poopo, Bolivia *2,800 sq km (1,100 sq mi)*
3   Lake Mar Chiquita, Argentina *2,000 sq km (780 sq mi)*
4   Lake General Carrera (Buenos Aires), Argentina/Chile *1,850 sq km (720 sq mi)*
5   Lake Argentino, Argentina *1,470 sq km (575 sq mi)*

Largest Islands
1   Tierra del Fuego, Argentina/Chile *47,000 sq km (18,100 sq mi)*
2   Chiloe, Chile *8,400 sq km (3,235 sq mi)*
3   Falkland Is. (East), Atlantic Ocean *6,800 sq km (2,600 sq mi)*
4   Wellington, Chile *5,560 sq km (2,140 sq mi)*
5   Riesco, Chile *5,110 sq km (1,970 sq mi)*

COUNTRIES: WEALTH

	Country/Territory	Annual Income (US$ per capita)
1	Falkland Islands (UK)	25,000
2	Argentina	15,000
3	Chile	12,700
4	Uruguay	10,700
5	Brazil	8,600
6	Colombia	8,400
7	French Guiana (France)	8,300
8	Venezuela	6,900
9	Peru	6,400
10	Guyana	4,700

World: Regions in the News

KASHMIR

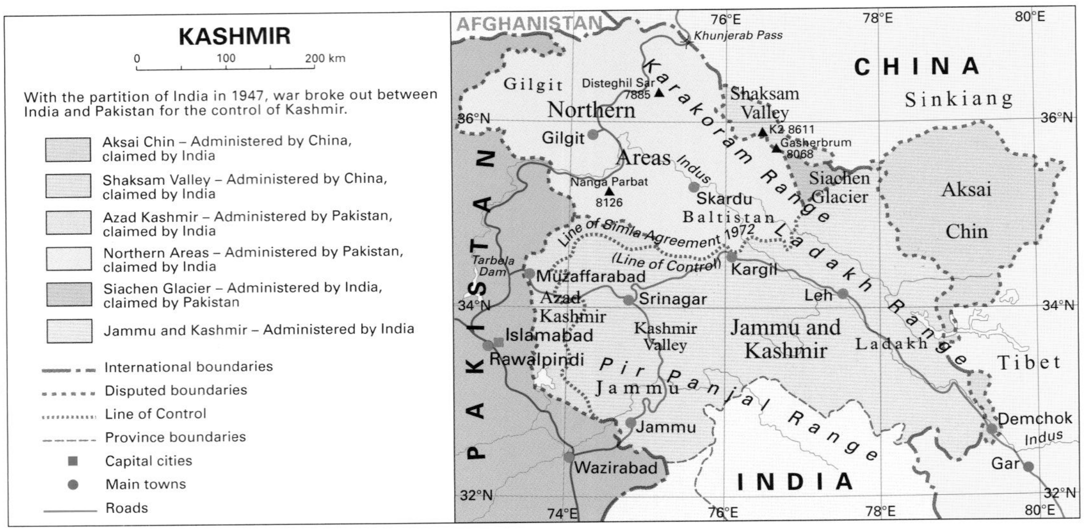

KASHMIR
0 100 200 km
Aksai Chin – Administered by China, claimed by India
Shaksam Valley – Administered by China, claimed by India
Azad Kashmir – Administered by Pakistan, claimed by India
Northern Areas – Administered by Pakistan, claimed by India
Siachen Glacier – Administered by India, claimed by Pakistan
Jammu and Kashmir – Administered by India
International boundaries
Disputed boundaries
Line of Control
Province boundaries
Capital cities
Main towns
Roads
AFGHANISTAN
CHINA
Sinkiang
Gilgit
Northern Areas
Shaksam Valley
K2 8611
Gasherbrum 8068
Disteghil Sar 7885
Khunjerab Pass
Karakoram Range
Nanga Parbat 8126
Skardu
Baltistan
Siachen Glacier
Aksai Chin
Ladakh Range
Line of Simla Agreement 1972 (Line of Control)
Kargil
Tarbela Dam
Muzaffarabad
Azad Kashmir
Srinagar
Leh
Islamabad
Rawalpindi
Kashmir Valley
Jammu and Kashmir
Ladakh
Tibet
Pir Panjal Range
Jammu
Demchok
Indus
Gar
Wazirabad
INDIA
PAKISTAN
76°E
78°E
80°E
74°E
36°N
34°N
32°N

With the partition of India in 1947, war broke out between India and Pakistan for the control of Kashmir.

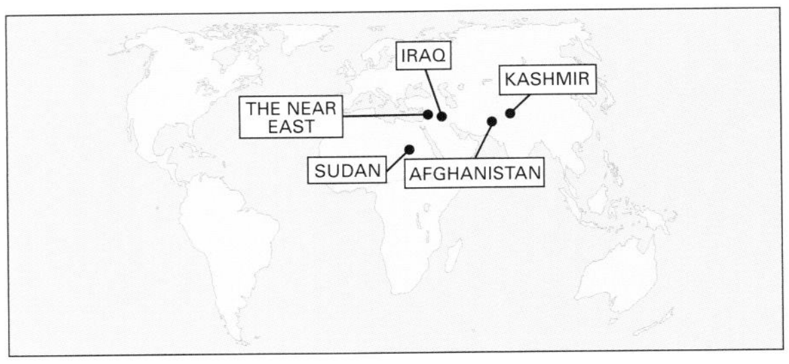

IRAQ
KASHMIR
THE NEAR EAST
SUDAN
AFGHANISTAN

IRAQ

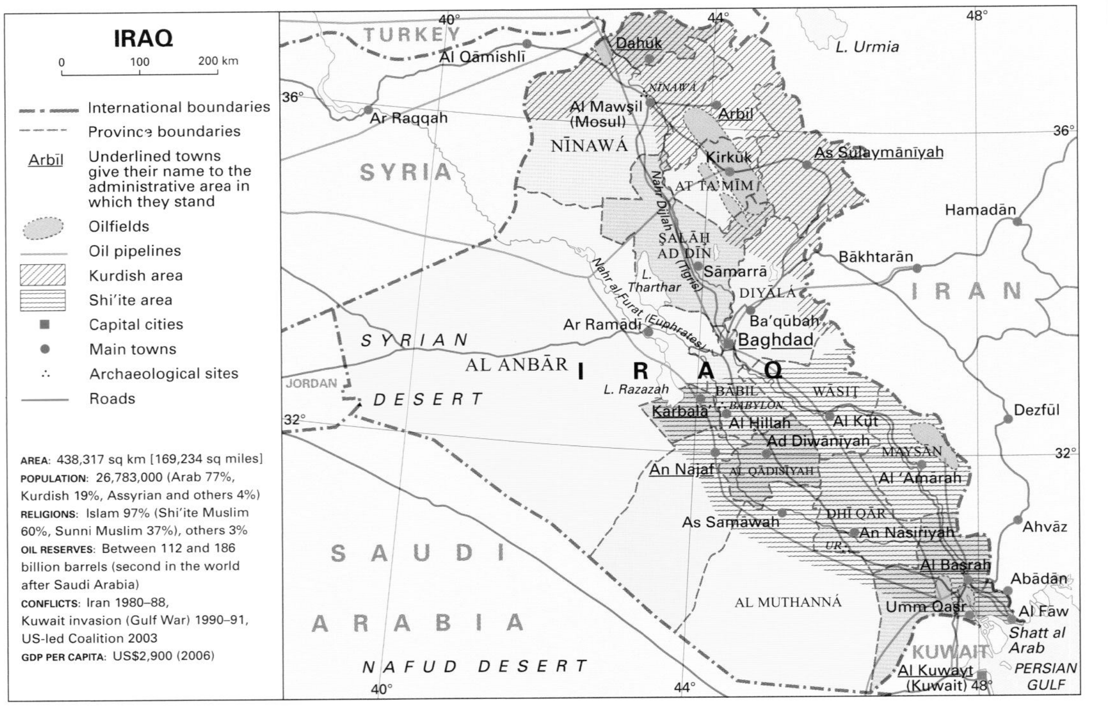

IRAQ
0 100 200 km
International boundaries
Province boundaries
Arbil Underlined towns give their name to the administrative area in which they stand
Oilfields
Oil pipelines
Kurdish area
Shi'ite area
Capital cities
Main towns
Archaeological sites
Roads
TURKEY
Al Qāmishlī
Dahūk
L. Urmia
NINAWĀ
Al Mawşil (Mosul)
Arbil
Ar Raqqah
Kirkūk
As Sulaymānīyah
SYRIA
AT TA'MĪM
Hamadān
ŞALĀH AD DĪN
Sāmarrā
Bākhtarān
L. Tharthar
DIYĀLĀ
IRAN
Ar Ramādī
Ba'qūbah
Baghdad
SYRIAN DESERT
AL ANBĀR
IRAQ
JORDAN
L. Razazah
BĀBIL
BABYLON
WĀSIT
Karbalā'
Al Hillah
Al Kūt
Dezfūl
Ad Dīwānīyah
MAYSĀN
An Najaf
AL QĀDISĪYAH
Al 'Amārah
DHĪ QĀR
As Samāwah
An Nāşirīyah
UR
Ahvāz
SAUDI ARABIA
Al Başrah
Abādān
AL MUTHANNĀ
Umm Qaşr
Al Fāw
Shatt al Arab
KUWAIT
Al Kuwayt (Kuwait)
PERSIAN GULF
NAFUD DESERT
40°
44°
48°
36°
32°

AREA: 438,317 sq km [169,234 sq miles]
POPULATION: 26,783,000 (Arab 77%, Kurdish 19%, Assyrian and others 4%)
RELIGIONS: Islam 97% (Shi'ite Muslim 60%, Sunni Muslim 37%), others 3%
OIL RESERVES: Between 112 and 186 billion barrels (second in the world after Saudi Arabia)
CONFLICTS: Iran 1980–88, Kuwait invasion (Gulf War) 1990–91, US-led Coalition 2003
GDP PER CAPITA: US$2,900 (2006)

THE NEAR EAST

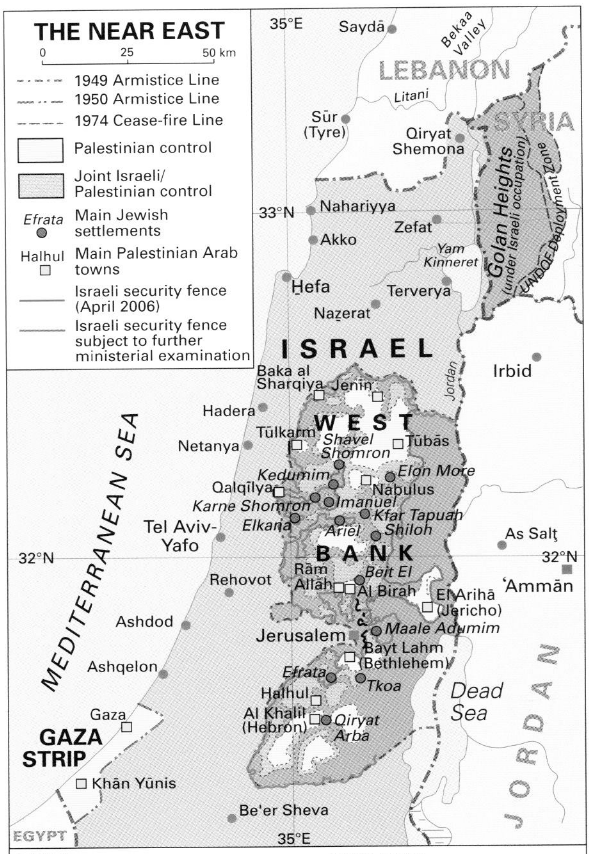

THE NEAR EAST
0 25 50 km
1949 Armistice Line
1950 Armistice Line
1974 Cease-fire Line
Palestinian control
Joint Israeli/ Palestinian control
Efrata Main Jewish settlements
Halhul Main Palestinian Arab towns
Israeli security fence (April 2006)
Israeli security fence subject to further ministerial examination
Saydā
Bekaa Valley
LEBANON
Litani
Şūr (Tyre)
Qiryat Shemona
SYRIA
Golan Heights (under Israeli occupation)
UNDOF Deployment Zone
Nahariyya
Akko
Zefat
Yam Kinneret
Hefa
Terverya
Nazerat
ISRAEL
Irbid
Baka al Sharqiya
Jenin
Hadera
Tūlkarm
Shavel Shomron
Tūbās
WEST BANK
Netanya
Kedumim
Elon More
Qalqīlya
Nabulus
Karne Shomron
Imanuel
Kfar Tapuah
Elkana
Ariel
Shiloh
Tel Aviv-Yafo
As Salţ
MEDITERRANEAN SEA
Rām Allāh
Beit El
Rehovot
Al Bīrah
Arīḥā (Jericho)
'Ammān
Ashdod
Jerusalem
Maale Adumim
Bayt Lahm (Bethlehem)
Ashqelon
Efrata
Tkoa
Halhul
Dead Sea
Gaza
Al Khalīl (Hebron)
Qiryat Arba
GAZA STRIP
Khān Yūnis
Be'er Sheva
EGYPT
JORDAN
35°E
33°N
32°N

ISRAEL
POPULATION: 6,352,000 (inc. Israeli settlers in West Bank and Golan Heights)
INFANT MORTALITY: 6.7 deaths per 1,000 births
RELIGIONS: Jewish 76.4%, Muslim 16%, Christian 2.1%
GDP PER CAPITA: US$26,200 (2006)

WEST BANK
POPULATION: 2,460,000 (Muslim 75%, Jewish 17%)
INFANT MORTALITY: 18.7 deaths per 1,000 births
GDP PER CAPITA: US$1,100 (2003)

GAZA STRIP
POPULATION: 1,429,000 (Muslim 98.7% Christian 0.7%, Jewish 0.6%)
INFANT MORTALITY: 21.9 deaths per 1,000 births
GDP PER CAPITA: US$600 (2003)

JORDAN
POPULATION: 5,907,000 (Palestinian Arab 50%)

LEBANON
POPULATION: 3,874,000 (Palestinian Arab 11%)

AFGHANISTAN

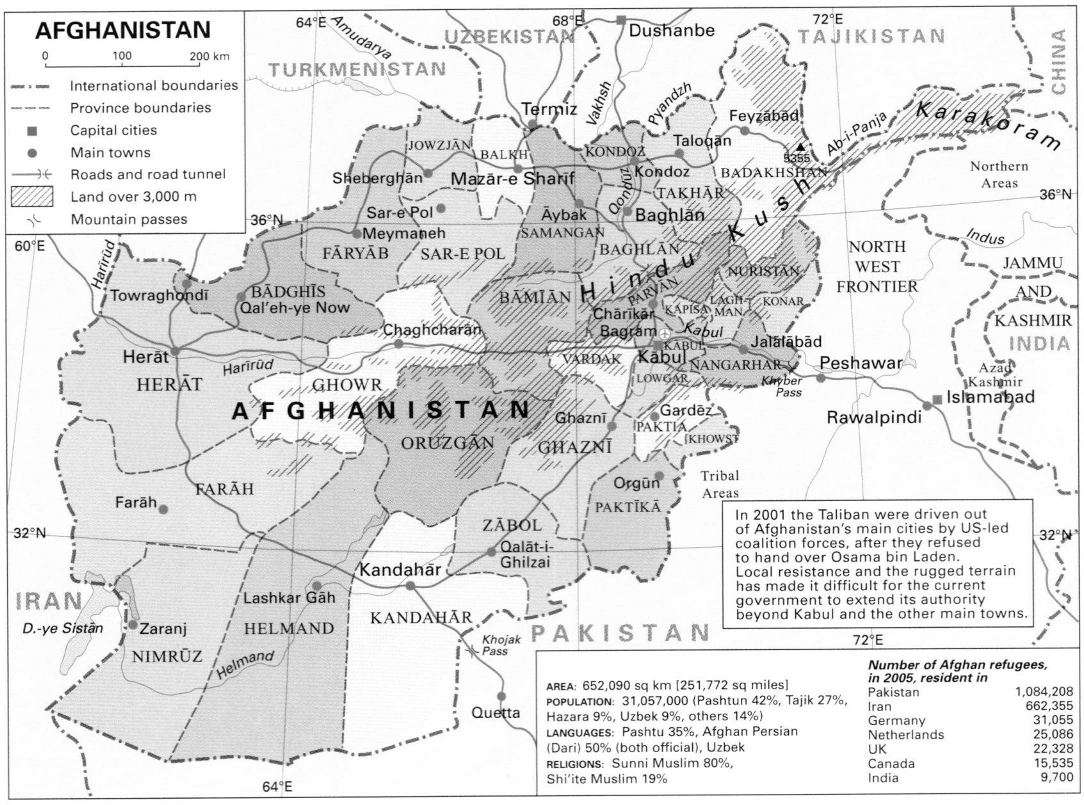

AFGHANISTAN
0 100 200 km
International boundaries
Province boundaries
Capital cities
Main towns
Roads and road tunnel
Land over 3,000 m
Mountain passes
UZBEKISTAN
TAJIKISTAN
TURKMENISTAN
CHINA
Amudarya
Dushanbe
Termiz
Vakhsh
Pyandzh
Feyzābād
Karakoram
Ab-i-Panja
JOWZJĀN
BALKH
KONDOZ
Taloqān
BADAKHSHĀN
Northern Areas
Sheberghān
Mazār-e Sharīf
Kondoz
TAKHĀR
Sar-e Pol
Āybak
Baghlān
SAMANGĀN
Meymaneh
FĀRYĀB
SAR-E POL
BAGHLĀN
Hindu Kush
NURISTĀN
NORTH WEST FRONTIER
Indus
JAMMU AND KASHMIR
INDIA
Towraghondī
BĀDGHĪS
Qal'eh-ye Now
BĀMĪĀN
PARVĀN
KAPISA
LAGHMAN
KONAR
Chārīkār
Bagrām
Chaghcharān
KABUL
Kabul
Jalālābād
Herāt
HERĀT
Harīrūd
GHOWR
VARDAK
NANGARHĀR
Peshawar
Khyber Pass
Azad Kashmir
Islamabad
AFGHANISTAN
LOWGAR
Gardēz
PAKTIA
KHOWST
Ghaznī
GHAZNĪ
ORUZGĀN
Rawalpindi
Orgūn
PAKTĪKĀ
Tribal Areas
Farāh
FARĀH
ZĀBOL
Qalāt-i-Ghilzai
Kandahār
Lashkar Gāh
IRAN
D.-ye Sīstān
Zaranj
HELMAND
KANDAHĀR
Khojak Pass
PAKISTAN
NIMRŪZ
Helmand
Quetta
60°E
64°E
68°E
72°E
36°N
32°N

In 2001 the Taliban were driven out of Afghanistan's main cities by US-led coalition forces, after they refused to hand over Osama bin Laden. Local resistance and the rugged terrain has made it difficult for the current government to extend its authority beyond Kabul and the other main towns.

AREA: 652,090 sq km [251,772 sq miles]
POPULATION: 31,057,000 (Pashtun 42%, Tajik 27%, Hazara 9%, Uzbek 9%, others 14%)
LANGUAGES: Pashtu 35%, Afghan Persian (Dari) 50% (both official), Uzbek
RELIGIONS: Sunni Muslim 80%, Shi'ite Muslim 19%

Number of Afghan refugees, in 2005, resident in	
Pakistan	1,084,208
Iran	662,355
Germany	31,055
Netherlands	25,086
UK	22,328
Canada	15,535
India	9,700

SUDAN

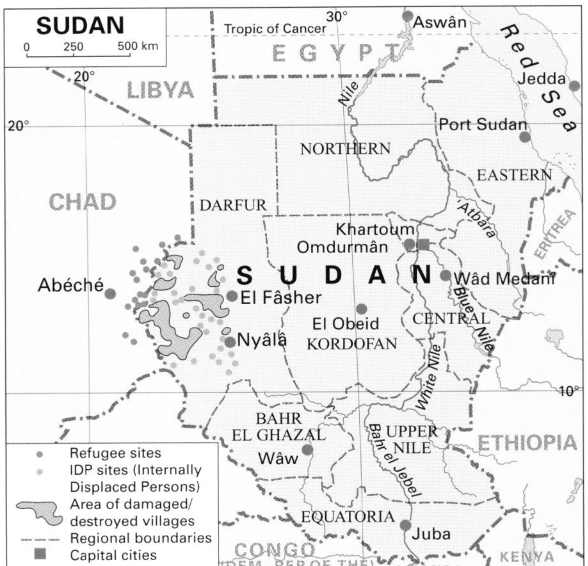

SUDAN
0 250 500 km
Tropic of Cancer
Aswân
EGYPT
Red Sea
LIBYA
Nile
Jedda
Port Sudan
NORTHERN
EASTERN
CHAD
DARFUR
Atbara
ERITREA
Khartoum
Omdurmân
Abéché
SUDAN
Wad Medani
El Fâsher
Blue Nile
CENTRAL
El Obeid
Nyâlâ
KORDOFAN
White Nile
BAHR EL GHAZAL
UPPER NILE
ETHIOPIA
Wâw
Bahr el Jebel
EQUATORIA
Juba
CONGO (DEM. REP. OF THE)
UGANDA
KENYA
Refugee sites
IDP sites (Internally Displaced Persons)
Area of damaged/ destroyed villages
Regional boundaries
Capital cities
Main towns
20°
30°
10°

AREA: 2,505,813 sq km [967,494 sq miles]
POPULATION: 41,236,000 (Black 52%, Arab 39%, Beja 6%, others 3%)
RELIGIONS: Sunni Muslim 70% (mostly in the north), indigenous beliefs 25%, Christian 5% (mostly in the south)

Sudan has more internally displaced people than any other country (5.3 million in 2006) and there are 229,000 Sudanese refugees in neighbouring Chad. Up to 400,000 people are estimated to have been killed since conflict began in the Darfur region in early 2003.

NATIONS OF THE WORLD

Country	Page
Afghanistan	18
Albania	18
Algeria	18
American Samoa	18
Andorra	18
Angola	18
Anguilla	19
Antigua and Barbuda	19
Argentina	19
Armenia	19
Aruba	19
Australia	19
Austria	20
Azerbaijan	20
Bahamas	20
Bahrain	20
Bangladesh	20
Barbados	20
Belarus	20
Belgium	21
Belize	21
Benin	21
Bermuda	21
Bhutan	21
Bolivia	21
Bosnia-Herzegovina	22
Botswana	22
Brazil	22
Brunei	23
Bulgaria	23
Burkina Faso	23
Burma (Myanmar)	23
Burundi	23
Cambodia	24
Cameroon	24
Canada	24
Cape Verde	25
Cayman Islands	25
Central African Republic	25
Chad	25
Chile	25
China	26
Colombia	26
Comoros	26
Congo	26
Congo (Dem. Rep. of the)	27
Costa Rica	27
Croatia	27
Cuba	27
Cyprus	28
Czech Republic	28
Denmark	28
Djibouti	29
Dominica	29
Dominican Republic	29
East Timor	29
Ecuador	29
Egypt	29
El Salvador	30
Equatorial Guinea	30
Eritrea	30
Estonia	30
Ethiopia	31
Falkland Islands	31
Færoe Islands	31
Fiji Islands	31
Finland	31
France	31
French Guiana	32
French Polynesia	32
Gabon	32
Gambia, The	32
Georgia	33
Germany	33
Ghana	33
Gibraltar	34
Greece	34
Greenland	34
Grenada	34
Guadeloupe	34
Guam	34
Guatemala	34
Guinea	34
Guinea-Bissau	35
Guyana	35
Haiti	35
Honduras	35
Hungary	36
Iceland	36
India	36
Indonesia	36
Iran	37
Iraq	37
Ireland	37
Israel	38
Italy	38
Ivory Coast	38
Jamaica	39
Japan	39
Jordan	39
Kazakhstan	39
Kenya	40
Kiribati	40
Korea, North	40
Korea, South	41
Kuwait	41
Kyrgyzstan	41
Laos	41
Latvia	41
Lebanon	42
Lesotho	42
Liberia	42
Libya	43
Liechtenstein	43
Lithuania	43
Luxembourg	43
Macedonia (FYROM)	43
Madagascar	44
Malawi	44
Malaysia	44
Maldives	45
Mali	45
Malta	45
Marshall Islands	45
Martinique	45
Mauritania	45
Mauritius	46
Mexico	46
Micronesia	46
Moldova	46
Monaco	46
Mongolia	46
Montenegro	47
Montserrat	47
Morocco	47
Mozambique	47
Namibia	47
Nauru	47
Nepal	48
Netherlands	48
Netherlands Antilles	48
New Caledonia	48
New Zealand	48
Nicaragua	49
Niger	49
Nigeria	49
Northern Mariana Islands	49
Norway	49
Oman	50
Pakistan	50
Palau	50
Panama	50
Papua New Guinea	50
Paraguay	51
Peru	51
Philippines	51
Pitcairn	51
Poland	51
Portugal	52
Puerto Rico	52
Qatar	52
Réunion	52
Romania	52
Russia	52
Rwanda	53
St Helena	53
St Kitts and Nevis	53
St Lucia	53
St Vincent and the Grenadines	53
Samoa	53
San Marino	54
São Tomé and Príncipe	54
Saudi Arabia	54
Senegal	54
Serbia	54
Seychelles	54
Sierra Leone	54
Singapore	55
Slovak Republic	55
Slovenia	55
Solomon Islands	56
Somalia	56
South Africa	56
Spain	56
Sri Lanka	57
Sudan	57
Suriname	57
Swaziland	57
Sweden	58
Switzerland	58
Syria	58
Taiwan	58
Tajikistan	59
Tanzania	59
Thailand	59
Togo	59
Tonga	60
Trinidad and Tobago	60
Tunisia	60
Turkey	60
Turkmenistan	60
Turks and Caicos Islands	61
Tuvalu	61
Uganda	61
Ukraine	61
United Arab Emirates	61
United Kingdom	61
United States of America	62
Uruguay	62
Uzbekistan	63
Vanuatu	63
Vatican City	63
Venezuela	63
Vietnam	63
Virgin Islands, British	64
Virgin Islands, US	64
Wallis and Futuna Islands	64
Yemen	64
Zambia	64
Zimbabwe	64

NOTE: This alphabetical list includes the principal countries and territories of the world. The area figures give the total area of land, inland water and ice. The population figures are 2006 estimates where available.

NATIONS OF THE WORLD

AFGHANISTAN

AREA 652,090 sq km [251,772 sq mi]
POPULATION 31,057,000
CAPITAL Kabul
GOVERNMENT Transitional
ETHNIC GROUPS Pashtun (Pathan) 44%, Tajik 25%, Hazara 10%, Uzbek 8%, others 13%
LANGUAGES Pashtu, Dari/Persian (both official), Uzbek
RELIGIONS Islam (Sunni Muslim 84%, Shi'ite Muslim 15%), others 1%
CURRENCY Afghani = 100 puls

GEOGRAPHY The Republic of Afghanistan is a landlocked, mountainous country in southern Asia. The central highlands reach a height of more than 7,000 m [22,966 ft] in the east and make up nearly three-quarters of Afghanistan. The main range is the Hindu Kush, which is cut by deep, fertile valleys.

In winter, northerly winds bring cold, snowy weather to the mountains, but summers are hot and dry.

POLITICS & ECONOMY The modern history of Afghanistan began in 1747, when the various tribes in the area united for the first time. In the 19th century, Russia and Britain struggled for control of the country. Following Britain's withdrawal in 1919, Afghanistan became fully independent. Soviet troops invaded Afghanistan in 1979 to support a socialist regime, but they withdrew in 1989. In the early 2000s, an Islamic group called the Taliban seized power. In 2001, when the Taliban government refused to hand over the terrorist leader Osama bin Laden, an international force overthrew the Taliban government. A coalition government was set up, led by the USA-backed Hamid Karzai. Under a new constitution, approved in 2004, Karzai was elected president. Parliamentary elections, the first in more than 35 years, were held in 2005, but fighting between NATO and Taliban forces continued into 2007.

Afghanistan is one of the world's poorest countries. About 70% of the people live by farming, many growing poppies to make opium. Others are semi-nomadic herders. Natural gas is produced. Exports include carpets, fruit and nuts, opium and wool.

ALBANIA

AREA 28,748 sq km [11,100 sq mi]
POPULATION 3,582,000
CAPITAL Tirana
GOVERNMENT Multiparty republic
ETHNIC GROUPS Albanian 95%, Greek 3%, Macedonian, Vlachs, Gypsy
LANGUAGES Albanian (official)
RELIGIONS Many people say they are non-believers; of the believers, 70% follow Islam and 30% follow Christianity (Orthodox 20%, Roman Catholic 10%)
CURRENCY Lek = 100 qindars

GEOGRAPHY The Republic of Albania lies in the Balkan peninsula, facing the Adriatic Sea. About 70% of the land is mountainous, but most Albanians live on the coastal lowlands. Albania's coastal areas have a typical Mediterranean climate, with fairly dry, sunny summers and cool, moist winters. The mountains have a severe climate, with heavy snowfalls in winter.

POLITICS & ECONOMY Albania is one of Europe's poorest nations. A former Communist country, Albania adopted a multiparty system in the early 1990s. The transition to democracy and closer integration into Europe has been difficult. The elections of 2005, which resulted in victory for the centre-right Democratic Party over the Socialists, were rated to be short of international standards.

Albania is Europe's poorest country. Agriculture employs about 50% of the workforce. Private ownership has been encouraged since 1991 and, in the 21st century, the economy began to expand, partly as a result of remittances by the million or so Albanians working abroad. Albania has some minerals. Chromite, copper and nickel are exported.

ALGERIA

AREA 2,381,741 sq km [919,590 sq mi]
POPULATION 32,930,000
CAPITAL Algiers
GOVERNMENT Socialist republic
ETHNIC GROUPS Arab-Berber 99%
LANGUAGES Arabic and Berber (official), French
RELIGIONS Sunni Muslim 99%
CURRENCY Algerian dinar = 100 centimes

GEOGRAPHY The People's Democratic Republic of Algeria is Africa's second largest country after Sudan. Most Algerians live in the north, on the fertile coastal plains and hill country bordering the Mediterranean Sea. Four-fifths of Algeria is in the Sahara. The coast has a Mediterranean climate, but the arid Sahara is hot by day and cool at night.

POLITICS & ECONOMY France ruled Algeria from 1830 until 1962, when the socialist FLN (National Liberation Front) formed a one-party government. Following the recognition of opposition parties in 1989, a Muslim group, the FIS (Islamic Salvation Front), won an election in 1991. The FLN cancelled the elections and civil conflict broke out. About 100,000 people were killed in the 1990s. In 1999, following the withdrawal of the other candidates who alleged fraud, Abdelaziz Bouteflika was elected president. Violence was reduced. In 2006, the government began releasing Islamic militants under an amnesty. However, violence returned when suicide bombings occurred in Algiers in April 2007.

Algeria is a developing country, whose chief resources are oil and natural gas. The natural gas reserves are among the world's largest, and gas and oil account for 90% of Algeria's exports. Cement, iron and steel, textiles and vehicles are manufactured.

AMERICAN SAMOA

AREA 199 sq km [77 sq mi]
POPULATION 58,000
CAPITAL Pago Pago

An 'unincorporated territory' of the United States, American Samoa lies in the south-central Pacific Ocean. Two islands are coral islands. The other five are extinct volcanoes. The US took control of the islands between 1900 and 1904. The main industry is tuna canning and fish products dominate the economy.

ANDORRA

AREA 468 sq km [181 sq mi]
POPULATION 71,000
CAPITAL Andorra La Vella

A mini-state situated in the Pyrenees Mountains, Andorra is a co-principality ruled by the 'princes' of Andorra – namely the Bishop of Urgel, Spain, and the government of France. However, Catalan is the official language. The first known ruler of Andorra was the Spanish Count of Urgel in the 9th century. Today, most Andorrans live in the six valleys (the Valls) that drain the River Valira. The chief activity is tourism, including skiing in winter.

ANGOLA

AREA 1,246,700 sq km [481,351 sq mi]
POPULATION 12,127,000
CAPITAL Luanda
GOVERNMENT Multiparty republic
ETHNIC GROUPS Ovimbundu 37%, Kimbundu 25%, Bakongo 13%, others 25%
LANGUAGES Portuguese (official), many others
RELIGIONS Traditional beliefs 47%, Roman Catholic 38%, Protestant 15%
CURRENCY Kwanza = 100 lwei

GEOGRAPHY The Republic of Angola is a large country in south-western Africa. Much of the country is part of the plateau that forms most of southern Africa, with a narrow coastal plain in the west.

Angola has a tropical climate, with temperatures of over 20°C [68°F] throughout the year, though the highest areas are cooler. The coastal regions are dry, but the rainfall increases to the east and north. Tropical savanna covers much of the country, with forests in the south and north-east.

POLITICS & ECONOMY The earliest inhabitants of Angola were probably hunter-gatherers, but Bantu-speaking peoples from the north displaced them in the 13th century. Later, several major kingdoms developed, including the Kong in the north and the Mbundu in the south. From the mid-17th century, the Portuguese controlled the coast from which they exported slaves to the Portuguese territory of Brazil. The Portuguese extended their control inland in the late 19th century and ruled the territory until independence was achieved in 1975, following a guerrilla war that began in the 1960s.

From 1975, rival nationalist groups fought for power. A long-running civil war ensued, which, despite a cease-fire in the mid-1990s, continued until 2002, when Jonas Savimbi, leader of the chief rebel group UNITA, was killed in action and his successors negotiated peace. Following the war, Angola has faced severe economic problems, despite its mineral wealth.

Angola is a developing country, where 70% of the people are poor farmers. The main food crops are cassava and maize. Coffee is exported. Angola has much economic potential. It has oil reserves near Luanda and in the Cabinda enclave, which is separated from Angola by a strip of land belonging to Congo (Dem. Rep.). Oil is the leading export. Angola also produces diamonds and has reserves of copper, manganese and phosphates.

ANGUILLA

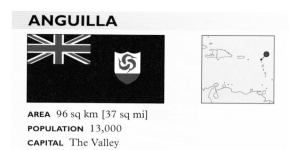

AREA 96 sq km [37 sq mi]
POPULATION 13,000
CAPITAL The Valley

A British colony in 1650, Anguilla was linked with St Kitts (then St Christopher) and Nevis in 1883. St Kitts and Nevis became a British associated state in 1967, but the people of Anguilla voted to become a British dependency (now a British overseas territory) in 1980. The main activity is tourism, although lobster still accounts for half of the island's exports.

ANTIGUA AND BARBUDA

AREA 442 sq km [171 sq mi]
POPULATION 69,000
CAPITAL St John's

Britain made Antigua a colony in 1632. The islands of Barbuda and Redonda were later added to the colony, which was known as Antigua. Britain brought African slaves to the colony and most of the population today is of African descent. Antigua and Barbuda became independent in 1981. Tourism is the main industry.

ARGENTINA

AREA 2,780,400 sq km [1,073,512 sq mi]
POPULATION 39,922,000
CAPITAL Buenos Aires
GOVERNMENT Federal republic
ETHNIC GROUPS European 97%, Mestizo, Amerindian
LANGUAGES Spanish (official)
RELIGIONS Roman Catholic 92%, Protestant 2%, Jewish 2%, others
CURRENCY Argentine peso = 10,000 australs

GEOGRAPHY The Argentine Republic is South America's second largest and the world's eighth largest country. The Andes range in the west contains Mount Aconcagua, the highest peak in the Americas. In the south, the Andes overlook Patagonia, an arid plateau region. In east-central Argentina lies a fertile, well-watered plain called the *pampas*. Temperatures vary from subtropical to temperate.

POLITICS & ECONOMY The earliest people of Argentina were American Indians, but they were relatively few in number. Today, about 86% of the population is of European ancestry. Spain took control of the country in the 16th century and ruled until independence was achieved in 1816. Argentina later suffered from instability and periods of military rule. In 1982, the government, led by the army chief General Leopoldo Galtieri, invaded the Falkland (Malvinas) Islands. But Britain regained the islands later that year and civilian rule was restored in 1983. In 1994, Argentina adopted a new constitution.

According to the World Bank, Argentina is an 'upper-middle-income' developing country. Large

areas are fertile and the main agricultural products are beef, maize and wheat. But about 90% of the people live in cities and towns. Industries include food processing and the manufacture of cars, electrical equipment and textiles. Oil is the chief natural resource. Major exports include meat, wheat, maize, vegetable oils, hides and skins, and wool. In 1991, Argentina, Brazil, Paraguay and Uruguay set up Mercosur, an alliance aimed to create a common market. In 2001, a major economic crisis occurred. The government worked to restore confidence and the economy continued to strengthen between 2003 and 2007.

ARMENIA

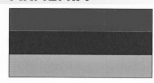

AREA 29,800 sq km [11,506 sq mi]
POPULATION 2,976,000
CAPITAL Yerevan
GOVERNMENT Multiparty republic
ETHNIC GROUPS Armenian 93%, Russian 2%, Azeri 1%, others (mostly Kurds) 4%
LANGUAGES Armenian (official)
RELIGIONS Armenian Apostolic 94%
CURRENCY Dram = 100 couma

GEOGRAPHY The Republic of Armenia is a land-locked country in south-western Asia. Most of Armenia consists of a rugged plateau, criss-crossed by long faults (cracks). Movements along the faults cause earthquakes. The highest point is Mount Aragats, at 4,090 m [13,419 ft] above sea level. Because of the high altitude, winters are severe and summers cool. The rainfall is generally low.

POLITICS & ECONOMY In 1920, Armenia became a Communist republic and, in 1922, it became, with Azerbaijan and Georgia, part of the Transcaucasian Republic within the Soviet Union. But the three territories became separate Soviet Socialist Republics in 1936. After the break-up of the Soviet Union in 1991, Armenia became an independent republic. Fighting broke out over Nagorno-Karabakh, an enclave within Azerbaijan where most people are Armenians. In 1992, Armenia occupied the area between it and the enclave. A cease-fire in 1994 left Armenia in control of about 20% of Azerbaijan's land area. With Azerbaijan and Turkey blocking its borders, Armenia became more dependent on Iran and Georgia for access to the outside world. Talks with Azerbaijan in 2006 again ended in failure.

The World Bank classifies Armenia as a 'lower-middle-income' economy. After 1992, the government encouraged free enterprise, but the conflict with Azerbaijan damaged the economy.

ARUBA

AREA 193 sq km [75 sq mi]
POPULATION 72,000
CAPITAL Oranjestad

Formerly part of the Netherlands Antilles, Aruba became a separate self-governing Dutch territory in 1986. The Netherlands is responsible for Aruba's defence and foreign affairs. Aruba is a hilly island with little agriculture. However, its warm, dry climate and fine beaches make tourism a major activity.

AUSTRALIA

AREA 7,741,220 sq km [2,988,885 sq mi]
POPULATION 20,264,000
CAPITAL Canberra
GOVERNMENT Federal constitutional monarchy
ETHNIC GROUPS Caucasian 92%, Asian 7%, Aboriginal 1%
LANGUAGES English (official)
RELIGIONS Roman Catholic 26%, Anglican 26%, other Christian 24%, non-Christian 24%
CURRENCY Australian dollar = 100 cents

GEOGRAPHY The Commonwealth of Australia, the world's sixth largest country, is also a continent. Australia is the flattest of the continents and the main highland area is in the east. Here the Great Dividing Range separates the eastern coastal plains from the Central Plains. This range extends from the Cape York Peninsula to Victoria in the far south. The longest rivers, the Murray and Darling, drain the south-eastern part of the Central Plains. The Western Plateau makes up two-thirds of Australia. A few mountain ranges break the monotony of the generally flat landscape.

Only 10% of Australia has an average yearly rainfall of more than 1,000 mm [39 in]. These areas include the tropical north, the north-east coast, and the south-east. However, the south-east, including the Murray–Darling basin, which produces about 40% of Australia's farm produce, suffered severe drought between 2001 and 2007. The western interior is arid. Deserts cover about a third of the country.

POLITICS & ECONOMY The Aboriginal people of Australia entered the continent from South-east Asia more than 50,000 years ago. The first European explorers were Dutch in the 17th century, but they did not settle. In 1770, the British Captain Cook explored the east coast and, in 1788, the first British settlement was established for convicts on the site of what is now Sydney. Australia has strong ties with the British Isles. But in the last 50 years, people from other parts of Europe and, most recently, from Asia have settled in Australia. Ties with Britain were also weakened by Britain's membership of the European Union. Many Australians believe that they should become more involved with the nations of eastern Asia and the Americas rather than with Europe. In 1999, Australia held a referendum on whether the country should become a republic or remain a constitutional monarchy. By a majority of about 55 to 45, the country retained its status as a monarchy, with Queen Elizabeth II remaining its titular head of state. In 2003, Australian troops joined the coalition forces in the invasion of Iraq. In 2004, the conservative prime minister John Howard won a fourth successive general election victory.

Australia is a prosperous country. Crops can be grown on only 6% of the land, but dry pasture covers another 58%. Yet the country remains a major producer and exporter of farm products, particularly cattle, wheat and wool. Grapes grown for wine-making are also important. The country is a major producer of minerals, including bauxite, coal, copper, diamonds, gold, iron ore, manganese, nickel, silver, tin, tungsten and zinc. Australia also produces oil and natural gas. Metals, minerals and farm products account for the bulk of exports. Australia's imports are mostly manufactured products, although the country makes many factory products, especially consumer goods. Imports include machinery.

NATIONS OF THE WORLD

AUSTRIA

AREA 83,859 sq km [32,378 sq mi]
POPULATION 8,193,000
CAPITAL Vienna
GOVERNMENT Federal republic
ETHNIC GROUPS Austrian 90%, Croatian, Slovene, others
LANGUAGES German (official)
RELIGIONS Roman Catholic 78%, Protestant 5%, Islam and others 17%
CURRENCY Euro = 100 cents

GEOGRAPHY Austria is a landlocked country in Europe. Northern Austria contains the valley of the River Danube, which flows from Germany to the Black Sea, and the Vienna basin. Southern Austria contains ranges of the Alps, their highest point at Grossglockner, 3,797 m [12,457 ft] above sea level.

The climate is influenced by westerly and easterly winds. Moist westerly winds bring rain and snow, and moderate temperatures. Dry easterly winds bring cold weather in winter and hot weather in summer.

POLITICS & ECONOMY Formerly part of the monarchy of Austria–Hungary, which collapsed in 1918, Austria was annexed by Germany in 1938. After World War II, the Allies partitioned and occupied the country. In 1955, Austria became a neutral federal republic. It joined the European Union on 1 January 1995. In 2004, a Social Democrat, Dr Heinz Fischer, was elected president of Austria. Although the Social Democratic Party had won the most seats in a general election in 2006, it was forced in 2007 to form a coalition with the conservative People's Party.

Austria has a highly developed economy, with plenty of hydroelectric power and some oil, gas and coal reserves. The chief activity is manufacturing metals or metal products. Crops are grown on 18% of the land, and another 24% is pasture. Farming products include dairy and livestock products, barley, potatoes, rye, sugar beet and wheat. Tourism is a major activity.

AZERBAIJAN

AREA 86,600 sq km [33,436 sq mi]
POPULATION 7,962,000
CAPITAL Baku
GOVERNMENT Federal multiparty republic
ETHNIC GROUPS Azeri 90%, Dagestani 3%, Russian, Armenian, others
LANGUAGES Azerbaijani (official), Russian, Armenian
RELIGIONS Islam 93%, Russian Orthodox 2%, Armenian Orthodox 2%
CURRENCY Azerbaijani manat = 100 gopik

GEOGRAPHY The Azerbaijani Republic is a country in the south-west of Asia, facing the Caspian Sea to the east. It includes an area called the Naxçivan Autonomous Republic, which is completely cut off from the rest of Azerbaijan by Armenian territory. The Caucasus Mountains border Russia in the north.

Azerbaijan has hot summers and cool winters. The plains are fairly dry, but the mountains are rainy.

POLITICS & ECONOMY After the Russian Revolution of 1917, attempts were made to form a Transcaucasian Federation made up of Armenia, Azerbaijan and Georgia. When this failed, Azerbaijanis set up an independent state. But Russian forces occupied the area in 1920. In 1922, the Communists set up a Transcaucasian Republic consisting of Armenia, Azerbaijan and Georgia under Russian control. In 1936, the three areas became separate Soviet Socialist Republics within the Soviet Union. In 1991, following the break-up of the Soviet Union, Azerbaijan became an independent nation. After independence, the country's economic progress was slow, partly because of the conflict with Armenia over the enclave of Nagorno-Karabakh, a region in Azerbaijan where the majority of people are Armenians. A cease-fire in 1994 left Armenia in control of about 20% of Azerbaijan's area, including Nagorno-Karabakh. Talks with Armenia in 2006 again failed to break the deadlock.

In the mid-1990s, the World Bank classified Azerbaijan as a 'lower-middle-income' economy. Yet Azerbaijan has enormous oil reserves. In 2006, an oil pipeline came into operation, extending from Baku, through Georgia, to Ceyhan in Turkey. Oil extraction and manufacturing, including oil refining and the production of chemicals, machinery and textiles, are the most valuable economic activities.

BAHAMAS

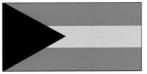

AREA 13,878 sq km [5,358 sq mi]
POPULATION 304,000
CAPITAL Nassau

A coral-limestone archipelago off the coast of Florida, the Bahamas became independent from Britain in 1973, and has since developed strong ties with the United States. Tourism and banking are major activities.

BAHRAIN

AREA 694 sq km [268 sq mi]
POPULATION 699,000
CAPITAL Manama

The Kingdom of Bahrain, an island nation in the Gulf, became independent from the UK in 1971. Oil accounts for about 70% of Bahrain's exports.

BANGLADESH

AREA 143,998 sq km [55,598 sq mi]
POPULATION 147,365,000
CAPITAL Dhaka
GOVERNMENT Multiparty republic
ETHNIC GROUPS Bengali 98%, tribal groups
LANGUAGES Bengali (official), English
RELIGIONS Islam 83%, Hinduism 16%
CURRENCY Taka = 100 paisas

GEOGRAPHY The People's Republic of Bangladesh is one of the world's most densely populated countries. Apart from hilly regions in the far north-east and south-east, most of the land is flat and covered by fertile alluvium spread over the land by the Ganges, Brahmaputra and Meghna rivers. Bangladesh has a tropical monsoon climate. Dry northerly winds blow in winter, but, in summer, moist winds from the south bring monsoon rains. Floods occur when rivers overflow or cyclones (hurricanes) batter the coast, though Bangladesh emerged relatively unscathed by the tsunami in the Indian Ocean in December 2004.

POLITICS & ECONOMY In 1947, British India was partitioned between the mainly Hindu India and the Muslim Pakistan. Pakistan consisted of two parts, West and East Pakistan, which were separated by about 1,600 km [1,000 mi] of Indian territory. Differences developed between West and East Pakistan. In 1971, the East Pakistanis rebelled. After a nine-month civil war, they declared East Pakistan to be a separate nation named Bangladesh.

A famine in 1974 and a coup in 1975 were followed by many upheavals. In 2007, following mass protests, planned elections were postponed. The army intervened, declaring a state of emergency. Some leading politicians were arrested.

Bangladesh is one of the world's poorest countries. Its economy depends mainly on agriculture, which employs over half the population.

BARBADOS

AREA 430 sq km [166 sq mi]
POPULATION 280,000
CAPITAL Bridgetown

Britons settled on Barbados in 1615 and the island became a British colony in 1652. The island became independent as a constitutional monarchy in 1966. However, in 2000, moves began to make the country a republic. The most easterly of the Caribbean islands, Barbados is also one of the region's most prosperous, with agriculture, manufacturing and tourism all making contributions to the economy.

BELARUS

AREA 207,600 sq km [80,154 sq mi]
POPULATION 10,293,000
CAPITAL Minsk
GOVERNMENT Multiparty republic
ETHNIC GROUPS Belarusian 81%, Russian 11%, Polish, Ukrainian, others
LANGUAGES Belarusian, Russian (both official)
RELIGIONS Eastern Orthodox 80%, others 20%
CURRENCY Belarusian rouble = 100 kopecks

GEOGRAPHY The Republic of Belarus is a landlocked country in Eastern Europe. The land is low-lying and mostly flat. In the south, much of the land is marshy and this area contains Europe's largest marsh and peat bog, the Pripet Marshes. The climate is affected by both the moderating influence of the Baltic Sea and continental conditions to the east. The winters are cold and the summers warm.

POLITICS & ECONOMY In 1918, Belarus (White Russia) became an independent republic, but Russia invaded the country and, in 1919, a Communist state was set up. In 1922, Belarus became a founder republic of the Soviet Union. In 1991, Belarus again became an independent republic. As part of the Soviet Union, Belarus prospered, but its economy declined in the 1990s and most economic activities remain under government control. President Alexander Lukashenko, who was elected in flawed elections in 1994, 2001 and 2006, favours union with Russia, but little progress has been achieved. His government's poor record on human rights and suppression of freedom of speech has provoked international criticism.

The World Bank classifies Belarus as an 'upper-middle-income' economy. Its economy is closely tied to that of Russia, especially in its dependence on Russian gas to meet its energy needs.

BELGIUM

AREA 30,528 sq km [11,787 sq mi]
POPULATION 10,379,000
CAPITAL Brussels
GOVERNMENT Federal constitutional monarchy
ETHNIC GROUPS Belgian 89% (Fleming 58%, Walloon 31%), others 11%
LANGUAGES Dutch, French, German (all official)
RELIGIONS Roman Catholic 75%, others 25%
CURRENCY Euro = 100 cents

GEOGRAPHY The Kingdom of Belgium is a densely populated country in western Europe. Behind the coastline on the North Sea, which is 63 km [39 mi] long, lie its coastal plains. Central Belgium consists of low plateaux and the only highland region is the Ardennes in the south-east.

Belgium has a cool, temperate climate. Moist winds from the Atlantic Ocean bring fairly heavy rain, especially in the Ardennes. In January and February much snow falls on the Ardennes.

POLITICS & ECONOMY In 1815, Belgium and the Netherlands united as the 'low countries', but Belgium became independent in 1830. Belgium's economy was weakened by the two World Wars, but, from 1945, the country recovered quickly, first through collaboration with the Netherlands and Luxembourg, which formed a customs union called Benelux, and later through its membership of the European Union.

A central political problem in Belgium has been the tension between the Dutch-speaking Flemings and the French-speaking Walloons. In the 1970s, the government divided the country into three economic regions: Dutch-speaking Flanders, French-speaking Wallonia and bilingual Brussels. In 1993, Belgium adopted a federal constitution, with each region having its own parliament. Elections under this system were held in 1995, 1999 and 2003. The 2003 elections were won comfortably by the ruling centre-left coalition, which was headed by Prime Minister Guy Verhofstadt.

Belgium is a major trading nation, with a highly developed economy. Its main products include chemicals, processed food and steel. The textile industry is important. It has existed since medieval times in the Belgian province of Flanders. The steel industry was once based on Belgium's coalfields, but today the steelworks lie near to ports because they are powered by petroleum. In 2002, the parliament voted to phase out the use of nuclear energy by 2025.

Agriculture employs less than 2% of the people, but Belgian farmers produce most of the food needed by the people. The chief crops are barley and wheat, but the most valuable activities are dairy farming and livestock rearing.

BELIZE

AREA 22,966 sq km [8,867 sq mi]
POPULATION 288,000
CAPITAL Belmopan
GOVERNMENT Constitutional monarchy
ETHNIC GROUPS Mestizo 49%, Creole 25%, Mayan Indian 11%, Garifuna 6%, others 9%
LANGUAGES English (official), Spanish, Creole
RELIGIONS Roman Catholic 50%, Protestant 27%, others
CURRENCY Belizean dollar = 100 cents

GEOGRAPHY Behind the southern coastal plain, the land rises to the Maya Mountains, which reach 1,120 m [3,674 ft] at Victoria Peak. The north is mostly low-lying and swampy. Temperatures are high all year round, while the average annual rainfall ranges from 1,300 mm [51 in] in the north to over 3,800 mm [150 in] in the south. Hurricanes sometimes occur. One in 2001 killed 22 people and left 12,000 homeless.

POLITICS & ECONOMY From 1862, Belize (then called British Honduras) was a British colony. Full independence was achieved in 1981, but Guatemala, which had claimed the area since the early 19th century, opposed Belize's independence and British troops remained to prevent a possible invasion. In 1983, Guatemala reduced its claim to the southern fifth of Belize. Improved relations in the early 1990s led Guatemala to recognize Belize's independence. Hurricanes caused considerable damage in the 1990s and 2000s, but tourism has steadily increased.

The World Bank classifies Belize as a 'lower-middle-income' developing country. Its economy is based on agriculture, and sugar cane is the chief commercial crop and export. Other crops include bananas, beans, citrus fruits, maize and rice. Forestry, fishing and tourism are other important activities.

BENIN

AREA 112,622 sq km [43,483 sq mi]
POPULATION 7,863,000
CAPITAL Porto-Novo
GOVERNMENT Multiparty republic
ETHNIC GROUPS Fon, Adja, Bariba, Yoruba, Fulani
LANGUAGES French (official), Fon, Adja, Yoruba
RELIGIONS Traditional beliefs 50%, Christianity 30%, Islam 20%
CURRENCY CFA franc = 100 centimes

GEOGRAPHY The Republic of Benin is one of Africa's smallest countries. It extends north–south for about 620 km [390 mi]. Lagoons line the short coastline, and the country has no natural harbours.

Benin has a hot, wet climate. The average annual temperature on the coast is about 25°C [77°F], and the average rainfall is about 1,330 mm [52 in]. The inland plains are wetter than the coast.

POLITICS & ECONOMY After slavery was ended in the 19th century, the French began to gain influence in the area. Benin became self-governing in 1958 and fully independent in 1960. After much instability and many changes of government, a military group took over in 1972. The country, renamed Benin in 1975, became a one-party socialist state. Socialism was

abandoned in 1989. Benin then developed into one of Africa's most stable nations. In 2006, Yayi Boni, a former banker, was elected president.

Benin is a developing country. About half of the people live by farming, mainly at subsistence level. Exports include cotton, petroleum and palm products.

BERMUDA

AREA 53 sq km [21 sq mi]
POPULATION 66,000
CAPITAL Hamilton

A group of about 150 small islands situated 920 km [570 miles] east of the United States. British settlers first arrived in 1610 and the islands became a British colony in 1684. Bermuda has a long tradition of self-rule. Tourism is the leading industry.

BHUTAN

AREA 47,000 sq km [18,147 sq mi]
POPULATION 2,280,000
CAPITAL Thimphu
GOVERNMENT Constitutional monarchy
ETHNIC GROUPS Bhutanese 50%, Nepalese 35%
LANGUAGES Dzongkha (official)
RELIGIONS Buddhism 75%, Hinduism 25%
CURRENCY Ngultrum = 100 chetrum

GEOGRAPHY A mountainous, isolated Himalayan country located between India and Tibet. The climate is similar to that of Nepal, being dependent on altitude and affected by monsoonal winds.

POLITICS & ECONOMY The monarch of Bhutan is head of both state and government and this predominantly Buddhist country remains, even in the Asian context, both conservative and poor. About 80% of the population lives in rural areas and is dependent on agriculture. In 2005, the king announced that he would step down in favour of the crown prince in 2008, when the first-ever democratic elections would be held.

BOLIVIA

AREA 1,098,581 sq km [424,162 sq mi]
POPULATION 8,989,000
CAPITAL La Paz (seat of government); Sucre (legal capital/seat of judiciary)
GOVERNMENT Multiparty republic
ETHNIC GROUPS Mestizo 30%, Quechua 30%, Aymara 25%, White 15%
LANGUAGES Spanish, Aymara, Quechua (all official)
RELIGIONS Roman Catholic 95%
CURRENCY Boliviano = 100 centavos

GEOGRAPHY The Republic of Bolivia is a land-locked country which straddles the Andes Mountains in central South America. The Andes rise to a height of 6,520 m [21,399 ft] at Nevado Sajama in the west. About 40% of Bolivians live on a high plateau called the Altiplano in the Andean region, while the sparsely populated east is essentially a vast lowland plain. The Andean peaks are permanently snow-covered, while the eastern plains are hot and humid.

POLITICS & ECONOMY American Indians have lived in Bolivia for at least 10,000 years. The main groups today are the Aymara and Quechua people.

In the last 50 years, Bolivia, an independent country since 1825, has been ruled by a succession of civilian and military governments. Democracy was restored in 1982. Economic problems in the 1980s led to a widening of the gap between rich and poor. In 2005, Evo Morales, a left-wing Aymara farmer, was elected president. In 2006, he nationalized the oil and natural gas industries, and launched a land reform programme aimed at redistributing land considered unproductive or illegally owned to poor peasant communities.

Bolivia is one of South America's poorest countries. Its resources include natural gas, silver, tin and zinc, but the main activity is agriculture. Soybeans and soybean products are major exports.

BOSNIA-HERZEGOVINA

AREA 51,197 sq km [19,767 sq mi]
POPULATION 4,499,000
CAPITAL Sarajevo
GOVERNMENT Federal republic
ETHNIC GROUPS Bosnian 48%, Serb 37%, Croat 14%
LANGUAGES Bosnian, Serbian, Croatian
RELIGIONS Islam 40%, Serbian Orthodox 31%, Roman Catholic 15%, others 14%
CURRENCY Convertible marka = 100 convertible pfenniga

GEOGRAPHY The Republic of Bosnia-Herzegovina is one of the five republics to emerge from the former Federal People's Republic of Yugoslavia. Much of the country is mountainous or hilly, with an arid limestone plateau in the south-west. The River Sava, which forms most of the northern border with Croatia, is a tributary of the River Danube. Because of the country's odd shape, the coastline is limited to a stretch of 20 km [13 mi] on the Adriatic coast.

A Mediterranean climate, with dry, sunny summers and moist, mild winters, prevails only near the coast. Inland, the weather becomes more severe, with hot, dry summers and bitterly cold, snowy winters.

POLITICS & ECONOMY In 1918, Bosnia-Herzegovina became part of the Kingdom of the Serbs, Croats and Slovenes, which was renamed Yugoslavia in 1929. Germany occupied the area during World War II (1939–45). From 1945, Communist governments ruled Yugoslavia as a federation containing six republics, one of which was Bosnia-Herzegovina. In the 1980s, Communist policies proved unsuccessful and differences arose between ethnic groups.

Free elections were held in Bosnia-Herzegovina in 1990 and the non-Communists won a majority. A Muslim, Alija Izetbegovic, was elected president. In 1991, Croatia and Slovenia, other parts of the former Yugoslavia, declared themselves independent. In 1992, Bosnia-Herzegovina held a vote on independence. Most Bosnian Serbs boycotted the vote, while the Muslims and Bosnian Croats voted in favour. Many Bosnian Serbs, opposed to independence, started a war against the non-Serbs. They soon occupied more than two-thirds of the land. The Bosnian Serbs were accused of 'ethnic cleansing' – that is, the killing or expulsion of other ethnic groups from Serb-occupied areas. The war was later extended when Croat forces seized other parts of the country.

In 1995, the warring parties agreed to a solution to the conflict. This involved keeping the present boundaries of Bosnia-Herzegovina, but dividing it into two self-governing provinces, one Bosnian Serb and the other Muslim-Croat, under a central unified government. With the help of a NATO-led force, it soon became stable. In 2005, the government announced reforms aimed at paving the way for the country's future entry into NATO and the European Union. In 2007, following elections in 2006, the European Union announced a cut in its peace-keeping force.

The economy of Bosnia-Herzegovina, the least developed of the six republics of the former Yugoslavia apart from Macedonia, was shattered by the war in the early 1990s. Before the war, manufactures were the main exports, including electrical equipment, machinery and transport equipment, and textiles. Farm products include fruits, maize, tobacco, vegetables and wheat, but the country has to import food.

BOTSWANA

AREA 581,730 sq km [224,606 sq mi]
POPULATION 1,640,000
CAPITAL Gaborone
GOVERNMENT Multiparty republic
ETHNIC GROUPS Tswana (or Setswana) 79%, Kalanga 11%, Basarwa 3%, others
LANGUAGES English (official), Setswana
RELIGIONS Traditional beliefs 85%, Christianity 15%
CURRENCY Pula = 100 thebe

GEOGRAPHY The Republic of Botswana is a landlocked country in southern Africa. The Kalahari, a semi-desert area covered mostly by grasses and thorn scrub, covers much of the country. Most of the south has no permanent streams, but large depressions in the north are inland drainage basins. In one of them, the Okavango River, which rises in Angola, forms a large, swampy delta.

Temperatures are high in the summer months (October to April), but the winter months are much cooler. In winter, night-time temperatures sometimes drop below freezing point. The average annual rainfall ranges from over 400 mm [16 in] in the east to less than 200 mm [8 in] in the south-west.

POLITICS & ECONOMY Around 20,000 years ago, the area that is now Botswana was occupied by nomadic Khoisan people. Some of them, the Khoikhoi, developed a cattle-rearing culture, while others, the San (also called Bushmen) were nomadic hunters and gatherers. During the first millennium AD, Bantu-speaking peoples moved into the area, displacing the Khoisan and introducing a farming culture. Today, the main group of people in Botswana are Bantu-speaking Tswana, though there is a small San minority. The Khoikhoi are now extinct as a separate ethnic group.

Britain ruled the area as the Bechuanaland Protectorate between 1885 and 1966, when the country became independent and was renamed Botswana. Since then, the country has been a stable, multiparty democracy. But in the early 21st century, health officials reported that 25% of the people of Botswana were infected with HIV/AIDS. In 2006, fees for secondary education in state schools had to be restored because of the mounting cost of health services.

In 1966, Botswana depended on meat and live cattle for its exports. But the discovery of minerals, including coal, cobalt, copper, diamonds and nickel, boosted the economy. Agriculture now employs about 10% of the people and industries process farm products.

BRAZIL

AREA 8,514,215 sq km [3,287,338 sq mi]
POPULATION 188,078,000
CAPITAL Brasília
GOVERNMENT Federal republic
ETHNIC GROUPS White 55%, Mulatto 38%, Black 6%, others 1%
LANGUAGES Portuguese (official)
RELIGIONS Roman Catholic 80%
CURRENCY Real = 100 centavos

GEOGRAPHY The Federative Republic of Brazil is the world's fifth largest country. It contains three main regions. The Amazon basin in the north covers more than half of Brazil. The Amazon, the world's second longest river, has a far greater volume than any other river. The second region, the north-east, consists of a coastal plain and the *sertão*, which is the name for the inland plateaux and hill country. The main river in this region is the São Francisco. The third region is made up of the plateaux in the south-east. This region, which covers about a quarter of the country, is the most developed and densely populated part of Brazil. Its main river is the Paraná, which flows south through Argentina.

Manaus has high temperatures all through the year. The rainfall is heavy, though the period from June to September is drier than the rest of the year. The capital, Brasília, and the city Rio de Janeiro also have tropical climates, with much more marked dry seasons than Manaus. The far south has a temperate climate. The north-eastern interior is the driest region, with an average annual rainfall of only 250 mm [10 in] in places. The rainfall is also unreliable and severe droughts are common in this region.

POLITICS & ECONOMY The Portuguese explorer Pedro Alvarez Cabral claimed Brazil for Portugal in 1500. With Spain occupied in western South America, the Portuguese began to develop their colony, which was more than 90 times as big as Portugal. To do this, they enslaved many local Amerindian people and introduced about 4 million African slaves. Brazil declared itself an independent empire in 1822 and a republic in 1889. From the 1930s, Brazil faced periods of military rule and widespread corruption. Civilian rule was restored in 1985, and a new constitution was adopted in 1988.

The United Nations has described Brazil as a 'Rapidly Industrializing Country', or RIC. Its total volume of production is one of the largest in the world. But many people, including poor farmers and residents of the *favelas* (city slums), lived in poverty. Poverty, inflation and unemployment led to the election as president of Luiz Inácio Lula da Silva (popularly known as 'Lula') in 2002. Despite revelations about political corruption in his government, Lula was re-elected president in 2006.

By the early 1990s, industry was the chief economic activity. Brazil is among the world's top producers of bauxite, chrome, gold, iron ore, manganese and tin. Major manufacturing products include aircraft, cars, chemicals, iron and steel, paper, textiles, and processed food, including raw sugar.

Brazil is one of the world's leading farming countries and agriculture employs 18% of the people. Coffee is a major export. Other leading products include bananas, citrus fruits, cocoa, maize, rice, soybeans and sugar cane. Brazil is also the top producer of eggs, meat and milk in South America. Forestry is a major industry, though many people fear that the exploitation of the rainforests, with 1.5% to 4% of Brazil's forest being destroyed every year, is a disaster for the entire world.

BRUNEI

AREA 5,765 sq km [2,226 sq mi]
POPULATION 379,000
CAPITAL Bandar Seri Begawan

Brunei was a major trading centre on the north coast of Borneo around 1,400 years ago. The first sultan took power in the 13th century, but Britain took over the area in the 19th century. Brunei became a British protectorate in 1888 and it declined in importance. But the discovery of oil in 1929 revived the economy and Brunei became independent on 1 January 1984. The modern Islamic Republic of Brunei is prosperous, the result of its abundant oil and natural gas, and the Sultan is said to be one of the world's richest men. The climate is tropical and rainforests cover large areas.

BULGARIA

AREA 110,912 sq km [42,823 sq mi]
POPULATION 7,385,000
CAPITAL Sofia
GOVERNMENT Multiparty republic
ETHNIC GROUPS Bulgarian 84%, Turkish 9%, Gypsy 5%, Macedonian, Armenian, others
LANGUAGES Bulgarian (official), Turkish
RELIGIONS Bulgarian Orthodox 83%, Islam 12%, Roman Catholic 2%, others
CURRENCY Lev = 100 stotinki

GEOGRAPHY The Republic of Bulgaria is a country in the Balkan peninsula, facing the Black Sea in the east. The heart of Bulgaria is mountainous. The main ranges are the Balkan Mountains in the centre and the Rhodope (or Rhodopi) Mountains in the south.

Summers are hot and winters are cold, though seldom severe. The rainfall is moderate.
POLITICS & ECONOMY Ottoman Turks ruled Bulgaria from 1396 and ethnic Turks still form a sizeable minority in the country. In 1879, Bulgaria became a monarchy, and in 1908 it became fully independent. Bulgaria was an ally of Germany in World War I (1914–18) and again in World War II (1939–45). In 1944, Soviet troops invaded Bulgaria and, after the war, the monarchy was abolished and the country became a Communist ally of the Soviet Union. In the late 1980s, reforms in the Soviet Union led Bulgaria's government to introduce a multiparty system in 1990. A non-Communist government was elected in 1991, the first free elections in 44 years. In 2001, a coalition led by the former King Siméon, who had left Bulgaria in 1948, won the elections. Siméon served as prime minister until 2005. Bulgaria became a member of NATO in 2004 and a member of the European Union on 1 January 2007.

According to the World Bank, Bulgaria in the 1990s was a 'lower-middle-income' developing country. Bulgaria has some deposits of minerals, including brown coal, manganese and iron ore. But manufacturing is the leading economic activity, though problems arose in the early 1990s because much of the industrial technology was outdated. The main products are chemicals, processed foods, metal products, machinery and textiles. Manufactures are Bulgaria's leading exports.

BURKINA FASO

AREA 274,000 sq km [105,791 sq mi]
POPULATION 13,903,000
CAPITAL Ouagadougou
GOVERNMENT Multiparty republic
ETHNIC GROUPS Mossi 40%, Gurunsi, Senufo, Lobi, Bobo, Mande, Fulani
LANGUAGES French (official), Mossi, Fulani
RELIGIONS Islam 50%, traditional beliefs 40%, Christianity 10%
CURRENCY CFA franc = 100 centimes

GEOGRAPHY The Democratic People's Republic of Burkina Faso is a landlocked country in West Africa. It consists of a plateau, between about 300 m and 700 m [650 ft to 2,300 ft] above sea level.

The capital city, Ouagadougou, in central Burkina Faso, has high temperatures throughout the year. Most of the rain falls between May and September, but the rainfall is erratic and droughts are common.
POLITICS & ECONOMY The people of Burkina Faso are divided into two main groups. The Voltaic group includes the Mossi, who form the largest single group, and the Bobo. The French conquered the Mossi capital of Ouagadougou in 1897 and they made the area a protectorate. In 1919, the area became a French colony called Upper Volta. After independence in 1960, Upper Volta became a one-party state. But it was unstable – military groups seized power several times and political killings took place. In 1984, the country's name was changed to Burkina Faso. In 1991, 1998 and 2005, the former military leader, Blaise Compaoré, was elected president, but the military continued to have influence in government.

Burkina Faso is one of the world's 20 poorest countries and is highly dependent on foreign aid. The main food crops are beans, maize, millet, rice and sorghum. Cotton, groundnuts and shea nuts are grown for export. Cattle are also exported.

The country has few resources and manufacturing is on a small scale. There are some deposits of manganese, zinc, lead and nickel in the north of the country, but exploitation awaits improvements to the transport system there. Many young men seek jobs abroad in Ghana and Ivory Coast. The money they send home is important to the country's economy.

BURMA (MYANMAR)

AREA 676,578 sq km [261,227 sq mi]
POPULATION 47,383,000
CAPITAL Rangoon (Yangon); Naypyidaw (administrative capital)
GOVERNMENT Military regime
ETHNIC GROUPS Burman 68%, Shan 9%, Karen 7%, Rakhine 4%, Chinese, Indian, Mon
LANGUAGES Burmese (official); minority ethnic groups have their own languages
RELIGIONS Buddhism 89%, Christianity, Islam
CURRENCY Kyat = 100 pyas

GEOGRAPHY The Union of Burma is now officially known as the Union of Myanmar; its name was changed in 1989. Mountains border the country in the east and west, with the highest mountains in the north. Burma's highest mountain is Hkakabo Razi, which is 5,881 m [19,294 ft] high. Between these ranges is central Burma, which contains the fertile valleys of the Irrawaddy and Sittang rivers. The Irrawaddy delta on the Bay of Bengal is one of the world's leading rice-growing areas. Burma also includes the long Tenasserim coast in the south-east.

Burma has a tropical monsoon climate, with three seasons. The rainy season runs from late May to mid-October. A cool, dry season follows, between late October and the middle part of February. The hot season lasts from late February to mid-May, though temperatures remain high during the humid rainy season.
POLITICS & ECONOMY Many groups settled in Burma in ancient times. Some, called the hill peoples, live in remote mountain areas where they have retained their own cultures. The ancestors of the country's main ethnic group today, the Burmese, arrived in the 9th century AD.

Britain conquered Burma in the 19th century and made it a province of British India. But, in 1937, the British granted Burma limited self-government. Japan conquered Burma in 1942, but the Japanese were driven out in 1945. Burma became a fully independent country in 1948.

Revolts by Communists and various hill people led to instability in the 1950s. In 1962, Burma became a military dictatorship and, in 1974, a one-party state. Attempts to control minority liberation movements and the opium trade led to repressive rule. The National League for Democracy led by Aung San Suu Kyi won the elections in 1990, but the military continued their repressive rule, earning Burma the reputation for having one of the world's worst human rights record. In 2004, a United Nations report criticized the regime for holding more than 1,800 political detainees and for its failure to release opposition leader Aung San Suu Kyi from house arrest. In 2005, the government announced that a new administrative capital, called Naypyidaw ('Abode of Kings'), was being built in the north.

Agriculture is the main activity, employing 66% of the people. The chief crop is rice. Maize, pulses, oilseeds and sugar cane are other major products. Forestry is important. Teak and rice together make up about two-thirds of the total value of the exports. Burma has many mineral resources, though they are mostly undeveloped, but the country is famous for its precious stones, especially rubies. Manufacturing is mostly on a small scale.

BURUNDI

AREA 27,834 sq km [10,747 sq mi]
POPULATION 8,090,000
CAPITAL Bujumbura
GOVERNMENT Republic
ETHNIC GROUPS Hutu 85%, Tutsi 14%, Twa (Pygmy) 1%
LANGUAGES French and Kirundi (both official)
RELIGIONS Roman Catholic 62%, traditional beliefs 23%, Islam 10%, Protestant 5%
CURRENCY Burundi franc = 100 centimes

GEOGRAPHY The Republic of Burundi is the fifth smallest country in mainland Africa. It is also the second most densely populated after its northern neighbour, Rwanda. Part of the Great African Rift Valley, which runs throughout eastern Africa into south-western Asia, lies in western Burundi. It includes part of Lake Tanganyika.

NATIONS OF THE WORLD

The capital city, Bujumbura, on the shores of Lake Tanganyika, has a warm climate. A dry season runs from June to September, but the rest of the year is rainy. The highlands are cooler and wetter, though the rainfall decreases to the east.

POLITICS & ECONOMY The Twa, a pygmy people, were the first known inhabitants of Burundi. About 1,000 years ago, the Hutu, a people who speak a Bantu language, gradually began to settle the area, pushing the Twa into remote areas.

From the 15th century, the Tutsi, a cattle-owning people from the north-east, gradually took over the country. The Hutu, although greatly outnumbering the Tutsi, were forced to serve the Tutsi overlords.

Germany conquered the area that is now Burundi and Rwanda in the late 1890s. The area, called Ruanda-Urundi, was taken by Belgium during World War I (1914–18). In 1961, the people of Urundi voted to become a monarchy, while the people of Ruanda voted to become a republic. The two territories became fully independent as Burundi and Rwanda in 1962. After 1962, the rivalries between the Hutu and Tutsi led to periodic outbreaks of fighting. The Tutsi monarchy was ended in 1966 and Burundi became a republic. Instability continued, with massacres of thousands of people in ethnic violence. In 2001, a power-sharing agreement was reached, though conflict continued in some areas. Parliamentary and presidential elections were held in 2005 under a new constitution.

Burundi is one of the world's ten poorest countries. About 93% of the people are farmers who live mostly at subsistence level. The main food crops are beans, cassava, maize and sweet potatoes. Cattle, goats and sheep are raised and fishing is also important. However, Burundi has to import food.

CAMBODIA

AREA 181,035 sq km [69,898 sq mi]
POPULATION 13,881,000
CAPITAL Phnom Penh
GOVERNMENT Constitutional monarchy
ETHNIC GROUPS Khmer 90%, Vietnamese 5%, Chinese 1%, others
LANGUAGES Khmer (official), French, English
RELIGIONS Buddhism 95%, others 5%
CURRENCY Riel = 100 sen

GEOGRAPHY The Kingdom of Cambodia is a country in South-east Asia. Low mountains border the country except in the south-east. But most of Cambodia consists of plains drained by the River Mekong, which enters Cambodia from Laos in the north and exits through Vietnam in the south-east. The north-west contains Tonlé Sap (or Great Lake). In the dry season, this lake drains into the River Mekong. But in the wet season, the level of the Mekong rises and water flows in the opposite direction from the river into Tonlé Sap – the lake then becomes the largest freshwater lake in Asia.

Cambodia has a tropical monsoon climate, with high temperatures all through the year. The dry season, when winds blow from the north or north-east, runs from November to April. During the rainy season, from May to October, moist winds blow from the south and south-east. The high humidity and heat often make conditions unpleasant. The rainfall is heaviest near the coast, and rather lower inland.

POLITICS & ECONOMY From 802 to 1432, the Khmer people ruled a great empire, which reached its peak in the 12th century. The Khmer capital was at Angkor. The Hindu stone temples built there and at nearby Angkor Wat form the world's largest group of religious buildings. France ruled the country between 1863 and 1954, when the country became an independent monarchy. But the monarchy was abolished in 1970 and Cambodia became a republic.

In 1970, US and South Vietnamese troops entered Cambodia but left after destroying North Vietnamese Communist camps in the east. The country became involved in the Vietnamese War, and then in a civil war as Cambodian Communists of the Khmer Rouge organization fought for power. The Khmer Rouge took over Cambodia in 1975 and launched a reign of terror in which between 1 million and 2.5 million people were killed. In 1979, Vietnamese and Cambodian troops overthrew the Khmer Rouge government. But fighting continued between several factions. Vietnam withdrew in 1989, and in 1991 Prince Sihanouk was recognized as head of state. Elections were held in May 1993, and in September 1993 the monarchy was restored, with Sihanouk as king. Elections were held in 1998 and 2003. In 2001, the government set up courts to try leaders of the Khmer Rouge. In 2004, Sihanouk abdicated because of ill health and his son, Prince Norodom Sihamoni, succeeded him.

Cambodia is a poor country whose economy has been wrecked by war. Until the 1970s, the country's farmers produced most of the food needed by the people. But by 1986, it was only able to supply 80% of its needs. Recovery was slow. Farming is still the main activity. Rice, rubber and maize are important. Manufacturing is on a small scale, but the discovery of oil reserves and an increase in tourism have recently boosted the economy.

CAMEROON

AREA 475,442 sq km [183,568 sq mi]
POPULATION 17,341,000
CAPITAL Yaoundé
GOVERNMENT Multiparty republic
ETHNIC GROUPS Cameroon Highlanders 31%, Bantu 27%, Kirdi 11%, Fulani 10%, others
LANGUAGES French and English (both official), many others
RELIGIONS Christianity 40%, traditional beliefs 40%, Islam 20%
CURRENCY CFA franc = 100 centimes

GEOGRAPHY The Republic of Cameroon in West Africa derived its name from the Portuguese word *camarões*, or prawns. This name was used by Portuguese explorers who fished for prawns along the coast. Behind the narrow coastal plains on the Gulf of Guinea, the land rises to a series of plateaux, with a mountainous region in the south-west where the volcano Mount Cameroun is situated. In the north, the land slopes down towards the Lake Chad basin.

The rainfall is heavy, especially in the highlands. The rainiest months near the coast are June to September. The rainfall decreases to the north and the far north has a hot, dry climate. Temperatures are high on the coast, whereas the inland plateaux are cooler.

POLITICS & ECONOMY Germany lost Cameroon during World War I (1914–18). The country was then divided into two parts, one ruled by Britain and the other by France. In 1960, French Cameroon became the independent Cameroon Republic. In 1961, after a vote in British Cameroon, part of the territory joined the Cameroon Republic to become the Federal Republic of Cameroon – the other part joined Nigeria. In 1972, Cameroon became a unitary state called the United Republic of Cameroon. It adopted the name Republic of Cameroon in 1984, but the country had two official languages. In 2002, the International Court of Justice gave Cameroon sovereignty over the oil-rich Bakassi peninsula. Nigeria finally withdrew in 2006, although it will keep control of the southern part of the peninsula until 2008.

Like most countries in tropical Africa, Cameroon's economy is based on agriculture, which employs more than half of the people. Food crops include maize, millet, sweet potatoes and yams, and coffee and cocoa are exported. Cameroon has some oil, which has become the chief export, and bauxite. There are few manufactures, but the mineral exports and self-sufficiency in food production make it one of tropical Africa's better-off countries.

CANADA

AREA 9,970,610 sq km [3,849,653 sq mi]
POPULATION 33,099,000
CAPITAL Ottawa
GOVERNMENT Federal multiparty constitutional monarchy
ETHNIC GROUPS British origin 28%, French origin 23%, other European 15%, Amerindian/Inuit 2%, others
LANGUAGES English and French (both official)
RELIGIONS Roman Catholic 46%, Protestant 36%, Judaism, Islam, Hinduism
CURRENCY Canadian dollar = 100 cents

GEOGRAPHY Canada is the world's second largest country after Russia. It is thinly populated, however, with much of the land too cold or too mountainous for human settlement. Most Canadians live within 300 km [186 mi] of the southern border.

Western Canada is rugged. It includes the Pacific ranges and the mighty Rocky Mountains. East of the Rockies are the interior plains. In the north lie the bleak Arctic islands, while to the south lie the densely populated lowlands around lakes Erie and Ontario and in the St Lawrence River valley.

Canada has a cold climate. In winter, temperatures fall below freezing point throughout most of Canada. But the south-western coast has a relatively mild climate. Along the Arctic Circle, mean temperatures are below freezing for seven months a year.

Western and south-eastern Canada experience high rainfall, but the prairies are dry with 250 mm to 500 mm [10 in to 20 in] of rain every year.

POLITICS & ECONOMY Canada's first people, the ancestors of the Native Americans, or Indians, arrived in North America from Asia around 40,000 years ago. Later arrivals were the Inuit (Eskimos), who also came from Asia. Europeans reached the Canadian coast in 1497 and a race began between Britain and France for control of the territory.

France gained an initial advantage, and the French founded Québec in 1608. But the British later occupied eastern Canada. In 1867, Britain passed the British North America Act, which set up the Dominion of Canada, which was made up of Québec, Ontario, Nova Scotia and New Brunswick. Other areas were added, the last being Newfoundland in 1949. Canada fought alongside Britain in both World Wars and many Canadians feel close ties with Britain. Canada is a constitutional monarchy, and the British monarch is Canada's head of state.

Rivalries between French- and English-speaking Canadians continue. In 1995, Québeckers voted narrowly against a move to make Québec a sovereign state. In 2006, the national parliament voted to recognize Québec as a nation within a united Canada – a symbolic act of reconciliation.

Another major issue concerns the rights of Aboriginal minorities. In 1999, Canada created the territory of Nunavut for the Inuit population. Nunavut covers about 64% of what was formerly the eastern part of the Northwest Territories. In 2006, the Conservative Party led by Stephen Harper was returned to power, ending 12 years of Liberal Party rule.

Canada is a highly developed and prosperous country. Although farmland covers only 8% of the country, Canadian farms are highly productive. Canada is one of the world's leading producers of barley, wheat, meat and milk. Forestry and fishing are other important industries. It is rich in natural resources, especially oil and natural gas. Canada exports minerals, including copper, gold, iron ore, uranium and zinc. Manufacturing is important, mainly in the cities where 80% of the people live. Canada processes farm and mineral products. It also produces cars, chemicals, electronic goods, machinery, paper and timber products.

CAPE VERDE

AREA 4,033 sq km [1,557 sq mi]
POPULATION 421,000
CAPITAL Praia

Cape Verde consists of ten large and five small islands, and is situated 560 km [350 mi] west of Dakar in Senegal. The islands have a tropical climate, with high temperatures throughout the year.

Portuguese explorers discovered the islands in the 15th century. They became an assembly point for African slaves, but the abolition of slavery in the 19th century, combined with severe droughts, ended the islands' prosperity. In 1951, Cape Verde became an overseas province of Portugal, but it became a fully independent republic in 1975. The World Bank rates Cape Verde as a 'low-income' developing country. Only 10% to 15% of the land is suitable for farming.

CAYMAN ISLANDS

AREA 264 sq km [102 sq mi]
POPULATION 45,000
CAPITAL George Town

The Cayman Islands are an overseas territory of the UK. There are three low-lying islands: Grand Cayman, Little Cayman and Cayman Brac. Discovered by Christopher Columbus in 1503, they were recognized as British possessions in 1670. The islands were governed as part of Jamaica from 1863, but they became a separate dependency when Jamaica became independent in 1962. Financial services are the main economic activity and the islands offer a tax haven to many companies and banks. Farm production is limited and food is imported.

CENTRAL AFRICAN REPUBLIC

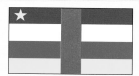

AREA 622,984 sq km [240,534 sq mi]
POPULATION 4,303,000
CAPITAL Bangui
GOVERNMENT Multiparty republic
ETHNIC GROUPS Baya 33%, Banda 27%, Mandjia 13%, Sara 10%, Mboum 7%, Mbaka 4%, others
LANGUAGES French (official), Sangho
RELIGIONS Traditional beliefs 35%, Protestant 25%, Roman Catholic 25%, Islam 15%
CURRENCY CFA franc = 100 centimes

GEOGRAPHY The Central African Republic consists mostly of a plateau lying between about 600 m and 800 m [1,970 ft to 2,620 ft] above sea level. The Ubangi drains the south, while the Chari (or Shari) River flows from the north to the Lake Chad basin.

The climate is warm throughout the year, while the annual average rainfall in the capital Bangui totals 1,574 mm [62 in]. The north is drier, with an average annual rainfall of about 800 mm [31 in].

POLITICS & ECONOMY France set up an outpost at Bangui in 1899 and ruled the country as a colony from 1894. Known as Ubangi-Shari, the country was ruled by France as part of French Equatorial Africa until it gained independence in 1960.

Central African Republic became a one-party state in 1962, but army officers seized power in 1966. The head of the army, Jean-Bedel Bokassa, made himself emperor in 1976. The country was renamed the Central African Empire, but after a brutal reign, the tyrannical Bokassa was overthrown in a military coup in 1979. The country again became a republic.

The country adopted a new constitution in 1991, but a coup in 2003 brought General François Bozize to power. Bozize was elected president in 2005, but rebel activities in 2006–7 led to the movement of thousands of refugees to Chad and Cameroon.

The World Bank classifies Central African Republic as a 'low-income' developing country. Over 80% of the people are farmers, mostly at subsistence level. Bananas, maize, manioc, millet and yams are food crops, while cotton, timber and tobacco are exported. The country depends on aid, especially from France.

CHAD

AREA 1,284,000 sq km [495,752 sq mi]
POPULATION 9,944,000
CAPITAL Ndjamena
GOVERNMENT Multiparty republic
ETHNIC GROUPS 200 distinct groups: mostly Muslim in the north and centre; mostly Christian or animist in the south
LANGUAGES French and Arabic (both official), many others
RELIGIONS Islam 51%, Christianity 35%, animist 7%
CURRENCY CFA franc = 100 centimes

GEOGRAPHY The Republic of Chad is a landlocked country in north-central Africa. It is Africa's fifth largest country. Ndjamena in central Chad has a hot, tropical climate, with a dry season from November to April. The south of the country is wetter, with an average yearly rainfall of around 1,000 mm [39 in].

The hot desert in the north has an average yearly rainfall of less than 130 mm [5 in].

POLITICS & ECONOMY Chad straddles two worlds. Muslim Arabs and Berbers live in the north, while black Africans, followers of traditional beliefs or Christianity, live in the south.

France made Chad a colony in 1902. The country became independent in 1960, but the 1970s were marked by ethnic conflict that led to civil wars, coups and conflict with Libya, which supported rebel factions. Chad and Libya agreed a truce in 1987 and, in 1994, the International Court of Justice ruled against Libya's claim on the Aozou Strip. From 2004, Chad forces clashed with pro-Sudanese militias as the conflict in Sudan's Darfur province spilled over the border. In 2006, an attempt to overthrow the government of President Idriss Déby failed.

Hit by drought and civil war, Chad is one of the world's poorest countries. Farming, fishing and livestock raising employ 83% of the people. Groundnuts, millet, rice and sorghum are major food crops in the south, but the chief export crop is cotton. Chad has few manufacturing industries, but its oil reserves hold out hope for development in the 21st century.

CHILE

AREA 756,626 sq km [292,133 sq mi]
POPULATION 16,134,000
CAPITAL Santiago
GOVERNMENT Multiparty republic
ETHNIC GROUPS Mestizo 95%, Amerindian 3%
LANGUAGES Spanish (official)
RELIGIONS Roman Catholic 89%, Protestant 11%
CURRENCY Chilean peso = 100 centavos

GEOGRAPHY The Republic of Chile stretches about 4,260 km [2,650 mi] from north to south, although the maximum east–west distance is only about 430 km [267 mi]. The high Andes Mountains form Chile's eastern borders with Argentina and Bolivia. To the west are basins and valleys, with coastal uplands overlooking the shore. Most people live in the central valley, where Santiago is situated.

Santiago has a Mediterranean climate, with hot, dry summers and mild, moist winters. The Atacama Desert in the north is one of the world's driest places, while southern Chile is cold and stormy.

POLITICS & ECONOMY Amerindian people reached the southern tip of South America 8,000 years ago. In 1520, Portuguese navigator Ferdinand Magellan was the first European to sight Chile. The country became a Spanish colony in the 1540s. Chile became independent in 1818. During a war (1879–83), it gained mineral-rich areas from Peru and Bolivia.

In 1970, Salvador Allende became the first Communist leader to be elected democratically. He was overthrown in 1973 by army officers, who were supported by the CIA. General Augusto Pinochet then ruled as a dictator. A new constitution was introduced in 1981 and elections were held in 1989. Attempts to prosecute General Pinochet continued in the 1990s and 2000s, but he died in December 2006 before being brought to trial. Earlier in 2006, Michelle Bachelet, a centre-left, former torture victim under the Pinochet regime, was elected president of Chile.

The World Bank classifies Chile as a 'lower-middle-income' developing country. Copper is mined and minerals are exported. The main activity is manufacturing, including processed foods, metals, iron and steel, transport equipment and textiles.

NATIONS OF THE WORLD

CHINA

AREA 9,596,961 sq km [3,705,387 sq mi]
POPULATION 1,313,974,000
CAPITAL Beijing
GOVERNMENT Single-party Communist republic
ETHNIC GROUPS Han Chinese 92%, many others
LANGUAGES Mandarin Chinese (official)
RELIGIONS Atheist (official)
CURRENCY Renminbi yuan = 10 jiao = 100 fen

GEOGRAPHY The People's Republic of China is the world's third largest country. Most people live in the east – on the coastal plains or in the fertile valleys of the Huang He (Hwang Ho or Yellow River), the Chang Jiang (Yangtze Kiang), which is Asia's longest river at 6,380 km [3,960 mi], and the Xi Jiang (Si Kiang).

Western China is thinly populated. It includes the bleak Tibetan plateau which is bounded by the Himalaya, the world's highest mountain range. Other ranges include the Kunlun Shan, the Altun Shan and the Tian Shan. Deserts include the Gobi Desert along the Mongolian border and the Taklimakan Desert in the far west.

Beijing in north-eastern China has cold winters and warm summers, with a moderate rainfall. Shanghai, in the east-central region of China, has milder winters and more rain. The south-east has a wet, subtropical climate. In the west, the climate is severe. Lhasa has very cold winters and a low rainfall.

POLITICS & ECONOMY China is one of the world's oldest civilizations, going back 3,500 years. Under the Han dynasty (202 BC to AD 220), the Chinese empire was as large as the Roman empire. Mongols conquered China in the 13th century, but Chinese rule was restored in 1368. The Manchu people of Mongolia ruled the country from 1644 to 1912, when the country became a republic.

War with Japan (1937–45) was followed by civil war between the nationalists and the Communists. The Communists triumphed in 1949, setting up the People's Republic of China. In the 1980s, following the death of the revolutionary leader Mao Zedong (Mao Tse-tung) in 1976, China encouraged formerly forbidden policies, namely private enterprise and foreign investment. But the Communist leaders have not permitted political freedom. Opponents are still harshly treated, while attempts to negotiate some degree of autonomy for Tibet have been rejected.

China's economy has expanded greatly since the 1970s, with many Communist policies being abandoned. Foreign investors have helped to set up many new industries in the east. Between 1989 and 2006, the economy grew by an average of more than 9% per year. By 2006, China had the world's fourth largest economy. Only the United States, Japan and Germany had larger GDPs. In 2005–6, China expanded its economic ties with Africa.

China has benefited from the return of Hong Kong in 1997 and its admission to the World Trade Organization in 2001. China would also like to regain the island of Taiwan, which it regards as a renegade province. This seems unlikely in the near future, although its economy is closely tied to the mainland. In 2006, the 56-year ban on direct passenger flights from mainland China to Taiwan was ended.

Despite its recent success, China remains a poor country. In the early 2000s, agriculture still employed 43% of the workforce, although only 10% of the land is farmed. In 2006, the government announced plans

to help the 800 million people living in the countryside catch up economically with people in the cities.

Farm products include rice, sweet potatoes, tea and wheat, and many fruits and vegetables. Livestock farming is also important. Pork is popular and China has more than a third of the world's pigs.

Resources include coal, iron ore and other metals. Leading manufactures include cement, chemicals, fertilizers, machinery, telecommunications and recording equipment, and textiles. The recent shift in emphasis from heavy industry to the production of consumer goods has enabled China to become a major player in world trade.

COLOMBIA

AREA 1,138,914 sq km [439,735 sq mi]
POPULATION 43,593,000
CAPITAL Bogotá
GOVERNMENT Multiparty republic
ETHNIC GROUPS Mestizo 58%, White 20%, Mulatto 14%, Black 4%
LANGUAGES Spanish (official)
RELIGIONS Roman Catholic 90%
CURRENCY Colombian peso = 100 centavos

GEOGRAPHY The Republic of Colombia, in northeastern South America, is the only country in the continent to have coastlines on both the Pacific and the Caribbean Sea. Colombia also contains the northernmost ranges of the Andes Mountains.

There is a tropical climate in the lowlands. But the altitude greatly affects the climate of the Andes. The capital, Bogotá, which stands on a plateau in the eastern Andes at about 2,800 m [9,200 ft] above sea level, has mild temperatures throughout the year. The rainfall is heavy, especially on the Pacific coast.

POLITICS & ECONOMY Amerindian people have lived in Colombia for thousands of years. But today, only a small proportion of the people are of unmixed Amerindian ancestry. Mestizos (people of mixed white and Amerindian ancestry) form the largest group, followed by whites and mulattos (people of mixed European and African ancestry).

Spaniards opened up the area in the early 16th century. They set up a territory known as the Viceroyalty of the New Kingdom of Granada, including Colombia, Ecuador, Panama and Venezuela. In 1819, the area became independent, but Ecuador and Venezuela soon split away, followed by Panama in 1903. Instability has marked its recent history. Political rivalries led to civil wars in 1899–1902 and 1949–57, when a coalition government was formed. The coalition ended in 1986 when the Liberal Party was elected. Colombia faces economic and security problems, notably combating left-wing guerrillas and right-wing paramilitaries, while controlling a large illicit drug industry. In the early 2000s, the US provided aid to help Colombia fight drug-trafficking. Andrés Pastrana, who had been elected president in 1998, tried hard to end the guerrilla war, but peace talks collapsed in 2002 and conflict resumed. His successor, Alvaro Uribe, elected in 2002 and again in 2006, pursued a tough line against the rebels.

The World Bank classifies Colombia as a 'lower-middle-income' developing country. Agriculture is important and coffee is the leading export crop. Other crops include bananas, cocoa, maize and tobacco. Colombia exports coal and oil, and it also produces emeralds and gold. The main manufacturing centre is the capital, Bogotá, together with Cali and Medellín.

COMOROS

AREA 2,235 sq km [863 sq mi]
POPULATION 691,000
CAPITAL Moroni

The Union des Isles Comores, as the Comoros is officially called, consists of three large volcanic islands and some smaller ones, lying at the northern end of the Mozambique Channel in the Indian Ocean. France took over one of the islands, Mayotte, in 1843, and, in 1886, the other islands came under French protection.

The Comoros became independent in 1974, but the people of Mayotte opted to remain French. In the late 1990s, separatists on the islands of Anjouan and Mohéli sought to secede, but, in 2004, each of the large islands was granted autonomy, with its own president and legislature.

The Comoros is a poor country. Most people are subsistence farmers. The main exports are cloves, perfume oils and vanilla.

CONGO

AREA 342,000 sq km [132,046 sq mi]
POPULATION 3,702,000
CAPITAL Brazzaville
GOVERNMENT Military regime
ETHNIC GROUPS Kongo 48%, Sangha 20%, Teke 17%, M'bochi 12%
LANGUAGES French (official), many others
RELIGIONS Christianity 50%, animist 48%, Islam 2%
CURRENCY CFA franc = 100 centimes

GEOGRAPHY The Republic of Congo is a country on the River Congo in west-central Africa. The Equator runs through the centre of the country. Congo has a narrow coastal plain on which its main port, Pointe Noire, stands. Behind the plain are uplands through which the River Niari has carved a fertile valley. Central Congo consists of high plains. The north contains large swampy areas in the valleys of the tributaries of the River Congo.

Congo has a hot, wet equatorial climate. Brazzaville has a dry season between June and September. The coast is drier and cooler than the rest of Congo, because of the cold offshore Benguela ocean current.

POLITICS & ECONOMY Part of the huge Kongo kingdom between the 15th and 18th centuries, the coast of the Congo later became a centre of the European slave trade. The area came under French protection in 1880. It was later governed as part of a larger region called French Equatorial Africa. The country remained under French control until 1960.

Congo became a one-party state in 1964 and a military group took over the government in 1968. In 1970, Congo declared itself a Communist country, though it continued to seek aid from Western countries. The government officially abandoned its Communist policies in 1990. Multiparty elections were held in 1992, but the elected president, Pascal Lissouba, was overthrown in 1997 by former president Denis Sassou-Nguesso. Civil war again occurred in January 1999, but peace was restored and a peace accord was signed in 2003.

The World Bank classifies Congo as a 'lower-middle-income' developing country. Agriculture is the most important activity, employing about 60% of the people. But many farmers produce little more than they need to feed their families. Major food crops include bananas, cassava, maize and rice, while the leading cash crops are coffee and cocoa. Congo's main exports are oil (which makes up 90% of the total) and timber. Manufacturing is relatively unimportant at the moment, still hampered by poor transport links. Inland, rivers form the main lines of communication, and Brazzaville is linked to the port of Pointe-Noire by the Congo-Ocean Railway.

CONGO (DEM. REP. OF THE)

AREA 2,344,858 sq km [905,350 sq mi]
POPULATION 62,661,000
CAPITAL Kinshasa
GOVERNMENT Single-party republic
ETHNIC GROUPS Over 200; the largest are Mongo, Luba, Kongo, Mangbetu-Azande
LANGUAGES French (official), tribal languages
RELIGIONS Roman Catholic 50%, Protestant 20%, Islam 10%, others
CURRENCY Congolese franc = 100 centimes

GEOGRAPHY The Democratic Republic of the Congo, formerly known as Zaïre, is the world's 12th largest country. Much of the country lies within the drainage basin of the huge River Congo. The river reaches the sea along the country's coastline, which is 40 km [25 mi] long. Mountains rise in the east, where the country's borders run through lakes Tanganyika, Kivu, Edward and Albert.

The equatorial region has high temperatures and heavy rainfall throughout the year.

POLITICS & ECONOMY Pygmies were the first inhabitants of the region, with Portuguese navigators not reaching the coast until 1482, but the interior was not explored until the late 19th century. In 1885, the country, called Congo Free State, became the personal property of King Léopold II of Belgium. In 1908, the country became a Belgian colony.

The Belgian Congo became independent in 1960 and was renamed Zaïre in 1971. Ethnic rivalries caused instability until 1965, when the country became a one-party state, ruled by President Mobutu. The government allowed the formation of political parties in 1990, but elections were repeatedly postponed. In 1996, fighting broke out in eastern Zaïre, as the Tutsi–Hutu conflict in Burundi and Rwanda spilled over. The rebel leader Laurent Kabila took power in 1997, ousting Mobutu and renaming the country. A rebellion against Kabila broke out in 1998. Rwanda and Uganda supported the rebels, while Angola, Chad, Namibia and Zimbabwe assisted Kabila. A peace treaty was signed in 1999, but fighting continued. Kabila was assassinated in 2001. His son, Major-General Joseph Kabila, who became president, worked to end a war which, by early 2003, had claimed over 2 million lives. Under a new constitution (2005), elections were held in 2006 and Kabila was elected president. Hopes for stability were high, but sporadic fighting continued in the east.

The World Bank classifies the Democratic Republic of the Congo as a 'low-income' developing country, despite its reserves of copper, the main export, and other minerals. Agriculture, mainly at subsistence level, employs about 60% of the people.

COSTA RICA

AREA 51,100 sq km [19,730 sq mi]
POPULATION 4,075,000
CAPITAL San José
GOVERNMENT Multiparty republic
ETHNIC GROUPS White (including Mestizo) 94%, Black 3%, Amerindian 1%, Chinese 1%, others
LANGUAGES Spanish (official), English
RELIGIONS Roman Catholic 76%, Evangelical 14%
CURRENCY Costa Rican colón = 100 céntimos

GEOGRAPHY The Republic of Costa Rica in Central America has coastlines on the Pacific Ocean and the Caribbean Sea. Mountain ranges, plateaux and volcanoes lie inland where the tropical climate is tempered by the altitude. Heavy rain occurs on the Caribbean coast, but the highlands and the Pacific coast are less rainy.

POLITICS & ECONOMY Christopher Columbus reached the Caribbean coast in 1502 and rumours of treasure soon attracted many Spaniards to settle in the country. Spain ruled the country until 1821, when Spain's Central American colonies broke away to join Mexico in 1822. In 1823, the Central American states broke with Mexico and set up the Central American Federation. Later, this large union broke up and Costa Rica became fully independent in 1838. From the late 19th century, Costa Rica experienced a number of revolutions, dictatorships and periods of democracy. In 1948 the army was abolished. Since then, Costa Rica has been a stable democracy, though its reputation was tarnished in the 2000s by charges of corruption against some politicians. In 2006, Nobel Peace Prize winner Oscar Arias was elected president.

The World Bank rates Costa Rica as a 'lower-middle-income' developing country. It is one of Central America's most prosperous nations with high educational standards and an average life expectancy of 78 years. Agriculture employs 15% of the people. Costa Rica's resources include its forests, but it lacks minerals apart from some bauxite and manganese. Manufacturing and tourism are increasing. The United States is Costa Rica's chief trading partner.

CROATIA

AREA 56,538 sq km [21,829 sq mi]
POPULATION 4,495,000
CAPITAL Zagreb
GOVERNMENT Multiparty republic
ETHNIC GROUPS Croat 90%, Serb 5%, others
LANGUAGES Croatian 96%
RELIGIONS Roman Catholic 88%, Orthodox 4%, Islam 1%, others
CURRENCY Kuna = 100 lipas

GEOGRAPHY The Republic of Croatia was one of the six republics that made up the former Communist country of Yugoslavia until it became independent in 1991. The region bordering the Adriatic Sea is called Dalmatia. It includes the coastal ranges, which contain large areas of bare limestone. Most of the rest of the country consists of the fertile Pannonian plains.

The coastal area has a typical Mediterranean climate, with hot, dry summers and mild, moist winters. Inland, the climate becomes more continental. Winters are cold, while temperatures often soar to 38°C [100°F] in the summer months.

POLITICS & ECONOMY Slav people settled in the area around 1,400 years ago. In 803, Croatia became part of the Holy Roman empire and the Croats soon adopted Christianity. Croatia was an independent kingdom in the 10th and 11th centuries. In 1102, the king of Hungary also became king of Croatia, creating a union that lasted 800 years. In 1526, part of Croatia came under the Turkish Ottoman empire, while the rest came under the Austrian Habsburgs.

After Austria–Hungary was defeated in World War I (1914–18), Croatia became part of the new Kingdom of the Serbs, Croats and Slovenes. This kingdom was renamed Yugoslavia in 1929. Germany occupied Yugoslavia during World War II (1939–45). Croatia was proclaimed independent, but it was really ruled by the invaders.

After the war, Communists took power with Josip Broz Tito as the country's leader. Despite ethnic differences between the people, Tito held Yugoslavia together until his death in 1980. In the 1980s, economic and ethnic problems, including a deterioration in relations with Serbia, threatened stability. In the 1990s, Yugoslavia split into five nations, one of which was Croatia, which declared itself independent in 1991.

After Serbia supplied arms to Serbs living in Croatia, war broke out between the two republics, causing great damage. Croatia lost more than 30% of its territory. But in 1992, the United Nations sent a peacekeeping force to Croatia, which effectively ended the war with Serbia. In 1992, when war broke out in Bosnia-Herzegovina, Bosnian Croats occupied parts of the country. But, in 1994, Croatia helped to end Croat–Muslim conflict, and, in 1995, it helped to draw up the Dayton Peace Accord which ended the civil war there.

The wars of the early 1990s disrupted Croatia's economy, but following the election of a pro-democratic coalition government in 2000, stability, which is so vital for the valuable tourist industry, appeared to be increasing. Manufacturing is the main activity. In 2004, the European Union agreed that accession talks with Croatia would begin in 2005, but many problems stood in the way.

CUBA

AREA 110,861 sq km [42,803 sq mi]
POPULATION 11,383,000
CAPITAL Havana
GOVERNMENT Socialist republic
ETHNIC GROUPS Mulatto 51%, White 37%, Black 11%
LANGUAGES Spanish (official)
RELIGIONS Christianity
CURRENCY Cuban peso = 100 centavos

GEOGRAPHY The Republic of Cuba is the largest island country in the Caribbean Sea. It consists of one large island, Cuba, the Isle of Youth (Isla de la Juventud) and about 1,600 small islets. Mountains and hills cover about a quarter of Cuba. The highest mountain range, the Sierra Maestra in the south-east, reaches 2,000 m [6,562 ft] above sea level. The rest of the land consists of gently rolling country or coastal plains, crossed by the short, fertile valleys carved by the short, mostly shallow and narrow rivers.

Cuba lies in the tropics. But sea breezes moderate the temperature, warming the land in winter and cooling it in summer.

NATIONS OF THE WORLD

POLITICS & ECONOMY Christopher Columbus discovered the island in 1492 and Spaniards began to settle there from 1511. Spanish rule ended in 1898, when the United States defeated Spain in the Spanish–American War. American influence in Cuba remained strong until 1959, when revolutionary forces under Fidel Castro overthrew the dictatorial government of Fulgencio Batista.

The United States opposed Castro's policies, when he turned to the Soviet Union for assistance. In 1961, Cuban exiles attempting an invasion were defeated. In 1962, the US learned that nuclear missile bases armed by the Soviet Union had been established in Cuba. The US ordered the Soviet Union to remove the missiles and bases and, after a few days, when many people feared that a world war might break out, the Soviet Union agreed to the American demands.

Cuba's relations with the Soviet Union remained strong until 1991, when the Soviet Union was broken up. The loss of Soviet aid greatly damaged Cuba's economy, but Castro maintained his left-wing policies. In 2000, the United States lifted its food embargo on Cuba, but, in 2004, following a United States crackdown on currency and travel, Cuba declared that US dollars would no longer be accepted as payments for goods and services.

The government runs Cuba's economy and owns 70% of the farmland. Agriculture is important and sugar is the chief export, followed by refined nickel ore. Other exports include cigars, citrus fruits, fish, medical products and rum. Before 1959, US companies owned most businesses. Under Castro, the government took them over. After the collapse of the Soviet Union in 1991, Cuba worked to increase its trade with Latin America and China.

CYPRUS

AREA 9,251 sq km [3,572 sq mi]
POPULATION 784,000
CAPITAL Nicosia
GOVERNMENT Multiparty republic
ETHNIC GROUPS Greek Cypriot 77%, Turkish Cypriot 18%, others
LANGUAGES Greek and Turkish (both official), English
RELIGIONS Greek Orthodox 78%, Islam 18%
CURRENCY Cypriot pound = 100 cents

GEOGRAPHY The Republic of Cyprus is an island nation in the north-eastern Mediterranean Sea. Geographers regard it as part of Asia, but it resembles southern Europe in many ways. Its scenic mountain ranges include the southern Troodos Mountains, which reach 1,951 m [6,401 ft] at Mount Olympus, and the Kyrenia range in the north. Between them lies the broad Mesaoria plain.

The climate is Mediterranean, with hot dry summers and mild, moist winters. But the island's proximity to south-western Asia makes it hotter than places in the western Mediterranean.

POLITICS & ECONOMY Greeks settled on Cyprus around 3,200 years ago. From AD 330, the island was part of the Byzantine empire. In the 1570s, Cyprus became part of the Turkish Ottoman empire. Turkish rule continued until 1878 when Cyprus was leased to Britain. Britain annexed the island in 1914 and proclaimed it a colony in 1925.

In the 1950s, Greek Cypriots, who made up four-fifths of the population, began a campaign for *enosis* (union) with Greece. Their leader was

the Greek Orthodox Archbishop Makarios. A secret guerrilla force called EOKA attacked the British, who exiled Makarios. Cyprus became an independent country in 1960, although Britain retained two military bases. Independent Cyprus had a constitution which provided for power-sharing between the Greek and Turkish Cypriots. But the constitution proved unworkable and fighting broke out. In 1964, the United Nations sent in a peacekeeping force, but communal clashes recurred in 1967.

In 1974, Cypriot forces led by Greek officers overthrew Makarios. This led Turkey to invade northern Cyprus, a territory occupying about 40% of the island. Many Greek Cypriots fled from the north which, in 1979, was proclaimed an independent state called the Turkish Republic of Northern Cyprus, but the only country to recognize it was Turkey.

In 2002, the European Union invited Cyprus to become a member in 2004. In April 2004, the people voted on a UN plan to reunify the island. The Turkish-Cypriots voted in favour of the plan, but the Greek-Cypriots in the south voted against. Hence, only the south was admitted to membership of the EU on 1 May 2004.

Cyprus got its name from the Greek word *kypros*, meaning copper. But little copper remains and the chief minerals today are asbestos and chromium. However, the most valuable activity in Cyprus is tourism. In the early 1990s, the United Nations reclassified Cyprus as a developed rather than a developing country. But the economy of the Turkish-Cypriot north lags behind that of the more prosperous Greek-Cypriot south.

CZECH REPUBLIC

AREA 78,866 sq km [30,450 sq mi]
POPULATION 10,235,000
CAPITAL Prague
GOVERNMENT Multiparty republic
ETHNIC GROUPS Czech 81%, Moravian 13%, Slovak 3%, Polish, German, Silesian, Gypsy, Hungarian, Ukrainian
LANGUAGES Czech (official)
RELIGIONS Atheist 40%, Roman Catholic 39%, Protestant 4%, Orthodox 3%, others
CURRENCY Czech koruna = 100 haler

GEOGRAPHY The Czech Republic is the western three-fifths of the former country of Czechoslovakia. It contains two regions: Bohemia in the west and Moravia in the east. Mountains border much of the country in the west. The Bohemian basin in the north-centre is a fertile lowland region, with Prague, the capital city, as its main centre. Highlands cover much of the centre of the country, with lowlands in the south-east.

The climate is influenced by its landlocked position in east-central Europe. Prague has warm, sunny summers and cold winters. The average rainfall is moderate, with 500 mm to 750 mm [20 in to 30 in] every year in lowland areas.

POLITICS & ECONOMY After World War I (1914–18), Czechoslovakia was created. Germany seized the country in World War II (1939–45). In 1948, Communist leaders took power and Czechoslovakia was allied to the Soviet Union. When democratic reforms were introduced in the Soviet Union in the late 1980s, the Czechs also demanded reforms. Free elections were held in 1990, but differences between the Czechs and the Slovaks led

to the partitioning of the country on 1 January 1993. The government continued to develop ties with Western Europe when it became a member of NATO in 1992. On 1 May 2004, the Czech Republic became a member of the European Union. This followed a referendum in 2003 in which 77% of Czechs voted in favour of their country joining the EU.

Under Communist rule the Czech Republic became one of the most industrialized parts of Eastern Europe. The country has deposits of coal, uranium, iron ore, magnesite, tin and zinc. Manufacturing employs about 25% of the Czech Republic's entire workforce. Farming is also important. Under Communism, the government owned the land, but private ownership is now being restored. The country was admitted into the OECD in 1995.

DENMARK

AREA 43,094 sq km [16,639 sq mi]
POPULATION 5,451,000
CAPITAL Copenhagen
GOVERNMENT Parliamentary monarchy
ETHNIC GROUPS Scandinavian, Inuit, Færoese, German
LANGUAGES Danish (official), English, Færoese
RELIGIONS Evangelical Lutheran 95%
CURRENCY Danish krone = 100 øre

GEOGRAPHY The Kingdom of Denmark is the smallest country in Scandinavia. It consists of a peninsula, called Jutland (or Jylland), which is joined to Germany, and more than 400 islands, 89 of which are inhabited.

The land is flat and mostly covered by rocks dropped there by huge ice-sheets during the last Ice Age. The highest point in Denmark is on Jutland. It is only 173 m [568 ft] above sea level.

Denmark has a cool but pleasant climate, except during cold spells in the winter when The Sound between Sjælland and Sweden may freeze over. Summers are warm. Rainfall occurs all through the year.

POLITICS & ECONOMY Danish Vikings terrorized much of Western Europe for about 300 years after AD 800. Danish kings ruled England in the 11th century. In the late 14th century, Denmark formed a union with Norway and Sweden (which included Finland). Sweden broke away in 1523, while Denmark lost Norway to Sweden in 1814.

After 1945, Denmark played an important part in European affairs, becoming a member of the North Atlantic Treaty Organization (NATO). In 1973, Denmark joined the European Union, although it rejected the adoption of the euro in 2000. The Danes now enjoy some of the world's highest living standards, although economic problems led to cutbacks in the early 2000s. Under Prime Minister Anders Fogh Rasmussen, who won a second term in 2005, the government tightened immigration controls. In 2006, published caricatures of the Prophet Muhammad by Danish artists provoked protests by Muslims, while anti-Danish protests occurred abroad.

Denmark has few natural resources apart from some oil and gas from wells deep under the North Sea. But the economy is highly developed. Manufacturing industries, which employ about 15% of all workers, produce a wide variety of products, including furniture, processed food, machinery, television sets and textiles. Farms cover about three-quarters of the land. Farming employs only 3% of the workers, but it is highly scientific and productive. Meat and dairy farming are the chief activities.

DJIBOUTI

AREA 23,200 sq km [8,958 sq mi]
POPULATION 487,000
CAPITAL Djibouti
GOVERNMENT Multiparty republic
ETHNIC GROUPS Somali 60%, Afar 35%
LANGUAGES Arabic and French (both official)
RELIGIONS Islam 94%, Christianity 6%
CURRENCY Djiboutian franc = 100 centimes

GEOGRAPHY The Republic of Djibouti in eastern Africa occupies a strategic position where the Red Sea meets the Gulf of Aden. Djibouti has one of the world's hottest and driest climates.
POLITICS & ECONOMY France set up a territory called French Somaliland in 1888. Its capital, Djibouti, became important when a railway was built to Addis Ababa and Djibouti became the main outlet for Ethiopian trade. In 1967, France renamed the dependency the French Territory of the Afars and Issas, but it became Djibouti on independence in 1977.

Djibouti became a one-party state in 1981, but a new constitution (1992) permitted four parties which had to maintain a balance between the country's ethnic groups. Conflict flared up between the Afars and the Issas in 1992, but a peace agreement was signed in 1994. The economy is based largely on the revenue it gets from its port and railway.

DOMINICA

AREA 751 sq km [290 sq mi]
POPULATION 69,000
CAPITAL Roseau

The Commonwealth of Dominica, a former British colony, became independent in 1978. The island has a mountainous spine and less than 10% of the land is cultivated. Yet agriculture employs a substantial proportion of the people. Manufacturing, mining and tourism are other minor activities.

DOMINICAN REPUBLIC

AREA 48,511 sq km [18,730 sq mi]
POPULATION 9,184,000
CAPITAL Santo Domingo
GOVERNMENT Multiparty republic
ETHNIC GROUPS Mulatto 73%, White 16%, Black 11%
LANGUAGES Spanish (official)
RELIGIONS Roman Catholic 95%
CURRENCY Dominican peso = 100 centavos

GEOGRAPHY Second largest of the Caribbean nations in both area and population, the Dominican Republic shares the island of Hispaniola with Haiti. The country is mountainous, and the generally hot and humid climate eases with altitude.
POLITICS & ECONOMY The Dominican Republic has chaotic origins, having been held by Spain, France, Haiti and the United States at various times. Civil war broke out in 1966 but the conflict soon ended after US intervention. Since 1966, a young democracy has survived violent elections under the watchful eye of the USA.

EAST TIMOR

AREA 14,874 sq km [5,743 sq mi]
POPULATION 1,063,000
CAPITAL Dili

The Republic of East Timor (or Timor-Leste) became fully independent on 20 May 2002. The land is mainly rugged. Temperatures are generally high and the rainfall is moderate. Portugal ruled the territory from the late 19th century, when it was called Portuguese Timor. Portugal withdrew in 1975 and Indonesia seized the area. Guerrilla activity mounted under Indonesian rule and, in 1999, the people voted for independence. Timor is the poorest country in South-east Asia. But, in 2006, East Timor and Australia signed a deal to share the revenue from the oil and natural gas deposits under the Timor Sea.

ECUADOR

AREA 283,561 sq km [109,483 sq mi]
POPULATION 13,548,000
CAPITAL Quito
GOVERNMENT Multiparty republic
ETHNIC GROUPS Mestizo (mixed White/Amerindian) 65%, Amerindian 25%, White 7%, Black 3%
LANGUAGES Spanish (official), Quechua
RELIGIONS Roman Catholic 95%
CURRENCY US dollar = 100 cents

GEOGRAPHY The Republic of Ecuador straddles the Equator on the west coast of South America. Three ranges of the high Andes Mountains form the backbone of the country. Between the towering, snow-capped peaks of the mountains, some of which are volcanoes, lie a series of high plateaux, or basins. Nearly half of Ecuador's population lives on these plateaux.

The climate in Ecuador depends on the height above sea level. Though the coastline is cooled by the cold Peruvian Current, temperatures are between 23°C and 25°C [73°F to 77°F] all through the year. In Quito, at 2,500 m [8,200 ft] above sea level, temperatures are 14°C to 15°C [57°F to 59°F], though the city is just south of the Equator.
POLITICS & ECONOMY The Inca people of Peru conquered much of what is now Ecuador in the late 15th century. They introduced their language, Quechua, which is widely spoken today. Spanish forces defeated the Incas in 1533 and took control of Ecuador. The country became independent in 1822, following the defeat of a Spanish force in a battle near Quito. In the 19th and 20th centuries, Ecuador suffered from political instability, while successive governments failed to tackle the country's social and economic problems. A war with Peru in 1941 led to a loss of territory. Disputes continued until 1995, but a border agreement was signed in January 1998. The leftist Rafael Correa was elected president in 2006 and, in 2007, the people voted in favour of overhauling the political system.

The World Bank classifies Ecuador as a 'lower-middle-income' developing country. Agriculture employs 8% of the people and bananas, cocoa and coffee are all important crops. Fishing, forestry, mining and manufacturing are other activities.

EGYPT

AREA 1,001,449 sq km [386,659 sq mi]
POPULATION 78,887,000
CAPITAL Cairo
GOVERNMENT Republic
ETHNIC GROUPS Egyptians/Bedouins/Berbers 99%
LANGUAGES Arabic (official), French, English
RELIGIONS Islam (mainly Sunni Muslim) 94%, Christianity (mainly Coptic Christian) and others 6%
CURRENCY Egyptian pound = 100 piastres

GEOGRAPHY The Arab Republic of Egypt is Africa's second largest country by population after Nigeria, though it ranks 13th in area. Most of Egypt is desert. Almost all the people live either in the Nile Valley and its fertile delta or along the Suez Canal, the artificial waterway between the Mediterranean and Red seas. This canal shortens the sea journey between the United Kingdom and India by 9,700 km [6,027 mi]. Recent attempts have been made to irrigate parts of the western desert.

Apart from the Nile Valley, Egypt has three other main regions. The Western and Eastern deserts are parts of the Sahara. The Sinai peninsula (Es Sina), to the east of the Suez Canal, is a mountainous desert region, geographically within Asia. It contains Egypt's highest peak, Gebel Katherina (2,637 m [8,650 ft]); few people live in this area.

Egypt is a dry country. The low rainfall occurs, if at all, in winter and the country is one of the sunniest places on Earth.
POLITICS & ECONOMY Ancient Egypt, which was founded about 5,000 years ago, was one of the great early civilizations. Throughout the country, pyramids, temples and richly decorated tombs are memorials to its great achievements. After Ancient Egypt declined, the country came under successive foreign rulers. Arabs occupied Egypt in AD 639–42. They introduced the Arabic language and Islam. Their influence was so great that most Egyptians now regard themselves as Arabs.

Egypt came under British rule in 1882, but it gained partial independence in 1922, becoming a monarchy. The monarchy was abolished in 1952, when Egypt became a republic. The creation of Israel in 1948 led Egypt into a series of wars in 1948–9, 1956, 1967 and 1973. Since the late 1970s, Egypt has sought for peace. In 1979, Egypt signed a peace treaty with Israel and regained the Sinai region which it had lost in a war in 1967. Extremists opposed contacts with Israel and, in 1981, President Sadat, who had signed the treaty, was assassinated.

While Egypt plays a major part in Arab affairs, most of its people are poor. Some Islamic fundamentalists, who dislike Western influences on their way of life, have resorted to violence. In the 1990s, attacks on foreign visitors caused a decline in the valuable tourist industry. In 1999, Hosni Mubarak, president since 1981, was himself attacked by extremists, but he was re-elected to a fourth term in office. He was re-elected in 2005, though supporters of the banned Muslim Brotherhood made gains in parliamentary elections.

Most people are poor, although Egypt is Africa's second most industrialized country. Oil and textiles are exported.

EL SALVADOR

AREA 21,041 sq km [8,124 sq mi]
POPULATION 6,822,000
CAPITAL San Salvador
GOVERNMENT Republic
ETHNIC GROUPS Mestizo (mixed White and Amerindian) 90%, White 9%, Amerindian 1%
LANGUAGES Spanish (official)
RELIGIONS Roman Catholic 83%
CURRENCY US dollar = 100 cents

GEOGRAPHY The Republic of El Salvador is the only country in Central America which does not have a coast on the Caribbean Sea. El Salvador has a narrow coastal plain along the Pacific Ocean. Behind the coastal plain, the coastal range is a zone of rugged mountains, including volcanoes, which overlooks a densely populated inland plateau. Beyond the plateau, the land rises to the sparsely populated interior highlands.

The coast has a hot, tropical climate. Inland, the climate is moderated by the altitude. Rain falls on practically every afternoon between May and October.
POLITICS & ECONOMY Amerindians have lived in El Salvador for thousands of years. The ruins of Mayan pyramids built between AD 100 and 1000 are found in the west. Spanish soldiers conquered the area in 1524–5 and Spain ruled until 1821.

In 1823, all the Central American countries, apart from Panama, set up a Central American Federation. El Salvador withdrew in 1840 and declared its independence in 1841. Instability plagued El Salvador in the 19th century. The 20th century saw some improvements, but, from 1931, military dictatorships alternated with elected governments.

In the 1970s, El Salvador was plagued by conflict as protesters demanded that the government introduce reforms to help the poor. Kidnappings and murders committed by left- and right-wing groups caused instability. A civil war broke out in 1979 between the US-backed, right-wing government forces and left-wing guerrillas. In 12 years, 750,000 people died. A cease-fire was agreed in 1992 and, by 2003, the economy had shown signs of recovery.

The World Bank classifies El Salvador as a 'lower-middle-income' economy. About 70% of the land is farmed. Coffee is the main export, followed by sugar and cotton. Fishing for lobsters and shrimps is important, but manufacturing is on a small scale.

EQUATORIAL GUINEA

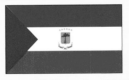

AREA 28,051 sq km [10,830 sq mi]
POPULATION 540,000
CAPITAL Malabo
GOVERNMENT Multiparty republic (transitional)
ETHNIC GROUPS Bubi (on Bioko), Fang (in Rio Muni)
LANGUAGES Spanish and French (both official)
RELIGIONS Christianity
CURRENCY CFA franc = 100 centimes

GEOGRAPHY The Republic of Equatorial Guinea is a small republic in west-central Africa. It consists of a mainland territory which makes up 90% of the land area, called Rio Muni, between Cameroon and Gabon, and five offshore islands in the Bight of Bonny, the largest of which is Bioko. The island of Annobon lies 560 km [350 mi] south-west of Rio Muni. Rio Muni consists mainly of hills and plateaux behind the coastal plains.

The climate is hot and humid. Bioko is mountainous, with the land rising to 3,008 m [9,869 ft], and hence it is particularly rainy. However, there is a marked dry season between the months of December and February. Mainland Rio Muni has a similar climate, though the rainfall diminishes inland.
POLITICS & ECONOMY Portuguese navigators reached the area in 1471. In 1778, Portugal granted Bioko, together with rights over Rio Muni, to Spain.

In 1959, Spain made Bioko and Rio Muni provinces of overseas Spain and, in 1963, it gave the provinces a degree of self-government. Equatorial Guinea became independent in 1968.

The first president of Equatorial Guinea, Francisco Macias Nguema, proved to be a tyrant. He was overthrown in 1979 and a group of officers, led by Lt.-Col. Teodoro Obiang Nguema Mbasogo, set up a Supreme Military Council to rule the country. In 1991, the people voted to set up a multiparty democracy. Elections were held in the 1990s, but accusations of human rights abuses continued. In 2004, a coup attempt by mercenaries was foiled and its leaders were arrested.

Agriculture employs about half of the people and the most valuable crop is coffee. However, oil has been produced since 1966 and, by the 2000s, it was by far the most important export. Other exports include methanol, wood and cocoa beans. Yet despite the rapid expansion of the economy, about two-thirds of the population live in poverty.

ERITREA

AREA 117,600 sq km [45,405 sq mi]
POPULATION 4,787,000
CAPITAL Asmara
GOVERNMENT Transitional government
ETHNIC GROUPS Tigrinya 50%, Tigre and Kunama 40%, Afar 4%, Saho 3%, others
LANGUAGES Afar, Arabic, Tigre and Kunama, Tigrinya
RELIGIONS Islam, Coptic Christian, Roman Catholic
CURRENCY Nakfa = 100 cents

GEOGRAPHY The State of Eritrea consists of a hot, dry coastal plain facing the Red Sea, with a fairly mountainous area in the centre. Most people live in the cooler highland area.
POLITICS & ECONOMY From the 1st century AD, Eritrea formed part of the ancient Kingdom of Axum, which adopted Christianity in the 4th century. Axum reached its greatest period of prosperity in the 4th century, but it began to decline in the 7th century. The Ottoman Turks took over the area in the 16th century and, in the 1880s, it became an Italian colony. The Italians were driven out in 1941 and, in 1952, it became part of Ethiopia.

A guerrilla struggle launched in 1961 ended in 1993, when Eritrea became independent. But economic recovery was hampered by conflict with Yemen over three islands in the Red Sea. Then, in 1998–9, clashes with Ethiopia flared up along the border. Despite a peace agreement in 2000, tensions grew in 2005 and 2006 following Ethiopia's refusal to accept an international ruling that the disputed border town of Badme should be in Eritrea. Farming and livestock rearing are the main activities in Eritrea. Most of the few manufacturing industries are based in Asmara.

ESTONIA

AREA 45,100 sq km [17,413 sq mi]
POPULATION 1,324,000
CAPITAL Tallinn
GOVERNMENT Multiparty republic
ETHNIC GROUPS Estonian 65%, Russian 28%, Ukrainian 3%, Belarusian 2%, Finnish 1%
LANGUAGES Estonian (official), Russian
RELIGIONS Lutheran, Russian and Estonian Orthodox, Methodist, Baptist, Roman Catholic
CURRENCY Estonian kroon = 100 senti

GEOGRAPHY The Republic of Estonia is the smallest of the three states on the Baltic Sea, which were formerly part of the Soviet Union, but which became independent in the early 1990s. Estonia consists of a generally flat plain which was covered by ice-sheets during the Ice Age. The land is strewn with moraine (rocks deposited by the ice).

The country is dotted with more than 1,500 small lakes, and water, including the large Lake Peipus (Chudskoye Ozero) and the River Narva makes up much of Estonia's eastern border with Russia. Estonia has more than 800 islands, which together make up about a tenth of the country. The largest island is Saaremaa (Sarema).

Despite its northerly position, Estonia has a fairly mild climate because of its nearness to the sea. This is because sea winds tend to warm the land in winter and cool it in summer.
POLITICS & ECONOMY The ancestors of the Estonians, who are related to the Finns, settled in the area several thousand years ago. German crusaders, known as the Teutonic Knights, introduced Christianity in the early 13th century. By the 16th century, German noblemen owned much of the land in Estonia. In 1561, Sweden took the northern part of the country and Poland the south. From 1625, Sweden controlled the entire country until Sweden handed it over to Russia in 1721.

Estonian nationalists campaigned for their independence from around the mid-19th century. Finally, Estonia was proclaimed independent in 1918. In 1919, the government began to break up the large estates and distribute land among the peasants.

In 1939, Germany and the Soviet Union agreed to take over parts of Eastern Europe. In 1940, Soviet forces occupied Estonia, but they were driven out by the Germans in 1941. Soviet troops returned in 1944 and Estonia became one of the 15 Soviet Socialist Republics of the Soviet Union. The Estonians strongly opposed Soviet rule. Many of them were deported to Siberia.

Political changes in the Soviet Union in the late 1980s led to renewed demands for freedom. In 1990, the Estonian government declared the country independent and, finally, the Soviet Union recognized this act in September 1991, shortly before the Soviet Union was dissolved. Estonia adopted a new constitution in 1992, when multiparty elections were held for a new national assembly. In 1993, Estonia negotiated an agreement with Russia to withdraw its troops.

Under Soviet rule, Estonia was the most prosperous of the three Baltic states. Since 1988, Estonia has restructured its economy. Turning increasingly to the West, it became a member of NATO and the European Union in 2004. Its industries produce fertilizers, processed food, machinery, petrochemical products, wood products and textiles. Agriculture and fishing are also important.

ETHIOPIA

AREA 1,104,300 sq km [426,370 sq mi]
POPULATION 74,778,000
CAPITAL Addis Ababa
GOVERNMENT Federation of nine provinces
ETHNIC GROUPS Oromo 40%, Amhara and Tigre 32%, Sidamo 9%, Shankella 6%, Somali 6%, others
LANGUAGES Amharic (official), many others
RELIGIONS Islam 47%, Ethiopian Orthodox 40%, traditional beliefs 12%
CURRENCY Birr = 100 cents

GEOGRAPHY Ethiopia is a landlocked country in north-eastern Africa. The land is mainly mountainous, though there are extensive plains in the east, bordering southern Eritrea, and in the south, bordering Somalia. The highlands are divided into two blocks by the Great Rift Valley.

The climate in Ethiopia is greatly affected by the altitude. Addis Ababa, at 2,450 m [8,000 ft], has an average yearly temperature of 20°C [68°F]. The rainfall is generally more than 1,000 mm [39 in]. But the lowlands are hot and arid.

POLITICS & ECONOMY Ethiopia was the home of an ancient monarchy, which became Christian in the 4th century. In the 7th century, Muslims gained control of the lowlands, but Christianity survived in the highlands. Ethiopia resisted attempts to colonize it, but Italy invaded the country in 1935. The Italians were driven out in 1941 during World War II.

In 1952, Eritrea, on the Red Sea coast, was federated with Ethiopia. But in 1961, Eritrean nationalists demanded their freedom, beginning a struggle that ended in their independence in 1993. In 1995, in recognition of Ethiopia's ethnic diversity, the country was divided into nine provinces, each with its own assembly. Clashes along the border with Eritrea occurred in the late 1990s. A peace agreement was signed in 2000, but Ethiopia later refused to accept an international ruling that Badme, the town where the conflict began, belonged to Eritrea. In 2005, Meles Zenawi, prime minister since 1995, led his party, the Ethiopian Revolutionary Democratic Front, to victory in national elections, but claims of vote-rigging led to violence in several cities. In 2006–7, Ethiopian forces intervened on behalf of the provisional government in Somalia, opposing the Islamist Union of Islamic Courts which had taken control of Mogadishu.

Ethiopia is one of the world's poorest countries. Since the 1970s, it has been plagued by droughts and civil conflict. Agriculture remains the chief activity.

FALKLAND ISLANDS

AREA 12,173 sq km [4,700 sq mi]
POPULATION 3,000
CAPITAL Stanley

Comprising two main islands and over 200 small islands, the Falkland Islands lie 480 km [300 mi] from South America. Sheep farming is the main activity, though the search for oil and diamonds holds out hope for the future of this treeless environment. Argentina claims the islands, which it calls Las Malvinas, and occupied them briefly in 1982.

FÆROE ISLANDS

AREA 1,399 sq km [540 sq mi]
POPULATION 47,000
CAPITAL Tórshavn

The Færoe Islands are a group of 18 volcanic islands and some reefs in the North Atlantic Ocean. The islands have been Danish since 1380 when they, and Norway, passed to Danish control. They were administratively separated from Norway in 1709. Since 1948, the islands have been largely self-governing. In 2001, a referendum on independence was called off when the Danish prime minister said that subsidies would end four years after the islands became independent.

FIJI ISLANDS

AREA 18,274 sq km [7,056 sq mi]
POPULATION 906,000
CAPITAL Suva

The Fiji Islands is a republic, comprising more than 800 Melanesian islands. The two largest islands are Viti Levu and Vanua Levu. Together they make up 87% of the land area. The climate is tropical, with south-east trade winds blowing throughout the year.

A former British colony, Fiji became independent in 1970 and a republic in 1987. Coups occurred in 1987, 2000 and 2006, as ethnic Fijians sought to stop members of the ethnic Indian community from holding senior cabinet posts. Their actions provoked international criticism. The country's name was changed from Fiji to Fiji Islands in 1998.

FINLAND

AREA 338,145 sq km [130,558 sq mi]
POPULATION 5,231,000
CAPITAL Helsinki
GOVERNMENT Multiparty republic
ETHNIC GROUPS Finnish 93%, Swedish 6%
LANGUAGES Finnish and Swedish (both official)
RELIGIONS Evangelical Lutheran 89%
CURRENCY Euro = 100 cents

GEOGRAPHY The Republic of Finland is a beautiful country in northern Europe. In the south, behind the coastal lowlands where most Finns live, lies a region of sparkling lakes worn out by ice-sheets in the Ice Age. The thinly populated northern uplands cover about two-fifths of the country.

Helsinki, the capital city, has warm summers, but the average temperatures between the months of December and March are below freezing point. Snow covers the land in winter. The north has less precipitation than the south, but it is much colder.

POLITICS & ECONOMY Between 1150 and 1809, Finland was under Swedish rule. The close links between the countries continue today. Swedish remains an official language in Finland and many towns have Swedish as well as Finnish names.

In 1809, Finland became a grand duchy of the Russian empire. It finally declared itself independent in 1917, after the Russian Revolution and the collapse of the Russian empire. But during World War II (1939–45), the Soviet Union declared war on Finland and took part of Finland's territory. Finland allied itself with Germany, but it lost more land to the Soviet Union at the end of the war.

After World War II, Finland became a neutral country and negotiated peace treaties with the Soviet Union. Finland also strengthened its relations with other northern European countries and became an associate member of the European Free Trade Association (EFTA) in 1961. Finland became a full member of EFTA in 1986, but in 1992, along with most of its fellow EFTA members, it applied for membership of the European Union, which it finally achieved on 1 January 1995. On 1 January 2002, the euro became Finland's sole official unit of currency. Finland has also discussed the possibility of joining NATO, but the re-election of the centre-left Tarja Halonen in 2006 suggested that NATO membership was unlikely during her six-year term.

Forests are Finland's most valuable natural resource, and wood, wood products and paper once dominated the economy. They still make up about a quarter of the country's exports, but, since World War II, Finland has set up many new industries, producing machinery and transport equipment. As a result, the economy has expanded quickly. Machinery and apparatus now account for more than a third of the exports.

FRANCE

AREA 551,500 sq km [212,934 sq mi]
POPULATION 60,876,000
CAPITAL Paris
GOVERNMENT Multiparty republic
ETHNIC GROUPS Celtic, Latin, Arab, Teutonic, Slavic
LANGUAGES French (official)
RELIGIONS Roman Catholic 85%, Islam 8%, others
CURRENCY Euro = 100 cents

GEOGRAPHY The Republic of France is the largest country in Western Europe. The scenery is extremely varied. The Vosges Mountains overlook the Rhine valley in the north-east, the Jura Mountains and the Alps form the borders with Switzerland and Italy in the south-east, while the Pyrenees straddle France's border with Spain. The only large highland area entirely within France is the Massif Central in southern France.

Brittany (Bretagne) and Normandy (Normande) form a scenic hill region. Fertile lowlands cover most of northern France, including the densely populated Paris basin. Another major lowland area, the Aquitanian basin, is in the south-west, while the Rhône-Saône valley and the Mediterranean lowlands are in the south-east.

The climate of France varies from west to east and from north to south. The west comes under the moderating influence of the Atlantic Ocean, giving generally mild weather. To the east, summers are warmer and winters colder. The climate also becomes warmer as one travels from north to south. The Mediterranean Sea coast has hot, dry summers and mild, moist winters. The Alps, Jura and Pyrenees mountains have snowy winters. Winter sports centres are found in all three areas. Large glaciers occupy high valleys in the Alps.

POLITICS & ECONOMY The Romans conquered France (then called Gaul) in the 50s BC. Roman rule began to decline in the 5th century AD and, in 486, the Frankish realm (as France was called) became independent under a Christian king, Clovis. In 800, Charlemagne, who had been king since 768, became emperor of the Romans. He extended France's boundaries, but, in 843, his empire was divided into three parts and the area of France contracted. After the Norman invasion of England in 1066, large areas of France came under English rule, but this was finally ended in 1453.

France later became a powerful monarchy. But the French Revolution (1789–99) ended absolute rule by French kings. In 1799, Napoleon Bonaparte took power and fought a series of brilliant military campaigns before his final defeat in 1815. The monarchy was restored until 1848, when the Second Republic was founded. In 1852, Napoleon's nephew became Napoleon III, but the Third Republic was established in 1875. France was the scene of much fighting during World War I (1914–18) and World War II (1939–45), causing great loss of life and much damage to the economy.

In 1946, France adopted a new constitution, establishing the Fourth Republic. But political instability and costly colonial wars slowed France's post-war recovery. In 1958, Charles de Gaulle was elected president and he introduced a new constitution, giving the president extra powers and inaugurating the Fifth Republic.

Since the 1960s, France has made rapid economic progress, becoming one of the most prosperous nations in the European Union. But France's government faced a number of problems, including unemployment, pollution and the growing number of elderly people, who find it difficult to live when inflation rates are high. One social problem concerns the presence in France of large numbers of immigrants from Africa and southern Europe, many of whom live in poor areas.

A socialist government under Lionel Jospin was elected in June 1997. Under Jospin, France adopted the euro, the single European currency, and shortened the working week. The French system of high social security seemed likely to continue. However, in 2002, centre-right parties won a resounding victory and Jean-Pierre Raffarin replaced Jospin as prime minister. France has a long record of independence in foreign affairs and, in 2003, it angered the US and some of its allies in the European Union by opposing the invasion of Iraq. In 2005, the people voted in a referendum against a proposed constitution for the European Union. Later in 2005, France was rocked by inter-ethnic urban violence. In 2007, the right-wing Nicolas Sarkozy was elected president, defeating his socialist rival, Ségolène Royal.

France is one of the world's most developed countries. Its natural resources include its fertile soil, together with deposits of bauxite, coal, iron ore, oil and natural gas, and potash. France is also one of the world's top manufacturing nations, and it has often innovated in bold and imaginative ways. The TGV, Concorde and hypermarkets are all typical examples. Paris is a world centre of fashion industries, but France has many other industrial towns and cities. Major manufactures include aircraft, cars, chemicals, electronic products, machinery, metal products, processed food, steel and textiles.

Agriculture employs 3% of the people, but France is the largest producer of farm products in Western Europe, producing most of the food it needs. Wheat is the leading crop and livestock farming is of major importance. Fishing and forestry are leading industries. Tourism is also important. Paris is one of the world's great cities and major cultural centres, with many magnificent public buildings.

FRENCH GUIANA

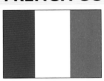

AREA 90,000 sq km [34,749 sq mi]
POPULATION 200,000
CAPITAL Cayenne
GOVERNMENT Overseas department of France
ETHNIC GROUPS Black or Mulatto 66%, East Indian/Chinese and Amerindian 12%, White 12%, others 10%
LANGUAGES French (official)
RELIGIONS Roman Catholic
CURRENCY Euro = 100 cents

GEOGRAPHY French Guiana is the smallest country in mainland South America. The coastal plain is swampy in places, but some dry areas are cultivated. Inland lies a plateau, with the low Tumachumac Mountains in the south. Most of the rivers run north towards the Atlantic Ocean.

French Guiana has a hot, equatorial climate, with high temperatures throughout the year. The rainfall is heavy, especially between December and June, but it is dry between August and October. The north-east trade winds blow constantly across the country.

POLITICS & ECONOMY The first people to live in what is now French Guiana were Amerindians. Today, only a few of them survive in the interior. The first Europeans to explore the coast arrived in 1500 and French merchants founded Cayenne in 1637. The area became a French colony in the late 17th century. France used the colony as a penal settlement for political prisoners from the times of the French Revolution in the 1790s. From the 1850s to 1945, the country became notorious for the harsh treatment of prisoners.

In 1946, French Guiana became an overseas department of France, and in 1974 it also became an administrative region. An independence movement developed in the 1980s, but most people want to retain their links with France and continue to obtain financial aid to develop their territory.

Although it has rich forest and mineral resources, such as bauxite (aluminium ore), French Guiana is a developing country. It depends greatly on France for money to run its services and the government is the country's biggest employer. Since 1968, Kourou in French Guiana, the European Space Agency's rocket-launching site, has earned money for France by sending communications satellites into space.

FRENCH POLYNESIA

AREA 4,000 sq km [1,544 sq mi]
POPULATION 275,000
CAPITAL Papeete

French Polynesia consists of 130 islands, scattered over 2.5 million sq km [1 million sq mi] of the Pacific Ocean. Tribal chiefs in the area agreed to a French protectorate in 1843. They gained increased autonomy in 1984, but the links with France ensure a high standard of living. However, some people favour independence. Following a struggle for power in 2004, the pro-independence Union for Democracy Party, led by Oscar Timaru, ousted the pro-French ruling party led by Gaston Flosse.

GABON

AREA 267,668 sq km [103,347 sq mi]
POPULATION 1,425,000
CAPITAL Libreville
GOVERNMENT Multiparty republic
ETHNIC GROUPS Four major Bantu tribes: Fang, Bapounou, Nzebi and Obamba
LANGUAGES French (official), Fang, Myene, Nzebi, Bapounou/Eschira, Bandjabi
RELIGIONS Christianity 75%, animist, Islam
CURRENCY CFA franc = 100 centimes

GEOGRAPHY The Gabonese Republic lies on the Equator in west-central Africa. Behind the narrow, partly lagooned 800 km [500 mi] long coastline, the land rises to hills, plateaux and mountains divided by deep valleys carved by the River Ogooué.

Most of Gabon has an equatorial climate, with high temperatures and humidity throughout the year. The rainfall is heavy and the skies are often cloudy.

POLITICS & ECONOMY Gabon became a French colony in the 1880s, but it achieved full independence in 1960. In 1964, an attempted coup was put down when French troops intervened and crushed the revolt. In 1967, Bernard-Albert Bongo, who later renamed himself El Hadj Omar Bongo, became president. He declared Gabon a one-party state in 1968. Opposition parties were legalized in 1991 and Bongo won successive victories in presidential elections. In 2003, constitutional changes enabled Bongo to stand again in 2005, when he was re-elected.

Gabon's abundant natural resources include its forests, oil and gas deposits near Port Gentil, together with manganese and uranium. These mineral deposits make Gabon one of Africa's better-off countries. But agriculture still employs about 34% of the population and many farmers produce little more than they need to support their families.

GAMBIA, THE

AREA 11,295 sq km [4,361 sq mi]
POPULATION 1,642,000
CAPITAL Banjul
GOVERNMENT Military regime
ETHNIC GROUPS Mandinka 42%, Fula 18%, Wolof 16%, Jola 10%, Serahuli 9%, others
LANGUAGES English (official), Mandinka, Wolof, Fula
RELIGIONS Islam 90%, Christianity 9%, traditional beliefs 1%
CURRENCY Dalasi = 100 butut

GEOGRAPHY The Republic of The Gambia is the smallest country in mainland Africa. It consists of a narrow strip of land bordering the River Gambia. The Gambia is almost entirely enclosed by Senegal, except along the short Atlantic coastline.

The Gambia has hot and humid summers, but the winter temperatures (November to May) drop to around 16°C [61°F]. In the summer, moist south-westerlies bring rain, which is heaviest on the coast.

POLITICS & ECONOMY English traders bought rights to trade on the River Gambia in 1588, and in 1664 the English established a settlement on an island in the river estuary. In 1765, the British founded a colony called Senegambia, which included parts of The Gambia and Senegal. In 1783, Britain handed this colony over to France.

In the 1860s and 1870s, Britain and France discussed the exchange of The Gambia for some other French territory. But no agreement was reached and Britain made The Gambia a British colony in 1888. It remained under British rule until it achieved full independence in 1965. In 1970, The Gambia became a republic. In 1981, a coup in The Gambia was put down with the help of Senegalese troops. In 1982, The Gambia and Senegal set up a defence alliance, called the Confederation of Senegambia. But this alliance was dissolved in 1989. In July 1994, a military group overthrew the president, Sir Dawda Jawara, who fled into exile. Captain Yahya Jammeh, who took power, was elected president in 1996 and re-elected in 2001 and 2006.

Agriculture is the main activity, though the government announced in 2004 that large oil reserves had been discovered. Food crops include cassava, millet and sorghum. Groundnuts and groundnut products are the chief exports. Tourism is a growing industry.

GEORGIA

AREA 69,700 sq km [26,911 sq mi]
POPULATION 4,661,000
CAPITAL Tbilisi
GOVERNMENT Multiparty republic
ETHNIC GROUPS Georgian 70%, Armenian 8%, Russian 6%, Azeri 6%, Ossetian 3%, Greek 2%, Abkhaz 2%, others 3%
LANGUAGES Georgian (official), Russian
RELIGIONS Georgian Orthodox 65%, Islam 11%, Russian Orthodox 10%, Armenian Apostolic 8%
CURRENCY Lari = 100 tetri

GEOGRAPHY Georgia is a country on the borders of Europe and Asia, facing the Black Sea. The land is rugged with the Caucasus Mountains forming its northern border. The highest mountain in this range, Mount Elbrus (5,642 m [18,510 ft]), lies over the border in Russia. The Black Sea plains have hot summers and mild winters. The rainfall is heavy, though inland areas are drier.

POLITICS & ECONOMY The first Georgian state was set up nearly 2,500 years ago. But for much of its history, the area was ruled by various conquerors. Christianity was introduced in AD 330. Georgia freed itself of foreign rule in the 11th and 12th centuries, but Mongol armies attacked in the 13th century. From the 16th to the 18th centuries, Iran and the Turkish Ottoman empire struggled for control of the area, and in the late 18th century Georgia sought the protection of Russia and, by the early 19th century, Georgia was part of the Russian empire. After the Russian Revolution of 1917, Georgia declared its independence, but Russia invaded, making the country part of the Soviet regime. Georgia declared itself independent in 1991. It became a separate country when the Soviet Union was dissolved in December 1991.

Georgia contains three regions containing minority peoples: Abkhazia in the north-west, South Ossetia in north-central Georgia, and Adjaria (also spelled Adzharia) in the south-west. Civil war broke out in South Ossetia in the early 1990s, while fierce fighting continued in Abkhazia until the late 1990s. In 2000, Georgia agreed to recognize Adjaria's autonomy in

the country's constitution. In 2002, Russian and Georgian troops attacked Chechen rebels in Pankisi Gorge in north-eastern Georgia. The USA also alleged that other Islamic terrorists were hiding in the area. In 2006, relations with Russia deteriorated when Georgia's president, Mikhail Saakashvili, accused Russia of supporting the secessionists.

Georgia is a developing country. Agriculture is important. Major products include barley, citrus fruits, grapes for wine-making, vegetables, maize, tobacco and tea. Food processing and silk and perfume-making are other important activities. Sheep and cattle are reared.

GERMANY

AREA 357,022 sq km [137,846 sq mi]
POPULATION 82,422,000
CAPITAL Berlin
GOVERNMENT Federal multiparty republic
ETHNIC GROUPS German 92%, Turkish 3%, Serbo-Croatian, Italian, Greek, Polish, Spanish
LANGUAGES German (official)
RELIGIONS Protestant (mainly Lutheran) 34%, Roman Catholic 34%, Islam 4%, others
CURRENCY Euro = 100 cents

GEOGRAPHY The Federal Republic of Germany is the fourth largest country in Western Europe, after France, Spain and Sweden. The North German plain borders the North Sea in the north-west and the Baltic Sea in the north-east. Major rivers draining the plain include the Weser, Elbe and Oder.

The central highlands contain plateaux and highlands, including the Harz Mountains, the Thuringian Forest (Thüringer Wald), the Ore Mountains (Erzgebirge), and the Bohemian Forest (Böhmerwald) on the Czech border. South Germany is largely hilly, but the land rises in the south to the Bavarian Alps, which contain Germany's highest peak, Zugspitze, at 2,962 m [9,718 ft] above sea level. The scenic Black Forest (Scharzwald) overlooks the River Rhine, which flows through a rift valley in the south-west. The Black Forest contains the source of the River Danube.

North-western Germany has a mild climate, but the Baltic coastlands are cooler. To the south, the climate becomes more continental, especially in the highlands. The precipitation is greatest on the uplands, many of which are snow-capped in winter.

POLITICS & ECONOMY Germany and its allies were defeated in World War I (1914–18) and the country became a republic. Adolf Hitler came to power in 1933 and ruled as a dictator. His order to invade Poland led to the start of World War II (1939–45), which ended with Germany in ruins.

In 1945, Germany was divided into four military zones. In 1949, the American, British and French zones were amalgamated to form the Federal Republic of Germany (West Germany), while the Soviet zone became the German Democratic Republic (East Germany), a Communist state. Berlin, which had also been partitioned, became a divided city. West Berlin was part of West Germany, while East Berlin became the capital of East Germany. Bonn was the capital of West Germany.

Tension between East and West mounted during the Cold War, but West Germany rebuilt its economy quickly. In East Germany, the recovery was less rapid. In the late 1980s, reforms in the Soviet Union led to unrest in East Germany. Free elections were held in East Germany in 1990 and, on 3 October 1990, Germany was reunited.

The united Germany adopted West Germany's official name, the Federal Republic of Germany. Elections in December 1990 returned Helmut Kohl, West Germany's Chancellor (head of government) since 1982, to power. In 1998, Kohl was succeeded by Social Democrat Gerhard Schröder.

Since reunification, Germany has faced many problems, some arising from the weak economy of eastern Germany and others involving racist violence and the resurgence of far-right groups. In 2005, Angela Merkel became the first female Chancellor, when she led the Christian Democratic Union to a narrow victory over Schröder's Social Democrats. She headed a broad left-right coalition government.

Germany is one of the world's leading economic powers. However, in the early 2000s, the economy became sluggish and Schröder introduced unpopular cuts in the welfare system. Manufacturing is the main economic sector and manufactures make up the bulk of Germany's exports. Leading manufactures include cars and other vehicles, cement, chemicals, computers, electrical equipment, processed food, machinery, scientific instruments, ships, steel, textiles and tools. Germany has some coal, potash and rock salt deposits, but it imports many raw materials.

Germany also imports food. Major agricultural products include fruits, grapes for wine-making, potatoes, sugar beet and vegetables. Beef and dairy cattle are raised, together with many other livestock.

GHANA

AREA 238,533 sq km [92,098 sq mi]
POPULATION 22,410,000
CAPITAL Accra
GOVERNMENT Republic
ETHNIC GROUPS Akan 44%, Moshi-Dagomba 16%, Ewe 13%, Ga 8%, Gurma 3%, Yoruba 1%
LANGUAGES English (official), Akan, Moshi-Dagomba, Ewe, Ga
RELIGIONS Christianity 63%, traditional beliefs 21%, Islam 16%
CURRENCY Cedi = 100 pesewas

GEOGRAPHY The Republic of Ghana faces the Gulf of Guinea in West Africa. It was formerly called the Gold Coast. Behind the thickly populated southern plains lies a plateau in the south-west. Lying just north of the Equator, it has a hot tropical climate. The south is rainy, but the north is drier.

POLITICS & ECONOMY Portuguese explorers reached the area in 1471 and named it the Gold Coast. The area became a centre of the slave trade in the 17th century. The slave trade was ended in the 1860s and, gradually, the British took control of the area. After independence in 1957, attempts were made to develop the economy by creating large state-owned manufacturing industries. But debt and corruption, together with falls in the price of cocoa, the chief export, caused economic problems. This led to instability and frequent coups. In 1981, power was invested in a Provisional National Defence Council, led by Flight-Lieutenant Jerry Rawlings.

The government steadied the economy and, in 1992, it reintroduced multiparty elections. Rawlings was elected president in 1992 and served until his retirement in 2000. He was succeeded by John Kufuor, who was re-elected in 2004.

The World Bank classifies Ghana as a 'low-income' developing country. Most people are poor and farming employs 50% of the population.

NATIONS OF THE WORLD

GIBRALTAR

AREA 6 sq km [2.3 sq mi]
POPULATION 28,000
CAPITAL Gibraltar Town

Gibraltar occupies a strategic position on the south coast of Spain where the Mediterranean meets the Atlantic. Formerly held by Moors from North Africa and later by Spain, it was recognized as a British possession in 1713. Despite Spanish claims, its population has consistently voted to retain its contacts with Britain.

GREECE

AREA 131,957 sq km [50,949 sq mi]
POPULATION 10,688,000
CAPITAL Athens
GOVERNMENT Multiparty republic
ETHNIC GROUPS Greek 98%
LANGUAGES Greek (official)
RELIGIONS Greek Orthodox 98%
CURRENCY Euro = 100 cents

GEOGRAPHY The Hellenic Republic, as Greece is officially called, is a rugged country situated at the southern end of the Balkan peninsula. Olympus, at 2,917 m [9,570 ft], is the highest peak. Islands make up about a fifth of the land. Greece has a typical Mediterranean climate, with mild, moist winters and hot, dry summers. The east coast has only about a half of the rainfall of the west. The mountains have a more severe climate than the lowlands.

POLITICS & ECONOMY Around 2,500 years ago, Greece became the birthplace of Western civilization. Ancient Greek ruins and art still attract millions of tourists to the country. The first civilization – the Minoan, centred on Crete – flourished between about 3000 and 1400 BC. Following the end of the related Mycaenean period on the mainland(1580–1100 BC), a 'dark age' lasted until about 800 BC. But from 750 BC, Greeks became rich traders and the city-state of Athens reached its peak in 461–431 BC. Greece became a Roman province in 146 BC and, in AD 365, it became part of the Byzantine Empire.

The Byzantine Empire fell to the Turks in 1453. But Greece became an independent monarchy in 1830. After World War II (1939–45), when Germany ruled Greece, a civil war broke out between Communists and nationalists. It ended in 1949 and a military dictatorship took power in 1967. The monarchy was abolished in 1973 and democracy was resumed in 1974. Greece joined the European Community (now the EU) in 1981. On 1 January 2002, the euro became the sole unit of currency.

Greece is one of Europe's poorer nations and, in 2006, researchers reported that 21% of the people lived below the poverty line. Greece mines lignite (brown coal), bauxite and chromite. Manufactured products include processed food, cement, chemicals, metal products, textiles and tobacco. Farmland covers about a third of the country and grazing land another 40%. Crops include barley, grapes for wine-making, fruits, olives, potatoes, sugar beet and wheat. Livestock farming is important, as is tourism.

GREENLAND

AREA 2,175,600 sq km [838,999 sq mi]
POPULATION 56,000
CAPITAL Nuuk (Godthåb)

Greenland is the world's largest island. Settlements are confined to the coast, because an ice-sheet covers four-fifths of the land. Greenland became a Danish possession in 1380. Full internal self-government was granted in 1981 and, in 1997, Danish place names were superseded by Inuit name forms. Its official name in the local language is Kalaallit Nunaat. However, Greenland remains heavily dependent on Danish subsidies.

GRENADA

AREA 344 sq km [133 sq mi]
POPULATION 90,000
CAPITAL St George's

The most southerly of the Windward Islands in the Caribbean Sea, Grenada became independent from the UK in 1974. A military group seized power in 1983, when the prime minister was killed. US troops intervened and restored order. Agriculture and tourism are the chief activities. Exports include bananas, cocoa, mace, nutmeg and textiles. In 2004 and 2005, hurricanes caused great damage.

GUADELOUPE

AREA 1,705 sq km [658 sq mi]
POPULATION 453,000
CAPITAL Basse-Terre

Guadeloupe is a French overseas department which includes seven Caribbean islands, the largest of which is Basse-Terre. French settlers arrived in 1635 and Guadeloupe has remained French except for a period of British rule in 1759–1813. French aid has helped to maintain reasonable living standards for the people.

GUAM

AREA 549 sq km [212 sq mi]
POPULATION 171,000
CAPITAL Agana

Guam, a strategically important 'unincorporated territory' of the USA, is the largest of the Mariana Islands in the Pacific Ocean. It is composed of a coralline limestone plateau. Guam was ruled by Spain from 1668 until it was ceded to the United States in 1898 after the Spanish–American War.

GUATEMALA

AREA 108,889 sq km [42,042 sq mi]
POPULATION 12,294,000
CAPITAL Guatemala City
GOVERNMENT Republic
ETHNIC GROUPS Ladino (mixed Hispanic and Amerindian) 55%, Amerindian 43%, others 2%
LANGUAGES Spanish (official), Amerindian languages
RELIGIONS Christianity, indigenous Mayan beliefs
CURRENCY US dollar; Quetzal = 100 centavos

GEOGRAPHY The Republic of Guatemala in Central America contains a thickly populated mountain region, with fertile soils. The mountains, which run in an east–west direction, contain many volcanoes, some of which are active. Volcanic eruptions and earthquakes are common in the highlands. South of the mountains lie the thinly populated Pacific coastlands, while a large inland plain occupies the north.

Guatemala lies in the tropics. The lowlands are hot and rainy. But the central mountain region is cooler and drier. Guatemala City, at about 1,500 m [5,000 ft] above sea level, has a pleasant, warm climate, with a marked dry season between November and April.

POLITICS & ECONOMY In 1823, Guatemala joined the Central American Federation. But it became fully independent in 1839. Since independence, Guatemala has been plagued by instability and violence.

Guatemala has a long-standing claim over Belize, but this was reduced in 1983 to the southern fifth of the country. Violence became widespread in Guatemala from the early 1960s, because of conflict between left-wing groups and government forces. A peace accord was signed in 1996, ending a 36-year war that had claimed perhaps 200,000 lives. In 2004, the government paid US$3.5 million in damages to victims of state-sponsored oppression.

The World Bank classifies Guatemala as a 'lower-middle-income' developing country. Agriculture employs nearly 40% of the population and coffee, sugar, bananas and beef are the leading exports. Other important crops include the spice cardamom and cotton, while maize is the chief food crop. But Guatemala still has to import food to feed the people.

GUINEA

AREA 245,857 sq km [94,925 sq mi]
POPULATION 9,690,000
CAPITAL Conakry
GOVERNMENT Multiparty republic
ETHNIC GROUPS Peuhl 40%, Malinke 30%, Soussou 20%, others 10%
LANGUAGES French (official)
RELIGIONS Islam 85%, Christianity 8%, traditional beliefs 7%
CURRENCY Guinean franc = 100 cauris

GEOGRAPHY The Republic of Guinea faces the Atlantic Ocean in West Africa. A flat, swampy plain borders the coast. Behind this plain, the land rises to a plateau region called Fouta Djalon. The Upper Niger plains are in the north-east.

Guinea has a tropical climate and Conakry, on the coast, has heavy rains between May and November.

This is also the coolest period in the year. During the dry season, hot, dry harmattan winds blow south-westwards from the Sahara Desert.

POLITICS & ECONOMY Guinea became independent in 1958. Its president, Sékou Touré, pursued socialist policies, though he had to resort to repressive policies to hold on to power. After his death in 1984, a military government, under President Lansana Conté, introduced free-enterprise policies. A multiparty system was restored in 1992 and Conté was elected president in 1993. He was re-elected in 1998 and 2002. From the late 1990s, Guinea was drawn into the civil conflicts in Liberia and Sierra Leone. In 2005, Conté survived an assassination attempt.

The World Bank classifies Guinea as a 'low-income' developing country. It has several natural resources, including bauxite (aluminium ore), diamonds, gold, iron ore and uranium. Bauxite and alumina (processed bauxite) account for 60% of the value of the exports. Agriculture, however, employs 74% of the people, many of whom produce little more than they need for their own families. Guinea has some manufacturing industries. Products include alumina, processed food and textiles.

GUINEA-BISSAU

AREA 36,125 sq km [13,948 sq mi]
POPULATION 1,442,000
CAPITAL Bissau
GOVERNMENT 'Interim' government
ETHNIC GROUPS Balanta 30%, Fula 20%, Manjaca 14%, Mandinga 13%, Papel 7%
LANGUAGES Portuguese (official), Crioulo
RELIGIONS Traditional beliefs 50%, Islam 45%, Christianity 5%
CURRENCY CFA franc = 100 centimes

GEOGRAPHY The Republic of Guinea-Bissau, formerly known as Portuguese Guinea, is a small country in West Africa. The land is mostly low-lying, with a broad, swampy coastal plain and many flat offshore islands, including the Bijagós Archipelago.

The country has a tropical climate, with one dry season (December to May) and a rainy season from June to November.

POLITICS & ECONOMY Portugal appointed a governor to administer Guinea-Bissau and the Cape Verde Islands in 1836, but in 1879 the two territories were separated and Guinea-Bissau became a colony, then called Portuguese Guinea. But development was slow, partly because the territory did not attract settlers on the same scale as Portugal's much healthier African colonies of Angola and Mozambique.

In 1956, African nationalists in Portuguese Guinea and Cape Verde founded the African Party for the Independence of Guinea and Cape Verde (PAIGC). Because Portugal seemed determined to hang on to its overseas territories, the PAIGC began a guerrilla war in 1963. By 1968, it held two-thirds of the country. In 1972, a rebel National Assembly, elected by the people in the PAIGC-controlled area, voted to make the country independent as Guinea-Bissau.

The independent nation faced many problems arising from its under-developed economy and its lack of trained personnel. Its leaders wanted to unite their country with Cape Verde, but, in 1980, military leaders seized power. The Revolutionary Council, which took over, opposed unification with Cape Verde. Guinea-Bissau ceased to be a one-party state in 1991 and elections were held in 1994. Civil war

broke out in 1998 and a military coup occurred in 1999. Kumba Ialá was elected president in 2000, but he was overthrown in a coup in 2003. Civilian rule was restored in 2004. In 2005, former military leader João Bernardo Vieira was elected president.

Guinea-Bissau is a poor country. Agriculture employs 76% of the people, but most farming is at subsistence level. Major crops include beans, coconuts, groundnuts, maize and rice.

GUYANA

AREA 214,969 sq km [83,000 sq mi]
POPULATION 767,000
CAPITAL Georgetown
GOVERNMENT Multiparty republic
ETHNIC GROUPS East Indian 50%, Black 36%, Amerindian 7%, others 7%
LANGUAGES English (official), Creole, Hindi, Urdu
RELIGIONS Christianity 50%, Hinduism 35%, Islam 10%, others
CURRENCY Guyanese dollar = 100 cents

GEOGRAPHY The Co-operative Republic of Guyana is a country facing the Atlantic Ocean in north-eastern South America. The coastal plain is flat and much of it is below sea level.

The climate is hot and humid, though the interior highlands are cooler than the coast. The rainfall is heavy, occurring on more than 200 days a year.

POLITICS & ECONOMY Britain gained control of the area in 1814 and set up the colony of British Guiana in 1831. British Guiana became independent as Guyana in 1966. A black lawyer, Forbes Burnham, became the first prime minister. Under a new constitution adopted in 1980, the president's powers were increased. Burnham became president until he died in 1985. He was succeeded by Hugh Desmond Hoyte, who was defeated in 1993 by an ethnic Indian, Cheddi Jagan. Jagan died in 1997 and was succeeded by his wife, Janet. In 1999, Bharrat Jagdeo was elected president. He was re-elected in 2001.

Guyana is a poor country. Its resources include gold, bauxite (aluminium ore) and other minerals, forests and fertile soils. Sugar cane and rice are leading crops. Electric power is in short supply, although the country has great potential for producing hydroelectricity from its many rivers.

HAITI

AREA 27,750 sq km [10,714 sq mi]
POPULATION 8,309,000
CAPITAL Port-au-Prince
GOVERNMENT Multiparty republic
ETHNIC GROUPS Black 95%, Mulatto/White 5%
LANGUAGES French and Creole (both official)
RELIGIONS Roman Catholic 80%, Voodoo
CURRENCY Gourde = 100 centimes

GEOGRAPHY The Republic of Haiti occupies the western third of Hispaniola in the Caribbean. The land is mainly mountainous. The climate is hot and humid, though the northern highlands, with about 200 mm [79 in], have more than twice as much rainfall as the southern coast.

POLITICS & ECONOMY Visited by Christopher Columbus in 1492, Haiti was later developed by the French. The African slaves revolted in 1791 and the country became independent in 1804. Since independence, Haiti has suffered from instability, violence and dictatorial rule. Elections in 1990 returned Jean-Bertrand Aristide as president, but he was overthrown in 1991. Following US intervention, he returned in 1994. In 1995, René Préval was elected president, but Aristide was again elected president in 2000. In 2004, rebel activity forced Aristide to flee the country. A US-backed government was set up to restore order and, in 2006, René Préval was re-elected president in national elections. Haiti suffered much hurricane damage in 2004 and 2005.

Haiti is the poorest country in the Americas. More than half of the people work on farms, producing barely enough to feed their families. Haiti has few industries.

HONDURAS

AREA 112,088 sq km [43,277 sq mi]
POPULATION 7,326,000
CAPITAL Tegucigalpa
GOVERNMENT Republic
ETHNIC GROUPS Mestizo 90%, Amerindian 7%, Black (including Black Carib) 2%, White 1%
LANGUAGES Spanish (official), Amerindian dialects
RELIGIONS Roman Catholic 97%
CURRENCY Honduran lempira = 100 centavos

GEOGRAPHY The Republic of Honduras is the second largest country in Central America. The northern coast on the Caribbean Sea extends more than 600 km [373 mi], but the Pacific coast in the south-east is only about 80 km [50 mi] long.

Honduras has a tropical climate, but the highlands, where the capital Tegucigalpa is situated, have a cooler climate than the hot coastal plains. The months between May and November are the rainiest. Hurricanes often strike the coast. In 1998, Hurricane Mitch caused great destruction.

POLITICS & ECONOMY Western Honduras was part of the Maya civilization and the ancient ruins of Copán in Honduras are testimony to the greatness of the Mayas. In 1502, Christopher Columbus claimed the land for Spain and Spain ruled the country from 1625 until 1821. It became part of the Central American Federation but it withdrew in 1838.

In the 1890s, American companies developed plantations in Honduras to grow bananas, which soon became the country's chief source of income. The companies exerted great political influence in Honduras and the country became known as a 'banana republic', a name that was later applied to several other Latin American nations.

Instability has continued to mar the country's progress. In 1969, Honduras fought the short 'Soccer War' with El Salvador. The war was sparked off by the treatment of fans during a World Cup soccer series. However, the real reason was that Honduras had forced Salvadoreans in Honduras to give up land. Since 1980, civilian governments have ruled Honduras, though the military remain influential.

Honduras is a developing country – one of the poorest in the Americas and the least industrialized in Central America. It has few resources besides some silver, lead and zinc, and agriculture dominates the economy. Bananas and coffee are the leading exports, and maize is the main food crop. Manufactures include processed food, textiles, and a variety of wood products.

NATIONS OF THE WORLD

HUNGARY

AREA 93,032 sq km [35,920 sq mi]
POPULATION 9,981,000
CAPITAL Budapest
GOVERNMENT Multiparty republic
ETHNIC GROUPS Magyar 90%, Gypsy, German, Serb, Romanian, Slovak
LANGUAGES Hungarian (official)
RELIGIONS Roman Catholic 68%, Calvinist 20%, Lutheran 5%, others
CURRENCY Forint = 100 fillér

GEOGRAPHY The Hungarian Republic is a land-locked country in central Europe. The land is mostly low-lying and drained by the Danube (Duna) and its tributary, the Tisza. Most of the land east of the Danube belongs to a region called the Great Plain (Nagyalföld), which covers about half of Hungary.

Hungary lies far from the moderating influence of the sea. As a result, summers are warmer and sunnier, and the winters colder than in Western Europe.

POLITICS & ECONOMY Hungary entered World War II (1939–45) in 1941, as an ally of Germany, but the Germans occupied the country in 1944. The Soviet Union invaded Hungary in 1944 and, in 1946, the country became a republic. The Communists gradually took over the government, taking complete control in 1949. From 1949, Hungary was an ally of the Soviet Union. In 1956, Soviet troops crushed an anti-Communist revolt. But in the 1980s, reforms in the Soviet Union led to the growth of anti-Communist groups in Hungary. In 1989, Hungary adopted a new constitution making it a multiparty state. Elections held in 1990 led to a victory for the non-Communist Democratic Forum. In 2002, the Hungarian Socialist Party, in alliance with the liberal Free Democrats, won a majority in parliament. In 2004, Hungary became a member of NATO and the EU.

Before World War II, Hungary's economy was based mainly on agriculture. But the Communists set up many manufacturing industries. The new factories were owned by the government, as also was most of the land. From the late 1980s, the government worked to increase private ownership. This created many problems. Manufacturing is the chief economic activity. Products include aluminium, chemicals, and electrical and electronic goods.

ICELAND

AREA 103,000 sq km [39,768 sq mi]
POPULATION 299,000
CAPITAL Reykjavik
GOVERNMENT Multiparty republic
ETHNIC GROUPS Icelandic 97%, Danish 1%
LANGUAGES Icelandic (official)
RELIGIONS Evangelical Lutheran 87%, other Protestant 4%, Roman Catholic 2%, others
CURRENCY Icelandic króna = 100 aurar

GEOGRAPHY The Republic of Iceland, in the North Atlantic Ocean, is closer to Greenland than Scotland. Iceland sits astride the Mid-Atlantic Ridge. It is slowly getting wider as the ocean is being stretched apart by continental drift.

Iceland has around 200 volcanoes, and eruptions are frequent. An eruption under the Vatnajökull ice-cap in 1996 created a subglacial lake which subsequently burst, causing severe flooding. Geysers and hot springs are other features. Ice-caps and glaciers cover about an eighth of the land. The only habitable areas are the coastal lowlands.

Although it lies far to the north, Iceland's climate is moderated by the warm waters of the Gulf Stream. The port of Reykjavik is ice-free all the year round.

POLITICS & ECONOMY Norwegian Vikings colonized Iceland in AD 874, and in 930 the settlers founded the world's oldest parliament, the Althing.

Iceland united with Norway in 1262. But when Norway united with Denmark in 1380, Iceland came under Danish rule. Iceland became a self-governing kingdom, united with Denmark, in 1918. It became a fully independent republic in 1944, following a referendum in which 97% of the people voted to break their country's ties with Denmark.

Iceland has played an important part in European affairs and is a member of the North Atlantic Treaty Organization. But Iceland has been involved in fishing disputes. In 1992, it left the International Whaling Commission because of its alleged anti-whaling policy. It rejoined in 2002, but, in 2003, it undertook its first whale hunt for 15 years, stating that it was a 'scientific catch' to study the impact of whales on fish stocks.

Iceland has few resources besides the fishing grounds which surround it, but it is one of Europe's richest countries. Fishing and fish processing are important and they dominate Iceland's overseas trade. Barely 1% of the land is used to grow crops, but 23% of the country can be used for grazing sheep and cattle.

INDIA

AREA 3,287,263 sq km [1,269,212 sq mi]
POPULATION 1,095,352,000
CAPITAL New Delhi
GOVERNMENT Multiparty federal republic
ETHNIC GROUPS Indo-Aryan (Caucasoid) 72%, Dravidian (Aboriginal) 25%, others (mainly Mongoloid) 3%
LANGUAGES Hindi, English, Telugu, Bengali, Marathi, Tamil, Urdu, Gujarati, Malayalam, Kannada, Oriya, Punjabi, Assamese, Kashmiri, Sindhi and Sanskrit are all official languages
RELIGIONS Hinduism 82%, Islam 12%, Christianity 2%, Sikhism 2%, Buddhism and others
CURRENCY Indian rupee = 100 paisa

GEOGRAPHY The Republic of India is the world's seventh largest country. In population, it ranks second only to China. The north is mountainous, with mountains and foothills of the Himalayan range. Rivers, such as the Brahmaputra and Ganges (Ganga), rise in the Himalaya and flow across the fertile northern plains. Southern India consists of a large plateau, called the Deccan. The Deccan is bordered by two mountain ranges, the Western Ghats and the Eastern Ghats.

India has three main seasons. The cool season runs from October to February. The hot season runs from March to June. The rainy monsoon season starts in the middle of June and continues into September. Delhi has a moderate rainfall, with about 640 mm [25 in] a year. The south-western coast and the north-east have far more rain. Darjeeling in the north-east has an average annual rainfall of 3,040 mm [120 in]. But parts of the Thar Desert in the north-west have only 50 mm [2 in] of rain per year.

POLITICS & ECONOMY In southern India, most of the people are descendants of the dark-skinned Dravidians, who were among India's earliest people. Most northerners are descendants of lighter-skinned Aryans who arrived around 3,500 years ago.

India was the birthplace of several major religions, including Hinduism, Buddhism and Sikhism. Islam was introduced from about AD 1000. The Muslim Mughal empire was founded in 1526. From the 17th century, Britain began to gain influence. From 1858 to 1947, India was ruled as part of the British empire. An independence movement began after the Sepoy Rebellion (1857–9) and, in 1885, the Indian National Congress was formed. In 1920, Mohandas K. Gandhi became its leader and it soon became a mass movement. When independence was finally achieved in 1947, British India was divided into modern India and Muslim Pakistan. Partition was marred by mass slaughter as Hindus and Sikhs fled from Pakistan, and Indian Muslims poured into Pakistan. In the ensuing disputes, some 1 million people were killed.

Although India has 15 major languages and hundreds of minor ones, together with many religions, the country remains the world's largest democracy. It has faced many problems, especially with Pakistan, over the disputed territory of Jammu and Kashmir. Two wars in 1965 and 1972 failed to alter greatly the 1948 cease-fire lines. In the late 1980s, Kashmiri nationalists in the Indian-controlled area waged a campaign, demanding either integration into Pakistan or independence. India sent in troops and accused Pakistan of intervention. In the 1990s, Pakistani-backed guerrillas fought to break India's hold on the Srinigar valley, Kashmir's most populous region. The situation was aggravated when both India and Pakistan tested nuclear devices in 1998. Between 2003 and 2007, the countries launched a series of peace moves, but conflict continued on the ground.

Economic development has been a major problem and, according to the World Bank, India is a 'low-income' developing country. After socialist policies failed to raise the living standards of the poor, the government introduced private enterprise. Farming employs 52% of the people. The main crops are rice, wheat, millet, sorghum, peas and beans. India has more cattle than any other country. Milk is produced but Hindus do not eat beef. India has reserves of coal, iron ore and oil, and manufacturing has expanded greatly since 1947. By 2005, India had the world's 11th largest economy, producing high-tech goods, iron and steel, machinery, refined petroleum, textiles, jewellery and transport equipment.

INDONESIA

AREA 1,904,569 sq km [735,354 sq mi]
POPULATION 245,453,000
CAPITAL Jakarta
GOVERNMENT Multiparty republic
ETHNIC GROUPS Javanese 45%, Sundanese 14%, Madurese 7%, coastal Malays 7%, approximately 300 others
LANGUAGES Bahasa Indonesian (official), many others
RELIGIONS Islam 88%, Roman Catholic 3%, Hinduism 2%, Buddhism 1%
CURRENCY Indonesian rupiah = 100 sen

GEOGRAPHY The Republic of Indonesia is an island nation in South-east Asia. In all, Indonesia contains about 13,600 islands, less than 6,000 of which are inhabited. Three-quarters of the country is made up of five main areas: the islands of Sumatra, Java and Sulawesi (Celebes), together with Kalimantan (southern Borneo) and Irian Jaya (western New Guinea). The islands are generally mountainous and volcanic. The larger islands have extensive coastal lowlands. The climate is hot and humid, with a high rainfall. Only Java and the Sunda Islands have relatively dry seasons.

POLITICS & ECONOMY Indonesia is the world's most populous Muslim nation, though Islam was introduced as recently as the 15th century. The Dutch became active in the area in the early 17th century and Indonesia became a Dutch colony in 1799. After a long struggle, the Netherlands recognized Indonesia's independence in 1949. The economy has expanded, but ethnic and religious conflict have slowed down economic progress.

In the early 21st century, Indonesia faced considerable internal disorder. Separatists were operating in Aceh province in northern Sumatra and in West Papua (formerly Irian Jaya), Christian–Muslim clashes led to loss of life in the Moluccas, while East (formerly Portuguese) Timor became independent in 2002.

In December 2004, more than 120,000 people were killed in Indonesia by a tsunami. Worst hit was Aceh, where the tragedy provoked talks which led to autonomy for Aceh province in 2006.

Indonesia is a developing country. Its resources include oil, natural gas, tin and other minerals, its fertile volcanic soils and its forests. Oil and gas are major exports. Timber, textiles, rubber, coffee and tea are also exported. The principal food crop is rice. Manufacturing is increasing, particularly on Java.

IRAN

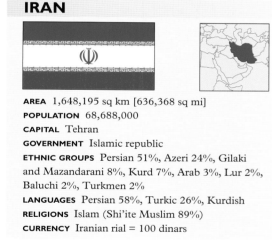

AREA 1,648,195 sq km [636,368 sq mi]
POPULATION 68,688,000
CAPITAL Tehran
GOVERNMENT Islamic republic
ETHNIC GROUPS Persian 51%, Azeri 24%, Gilaki and Mazandarani 8%, Kurd 7%, Arab 3%, Lur 2%, Baluchi 2%, Turkmen 2%
LANGUAGES Persian 58%, Turkic 26%, Kurdish
RELIGIONS Islam (Shi'ite Muslim 89%)
CURRENCY Iranian rial = 100 dinars

GEOGRAPHY The Republic of Iran contains a barren central plateau which covers about half of the country. It includes the Dasht-e-Kavir (Great Salt Desert) and the Dasht-e-Lut (Great Sand Desert). The Elburz Mountains north of the plateau contain Iran's highest peak, Damavand, while narrow lowlands lie between the mountains and the Caspian Sea. West of the plateau are the Zagros Mountains, beyond which the land descends to the Persian Gulf.

Much of Iran has a severe, dry climate, with hot summers and cold winters. In Tehran, rain falls on only about 30 days in the year and the annual temperature range is more than 25°C [45°F]. The climate in the lowlands, however, is generally milder.

POLITICS & ECONOMY Iran was called Persia until 1935. The empire of Ancient Persia flourished between 550 and 350 BC, when it fell to Alexander the Great. Islam was introduced in AD 641.

Britain and Russia competed for influence in the area in the 19th century, and in the early 20th century the British began to develop the country's oil resources. In 1925, the Pahlavi family took power. Reza Khan became shah (king) and worked to modernize the country. The Pahlavi dynasty was

ended in 1979 when a religious leader, Ayatollah Ruhollah Khomeini, made Iran an Islamic republic. In 1980–8, Iran and Iraq fought a war over disputed borders. Khomeini died in 1989, but his anti-Western views continued to dominate politics. In 2005, a hardliner, Mahmoud Ahmadinejad, was elected president. His government's support for Iran's nuclear programme, which many in the West considered was intended to develop nuclear weapons, led to sanctions being applied against Iran in 2006–7.

Iran's prosperity is based on its oil production and oil accounts for 85% of the country's exports. However, the economy was severely damaged by the Iran–Iraq war in the 1980s. Oil revenues have been used to develop a growing manufacturing sector. Agriculture is important even though farms cover only a tenth of the land. The main crops are wheat and barley. Livestock farming and fishing are other important activities, although Iran has to import much of the food it needs.

IRAQ

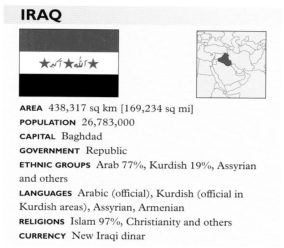

AREA 438,317 sq km [169,234 sq mi]
POPULATION 26,783,000
CAPITAL Baghdad
GOVERNMENT Republic
ETHNIC GROUPS Arab 77%, Kurdish 19%, Assyrian and others
LANGUAGES Arabic (official), Kurdish (official in Kurdish areas), Assyrian, Armenian
RELIGIONS Islam 97%, Christianity and others
CURRENCY New Iraqi dinar

GEOGRAPHY The Republic of Iraq is a south-west Asian country at the head of the Gulf. Rolling deserts cover western and south-western Iraq, with mountains in the north-east. The northern plains, across which flow the rivers Euphrates (Nahr al Furat) and Tigris (Nahr Dijlah), are dry. But the southern plains, including Mesopotamia, and the delta of the Shatt al Arab, the river formed south of Al Qurnah by the combined Euphrates and Tigris, contain irrigated farmland, together with marshes. The climate of Iraq ranges from temperate in the north to subtropical in the south.

POLITICS & ECONOMY Mesopotamia was the home of several great civilizations, including Sumer, Babylon and Assyria. It later became part of the Persian empire. Islam was introduced in AD 637 and Baghdad became the brilliant capital of the powerful Arab empire. But Mesopotamia declined after the Mongols invaded it in 1258. From 1534, Mesopotamia became part of the Turkish Ottoman empire. Britain invaded the area in 1916. In 1921, Britain renamed the country Iraq and set up an Arab monarchy. Iraq finally became independent in 1932.

By the 1950s, oil dominated Iraq's economy. In 1952, Iraq agreed to take 50% of the profits of the foreign oil companies. This revenue enabled the government to pay for welfare services and development projects. But many Iraqis felt that they should benefit more from their oil.

Since 1958, when army officers killed the king and made Iraq a republic, the country has undergone turbulent times. In the 1960s, the Kurds, who live in northern Iraq and also in Iran, Turkey, Syria and Armenia, asked for self-rule. The government rejected their demands and war broke out. A peace treaty was signed in 1975, but conflict has continued.

In 1979, Saddam Hussein became Iraq's president.

Under his leadership, Iraq invaded Iran in 1980, starting an eight-year war. Iraqi Kurds supported Iran and the Iraqi government attacked Kurdish villages with poison gas. In 1990, Iraqi troops occupied Kuwait, but an international force drove them out in 1991. Since 1991, Iraqi troops have attacked Shi'ite Marsh Arabs and Kurds. In 1998, Iraq's failure to permit UN inspectors, charged with disposing of Iraq's deadliest weapons, access to suspect sites led to the Western bombardment of Iraqi military sites. Another major offensive occurred in February 2001.

In 2002 and 2003, pressure mounted on Iraq to dispose of its alleged weapons of mass destruction. Its failure to do so led to a coalition force, headed by the United States and the UK, to invade Iraq and overthrow the Saddam regime in March–April 2003. Violence continued after the successful military operation, partly because of the conflict between the majority Shia Muslims and the Sunni Muslims, who make up about a sixth of the population. However, parliamentary elections were held under a new constitution in 2005. Nouri al-Maliki, a Shia, became prime minister.

War damage, UN sanctions and mismanagement have all contributed to weakening the economy. Oil remains Iraq's chief resource. Farmland, including pasture, covers about a fifth of the land. Products include barley, cotton, dates, fruit, livestock, wheat and wool, but Iraq still has to import food. Industries include oil refining and the manufacture of petrochemicals and consumer goods.

IRELAND

AREA 70,273 sq km [27,132 sq mi]
POPULATION 4,062,000
CAPITAL Dublin
GOVERNMENT Multiparty republic
ETHNIC GROUPS Irish 94%
LANGUAGES Irish (Gaelic) and English (both official)
RELIGIONS Roman Catholic 92%, Protestant 3%
CURRENCY Euro = 100 cents

GEOGRAPHY The Republic of Ireland occupies five-sixths of the island of Ireland. The country consists of a large lowland region surrounded by a broken rim of low mountains. The uplands include the Mountains of Kerry where Carrauntoohill, Ireland's highest peak at 1,041 m [3,415 ft], is situated. The River Shannon is the longest in Ireland, flowing through three large lakes, loughs Allen, Ree and Derg.

Ireland has a mild, damp climate greatly influenced by the warm Gulf Stream current that washes its shores. The effects of the Gulf Stream are greatest in the west. Dublin in the east is cooler than places on the west coast. Rain occurs throughout the year.

POLITICS & ECONOMY In 1801, the Act of Union created the United Kingdom of Great Britain and Ireland. But Irish discontent intensified in the 1840s when a potato blight caused a famine in which a million people died and nearly a million emigrated. Britain was blamed for not having done enough to help. In 1916, an uprising in Dublin was crushed, but between 1919 and 1922 civil war occurred. In 1922, the Irish Free State was created as a Dominion in the British Commonwealth. But Northern Ireland remained part of the UK.

Ireland became a republic in 1949. Since then, Irish governments have sought to develop the economy, and it was for this reason that Ireland joined the

European Community in 1973. In 1998, Ireland took part in the negotiations to produce a constitutional settlement in Northern Ireland. As part of this 'Good Friday Agreement', Ireland agreed to give up its constitutional claim on Northern Ireland. The agreement proved difficult to implement, but, in 2007, a power-sharing government was set up in the north.

Major farm products in Ireland include barley, cattle and dairy products, pigs, potatoes, poultry, sheep, sugar beet and wheat, while fishing provides another valuable source of food. Farming is now profitable, aided by European Union grants, but manufacturing is the leading economic sector. Many factories produce food and beverages. Chemicals and pharmaceuticals, electronic equipment, machinery, paper and textiles are also important.

ISRAEL

AREA 20,600 sq km [7,954 sq mi]
POPULATION 6,352,000
CAPITAL Jerusalem
GOVERNMENT Multiparty republic
ETHNIC GROUPS Jewish 80%, Arab and others 20%
LANGUAGES Hebrew and Arabic (both official)
RELIGIONS Judaism 80%, Islam (mostly Sunni) 14%, Christianity 2%, Druze and others 2%
CURRENCY New Israeli shekel = 100 agorat

GEOGRAPHY The State of Israel is a small country in the eastern Mediterranean. It includes a fertile coastal plain, where Israel's main industrial cities, Haifa (Hefa) and Tel Aviv-Jaffa are situated. Inland lie the Judaeo-Galilean highlands, which run from northern Israel to the northern tip of the Negev Desert. To the east lies part of the Great Rift Valley which contains the River Jordan, the Sea of Galilee and the Dead Sea.

Summers are hot and dry. Winters on the coast are mild and moist, but the rainfall decreases from west to east and from north to south.

POLITICS & ECONOMY Israel is part of a region called Palestine. Some Jews have always lived in the area, though most modern Israelis are descendants of immigrants who began to settle there from the 1880s. Britain ruled Palestine from 1917. Large numbers of Jews escaping Nazi persecution arrived in the 1930s, provoking an Arab uprising against British rule. In 1947, the UN agreed to partition Palestine into an Arab and a Jewish state. Fighting broke out after Arabs rejected the plan. The State of Israel came into being in May 1948, but fighting continued into 1949. Other Arab–Israeli wars in 1956, 1967 and 1973 led to land gains for Israel.

In 1978, Israel signed a treaty with Egypt which led to the return of the occupied Sinai peninsula to Egypt in 1979. But conflict continued between Israel and the PLO (Palestine Liberation Organization). In 1993, the PLO and Israel agreed to establish Palestinian self-rule in two areas: the occupied Gaza Strip, and in the town of Jericho in the occupied West Bank. The agreement was extended in 1995 to include more than 30% of the West Bank. Israel's prime minister, Yitzhak Rabin, was assassinated in 1995. In 1996, Benjamin Netanyahu was elected prime minister. The peace process stalled until Ehud Barak defeated Netanyahu in 1999. But, following renewed violence, Barak resigned and Ariel Sharon succeeded him in 2001. In 2005, Sharon ordered the withdrawal of Israeli forces and the dismantlement of Israeli settlements in the Gaza Strip, which came under the Palestinian Authority. Sharon formed a new party, Kadima. But after Sharon suffered a stroke, Ehud Olmert took over and led Kadima to electoral victory in 2006. Arab-Israeli tensions mounted when Hamas, a militant party which refused to recognize Israel, won elections in the Palestine Authority.

Israel's most valuable activity is manufacturing and the country's products include chemicals, electronic equipment, fertilizers, military equipment, plastics, processed food, scientific instruments and textiles. Fruits and vegetables are leading exports.

ITALY

AREA 301,318 sq km [116,339 sq mi]
POPULATION 58,134,000
CAPITAL Rome
GOVERNMENT Multiparty republic
ETHNIC GROUPS Italian 94%, German, French, Albanian, Slovene, Greek
LANGUAGES Italian (official), German, French, Slovene
RELIGIONS Predominantly Roman Catholic
CURRENCY Euro = 100 cents

GEOGRAPHY The Republic of Italy is famous for its history and traditions, its art and culture, and its beautiful scenery. Northern Italy is bordered in the north by the high Alps, with their many climbing and skiing resorts. The Alps overlook the northern plains – Italy's most fertile and densely populated region – drained by the River Po. The rugged Apennines form the backbone of southern Italy. The south also contains a string of active volcanoes, including Etna on Sicily, Italy's largest island.

Northern Italy has cold, often snowy, winters, but the summer months are warm and sunny, with brief summer thunderstorms. Rainfall is abundant. The south has mild, moist winters and warm, dry summers.

POLITICS & ECONOMY Magnificent ruins throughout Italy testify to the glories of the ancient Roman Empire, which was founded, according to legend, in 753 BC. It reached its peak in the AD 100s. It finally collapsed in the 400s, although the Eastern Roman empire, also called the Byzantine empire, survived for another 1,000 years.

In the Middle Ages, Italy was split into many tiny states. These states made a great contribution to the revival of art and learning, called the Renaissance, in the 14th to 16th centuries. Beautiful cities, such as Florence (Firenze) and Venice (Venézia), testify to the artistic achievements of this period.

Italy finally became a united kingdom in 1861, although the Papal Territories (a large area ruled by the Roman Catholic Church) was not added until 1870. The Pope and his successors disputed the take-over of the Papal Territories. The dispute was finally resolved in 1929, when the Vatican City was set up in Rome as a fully independent state.

Italy fought in World War I (1914–18) alongside the Allies – Britain, France and Russia. In 1922, the dictator Benito Mussolini, leader of the Fascist Party, took power. Under Mussolini, Italy conquered Ethiopia. During World War II (1939–45), Italy at first fought on Germany's side against the Allies. But in late 1943, Italy declared war on Germany. Italy became a republic in 1946. It has played an important part in European affairs. It was a founder member of the North Atlantic Treaty Organization (NATO) in 1949 and also of what has now become the European Union in 1958.

After the setting up of the European Union, Italy's economy developed quickly. But the country faced many problems. For example, much of the economic development was in the north. This forced many people to leave the poor south to find jobs in the north or abroad. Social problems, corruption at high levels of society, and a succession of weak coalition governments all contributed to instability. Elections in 1996 were won by the left-wing Olive Tree Alliance led by Romano Prodi. However, in 2001, a centre-right coalition led by media tycoon Silvio Berlusconi was elected with a large majority. In 2006, a centre-left coalition, led by Romano Prodi, defeated Berlusconi's centre-right House of Liberties by a narrow majority.

Only 50 years ago, Italy was a mainly agricultural society – today it is a leading industrial power. It lacks mineral resources, and imports most of the raw materials used in industry. Manufactures include textiles, processed food, machinery, cars and chemicals. The chief industrial region is in the north-west.

Farmland covers around 42% of the land, pasture 17%, and forest and woodland 22%. Major crops include citrus fruits, grapes which are used to make wine, olive oil, sugar beet and vegetables. Livestock farming is important, though meat is imported.

IVORY COAST

AREA 322,463 sq km [124,503 sq mi]
POPULATION 17,655,000
CAPITAL Yamoussoukro
GOVERNMENT Multiparty republic
ETHNIC GROUPS Akan 42%, Voltaiques 18%, Northern Mandes 16%, Krous 11%, Southern Mandes 10%
LANGUAGES French (official), many native dialects
RELIGIONS Islam 40%, Christianity 30%, traditional beliefs 30%
CURRENCY CFA franc = 100 centimes

GEOGRAPHY The Republic of the Ivory Coast, in West Africa, is officially known as Côte d'Ivoire. The south-east coast is bordered by sand bars that enclose lagoons. The south-west coast is lined by rocky cliffs.

Ivory Coast has a hot and humid tropical climate, with high temperatures all year. The south has two rainy seasons: between May and July, and from October to November. Inland, the rainfall decreases and the north has one dry and one rainy season.

POLITICS & ECONOMY From 1895, Ivory Coast was governed as part of French West Africa, a massive union which also included what are now Benin, Burkina Faso, Guinea, Mali, Mauritania, Niger and Senegal. In 1946, Ivory Coast became a territory in the French Union.

Ivory Coast became fully independent in 1960. Its first president, Félix Houphouët-Boigny, became the longest serving head of state in Africa with an uninterrupted period in office which ended with his death in 1993. Houphouët-Boigny, a pro-Western leader, made Ivory Coast a one-party state. In 1983, the National Assembly voted to make Yamoussoukro, the president's birthplace, the new capital. In 1999, a military coup occurred, but civilian rule was restored in 2000, when Laurent Gbagbo was elected president. However, conflict from 2002 led to the division of the country into the government-held south and the rebel-held, mainly Muslim, north. In 2007, the government agreed a peace deal, holding out hopes of a settlement.

Agriculture employs about half of the people, and farm products make up nearly half the value of the exports. Manufactures include fertilizers, processed food, refined oil, textiles and timber.

JAMAICA

AREA 10,991 sq km [4,244 sq mi]
POPULATION 2,758,000
CAPITAL Kingston
GOVERNMENT Constitutional monarchy
ETHNIC GROUPS Black 91%, Mixed 7%, East Indian 1%
LANGUAGES English (official), patois English
RELIGIONS Protestant 61%, Roman Catholic 4%
CURRENCY Jamaican dollar = 100 cents

GEOGRAPHY Third largest of the Caribbean islands, half of Jamaica lies above 300 m [1,000 ft] and moist south-east trade winds bring rain to the central mountain range. The 'cockpit country' in the north-west of the island is an inaccessible limestone area of steep broken ridges and isolated basins.

POLITICS & ECONOMY Christopher Columbus reached the island in 1494 and claimed it for Spain. Britain took Jamaica from Spain in the 17th century and, despite slave and peasant revolts, the island did not achieve independence until 1962. Power has alternated between the People's National Party (PNP) and Jamaica Labour Party. In 2006, Prime Minister Percival Patterson stepped down and was succeeded by the new PNP leader, Portia Simpson-Miller.

Jamaica has an important tourist industry. Farming is important and sugar cane is the chief crop. But alumina and bauxite make up 60% of the exports.

JAPAN

AREA 377,829 sq km [145,880 sq mi]
POPULATION 127,464,000
CAPITAL Tokyo
GOVERNMENT Constitutional monarchy
ETHNIC GROUPS Japanese 99%, Chinese, Korean, Brazilian and others
LANGUAGES Japanese (official)
RELIGIONS Shintoism and Buddhism 84% (most Japanese consider themselves to be both Shinto and Buddhist), others
CURRENCY Yen = 100 sen

GEOGRAPHY Japan's four largest islands – Honshu, Hokkaido, Kyushu and Shikoku – make up 98% of the country. But Japan contains thousands of small islands. The four largest islands are mainly mountainous, while many of the small islands are the tips of volcanoes. Japan has more than 150 volcanoes, about 60 of which are active. Volcanic eruptions, earthquakes and tsunamis (destructive sea waves triggered by underwater earthquakes and eruptions) are common because the islands lie in an unstable part of our planet, where continental plates are always on the move. One powerful recent earthquake killed more than 5,000 people in Kobe in 1995.

The climate of Japan varies greatly from north to south. Hokkaido in the north has cold, snowy winters. At Sapporo, temperatures below –20°C [4°F] have been recorded between December and March. But summers are warm, with temperatures sometimes exceeding 30°C [86°F]. Rain falls throughout the year, though Hokkaido is one of the driest parts of Japan. Tokyo has higher rainfall and temperatures, while the southern islands of Shikoku and Kyushu

have warm temperate climates. Summers are long and hot. Winters are cold.

POLITICS & ECONOMY In the late 19th century, Japan began a programme of modernization. Under its new imperial leaders, it began to look for lands to conquer. In 1894–5, it fought a war with China and, in 1904–5, it defeated Russia. Soon its overseas empire included Korea and Taiwan. In 1930, Japan invaded Manchuria (north-east China) and, in 1937, it began a war against China. In 1941, Japan launched an attack on the US base at Pearl Harbor in Hawai'i. This drew both Japan and the United States into World War II.

Japan surrendered in 1945 when the Americans dropped atomic bombs on two cities, Hiroshima and Nagasaki. The United States occupied Japan until 1952. During this period, Japan adopted a democratic constitution. The emperor, who had previously been regarded as a god, became a constitutional monarch. Power was vested in the prime minister and cabinet, who are chosen from the Diet (elected parliament).

From the 1960s, Japan experienced many changes as the country rapidly built up new industries. By the early 1990s, Japan had become the world's second richest economic power after the US. But economic success has brought problems. For example, the rapid growth of cities has led to housing shortages and pollution. Another problem is that the proportion of people over 65 years of age is steadily increasing.

Japan has the world's second highest gross domestic product (GDP) after the United States. [The GDP is the total value of all goods and services produced in a country in one year.] The most important sector of the economy is industry. Yet Japan has to import most of the raw materials and fuels it needs for its industries. Its success is based on its use of the latest technology, its skilled and hard-working labour force, its vigorous export policies and its comparatively small government spending on defence. Manufactures dominate its exports, which include machinery, electrical and electronic equipment, vehicles and transport equipment, iron and steel, chemicals, textiles and ships. Japan experienced an economic slowdown in the 1990s and a recession in the early 2000s. But signs of recovery were evident by 2006–7.

Japan is one of the world's top fishing nations and fish is an important source of protein. Because the land is so rugged, only 15% of the country can be farmed. Yet Japan produces about 70% of the food it needs. Rice is the chief crop, taking up about half of the total farmland. Other major products include fruits, sugar beet, tea and vegetables. Livestock farming has increased since the 1950s.

JORDAN

AREA 89,342 sq km [34,495 sq mi]
POPULATION 5,907,000
CAPITAL Amman
GOVERNMENT Constitutional monarchy
ETHNIC GROUPS Arab 98%, of which Palestinians make up roughly half
LANGUAGES Arabic (official)
RELIGIONS Islam (mostly Sunni) 94%, Christianity (mostly Greek Orthodox) 6%
CURRENCY Jordanian dinar = 1,000 fils

GEOGRAPHY The Hashemite Kingdom of Jordan is an Arab country in south-western Asia. The Great Rift Valley in the west contains the River Jordan and the Dead Sea, which Jordan shares with Israel. East

of the Rift Valley is the Transjordan plateau, where most Jordanians live. To the east and south lie vast areas of desert.

Amman has a much lower rainfall and longer dry season than the Mediterranean lands to the west. The Transjordan plateau, on which Amman stands, is a transition zone between the Mediterranean climate zone to the west and the desert climate to the east.

POLITICS & ECONOMY In 1921, Britain created a territory called Transjordan east of the River Jordan. In 1923, Transjordan became self-governing, but Britain retained control of its defences, finances and foreign affairs. This territory became fully independent as Jordan in 1946.

Jordan has suffered from instability arising from the Arab–Israeli conflict since the creation of the State of Israel in 1948. After the first Arab–Israeli War in 1948–9, Jordan acquired East Jerusalem and a fertile area called the West Bank. In 1967, Israel occupied this area. In Jordan, the presence of Palestinian refugees led to civil war in 1970–1.

In 1974, Arab leaders declared that the PLO (Palestine Liberation Organization) was the sole representative of the Palestinian people. In 1988, King Hussein of Jordan renounced Jordan's claims to the West Bank and passed responsibility for it to the PLO. Opposition parties were legalized in 1991 and elections were held in 1993. In October 1994, Jordan and Israel signed a peace treaty, ending a state of war that had lasted more than 40 years. Jordan's King Hussein commanded respect for his role in Middle Eastern affairs until his death in 1999. He was succeeded by his eldest son who became Abdullah II.

Following the path of his father, Abdullah has sought to further the Israeli–Palestinian peace process, while consolidating Jordan's relations with other Middle Eastern countries. Jordan supported the US-led war on terrorism. But its reputation as one of the safest countries in the Middle East was damaged in 2005 by suicide bombings on hotels in Amman. An Islamic group based in Iraq but led by a Jordanian-born militant claimed responsibility.

Jordan lacks natural resources, apart from phosphates and potash, and the economy depends substantially on aid. The World Bank classifies Jordan as a 'lower-middle-income' developing country. Less than 6% of the land is farmed or used as pasture. Jordan has an oil refinery and manufactures include cement, ceramics, pharmaceuticals, processed food, fertilizers, shoes and textiles. Jordan depends on foreign aid and remittances sent home by Jordanians who have taken jobs abroad. Service industries, including tourism, employ more than 70% of the people.

KAZAKHSTAN

AREA 2,724,900 sq km [1,052,084 sq mi]
POPULATION 15,233,000
CAPITAL Astana
GOVERNMENT Multiparty republic
ETHNIC GROUPS Kazakh 53%, Russian 30%, Ukrainian 4%, German 2%, Uzbek 2%
LANGUAGES Kazakh (official); Russian, the former official language, is widely spoken
RELIGIONS Islam 47%, Russian Orthodox 44%
CURRENCY Tenge = 100 tiyn

GEOGRAPHY Kazakhstan is a large country in west-central Asia. In the west, the Caspian Sea lowlands include the Karagiye depression, which reaches 132 m [433 ft] below sea level. The lowlands extend eastwards through the Aral Sea area. The north contains high plains, but the highest land is along the eastern and southern borders. These areas include parts of the Altai and Tian Shan mountain ranges.

Eastern Kazakhstan contains several freshwater lakes, the largest of which is Lake Balkhash. The water in the rivers has been used for irrigation, causing ecological problems. For example, the Aral Sea, deprived of water, shrank from 66,900 sq km [25,830 sq mi] in 1960 to 33,642 sq km [12,989 sq mi] in 1993. Large areas are now barren desert.

Kazakhstan has an extreme climate. Winters are cold and snow covers the land for about 100 days at Almaty. The rainfall is generally low.

POLITICS & ECONOMY After the Russian Revolution of 1917, many Kazakhs wanted to make their country independent. But the Communists prevailed and in 1936 Kazakhstan became a republic of the Soviet Union, called the Kazakh Soviet Socialist Republic. During World War II and also after the war, the Soviet government moved many people from the west into Kazakhstan. From the 1950s, people were encouraged to work on a 'Virgin Lands' project, which involved bringing large areas of grassland under cultivation.

Reforms in the Soviet Union in the 1980s led to the break-up of the country in December 1991. Kazakhstan maintained contacts with Russia through the Commonwealth of Independent States (CIS). In 1997, the government moved its capital from Almaty to Aqmola (later renamed Astana), a town in the Russian-dominated north. By the mid-2000s, Kazakhstan's economy was in better shape than the other ex-Soviet republics in Central Asia. But its President Nursultan Nazarbaev was criticized for his authoritarian rule. In 2005, Nazarbaev took 91% of the vote in a widely criticized presidential election. In 2006, the government was accused of operating death squads to eliminate opposition leaders.

The World Bank classifies Kazakhstan as a 'lower-middle-income' developing country. Livestock farming, especially sheep and cattle, is an important activity, and major crops include barley, cotton, rice and wheat. The country is rich in mineral resources, including coal and oil reserves, together with bauxite, copper, lead, tungsten and zinc. Manufactures include chemicals, food products, machinery and textiles. Oil is exported via a pipeline through Russia, though, to reduce dependence on Russia, Kazakhstan signed an agreement in 1997 to build a new pipeline to China. Other exports include metals, chemicals, grain, wool and meat.

KENYA

AREA 580,367 sq km [224,080 sq mi]
POPULATION 34,708,000
CAPITAL Nairobi
GOVERNMENT Multiparty republic
ETHNIC GROUPS Kikuyu 22%, Luhya 14%, Luo 13%, Kalenjin 12%, Kamba 11%, others
LANGUAGES Kiswahili and English (both official)
RELIGIONS Protestant 45%, Roman Catholic 33%, traditional beliefs 10%, Islam 10%
CURRENCY Kenyan shilling = 100 cents

GEOGRAPHY The Republic of Kenya is a country in East Africa which straddles the Equator. It is slightly larger in area than France. Behind the narrow coastal plain on the Indian Ocean, the land rises to high plains and highlands, broken by volcanic mountains,

including Mount Kenya, the country's highest peak at 5,199 m [17,057 ft]. Crossing the country is an arm of the Great Rift Valley, on the floor of which are several lakes, including Baringo, Magadi, Naivasha, Nakuru and, on the northern frontier, Lake Turkana (formerly Lake Rudolf).

Mombasa on the coast is hot and humid. But inland, the climate is moderated by the height of the land. As a result, Nairobi, in the thickly populated south-western highlands, has summer temperatures which are 10°C [18°F] lower than Mombasa. Nights can be cool, but temperatures do not fall below freezing. Nairobi's main rainy season is from April to May, with 'little rains' in November and December. However, only about 15% of the country has a reliable rainfall of 800 mm [31 in].

POLITICS & ECONOMY The Kenyan coast has been a trading centre for more than 2,000 years. Britain took over the coast in 1895 and soon extended its influence inland. In the 1950s, a secret movement, called Mau Mau, launched an armed struggle against British rule. Although Mau Mau was eventually defeated, Kenya became independent in 1963.

Many Kenyans felt that Kenya should have a strong central government, and Kenya was a one-party state for much of the time since 1963. But democracy was restored in the early 1990s and elections were held in 1992, 1997 and 2002. In 1999, Kenya, with Tanzania and Uganda, set up an East African Community, which aimed to create a customs union, a common market, a monetary union, and, ultimately, a political union.

When it became a republic in 1964, Kenya's first president was the nationalist veteran Jomo Kenyatta, who died in 1978. His successor, Daniel arap Moi, was criticized for his autocratic rule. In 2002, a veteran politician, Mwai Kibaki, was elected president. Kibaki promised to make Kenya more democratic and combat corruption. But, in 2005 and 2006, Kenya was hit by a severe drought, and Kibaki's government was widely criticized for its failure to halt corruption. Voters also rejected a draft constitution. Many argued that it conferred too many powers on the president.

Kenya has the largest economy of the countries of East Africa, but it remains a 'low-income' developing country. Many Kenyans are subsistence farmers. The chief food crop is maize. The main cash crops and leading exports are coffee and tea. Manufactures include chemicals, leather and footwear, processed food, petroleum products and textiles.

KIRIBATI

AREA 726 sq km [280 sq mi]
POPULATION 105,000
CAPITAL Tarawa

The Republic of Kiribati comprises three groups of low-lying coral atolls scattered over 5 million sq km [2 million sq mi], which are threatened by global warming and consequent rising sea levels. Kiribati straddles the Equator and temperatures are high throughout the year. The rainfall is abundant.

The Gilbert and Ellice Islands became a British protectorate in 1892 and a colony in 1915. In 1975, the Ellice Islands, following a referendum, officially severed its links with the Gilbert Islands and became a separate territory called Tuvalu in 1978. In 1979, the Gilbert Islands became fully independent as the Republic of Kiribati. The main export is copra and the country depends heavily on foreign aid.

KOREA, NORTH

AREA 120,538 sq km [46,540 sq mi]
POPULATION 23,113,000
CAPITAL Pyŏngyang
GOVERNMENT Single-party people's republic
ETHNIC GROUPS Korean 99%
LANGUAGES Korean (official)
RELIGIONS Buddhism and Confucianism
CURRENCY North Korean won = 100 chon

GEOGRAPHY The Democratic People's Republic of Korea occupies the northern part of the Korean peninsula which extends south from north-eastern China. Mountains form the heart of the country, with the highest peak, Paektu-san, reaching 2,744 m [9,003 ft] on the northern border. In winter, winds blow from across central Asia, bringing snow and freezing conditions. In summer, moist oceanic winds bring rain.

POLITICS & ECONOMY North Korea was created in 1945, when the peninsula, a Japanese colony since 1910, was divided into two parts. Soviet forces occupied the north, with US forces in the south. Soviet occupation led to a Communist government being established in 1948 under the leadership of Kim Il Sung. He created a Stalinist regime and ruled as a dictator. He also became the world's most durable Communist leader.

The Korean War began in June 1950 when North Korean troops invaded the south. North Korea, aided by China and the Soviet Union, fought with South Korea, which was supported by troops from the United States and other UN members. The war ended in July 1953. An armistice was signed but no permanent peace treaty was agreed. After the war, North Korea adopted a hostile policy towards South Korea in pursuit of its policy of reunification.

The ending of the Cold War in the late 1980s eased the situation and both North and South Korea joined the United Nations in 1991. The two countries made several agreements, including one in which they agreed not to use force against each other. However, North Korea remained as isolated as ever.

In 1993, North Korea began a new international crisis by announcing that it was withdrawing from the Nuclear Non-Proliferation Treaty. This led to suspicions that North Korea, which had signed the Treaty in 1985, was developing its own nuclear weapons. Kim Il Sung, who had ruled as a virtual dictator from 1948 until his death in 1994, was succeeded by his son, Kim Jong Il.

In the early 2000s, attempts were made to reconcile the two Koreas, though the prospect of reunification seemed remote. In 2003, North Korea's relations with the United States deteriorated when the US accused the country of having a secret nuclear weapons programme. In 2006, North Korea conducted its first nuclear test, but in 2007 it agreed to a nuclear freeze in return for foreign aid.

North Korea has considerable resources, including coal, copper, iron ore, lead, tin, tungsten and zinc. Under Communism, North Korea has concentrated on developing heavy, state-owned industries. Manufactures include chemicals, iron and steel, machinery, processed food and textiles. Agriculture employs about a third of the people of North Korea and rice is the leading crop. Economic decline and mismanagement, aggravated by three successive crop failures caused by floods in 1995 and 1996 and a drought in 1997, led to famine on a large scale.

KOREA, SOUTH

AREA 99,268 sq km [38,327 sq mi]
POPULATION 48,847,000
CAPITAL Seoul
GOVERNMENT Multiparty republic
ETHNIC GROUPS Korean 99%
LANGUAGES Korean (official)
RELIGIONS No affiliation 46%, Christianity 26%,
Buddhism 26%, Confucianism 1%
CURRENCY South Korean won = 100 chon

GEOGRAPHY The Republic of Korea, as South Korea is officially known, occupies the southern part of the Korean peninsula. Mountains cover much of the country. The southern and western coasts are major farming regions. Many islands are found along the west and south coasts. The largest is Cheju-do, which contains South Korea's highest peak, which rises to 1,950 m [6,398 ft].

Like North Korea, South Korea is chilled in winter by cold, dry winds blowing from central Asia. Snow often covers the mountains in the east. The summers are hot and wet, especially in July and August.

POLITICS & ECONOMY After Japan's defeat in World War II (1939–45), North Korea was occupied by troops from the Soviet Union, while South Korea was occupied by United States forces. Attempts to reunify Korea failed and, in 1948, a National Assembly was elected in South Korea. This Assembly created the Republic of Korea, while North Korea became a Communist state. North Korean troops invaded the South in June 1950, sparking off the Korean War (1950–3).

In the 1950s, South Korea had a weak economy, which had been further damaged by the destruction caused by the Korean War. From the 1960s to the 1980s, South Korean governments worked to industrialize the economy. The governments were dominated by military leaders, who often used authoritarian methods and flouted human rights. In 1987, a new constitution was approved, enabling presidential elections to be held every five years. In 1991, South and North Korea became members of the United Nations and they signed agreements, including one in which they agreed not to use force against each other. In the 2000s, South Korea worked to engage the North in closer relations. However, in 2006, following the North's nuclear test, it imposed sanctions against its neighbour.

The World Bank classifies South Korea as an 'upper-middle-income' developing country. It is also one of the world's fastest growing industrial economies. The country's resources include coal and tungsten, and its main manufactures are processed food and textiles. Since partition, heavy industries have been built up, making chemicals, fertilizers, iron and steel, and ships. South Korea has also developed the production of such things as computers, cars and television sets. In late 1997, however, the dramatic expansion of the economy was halted by a market crash which affected many of the booming economies of Asia. However, South Korea recovered faster than any other country in the region, and huge inflows of foreign investment and strict financial measures, including the restructuring of its short-term debt, led to the restoration of confidence and economic growth.

Farming remains important in South Korea. Rice is the chief crop, together with fruit, grains and vegetables, while fishing provides a major source of protein.

KUWAIT

AREA 17,818 sq km [6,880 sq mi]
POPULATION 2,418,000
CAPITAL Kuwait City

The State of Kuwait at the north end of the Persian Gulf is largely made up of desert. Temperatures are high and the rainfall low. Kuwait became independent from Britain in 1961 and revenues from its oil wells have made it prosperous. Iraq invaded Kuwait in 1990 and much damage was inflicted in the conflict in 1991 when Kuwait was liberated. In 2004, the government announced draft legislation for women to vote and stand for parliament.

KYRGYZSTAN

AREA 199,900 sq km [77,181 sq mi]
POPULATION 5,214,000
CAPITAL Bishkek
GOVERNMENT Multiparty republic
ETHNIC GROUPS Kyrgyz 65%, Russian 13%, Uzbek 13%, Ukrainian 1%, others
LANGUAGES Kyrgyz and Russian (both official)
RELIGIONS Islam 75%, Russian Orthodox 20%
CURRENCY Kyrgyzstani som = 100 tyiyn

GEOGRAPHY The Republic of Kyrgyzstan is a land-locked country between China, Tajikistan, Uzbekistan and Kazakhstan. The country is mountainous, with spectacular scenery. The highest mountain, Pik Pobedy in the Tian Shan range, reaches 7,439 m [24,406 ft] in the east. The lowlands have warm summers and cold winters. But January temperatures in the mountains plummet to –28°C [–18°F]. Kyrgyzstan has a low annual rainfall.

POLITICS & ECONOMY In 1876, Kyrgyzstan became a province of Russia and Russian settlement in the area began. In 1916, Russia crushed a rebellion among the Kyrgyz, and many subsequently fled to China. In 1922, the area became an autonomous *oblast* (self-governing region) of the newly formed Soviet Union but, in 1936, it became one of the Soviet Socialist Republics. Under Communist rule, local customs and religious worship were suppressed, but education and health services were greatly improved.

In 1991, Kyrgyzstan became an independent country following the break-up of the Soviet Union. The Communist Party was dissolved, but the country maintained ties with Russia through an organization called the Commonwealth of Independent States. Massive protests followed parliamentary elections in 2005. Askar Akayev, who had been president since 1990, but who had monopolized power, fled the country. In 2006, his successor, Kurmanbek Bakiyev, signed a new constitution reducing the president's powers, in an attempt to placate the opposition.

In the early 1990s, when Kyrgyzstan was working to reform its economy, the World Bank classified it as a 'lower-middle-income' developing country. Agriculture, especially livestock rearing, is the chief activity. The chief products include cotton, eggs, fruits, grain, tobacco, vegetables and wool. But food must be imported. Industries are mainly concentrated around the capital Bishkek.

LAOS

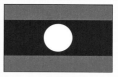

AREA 236,800 sq km [91,428 sq mi]
POPULATION 6,368,000
CAPITAL Vientiane
GOVERNMENT Single-party republic
ETHNIC GROUPS Lao Loum 68%, Lao Theung 22%, Lao Soung 9%
LANGUAGES Lao (official), French, English
RELIGIONS Buddhism 60%, traditional beliefs and others 40%
CURRENCY Kip = 100 at

GEOGRAPHY The Lao People's Democratic Republic is a landlocked country in South-east Asia. Mountains and plateaux cover much of Laos. Most people live on the plains bordering the River Mekong and its tributaries. The Mekong, one of Asia's longest rivers, forms much of the country's western borders.

Laos has a tropical monsoon climate. Winters are dry and sunny, with winds blowing from the north-east. The temperatures rise until April, when the wind directions are reversed. Moist south-westerly winds then arrive, heralding the start of the wet monsoon season.

POLITICS & ECONOMY France made Laos a protectorate in the late 19th century and ruled it as part of French Indo-China, a region which also included Cambodia and Vietnam. Laos became a member of the French Union in 1948 and an independent kingdom in 1954.

After independence, Laos suffered from instability caused by a long power struggle between royalist government forces and a pro-Communist group called the Pathet Lao. A civil war broke out in 1960 and continued into the 1970s. The Pathet Lao took control in 1975 and the king abdicated. Laos then came under the influence of Communist Vietnam, which had used Laos as a supply base during the Vietnam War (1957–75). From the early 1980s, the economy deteriorated. Bombings occurred in Vientiane in 2000. Some experts attributed them to the minority Hmong people who had been engaged in a low-level rebellion since 1975.

Laos is one of the world's poorest countries. Agriculture employs 78% of the people. Rice is the main crop, and timber and coffee are exported. But the most valuable export is electricity, which is produced at hydroelectric power stations on the River Mekong and is exported to Thailand. Laos also produces opium.

LATVIA

AREA 64,600 sq km [24,942 sq mi]
POPULATION 2,275,000
CAPITAL Riga
GOVERNMENT Multiparty republic
ETHNIC GROUPS Latvian 58%, Russian 30%, Belarusian, Ukrainian, Polish, Lithuanian
LANGUAGES Latvian (official), Lithuanian, Russian
RELIGIONS Lutheran, Roman Catholic, Russian Orthodox
CURRENCY Latvian lat = 10 santimi

GEOGRAPHY The Republic of Latvia is one of three states on the south-eastern corner of the Baltic Sea which were ruled as parts of the Soviet Union between 1940 and 1991. Latvia consists mainly of flat plains separated by low hills.

Riga has warm summers, but temperatures between December and March are subzero. Moderate rainfall occurs throughout the year, with light snow in winter.

POLITICS & ECONOMY In 1800, Russia was in control of Latvia, but Latvians declared their independence after World War I. In 1940, under a German-Soviet pact, Soviet troops occupied Latvia, but they were driven out by the Germans in 1941. Soviet troops returned in 1944 and Latvia became part of the Soviet Union. Under Soviet rule, many Russian immigrants settled in Latvia and many Latvians feared that the Russians would become the dominant ethnic group.

In the late 1980s, when reforms were being introduced in the Soviet Union, Latvia's government ended absolute Communist rule and made Latvian the official language. In 1990, it declared the country to be independent, an act which was finally recognized by the Soviet Union in September 1991.

Latvia held its first free elections to its parliament (the Saeima) in 1993. Voting was limited only to citizens of Latvia on 17 June 1940 and their descendants. This meant that about 34% of Latvian residents were unable to vote. In 1994, Latvia restricted the naturalization of non-Latvians, including many Russian settlers, who were not allowed to vote or own land. However, in 1998, the government agreed that all children born since independence should have automatic citizenship. Its cultivation of closer ties to the West proved successful in 2004, when Latvia was admitted to membership of both the North Atlantic Treaty Organization (NATO) and the European Union (EU).

The World Bank classifies Latvia as a 'lower-middle-income' country and, in the 1990s, it faced many problems in turning its economy into a free-market system. Products include electronic goods, farm machinery, fertilizers, processed food, plastics, radios and vehicles. Latvia produces only about a tenth of the electricity it needs. It imports the rest from Belarus, Russia and Ukraine.

LEBANON

AREA 10,400 sq km [4,015 sq mi]
POPULATION 3,874,000
CAPITAL Beirut
GOVERNMENT Multiparty republic
ETHNIC GROUPS Arab 95%, Armenian 4%, others
LANGUAGES Arabic (official), French, English, Armenian
RELIGIONS Islam 70%, Christianity 30%
CURRENCY Lebanese pound = 100 piastres

GEOGRAPHY The Republic of Lebanon is a country on the eastern shores of the Mediterranean Sea. Behind the coastal plain are the rugged Lebanon Mountains (Jabal Lubnan). Between this range and the Anti-Lebanon Mountains (Al Jabal ash Sharqi) lies the fertile Bekaa (Beqaa) Valley. The coast has hot dry summers and mild wet winters. Inland, in winter, onshore winds bring heavy rain and snow to the western slopes of the mountains.

POLITICS & ECONOMY Lebanon was ruled by Turkey from 1516 until World War I. France ruled the country from 1923, but Lebanon became independent in 1946. After independence, the Muslims and Christians agreed to share power, and Lebanon made rapid economic progress. But from the late

1950s, development was slowed by periodic conflict between Sunni and Shia Muslims, Druze and Christians. The situation was further complicated by the presence of Palestinian refugees who used bases in Lebanon to attack Israel.

In 1975, civil war broke out as private armies representing the many factions struggled for power. This led to intervention by Israel in the south and Syria in the north. UN peacekeeping forces arrived in 1978, but bombings, assassinations and kidnappings became almost everyday events in the 1980s. From 1991, Lebanon enjoyed an uneasy peace. But, Israel continued to occupy an area in the south. In the 1990s, Israel clashed with Hezbollah guerrillas in Lebanon, but Israeli troops left in 2000. In 2005, the assassination of Rafik Hariri, former prime minister, was blamed on Syria, which then withdrew its forces from Lebanon. In 2006, another devastating conflict occurred when Israeli troops again clashed with Hezbollah guerrillas in southern Lebanon.

Lebanon's civil war almost destroyed valuable trade and financial services that had been Lebanon's chief source of income, together with tourism. Manufacturing, which had formerly been a major activity, was badly hit.

LESOTHO

AREA 30,355 sq km [11,720 sq mi]
POPULATION 2,022,000
CAPITAL Maseru
GOVERNMENT Constitutional monarchy
ETHNIC GROUPS Sotho 99%
LANGUAGES Sesotho and English (both official)
RELIGIONS Christianity 80%, traditional beliefs 20%
CURRENCY Loti = 100 lisente

GEOGRAPHY The Kingdom of Lesotho is a land-locked country, completely enclosed by South Africa. The land is mountainous, rising to 3,482 m [11,424 ft] on the north-eastern border. The Drakensberg range covers most of the country.

The climate of Lesotho is greatly affected by the altitude, because most of the country lies above 1,500 m [4,920 ft]. Maseru has warm summers, but the temperatures fall below freezing in the winter. The mountains are colder. The rainfall varies, averaging around 700 mm [28 in].

POLITICS & ECONOMY The Basotho nation was founded in the 1820s by King Moshoeshoe I, who united various groups fleeing from tribal wars in southern Africa. Britain made the area a protectorate in 1868 and, in 1871, placed it under the British Cape Colony in South Africa. But in 1884, Basutoland, as the area was called, was reconstituted as a British protectorate, where whites were not allowed to own land.

The country finally became independent in 1966 as the Kingdom of Lesotho, with Moshoeshoe II, great-grandson of Moshoeshoe I, as its king. Since independence, Lesotho has suffered instability. The military seized power in 1986 and stripped Moshoeshoe II of his powers in 1990, installing his son, Letsie III, as monarch. After elections in 1993, Moshoeshoe II was restored to office in 1995. But after his death in a car crash in 1996, Letsie III again became king. In 1998, an army revolt, following an election in which the ruling party won 79 out of the 80 seats, caused damage to the economy and, in 2004, the government declared a state of emergency following three years of drought. In 2005, the govern-

ment offered HIV tests to all citizens – 25% of the people are thought to be infected.

Lesotho lacks natural resources, and the UN has described 40% of its population as 'ultra-poor'. One-fifth of the people live by farming, mostly at subsistence level. Other sources of income include light manufacturing and remittances sent home by Basotho working abroad.

LIBERIA

AREA 111,369 sq km [43,000 sq mi]
POPULATION 3,042,000
CAPITAL Monrovia
GOVERNMENT Multiparty republic
ETHNIC GROUPS Indigenous African tribes 95% (including Kpelle, Bassa, Grebo, Gio, Kru, Mano)
LANGUAGES English (official), ethnic languages
RELIGIONS Christianity 40%, Islam 20%, traditional beliefs and others 40%
CURRENCY Liberian dollar = 100 cents

GEOGRAPHY The Republic of Liberia is a country in West Africa. Behind the coastline, 500 km [311 mi] long, lies a narrow coastal plain. Beyond, the land rises to a plateau region, with the highest land along the border with Guinea.

Liberia has a tropical climate with high temperatures and high humidity all through the year. The rainfall is abundant all year round, but there is a particularly wet period from June to November. The rainfall generally increases from east to west.

POLITICS & ECONOMY In the late 18th century, some white Americans in the United States wanted to help freed black slaves to return to Africa. In 1816, they set up the American Colonization Society, which bought land in what is now Liberia.

In 1822, the Society landed former slaves at a settlement on the coast which they named Monrovia. In 1847, Liberia became a fully independent republic with a constitution much like that of the United States. For many years, the Americo-Liberians controlled the country's government. US influence remained strong and the American Firestone Company, which ran Liberia's rubber plantations, was especially influential. Foreign companies were also involved in exploiting Liberia's mineral resources, including its huge iron-ore deposits.

In 1980, a military group composed of people from the local population killed the Americo-Liberian president, William R. Tolbert. An army sergeant, Samuel K. Doe, was made president of Liberia. Elections held in 1985 resulted in victory for Doe.

From 1989, the country was plunged into civil war between various ethnic groups. Doe was assassinated in 1990 and the struggle with rebel groups continued. A cease-fire was agreed in 1995. A council of state was set up and, in 1997, a warlord, Charles Taylor, became president. Taylor fled the country in 2003 and, in 2006, he was extradited and charged with war crimes. In 2005, elections were held. Ellen Sirleaf-Johnson, a former minister, was elected president. She became the first woman president in Africa.

Liberia's civil war devastated its economy. More than half of the people depend on agriculture, though many of them grow little more than they need to feed their families. Major food crops include cassava, rice and sugar cane, while rubber, cocoa and coffee are exported. But the most valuable export is iron ore.

Liberia also obtains revenue from its 'flag of convenience', which is used by about one-sixth of the world's commercial shipping, exploiting low taxes.

LIBYA

AREA 1,759,540 sq km [679,358 sq mi]
POPULATION 5,901,000
CAPITAL Tripoli
GOVERNMENT Single-party socialist state
ETHNIC GROUPS Libyan Arab and Berber 97%
LANGUAGES Arabic (official), Berber
RELIGIONS Islam (Sunni Muslim) 97%
CURRENCY Libyan dinar = 1,000 dirhams

GEOGRAPHY The Socialist People's Libyan Arab Jamahiriya, as Libya is officially called, is a large country in North Africa. Most people live on the coastal plains in the north-east and north-west. The Sahara, which occupies 95% of Libya, reaches the Mediterranean coast along the Gulf of Sidra (Khalij Surt). The north-eastern and north-western coastal plains have Mediterranean climates, with hot, dry summers and mild, moist winters. Inland, the average annual rainfall drops to 100 mm [4 in] or less.

POLITICS & ECONOMY Italy took over Libya in 1911, but lost it during World War II. Britain and France then jointly ruled Libya until 1951, when the country became an independent kingdom.

In 1969, a military group headed by Colonel Muammar Gaddafi deposed the king and set up a military government. Under Gaddafi, the government took control of the economy and used money from oil exports to finance welfare services and development projects. Gaddafi was criticized for supporting terrorist groups around the world, and Libya became isolated from the mid-1980s. In 1998, he tried to restore Libya's reputation by surrendering for trial two Libyans suspected of planting a bomb on a PanAm plane which exploded over the Scottish town of Lockerbie in 1988. In 2003, Libya announced an agreement to pay compensation to victims of the bombing. In 2004, Libya announced that it was abandoning programmes to produce weapons of mass destruction. In 2006, the United States rescinded its designation of Libya as a state sponsor of terrorism.

The discovery of oil and natural gas in 1959 led to the transformation of Libya's economy. Once one of the world's poorest countries, it has become Africa's richest in terms of its per capita income. It remains a developing country because of its dependence on oil, which accounts for nearly all of its export revenues.

Agriculture is important, although Libya has to import food. Crops include barley, citrus fruits, dates, olives, potatoes and wheat. Cattle, sheep and poultry are raised. Libya has oil refineries and petrochemical plants. Other manufactures include cement and steel.

LIECHTENSTEIN

AREA 160 sq km [62 sq mi]
POPULATION 34,000
CAPITAL Vaduz

The tiny Principality of Liechtenstein is sandwiched between Switzerland and Austria. The River Rhine flows along its western border, while Alpine peaks rise in the east and south. The climate is relatively mild, with the annual precipitation averaging about 890 mm [35 in].

Liechtenstein has been an independent principality since 1719, except for a brief period in the early 19th century when it was controlled by Napoleon I of France. After World War I (1914–18), Switzerland represented Liechtenstein abroad and Swiss currency was adopted in 1921. Since 1924, Liechtenstein has been in a customs union with Switzerland. Taxation is low and the country is a haven for foreign companies. In 2003, the people voted to give their head of state, Prince Hans Adam III, sovereign powers. In 2004, he handed over the running of the country to his son, Prince Alois, while remaining the titular head of state.

LITHUANIA

AREA 65,200 sq km [25,174 sq mi]
POPULATION 3,586,000
CAPITAL Vilnius
GOVERNMENT Multiparty republic
ETHNIC GROUPS Lithuanian 80%, Russian 9%, Polish 7%, Belarusian 2%
LANGUAGES Lithuanian (official), Russian, Polish
RELIGIONS Mainly Roman Catholic
CURRENCY Litas = 100 centai

GEOGRAPHY The Republic of Lithuania is the southernmost of the three Baltic states which were ruled as part of the Soviet Union between 1940 and 1991. Much of the land is flat or gently rolling, with the highest land in the south-east.

Winters are cold. January's temperatures average –3°C [27°F] in the west and –6°C [21°F] in the east. Summers are warm, with average temperatures in July of 17°C [63°F]. The average rainfall in the west is about 630 mm [25 in]. Inland areas are drier.

POLITICS & ECONOMY The Lithuanian people were united into a single nation in the 12th century, and later joined a union with Poland. In 1795, Lithuania came under Russian rule. After World War I (1914–18), Lithuania declared itself independent, and in 1920 it signed a peace treaty with the Russians, though Poland held Vilnius until 1939. In 1940, the Soviet Union occupied Lithuania, but the Germans invaded in 1941. Soviet forces returned in 1944, and Lithuania was integrated into the Soviet Union. In 1988, when the Soviet Union was introducing reforms, the Lithuanians demanded independence. Their language is one of the oldest in the world, and the country was always the most homogenous of the Baltic states, staunchly Catholic and resistant of attempts to suppress their culture. Pro-independence groups won the national elections in 1990 and, in 1991, the Soviet Union recognized Lithuania's independence.

Since 1991, Lithuania has sought to reform its economy and introduce a private enterprise system, which was close to completion a decade later. Lithuania has also drawn closer to the West and, in 2004, Lithuania became a member of the North Atlantic Treaty Organization (NATO) and, on 1 May, a member of the European Union.

The World Bank classifies Lithuania as a 'middle-income' country. In 2005, agriculture employed 12% of the people and accounted for 5% of the gross domestic product, industry 20% and services 58%. Lithuania's main exports include mineral fuels, farm and food products, machinery and apparatus, textiles and clothing, and transport equipment. The main trading partners are Russia, Germany and Latvia.

LUXEMBOURG

AREA 2,586 sq km [998 sq mi]
POPULATION 474,000
CAPITAL Luxembourg
GOVERNMENT Constitutional monarchy (Grand Duchy)
ETHNIC GROUPS Luxembourger 71%, Portuguese, Italian, French, Belgian, Slavs
LANGUAGES Luxembourgish (official), French, German
RELIGIONS Roman Catholic 87%, others 13%
CURRENCY Euro = 100 cents

GEOGRAPHY The Grand Duchy of Luxembourg is one of the smallest and oldest countries in Europe. The north belongs to an upland region which includes the Ardenne in Belgium and Luxembourg, and the Eifel highlands in Germany.

Luxembourg has a temperate climate. The south has warm summers and autumns, when grapes ripen in sheltered south-eastern valleys. Winters are sometimes severe, especially in upland areas.

POLITICS & ECONOMY Germany occupied Luxembourg in World Wars I and II. In 1944–5, northern Luxembourg was the scene of the famous Battle of the Bulge. In 1948, Luxembourg joined Belgium and the Netherlands in a union called Benelux and, in the 1950s, it was one of the six founders of what is now the European Union. Luxembourg has played a major role in Europe. Its capital contains the headquarters of the European Court of Justice. In 2005, the people of Luxembourg voted in favour of a proposed new European Union constitution, which had already been rejected by French and Dutch voters.

Luxembourg has iron-ore reserves and is a major steel producer. It also has many high-technology industries, producing electronic goods and computers. Steel and other manufactures, including chemicals, rubber products, glass and aluminium, dominate the country's exports. Other major activities include tourism and financial services.

MACEDONIA (FYROM)

AREA 25,713 sq km [9,928 sq mi]
POPULATION 2,051,000
CAPITAL Skopje
GOVERNMENT Multiparty republic
ETHNIC GROUPS Macedonian 64%, Albanian 25%, Turkish 4%, Romanian 3%, Serb 2%
LANGUAGES Macedonian and Albanian (official)
RELIGIONS Macedonian Orthodox 70%, Islam 29%
CURRENCY Macedonian denar = 100 paras

GEOGRAPHY The Republic of Macedonia is a country in south-eastern Europe, which was once one of the six republics that made up the former Federal People's Republic of Yugoslavia. This landlocked country is largely mountainous or hilly.

Macedonia has hot summers, though highland areas are cooler. Winters are cold and snowfalls are often heavy. The climate is fairly continental in character and rain occurs throughout the year.

POLITICS & ECONOMY Until the 20th century, Macedonia's history was closely tied to a larger area, also called Macedonia, which included parts of northern Greece and south-western Bulgaria. This region reached its peak in power at the time of Philip II (382–336 BC) and his son Alexander the Great (336–323 BC). After Alexander's death, his empire was split up and it gradually declined. The area became a Roman province in the 140s BC and part of the Byzantine Empire from AD 395.

In the 6th century, Slavs from eastern Europe settled in the area, followed by the Bulgars from central Asia in the 9th century. The Byzantine Empire regained control in 1018, but Serbia took Macedonia in the early 14th century. In 1371, the Ottoman Turks conquered the area and ruled it for more than 500 years. The Ottoman Empire began to collapse in the late 19th century. In 1913, at the end of the Balkan Wars, the area was divided between Serbia, Bulgaria and Greece. At the end of World War I, Serbian Macedonia became part of the Kingdom of the Serbs. Croats and Slovenes, which was renamed Yugoslavia in 1929. After World War II, Yugoslavia became a Communist country under ex-partisan leader Josip Broz Tito.

Tito died in 1980 and, in the early 1990s, the country broke up into five separate republics. Macedonia declared its independence in September 1991. Greece objected to this territory using the name Macedonia, which it considered to be a Greek name. It also objected to a symbol on Macedonia's flag and a reference in the constitution to the desire to reunite the three parts of the old Macedonia. In 1993, the United Nations accepted the new republic as a member under the name of The Former Yugoslav Republic of Macedonia (FYROM).

By the end of 1993, all the countries of the EU, except Greece, were establishing diplomatic relations with the FYROM. In 1995, Greece lifted its trade ban, when Macedonia agreed to redesign its flag and remove territorial claims from its constitution. In 2001, fighting along the Kosovo border spilled over into Macedonia. It was attributed to nationalists who wanted to create a Greater Albania. The uprising ended when Macedonian Albanian-speakers were given increased rights. In 2004, the USA recognized the name Republic of Macedonia instead of FYROM. Despite objections by Greece, other nations soon followed this lead.

The World Bank describes Macedonia as a 'lower-middle-income' developing country. Manufactures dominate the country's exports. Macedonia mines coal, but imports all its oil and natural gas. The country is self-sufficient in its basic food needs.

MADAGASCAR

AREA 587,041 sq km [226,657 sq mi]
POPULATION 18,595,000
CAPITAL Antananarivo
GOVERNMENT Republic
ETHNIC GROUPS Merina, Betsimisaraka, Betsileo, Tsimihety, Sakalava and others
LANGUAGES Malagasy and French (both official)
RELIGIONS Traditional beliefs 52%, Christianity 41%, Islam 7%
CURRENCY Malagasy franc = 100 centimes

GEOGRAPHY The Democratic Republic of Madagascar, in south-eastern Africa, is an island nation, which has a larger area than France. Behind the narrow coastal plains in the east lies a highland zone, mostly between 610 m and 1,220 m [2,000 ft to 4,000 ft] above sea level. Broad plains border the Mozambique Channel in the west.

Temperatures in the highlands are moderated by the altitude. The winters (from April to September) are dry, but heavy rains occur in summer. The eastern coastlands are warm and humid. The west is drier and the south and south-west are hot and dry.

POLITICS & ECONOMY People from South-east Asia began to settle on Madagascar around 2,000 years ago. Subsequent influxes from Africa and Arabia added to the island's diverse heritage, culture and language.

French troops defeated a Malagasy army in 1895 and Madagascar became a French colony. In 1960, it achieved full independence as the Malagasy Republic. In 1972, army officers seized control and, in 1975, under the leadership of Lt-Commander Didier Ratsiraka, the country was renamed Madagascar. Parliamentary elections were held in 1977, but Ratsiraka remained president of a one-party socialist state. In 2002, the country came close to civil war when Ratsiraka and his opponent, Marc Ravalomanana, both claimed victory in presidential elections. Ravalomanana was finally recognized as president. Re-elected in 2006, he has introduced many economic reforms.

Madagascar is a poor country. Poverty and increased population have put pressure on the dwindling forests and its unique wildlife, as well as causing severe soil erosion. Farming, fishing and forestry employ more than 70% of the people. Food crops include bananas, cassava, rice and sweet potatoes. Coffee is exported.

MALAWI

AREA 118,484 sq km [45,747 sq mi]
POPULATION 13,014,000
CAPITAL Lilongwe
GOVERNMENT Multiparty republic
ETHNIC GROUPS Chewa, Nyanja, Tonga, Tumbuka, Lomwe, Yao, Ngoni and others
LANGUAGES Chichewa and English (both official)
RELIGIONS Protestant 55%, Roman Catholic 20%, Islam 20%
CURRENCY Malawian kwacha = 100 tambala

GEOGRAPHY The Republic of Malawi includes part of Lake Malawi, which is drained by the River Shire, a tributary of the River Zambezi. The land is mostly mountainous. The highest peak, Mulanje, reaches 3,000 m [9,843 ft] in the south-east.

While the low-lying areas of Malawi are hot and humid all year round, the uplands have a pleasant climate. Lilongwe, at about 1,100 m [3,609 ft] above sea level, has a warm and sunny climate. Frosts may occur in July and August, during the long dry season.

POLITICS & ECONOMY Malawi, then called Nyasaland, became a British protectorate in 1891. In 1953, Britain established the Federation of Rhodesia and Nyasaland, which also included what are now Zambia and Zimbabwe. Black African opposition, led in Nyasaland by Dr Hastings Kamuzu Banda, led to the dissolution of the federation in 1963.

In 1964, Nyasaland became independent as Malawi, with Banda as prime minister. Banda became president when the country became a republic in 1966 and, in 1971, he was made president for life. Banda was an autocratic ruler, but a multiparty system was restored in 1993. Bakili Muluzi became president and, in 2004, he was succeeded by Bingu wa Mutharika, leader of the United Democratic Front (UDF). In office, he resigned from the UDF and set up a new Democratic Progressive Party.

Malawi is one of the world's poorest countries. More than 80% of the people are farmers, but many grow little more than they need to feed their families. Crops include cotton, groundnuts, maize, sorghum and sugar cane. The leading exports are tobacco, sugar and tea. Malawi has few manufacturing industries.

MALAYSIA

AREA 329,758 sq km [127,320 sq mi]
POPULATION 24,386,000
CAPITAL Kuala Lumpur; Putrajaya (administrative capital awaiting completion)
GOVERNMENT Federal constitutional monarchy
ETHNIC GROUPS Malay and other indigenous groups 58%, Chinese 24%, Indian 8%, others
LANGUAGES Malay (official), Chinese, English
RELIGIONS Islam, Buddhism, Daoism, Hinduism, Christianity, Sikhism
CURRENCY Ringgit = 100 cents

GEOGRAPHY The Federation of Malaysia consists of two main parts. Peninsular Malaysia, which is joined to mainland Asia, contains about 80% of the population. The other main regions, Sabah and Sarawak, are in northern Borneo, an island which Malaysia shares with Indonesia. Much of the land is mountainous, with coastal lowlands bordering the rugged interior. The highest peak, Kinabalu, reaches 4,101 m [13,455 ft] in Sabah.

Malaysia has a hot equatorial climate. The temperatures are high all through the year, though the mountains are much cooler than the lowland areas. The rainfall is heavy throughout the year.

POLITICS & ECONOMY The Malay peninsula has long been a crossroads for trade. Around 1,200 years ago, Indian traders introduced Hinduism and Buddhism to the area, while Arab traders introduced Islam in the 15th century. Portuguese traders reached Melaka in 1509 and the Dutch took over in 1641. The British East India Company became established in the area in 1786. Britain gradually extended its control in the 19th century. Japan occupied the area during World War II (1939–45), but British rule was re-established in 1945. In the 1940s and 1950s, British troops fought against Communist guerrillas, but Peninsular Malaysia (then called Malaya) became independent in 1957. Malaysia was created in 1963, when Malaya, Singapore, Sabah and Sarawak agreed to unite, but Singapore withdrew in 1965.

From the 1970s, Malaysia achieved rapid economic progress and, by the mid-1990s, it was playing a major part in regional affairs, especially through its membership of ASEAN (Association of South-east Asian Nations). However, together with several other countries in eastern Asia, Malaysia was hit by economic recession in 1997, including a major fall in stock market values. In response to the crisis, the government ordered the repatriation of many temporary foreign workers and initiated a series of austerity measures. In 2003, Mahathir bin Mohamad, who had served as prime minister since 1981, handed over power to Abdullah Ahmad Badawi, who won a landslide election victory in 2004.

The World Bank classifies Malaysia as an 'upper-middle-income' developing country. Malaysia is a leading producer of palm oil, rubber and tin. Manufacturing now plays a major part in the economy. Manufactures are diverse, including cars, chemicals, a wide range of electronic goods, plastics, textiles, rubber and wood products.

MALDIVES

AREA 298 sq km [115 sq mi]
POPULATION 359,000
CAPITAL Malé

The Republic of the Maldives, Asia's smallest independent country, consists of about 1,200 low-lying coral islands, south of India. The highest point is 24 m [79 ft] above sea level. From the 16th century, the islands came under Portuguese and, later, Dutch rule, before the islands officially became a British territory until independence in 1965. Various crops are grown, but tourism and fishing are the main industries and fish are the main export. A tsunami struck the islands in December 2004, killing 82 people. In 2005, President Maumoon Abdul Gayoom, who had been in office since 1978, announced plans to introduce a multiparty democracy.

MALI

AREA 1,240,192 sq km [478,838 sq mi]
POPULATION 11,717,000
CAPITAL Bamako
GOVERNMENT Multiparty republic
ETHNIC GROUPS Mande 50% (Bambara, Malinke, Soninke), Peul 17%, Voltaic 12%, Songhai 6%, Tuareg and Moor 10%, others
LANGUAGES French (official), many African languages
RELIGIONS Islam 90%, traditional beliefs 9%, Christianity 1%
CURRENCY CFA franc = 100 centimes

GEOGRAPHY The Republic of Mali is a landlocked country in northern Africa. The land is generally flat, with the highest land in the Adrar des Iforhas on the border with Algeria.

Northern Mali is part of the Sahara, with a hot, practically rainless climate. But the south has enough rain for farming.

POLITICS & ECONOMY Between the 4th and 16th centuries, present-day Mali formed part of three major African empires which grew rich because of trans-Saharan trade. They were ancient Ghana, ancient Mali and Songhay. Islam was introduced from North Africa around 1,000 years ago and Tombouctou (Timbuktu) became a great centre of Muslim learning. However, following the defeat of the Songhay empire by Morocco in 1591, the area was divided into small kingdoms. France ruled the area, then known as French Sudan, from 1893 until the country achieved independence as Mali in 1960.

The first socialist government was overthrown in 1968 by an army group led by Moussa Traoré, but he was ousted in 1991. Multiparty democracy was restored in 1992. Alpha Oumar Konaré became president. He stood down in 2002 and Ahmadou Touré, who had restored democracy in 1992, was elected president. He was re-elected in 2007.

Mali is one of the world's poorest countries and 70% of the land is desert or semi-desert. Only about 2% of the land is used for growing crops, while 25% is used for grazing animals. Despite this, agriculture employs nearly 80% of the people, many of whom still subsist by nomadic livestock rearing.

MALTA

AREA 316 sq km [122 sq mi]
POPULATION 400,000
CAPITAL Valletta
GOVERNMENT Multiparty republic
ETHNIC GROUPS Maltese 96%, British 2%
LANGUAGES Maltese and English (both official)
RELIGIONS Roman Catholic 98%
CURRENCY Maltese lira = 100 cents

GEOGRAPHY The Republic of Malta consists of two main islands, Malta and Gozo, a third, much smaller island called Comino lying between the two large islands, and two tiny islets. Malta's climate is typically Mediterranean, with hot, dry summers and mild, wet winters. The sirocco, a hot wind from North Africa, may raise temperatures considerably during spring.

POLITICS & ECONOMY Malta's colourful history dates back to the Stone and Bronze Age remains that have been found there. The islands later came under Phoenician, Greek, Carthaginian, Roman and Arab rule. In about 1090, Malta came under the Norman kings of Sicily and, from 1530, the Knights Hospitallers. France took the islands in 1798, but the British drove them out in 1800. British rule was officially recognized in 1815.

During World War I (1914–18), Malta was an important British naval base. In World War II (1939–45), Italian and German aircraft bombed the islands. In recognition of the bravery of the Maltese, the British King George VI awarded the George Cross to Malta in 1942. In 1953, Malta became a base for NATO (North Atlantic Treaty Organization). Malta became independent in 1964 and it became a republic in 1974. In 1979, Britain's military agreement with Malta expired and Malta ceased to be a British military base. In the 1980s, Malta was declared a neutral country. On 1 May 2004, it became a member of the European Union.

The World Bank classifies Malta as an 'upper-middle-income' developing country. It lacks natural resources, and most people work in the former naval dockyards, which are now used for commercial shipbuilding and repairs, in manufacturing, and in tourism. Manufactures include chemicals, processed food and chemicals. Farming is difficult, because of the rocky soils. Crops include barley, fruits, potatoes and wheat. Fishing is also important.

MARSHALL ISLANDS

AREA 181 sq km [70 sq mi]
POPULATION 60,000
CAPITAL Majuro

The Republic of the Marshall Islands consists of 31 coral atolls, five single islands and more than 1,000 islets. It lies north of Kiribati in a region called Micronesia. The islands came under German rule in 1885 and became a Japanese mandate after World War I (1914–18). US forces took the main islands in 1944 and the territory became a US Trust Territory in 1947. Independence was achieved in 1991, but the islands remain heavily dependent on US aid. The main activities are agriculture and tourism.

MARTINIQUE

AREA 1,102 sq km [425 sq mi]
POPULATION 436,000
CAPITAL Fort-de-France

Martinique, a volcanic island nation in the Caribbean, was visited by Christopher Columbus in 1502 and colonized by France in 1635. It became a French department in 1946. Tourism and agriculture are major activities. French government aid makes up a substantial part of the gross domestic product, allowing for a good standard of living.

MAURITANIA

AREA 1,025,520 sq km [395,953 sq mi]
POPULATION 3,177,000
CAPITAL Nouakchott
GOVERNMENT Multiparty Islamic republic
ETHNIC GROUPS Mixed Moor/Black 40%, Moor 30%, Black 30%
LANGUAGES Arabic and Wolof (both official), French
RELIGIONS Islam
CURRENCY Ouguiya = 5 khoums

GEOGRAPHY The Islamic Republic of Mauritania in north-western Africa is nearly twice the size of France. But France has more than 28 times as many people. Part of the world's largest desert, the Sahara, covers northern Mauritania and most Mauritanians live in the south-west.

The amount of rainfall and the length of the rainy season increase from north to south. Much of the land is desert, with dry north-east and easterly winds throughout the year. But south-westerly winds bring summer rain to the south.

POLITICS & ECONOMY Originally part of the great African empires of Ghana and Mali, France set up a protectorate in Mauritania in 1903, attempting to exploit the trade in gum arabic. The country became a territory of French West Africa and a French colony in 1920. French West Africa was a huge territory, which included present-day Benin, Burkina Faso, Guinea, Ivory Coast, Mali, Niger and Senegal, as well as Mauritania. In 1958, Mauritania became a self-governing territory in the French Union and it became fully independent in 1960.

In 1976, Spain withdrew from Spanish (now Western) Sahara, a territory bordering Mauritania to the north. Morocco occupied the northern two-thirds of this territory, while Mauritania took the rest. But Saharan guerrillas belonging to POLISARIO (the Popular Front for the Liberation of Saharan Territories) began an armed struggle for independence. In 1979, Mauritania withdrew from Western Sahara. In 1991, the country adopted a new constitution aimed at creating a multiparty democracy. A military group overthrew the government in 2005. However, democratic elections were held in 2007 and Sidi Ould Sheikh Abdallahi was elected president.

The World Bank classifies Mauritania as a 'low-income' developing country. Nearly half of the people are engaged in agriculture. In 2006, Mauritania became Africa's newest oil producer, when an offshore platform came online for the first time.

NATIONS OF THE WORLD

MAURITIUS

AREA 2,040 sq km [788 sq mi]
POPULATION 1,241,000
CAPITAL Port Louis

The Republic of Mauritius, an Indian Ocean nation lying to the east of Madagascar, was previously ruled by France and Britain until it achieved independence in 1968. It became a republic in 1992. Sugar production is in decline but tourism is vital to the economy.

MEXICO

AREA 1,958,201 sq km [756,061 sq mi]
POPULATION 107,450,000
CAPITAL Mexico City
GOVERNMENT Federal republic
ETHNIC GROUPS Mestizo 60%, Amerindian 30%, White 9%
LANGUAGES Spanish (official)
RELIGIONS Roman Catholic 90%, Protestant 6%
CURRENCY Mexican peso = 100 centavos

GEOGRAPHY The United Mexican States, as Mexico is officially named, is the world's most populous Spanish-speaking country. Much of the land is mountainous, although most people live on the central plateau. Mexico contains two large peninsulas, Lower (or Baja) California in the north-west and the flat Yucatán peninsula in the south-east.

The climate varies according to the altitude. The resort of Acapulco on the south-west coast has a dry and sunny climate. Mexico City, at about 2,300 m [7,546 ft] above sea level, is much cooler. Most rain occurs between June and September. The rainfall decreases north of Mexico City and northern Mexico is mainly arid.

POLITICS & ECONOMY In the mid-19th century, Mexico lost land to the United States, and between 1910 and 1921 violent revolutions created chaos.

Reforms were introduced in the 1920s and, in 1929, the Institutional Revolutionary Party (PRI) was formed. The PRI ruled Mexico effectively as a one-party state until it was finally defeated in 2001. President Vicente Fox was succeeded in 2006 by Felipe Calderón, who won the presidential poll by 234,000 votes out of the 41.6 million ballots cast. Opposition supporters contested the result, but Calderón finally took up his office in December 2006.

The World Bank classifies Mexico as an 'upper-middle-income' developing country. Agriculture is important. Food crops include beans, maize, rice and wheat, while cash crops include coffee, cotton, fruits and vegetables. Beef cattle, dairy cattle and other livestock are raised and fishing is also important.

But oil and oil products are the chief exports, while manufacturing is the most valuable activity. Many factories near the northern border assemble goods, such as car parts and electrical products, for US companies. These factories are called *maquiladoras*. Hope for the future lies in increasing economic co-operation with the USA and Canada through NAFTA (North American Free Trade Agreement), which came into being on 1 January 1994.

MICRONESIA

AREA 702 sq km [271 sq mi]
POPULATION 108,000
CAPITAL Palikir

The Federated States of Micronesia consist of about 600 islands spread across a vast area in the western Pacific. US forces took the islands in World War II (1939–45). From 1947, they were ruled by the United States, becoming fully independent in 1991. Copra is exported. Fishing and tourism are also important.

MOLDOVA

AREA 33,851 sq km [13,070 sq mi]
POPULATION 4,467,000
CAPITAL Chişinău
GOVERNMENT Multiparty republic
ETHNIC GROUPS Moldovan/Romanian 65%, Ukrainian 14%, Russian 13%, others
LANGUAGES Moldovan/Romanian and Russian (official)
RELIGIONS Eastern Orthodox 98%
CURRENCY Moldovan leu = 100 bani

GEOGRAPHY The Republic of Moldova is a small country sandwiched between Ukraine and Romania. It was formerly one of the 15 republics that made up the Soviet Union. Much of the land is hilly and the highest areas are near the centre of the country.

Moldova has a moderately continental climate, with warm summers and fairly cold winters. Most of the rain comes in the warmer months.

POLITICS & ECONOMY In the 14th century, the Moldavians formed a state called Moldavia. It included part of Romania and Bessarabia (now the modern country of Moldova). The Ottoman Turks took the area in the 16th century, but in 1812 Russia took over Bessarabia. In 1861, Moldavia and Walachia united to form Romania. Russia retook southern Bessarabia in 1878.

After World War I (1914–18), all of Bessarabia was returned to Romania, but the Soviet Union did not recognize this act. From 1944, the Moldovan Soviet Socialist Republic was part of the Soviet Union.

In 1989, the Moldovans asserted their independence and ethnicity by making Romanian the official language and, at the end of 1991, Moldova became an independent nation. But Trans-Dniester, an area east of the River Dniester, has sought autonomy. In 2006, its people voted for independence and union with Russia. This vote was not recognized internationally.

Multiparty elections were held in 1994, but economic problems made the government unpopular. In 2001, Moldova became the first former Soviet republic to return the Communist Party to power in a general election. The Communist Party was re-elected in 2005, though it now advocates close ties with the West, a matter of some concern to Russia.

In terms of its GNP per capita, Moldova is Europe's poorest country. Agriculture is the leading activity and products include fruits, maize, tobacco and wine. Moldova has few natural resources and it imports materials and fuels for its industries. Light industries, such as food processing and factories making household appliances, are increasing.

MONACO

AREA 1 sq km [0.4 sq mi]
POPULATION 33,000
CAPITAL Monaco

The tiny Principality of Monaco consists of a narrow strip of coastline and a rocky peninsula on the French Riviera. Its considerable wealth is derived largely from banking, finance, gambling and tourism, with such attractions as the Monaco Grand Prix. Monaco's citizens do not pay any state tax. The reigning prince is Albert II, son of Prince Rainier III, who died in 2005, and his wife, the actress Grace Kelly.

MONGOLIA

AREA 1,566,500 sq km [604,826 sq mi]
POPULATION 2,832,000
CAPITAL Ulan Bator
GOVERNMENT Multiparty republic
ETHNIC GROUPS Khalkha Mongol 85%, Kazakh 6%
LANGUAGES Khalkha Mongolian (official), Turkic, Russian
RELIGIONS Tibetan Buddhist Lamaism 96%
CURRENCY Tugrik = 100 möngös

GEOGRAPHY The State of Mongolia is the world's largest landlocked country. It consists mainly of high plateaux, with the Gobi Desert in the south-east. Ulan Bator has bitterly cold winters. Summer temperatures are moderated by the altitude.

POLITICS & ECONOMY In the 13th century, Genghis Khan united the Mongolian peoples and built up a great empire. Under his grandson, Kublai Khan, the Mongol empire extended from Korea and China to eastern Europe and present-day Iraq.

The Mongol empire broke up in the late 14th century. In the early 17th century, Inner Mongolia came under Chinese control, and by the late 17th century Outer Mongolia had become a Chinese province. In 1911, the Mongolians drove the Chinese out of Outer Mongolia and made the area a Buddhist kingdom. But in 1924, under Russian influence, the Communist Mongolian People's Republic was set up. From the 1950s, Mongolia supported the Soviet Union in its disputes with China. In 1990, the people demonstrated for more freedom, and free elections in June 1990, resulted in victory for the Communist Mongolian People's Revolutionary Party (MPRP). The Democratic Union coalition won power over the Communists in 1996, but the MPRP regained power in 2000. In 2004, after disputed elections, a coalition government was set up. In 2005, the MPRP candidate, Nambaryn Enkhbayar, was elected president.

The World Bank classifies Mongolia as a 'lower-middle-income' developing country. Most people were once nomads, who moved around with their herds of sheep, cattle, goats and horses. Under Communist rule, most people were moved into permanent homes on government-owned farms. But livestock and animal products remain leading exports. The Communists also developed industry, especially the mining of coal, copper, gold, molybdenum, tin and tungsten, and manufacturing. Minerals and fuels now account for around half of Mongolia's exports.

MONTENEGRO

AREA 14,026 sq km [5,415 sq mi]
POPULATION 631,000
CAPITAL Podgorica
GOVERNMENT Republic
ETHNIC GROUPS Montenegrin 43%, Serb 32%, Bosnian 8%, Albanian 5%, others
LANGUAGES Serbian (official), Bosnian, Albanian, Croatian
RELIGIONS Orthodox, Islam, Roman Catholic
CURRENCY Euro = 100 cents

The Republic of Montenegro became fully independent in 2006. It was formerly part of the Union of Serbia and Montenegro and, before 2003, part of Yugoslavia. The smallest country in the Balkan peninsula, its coast has a Mediterranean climate, while the Dinaric Alps inland have a more extreme climate.

Serbia fell under Turkish rule in the 14th century, but Montenegro remained Christian. Montenegro was absorbed into Serbia in 1918. It became part of the Kingdom of the Serbs, Croats and Slovenes, which was renamed Yugoslavia in 1929. After World War II, Montenegro was recognized as one of the six republics in the Federal People's Republic of Yugoslavia.

Manufacturing is the leading activity, and steel and aluminium are major products. But farming remains important. Forests cover more than half of the land.

MONTSERRAT

AREA 102 sq km [39 sq mi]
POPULATION 9,000
CAPITAL Plymouth

Monserrat is a British overseas territory in the Caribbean Sea. It was colonized by Britain in 1632 and settled initially by Irish people. The climate is tropical and hurricanes cause much damage. Periodic eruptions of the Soufrière Hills volcano between 1995 and 1998, and again in 2003, led to large-scale emigration and the virtual destruction of the capital, Plymouth. A new airport was opened in 2005.

MOROCCO

AREA 446,550 sq km [172,413 sq mi]
POPULATION 33,241,000
CAPITAL Rabat
GOVERNMENT Constitutional monarchy
ETHNIC GROUPS Arab-Berber 99%
LANGUAGES Arabic (official), Berber dialects, French
RELIGIONS Islam 99%
CURRENCY Moroccan dirham = 100 centimes

GEOGRAPHY The Kingdom of Morocco lies in north-western Africa. Its name comes from the Arabic Maghreb-el-Aksa, meaning 'the farthest west'. Behind the western coastal plain, the land rises to the Atlas Mountains. East of the mountains, the land descends to the arid Sahara. The Atlantic coast is cooled by the Canaries Current. Inland, summers are hot and dry, but winters are mild and rainy. Snow often falls on the High Atlas Mountains.

POLITICS & ECONOMY The original people of Morocco were the Berbers. But in the 680s, Arab invaders introduced Islam and the Arabic language. By the early 20th century, France and Spain controlled Morocco, which became an independent kingdom in 1956. Although Morocco is a constitutional monarchy, King Hassan II ruled the country in a generally authoritarian way from the time of his accession to the throne in 1961 to his death in 1999. His son and successor, Mohamed VI, faced several problems, including the future of Western Sahara which Hassan II had vigorously claimed for Morocco. Relations with Spain became strained in 2002 over the disputed island of Leila (Perejil in Spanish) in the Strait of Gibraltar. But diplomatic relations were restored in 2003. Another problem faced by Morocco is activity by Islamic extremists. Its opposition to extremism led the United States to designate Morocco as a major non-NATO ally in 2004.

Morocco is classified as a 'lower-middle-income' developing country. It is the world's third largest producer of phosphate rock, which is used to make fertilizer. One of the reasons why Morocco wants to keep Western Sahara is that it, too, has large phosphate reserves. Farming employs 40% of Moroccans. Crops include barley, beans, citrus fruits, maize and wheat. Tourism is also important.

MOZAMBIQUE

AREA 801,590 sq km [309,494 sq mi]
POPULATION 19,687,000
CAPITAL Maputo
GOVERNMENT Multiparty republic
ETHNIC GROUPS Indigenous tribal groups (Shangaan, Chokwe, Manyika, Sena, Makua, others) 99%
LANGUAGES Portuguese (official), many others
RELIGIONS Traditional beliefs, Christianity, Islam
CURRENCY Metical = 100 centavos

GEOGRAPHY The Republic of Mozambique borders the Indian Ocean in south-eastern Africa. The coastal plains are narrow in the north but broaden in the south. Inland lie plateaux and hills, which make up another two-fifths of the land. Most of the country has a tropical climate.

POLITICS & ECONOMY In 1885, when the European powers divided Africa, Mozambique was recognized as a Portuguese colony. But black African opposition to European rule gradually increased. In 1961, the Front for the Liberation of Mozambique (FRELIMO) was founded to oppose Portuguese rule. A guerrilla war began in 1964 and continued for ten years. Mozambique became independent in 1975.

After independence, Mozambique became a one-party state. Its government aided African nationalists in Rhodesia (now Zimbabwe) and South Africa. But the white governments of these countries helped an opposition group, the Mozambique National Resistance Movement (RENAMO), to lead an armed struggle against Mozambique's government. Civil war, combined with droughts, caused much suffering in the 1980s. In 1989, FRELIMO declared that it had dropped its Communist policies and ended one-party rule. The war ended in 1992 and multiparty elections in 1994, 1999 and 2004 were all won by FRELIMO. In 1995, Mozambique became the 53rd member of the Commonwealth.

In the early 1990s, the UN rated Mozambique as one of the world's poorest countries. The second half of the 1990s saw a surge in economic growth, but huge floods in 2000 and 2001 proved to be a major setback. About 80% of the people are poor and agriculture is the main activity. Crops include cassava, cotton, maize, rice and tea.

NAMIBIA

AREA 824,292 sq km [318,259 sq mi]
POPULATION 2,044,000
CAPITAL Windhoek
GOVERNMENT Multiparty republic
ETHNIC GROUPS Ovambo 50%, Kavango 9%, Herero 7%, Damara 7%, White 6%, Nama 5%
LANGUAGES English (official), Afrikaans, German, indigenous dialects
RELIGIONS Christianity 90% (Lutheran 51%)
CURRENCY Namibian dollar = 100 cents

GEOGRAPHY The Republic of Namibia was formerly ruled by South Africa, which called it South West Africa. The country became independent in 1990. The coastal region contains the arid Namib Desert, which is virtually uninhabited. Inland is a central plateau, bordered by a rugged spine of mountains stretching north–south. Eastern Namibia contains part of the Kalahari Desert. Namibia is a warm, arid country. Windhoek has an average annual rainfall of 370 mm [15 in]. Thunderstorms often occur in summer.

POLITICS & ECONOMY During World War I, South African troops defeated the Germans who ruled what is now Namibia. After World War II, many people challenged South Africa's right to govern the territory and a civil war began in the 1960s between African guerrillas and South African troops. A cease-fire was agreed in 1989 and Namibia became independent in 1990. The coastal enclave of Walvis Bay (Walvisbaai) was part of South Africa until 1994, when it was transferred to Namibia. In 2004, Sam Nujoma, president since independence, retired and was succeeded by Hifikepunye Pohamba.

Namibia is rich in mineral reserves, including diamonds, uranium, zinc and copper. Minerals are major exports, but farming employs about 20% of the people. In 2003–4, the government revealed that it planned to speed up land reform by transferring commercial farmland from white to black Namibians, and, in 2005, the government began to expropriate white-owned farms as part of the land reform programme. Sea fishing is important, but the country has few industries. Tourism is increasing.

NAURU

AREA 21 sq km [8 sq mi]
POPULATION 13,000
CAPITAL Yaren

A former UN Trust Territory ruled by Australia, Nauru became independent in 1968. Located in the western Pacific, close to the Equator, it is the world's smallest republic. Nauru's prosperity is based on phosphate mining, but the reserves are running out.

NATIONS OF THE WORLD

NEPAL

AREA 147,181 sq km [56,827 sq mi]
POPULATION 28,287,000
CAPITAL Katmandu
GOVERNMENT Constitutional monarchy
ETHNIC GROUPS Brahman, Chetri, Newar, Gurung,
Magar, Tamang, Sherpa and others
LANGUAGES Nepali (official), local languages
RELIGIONS Hinduism 86%, Buddhism 8%, Islam 4%
CURRENCY Nepalese rupee = 100 paisa

GEOGRAPHY Over three-quarters of Nepal lies in the Himalayan region, culminating in the world's highest peak (Mount Everest, or Chomolongma in Nepali) at 8,850 m [29,035 ft]. As a result, climatic conditions vary widely according to the altitude.

POLITICS & ECONOMY Nepal was united in the late 18th century, although its complex topography has ensured that it remains a diverse patchwork of peoples. From the mid-19th century to 1951, power was held by the royal Rana family. Attempts to introduce a democratic system in the 1950s failed. The first democratic elections in 32 years were held in 1991, but, by the early 21st century, Nepal faced a major revolt by Maoist guerrillas. In 2005, King Gyanendra seized power and sacked the government. The fighting continued and, in 2006, Nepal's ruling parties combined with the Maoists to vest executive power in the prime minister, and not the king.

Agriculture remains the chief activity in this over-whelmingly rural country and the government is heavily dependent on aid. Tourism, centred around the high Himalaya, grows in importance each year, although Nepal was closed to foreigners until 1951. There are also plans to exploit the hydroelectric potential offered by the Himalayan rivers.

NETHERLANDS

AREA 41,526 sq km [16,033 sq mi]
POPULATION 16,491,000
CAPITAL Amsterdam; The Hague (seat of government)
GOVERNMENT Constitutional monarchy
ETHNIC GROUPS Dutch 83%, Indonesian, Turkish, Moroccan and others
LANGUAGES Dutch (official), Frisian
RELIGIONS Roman Catholic 31%, Protestant 21%, Islam 4%, others
CURRENCY Euro = 100 cents

GEOGRAPHY The Netherlands lies at the western end of the North European Plain, which extends to the Ural Mountains in Russia. Except for the far south-eastern corner, the Netherlands is flat and about 40% lies below sea level at high tide. To prevent flooding, the Dutch have built dykes (sea walls) to hold back the waves. Large areas which were once under the sea, but which have been reclaimed, are called polders. Because of its position on the North Sea, the Netherlands has a temperate climate, with mild, rainy winters.

POLITICS & ECONOMY Before the 16th century, the area that is now the Netherlands was under a succession of foreign rulers, including the Romans,

the Germanic Franks, the French and the Spanish. The Dutch declared their independence from Spain in 1581 and their status was finally recognized by Spain in 1648. In the 17th century, the Dutch built up a great overseas empire, especially in South-east Asia. But in the early 18th century, the Dutch lost control of the seas to England.

France controlled the Netherlands from 1795 to 1813. In 1815, the Netherlands, then containing Belgium and Luxembourg, became an independent kingdom. Belgium broke away in 1830 and Luxembourg followed in 1890.

The Netherlands was neutral in World War I (1914–18), but was occupied by Germany in World War II (1939–45). After the war, the Netherlands Indies became independent as Indonesia. The Netherlands became active in West European affairs. With Belgium and Luxembourg, it formed a customs union called Benelux in 1948. In 1949, it joined NATO (the North Atlantic Treaty Organization), and the European Coal and Steel Community (ECSC) in 1953. In 1957, it became a founder member of the European Economic Community (now the European Union) and, in 2002, it adopted the euro as its sole unit of currency.

The Netherlands is a highly industrialized country and industry and commerce are the most valuable activities. Its resources include natural gas, some oil, salt and china clay. Many materials used in its industries are imported and the Netherlands is a major trading nation. Manufactures include aircraft, chemicals, electronic equipment, machinery, textiles and vehicles. Agriculture employs 3% of the people, but yields are high. Dairy farming is the main activity. Major products include barley, flowers and bulbs, potatoes, sugar beet and wheat.

NETHERLANDS ANTILLES

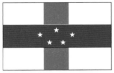

AREA 800 sq km [309 sq mi]
POPULATION 222,000
CAPITAL Willemstad

The Netherlands Antilles consists of two different island groups; one off the coast of Venezuela, and the other at the northern end of the Leeward Islands, some 800 km [500 mi] away. They remain a self-governing Dutch territory. The island of Aruba was once part of the territory, but it broke away in 1986 to become a separate Dutch territory. Oil refining and tourism are important activities.

NEW CALEDONIA

AREA 18,575 sq km [7,172 sq mi]
POPULATION 219,000
CAPITAL Nouméa

New Caledonia is the most southerly of the Melanesian countries in the Pacific. A French possession since 1853 and an Overseas Territory since 1958. In 1998, France announced an agreement with local Melanesians that a vote on independence would be postponed until 2014. The country is rich in mineral resources. Experts estimate that it has about a quarter of the world's nickel reserves.

NEW ZEALAND

AREA 270,534 sq km [104,453 sq mi]
POPULATION 4,076,000
CAPITAL Wellington
GOVERNMENT Constitutional monarchy
ETHNIC GROUPS New Zealand European 74%,
New Zealand Maori 10%, Polynesian 4%
LANGUAGES English and Maori (both official)
RELIGIONS Anglican 24%, Presbyterian 18%,
Roman Catholic 15%, others
CURRENCY New Zealand dollar = 100 cents

GEOGRAPHY New Zealand lies about 1,600 km [994 mi] south-east of Australia. It consists of two main islands and several other small ones. Much of the North Island is volcanic. Active volcanoes include Ngauruhoe and Ruapehu. Hot springs and geysers are common, and steam from the ground is used to produce electricity. South Island contains the Southern Alps, which include the country's highest peak, Aoraki Mount Cook, at 3,753 m [12,313 ft]. The Southern Alps form the backbone of South Island. Scenic fjords line the south-western coast, but the island also has some large, fertile plains. The third largest island, Stewart Island, lies off the south coast of South Island.

Auckland in the north has a warm, humid climate throughout the year. Wellington has cooler summers, while in Dunedin, in the south-east, temperatures sometimes dip below freezing in winter. The rainfall is heaviest on the western highlands.

POLITICS & ECONOMY Evidence suggests that early Maori settlers arrived in New Zealand more than 1,000 years ago. The Dutch navigator Abel Tasman reached New Zealand in 1642, but his discovery was not followed up. In 1769, the British Captain James Cook rediscovered the islands. In the early 19th century, British settlers arrived and, in 1840, under the Treaty of Waitangi, Britain took possession of the islands. Clashes occurred with the Maoris in the 1860s but, following the end of the New Zealand Wars in 1872, the Maoris were gradually integrated into society.

In 1907, New Zealand became a self-governing dominion in the British Commonwealth. The country's economy developed quickly and the people became increasingly prosperous. However, after Britain joined the European Economic Community in 1973, New Zealand's exports to Britain shrank and the country had to reassess its economic and defence strategies and seek new markets. The world recession led to cuts in welfare spending. The preservation of Maori culture and rights are other political issues.

Ties with Britain have been reduced and Helen Clark, leader of the Labour Party and prime minister since 1999, has expressed the view that New Zealand will eventually abolish the monarchy and become a republic. In 2005, the Labour Party won a narrow victory in national elections and formed a coalition with two minor parties.

New Zealand's economy has traditionally depended on agriculture, but manufacturing now employs nearly twice as many people as agriculture. Major manufactures include food products, machinery and apparatus, wood products and metals. Meat and dairy products are the most valuable items produced on farms. The importance of sheep, which once dominated New Zealand's agriculture, has declined, while the area under cattle, deer and vineyards has increased.

NICARAGUA

AREA 130,000 sq km [50,193 sq mi]
POPULATION 5,570,000
CAPITAL Managua
GOVERNMENT Multiparty republic
ETHNIC GROUPS Mestizo 69%, White 17%, Black 9%, Amerindian 5%
LANGUAGES Spanish (official)
RELIGIONS Roman Catholic 85%, Protestant
CURRENCY Córdoba oro (gold córdoba) = 100 centavos

GEOGRAPHY The Republic of Nicaragua contains a broad plain bordering the Caribbean Sea. The Central Highlands separate the Caribbean plain from the fertile western region, which contains about 40 volcanoes, many of which are active. Earthquakes are common in the west. The climate is tropical. Managua is hot throughout the year, with a marked rainy season from May to October. The Central Highlands are cooler and wetter. But the wettest region is the humid Caribbean plain.

POLITICS & ECONOMY In 1502, Christopher Columbus claimed the area for Spain, which ruled Nicaragua until 1821. In 1912, US forces entered the area to protect US interests. From 1927 to 1933, rebels under General Augusto César Sandino tried to drive out the US forces. In 1933, US marines set up a Nicaraguan army, the National Guard, to help defeat the rebels. Its leader, Anastasio Somoza Garcia, had Sandino murdered in 1934. From 1937, Somoza ruled Nicaragua as a dictator.

In the mid-1970s, many people began to protest against Somoza's rule. Many joined a guerrilla force, called the Sandinista National Liberation Front, named after General Sandino. The rebels defeated the Somoza regime in 1979. In the 1980s, the US-supported forces, called the 'Contras', launched a campaign against the Sandinista government. The US government opposed the Sandinista regime, under Daniel José Ortega Saavedra, claiming that it was a Communist dictatorship. The National Opposition Union defeated the Sandinistas in elections in 1990. Ortega was defeated in presidential elections in 2001, but he was re-elected president in 2006.

Nicaragua worked to rebuild its shattered economy in the 1990s. Agriculture is the main activity. Coffee, cotton and sugar are exported, while beans, maize and rice are the main food crops. Manufactures include processed food, textiles and clothing.

NIGER

AREA 1,267,000 sq km [489,189 sq mi]
POPULATION 12,525,000
CAPITAL Niamey
GOVERNMENT Multiparty republic
ETHNIC GROUPS Hausa 56%, Djerma 22%, Tuareg 8%, Fula 8%, others
LANGUAGES French (official), Hausa, Djerma
RELIGIONS Islam 80%, indigenous beliefs, Christianity
CURRENCY CFA franc = 100 centimes

GEOGRAPHY The Republic of Niger is a landlocked nation in north-central Africa. The northern plateaux lie in the Sahara Desert, while Central Niger contains the rugged Aïr Mountains. The most fertile, densely populated region is the Niger valley in the south-west.

Niger has a tropical climate and the south has a rainy season between June and September. The north is practically rainless.

POLITICS & ECONOMY Since independence in 1960, Niger, a French territory from 1900, has suffered severe droughts. Food shortages and the collapse of the traditional nomadic way of life of some of Niger's people have caused political instability. After a period of military rule, a multiparty constitution was adopted in 1992, but the military again seized power in 1996. Later that year, the coup leader, Col. Ibrahim Barre Mainassara, was elected president. He was assassinated in 1999, but parliamentary rule was rapidly restored and Tandja Mamadou was elected president. Mamadou was re-elected president in December 2004.

Niger's chief resource is uranium and it is the world's fourth largest producer. Tin and tungsten are also mined, although other mineral resources are largely untouched. Despite its resources, Niger is one of the world's poorest countries. Farming employs about three-quarters of the population, but only 3% of the land can be farmed while 8% is used for grazing.

NIGERIA

AREA 923,768 sq km [356,667 sq mi]
POPULATION 131,860,000
CAPITAL Abuja
GOVERNMENT Federal multiparty republic
ETHNIC GROUPS Hausa and Fulani 29%, Yoruba 21%, Ibo (or Igbo) 18%, Ijaw 10%, Kanuri 4%, many others
LANGUAGES English (official), Hausa, Yoruba, Ibo
RELIGIONS Islam 50%, Christianity 40%, traditional beliefs 10%
CURRENCY Naira = 100 kobo

GEOGRAPHY The Federal Republic of Nigeria is the most populous nation in Africa. The country's main rivers are the Niger and Benue, which meet in central Nigeria. North of the two river valleys are high plains and plateaux. The Lake Chad basin is in the north-east, with the Sokoto plains in the north-west. The south contains hilly areas and coastal plains. The south is hot and rainy throughout the year. The north is drier but often hotter than the south.

POLITICS & ECONOMY Nigeria has a long artistic tradition. Major cultures include the Nok (500 BC to AD 200), Ife, which developed about 1,000 years ago, and Benin, which flourished between the 15th and 17th centuries. Britain gradually extended its influence over the area in the second half of the 19th century.

Nigeria became independent in 1960 and a federal republic in 1963. A federal constitution dividing the country into regions was necessary because Nigeria contains more than 250 ethnic and linguistic groups, as well as several religious ones. Local rivalries have long been a threat to national unity, and six new states were created in 1996 in an attempt to overcome this. Civil war occurred between 1967 and 1970, when the people of the south-east attempted unsuccessfully to secede during the Biafran War. Between 1960 and 1998, Nigeria had only nine years of civilian government. In 1998–9, civilian rule was restored. A former general, Olusegun Obasanjo, was elected president, and he was re-elected in 2003. Nigeria faced many problems, including ongoing religious conflict and violence in the Niger delta region. Presidential elections in 2007 were marked by violence and allegations of vote-rigging and fraud. The victor was Umar Yar-dua, the Muslim governor of the northern state of Katsina.

Nigeria is a developing country with great potential. Its chief natural resource is oil, which accounts for most of its exports. Agriculture employs 43% of the people and the country is a major producer of cocoa, palm oil and palm kernels, groundnuts and rubber.

NORTHERN MARIANA ISLANDS

AREA 464 sq km [179 sq mi]
POPULATION 82,000
CAPITAL Saipan

The Commonwealth of the Northern Mariana Islands contains 16 mountainous islands north of Guam in the western Pacific Ocean. In a 1975 plebiscite, the islanders voted for Commonwealth status in union with the USA and, in 1986, they were granted US citizenship.

NORWAY

AREA 323,877 sq km [125,049 sq mi]
POPULATION 4,611,000
CAPITAL Oslo
GOVERNMENT Constitutional monarchy
ETHNIC GROUPS Norwegian 97%
LANGUAGES Norwegian (official)
RELIGIONS Evangelical Lutheran 86%
CURRENCY Norwegian krone = 100 ore

GEOGRAPHY The Kingdom of Norway forms the western part of the rugged Scandinavian peninsula. The deep inlets along the highly indented coastline were worn out by glaciers during the Ice Age.

The warm North Atlantic Drift off the coast of Norway moderates the climate, with mild winters and cool summers. Nearly all the ports are ice-free throughout the year. Inland, winters are colder and snow cover lasts for at least three months a year.

POLITICS & ECONOMY From about AD 800, for a period lasting about 300 years, Norwegian Vikings ravaged western Europe. Norway's first king, Harold I, united Norway in about 900. In 1380, Norway was united with Denmark. But under a treaty of 1814, Denmark handed Norway over to Sweden, though it kept Norway's colonies – Greenland, Iceland and the Færoe Islands. Norway briefly became independent, but Swedish forces defeated the Norwegians and Norway had to accept Sweden's king as its ruler.

The union between Norway and Sweden ended in 1903. During World War II (1939–45), Germany occupied Norway. Norway's economy developed quickly after the war and the country now enjoys one of the world's highest standards of living. In 1994, Norwegians voted against joining the EU. In the 1990s and 2000s, Norwegian diplomats sought to broker peace deals in Palestine and Sri Lanka.

Norway's chief resources and exports are oil and natural gas which come from wells under the North Sea. Farmland covers only 3% of the land. Dairy farming and meat production are important, but Norway has to import food. Norway has many industries powered by cheap hydroelectricity.

OMAN

AREA 309,500 sq km [119,498 sq mi]
POPULATION 3,102,000
CAPITAL Muscat
GOVERNMENT Monarchy with consultative council
ETHNIC GROUPS Arab, Baluchi, Indian, Pakistani
LANGUAGES Arabic (official), Baluchi, English
RELIGIONS Islam (mainly Ibadhi), Hinduism
CURRENCY Omani rial = 100 baizas

GEOGRAPHY The Sultanate of Oman faces the Red Sea. It includes the tip of the Musandam peninsula. It has a hot tropical climate.

POLITICS & ECONOMY British influence in Oman dates back to the end of the 18th century, but the country became fully independent in 1971. Since then, using revenue from oil, which was discovered in 1964, the absolute ruler, Qaboos ibn Said, and his government have sought to modernize Oman. In 2000, elections to a consultative assembly were held and, in 2004, the first woman minister was appointed. In 2005, 31 Islamists were convicted of trying to overthrow the government; they were later acquitted.

Oil accounts for the bulk of Oman's exports. Crops include alfalfa, bananas, coconuts, dates, limes, tobacco, vegetables and wheat. Fishing is also important, but Oman has to import food.

PAKISTAN

AREA 796,095 sq km [307,372 sq mi]
POPULATION 165,804,000
CAPITAL Islamabad
GOVERNMENT Military regime
ETHNIC GROUPS Punjabi, Sindhi, Pashtun (Pathan), Baluchi, Muhajir
LANGUAGES Urdu (official), many others
RELIGIONS Islam 97%, Christianity, Hinduism
CURRENCY Pakistani rupee = 100 paisa

GEOGRAPHY The Islamic Republic of Pakistan contains high mountains, fertile plains and rocky deserts. The Karakoram range, which contains K2, the world's second highest peak, lies in the northern part of Jammu and Kashmir, which is occupied by Pakistan but claimed by India. Other mountains rise in the west. Plains, drained by the River Indus and its tributaries, occupy much of the east. Most of Pakistan has hot summers and mild winters. The rainfall is sparse and deserts cover large areas.

POLITICS & ECONOMY Pakistan was the site of the Indus Valley civilization which developed about 4,500 years ago. But Pakistan's modern history dates from 1947, when British India was divided into India and Pakistan. Muslim Pakistan was divided into two parts: East and West Pakistan, but East Pakistan broke away in 1971 to become Bangladesh. In 1948–9, 1965 and 1971, Pakistan and India clashed over the disputed territory of Kashmir. In 1998, Pakistan responded in kind to a series of Indian nuclear weapon tests, provoking global controversy. However, in 2003–5, Pakistan launched a series of peace moves, raising hopes of a settlement in the disputed area, though militant activity continued on the ground.

Pakistan has been subject to several periods of military rule, but elections in 1988 led to Benazir Bhutto becoming prime minister. She was removed from office in 1990, but she returned as prime minister between 1993 and 1996. In 1997, Narwaz Sharif was elected prime minister, but a military coup in 1999 brought General Pervez Musharraf to power. In 2001, Pakistan supported the Western assault on Taliban forces in Afghanistan. Musharraf's powers were increased by constitutional changes in 2002, but Islamic parties received substantial support in subsequent national elections. Pakistan's opposition to international terrorism also provoked a backlash among Islamists. In 2004, President Musharraf announced that he would remain the army chief, despite criticism. In 2006–7, an uprising in Baluchistan and the activities of al Qaida and the Taliban in frontier regions caused much turmoil.

According to the World Bank, Pakistan is a 'low-income' developing country. The economy is based on farming or rearing goats and sheep. Agriculture employs nearly four-fifths of the people. Major crops include cotton, fruits, rice, sugar cane and wheat.

PALAU

AREA 459 sq km [177 sq mi]
POPULATION 21,000
CAPITAL Koror

The Republic of Palau became fully independent in 1994, after the USA refused to accede to a 1979 referendum that declared this island nation a nuclear-free zone. The economy relies on US aid, tourism, fishing and subsistence agriculture. The main crops include cassava, coconuts and copra.

PANAMA

AREA 75,517 sq km [29,157 sq mi]
POPULATION 3,191,000
CAPITAL Panamá
GOVERNMENT Multiparty republic
ETHNIC GROUPS Mestizo 70%, Black and Mulatto 14%, White 10%, Amerindian 6%
LANGUAGES Spanish (official), English
RELIGIONS Roman Catholic 85%, Protestant 15%
CURRENCY US dollar; Balboa = 100 centésimos

GEOGRAPHY The Republic of Panama forms an isthmus linking Central America to South America. The Panama Canal, which is 81.6 km [50.7 mi] long, has made the country a major transport centre. Panama has a tropical climate and temperatures are high on the coastal plains. The main rainy season is between May and December.

POLITICS & ECONOMY Christopher Columbus landed in Panama in 1502 and Spain soon took control of the area. In 1821, Panama became independent from Spain and a province of Colombia.

In 1903, Colombia refused a request by the United States to build a canal. Panama then revolted against Colombia, and became independent. The United States then began to build the canal, which was opened in 1914. The United States administered the Panama Canal Zone, a strip of land along the canal. But many Panamanians resented US influence and, in 1979, the Canal Zone was returned to Panama. Control of the canal itself was handed over by the USA to Panama on 31 December 1999.

Panama's government has changed many times since independence, and there have been periods of military dictatorships. In 1983, General Manuel Antonio Noriega became Panama's leader. In 1988, two US grand juries in Florida indicted Noriega on charges of drug trafficking. In 1989, Noriega was apparently defeated in a presidential election, but the government declared the election invalid. After the killing of a US marine, US troops entered Panama and arrested Noriega, who was convicted by a Miami court of drug offences in 1992. In 1999, Mireya Moscoso became Panama's first woman president. She was succeeded in 2004 by Martin Torrijos, son of a former military dictator.

The World Bank classifies Panama as a 'lower-middle-income' developing country. The Panama Canal is an important source of revenue and it generates many jobs in commerce, trade, manufacturing and transport. Away from the canal, the main activity is agriculture, which employs 14% of the people.

PAPUA NEW GUINEA

AREA 462,840 sq km [178,703 sq mi]
POPULATION 5,671,000
CAPITAL Port Moresby
GOVERNMENT Constitutional monarchy
ETHNIC GROUPS Papuan, Melanesian, Micronesian
LANGUAGES English (official), Melanesian Pidgin, more than 700 other indigenous languages
RELIGIONS Traditional beliefs 34%, Roman Catholic 22%, Lutheran 16%, others
CURRENCY Kina = 100 toea

GEOGRAPHY Papua New Guinea is an independent country in the Pacific Ocean, north of Australia. It is part of a Pacific island region called Melanesia. Papua New Guinea includes the eastern part of New Guinea, the Bismarck Archipelago, the northern Solomon Islands, the D'Entrecasteaux Islands and the Louisiade Archipelago. The land is largely mountainous. The climate is tropical. Most of the rain occurs during the monsoon season (December–April), when winds blow from the north-east. During the dry season, the winds blow from the south-west.

POLITICS & ECONOMY The Dutch took western New Guinea (now part of Indonesia) in 1828, but it was not until 1884 that Germany took north-eastern New Guinea and Britain took the south-east. In 1906, Britain handed the south-east over to Australia. It then became known as the Territory of Papua. When World War I broke out in 1914, Australia took German New Guinea and, in 1921, the League of Nations gave Australia a mandate to rule the area, which was named the Territory of New Guinea.

Japan invaded New Guinea in 1942, but the Allies reconquered the area in 1944. In 1949, Papua and New Guinea were combined. Papua New Guinea became independent in 1975. The new nation sought to develop its mineral reserves. One of the most valuable mines was on Bougainville, in the northern Solomon Islands, but a secessionist group declared the island independent. Under a peace treaty in 2001, Bougainville became autonomous and held its first elections in 2005. In 2004, Australia sent police to Papua New Guinea to help fight crime, but they were withdrawn in 2005 following a Supreme Court ruling that their presence was unconstitutional.

Papua New Guinea has a 'lower-middle-economy'. Agriculture employs 70% of the people, but most of them live at subsistence level. Petroleum and minerals, notably copper, are the leading exports.

PARAGUAY

AREA 406,752 sq km [157,047 sq mi]
POPULATION 6,506,000
CAPITAL Asunción
GOVERNMENT Multiparty republic
ETHNIC GROUPS Mestizo 95%
LANGUAGES Spanish and Guaraní (both official)
RELIGIONS Roman Catholic 90%, Protestant
CURRENCY Guaraní = 100 céntimos

GEOGRAPHY The Republic of Paraguay is a land-locked country and rivers, notably the Paraná, Pilco-mayo (Brazo Sur) and Paraguay, form most of its borders. A flat region called the Gran Chaco lies in the north-west, while the south-east contains plains, hills and plateaux.

Northern Paraguay lies in the tropics, while the south is subtropical. Most of the country has a warm, humid climate.

POLITICS & ECONOMY In 1776, Paraguay became part of a large colony called the Vice-royalty of La Plata, with Buenos Aires as the capital. Paraguayans opposed this move and the country declared its independence in 1811.

For many years, Paraguay was torn by internal strife and conflict with its neighbours. A war against Brazil, Argentina and Uruguay (1865–70) led to the deaths of more than half of Paraguay's population, and a great loss of territory.

General Alfredo Stroessner took power in 1954 and ruled as a dictator. His government imprisoned many opponents. Stroessner was overthrown in 1989. Free multiparty elections were held in 1993, 1998 and 2003. However, the return to democracy often seemed precarious because of rivalries between politicians and army leaders, together with economic recession which arose partly from the problems experienced in neighbouring Argentina and Brazil.

The World Bank classifies Paraguay as a 'lower-middle-income' developing country. Farming and forestry are leading activities. Paraguay produces hydroelectricity and exports power to its neighbours.

PERU

AREA 1,285,216 sq km [496,222 sq mi]
POPULATION 28,303,000
CAPITAL Lima
GOVERNMENT Transitional republic
ETHNIC GROUPS Amerindian 45%, Mestizo 37%, White 15%
LANGUAGES Spanish and Quechua (both official), Aymara, other Amazonian languages
RELIGIONS Roman Catholic 90%
CURRENCY New sol = 100 centavos

GEOGRAPHY The Republic of Peru lies in the tropics in western South America. A narrow coastal plain borders the Pacific Ocean in the west. Inland are ranges of the Andes Mountains, which rise to

6,768 m [22,205 ft] at Mount Huascarán, an extinct volcano. East of the Andes lies the Amazon basin.

Lima, on the coastal plain, has an arid climate. The coastal region is chilled by the cold, offshore Humboldt Current. The rainfall increases inland and many mountains in the high Andes are snow-capped.
POLITICS & ECONOMY Spanish conquistadors conquered Peru in the 1530s. In 1820, an Argentinian, José de San Martín, led an army into Peru and declared it independent. But Spain still held large areas. In 1823, the Venezuelan Simon Bolívar led another army into Peru and, in 1824, one of his generals defeated the Spaniards at Ayacucho. The Spaniards surrendered in 1826. Peru suffered much instability throughout the 19th century.

Instability continued in the 20th century. In 1980, when civilian rule was restored, a left-wing group called the Sendero Luminoso, or the 'Shining Path', began guerrilla warfare against the government. In 1990, Alberto Fujimori, son of Japanese immigrants, became president. In 1992, he suspended the constitution and dismissed the legislature. The guerrilla leader, Abimael Guzmán, was arrested in 1992, but instability continued. Following his victory in disputed presidential elections in 2000, Fujimori resigned and left the country. Between 2001 and 2006, Alejandro Toledo became the first Peruvian of Amerindian descent to serve as president. In 2006, a state of emergency was declared in six central provinces after suspected 'Shining Path' guerrilla activity. Later that year, Abimael Guzmán was found guilty of terrorism and sentenced to life imprisonment.

The World Bank classifies Peru as a 'lower-middle-income' developing country. Major food crops include beans, maize, potatoes and rice. Fish products are exported, but the most valuable export is copper. Peru also produces lead, silver, zinc and iron ore.

PHILIPPINES

AREA 300,000 sq km [115,830 sq mi]
POPULATION 89,469,000
CAPITAL Manila
GOVERNMENT Multiparty republic
ETHNIC GROUPS Christian Malay 92%, Muslim Malay 4%, Chinese and others
LANGUAGES Filipino (Tagalog) and English (both official), Spanish, many others
RELIGIONS Roman Catholic 83%, Protestant 9%, Islam 5%
CURRENCY Philippine peso = 100 centavos

GEOGRAPHY The Republic of the Philippines is an island country in south-eastern Asia. It includes about 7,100 islands, of which 2,770 are named and about 1,000 are inhabited. Luzon and Mindanao, the two largest islands, make up more than two-thirds of the country. The land is mainly mountainous.

The country has a hot tropical climate. The dry season runs from December to April. The rest of the year is wet. Much of the rainfall comes from the typhoons which periodically strike the east coast.
POLITICS & ECONOMY The first European to reach the Philippines was the Portuguese navigator Ferdinand Magellan in 1521. Spanish explorers claimed the region in 1565 when they established a settlement on Cebu. The Spaniards ruled the country until 1898, when the United States took over at the end of the Spanish–American War. Japan invaded the Philippines in 1941, but US forces returned in

1944. The country became fully independent as the Republic of the Philippines in 1946.
POLITICS & ECONOMY The first European to reach the Philippines was the Portuguese navigator Ferdinand Magellan in 1521. Spanish explorers claimed the region in 1565 when they established a settlement on Cebu. The Spaniards ruled the country until 1898, when the United States took over at the end of the Spanish–American War. Japan invaded the Philippines in 1941, but US forces returned in 1944. The country became fully independent as the Republic of the Philippines in 1946.

Since independence, the country's problems have included armed uprisings by left-wing guerrillas demanding land reform, and Muslim separatist groups, crime, corruption and unemployment. The dominant figure in recent times was Ferdinand Marcos, who ruled in a dictatorial manner from 1965 to 1986. His successors were Corazon Aquino (1986–92), Fidel Ramos (1992–8), and Joseph Estrada, who resigned after massive public protests against his alleged corruption in 2001. He was succeeded by Vice-President Gloria Arroyo. She faced continuing problems in trying, with American help, to defeat the Muslim terrorist groups in the south. In 2003, the government put down a military rebellion. Arroyo was re-elected president in 2004. Conflict continued in the south and, in 2006, the government declared a state of emergency after the army said that it had prevented a planned coup.

The Philippines is a developing country. Agriculture employs around 30% of the people. The main foods are rice and maize, while such crops as bananas, cocoa, coconuts, coffee, sugar cane and tobacco are all grown commercially. Manufacturing now plays an increasingly important role in the economy.

PITCAIRN

AREA 55 sq km [21 sq mi]
POPULATION 45
CAPITAL Adamstown

Pitcairn Island is a British overseas territory in the Pacific Ocean. Its inhabitants are descendants of the original settlers – nine mutineers from HMS *Bounty* and 18 Tahitians who arrived on this formerly uninhabited island in 1790.

POLAND

AREA 323,250 sq km [124,807 sq mi]
POPULATION 38,537,000
CAPITAL Warsaw
GOVERNMENT Multiparty republic
ETHNIC GROUPS Polish 97%, Belarusian, Ukrainian, German
LANGUAGES Polish (official)
RELIGIONS Roman Catholic 95%, Eastern Orthodox
CURRENCY Zloty = 100 groszy

GEOGRAPHY The Republic of Poland faces the Baltic Sea and, behind its lagoon-fringed coast, lies a broad plain. A plateau lies in the south-east, while the Sudeten Highlands straddle part of the border with the Czech Republic. Part of the

Carpathian Range (the Tatra) lies in the south-east.

Poland's climate is influenced by its position in Europe. Warm, moist air masses come from the west, while cold air masses come from the north and east. Summers are warm, but winters are cold and snowy.

POLITICS & ECONOMY Poland's boundaries have changed several times in the last 200 years, partly as a result of its geographical location between the powers of Germany and Russia. It disappeared from the map in the late 18th century, when a Polish state called the Grand Duchy of Warsaw was set up. But in 1815, the country was partitioned, between Austria, Prussia and Russia. Poland became independent in 1918, but in 1939 it was divided between Germany and the Soviet Union. The country again became independent in 1945, when it lost land to Russia but gained some from Germany. Communists took power in 1948, but opposition mounted and eventually became focused through an organization called Solidarity.

Solidarity was led by a trade unionist, Lech Walesa. A coalition government was formed between Solidarity and the Communists in 1989. In 1990, the Communist Party was dissolved and Walesa became president. But Walesa faced many problems in turning Poland towards a market economy. In presidential elections in 1995, Walesa was defeated by ex-Communist Aleksander Kwasniewski. However, Poland continued to follow westward-looking policies. Poland joined NATO in 1999 and the European Union on 1 May 2004. In 2005, a nationalist, Lech Kaczynski, became president. In 2006, his twin brother, Jaroslaw, was appointed prime minister.

Poland has large reserves of coal and deposits of various minerals which are used in its factories. Manufactures include chemicals, processed food, machinery, ships, steel and textiles.

PORTUGAL

AREA 88,797 sq km [34,285 sq mi]
POPULATION 10,606,000
CAPITAL Lisbon
GOVERNMENT Multiparty republic
ETHNIC GROUPS Portuguese 99%
LANGUAGES Portuguese (official)
RELIGIONS Roman Catholic 94%, Protestant
CURRENCY Euro = 100 cents

GEOGRAPHY The Republic of Portugal is the most westerly of Europe's mainland countries. The land rises from the coastal plains on the Atlantic Ocean to the western edge of the huge plateau, or Meseta, which occupies most of the Iberian peninsula. Portugal also contains two autonomous regions, the Azores and Madeira island groups.

The climate is moderated by winds blowing from the Atlantic Ocean. Summers are cooler and winters are milder than in other Mediterranean lands.

POLITICS & ECONOMY Portugal became a separate country, independent of Spain, in 1143. In the 15th century, Portugal led the 'Age of European Exploration'. This led to the growth of a large Portuguese empire, with colonies in Africa, Asia and, most valuable of all, Brazil in South America. Portuguese power began to decline in the 16th century and, between 1580 and 1640, Portugal was ruled by Spain. Portugal lost Brazil in 1822 and, in 1910, Portugal became a republic. Instability hampered progress and army officers seized power in 1926. In 1928, they chose Antonio de Salazar to be minister of finance.

Salazar became prime minister in 1932 and ruled as a dictator from 1933 until 1968. In 1974, army officers mounted a coup. The new regime made most of Portugal's remaining colonies independent and free elections were held in 1978. Portugal joined the European Community (now the European Union) in 1986 and, on 1 January 2002, the euro replaced the escudo as the sole unit of currency. In 2005, the Socialists, led by a moderate, José Sócrates, won a decisive victory in parliamentary elections.

Agriculture and fishing were the mainstays of the economy until the mid-20th century. Forest products, including timber and cork, are important and Portugal faced a setback in 2003 and 2005 when forest fires caused extensive damage. Manufacturing is now the most valuable sector of the economy.

PUERTO RICO

AREA 8,875 sq km [3,427 sq mi]
POPULATION 3,927,000
CAPITAL San Juan

The Commonwealth of Puerto Rico, a mainly mountainous island, is the easternmost of the Greater Antilles chain. The climate is hot and wet. Puerto Rico is a dependent territory of the USA and the people are US citizens. In 1998, 50.2% of the population voted in a referendum on possible statehood to maintain the status quo. Puerto Rico is the most industrialized country in the Caribbean. Tax exemptions attract US companies to the island and manufacturing is expanding.

QATAR

AREA 11,000 sq km [4,247 sq mi]
POPULATION 885,000
CAPITAL Doha

The State of Qatar occupies a low, barren peninsula that extends northwards from the Arabian peninsula into the Persian Gulf. The climate is hot and dry. Qatar became a British protectorate in 1916, but it became independent in 1971. Oil, first discovered in 1939, is the main resource of this prosperous nation. A new constitution, which became effective in 2005, provided for a 45-member Consultative Council.

RÉUNION

AREA 2,510 sq km [969 sq mi]
POPULATION 788,000
CAPITAL St-Denis

Réunion is a French overseas department in the Indian Ocean. The land is mainly mountainous, though the lowlands are intensely cultivated. Sugar and sugar products are the main exports, but French aid, given to the island in return for its use as a military base, is important to the economy.

ROMANIA

AREA 238,391 sq km [92,043 sq mi]
POPULATION 22,304,000
CAPITAL Bucharest
GOVERNMENT Multiparty republic
ETHNIC GROUPS Romanian 89%, Hungarian 7%, Roma 2%, Ukrainian
LANGUAGES Romanian (official), Hungarian, German
RELIGIONS Eastern Orthodox 87%, Protestant 7%, Roman Catholic 5%
CURRENCY Leu = 100 bani

GEOGRAPHY Romania faces the Black Sea and the eastern and southern parts of the country form part of the Danube basin. The heart of the country, called Transylvania, is ringed by uplands which are part of the Carpathian mountain system. Romania has hot summers and cold winters. The rainfall is heaviest in spring and early summer.

POLITICS & ECONOMY The country's modern history began in 1861 when Walachia and Moldavia united. In 1918, after World War I, Romania, which was an ally of the victorious Allies, obtained large areas, including Transylvania, where most people were Romanians. This almost doubled Romania's size and population. Romania lost territory to Bulgaria, Hungary and the Soviet Union in 1939. Romania was allied with Germany in World War II. Soviet troops occupied the country in 1944. Hungary returned Transylvania to Romania in 1945, but Bulgaria and the Soviet Union kept former Romanian territory. In 1947, Romania became a Communist country.

In 1990, Romania held its first free elections since the end of World War II. The National Salvation Front, led by Ion Iliescu and containing many former Communists, won a large majority. In 1991, the country became a democratic republic. Fresh elections in 1992 again resulted in victory for Iliescu, whose party was renamed the Party of Social Democracy in 1993. Iliescu was defeated in 1996, but served again as president between 2000 and 2004, when he stood down. Romania strengthened its ties with the West. It became a member of NATO in 2004 and a member of the European Union on 1 January 2007.

Romania is a 'lower-middle-income' economy, according to the World Bank. Under Communist rule, industry, including mining and manufacturing, became more important than agriculture.

RUSSIA

AREA 17,075,400 sq km [6,592,812 sq mi]
POPULATION 142,894,000
CAPITAL Moscow
GOVERNMENT Federal multiparty republic
ETHNIC GROUPS Russian 82%, Tatar 4%, Ukrainian 3%, Chuvash 1%, more than 100 others
LANGUAGES Russian (official), many others
RELIGIONS Mainly Russian Orthodox, Islam, Judaism
CURRENCY Russian ruble = 100 kopeks

GEOGRAPHY Russia is the world's largest country. About 25% lies west of the Ural Mountains in European Russia, where 80% of the population lives. It is mostly flat or undulating, but the land rises to the

Caucasus Mountains in the south, where Russia's highest peak, Elbrus, at 5,633 m [18,481 ft], is found. Asian Russia, or Siberia, contains vast plains and plateaux, with mountains in the east and south. The Kamchatka peninsula in the far east has many active volcanoes. Russia contains many of the world's longest rivers, including the Yenisey-Angara and the Ob-Irtysh. It also includes part of the world's largest inland body of water, the Caspian Sea, and Lake Baikal, the world's deepest lake.

Moscow has a continental climate with cold and snowy winters and warm summers. Krasnoyarsk in south-central Siberia has a harsher, drier climate, but it is not as severe as parts of northern Siberia.

POLITICS & ECONOMY In the 9th century AD, a state called Kievan Rus was formed by a group of people called the East Slavs. Kiev, now capital of Ukraine, became a major trading centre, but, in 1237, Mongol armies conquered Russia and destroyed Kiev. Russia was part of the Mongol empire until the late 15th century. Under Mongol rule, Moscow became the leading Russian city.

In the 16th century, Moscow's grand prince was retitled 'tsar'. The first tsar, Ivan the Terrible, expanded Russian territory. In 1613, after a period of civil war, Michael Romanov became tsar, founding a dynasty which ruled until 1917. In the early 18th century, Tsar Peter the Great began to westernize Russia and, by 1812, when Napoleon failed to conquer the country, Russia was a major European power. But during the 19th century, many Russians demanded reforms and discontent was widespread.

In World War I (1914–18), the Russian people suffered great hardships and, in 1917, Tsar Nicholas II was forced to abdicate. In November 1917, the Bolsheviks seized power under Vladimir Lenin. In 1922, the Bolsheviks set up a new nation, the Union of Soviet Socialist Republics (also called the USSR or the Soviet Union).

From 1924, Joseph Stalin introduced a socialist economic programme, suppressing all opposition. In 1939, the Soviet Union and Germany signed a non-aggression pact, but Germany invaded the Soviet Union in 1941. Soviet forces pushed the Germans back, occupying eastern Europe. They reached Berlin in May 1945. From the late 1940s, tension between the Soviet Union and its allies and Western nations developed into a 'Cold War'. This continued until 1991, when the Soviet Union was dissolved.

The Soviet Union collapsed because of the failure of its economic policies. From 1991, President Boris Yeltsin introduced democratic and economic reforms. Yeltsin retired in 1999 and, in 2000, was succeeded by Vladimir Putin. Putin, who was re-elected by a landslide in 2004, has sought to develop increasing contacts with the West. He supported the US-declared war on terrorism, though he opposed the attack on Iraq in 2003. The secessionist conflict in Chechenia, including the occupation of a school by Muslim extremists in 2004, which led to more than 330 deaths, caused outrage. In 2005, violent incidents in the republics of Dagestan, Ingushetia and Kabardino-Balkaria further confirmed that Russia's size and diversity make national unity hard to achieve. In 2006, the situation in Chechenia stabilized following several victories over the rebels. Notable among these was the death of Shamil Basayev, the leading rebel leader.

Russia's economy was thrown into disarray after the collapse of the Soviet Union, and in the early 1990s the World Bank described Russia as a 'lower-middle-income' economy. Russia was admitted to the Council of Europe in 1997, essentially to discourage instability in the Caucasus. In 1997, Russia attended the G7 summit, suggesting that Russia was now counted among the world's leading economies. Industry is the chief activity, though, under Communist rule, manu-

facturing was less efficient than in the West, with an emphasis on heavy industry. Today, light industries producing consumer goods are becoming important.

Russia's resources include oil and natural gas, coal, timber, metal ores and hydroelectric power. In the mid-2000s, the high international prices for oil and natural gas buoyed the Russian economy, but the country still faced many problems, including population decline. Russia is a major producer of farms products, though it imports grains. Major crops include barley, flax, fruits, oats, rye, potatoes, sugar beet, sunflower seeds, vegetables and wheat.

RWANDA

AREA 26,338 sq km [10,169 sq mi]
POPULATION 8,648,000
CAPITAL Kigali
GOVERNMENT Republic
ETHNIC GROUPS Hutu 84%, Tutsi 15%, Twa 1%
LANGUAGES French, English and Kinyarwanda (all official)
RELIGIONS Roman Catholic 57%, Protestant 26%, Adventist 11%, Islam 5%
CURRENCY Rwandan franc = 100 centimes

GEOGRAPHY The Republic of Rwanda is a small, landlocked country in east-central Africa. Lake Kivu and the River Ruzizi in the Great African Rift Valley form Rwanda's western border. Temperatures are moderated by the altitude. The rainfall is abundant.
POLITICS & ECONOMY Germany conquered the area, called Ruanda-Urundi, in the 1890s. However, Belgium occupied the region during World War I (1914–18) and ruled it until 1961, when the people of Ruanda voted for their country to become a republic, called Rwanda. This decision followed a rebellion by the majority Hutu people against the Tutsi monarchy. About 150,000 deaths resulted from this conflict. Many Tutsis fled to Uganda, where they formed a rebel army. Burundi became independent as a monarchy, though it became a republic in 1966.

Relations between Hutus and Tutsis deteriorated and, in 1994, between 500,000 and 800,000 people were massacred. After the Tutsis had restored order, many Hutu rebels fled into the Democratic Republic of the Congo (then Zaïre). Rwanda intervened in the Congo in 1996–2002. In the 2000s, Paul Kagame, the country's effective leader since 1994, worked to create unity and restore stability in Rwanda.

According to the World Bank, Rwanda is a 'low-income' developing country. Most people are poor farmers. Food crops include bananas, beans, cassava and sorghum. Some cattle are raised.

ST HELENA

AREA 122 sq km [47 sq mi]
POPULATION 8,000
CAPITAL Jamestown

St Helena, which became a British colony in 1834, is an isolated volcanic island in the south Atlantic Ocean. Now a British overseas territory, it is also the administrative centre of Ascension to the north and Tristan da Cunha to the south.

ST KITTS AND NEVIS

AREA 261 sq km [101 sq mi]
POPULATION 39,000
CAPITAL Basseterre

The Federation of St Kitts and Nevis were settled by Britain in the 1620s, though British ownership was later disputed with France. The nation became independent in 1983. In 1998, a vote for the secession of Nevis did not meet the two-thirds required. The country's economy is based on sugar and tourism.

ST LUCIA

AREA 539 sq km [208 sq mi]
POPULATION 168,000
CAPITAL Castries

From the 16th century, St Lucia often changed hands between Britain and France, but it finally became British in 1814. It became independent in 1979. St Lucia is a mountainous, forested island of extinct volcanoes. It exports bananas and coconuts, and now attracts many tourists.

ST VINCENT AND THE GRENADINES

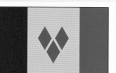

AREA 388 sq km [150 sq mi]
POPULATION 118,000
CAPITAL Kingstown

The island of St Vincent was settled in the 1620s by both British and French settlers. Its ownership was disputed, but it finally became a British territory. St Vincent and the Grenadines achieved independence in 1979. Tourism is growing, but this island country is less prosperous than its neighbours.

SAMOA

AREA 2,831 sq km [1,093 sq mi]
POPULATION 177,000
CAPITAL Apia

The Independent State of Samoa (formerly Western Samoa) comprises two islands in the South Pacific Ocean. The ownership of these Polynesian islands was disputed by European powers but Germany took control in 1900. Following Germany's defeat in World War I (1914–18), New Zealand governed Western Samoa from 1920 until 1961. The country became independent on 1 January 1962. The economy is based on agriculture, which employs more than 60% of the population, as well as fishing, copra, coconut oil and other coconut products.

NATIONS OF THE WORLD

SAN MARINO

AREA 61 sq km [24 sq mi]
POPULATION 29,000
CAPITAL San Marino

San Marino in northern Italy has been independent since 885 and a republic since the 14th century. It is the world's oldest republic. Tourism is the mainstay of the economy, followed by farming. San Marino also obtains revenue from its postage stamps and annual payment from Italy for certain privileges.

SÃO TOMÉ AND PRÍNCIPE

AREA 964 sq km [372 sq mi]
POPULATION 193,000
CAPITAL São Tomé

The Democratic Republic of São Tomé and Príncipe, a mountainous island territory west of Gabon, became Portuguese in 1522. After independence in 1975, the islands became a one-party Marxist state. Multiparty elections were held in 1991. The prospect of offshore oilfields holds out hope for the future.

SAUDI ARABIA

AREA 2,149,690 sq km [829,995 sq mi]
POPULATION 27,020,000
CAPITAL Riyadh
GOVERNMENT Absolute monarchy with consultative assembly
ETHNIC GROUPS Arab 90%, Afro-Asian 10%
LANGUAGES Arabic (official)
RELIGIONS Islam 100%
CURRENCY Saudi riyal = 100 halalas

GEOGRAPHY The Kingdom of Saudi Arabia occupies about three-quarters of the Arabian peninsula in south-west Asia. The land is mostly desert, with mountains in the west bordering the Red Sea plains. The climate is hot and dry.

POLITICS & ECONOMY Saudi Arabia contains the two holiest places in Islam – Mecca (or Makka), the birthplace of the Prophet Muhammad in AD 570, and Medina (Al Madinah) where Muhammad went in 622. These places are visited by many pilgrims.

The oil industry began to operate in the country in 1933 and oil revenues have been used to develop the country. Islamist activities disturbed Saudi Arabia in the 2000s. Many of the alleged terrorists involved in the attacks on the US on 11 September 2001 were Saudi nationals and, from 2003, Islamists launched attacks within Saudi Arabia. In 2007, the government arrested 172 people accused of planning air suicide attacks on oil installations and army bases.

Saudi Arabia has about 25% of the world's known oil reserves, and oil and oil products make up nearly 90% of its exports. Irrigation and desalination schemes have increased food production.

SENEGAL

AREA 196,722 sq km [75,954 sq mi]
POPULATION 11,987,000
CAPITAL Dakar
GOVERNMENT Multiparty republic
ETHNIC GROUPS Wolof 44%, Pular 24%, Serer 15%
LANGUAGES French (official), tribal languages
RELIGIONS Islam 94%, Christianity (mainly Roman Catholic) 5%, traditional beliefs 1%
CURRENCY CFA franc = 100 centimes

GEOGRAPHY The Republic of Senegal is on the north-west coast of Africa. The volcanic Cape Verde (Cap Vert), on which Dakar stands, is the most westerly point in Africa. Plains cover most of Senegal, though the land rises gently in the south-east.

Dakar has a tropical climate, with a short rainy season between July and October.

POLITICS & ECONOMY In 1882, Senegal became a French colony, and from 1895 it was ruled as part of French West Africa, the capital of which, Dakar, developed as a major port and city. In 1959, Senegal joined French Sudan (now Mali) to form the Federation of Mali. But Senegal withdrew in 1960 and became the separate Republic of Senegal. Its first president, Léopold Sédar Senghor, served until 1981, when he was succeeded by Abdou Diouf, who was later made 'president for life'. However, in 2000, Diouf was defeated in presidential elections by Abdoulaye Wade.

Senegal has usually enjoyed close relations with The Gambia, despite their differing traditions. In 1981, Senegalese troops put down an attempted coup in The Gambia and, in 1982, the countries set up a defence alliance, the Confederation of Senegambia, but it was dissolved in 1989. In 2005, a dispute with The Gambia over ferry tariffs on the border damaged the economies of both countries.

According to the World Bank, Senegal is a 'lower-middle-income' developing country. It was badly hit in the 1960s and 1970s by droughts, which caused starvation. Agriculture still employs 65% of the population though many farmers produce little more than they need to feed their families. Food crops include groundnuts, millet and rice. Phosphates are the country's chief resource, but Senegal also refines oil which it imports from Gabon and Nigeria. Dakar is a busy port and has many industries.

SERBIA

AREA 88,361 sq km [34,116 sq mi]
POPULATION 9,396,000
CAPITAL Belgrade
GOVERNMENT Republic
ETHNIC GROUPS Serb 66%, Albanian 17%, others
LANGUAGES Serbian (official), Albanian
RELIGIONS Serbian Orthodox, Islam, Roman Catholic, Protestant
CURRENCY New dinar = 100 paras

GEOGRAPHY The Republic of Serbia lies in the central Balkan peninsula. A landlocked country, it is mountainous in the south-east, while the Pannonian plains, drained by the River Danube, occupy much of the north. The centre and north have a continental climate, with heavy rain in the spring and autumn. The south-east has a more Mediterranean climate.

POLITICS & ECONOMY South Slavs moved into the area around 1,500 years ago. Each group founded its own state. Serbia came under the Turkish Ottoman Empire in the 15th century. In the 19th century, many Slavs worked for independence and Slavic unity. In 1914, Austria–Hungary declared war on Serbia, blaming it for the assassination of Archduke Franz Ferdinand of Austria–Hungary. In 1918, the South Slavs united in the Kingdom of the Serbs, Croats and Slovenes. The country was renamed Yugoslavia in 1929. Germany invaded Yugoslavia in 1941, but the Communist partisans, led by Josip Broz (Tito), emerged victorious in 1945.

From 1945, Communists ruled the country, which was called the Federal People's Republic of Yugoslavia. In 1991–2, the country split apart, with Bosnia-Herzegovina, Croatia, Macedonia and Slovenia proclaiming their independence. The two remaining republics, Serbia and Montenegro, retained the name Yugoslavia. In 2003, the two republics agreed to form the loose Union of Serbia and Montenegro. But, in 2006, the Montenegrins voted for full independence, and Serbia and Montenegro became separate republics. Serbia includes the province of Kosovo in the south. Most Albanian-speakers in Kosovo favour independence. In 2007, the UN put forward a plan to enable Kosovo to move towards independence, but Serbia opposed this plan.

Serbia's resources include bauxite, coal, copper and other metals, together with oil and natural gas. Manufacturing became important under Communist rule and products include aluminium, machinery, plastics, steel, textiles and vehicles. Crops include fruits, maize, potatoes, tobacco and wheat. Livestock include cattle, pigs and sheep.

SEYCHELLES

AREA 455 sq km [176 sq mi]
POPULATION 82,000
CAPITAL Victoria

The Republic of Seychelles in the western Indian Ocean achieved independence from Britain in 1976. Coconuts are the main cash crop and fishing and tourism are important.

SIERRA LEONE

AREA 71,740 sq km [27,699 sq mi]
POPULATION 6,005,000
CAPITAL Freetown
GOVERNMENT Single-party republic
ETHNIC GROUPS Native African tribes 90%
LANGUAGES English (official), Mende, Temne, Krio
RELIGIONS Islam 60%, traditional beliefs 30%, Christianity 10%
CURRENCY Leone = 100 cents

GEOGRAPHY The Republic of Sierra Leone in West Africa is about the same size as the Republic of Ireland. The coast contains several deep estuaries in the north, with lagoons in the south. The most prominent feature is the mountainous Freetown (or Sierra Leone) peninsula. Sierra Leone has a tropical climate, with heavy rainfall between April and November.

POLITICS & ECONOMY A former British territory, Sierra Leone became independent in 1961 and a republic in 1971. It became a one-party state in 1978, but, in 1991, the people voted for the restoration of democracy. The military seized power in 1992 and a civil war caused much destruction in 1994–5. Elections in 1996 were followed by another military coup. In 1998, the West African Peace Force restored the deposed President Ahmed Tejan Kabbah. In 1999, a peace agreement followed further conflict. As part of this agreement, Foday Sankoh, one of the rebel leaders, became vice-president. However, he was arrested in 2000 and charged with war crimes. (He later died in custody in hospital in 2003, while another rebel leader, Johnny Paul Koroma, who was also wanted to stand trial for crimes against humanity, was killed in Liberia.) Conflict resumed, but another cease-fire was agreed. Disarmament continued through 2001. In 2002, the conflict appeared to be over – rebel raids from Liberia in 2003 failed to disturb the fragile peace. In 2004, President Kabbah declared that disarmament had been successful. In December 2005, the last of the UN soldiers, who had been helping the peace process, left the country.

Sierra Leone has a 'low-income economy'. About 60% of the people live by farming, mainly at subsistence level. The most valuable exports are minerals, including diamonds, bauxite and rutile (titanium ore). The country has few manufacturing industries.

SINGAPORE

AREA 683 sq km [264 sq mi]
POPULATION 4,492,000
CAPITAL Singapore City
GOVERNMENT Multiparty republic
ETHNIC GROUPS Chinese 77%, Malay 14%, Indian 8%
LANGUAGES Chinese, Malay, Tamil and English (all official)
RELIGIONS Buddhism, Islam, Christianity, Hinduism
CURRENCY Singapore dollar = 100 cents

GEOGRAPHY The Republic of Singapore is an island country at the southern tip of the Malay peninsula. It consists of the large Singapore Island and 58 small islands, 20 of which are inhabited. The climate is hot and humid. Rainfall is heavy throughout the year.

POLITICS & ECONOMY In 1819, Sir Thomas Stamford Raffles (1781–1826), agent of the British East India Company, made a treaty with the Sultan of Johor allowing the British to build a settlement on Singapore Island. Singapore soon became the leading British trading centre in South-east Asia and it later became a naval base. Japanese forces seized the island in 1942, but British rule was restored in 1945. In 1963, Singapore became part of the Federation of Malaysia, which also included Malaya and the territories of Sabah and Sarawak on Borneo. In 1965, Singapore broke away and became independent.

The People's Action Party (PAP) has ruled Singapore since 1959. Its leader, Lee Kuan Yew, served as prime minister from 1959 until 1990, when he resigned and was succeeded by Goh Chok Tong. Under the PAP, the economy expanded rapidly, though some considered its rule rather dictatorial. In 2004, Lee Hsien Loong, eldest son of Lee Kuan Yew, succeeded Goh Chok Tong as prime minister and called for a more open society. He also called for

more people to marry and have babies, a reflection of the country's falling birth rate.

The World Bank classifies Singapore as a 'high-income' economy. A skilled workforce has created a fast-growing economy, but the recession in 1997–8 was a setback. Trade and finance are leading activities. Manufactures include electronic products, machinery, scientific instruments, textiles and ships. Singapore has a large oil refinery. Petroleum products and manufactures are the main exports.

SLOVAK REPUBLIC

AREA 49,012 sq km [18,924 sq mi]
POPULATION 5,439,000
CAPITAL Bratislava
GOVERNMENT Multiparty republic
ETHNIC GROUPS Slovak 86%, Hungarian 11%
LANGUAGES Slovak (official), Hungarian
RELIGIONS Roman Catholic 60%, Protestant 8%, Orthodox 4%, others
CURRENCY Slovak koruna = 100 halierov

GEOGRAPHY The Slovak Republic is a predominantly mountainous country, consisting of part of the Carpathian range. The highest peak is Gerlachovsky in the Tatra Mountains, which reaches 2,655 m [8,711 ft]. The south is a fertile lowland.

The Slovak Republic has cold winters and warm summers. Kosice, in the east, has average temperatures ranging from –3°C [27°F] in January to 20°C [68°F] in July. The highland areas are much colder. Snow or rain falls throughout the year. Kosice has an average annual rainfall of 600 mm [24 in], the wettest months being July and August.

POLITICS & ECONOMY Slavic peoples settled in the region in the 5th century AD. They were subsequently conquered by Hungary, beginning a millennium of Hungarian rule and suppression of Slovak culture.

In 1867, Hungary and Austria united to form Austria–Hungary, of which the present-day Slovak Republic was a part. Austria–Hungary collapsed at the end of World War I (1914–18). The Czech and Slovak people then united to form a new nation, Czechoslovakia. But Czech domination led to resentment by many Slovaks. In 1939, the Slovak Republic declared itself independent, but Germany occupied the country. At the end of World War II, the Slovak Republic again became part of Czechoslovakia.

The Communist Party took control in 1948. In the 1960s, many people sought reform, but they were crushed by the Russians. In the late 1980s, demands for democracy mounted and a non-Communist government took office in 1990. Elections in 1992 led to victory for the Movement for a Democratic Slovakia headed by a former Communist and nationalist, Vladimir Meciar, and the independent Slovak Republic came into existence on 1 January 1993.

Independence raised national aspirations among Slovakia's Magyar-speaking community, but relations with Hungary deteriorated when the Magyars felt that administrative changes under-represented them politically. The government also made Slovak the only official language. The government's autocratic rule and human rights record provoked international criticism. In 1998, Meciar's party was defeated and Mikulas Dzurinda replaced Meciar as prime minister. Dzurinda narrowly held on to power in parliamentary elections in 2002 and his government continued to strengthen its ties with the West, gaining membership of NATO and the European Union in 2004. After

elections in 2006, Robert Fico, leader of the opposition party Smer, became prime minister.

Before 1948, the Slovak Republic's economy was based on farming, but Communist governments developed manufacturing industries, producing such things as chemicals, machinery, steel and weapons. Since the late 1980s, many state-run businesses have been handed over to private owners.

SLOVENIA

AREA 20,256 sq km [7,821 sq mi]
POPULATION 2,010,000
CAPITAL Ljubljana
GOVERNMENT Multiparty republic
ETHNIC GROUPS Slovene 92%, Croat 1%, Serb, Hungarian, Bosniak
LANGUAGES Slovenian (official), Serbo-Croatian
RELIGIONS Mainly Roman Catholic
CURRENCY Euro = 100 cents

GEOGRAPHY The Republic of Slovenia was one of the six republics which made up the former Yugoslavia. Much of the land is mountainous, rising to 2,863 m [9,393 ft] at Mount Triglav in the Julian Alps (Julijske Alpe) in the north-west. Central Slovenia contains the limestone Karst region. The Postojna caves near Ljubljana are among the largest in Europe. The coast has a mild Mediterranean climate, but inland the climate is more continental. The mountains are snow-capped in winter.

POLITICS & ECONOMY In the last 2,000 years, the Slovene people have been independent as a nation for less than 50 years. The Austrian Habsburgs ruled over the region from the 13th century until World War I. Slovenia became part of the Kingdom of the Serbs, Croats and Slovenes (later called Yugoslavia) in 1918. During World War II, Slovenia was invaded and partitioned between Italy, Germany and Hungary, but, after the war, Slovenia again became part of Yugoslavia.

From the late 1960s, some Slovenes demanded independence, but the central government opposed the break-up of the country. In 1990, when Communist governments had collapsed throughout Eastern Europe, elections were held and a non-Communist coalition government was set up. Slovenia then declared itself independent. This led to fighting between Slovenes and the federal army, but Slovenia did not become a battlefield like other parts of the former Yugoslavia. The European Community recognized Slovenia's independence in 1992. The electors returned a coalition led by the Liberal Democrats in 1992, 1996 and 2000. In 2004, Slovenia became a member of the North Atlantic Treaty Organization and the European Union. In October 2004, the centre-right Slovenian Democratic Party topped the polls in parliamentary elections. A centre-right coalition was formed, stating that it would continue Slovenia's westward-leaning stance.

The reform of the formerly state-run economy caused problems for Slovenia. However, it has enjoyed considerable economic progress, with one of Europe's fastest growing economies. In 1992, the World Bank classified Slovenia's economy as 'upper-middle-income'. Manufacturing is the leading activity and manufactures are the main exports. Manufactures include chemicals, machinery and transport equipment, metal goods and textiles. Agriculture and forestry employ 8% of the people. Fruits, maize, potatoes and wheat are the main crops.

NATIONS OF THE WORLD

SOLOMON ISLANDS

AREA 28,896 sq km [11,157 sq mi]
POPULATION 552,000
CAPITAL Honiara

The Solomon Islands, a chain of mainly volcanic islands in the Pacific Ocean, were a British territory between 1893 and 1978. The chain extends for some 2,250 km [1,400 mi]. They were the scene of fierce fighting in World War II. In 2003, an Australian peace-keeping force went to the Solomon Islands, which, the government believed, were threatened with anarchy. Fish, coconuts and cocoa are leading products, though economic development is hampered by the mountainous, forested terrain.

SOMALIA

AREA 637,657 sq km [246,199 sq mi]
POPULATION 8,863,000
CAPITAL Mogadishu
GOVERNMENT Single-party republic, military dominated
ETHNIC GROUPS Somali 85%, Bantu, Arab and others
LANGUAGES Somali (official), Arabic, English, Italian
RELIGIONS Islam (Sunni Muslim)
CURRENCY Somali shilling = 100 cents

GEOGRAPHY The Somali Democratic Republic, or Somalia, is in a region known as the 'Horn of Africa'. It is more than twice the size of Italy, the country which once ruled the southern part of Somalia. The most mountainous part of the country is in the north, behind the coastal plains that border the Gulf of Aden. Rainfall is light. The wettest regions are the south and the northern mountains. Droughts are common, sometimes bringing famine. Temperatures are high on the low plateaux and plains.
POLITICS & ECONOMY European powers became interested in the Horn of Africa in the 19th century. In 1884, Britain made the northern part of what is now Somalia a protectorate, while Italy took the south in 1905. The new boundaries divided the Somalis into five areas: the two Somalilands, Djibouti (which was taken by France in the 1880s), Ethiopia and Kenya. Since then, many Somalis have longed for reunification in a Greater Somalia.

Italy entered World War II in 1940 and invaded British Somaliland. But British forces conquered the region in 1941 and ruled both Somalilands until 1950, when the United Nations asked Italy to take over the former Italian Somaliland for ten years. In 1960, both Somalilands became independent and united to become Somalia.

Somalia has faced many problems since independence. Economic problems led a military group to seize power in 1969. In the 1970s, Somalia supported an uprising of Somali-speaking people in the Ogaden region of Ethiopia. But Ethiopian forces prevailed and, in 1988, Somalia signed a peace treaty with Ethiopia. The cost of the fighting weakened Somalia's economy. In the 1990s, Somalia gradually broke apart. In 1991, the people in what was formerly British Somaliland set up the 'Somaliland Republic', although it never received international recognition.

The north-east, which was called Puntland, also seceded from Somalia, while civil war, based on clan rivalry, raged in the south. In 2004–5, a Somali parliament, with a president and prime minister, was set up in Kenya. In 2006, it moved to Baidoa, in Somalia, because Mogadishu was regarded as unsafe. Mogadishu was then taken over by the Islamist Union of Islamic Courts, which brought peace to the city. However, Somali forces supported by Ethiopian troops seized Mogadishu. Resistance by the Islamists continued into 2007, while the transitional government sought to replace the Ethiopian troops with a supporting African Union force.

Somalia is a developing country whose economy has been shattered by war, droughts and periodic floods. Many Somalis are nomads, who raise livestock. Live animals, meat and hides and skins are major exports, followed by bananas grown in the wetter south. Other crops include citrus fruits, cotton, maize and sugar cane. Mining and manufacturing remain relatively unimportant in the economy.

SOUTH AFRICA

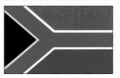

AREA 1,221,037 sq km [471,442 sq mi]
POPULATION 44,188,000
CAPITAL Cape Town (legislative); Tshwane/Pretoria (administrative); Bloemfontein (judiciary)
GOVERNMENT Multiparty republic
ETHNIC GROUPS Black 76%, White 13%, Coloured 9%, Asian 2%
LANGUAGES Afrikaans, English, Ndebele, Pedi, Sotho, Swazi, Tsonga, Tswana, Venda, Xhosa and Zulu (all official)
RELIGIONS Christianity 68%, Islam 2%, Hinduism 1%
CURRENCY Rand = 100 cents

GEOGRAPHY The Republic of South Africa is made up largely of the southern part of the huge plateau which makes up most of southern Africa. The highest peaks are in the Drakensberg range, which is formed by the uplifted rim of the plateau. The coastal plains include part of the Namib Desert in the north-west.

Most of South Africa has a mild, sunny climate. Much of the coastal strip, including the city of Cape Town, has warm, dry summers and mild, rainy winters. Inland, large areas are arid.
POLITICS & ECONOMY Early inhabitants in South Africa were the Khoisan. In the last 2,000 years, Bantu-speaking people moved into the area. Their descendants include the Zulu, Xhosa, Sotho and Tswana. The Dutch founded a settlement at the Cape in 1652, but Britain took over in the early 19th century, making the area a colony. The Dutch, called Boers or Afrikaners, resented British rule and moved inland. Rivalry between the groups led to Anglo-Boer Wars in 1880–1 and 1899–1902.

In 1910, the country was united as the Union of South Africa. In 1948, the National Party won power and introduced a policy known as apartheid, under which non-whites had no votes and their human rights were strictly limited. In 1990, Nelson Mandela, leader of the African National Congress (ANC), was released from prison. Multiracial elections were held in 1994 and Mandela became president. After Mandela's retirement in 1999, his successor, Thabo Mbeki, led the ANC to an emphatic victory in the elections in 1999 and again, by another landslide, in 2004. Its vote of almost 70% put it far ahead of its nearest rival, the Democratic Alliance, which

took only 13%. The government still faced massive problems of poverty and under-development and maintaining national unity – the ANC failed to win outright control of Kwazulu-Natal province, where it was opposed by the nationalist Inkatha Freedom Party, and Western Cape province. South Africa also faces a major health crisis, with about 11% of the population infected with the HIV virus. It has the world's highest number of infected people. Until 2004, the government refused to provide anti-retroviral drugs to slow down the effects of the disease, citing cost and safety.

South Africa is Africa's most developed country. However, most of the black people are poor, with low standards of living. Natural resources include diamonds, gold and many other metals. Mining and manufacturing are the most valuable activities. Products include chemicals, iron and steel, metal goods, processed food, and vehicles. Major crops include fruits, maize, potatoes, sugar cane, tobacco and wheat. Livestock products are also important.

SPAIN

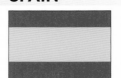

AREA 497,548 sq km [192,103 sq mi]
POPULATION 40,398,000
CAPITAL Madrid
GOVERNMENT Constitutional monarchy
ETHNIC GROUPS Composite of Mediterranean and Nordic types
LANGUAGES Castilian Spanish (official) 74%, Catalan 17%, Galician 7%, Basque 2%
RELIGIONS Roman Catholic 94%, others
CURRENCY Euro = 100 cents

GEOGRAPHY The Kingdom of Spain is the second largest country in Western Europe after France. It shares the Iberian peninsula with Portugal. A large plateau, called the Meseta, covers most of Spain. Much of the Meseta is flat, but it is crossed by several mountain ranges, called sierras.

The northern highlands include the Cantabrian Mountains (Cordillera Cantabrica) and the high Pyrenees, which form Spain's border with France. But Mulhacén, the highest peak on the Spanish mainland, is in the Sierra Nevada in the south-east. Spain also contains fertile coastal plains. Other major lowlands are the Ebro river basin in the north-east and the Guadalquivir river basin in the south-west. Spain also includes the Balearic Islands in the Mediterranean Sea and the Canary Islands off the north-west coast of Africa.

The Meseta has a continental climate, with hot summers and cold winters, when temperatures often fall below freezing point. Snow frequently covers the mountain ranges on the Meseta. The Mediterranean coasts have hot, dry summers and mild winters.
POLITICS & ECONOMY In the 16th century, Spain became a world power. At its peak, it controlled much of Central and South America, parts of Africa and the Philippines in Asia. Spain began to decline in the late 16th century. Its sea power was destroyed by a British fleet in the Battle of Trafalgar (1805). By the 20th century, it was a poor country.

Spain became a republic in 1931, but the republicans were defeated in the Spanish Civil War (1936–9). General Francisco Franco (1892–1975) became the country's dictator, though, technically, it was a monarchy. When Franco died, the monarchy was restored. Prince Juan Carlos became king.

Spain has several groups with their own languages

and cultures. Since the late 1970s, regional parliaments have been set up in the northern Basque Country (called Euskadi in the indigenous language and Pais Vasco in Spanish), in Catalonia in the north-east, and in Galicia in the north-west. From the 1960s, Eta, a Basque secessionist group, waged a violent campaign and, in 2003, Batasuna, the Basque separatist party, was banned. In March 2004, bombings attributed to al Qaida terrorists killed about 200 people in Madrid. The opposition socialists won the parliamentary elections that followed. In 2005, the government rejected proposals to make the Basque Country a 'free state' associated with Spain. In 2006, ETA declared a cease-fire, but an attack on Madrid airport in December 2006 ended negotiations.

The revival of Spain's economy, which was shattered by the Civil War, began in the 1950s and 1960s, especially through the growth of tourism and manufacturing. Since the 1950s, Spain has changed from a poor country, dependent on agriculture, to a fairly prosperous industrial nation.

By the early 2000s, agriculture employed about 5% of the people, as compared with industry, 15%. Farmland, including pasture, makes up about two-thirds of the land, with forest covering most of the rest. Major crops include barley, citrus fruits, grapes for wine-making, olives, potatoes and wheat.

Spain has some high-grade iron ore in the north, though otherwise it lacks natural resources. But it has many manufacturing industries. Manufactures include cars, chemicals, clothing, electronics, processed food, metal goods, steel and textiles. The leading manufacturing centres are Barcelona, Bilbao and Madrid.

SRI LANKA

AREA 65,610 sq km [25,332 sq mi]
POPULATION 20,222,000
CAPITAL Colombo
GOVERNMENT Multiparty republic
ETHNIC GROUPS Sinhalese 74%, Tamil 18%, Moor 7%
LANGUAGES Sinhala and Tamil (both official)
RELIGIONS Buddhism 70%, Hinduism 15%, Christianity 8%, Islam 7%
CURRENCY Sri Lankan rupee = 100 cents

GEOGRAPHY The Democratic Socialist Republic of Sri Lanka is an island nation, separated from the south-east coast of India by the Palk Strait. The land is mostly low-lying, surrounding mountains in the south-centre. Western Sri Lanka has a wet equatorial climate. Temperatures are high and the rainfall is heavy. The east is drier than the west.
POLITICS & ECONOMY From the early 16th century, Ceylon (as Sri Lanka was then known) was ruled successively by the Portuguese, Dutch and British. Independence was achieved in 1948 and the country was renamed Sri Lanka in 1972.

After independence, rivalries between the two main ethnic groups, the Sinhalese and Tamils, marred progress. In the 1950s, the government made Sinhala the official language. Following protests, the prime minister made provisions for Tamil to be used in some areas. In 1959, the prime minister was assassinated by a Sinhalese extremist and he was succeeded by Sirimavo Bandanaraike, who became the world's first woman prime minister.

Conflict between Tamils and Sinhalese continued in the 1970s and 1980s. In 1987, India helped to engineer a cease-fire. Indian troops arrived to enforce the agreement, but withdrew in 1990 after failing

to subdue the main guerrilla group, the Tamil Tigers, who wanted to set up an independent Tamil homeland in northern Sri Lanka. In 1993, the country's president was assassinated by a suspected Tamil separatist. Offensives against the Tamil Tigers continued until hopes of peace were raised in 2002, with the signing of a cease-fire. In late 2004, a tsunami, caused by a sudden movement of the plates underlying the eastern Indian Ocean, struck parts of the coast of Sri Lanka, killing more than 30,000 people. The tragedy failed to lead to a conciliation between the warring forces. Despite attempts to start peace talks, fighting intensified in 2006–7.

The World Bank classifies Sri Lanka as a 'low-income' developing country. Agriculture employs about 28% of the workforce, and coconuts, rubber and tea are exported. Rice is the chief food crop. Textiles and clothing, petroleum products, and precious and semi-precious stones are also exported.

SUDAN

AREA 2,505,813 sq km [967,494 sq mi]
POPULATION 41,236,000
CAPITAL Khartoum
GOVERNMENT Military regime
ETHNIC GROUPS Black 52%, Arab 39%, Beja 6%, others
LANGUAGES Arabic (official), Nubian, Ta Bedawie
RELIGIONS Islam 70%, traditional beliefs 25%
CURRENCY Sudanese dinar = 10 Sudanese pounds

GEOGRAPHY The Republic of Sudan is the largest country in Africa. From north to south, it spans a vast area extending from the arid Sahara in the north to the wet equatorial region in the south. The land is mostly flat, with the highest mountains in the far south. The climate of Khartoum represents a transition between the virtually rainless northern deserts and the equatorial lands in the south.
POLITICS & ECONOMY In the 19th century, Egypt gradually took over Sudan. In 1881, a Muslim religious teacher, the Mahdi ('divinely appointed guide'), led an uprising. Britain and Egypt put the rebellion down in 1898. In 1899, they agreed to rule Sudan jointly as a condominium.

After independence in 1952, the black Africans in the south, who were either Christians or followers of traditional beliefs, feared domination by the Muslim northerners. For example, they objected to the government declaring that Arabic was the only official language. In 1964, civil war broke out and continued until 1972, when the south was given regional self-government, though executive power was still vested in the military government in Khartoum.

In 1983, the government established Islamic law throughout the country. This sparked off further conflict when the Sudan People's Liberation Army (SPLA) in the south launched attacks on government installations. In 2005, an agreement was signed, bringing peace to the south. Since 2003, another conflict has raged in the western province of Darfur, where government-backed militias have attacked the population in an operation described as genocide and ethnic cleansing. Thousands of refugees fled into Chad and conflict spilled over the border in 2005–7.

Agriculture employs 60% of the people and cotton is the chief crop. Cotton, gum arabic and sesame seeds are exported, but the most valuable exports are oil and oil products. Manufacturing industries produce items mainly for home consumption.

SURINAME

AREA 163,265 sq km [63,037 sq mi]
POPULATION 439,000
CAPITAL Paramaribo
GOVERNMENT Multiparty republic
ETHNIC GROUPS Hindustani/East Indian 37%, Creole (mixed White and Black) 31%, Javanese 15%, Black 10%, Amerindian 2%, Chinese 2%, others
LANGUAGES Dutch (official), Sranang Tonga
RELIGIONS Hinduism 27%, Protestant 25%, Roman Catholic 23%, Islam 20%
CURRENCY Surinamese dollar = 100 cents

GEOGRAPHY The Republic of Suriname is sandwiched between French Guiana and Guyana in north-eastern South America. The narrow coastal plain was once swampy, but it has been drained and now consists mainly of farmland. Inland lie hills and low mountains, which rise to 1,280 m [4,199 ft].

Suriname has a hot, wet and humid climate. Temperatures are high throughout the year.
POLITICS & ECONOMY In 1667, the British handed Suriname to the Dutch in return for New Amsterdam, an area that is now the state of New York. Slave revolts and Dutch neglect hampered development. In the early 19th century, Britain and the Netherlands disputed the ownership of the area. The British gave up their claims in 1813. Slavery was abolished in 1863 and, soon afterwards, Indian and Indonesian labourers were introduced to work on the plantations.

Suriname became fully independent in 1975, but the economy was weakened when thousands of skilled people emigrated from Suriname to the Netherlands. Following a coup in 1980, Suriname was ruled by a military dictator, Dési Bouterse. The adoption of a new constitution led to the restoration of democracy in 1988, though another military coup occurred in 1990. Elections were held in 1996 and 2000. In 1999, Bouterse was convicted *in absentia* in the Netherlands of having led a cocaine-trafficking ring during and after his tenure in office. In 2000, elections were won by the New Front for Democracy headed by Ronald Venetiaan, who was re-elected president in 2005.

The World Bank classifies Suriname as an 'upper-middle-income' developing country. Its economy is based on mining and metal processing. Suriname is a leading producer of bauxite, from which the metal aluminium is made.

SWAZILAND

AREA 17,364 sq km [6,704 sq mi]
POPULATION 1,136,000
CAPITAL Mbabane
GOVERNMENT Monarchy
ETHNIC GROUPS African 97%, European 3%
LANGUAGES Siswati and English (both official)
RELIGIONS Zionist (a mix of Christianity and traditional beliefs) 40%, Roman Catholic 20%, Islam 10%
CURRENCY Lilangeni = 100 cents

GEOGRAPHY The Kingdom of Swaziland is a small, landlocked country in southern Africa. The country has four regions which run north–south. In the west, the Highveld, with an average height of

NATIONS OF THE WORLD

1,200 m [3,950 ft], makes up 30% of Swaziland. The Middleveld, between 350 m and 1,000 m [1,150 ft to 3,280 ft], covers 28% of the country. The Lowveld, with an average height of 270 m [886 ft], covers another 33%. Finally, the Lebombo Mountains reach 800 m [2,600 ft] in the east. The Lowveld is almost tropical, with an average annual temperature of 22°C [72°F] and low rainfall. The altitude moderates the climate in the west.

POLITICS & ECONOMY In 1894, Britain and the Boers of South Africa agreed to put Swaziland under the control of the South African Republic (the Transvaal). But at the end of the Anglo–Boer War (1899–1902), Britain took control of the country. In 1968, when Swaziland became fully independent as a constitutional monarchy, the head of state was King Sobhuza II. Sobhuza died in 1982 and was succeeded by one of his sons, Prince Makhosetive, who, in 1986, was installed as King Mswati III. Elections in 1993 and 1998, in which political parties were banned, failed to satisfy protesters who opposed the absolute monarchy. Mswati continued to rule by decree. In 2005, Mswati signed a new constitution, which combined traditional and Western values, but political parties remained banned. In the 2000s, Swaziland faced a major health crisis – it has the world's highest HIV infection rate of 42.6%.

The World Bank classifies Swaziland as a 'lower-middle-income' developing country. Agriculture employs 50% of the people, and farm products and processed foods are the chief exports. Many farmers live at subsistence level. Swaziland's economy is heavily dependent on South Africa and the two countries are linked through a customs union.

SWEDEN

AREA 449,964 sq km [173,731 sq mi]
POPULATION 9,017,000
CAPITAL Stockholm
GOVERNMENT Constitutional monarchy
ETHNIC GROUPS Swedish 91%, Finnish, Sami
LANGUAGES Swedish (official), Finnish, Sami
RELIGIONS Lutheran 87%, Roman Catholic, Orthodox
CURRENCY Swedish krona = 100 öre

GEOGRAPHY The Kingdom of Sweden is the largest of the countries of Scandinavia in both area and population. It shares the Scandinavian peninsula with Norway. The western part of the country, along the border with Norway, is mountainous. The highest point is Kebnekaise, which reaches 2,117 m [6,946 ft] in the north-west. The climate of Sweden becomes more severe from south to north. Stockholm has cold winters and cool summers. The far south is much milder.

POLITICS & ECONOMY Swedish Vikings plundered areas to the south and east between the 9th and 11th centuries. Sweden, Denmark and Norway were united in 1397, but Sweden regained its independence in 1523. In 1809, Sweden lost Finland to Russia, but, in 1814, it gained Norway from Denmark. The union between Sweden and Norway was dissolved in 1905. Sweden was neutral in World Wars I and II. Since 1945, Sweden has become a prosperous country. In 1995, it joined the European Union. However, many people were sceptical about the advantages of EU membership and Sweden did not adopt the euro, the single EU currency, in 1999.

Sweden has wide-ranging welfare services. But many people are concerned about the high cost of these services and the high taxes they must pay. In

1991, the Social Democrats, who had built up the welfare state, were defeated. But the Social Democrats returned to power in 1994. In office, they sought to control public spending and expand the economy. In 2003, Swedish voters rejected the adoption of the euro as the country's unit of currency by 56% to 42%. In a general election in 2006, a centre-right alliance won 178 out of the 349 seats in parliament, defeating the Social Democrats who had ruled Sweden for 65 of the past 74 years. Fredrick Reinfeldt replaced Göran Persson as prime minister.

Sweden is a highly developed industrial country. Major products include steel and steel goods. Steel is used in the engineering industry to manufacture aircraft, cars, machinery and ships. Sweden has some of the world's richest iron ore deposits. They are located near Kiruna in the far north. But most of this ore is exported, and Sweden imports most of the materials needed by its industries. In 1996, a decision was taken to decommission all of Sweden's nuclear power stations. The first reactor was shut down in 1999, followed by a second in 2005. Another ten reactors remain to be decommissioned.

SWITZERLAND

AREA 41,284 sq km [15,940 sq mi]
POPULATION 7,524,000
CAPITAL Bern
GOVERNMENT Federal republic
ETHNIC GROUPS German 65%, French 18%, Italian 10%, Romansch 1%, others
LANGUAGES French, German, Italian and Romansch (all official)
RELIGIONS Roman Catholic 46%, Protestant 40%
CURRENCY Swiss franc = 100 centimes

GEOGRAPHY The Swiss Confederation is a land-locked country in Western Europe. Much of the land is mountainous. The Jura Mountains lie along Switzerland's western border with France, while the Swiss Alps make up about 60% of the country in the south and east. Four-fifths of the people of Switzerland live on the fertile Swiss plateau, which contains most of Switzerland's large cities.

The climate varies according to the height of the land. The plateau region has warm summers and cold, snowy winters. Rain occurs throughout the year.
POLITICS & ECONOMY In 1291, three small cantons (states) united to defend their freedom against the Habsburg rulers of the Holy Roman Empire. They were Schwyz, Uri and Unterwalden, and they called the confederation they formed 'Switzerland'. Switzerland expanded and, in the 14th century, defeated Austria in three wars of independence. After a defeat by the French in 1515, the Swiss adopted a policy of neutrality, which they still follow. In 1815, the Congress of Vienna expanded Switzerland to 22 cantons and guaranteed its neutrality. Switzerland's 23rd canton, Jura, was created in 1979 from part of Bern. Neutrality combined with the vigour and independence of its people have made Switzerland prosperous. The Swiss have voted against joining the European Union, although, in 2002, the country joined the United Nations. In 2005, it also joined the Schengen group, a European passport-free zone.

Although lacking in natural resources, Switzerland is a wealthy, industrialized country. Many workers are highly skilled. Major products include chemicals, electrical equipment, machinery and machine tools, precision instruments, processed food, watches and

textiles. Farmers produce about three-fifths of the country's food – the rest is imported. Livestock raising, especially dairy farming, is the chief agricultural activity. Crops include fruits, potatoes and wheat. Tourism and banking are also important. Swiss banks attract investors from all over the world.

SYRIA

AREA 185,180 sq km [71,498 sq mi]
POPULATION 18,881,000
CAPITAL Damascus
GOVERNMENT Multiparty republic
ETHNIC GROUPS Arab 90%, Kurdish, Armenian, others
LANGUAGES Arabic (official), Kurdish, Armenian
RELIGIONS Sunni Muslim 74%, other Islam 16%
CURRENCY Syrian pound = 100 piastres

GEOGRAPHY The Syrian Arab Republic is a country in south-western Asia. The narrow coastal plain is overlooked by a low mountain range which runs north–south. Another range, the Jabal ash Sharqi, runs along the border with Lebanon. South of this range are the Golan Heights, which Israel has occupied since 1967. The coast has a Mediterranean climate, with dry, warm summers and wet, mild winters. The climate becomes drier towards the east.
POLITICS & ECONOMY After the collapse of the Turkish Ottoman empire in World War I, Syria was ruled by France. Since independence in 1946, Syria has been involved in the Arab–Israeli wars and, in 1967, it lost a strategic border area, the Golan Heights, to Israel. In 1970, Lieutenant-General Hafez al-Assad took power, establishing a stable but repressive regime. Following Assad's death in 2000, his son, Bashar Assad, succeeded him. The Israeli occupation of the Golan Heights continues to be one of Syria's main grievances. But Syria has been criticized for supporting Palestinian terrorists and keeping troops in Lebanon. Syrian troops withdrew from Lebanon in 2005, but Syria came under the suspicion that it had been involved in the killing of former Lebanese prime minister Rafik Hariri.

The World Bank classifies Syria as a 'lower-middle-income' developing country. But it has great potential for development. Its main resources are oil, hydro-electricity from the dam at Lake Assad, and fertile land. Oil is the main export; farm products, textiles and phosphates are also important. Agriculture employs about a quarter of the workforce.

TAIWAN

AREA 36,000 sq km [13,900 sq mi]
POPULATION 23,036,000
CAPITAL Taipei
GOVERNMENT Unitary multiparty republic
ETHNIC GROUPS Taiwanese 84%, mainland Chinese 14%
LANGUAGES Mandarin Chinese (official), Min, Hakka
RELIGIONS Buddhism, Taoism, Confucianism
CURRENCY New Taiwan dollar = 100 cents

GEOGRAPHY High mountain ranges run down the length of the island, with dense forest in many areas. The climate is warm, moist and suitable for agriculture.
POLITICS & ECONOMY Chinese settlers occupied

Taiwan from the 7th century. In 1895, Japan seized the territory from the Portuguese, who had named it Isla Formosa, or 'beautiful island'. China regained the island after World War II (1939–45). In 1949, China's Communists defeated the Nationalist forces under Chiang Kai-shek, who moved his government to Taiwan. Both regimes regarded themselves as China's legitimate rulers and that Taiwan was a province of China. In the early 1970s, the US favoured the admission of China to the United Nations. This led to the expulsion of the Nationalists from the UN. From the late 1980s, relations between Taiwan and mainland China began to improve. But in the early 21st century, some Taiwanese politicians wanted independence for Taiwan. China threatened to attack if Taiwan did not accept that it was part of China.

Since 1949, with US help, Taiwan has greatly expanded its economy. Despite its lack of natural resources, it produces a wide range of manufactured goods. Agriculture employs about 6% of the people, though only about a fourth of the land can be farmed.

TAJIKISTAN

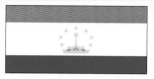

AREA 143,100 sq km [55,521 sq mi]
POPULATION 7,321,000
CAPITAL Dushanbe
GOVERNMENT Transitional democracy
ETHNIC GROUPS Tajik 65%, Uzbek 25%, Russian
LANGUAGES Tajik (official), Russian
RELIGIONS Islam (Sunni Muslim 85%)
CURRENCY Somoni = 100 dirams

GEOGRAPHY The Republic of Tajikistan is one of the five central Asian republics that formed part of the former Soviet Union. Only 7% of the land is below 1,000 m [3,280 ft], while almost all of eastern Tajikistan is above 3,000 m [9,840 ft]. Summers are hot and dry in the lower valleys, and winters are long and bitterly cold in the mountains.
POLITICS & ECONOMY Russia conquered parts of Tajikistan in the late 19th century and, by 1920, Russia took complete control. In 1924, Tajikistan became part of the Uzbek Soviet Socialist Republic, but, in 1929, it was expanded, taking in some areas populated by Uzbeks, becoming the Tajik Soviet Socialist Republic.

While the Soviet Union began to introduce reforms during the 1980s, many Tajiks demanded freedom. In 1989, the Tajik government made Tajik the official language instead of Russian and, in 1990, it stated that its local laws overruled Soviet laws. Tajikistan became fully independent in 1991, following the break-up of the Soviet Union. As the poorest of the ex-Soviet republics, Tajikistan faced many problems in trying to introduce a free-market system.

In 1992, civil war broke out between the government, which was run by former Communists, and an alliance of democrats and Islamic forces. A cease-fire was agreed in 1996, and in 1997 representatives of the opposition were brought into the government. In 2003, changes to the constitution enabled Emomali Rakhmanov, Tajikistan's president since 1994, to serve two more seven-year terms after elections in 2006, when he was re-elected with 79.3% of the vote.

The World Bank classifies Tajikistan as a 'low-income' developing country. Agriculture, mainly on irrigated land, is the main activity and cotton is the chief product. Other crops include fruits, grains and vegetables. The country has large hydroelectric power resources and it produces aluminium.

TANZANIA

AREA 945,090 sq km [364,899 sq mi]
POPULATION 37,445,000
CAPITAL Dodoma
GOVERNMENT Multiparty republic
ETHNIC GROUPS Native African 99% (Bantu 95%)
LANGUAGES Swahili (Kiswahili) and English (both official)
RELIGIONS Islam 35% (99% in Zanzibar), traditional beliefs 35%, Christianity 30%
CURRENCY Tanzanian shilling = 100 cents

GEOGRAPHY The United Republic of Tanzania consists of the former mainland country of Tanganyika and the island nation of Zanzibar, which also includes the island of Pemba. Behind a narrow coastal plain, most of Tanzania is a plateau, which is broken by arms of the Great African Rift Valley. In the west, this valley contains lakes Nyasa and Tanganyika. The highest peak is Kilimanjaro, Africa's tallest mountain.

The coast has a hot and humid climate, with the greatest rainfall in April and May. The inland plateaux and mountains are cooler and less humid.
POLITICS & ECONOMY Mainland Tanganyika became a German territory in the 1880s, while Zanzibar and Pemba became a British protectorate in 1890. Following Germany's defeat in World War I, Britain took over Tanganyika, which remained a British territory until its independence in 1961. In 1964, Tanganyika and Zanzibar united to form the United Republic of Tanzania. The country's president, Julius Nyerere, pursued socialist policies of self-help (*ujamaa*) and egalitarianism. Many of its social reforms were successful, though the country failed to make economic progress. Nyerere resigned as president in 1985, although he retained much influence until his death in 1999. His successors, Ali Hassan Mwinyi, Benjamin Mkapa and, from 2005, Jakaya Kikwete, introduced more liberal economic policies.

Tanzania is one of the world's poorest countries. Crops are grown on only 4.2% of the land, yet agriculture employs 78% of the people. Food crops include bananas, cassava, maize, millet and rice.

THAILAND

AREA 513,115 sq km [198,114 sq mi]
POPULATION 64,632,000
CAPITAL Bangkok
GOVERNMENT Constitutional monarchy
ETHNIC GROUPS Thai 75%, Chinese 14%, others 11%
LANGUAGES Thai (official), English, ethnic and regional dialects
RELIGIONS Buddhism 95%, Islam, Christianity
CURRENCY Baht = 100 satang

GEOGRAPHY The Kingdom of Thailand is one of the ten countries in South-east Asia. The highest land is in the north, where Doi Inthanon, the highest peak, reaches 2,565 m [8,415 ft]. The Khorat plateau, in the north-east, makes up about 30% of the country and is the most heavily populated part of Thailand. In the south, Thailand shares the finger-like Malay peninsula with Burma and Malaysia.

Thailand has a tropical climate. Monsoon winds from the south-west bring heavy rains between the months of May and October.
POLITICS & ECONOMY The first Thai state was set up in the 13th century. By 1350, it included most of what is now Thailand. European contact began in the early 16th century. But, in the late 17th century, the Thais, fearing interference in their affairs, forced all Europeans to leave. This policy continued for 150 years. In 1782, a Thai General, Chao Phraya Chakkri, became king, founding a dynasty which continues today. The country became known as Siam, and Bangkok became its capital. From the mid-19th century, contacts with the West were restored. In World War I, Siam supported the Allies. In 1941, the country was conquered by Japan and became its ally. However, after the end of World War II, it became an ally of the United States.

Since 1967, when Thailand became a member of ASEAN (the Association of South-east Asian Nations), its economy has grown, especially its manufacturing and service industries. From 1997, Thailand suffered economic recession. In 2001, a businessman, Thaksin Shinawatra, was elected prime minister. But, in 2006, protests occurred after Thaksin's party was re-elected. Thaksin stood down but returned to head a provisional government. A military junta took over in September.

Agriculture employs 40% of the people. Rice is the chief crop. Thailand also mines tin and other minerals. However, manufactures, including food products, machinery, timber products and textiles, are the main exports. Tourism is important, though the December 2004 tsunami, which killed more than 500 people, cast a shadow over its future growth.

TOGO

AREA 56,785 sq km [21,925 sq mi]
POPULATION 5,549,000
CAPITAL Lomé
GOVERNMENT Multiparty republic
ETHNIC GROUPS Native African 99% (largest tribes are Ewe, Mina and Kabre)
LANGUAGES French (official), African languages
RELIGIONS Traditional beliefs 51%, Christianity 29%, Islam 20%
CURRENCY CFA franc = 100 centimes

GEOGRAPHY The Republic of Togo is a long, narrow country in West Africa. From north to south, it extends about 500 km [311 mi]. Its coastline on the Gulf of Guinea is only 64 km [40 mi] long. Togo has a hot climate. The main wet season is March–July, with a minor wet season in October–November.
POLITICS & ECONOMY Togo became a German protectorate in 1884 but, in 1919, Britain took over the western third of the territory, while France took over the eastern two-thirds. In 1956, the people of British Togoland voted to join Ghana, while French Togoland became an independent republic in 1960.

A military regime took power in 1963. In 1967, General Gnassingbé Eyadéma became head of state and suspended the constitution. Under a new constitution, adopted in 1992, multiparty elections were held in 1994. In 1998, the count in presidential elections was stopped when it became clear that Eyadéma had been defeated. Leading opposition parties boycotted subsequent elections. Eyadéma died in 2005. His son, Faure Gnassingbé, was elected president amid claims that the polls were rigged.

Togo is a poor, developing country dependent on agriculture. Phosphate rock is the leading export.

NATIONS OF THE WORLD

TONGA

AREA 650 sq km [251 sq mi]
POPULATION 115,000
CAPITAL Nuku'alofa

Originally called the Friendly Islands, the Kingdom of Tonga became a British protectorate in 1900 and achieved independence in 1970. Situated in the South Pacific Ocean, it contains more than 170 islands, 36 of which are inhabited. Agriculture is the main activity – coconuts, copra, fruits and fish are leading products.

TRINIDAD AND TOBAGO

AREA 5,130 sq km [1,981 sq mi]
POPULATION 1,066,000
CAPITAL Port of Spain

Trinidad was captured from the French by the British in 1797, while Tobago was added in 1814. They became a single British colony in 1889. The Republic of Trinidad and Tobago became independent in 1962. These tropical islands, populated by people of African, Asian (mainly Indian) and European origin, are hilly and forested, though there are some fertile plains. Oil production is the main sector of the economy.

TUNISIA

AREA 163,610 sq km [63,170 sq mi]
POPULATION 10,175,000
CAPITAL Tunis
GOVERNMENT Multiparty republic
ETHNIC GROUPS Arab 98%, European 1%
LANGUAGES Arabic (official), French
RELIGIONS Islam 98%, Christianity 1%, others
CURRENCY Tunisian dinar = 1,000 millimes

GEOGRAPHY The Republic of Tunisia is the smallest country in North Africa. The mountains in the north are an eastwards and comparatively low extension of the Atlas Mountains. To the north and east of the mountains lie fertile plains, especially between Sfax, Tunis and Bizerte. In the south, low-lying regions contain a vast salt pan, called the Chott Djerid, and part of the Sahara Desert.

Northern Tunisia has a Mediterranean climate, with dry, sunny summers, and mild winters with a moderate rainfall. The average yearly rainfall decreases towards the south.
POLITICS & ECONOMY In 1881, France established a protectorate over Tunisia and ruled the country until 1956. The new parliament abolished the monarchy and declared Tunisia to be a republic in 1957, with the nationalist leader, Habib Bourguiba, as president. His government introduced many reforms, including votes for women, but various problems arose, including unemployment among the middle

class and fears that Western values introduced by tourists might undermine Muslim values. In 1987, the prime minister, Zine el Abidine Ben Ali, removed Bourguiba from office and succeeded him as president. He was elected in 1989 and re-elected in 1994, 1999 and 2004. His victories by landslide majorities provoked charges that the elections were not as democratic as they should have been.

The World Bank classifies Tunisia as a 'middle-income' developing country. The main resources and chief exports are phosphates and oil. Most industries are concerned with food processing. Agriculture employs about 18% of the people, the major crops being barley, dates, grapes, olives and wheat. Fishing is important, as is the tourist industry.

TURKEY

AREA 774,815 sq km [299,156 sq mi]
POPULATION 70,414,000
CAPITAL Ankara
GOVERNMENT Multiparty republic
ETHNIC GROUPS Turkish 80%, Kurdish 20%
LANGUAGES Turkish (official), Kurdish, Arabic
RELIGIONS Islam (mainly Sunni Muslim) 99%
CURRENCY New Turkish lira = 100 kurus

GEOGRAPHY The Republic of Turkey lies in two continents. European Turkey, also called Thrace, lies west of a waterway linking the Mediterranean and Black seas. Most of Asian Turkey consists of plateaux and mountains, which rise to 5,165 m [16,945 ft] at Mount Ararat (Agri Dagi) near the border with Armenia. Earthquakes are common.

Central Turkey has a dry climate, with hot, sunny summers and cold winters. The driest part of the central plateau lies south of the city of Ankara, around Lake Tuz. The west has a Mediterranean climate, but the Black Sea coast has cooler summers.
POLITICS & ECONOMY In AD 330, the Roman empire moved its capital to Byzantium, which it renamed Constantinople. Constantinople became capital of the East Roman (or Byzantine) empire in 395. Muslim Seljuk Turks from central Asia invaded Anatolia in the 11th century. In the 14th century, another group of Turks, the Ottomans, conquered the area. In 1453, the Ottoman Turks took Constantinople, which they called Istanbul.

The Ottoman Turks built up a large empire which finally collapsed during World War I (1914–18). In 1923, Turkey became a republic. Its leader Mustafa Kemal, or Atatürk ('father of the Turks'), launched policies to modernize and secularize the country.

Since the 1940s, Turkey has sought to strengthen its ties with Western powers. It joined NATO (North Atlantic Treaty Organization) in 1951 and it applied to join the European Economic Community in 1987. But Turkey's conflict with Greece, together with its invasion of northern Cyprus in 1974, have led many Europeans to treat Turkey's aspirations with caution. Political instability, military coups, conflict with Kurdish nationalists in eastern Turkey, and Turkey's human rights record are other problems.

Turkey has enjoyed democracy since 1983, though, in 1998, the government banned the Islamist Welfare Party, which it accused of violating secular principles. In 1999, the Muslim Virtue Party (successor to Islamist Welfare Party) lost ground. The largest numbers of parliamentary seats were won by the ruling Democratic Left Party and the far-right National Action Party. However, in the elections in

2002, the moderate Islamic Justice and Development Party (AKP) won 362 of the 500 seats in parliament, while none of the parties in the former ruling coalition won 10% of the vote. Turkey hopes to join the European Union. Negotiations began in 2005, but, because of opposition in several EU countries, the negotiations were expected to last around ten years.

The World Bank classifies Turkey as a 'lower-middle-income' developing country. Agriculture employs 26% of the people, and barley, cotton, fruits, maize, tobacco and wheat are major crops. Livestock farming is important and wool is a leading product.

Turkey produces chromium, but manufacturing is the chief activity. Manufactures include processed farm products and textiles, cars, fertilizers, iron and steel, machinery, metal products and paper products.

TURKMENISTAN

AREA 488,100 sq km [188,455 sq mi]
POPULATION 5,043,000
CAPITAL Ashkhabad
GOVERNMENT Single-party republic
ETHNIC GROUPS Turkmen 85%, Uzbek 5%, Russian 4%, others
LANGUAGES Turkmen (official), Russian, Uzbek, others
RELIGIONS Islam 89%, Eastern Orthodox 9%
CURRENCY Turkmen manat = 100 tenesi

GEOGRAPHY The Republic of Turkmenistan is one of the five central Asian republics which once formed part of the former Soviet Union. Most of the land is low-lying, with mountains lying on the southern and south-western borders. In the west lies the salty Caspian Sea. Most of Turkmenistan is arid and the Garagum, Asia's largest sand desert, covers about 80% of the country. Turkmenistan has a continental climate, with average annual rainfall varying from 80 mm [3 in] in the desert to 300 mm [12 in] in the mountains. Summer months are hot but winter temperatures drop well below freezing point.
POLITICS & ECONOMY Just over 1,000 years ago, Turkic people settled in the lands east of the Caspian Sea and the name 'Turkmen' comes from this time. Mongol armies conquered the area in the 13th century and Islam was introduced in the 14th century. Russia took over the area in the 1870s and 1880s. After the Russian Revolution of 1917, the area came under Communist rule and, in 1924, it became the Turkmen Soviet Socialist Republic. The Communists strictly controlled all aspects of life and discouraged religion. But they improved such services as education, health, housing and transport.

In the 1980s, when the Soviet Union began to introduce reforms, the Turkmen began to demand more freedom. In 1990, the Turkmen government stated that its laws overruled Soviet laws. In 1991, Turkmenistan became fully independent after the break-up of the Soviet Union. But the country kept ties with Russia through the Commonwealth of Independent States (CIS).

In 1992, Turkmenistan adopted a new constitution, allowing for the setting up of political parties, providing that they were not ethnic or religious in character. But, effectively, Turkmenistan remained a one-party state and, in 1992, Saparmurad Niyazov, the former Communist and then Democratic Party leader, was the only candidate. In 1999, parliament declared Niyazov president for life. Niyazov died in December 2006 and was succeeded by Gurbanguly

Berdymukhammedov. He was formally elected (no opposition candidates were allowed to stand) and was sworn in as president in 2007.

Faced with many economic problems, Turkmenistan began to look south rather than to the CIS for support. As part of this policy, it joined the Economic Co-operation Organization which had been set up in 1985 by Iran, Pakistan and Turkey. In 1996, the completion of a rail link from Turkmenistan to the Iranian coast was seen as an important step in the development of Central Asia. Oil and natural gas are Turkmenistan's chief resources, but agriculture is the main activity. Cotton is the main crop. Grain and vegetables are also important. Manufactures include cement, glass, petrochemicals and textiles.

TURKS AND CAICOS ISLANDS

AREA 430 sq km [166 sq mi]
POPULATION 21,000
CAPITAL Cockburn Town

The Turks and Caicos Islands, a British territory in the Caribbean since 1776, are a group of about 30 islands. Fishing and tourism are major activities and lobsters are exported.

TUVALU

AREA 26 sq km [10 sq mi]
POPULATION 12,000
CAPITAL Fongafale

Tuvalu, formerly called the Ellice Islands, was a British territory from the 1890s until it became independent in 1978. It consists of nine low-lying coral atolls in the southern Pacific Ocean. Copra is the chief export. Rising sea levels caused by global warming are threatening the future of the country.

UGANDA

AREA 241,038 sq km [93,065 sq mi]
POPULATION 28,196,000
CAPITAL Kampala
GOVERNMENT Republic in transition
ETHNIC GROUPS Baganda 17%, Ankole 8%, Basogo 8%, Iteso 8%, Bakiga 7%, Langi 6%, Rwanda 6%, Bagisu 5%, Acholi 4%, Lugbara 4% and others
LANGUAGES English and Swahili (both official), Ganda
RELIGIONS Roman Catholic 33%, Protestant 33%, traditional beliefs 18%, Islam 16%
CURRENCY Ugandan shilling = 100 cents

GEOGRAPHY The Republic of Uganda is a land-locked country on the East African plateau. It contains part of Lake Victoria, Africa's largest lake and a source of the River Nile, which occupies a shallow depression in the plateau.

The equator runs through Uganda and the country is warm throughout the year, though the high altitude moderates the temperature. The wettest regions are the area to the north of Lake Victoria and the western mountains, especially the high Ruwenzori range.

POLITICS & ECONOMY Little is known of the early history of Uganda. When Europeans first reached the area in the 19th century, many of the people were organized in kingdoms, the most powerful of which was Buganda, the home of the Baganda people. Britain took over the country between 1894 and 1914, and ruled it until 1962.

In 1967, Uganda became a republic and Buganda's Kabaka (king), Sir Edward Mutesa II, was made president. But tensions between the Kabaka and the prime minister, Apollo Milton Obote, led to the dismissal of the Kabaka in 1966. Obote also abolished the traditional kingdoms, including Buganda. Obote was overthrown in 1971 by an army group led by General Idi Amin Dada. Amin ruled as a dictator. He forced most Ugandan Asians to leave the country and had many of his opponents killed.

In 1978, a border dispute between Uganda and Tanzania led Tanzanian troops to enter Uganda. With help from Ugandan opponents of Amin, they overthrew Amin's government. In 1980, Obote led his party to victory in national elections. But after charges of fraud, Obote's opponents began guerrilla warfare. A military group overthrew Obote in 1985, though strife continued until 1986, when Yoweri Museveni's National Resistance Movement seized power.

In 1993, Museveni restored the traditional kingdoms. Elections were held in 1994, but political parties were forbidden. Museveni was elected in 1996 and 2001. He was re-elected in 2006, when political parties were again permitted. In the 2000s, Uganda has suffered from a conflict with a rebel force in the north, known as the Lord's Resistance Army. A truce was agreed in 2006, but a peace settlement proved difficult to achieve.

Internal strife since the 1960s has greatly damaged the economy, but conditions improved during the relative stability of the 1990s and 2000s. Agriculture dominates the economy, employing about 80% of the people. The chief export is coffee.

UKRAINE

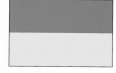

AREA 603,700 sq km [233,089 sq mi]
POPULATION 46,711,000
CAPITAL Kiev
GOVERNMENT Multiparty republic
ETHNIC GROUPS Ukrainian 78%, Russian 17%, Belarusian, Moldovan, Bulgarian, Hungarian, Polish
LANGUAGES Ukrainian (official), Russian
RELIGIONS Mostly Ukrainian Orthodox
CURRENCY Hryvnia = 100 kopiykas

GEOGRAPHY Ukraine is the second largest country in Europe after Russia. It was formerly part of the Soviet Union, which split apart in 1991. This mostly flat country faces the Black Sea in the south. The Crimean peninsula includes a highland region overlooking Yalta. Summers are warm, but winters are cold, becoming more severe from west to east. In summer, eastern Ukraine is often warmer than the west. The heaviest rainfall occurs in the summer.

POLITICS & ECONOMY Kiev was the original capital of the early Slavic civilization known as Kievan Rus. In the 17th and 18th centuries, parts of Ukraine came under Polish and Russian rule. But Russia gained most of Ukraine in the late 18th century. In 1918, Ukraine became independent, but in 1922 it became part of the Soviet Union. Millions of people died in the 1930s as a result of Soviet policies, while millions more died during the Nazi occupation (1941–4).

In the 1980s, Ukrainian people demanded more say over their affairs. The country became independent in 1991. Leonid Kuchma, who became president in 1994, came under fire in the early 2000s for mal-administration and for his alleged involvement in the murder of a journalist. In 2005, the pro-Western leader Victor Yuschenko was elected president. But, following economic problems and political infighting, a Russian-leaning party led by Viktor Yanukovich won the highest number of seats in parliamentary elections in 2006. Yuschenko was made prime minister.

The World Bank classifies Ukraine as a 'lower-middle-income' economy. Agriculture is important. Crops include wheat and sugar beet, which are the main exports. Livestock rearing and fishing are also important. But manufacturing is the chief economic activity. Manufactures include iron and steel, machinery and vehicles. Ukraine has large coalfields. The country imports oil and natural gas, but has hydro-electric and nuclear power stations. In 1986, an accident at the Chernobyl (Chornobyl) nuclear power plant caused widespread radiation. The plant was finally closed in 2000.

UNITED ARAB EMIRATES

AREA 83,600 sq km [32,278 sq mi]
POPULATION 2,603,000
CAPITAL Abu Dhabi

The United Arab Emirates were formed in 1971 when the seven Trucial States of the Gulf (Abu Dhabi, Dubai, Sharjah, Ajman, Umm al Qawayn, Ra's al Khaymah and Al Fujayrah) opted to join together and form an independent country. The economy of this hot and dry country depends on oil production, and oil revenues give the United Arab Emirates one of the highest per capita GNPs in Asia.

UNITED KINGDOM

AREA 241,857 sq km [93,381 sq mi]
POPULATION 60,609,000
CAPITAL London
GOVERNMENT Constitutional monarchy
ETHNIC GROUPS English 82%, Scottish 10%, Irish 2%, Welsh 2%, Ulster 2%, West Indian, Indian, Pakistani and others
LANGUAGES English (official), Welsh, Gaelic
RELIGIONS Christianity, Islam, Sikhism, Hinduism, Judaism
CURRENCY Pound sterling = 100 pence

GEOGRAPHY The United Kingdom (or UK) is a union of four countries. Three of them – England, Scotland and Wales – make up Great Britain. The fourth country is Northern Ireland. The Isle of Man and the Channel Islands, including Jersey and Guernsey, are not part of the UK. They are self-governing British dependencies.

The land is highly varied. Much of Scotland and Wales is mountainous, and the highest peak is

Scotland's Ben Nevis at 1,342 m [4,404 ft]. England has some highland areas, including the Cumbrian Mountains (or Lake District) and the Pennine range in the north. But England also has large areas of fertile lowland. Northern Ireland is also a mixture of lowlands and uplands. It contains the UK's largest lake, Lough Neagh.

The UK has a mild climate, influenced by the warm Gulf Stream which flows across the Atlantic from the Gulf of Mexico, then past the British Isles. Moist winds from the south-west bring rain, but the rainfall decreases from west to east. Winds from the east and north bring cold weather in winter.

POLITICS & ECONOMY In ancient times, Britain was invaded by many peoples, including Iberians, Celts, Romans, Angles, Saxons, Jutes, Norsemen, Danes, and Normans, who arrived in 1066. The evolution of the United Kingdom spanned hundreds of years. The Normans finally overcame Welsh resistance in 1282, when King Edward I annexed Wales and united it with England. Union with Scotland was achieved by the Act of Union of 1707. This created a country known as the United Kingdom of Great Britain.

Ireland came under Norman rule in the 11th century, and much of its later history was concerned with a struggle against English domination. In 1801, Ireland became part of the United Kingdom of Great Britain and Ireland. But in 1921, southern Ireland broke away to become the Irish Free State. Most of the people in the Irish Free State were Roman Catholics. In Northern Ireland, where the majority of the people were Protestants, most people wanted to remain citizens of the United Kingdom. As a result, the country's official name changed to the United Kingdom of Great Britain and Northern Ireland.

The modern history of the UK began in the 18th century when the British empire began to develop, despite the loss in 1783 of its 13 North American colonies which became the core of the modern United States. The other major event occurred in the late 18th century, when the UK became the first country to industrialize its economy.

The British empire broke up after World War II (1939–45), though the UK still administers many small, mainly island, territories around the world. The empire was transformed into the Commonwealth of Nations, a free association of independent countries which numbered 52 in 2007.

The UK has retained an important world role. For example, in 2001, it played a prominent role in creating a broad alliance to counter international terrorism following the attacks on the United States. It was also a prominent member of the coalition force which invaded Iraq in 2003. However, the UK has recognized that its economic future lies within Europe. It became a member of the European Economic Community (now the European Union) in 1973. In the early 21st century, most people accepted the importance of the EU to the UK's economic future. But some feared a loss of British identity should the EU ever evolve into a political federation.

The UK is a major industrial and trading nation. It lacks natural resources apart from coal, iron ore, oil and natural gas, and has to import most of the materials it needs for its industries. The UK also has to import food, because it produces only about two-thirds of the food it needs. In the first half of the 20th century, Britain was a major exporter of cars, ships, steel and textiles. But many industries have suffered from competition from other countries, with lower labour costs. Today, industries have to use high-technology in order to compete on the world market.

The UK is one of the world's most urbanized countries, and agriculture employs only 1% of the people.

Production is high because of the use of scientific methods and modern machinery. However, in the early 21st century, especially following the outbreak of foot-and-mouth disease in 2001, questions were raised about the future of rural industries. Major crops include barley, potatoes, sugar beet and wheat. Sheep are the leading livestock, but beef and dairy cattle, pigs and poultry are also important. Fishing is another major activity.

Service industries play a major part in the UK's economy. Financial and insurance services bring in much-needed foreign exchange, while tourism has become a major earner.

UNITED STATES OF AMERICA

AREA 9,629,091 sq km [3,717,792 sq mi]
POPULATION 298,444,000
CAPITAL Washington, DC
GOVERNMENT Federal republic
ETHNIC GROUPS White 77%, African American 13%, Asian 4%, Amerindian 2%, others
LANGUAGES English (official), Spanish, more than 30 others
RELIGIONS Protestant 56%, Roman Catholic 28%, Islam 2%, Judaism 2%
CURRENCY US dollar = 100 cents

GEOGRAPHY The United States of America is the world's fourth largest country in area and the third largest in population. It contains 50 states, 48 of which lie between Canada and Mexico, plus Alaska in north-western North America, and Hawai'i, a group of volcanic islands in the North Pacific Ocean. Densely populated coastal plains lie to the east and south of the Appalachian Mountains. The central lowlands drained by the Mississippi–Missouri rivers stretch from the Appalachians to the Rocky Mountains in the west. The Pacific region contains fertile valleys, separated by mountain ranges.

The climate varies greatly, ranging from the Arctic cold of Alaska to the intense heat of Death Valley, California. Of the 48 states between Canada and Mexico, winters are cold and snowy in the north, but mild in the south.

POLITICS & ECONOMY The first people in North America, the ancestors of the Native Americans (or American Indians) arrived perhaps 40,000 years ago from Asia. Although Vikings probably reached North America 1,000 years ago, European exploration proper did not begin until the late 15th century.

The first Europeans to settle in large numbers were the British, who founded settlements on the eastern coast in the early 17th century. British rule ended in the War of Independence (1775–83). The country expanded in 1803 when a vast territory in the south and west was acquired through the Louisiana Purchase, while the border with Mexico was fixed in the mid-19th century. The Civil War (1861–5) ended slavery and the serious threat that the nation might split into two parts. In the late 19th century, the West was opened up, while immigrants flooded in from Europe and elsewhere.

During the late 19th and early 20th centuries, industrialization led to the United States becoming the world's leading economic superpower and a pioneer in science and technology. It took on the mantle of the champion of Western democracy and, following the break-up of the former Soviet Union, it became the world's only superpower. But the attacks on the country on 11 September 2001 revealed its vulner-

ability to terrorists, especially those prepared to lose their lives in attacks, and also to the actions of rogue states. The response of the US government was vigorous. In 2001, it led a coalition force against the Taliban regime in Afghanistan, which was protecting al Qaida terrorists. Then, in 2003, it led another coalition force to overthrow the repressive regime of Saddam Hussein in Iraq. President George W. Bush was re-elected in 2004. In 2006, in elections, the Republican Party lost control of both houses of Congress to the Democrats, who had criticized his government's handling of the Iraq war.

The United States has the world's largest economy in terms of the total value of its production. Although agriculture employs only about 1.5% of the people, farming is highly mechanized and scientific, and the United States leads the world in farm production. Major products include beef and dairy cattle, together with such crops as cotton, fruits, groundnuts, maize, potatoes, soybeans, tobacco and wheat.

The country's natural resources include oil, natural gas and coal. There is also a wide range of metal ores that are used in manufacturing industries, together with timber, especially from the forests of the Pacific north-west. Manufacturing is the single most important activity, employing about 11% of the population. Major products include vehicles, food products, chemicals, machinery, printed goods, metal products and scientific instruments. California is now the leading manufacturing state. Many southern states, petroleum rich and climatically favoured, have also become highly prosperous in recent years.

URUGUAY

AREA 175,016 sq km [67,574 sq mi]
POPULATION 3,432,000
CAPITAL Montevideo
GOVERNMENT Multiparty republic
ETHNIC GROUPS White 88%, Mestizo 8%, Mulatto or Black 4%
LANGUAGES Spanish (official)
RELIGIONS Roman Catholic 66%, Protestant 2%, Judaism 1%
CURRENCY Uruguayan peso = 100 centésimos

GEOGRAPHY Uruguay is South America's second smallest independent country after Suriname. The land consists mainly of flat plains and hills. The River Uruguay, which forms the country's western border, flows into the Río de la Plata, a large estuary which leads into the South Atlantic Ocean.

Uruguay has a mild climate, with rain in every month, though droughts sometimes occur. Summers are pleasantly warm, especially near the coast. The weather remains relatively mild throughout the winter.

POLITICS & ECONOMY In 1726, Spanish settlers founded Montevideo in order to halt the Portuguese gaining influence in the area. By the late 18th century, Spaniards had settled in most of the country. Uruguay became part of a colony called the Viceroyalty of La Plata, which also included Argentina, Paraguay, and parts of Bolivia, Brazil and Chile. In 1820 Brazil annexed Uruguay, ending Spanish rule. In 1825, Uruguayans, supported by Argentina, began a struggle for independence. Finally, in 1828, Brazil and Argentina recognized Uruguay as an independent republic. Social and economic developments were slow in the 19th century, but, from 1903, Uruguay became stable and democratic.

From the 1950s, economic problems caused unrest. Terrorist groups, notably the Tupumaros, carried out murders and kidnappings. The army crushed the Tupumaros in 1972, but the army took over the government in 1973. Military rule continued until 1984 when elections were held. In the early 21st century, Uruguay faced many economic problems, many of which were the result of the economic crisis in Argentina. In 2005, Uruguay's first leftist president, Tabare Vasquez, was sworn in. He restored ties with Cuba and introduced measures to combat poverty.

The World Bank classifies Uruguay as an 'upper-middle-income' developing country. Agriculture employs only 4% of the people, but farm products, notably hides and leather goods, beef and wool, are the leading exports, while the leading manufacturing industries process farm products. The main crops include maize, potatoes, wheat and sugar beet.

UZBEKISTAN

AREA 447,400 sq km [172,741 sq mi]
POPULATION 27,307,000
CAPITAL Tashkent
GOVERNMENT Socialist republic
ETHNIC GROUPS Uzbek 80%, Russian 5%, Tajik 5%, Kazakh 3%, Tatar 2%, Kara-Kalpak 2%
LANGUAGES Uzbek (official), Russian
RELIGIONS Islam 88%, Eastern Orthodox 9%
CURRENCY Uzbekistani sum = 100 tiyin

GEOGRAPHY The Republic of Uzbekistan is one of the five republics in Central Asia which were once part of the Soviet Union. There are plains in the west and highlands in the east. The main rivers, the Amu (or Amu Darya) and Syr (or Syr Darya), drain into the Aral Sea. So much water has been taken from these rivers for irrigation that the Aral Sea is now only a quarter of its size in 1960. Much of the former sea is now desert. The climate is continental, with warm summers and cold winters. The west is arid, with an average annual rainfall of about 200 mm [8 in].

POLITICS & ECONOMY Russia took the area in the 19th century. After the Russian Revolution of 1917, the Communists took over and, in 1924, they set up the Uzbek Soviet Socialist Republic. Under Communism, all aspects of Uzbek life were controlled and religious worship was discouraged. But education, health, housing and transport were improved. In the late 1980s, the people demanded more freedom and, in 1990, the government stated that its laws overruled those of the Soviet Union. Uzbekistan became independent in 1991 when the Soviet Union broke up, but it retained links with Russia through the Commonwealth of Independent States. Islam Karimov, leader of the People's Democratic Party (formerly the Communist Party), was elected president in December 1991. In 1992–3, many opposition leaders were arrested because the government said that they threatened national stability. In 1994–5, the PDP was victorious in national elections and, in 1995, a referendum extended Karimov's term in office until 2000, when he was again re-elected. In 2001, Karimov allowed the United States to use bases in Uzbekistan for its military campaign in Afghanistan, but it demanded that US forces leave in 2005. International groups continued to criticize Uzbekistan's poor record on human rights.

Uzbekistan is a developing country where the government still controls most economic activity. The country produces coal, copper, gold, oil and natural gas.

VANUATU

AREA 12,189 sq km [4,706 sq mi]
POPULATION 209,000
CAPITAL Port-Vila

The Republic of Vanuatu, formerly the Anglo-French Condominium of the New Hebrides, became independent in 1980. (Vanuatu is a word meaning 'Our Land Forever'.) The republic consists of a chain of 80 islands in the South Pacific Ocean. Its economy is based on agriculture and it exports copra, beef and veal, timber and cocoa.

VATICAN CITY

AREA 0.44 sq km [0.17 sq mi]
POPULATION 1,000

Vatican City State, the world's smallest independent nation, is an enclave on the west bank of the River Tiber in Rome. It forms an independent base for the Holy See, the governing body of the Roman Catholic Church. Vatican City contains St Peter's Basilica and museums with priceless works of art.

VENEZUELA

AREA 912,050 sq km [352,143 sq mi]
POPULATION 25,730,000
CAPITAL Caracas
GOVERNMENT Federal republic
ETHNIC GROUPS Spanish, Italian, Portuguese, Arab, German, African, indigenous people
LANGUAGES Spanish (official), indigenous dialects
RELIGIONS Roman Catholic 96%
CURRENCY Bolívar = 100 céntimos

GEOGRAPHY The Bolivarian Republic of Venezuela, in northern South America, contains the Maracaibo lowlands around the oil-rich Lake Maracaibo in the west. Andean ranges enclose the lowlands and extend across most of northern Venezuela. The Orinoco river basin, containing tropical grasslands called *llanos*, lies between the northern highlands and the Guiana Highlands in the south-east.

Venezuela has a tropical climate. Temperatures are high throughout the year on the lowlands, though the mountains are much cooler. Rainfall is heaviest in the mountains, but much of the country has a marked dry season between December and April.

POLITICS & ECONOMY In the early 19th century, Venezuelans, such as Simón Bolívar and Francisco de Miranda, began a struggle against Spanish rule. Venezuela declared its independence in 1811. But it only became truly independent in 1821, when the Spanish were defeated in a battle near Valencia.

The development of Venezuela in the 19th and the first half of the 20th centuries was marred by instability, violence and periods of harsh dictatorial rule. But Venezuela has had elected governments since 1958.

The country has greatly benefited from its oil resources which were first exploited in 1917. In 1960, Venezuela helped to form OPEC (the Organization of Petroleum Exporting Countries) and, in 1976, the government of Venezuela took control of the entire oil industry. In 1999, Hugo Chavez, who had staged an unsuccessful coup in 1992, was elected president. Chavez survived an attempted coup in 2002 and, in 2004, he won a majority in a referendum that had been intended to remove him from office. He was re-elected in 2006 and his leftist policies continued to arouse US hostility.

Venezuela's economy is bolstered by oil production and oil accounts for 80% of the exports. Other exports include bauxite and aluminium, iron ore and farm products. Cattle ranching is another important activity. The chief industry is petroleum refining. Cement, steel and textiles are also manufactured.

VIETNAM

AREA 331,689 sq km [128,065 sq mi]
POPULATION 84,403,000
CAPITAL Hanoi
GOVERNMENT Socialist republic
ETHNIC GROUPS Vietnamese 87%, Chinese, Hmong, Thai, Khmer, Cham, mountain groups
LANGUAGES Vietnamese (official), English, Chinese
RELIGIONS Buddhism, Christianity, indigenous beliefs
CURRENCY Dong = 10 hao = 100 xu

GEOGRAPHY The Socialist Republic of Vietnam occupies an S-shaped strip of land facing the South China Sea in South-east Asia. The coastal plains include two densely populated, fertile delta regions: the Red (Hong) delta facing the Gulf of Tonkin in the north, and the Mekong delta in the south.

Vietnam has a tropical climate, though the driest months of January to March are a little cooler than the wet, hot summer months, when monsoon winds blow from the south-west. Typhoons (cyclones) sometimes hit the coast, causing much damage.

POLITICS & ECONOMY China dominated Vietnam for a thousand years before AD 939, when a Vietnamese state was founded. The French took over the area between the 1850s and 1880s. They ruled Vietnam as part of French Indo-China, which also included Cambodia and Laos.

Japan conquered Vietnam during World War II (1939–45). In 1946, war broke out between a nationalist group, called the Vietminh, and the French colonial government. France withdrew in 1954 and Vietnam was divided into a Communist North Vietnam, led by the Vietminh leader, Ho Chi Minh, and a non-Communist South.

A force called the Viet Cong rebelled against South Vietnam's government in 1957 and a war began, which gradually increased in intensity. The United States aided the South, but after it withdrew in 1975, South Vietnam surrendered. In 1976, the united Vietnam became a Socialist Republic. In 1978, Vietnam intervened in Cambodia to defeat the Khmer Rouge government, but it withdrew in 1989. In the 1990s, Vietnam launched reforms and its economy expanded rapidly in the 21st century. In 1995, the United States opened an embassy in Hanoi. In 2002, trade relations with the US were normalized and, in 2007, Vietnam became the 150th member of the World Trade Organization.

Agriculture is the main activity. Rice is the main food crop. Vietnam also produces chromium, oil (located off the south coast), tin and phosphates.

NATIONS OF THE WORLD

VIRGIN ISLANDS, BRITISH

AREA 151 sq km [58 sq mi]
POPULATION 23,000
CAPITAL Road Town

The British Virgin Islands, the most northerly of the Lesser Antilles, comprise four low-lying islands and 36 islets and cays. The islands were 'discovered' by Christopher Columbus in 1493. Dutch from 1648 but British since 1666, they are now a British overseas territory, with a substantial measure of self-government. Tourism is the chief source of income.

VIRGIN ISLANDS, US

AREA 347 sq km [134 sq mi]
POPULATION 109,000
CAPITAL Charlotte Amalie

The Virgin Islands of the United States, a group of three islands and 65 small islets, are a self-governing US territory. Purchased from Denmark in 1917, its residents are US citizens and they elect a non-voting delegate to the House of Representatives. The tropical climate is pleasant throughout the year.

WALLIS AND FUTUNA ISLANDS

AREA 200 sq km [77 sq mi]
POPULATION 16,000
CAPITAL Mata-Utu

The Wallis and Futuna Islands, in the South Pacific Ocean, form the smallest and the poorest of France's overseas territories. A French dependency since 1842, the territory comprises two groups of islands: the Isles de Hoorn, north-east of the Fiji Islands, which includes Futuna; and the Wallis Archipelago.

YEMEN

AREA 527,968 sq km [203,848 sq mi]
POPULATION 21,456,000
CAPITAL Sana'
GOVERNMENT Multiparty republic
ETHNIC GROUPS Predominantly Arab
LANGUAGES Arabic (official)
RELIGIONS Islam
CURRENCY Yemeni rial = 100 fils

GEOGRAPHY The Republic of Yemen faces the Red Sea and the Gulf of Aden in the south-western corner of the Arabian peninsula. Behind the narrow coastal plain along the Red Sea, the land rises to a mountain region called High Yemen.

The climate ranges from hot and often humid conditions on the coast to the cooler highlands. Most of the country is arid.

POLITICS & ECONOMY After World War I, northern Yemen, which had been ruled by Turkey, began to evolve into a separate state from the south, where Britain was in control. Britain withdrew in 1967 and a left-wing government took power in the south. North Yemen became a republic in 1962, when the monarchy was abolished.

Clashes occurred between the traditionalist Yemen Arab Republic in the north and the formerly British Marxist People's Democratic Republic of Yemen but, in 1990, the two Yemens merged to form a single country. Further conflict occurred in 1994, when southern secessionist forces were defeated. In 1998 and 1999, militants in the Aden-Abyan Islamic army sought to destabilize the country. In 2000, suicide bombers, thought to be part of the al Qaida network, killed 117 sailors on a US destroyer in Aden harbour. Hundreds of Yemenis were killed in 2004–5 during an uprising by Shia Muslims in the north. (Most Yemenis are Sunni Muslims.)

Yemen is a developing country and agriculture employs about half of the people. Sheep are reared and such crops as barley, fruits, wheat and vegetables are grown in highland valleys and around oases. Cash crops include coffee and cotton.

Imported oil is refined at Aden and petroleum extraction began in the north-west in the 1980s. Handicrafts, leather goods and textiles are manufactured. Remittances from Yemenis abroad are a major source of revenue.

ZAMBIA

AREA 752,618 sq km [290,586 sq mi]
POPULATION 11,502,000
CAPITAL Lusaka
GOVERNMENT Multiparty republic
ETHNIC GROUPS Native African (Bemba, Tonga, Maravi/Nyanja)
LANGUAGES English (official), Bemba, Kaonda, Nyanja and about 70 others
RELIGIONS Christianity 70%, Islam, Hinduism
CURRENCY Zambian kwacha = 100 ngwee

GEOGRAPHY The Republic of Zambia is a land-locked country in southern Africa. Zambia lies on the plateau that makes up most of southern Africa. Much of the land is between 900 m and 1,500 m [2,950 ft to 4,920 ft] above sea level. The Muchinga Mountains in the north-east rise above this flat land. Lakes include Bangweulu, which is entirely within Zambia, together with parts of lakes Mweru and Tanganyika in the north.

Zambia lies in the tropics, but temperatures are moderated by the altitude. The rainy season runs from November to March.

POLITICS & ECONOMY European contact with Zambia began in the 19th century, when the explorer David Livingstone crossed the River Zambezi. In the 1890s, the British South Africa Company, set up by Cecil Rhodes (1853–1902), the British financier and statesman, made treaties with local chiefs and gradually took over the area. In 1911, the Company named the area Northern Rhodesia. In 1924, Britain took over the government of the country.

In 1953, Britain formed a federation of Northern Rhodesia, Southern Rhodesia (now Zimbabwe) and Nyasaland (now Malawi). Because of African opposition, the federation was dissolved in 1963 and Northern Rhodesia became independent as Zambia in 1964. Kenneth Kaunda became president and one-party rule was introduced in 1972. Under a new constitution, Frederick Chiluba was elected president in 1996. He stood down in 2001 and Levy Mwanawasa became president. In 2005, the Supreme Court stated that the 2001 ballot had been flawed. In 2006, Mwanawasa was re-elected to a second term.

Copper is the main resource, accounting for half of Zambia's exports in 1998. Zambia also produces cobalt, lead, zinc and gemstones. Agriculture employs 69% of workers, as compared with 4% in industry and mining. Maize is the chief crop.

ZIMBABWE

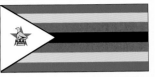

AREA 390,757 sq km [150,871 sq mi]
POPULATION 12,237,000
CAPITAL Harare
GOVERNMENT Multiparty republic
ETHNIC GROUPS Shona 82%, Ndebele 14%, other African groups 2%, mixed and Asian 1%
LANGUAGES English (official), Shona, Ndebele
RELIGIONS Christianity, traditional beliefs
CURRENCY Zimbabwean dollar = 100 cents

GEOGRAPHY The Republic of Zimbabwe is a land-locked country in southern Africa. Most of the country lies on a high plateau between the Zambezi and Limpopo rivers between 900 m to 1,500 m [2,950 ft to 4,920 ft] above sea level. From October to March, the weather is hot and wet. But daily temperatures may vary greatly in the winter.

POLITICS & ECONOMY The Shona people became dominant in the region about 1,000 years ago. The British South Africa Company, under the statesman Cecil Rhodes (1853–1902), occupied the area in the 1890s, after obtaining mineral rights from local chiefs. The area was named Rhodesia and later Southern Rhodesia. It became a self-governing British colony in 1923. Between 1953 and 1963, Southern and Northern Rhodesia (now Zambia) were joined to Nyasaland (Malawi) in the Central African Federation.

In 1965, the European government of Southern Rhodesia (then called Rhodesia) declared their country independent but Britain refused to accept this. Finally, after a civil war, the country became legally independent in 1980, though rivalries between the Shona and Ndebele people threatened stability. Order was restored when the Shona prime minister, Robert Mugabe, brought his Ndebele rivals into his government. In 1987, Mugabe became the country's executive president and, in 1991, the government renounced its Marxist ideology. Mugabe was re-elected president in 1990 and 1996. During the late 1990s, Mugabe threatened to seize white-owned farms without paying compensation to the owners. Despite international pressure, landless 'war veterans' began to occupy white farms. In 2002, Mugabe was re-elected amid accusations of electoral irregularities. The Commonwealth suspended Zimbabwe's membership and, in 2004, the European Union renewed sanctions against the country. In 2005, the US named Zimbabwe as one of the world's six 'outposts of tyranny'.

The World Bank classifies Zimbabwe as a 'low-income' developing country. In the 2000s, because of mismanagement, the economy was plunged into crisis with spiralling rates of inflation. However, the country has valuable mineral resources. Agriculture employs 56% of the people and maize is the chief crop.

IMAGES OF EARTH

IJSSELMEER, NETHERLANDS
This unique feature was created in the 13th century when the sea breached a protective sand bar, flooding all the low-lying land. The remnants of the bar can still be seen as the chain of Frisian Islands at the top of the image. Large-scale reclamation started in 1932 with the completion of the causeway in the north. Since then, four 'polders' have been drained and reclaimed. The city of Amsterdam can be seen at bottom left. *[Map page 17]*

IMAGES OF EARTH : EUROPE

▶ **ICELAND**

This winter image, captured in January, shows Iceland cloaked in snow, covering its four permanent ice-caps. The island sits astride the fault line between the North American and Eurasian tectonic plates. These plates are moving away from each other, resulting in a high level of volcanic activity, with much of the land covered in lava flows. Although situated just below the Arctic Circle, Iceland's climate in the south is modified by the relatively warm waters of the North Atlantic Drift Current. *[Map page 8]*

▼ **RHÔNE DELTA, FRANCE**

The river Rhône reaches the Mediterranean to the west of Marseilles (seen at bottom centre) after flowing from its source, the Rhône Glacier, in Switzerland. To the west of its mouth, protected by sand bars, are the salt lagoons and marshes of the Camargue, a UNESCO World Heritage site. On the opposite bank, to the east, is a large lake, the Étang de Berre. The pink area between the lake and the river is the arid, boulder-strewn Plaine de Crau. *[Map page 21]*

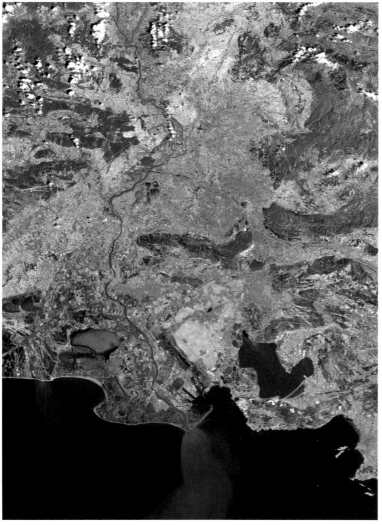

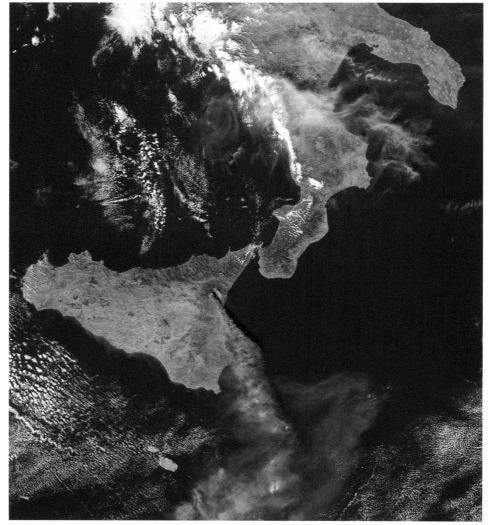

◄ **KANIN PENINSULA, RUSSIA**
The distinctive shape of this peninsula (Poluostrov Kanin in Russian) separates the White Sea (Beloye More) in the west from the Cheshskaya Guba in this false-colour image. Situated within the Arctic Circle, the area is flat, marshy tundra affected by permafrost, and serves as an important staging post for migrating birds. The local people are Nenets, with their own language and alphabet. Their traditional occupation is reindeer herding. [*Map page 52*]

◄ **MOUNT ETNA, SICILY**
The most active volcano in Europe, Mount Etna, 3,323 m [10,906 ft] high, is shown here during the 2002–3 eruption, its plume of ash and smoke spreading southwards over the Mediterranean. Activity from Etna has been traced back by geologists to 1500 BC. As with many other volcanoes, the volcanic debris has weathered to produce highly fertile soils, resulting in productive vineyards, banana plantations and citrus groves around its base. [*Map pages 42–3*]

▶ **WESTERN CRETE, GREECE**
Crete is largest of the Greek islands, stretching over 260 km [161 miles] long. The western end of the island is the most mountainous, with more than 50 peaks reaching over 2,000 m [6,564 ft]. Running north to south at right angles to the south coast, just to the west of the snow-capped mountains, can be seen one of Europe's longest gorges, 16 km [10 miles] long, now part of the Samaria National Park. On the bulbous peninsula to the north, the runways of Khanía airport are clearly visible. [*Map page 46*]

▲ DEAD SEA, ISRAEL/JORDAN

At 411 m [1,349 ft] below sea level, the Dead Sea is the lowest body of water on the Earth's surface. As a result, there is no outlet for the water that flows into it. Despite this, its water level is dropping steadily due to water abstraction for irrigation on both the Israeli and Jordanian sides of the River Jordan, the main source. Due to the high surface evaporation, the water in the Dead Sea is five times as saline as ocean water and nothing can live in it, hence its name. *[Map page 74]*

▶ RIYADH, SAUDI ARABIA

This false-colour image shows the Saudi Arabian capital in its desert setting, situated almost at the geographical centre of the kingdom. With a population of over 3 million people, water supply is of prime importance, and although dried-up river beds or 'wadis' can be identified in the image, most of the supply is drawn from underground aquifers. To the south-east, the green circles are in fact fields, irrigated by centre-pivot irrigation systems. *[Map page 75]*

◄ ABU DHABI, UAE
The green island at the centre of this image forms the core of the city of Abu Dhabi, the capital of the emirate of the same name. It is the richest of the United Arab Emirates and much effort has gone into the inclusion of many parks in the development of the capital. These are all irrigated with desalinated seawater. This part of the Persian Gulf coast is typified by its offshore islands and reefs. *[Map page 71]*

▼ MUSANDAM PENINSULA, OMAN
Jutting northwards into the Strait of Hormuz towards Iran, this peninsula is an enclave of Oman, surrounded by the UAE. The strait is only 64 km [40 miles] wide at this point, but is important strategically as much of the region's oil production is exported through these waters. The distinctive coastline shape to the north and east is caused by the tilting of the land and the submergence of the coast. *[Map page 71]*

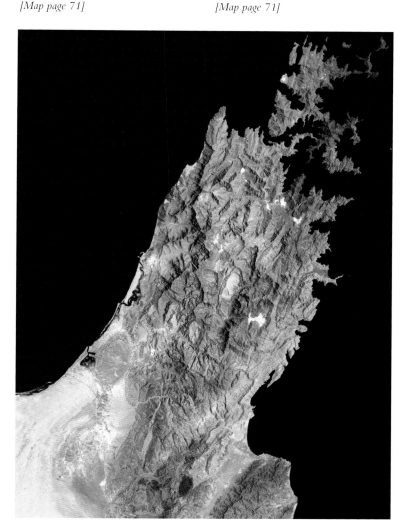

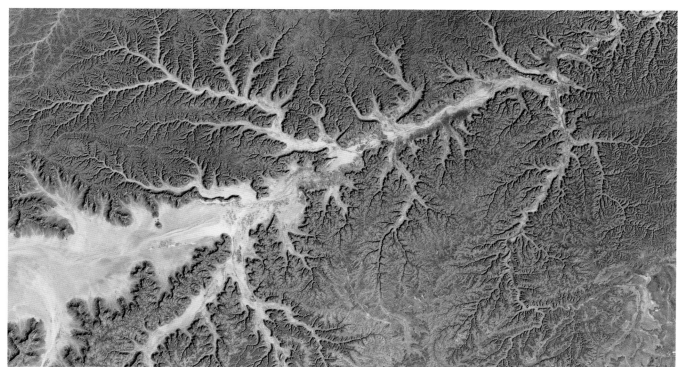

▲ GREAT SALT DESERT, IRAN
The area of this false-colour image is situated about 320 km [200 miles] south-east of Tehran. These amazing patterns are caused by the folding and subsequent wind erosion of layers of sediments. The blue salt lakes ('kavirs'), which dry out as salt flats in the hot season, can be seen in the south-west. An isolated road, crossing this otherwise uninhabited area from north to south, can also be identified. *[Map page 71]*

◄ WADI HADRAMAWT, YEMEN
Yemen is very arid, but images such as this show that its past was much wetter, enabling large river systems to evolve and carve out the deep, spectacular gorges and dried-up river beds seen here. These 'wadis' are still important for irrigation when it does rain in the interior mountains. This is one of the largest, stretching for over 550 km [340 miles] from the interior to the Gulf of Aden. *[Map page 75]*

▶ **TURFAN DEPRESSION, CHINA**
The dark green folded areas in the
north are the mountains of the Tian
Shan range, which change abruptly
into barren areas of overlapping
alluvial fans, shown in mauve.
Below these, steep rocky slopes fall
to the depression floor, some 154 m
[505 ft] below sea level. The yellow
area is a sand desert. Despite these
arid conditions, the dark green
areas are fields irrigated by an
ancient system of wells, growing
grapes, melons and other crops.
[Map page 60]

▲ **GANGES DELTA,
INDIA/BANGLADESH**
Over 300 km [186 miles] wide, this
is the world's largest delta, created
by the River Ganges depositing
sediment it has carried from the
Himalayas. It is extremely vulnerable
to frequent cyclones and tidal surges,
but is densely populated because
of the fertile land. On the western
side of the image is the mouth
of the Hugli, with the elongated
city of Kolkata (Calcutta) showing
as dark grey just to the north.
The large red area indicates the
presence of mangrove forests and
swamps, and is divided between the
countries of India and Bangladesh.
[Map page 69]

▼ **SINGAPORE**
Three separate countries can be seen
in this image. At the top, partially
covered by cloud, is the southern end
of Malaysia; the island in the centre
is the state of Singapore; and the
islands just visible at the bottom
of the image are part of Indonesia.
Singapore has developed a fast-
growing economy based on the
trans-shipment of goods between
the Far East and the West. As a
result, it is one of the world's major
ports and much new development
can be seen here, coloured grey.
[Map page 65]

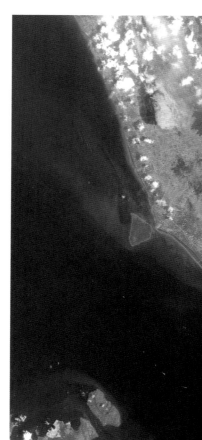

▶ **CHAIYAPHUM PROVINCE,
THAILAND**
Chaiyaphum is situated 332 km
[206 miles] north of Bangkok, in
a very fertile part of north-eastern
Thailand. Vegetation is shown
in red in this false-colour image,
highlighting the steep slopes of the
irregularly shaped plateau rising from
the surrounding plain and covered
with lush vegetation. On top of
this more resistant rock, there is a
dense patchwork of fields and lakes.
[Map page 64]

▲ **MOUNT KLYUCHEVSKAYA, RUSSIA**
The snow-covered peaks are seen here protruding through low cloud. Klyuchevskaya's almost perfectly shaped cone casts the longest shadow. At 4,750 m [15,589 ft], it is the highest of the 29 volcanoes located in one of the most active regions in the world, the remote Kamchatka Peninsula in eastern Siberia. It forms part of the 'Ring of Fire' that surrounds the Pacific Ocean.
[Map page 53]

► RICHAT STRUCTURE,
MAURITANIA
When first seen from space by the
Gemini spacecraft in 1965, this
striking circular structure, about
50 km [30 miles] in diameter in
north-eastern Mauritania, was
thought to be a meteorite crater.
Subsequent investigation, however,
has confirmed that it is the heavily
eroded remnant of a rock dome.
It is about 200 m [656 ft] above
the level of the desert, seen in the
top left-hand corner of this image.
[Map page 78]

▼ AL KUFRAH, LIBYA
The Al Kufrah region contains the
largest oases in the Libyan Desert.
Beneath the desert are enormous
freshwater reserves, which are held
in porous rock layers called aquifers.
This water collected when the
climate in the Saharan region was
much wetter. The false-colour image
shows the characteristic round 'fields'
that are irrigated by pumped water
fed into centre-pivot irrigation
systems, the crops showing up as red.
The smoke on the right is gas burn-
off from an oil well. *[Map page 79]*

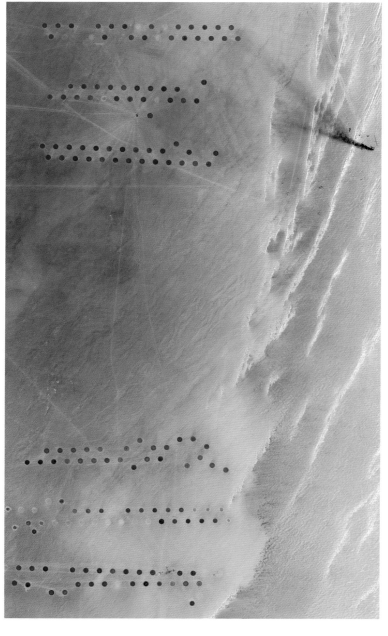

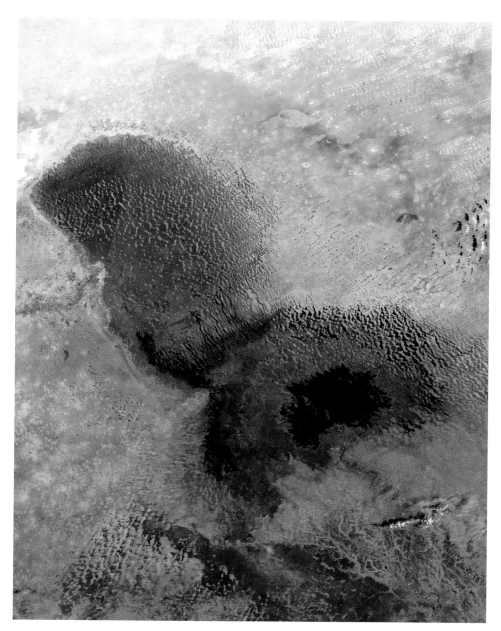

▲ VICTORIA FALLS, ZAMBIA/ZIMBABWE

At the top of the image, the Zambezi River plunges 105 m [345 ft] over a basalt cliff into a deep gorge. The falls are 1.6 km [1 mile] wide, but the chasm into which they fall is only 120 m [400 ft] wide, resulting in a fast turbulent torrent with many rapids. To the left of the river is Zimbabwe, with Zambia to its right. [Map page 87]

▼ CAPE PENINSULA, SOUTH AFRICA

The Cape Peninsula, seen running north to south on the far left of this image, is some 50 km [31 miles] long. Its southern extremity is the Cape of Good Hope, while the city of Cape Town sits at the northern end, beneath Table Mountain. Robben Island is clearly visible in Table Bay, to the north of the city. [Map page 88]

▲ LAKE CHAD

The lake, an inland drainage basin with no outlet to the sea, sits at the junction of four countries – Cameroon, Chad, Niger and Nigeria – and was once one of Africa's largest freshwater lakes, with an area of 25,000 sq km [9,650 sq miles] in 1963. However, sitting on the southern edge of the Sahara Desert, it has become susceptible to both the arid climate and increased abstraction of water for irrigation. By 2001, it had shrunk to only 1,350 sq km [839 sq miles] in area. [Map page 83]

◄ SUEZ CANAL, EGYPT

At the bottom of the image is the Gulf of Suez, at the northern end of the Red Sea. The port of Suez can be seen to the left of the line of the Suez Canal, which runs north to the Great Bitter Lakes, on its way to Port Said on the Mediterranean coast, 163 km [101 miles] away. Opened in 1869, the Suez Canal enables ships to travel between Europe and Asia without having to circumnavigate the whole of Africa. [Map page 80]

IMAGES OF EARTH : **AUSTRALIA AND OCEANIA**

▶ **ADMIRALTY GULF, AUSTRALIA**
Bordering the Timor Sea, the tropical coastline of this part of north-west Australia is one of the remotest on the continent. The rocks are very old and the cracks and fissures in them can clearly be seen in this image, enhanced by the vegetation growing along them. Western Australia, of which this is part, has an area of 2.5 million sq km [1 million sq miles], which makes it the largest state in the world. *[Map page 92]*

◀ **ULURU (AYERS ROCK), AUSTRALIA**
The remnant of a mountain range created some 500 million years ago and then eroded away, leaving only this huge outlier, Uluru rises 345 m [1,132 ft] above its surroundings and has a circumference of 9.4 km [5.8 miles]. The rock has been a centre of Aboriginal life for over 10,000 years. Its dramatic shape and coloration, caused by oxidized iron in the sandstone, now brings visitors from around the world to this remote site. The nearest town is Alice Springs, located 442 km [275 miles] to the east. *[Map page 93]*

▶ **NEW ZEALAND**
This fine natural colour image shows the whole of New Zealand, or 'Aotearoa' ('Land of the Long White Cloud') as it is known to the indigenous Maori people. It is situated approximately 2,000 km [1,250 miles] south-east of Australia. Its rocks are ancient and the islands split away some 800 million years ago from the other continental land masses, allowing a unique variety of animal species, such as the flightless Kiwi, to develop. Polynesians are believed to have been the first settlers here, about 900 years ago. *[Map page 91]*

Satellite image courtesy of Space Imaging/NPA Ltd (www.satmaps.com)

74

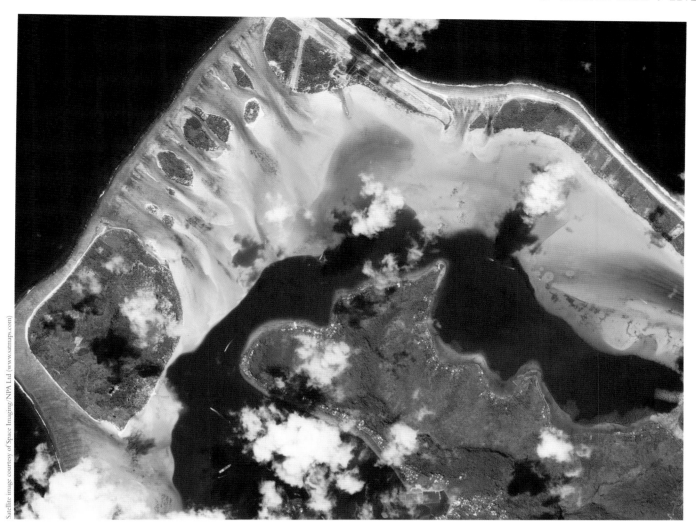

Satellite image courtesy of Space Imaging/NPA Ltd (www.satmaps.com)

◄ **BORA BORA, FRENCH POLYNESIA**
This image shows the northern tip of the island, its lagoon and fringing reef. The airport, visible at the top of the image, was built by US troops during World War II and can take international flights today. Situated 257 km [160 miles] north-west of Tahiti, Bora Bora is one of the Society Islands, part of French Polynesia. In the centre of the island, Mount Olemanu, the core of a long-extinct volcano, rises to a height of 725 m [2,380 ft]. *[Map page 97]*

▼ **CHRISTCHURCH, NEW ZEALAND**
Situated on the east coast of the South Island, the city of Christchurch, with more than 300,000 inhabitants, lies between the braided Waimakariri River and the spectacular Banks Peninsula. The latter was formed by the erosion of two ancient volcanic cones by glaciers and their subsequent inundation by the sea to create the two large harbours of Lyttelton to the north and Akaroa in the south, as well as numerous flooded valleys. Inland, to the west, lie the fertile Canterbury Plains, New Zealand's prime sheep-rearing area. *[Map page 91]*

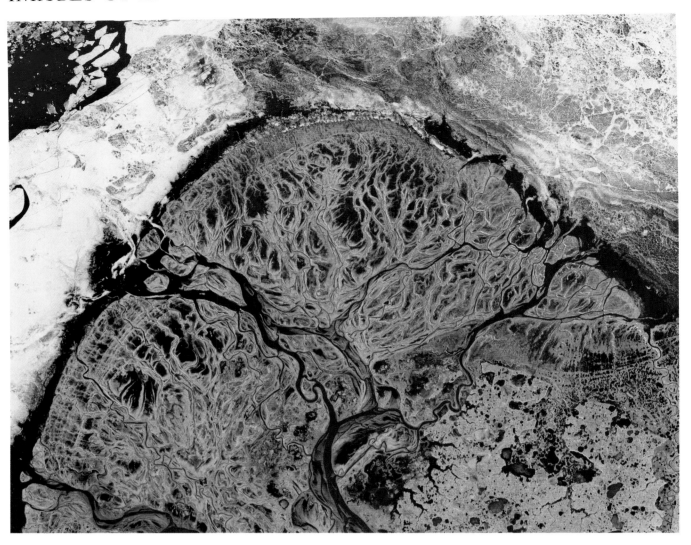

▶ LAKE MANICOUAGAN, CANADA
This circular lake in Québec, some 70 km [43 miles] in diameter, is believed to be the result of a meteorite hitting the Earth some 214 million years ago. The central core is an area of uplifted rock that readjusted after the removal of thousands of tonnes of material above it by the impact. The crater shape has been further modified by glacial erosion during the last Ice Age. It is now used as a reservoir for a hydroelectric power station on the river to the south and for recreation. *[Map page 105]*

▼ NEW ORLEANS, LOUISIANA
Sometimes called 'the Crescent City', the settlement is situated between the south bank of Lake Pontchartrain (the largest in this view) and the Mississippi River. The brown sediment-laden water of the latter can be seen meandering sluggishly across the image, and each year it deposits over a million tonnes of material in its lower reaches and delta, which is to the south-east of the city. The river has the third-largest drainage basin in the world, after the Amazon and Congo. *[Map page 113]*

▲ YUKON RIVER DELTA, ALASKA
At over 3,185 km [1,980 miles] long, the Yukon is one of North America's longest rivers, rising in Canada's McKenzie Mountains and flowing westwards across Alaska. It enters the Bering Sea via this complex delta, which is over 80 km [50 miles] wide. Lying just to the south of the Arctic Circle, sea ice can clearly be seen offshore, in light blue. *[Map page 100]*

▶ SAN FRANCISCO, CALIFORNIA
The whole of the 'Bay Area' is shown in this image: hilly San Francisco is at the top end of the southern peninsula, with the Golden Gate Bridge connecting it to Sausalito to the north. Alcatraz Island, former home of the infamous prison, can be seen as a small light area to the east of the bridge. On the opposite shore, connected by the double-decker Bay Bridge, are Oakland and Berkeley, while at the southern end of the bay is the city of San Jose. The bright green areas to the south of the bay are salt evaporation pans. *[Map page 110]*

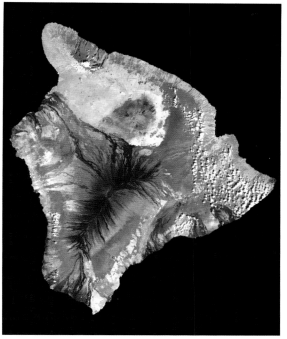

◄ HAWAI'I, USA
Hawai'i is the largest of this group of mid-Pacific islands. Situated over a 'hot spot' on the Earth's crust, they are either active, dormant or extinct volcanoes. The blackened area to the south is lava from the largest active volcano, Mauna Loa, at 4,169 m [13,683 ft] high. *[Map page 106]*

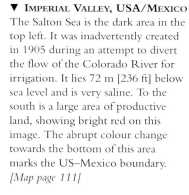

▼ IMPERIAL VALLEY, USA/MEXICO
The Salton Sea is the dark area in the top left. It was inadvertently created in 1905 during an attempt to divert the flow of the Colorado River for irrigation. It lies 72 m [236 ft] below sea level and is very saline. To the south is a large area of productive land, showing bright red on this image. The abrupt colour change towards the bottom of this area marks the US–Mexico boundary. *[Map page 111]*

► **BOLIVIA**
Bolivia has over 250,000 sq km [100,000 sq miles] of dry tropical forest, home to animals such as jaguars and ocelots. It is, however, being cleared at a rate of over 2% per annum. This false-colour image shows an area that has been almost completely cleared. The darkest areas are remnants of the original forest, some retained as wind breaks between newly created arable fields. The radial patterns are fields with new villages at their centres, part of a government resettlement scheme. *[Map page 124]*

▼ **SANTIAGO, CHILE**
The Chilean capital city, Santiago, lies in a fertile valley at the foot of the Andes, some 60 km [37 miles] south-east of the main port of Valparaíso on the Pacific coast. To the east, the mountains rise to over 6,000 m [20,000 ft]. The city has expanded rapidly to its current population of over 5 million inhabitants and this resulted in air-pollution problems in the 1980s, though measures have since been taken to counter this. *[Map page 126]*

▼ **WELLINGTON ISLAND, CHILE**
This image shows part of Wellington Island, which is situated off the coast of southern Chile. This large island is approximately 5,556 sq km [2,145 sq miles] in extent, but is almost totally uninhabited. Experts believe its highly fractured surface is not simply the result of glaciation, since the fissures, valleys and fjords all run in varying directions. A more likely explanation is that it is the result of a collision between two tectonic plates. *[Map page 128]*

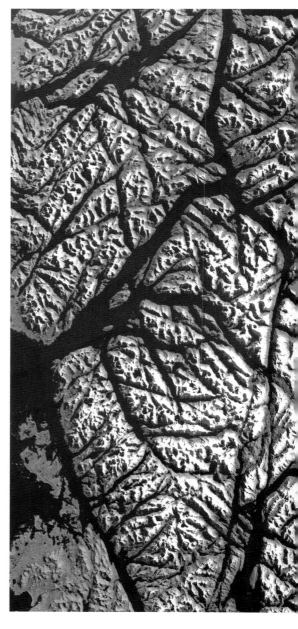

◀ **MANAUS, BRAZIL**
The town, with a population of almost 1.5 million, shows up in light blue at the confluence of the Rio Negro or Black River (to the north) with the Amazon (to the south), some 1,600 km [1,000 miles] from its mouth. The main branch of the river to the south, sometimes also called the Solimões, is carrying a heavy load of sediment from the Andes, hence the marked colour difference. Ocean-going vessels can navigate this far upstream, and indeed continue a further 2,100 km [1,300 miles] up the Amazon to Iquitos, in northern Peru. [Map page 124]

▼ **BUENOS AIRES, ARGENTINA**
Buenos Aires is situated where the continent's second-largest river system, the Paraná–Paraguay–Uruguay, flows into the flooded river valley that forms its estuary, the Río de la Plata (River Plate). The River Paraná flows in at the top left of the image. To the city's south and west is grazing land for livestock, while in the top right-hand corner, in Uruguay, wheat is the predominant crop grown locally. [Map page 126]

▲ PATAGONIA, CHILE
This false-colour image shows many classic glacial features. As it flows slowly from the mountains towards the coast, the glacier is covered in fissures and crevasses. The bright-red semi-circular ridge, a little distance from its end, consists of loose rock debris and was pushed there by the ice. It is called a 'terminal moraine'. The blue-green areas around the tongues of the glacier are meltwater lakes, the colour coming from suspended silt, and they contain ice floes. Rivers drain these lakes, cutting through the moraine on their way to the sea. [Map page 128]

WORLD
MAPS

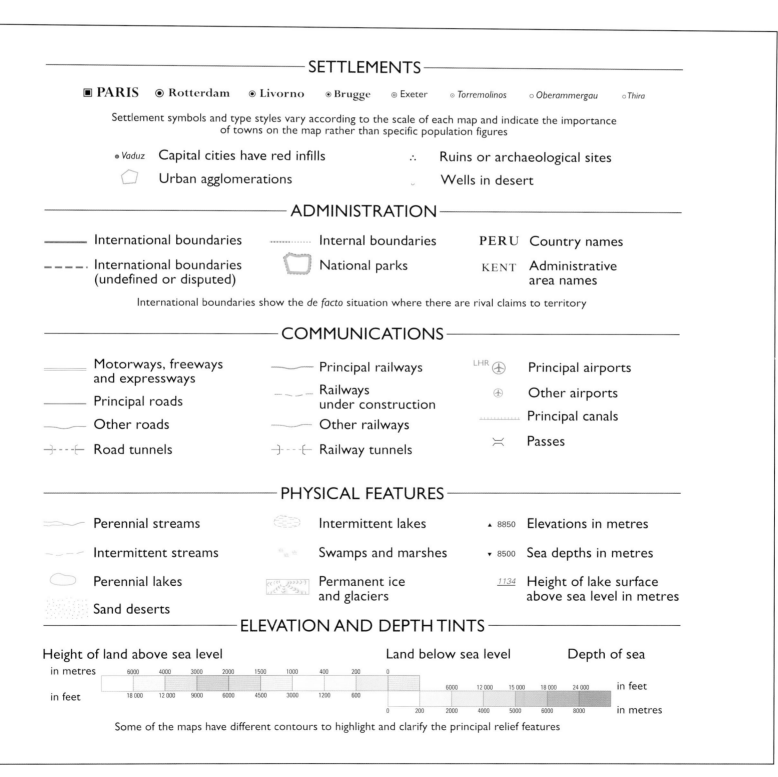

SETTLEMENTS

■ **PARIS**　◉ **Rotterdam**　◉ **Livorno**　◉ Brugge　◉ Exeter　○ *Torremolinos*　○ *Oberammergau*　○ *Thira*

Settlement symbols and type styles vary according to the scale of each map and indicate the importance
of towns on the map rather than specific population figures

● *Vaduz*　Capital cities have red infills

⬠　Urban agglomerations

∴　Ruins or archaeological sites

ᵛ　Wells in desert

ADMINISTRATION

——— International boundaries

- - - - - International boundaries
(undefined or disputed)

·········· Internal boundaries

National parks

PERU　Country names

KENT　Administrative
area names

International boundaries show the *de facto* situation where there are rival claims to territory

COMMUNICATIONS

——— Motorways, freeways
and expressways

——— Principal roads

——— Other roads

+ - - + Road tunnels

——— Principal railways

- - - - Railways
under construction

——— Other railways

+ - - + Railway tunnels

LHR ✈　Principal airports

⊕　Other airports

·········· Principal canals

≍　Passes

PHYSICAL FEATURES

~~~ Perennial streams

- - - Intermittent streams

Perennial lakes

Sand deserts

Intermittent lakes

Swamps and marshes

Permanent ice
and glaciers

▲ 8850　Elevations in metres

▼ 8500　Sea depths in metres

1134　Height of lake surface
above sea level in metres

ELEVATION AND DEPTH TINTS

Height of land above sea level

Land below sea level

Depth of sea

in metres　6000　4000　3000　2000　1500　1000　400　200　0

in feet　18 000　12 000　9000　6000　4500　3000　1200　600

6000　12 000　15 000　18 000　24 000　in feet

0　200　2000　4000　5000　6000　8000　in metres

Some of the maps have different contours to highlight and clarify the principal relief features

Beaufort Sea — Queen Elizabeth Islands — Parry Is. — Devon I. — Ellesmere I. — *Baffin Bay* — GREENLAND (KALAALLIT NUNAAT) *(Denmark)*

ALASKA *(U.S.A.)* — *Bering Strait* — Anchorage — Fairbanks — *Gulf of Alaska* — Kodiak I. — *Great Bear L.* — Yellowknife — *Great Slave L.* — Victoria I. — Banks I. — Mackenzie — Baffin I. — *Davis Strait* — Iqaluit — Nuuk — Reykjavik ICELAND — *Denmark Strait* — Jan Mayen *(Norway)* — *Norwegian Sea*

C A N A D A — Edmonton — Calgary — Winnipeg — *L. Winnipeg* — Nelson — Churchill — *Hudson Bay* — Newfoundland — St. John's — Halifax — Faroe Is. *(Den.)*

UNITED KINGDOM — Glasgow — Dublin — IRELAND — LONDON — Amsterdam — NETH. — Brussels — PARIS — FRANCE — *North Sea* — DENMARK — Hamburg — GER.

Queen Charlotte Is. — Vancouver — Vancouver I. — Seattle — Portland — Minneapolis-St. Paul — Milwaukee — CHICAGO — Detroit — Cleveland — Ottawa — Toronto — Montréal — Québec — Boston — NEW YORK — PHILADELPHIA — Pittsburgh — Baltimore — Washington D.C.

UNITED STATES — Sacramento — SAN FRANCISCO — Salt Lake City — Denver — Kansas City — St. Louis — Cincinnati — St. Petersburg — Bordeaux — Lyons — Milan — Marseilles — Madrid — Barcelona — PORTUGAL — SPAIN — Lisbon — *Mediterranean*

LOS ANGELES — San Diego — Las Vegas — Phoenix — El Paso — Dallas-Ft. Worth — Memphis — Atlanta — Jacksonville — Orlando — Tampa-St. Petersburg — New Orleans — Houston — San Antonio — Monterrey — Guadalupe *(Mex.)* — Ciudad Juárez — *Rio Grande*

Tropic of Cancer — Honolulu — HAWAII *(U.S.A.)* — Oahu — Hawai'i — Guadalajara — León — MEXICO — Puebla — *Gulf of Mexico* — Havana — CUBA — Nassau — BAHAMAS — Miami — Turks & Caicos Is. — Bermuda *(U.K.)* — Azores *(Port.)* — Madeira *(Port.)* — Tangier — Rabat — Casablanca — Marrakesh — MOROCCO — Algiers — Tunis

P A C I F I C — Revilla Gigedo Is. *(Mex.)* — MEXICO — Canary Is. *(Sp.)* — WESTERN SAHARA — El Aaiun — ALGERIA

MEXICO — GUATEMALA — BELIZE — Belmopan — Guatemala — HONDURAS — Tegucigalpa — San Salvador — EL SALVADOR — NICARAGUA — Managua — Cayman Is. *(U.K.)* — JAMAICA — Kingston — HAITI — Port-au-Prince — DOMINICAN REP. — Santo Domingo — PUERTO RICO *(U.S.A.)* — Virgin Is.*(U.S.A.-U.K.)* — ANTIGUA & BARBUDA — ST. KITTS-NEVIS — GUADELOUPE *(Fr.)* — DOMINICA — MARTINIQUE *(Fr.)* — ST. LUCIA — CAPE VERDE IS. — Praia — Nouakchott — MAURITANIA — MALI — Tombouctou — NIGER

O C E A N — *Caribbean Sea* — Barranquilla — San José — COSTA RICA — PANAMA — Panamá — NETH. ANTILLES — ST. VINCENT — BARBADOS — GRENADA — TRINIDAD & TOBAGO — Caracas — Georgetown — Paramaribo — Cayenne — Dakar — SENEGAL — GAMBIA — GUINEA-BISSAU — Bamako — Ouagadougou — Niamey — Conakry — GUINEA — BURKINA FASO — Freetown — SIERRA LEONE — Yamoussoukro — IVORY COAST — GHANA — Monrovia — LIBERIA — Abidjan — Accra — Ibadan — Lagos — NIGERIA — Abuja

Clipperton I. *(Fr.)* — Medellín — Bogotá — COLOMBIA — Cali — VENEZUELA — GUYANA — SURINAME — FRENCH GUIANA — *Orinoco* — *Gulf of Guinea* — EQUATORIAL GUINEA — SÃO TOMÉ & PRINCIPE — GABON

Palmyra Is. *(U.S.A.)* — Kiritimati — Galápagos *(Ecuador)* — Quito — ECUADOR — Guayaquil — *Japurá* — *Negro* — *Amazon* — Belém — Manaus — *Madeira* — Ascension I. *(U.K.)*

Equator — Jarvis I. *(U.S.A.)* — KIRIBATI — Starbuck I.

AMER. SAMOA *(U.S.A.)* — Penrhyn Is. — Manihiki — Marquesas Is. — PERU — Callao — LIMA — B R A Z I L — Recife — Natal — Fortaleza — Fernando de Noronha *(Brazil)*

Tropic of Capricorn — Tahiti — Society Is. — Niue *(N.Z.)* — Cook Is. *(N.Z.)* — Tubuai Is. — F R E N C H — *Tuamotu Is.* — POLYNESIA — Rapa — Easter I. *(Chile)* — Pitcairn I. *(U.K.)* — Ducie I. — Sala-y-Gómez *(Chile)* — BOLIVIA — Sucre — La Paz — Arequipa — *L. Titicaca* — Brasília — Belo Horizonte — *São Francisco* — Salvador — St. Helena *(U.K.)*

PARAGUAY — Asunción — Antofagasta — San Miguel de Tucumán — Curitiba — SÃO PAULO — RIO DE JANEIRO — Trindade *(Brazil)*

P O L Y N E S I A — San Felix *(Chile)* — San Ambrosio *(Chile)* — Córdoba — *Paraná* — URUGUAY — Pôrto Alegre — Rio Grande — Tristan da Cunha *(U.K.)*

SANTIAGO — Valparaíso — Rosario — BUENOS AIRES — Montevideo — Bahía Blanca — CHILE — ARGENTINA — *Uruguay*

Talcahuano — Chiloé I. — Falkland Is. *(U.K.)* — South Georgia *(U.K.)* — South Sandwich Is. *(U.K.)*

Punta Arenas — Tierra del Fuego — C. Horn — *Drake Passage* — South Shetland Is. — South Orkney Is. — *Scotia Sea* — Bouvet I. *(Norway)*

Antarctic Circle — *Amundsen Sea* — *Bellingshausen Sea* — *Weddell Sea*

A n t a r c t i c a

N O R T H A T L A N T I C O C E A N

S O U T H A T L A N T I C O C E A N

Projection: Winkel III

10 11 12 13 14 15 16 17 18

20 40 60 80 100 120 140 160 180

Franz Josef Land (Russia)

Severnaya Zemlya

ARCTIC OCEAN

Svalbard (Norway)

Barents Sea

Novaya Zemlya

Kara Sea

Laptev Sea

New Siberian Is.

East Siberian Sea

Wrangel I.

A

Arctic Circle

St. Lawrence I. (U.S.A.)

Murmansk

Arkhangelsk

Norilsk

Lena

Verkhoyansk

Magadan

Bering Sea

B

Yenisey

Yakutsk

Okhotsk

Petropavlovsk-Kamchatskiy

Aleutian Is. (U.S.A.)

ST. PETERSBURG

Helsinki

Salekhard

Ob

R U S S I A

Sea of Okhotsk

Komsomolsk

Sakhalin

Oslo

SWEDEN FINLAND

Stockholm

Copenhagen ESTONIA

LATVIA

MOSCOW

Volga

Perm

Yekaterinburg

Tomsk

Krasnoyarsk

L. Baikal

Irkutsk

Ulan Ude

Amur

Khabarovsk

Vladivostok

Sapporo

Kuril Is. (Russia)

POLAND BELARUS

Minsk

Kazan

Omsk

Novosibirsk

Barnaul

Ulan Bator

Harbin

Changchun

SHENYANG

Kitakyūshū

Osaka

TŌKYŌ

C

PACIFIC

Berlin Warsaw

Prague Kiev

Saratov

Chelyabinsk

Astana

MONGOLIA

NORTH KOREA

Pyongyang

SEOUL

SOUTH KOREA

JAPAN

Vienna HUNGARY

Budapest

UKRAINE

Volgograd

Astrakhan

KAZAKHSTAN

Almaty

Ürümqi

BEIJING TIANJIN

Dalian

Midway Is. (U.S.A.)

ROMANIA

Odessa

Black Sea

Aral Sea

L. Balkhash

Bishkek

Taiyuan

Lanzhou

Xi'an

Hwang Ho

Nanjing

SHANGHAI

Bonin Is. (Japan)

Belgrade Bucharest

GEORGIA

Tbilisi

Caspian Sea

Baku

UZBEKISTAN

KYRGYZSTAN

Samarkand

SINKIANG

C H I N A

Chengdu

CHONGQING

Wuhan

Yangtze

East China's Sea

Volcano Is. (Japan)

Tropic of Cancer

Sofia BULGARIA

İSTANBUL

Ankara

Yerevan

TURKMENISTAN

Ashkhabad

TAJIKISTAN

Dushanbe

TIBET

Lhasa

Kunming

Fuzhou

Taipei

Ryukyu Is.

İzmir

T U R K E Y

AZER.

TEHRĀN

Mashhad

Kābul

Islamabad

JAMMU

KASHMIR

GUANGZHOU

TAIWAN

20

CYPRUS

Beirut

SYRIA

IRAQ

Baghdad

Eşfahān

AFGHANISTAN

Lahore

NEPAL

DELHI

BHUTAN

Thimphu

BANGLADESH

Hwang

HONG KONG

Hainan

NORTHERN MARIANAS (U.S.A.)

OCEAN

Tripoli

Crete

Athens GREECE

ISRAEL

Jerusalem

Damascus

Amman

JORDAN

I R A N

Shīrāz

Tabriz

PAKISTAN

New Delhi

Kanpur

Katmandu

KOLKATA (Calcutta)

DHAKA

Nagpur

BURMA (MYANMAR)

Naypyidaw

Hanoi

Benghazi

Alexandria

CAIRO

KUWAIT

Kuwait

BAHRAIN

QATAR

Doha

Abu Dhabi

UNITED ARAB EMIRATES

Muscat

Ahmadabad

MUMBAI (Bombay)

I N D I A

Hyderabad

Rangoon

Vientiane

THAILAND

BANGKOK

VIETNAM

CAMBODIA

MANILA

PHILIPPINES

Yap

Caroline Is.

Truk Pohnpei

FED. STATES OF MICRONESIA

MARSHALL IS.

D

LIBYA

EGYPT

Aswan

SAUDI

Riyadh

Mecca

Red Sea

OMAN

Bay of Bengal

Bangalore (Bengaluru)

CHENNAI (Madras)

Andaman Is. (India)

Phnom Penh

Ho Chi Minh City

South China Sea

PALAU

SUDAN

Omdurmán

Khartoum

Blue Nile

ARABIA

YEMEN

Sana'

Socotra (Yemen)

Lakshadweep Is. (India)

Nicobar Is. (India)

CHAD

L. Chad

Ndjamena

ERITREA

Asmera

Aden

Gulf of Aden

DJIBOUTI

Addis Ababa

SRI LANKA

Colombo

MALDIVES

MALAYSIA

Kuala Lumpur

SABAH

Bandar Seri Begawan

BRUNEI

SARAWAK

Equator

KIRIBATI

CENTRAL AFRICAN REP.

Bangui

ETHIOPIA

SOMALI REP.

Mogadishu

Medan

Kuala Lumpur

SINGAPORE

Palembang

Banjarmasin

Borneo

Celebes

Papua

New Ireland

NAURU

New Britain

Phoenix Is.

CAMEROON

Yaoundé

GABON

CONGO

Congo

UGANDA

Kampala

KENYA

Nairobi

L. Turkana

Amirante Is. (Seychelles)

Chagos Arch. (U.K.)

JAKARTA

Bandung

Java

I N D O N E S I A

Surabaya

Ujung Pandang

Dili

EAST TIMOR

Arafura Sea

PAPUA NEW GUINEA

Honiara

SOLOMON IS.

TUVALU

Tokelau Is. (N.Z.)

SAMOA

E

CONGO (DEM. REP. OF THE)

Kinshasa

Kananga

RWANDA

Kigali

BURUNDI

Bujumbura

TANZANIA

Dodoma

L. Victoria

Mombasa

Zanzibar

Dar es Salaam

SEYCHELLES

Aldabra Is. (Seychelles)

Agalega Is. (Mauritius)

Cocos Is. (Austral.)

Christmas I. (Austral.)

C. York

Darwin

Port Moresby

Santa Cruz Is.

Wallis & Futuna Is. (Fr.)

ANGOLA

Luanda

Lubumbashi

L. Malawi

L. Tanganyika

COMOROS

Mayotte (Fr.)

MADAGASCAR

Cairns

Townsville

VANUATU

Port Vila

NEW CALEDONIA (Fr.)

FIJI

Suva

TONGA

Benguela

ZAMBIA

Lusaka

MALAWI

Lilongwe

Antananarivo

MAURITIUS

Rodriguez (Mauritius)

Cargados Carajos (Mauritius)

Alice Springs

Rockhampton

Norfolk I. (Austral.)

Tropic of Capricorn

NAMIBIA

ZIMBABWE

Harare

Bulawayo

MOZAMBIQUE

Mozambique Channel

RÉUNION (Fr.)

Geraldton

AUSTRALIA

Kalgoorlie-Boulder

Brisbane

Lord Howe I. (Austral.)

Kermadec Is. (N.Z.)

F

Windhoek

BOTSWANA

Gaborone

Pretoria

Maputo

SWAZ.

Johannesburg

LES.

Durban (eThekwini)

INDIAN OCEAN

Perth

Fremantle

Great Australian Bight

Darling

Adelaide

Newcastle

Sydney

Canberra

Melbourne

Tasman Sea

Auckland

North I.

Cape Town

C. of Good Hope

SOUTH AFRICA

Port Elizabeth

Amsterdam I. (Fr.)

St. Paul I. (Fr.)

Crozet Is. (Fr.)

Tasmania

Hobart

NEW ZEALAND

Wellington

40

Prince Edward Is. (S. Africa)

Kerguelen (Fr.)

South I.

Christchurch

Chatham Is. (N.Z.)

G

McDonald Is. (Austral.)

Heard I. (Austral.)

Dunedin

Bounty Is. (N.Z.)

Antipodes Is. (N.Z.)

Auckland Is. (N.Z.)

SOUTHERN OCEAN

Macquarie Is. (Austral.)

Campbell I. (N.Z.)

Antarctic Circle

H

Ross Sea

rctica

80

180

0 / 0

600 / 200

6 000 / 2000

12 000 / 4000

15 000 / 5000

18 000 / 6000

24 000 / 8000

ft / m

60

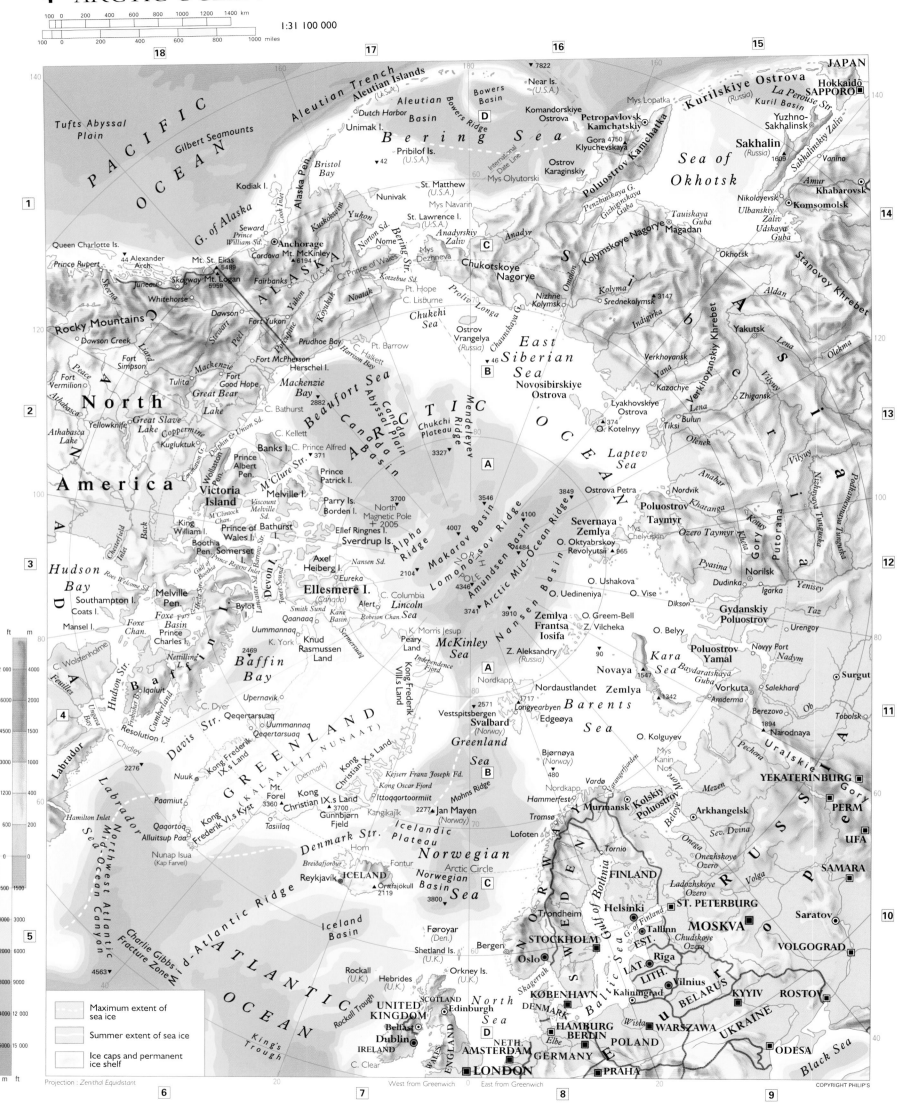

1:31 100 000

100 0 200 400 600 800 1000 1200 1400 km

100 0 200 400 600 800 1000 miles

Projection : Zenithal Equidistant

Maximum extent of sea ice

Summer extent of sea ice

Ice caps and permanent ice shelf

COPYRIGHT PHILIP'S

ANTARCTICA 5

1:31 100 000

Scale: 100 0 200 400 600 800 1000 1200 1400 km
100 0 200 400 600 800 1000 miles

West from Greenwich | East from Greenwich

Oceans and Seas

ATLANTIC OCEAN
SOUTHERN OCEAN
PACIFIC OCEAN
INDIAN OCEAN
Weddell Sea
Ross Sea
Bellingshausen Sea
Amundsen Sea
Scotia Sea
Lazarev Sea
Riiser-Larsen Sea
Cosmonaut Sea
Davis Sea
Dumont D'Urville Sea
Tasman Sea
Drake Passage

Selected labels

South Sandwich Trench 8325
Georgia Basin
South Georgia
Bird I. (U.K.)
Leskov I.
Zavodovski I.
Visokoi I.
Candlemas I.
Saunders I.
Montagu I.
Bristol I.
South Sandwich Is. (U.K.)
America-Antarctic Ridge
Atlantic-Indian Ridge
Prince Edward Fracture Zone
Conrad Rise 6739
Maud Rise
Enderby Abyssal Plain
Atlantic-Indian Basin

Bases on King George Island:
Jubany (Argentina)
Com. Ferraz (Brazil)
Ten. Rodolfo Marsh (Chile)
Great Wall (China)
King Sejong (Korea)
Arctowski (Poland)
Artigas (Uruguay)
Bellingshausen (Russia)

Stanley
Falkland Is. (U.K.)
Orcadas (Arg.) 5552
Signy I. (U.K.)
Coronation I.
South Orkney Is.
Antarctic Circle
Weddell Abyssal Plain

ARGENTINA
Shackleton Fracture Zone
Elephant I.
Clarence I.
King George I.
Joinville I.
South Shetland Is.
Esperanza (Arg.)
Marambio (Arg.)
James Ross I.
Robertson I.
Gen. Bernardo O'Higgins (Chile)
Capt. Arturo Prat (Chile)
Deception I.
Brunsfield Str.
Tierra del Fuego
Estr. de Le Maire
Ushuaia
C. de Hornos (C. Horn)
I. Hoste
CHILE
Graham Land
Palmer Arch.
Palmer (U.S.A.)
Anvers I.
Vernadsky (U.K.)
Larsen Ice Shelf
Antarctic Pen.
Palmer Land
Biscoe Is.
Adelaide I.
Rothera (U.K.)
San Martin (Arg.)
Dyer Plateau
George VI Sound 4191
Alexander I.
Charcot I.
C. Byrd
2987
2896
3658 975
Ronne Ice Shelf
Berkner I.
Filchner Ice Shelf
Vahsel Bay

Maitri (India)
Sanae IV (S.Afr.)
Neumayer (Germany)
Novolazarevskaya (Russia)
Syowa (Japan)
Molodezhnaya (Russia)
Fimbul Ice Shelf
Prinsesse Martha Kyst
Prinsesse Astrid Kyst
Prinsesse Ragnhild Kyst
Prins Harald Kyst
Kronprins Olav Kyst
Lützow Holmbukta
Mühlig Hofmann fjell
Sør-Rondane 3630
Dronning Maud Land
Riiser-Larsen Ice Shelf
Caird Coast
Coats Land
Lyddan I.
Brunt Ice Shelf
Halley (U.K.)
Belgrano (Arg.)
Luitpold Coast
Riiser-Larsen-halvøya
Kronprinsesse Martha Kyst
2717
3212 3039
2311 1431
3318 2990
3556 2600
Dome Fuji (Japan)
Enderby Land
C. Borley
Kemp Land
Stefansson Bay
Mawson (Austr.)
Valdivia Abyssal Plain
C. Darnley
MacRobertson Land 2645
Prince Charles Mts 3355
Lambert Glacier
Amery Ice Shelf
Amery Basin
Prydz Bay
Zhongshan (China)
Davis (Austr.)
Ingrid Christensen Coast
Mawson Coast
Progress (Russia)
West Ice Shelf
Princess Elizabeth Trough
Wilhelm II Coast
1800

Dome Argus 4030 1040
American Highland
East Antarctica
SOUTH POLE
Amundsen-Scott (U.S.A.) 2773 2407
Queen Mary Land 3030
Mirnyy (Russia)
Drygalski I.
Davis Sea
Masson I.
Shackleton Ice Shelf
Vostok (Russia) 3488 3700
Dome C
Concordia (France/Italy) 2407 3087
Mill I.
Bowman I.
Queen Maud Mts
Horlick Mts 3810
Beardmore Glacier
Queen Alexandra Range
Mt. Markham 4349
2801
Knox Coast
Scott Glacier
Denman Glacier
Budd Coast
Vincennes B.
Casey (Austr.)
Sabrina Coast
Totten Glacier
C. Poinsett
Wilkes Land
Banzare Coast
Paulding Bay
Porpoise Bay
Clarie Coast
4650
Australian-Antarctic Basin

West Antarctica
Ellsworth Land
Marie Byrd Land
Ellsworth Mts
Vinson Massif 4897
Thiel Mts 3657
Patriot Hills (Chile)
Siple (U.S.A.)
Pensacola Mts
Transantarctic Mts
Bentley Subglacial Trench
Hudson Mts
Thurston I. 1036
C. Flying Fish
Peter I Øy
Abbot Ice Shelf
2677 4335
3022
1797
4176
4528
Kohler Ra.
Mt. Sidley 4181
Rockefeller Plateau
Getz Ice Shelf
Hobbs Coast 3496
Edward VII Land
Bakutis Coast
Walgreen Coast
Amundsen Ridges
Amundsen Abyssal Plain
Bellingshausen Abyssal Plain

Ross Ice Shelf
Roosevelt I.
Sulzberger Ice Shelf
Bay of Whales
C. Colbeck
Ross Dep.
Ross I.
Mt. Erebus 3743
McMurdo (U.S.A.)
Scott (N.Z.)
Mt. Lister 4023
McMurdo Sd.
Franklin I.
Drygalski Ice Tongue
David Glacier
Mt. Murchison
Prince Albert Mts
Victoria Land
Coulman I. 3502
Possession I. 4163
Renwick Glacier
George V Land
Terre Adélie
Dumont d'Urville (Fr.)
Commonwealth Bay
South Magnetic Pole 2005
C. Adare
C. Freshfield
C. Hudson
Oates Land
2216 2798
2436 4776
Shackleton Inlet
Dome Concordia

Pacific-Antarctic Ridge
Antarctic Circle
Scott I.
Balleny Is.
Southeast Pacific Basin
Southeast Indian Ridge
Hjort Trench 6800
Macquarie Ridge
Macquarie Is. (Austr.)
Tharp Fracture Zone
Udintsev Fracture Zone
Eltanin Fracture Zone System
International Date Line
6240
Southwest Pacific Basin
Campbell I. (N.Z.)
Auckland Is. (N.Z.)
South Tasman Rise
Tasman Sea
Hobart
Launceston
Tasmania
Bass Str.
MELBOURNE
AUSTRALIA
Antipodes Is.
Bounty Is. (N.Z.)
Stewart I.
Campbell Plateau
Invercargill
Dunedin
NEW ZEALAND

Projection: Zenithal Equidistant

COPYRIGHT PHILIP'S

Legend

- Ice cap
- Permanent ice shelf
- Maximum extent of sea ice
- March (Summer) extent of sea ice
- ▲ 3488 / 3700 — Surface elevation and depth of ice (in metres)
- • Stanley (U.K.) — Permanent bases

Elevation scale:
ft | m
12 000 | 4000
| 2000
6000 | 2000
| 1500
4500 |
3000 | 1000
1200 | 400
600 | 200
0 | 0
500 | 1500
1000 | 3000
2000 | 6000
3000 | 9000
4000 | 12 000
5000 | 15 000
m | ft

Notes

The Antarctic Treaty was signed in Washington in 1959 so that scientific and technical research could continue unhampered by international politics.

All territorial claims covering land areas south of latitude 60°S have been suspended. Those claims were:

Norwegian claim (Dronning Maud Land)	45°E - 20°W
Australian claims	45°E - 136°E / 142°E - 160°E
French claim (Terre Adélie)	136°E - 142°E
New Zealand claim (Ross Dependency)	160°E - 150°W
British claim	80°W - 20°W
Argentine claim	74°W - 53°W
Chilean claim	90°W - 53°W

6 EUROPE : Physical

100 0 100 200 300 400 500 600 700 800 km

1:17 800 000

100 0 100 200 300 400 500 miles

ROCKALL Sea areas named in weather forecasts

ATLANTIC OCEAN

Norwegian Sea

Iceland

British Isles

Ireland

Great Britain

North Sea

Scandinavia

Lapland

Finland

Russia

Ural Mountains

West Siberian Lowlands

Central Russian Uplands

Ukraine

Black Sea

Caucasus

Transcaucasia

Anatolia (Asia Minor)

Kurdistan

Armenia

Mesopotamia

Caspian Sea

Caspian Depression

Kirgiziya Steppe

Volga Hts.

Carpathians

Balkans

Plain of Hungary

Wallachia

Rhodope

Pindus

Dinaric Alps

Adriatic Sea

Apennines

Ionian Sea

Tyrrhenian Sea

Ligurian Sea

Alps

Pyrenees

Iberian Peninsula

Sierra Nevada

Andalusia

Mediterranean Sea

Africa

Plateau of the Shotts

Bay of Biscay

English Channel

Brittany

Massif Central

Celtic Sea

Projection Bonne   West from Greenwich 0 East from Greenwich

ft 15 000 12 000 6000 3000 1200 600 200 0 200 600 1000 3000 6000 12 000 m
    5000 4000 2000 1000 400 200 0 1000 2000 4000

1:17 800 000

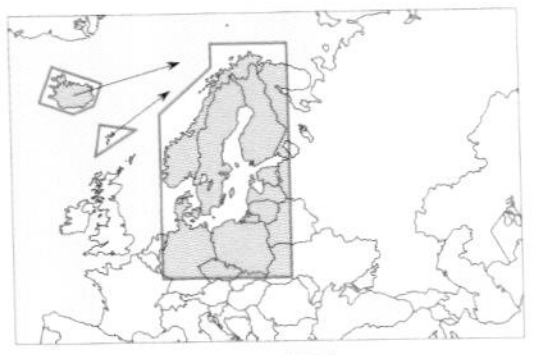

BARENTS SEA

RUSSIA

KARELIA

FINLAND

Lapland

NORWAY

SWEDEN

ATLANTIC OCEAN

NORWEGIAN SEA

Gulf of Bothnia

ICELAND
on same scale

FÆROE ISLANDS
on same scale

Føroyar (Faeroe Is.) (Den.)

Murmansk
Oulu
Tornio
Kemi
Rovaniemi
Luleå
Kiruna
Narvik
Tromsø
Trondheim
Östersund
Sundsvall
Bodø
Reykjavik

| 50 | | 0 | 25 | 50 | 75 | 100 | 125 | 150 | 175 km |

| 50 | | 0 | 25 | 50 | 75 | 100 | 125 miles |

1:5 300 000

1:1 800 000

10 0 10 20 30 40 50 60 70 80 km
10 0 10 20 30 40 50 miles

A T L A N T I C   O C E A N

NORTHERN IRELAND

Londonderry · LONDONDERRY · ANTRIM · Belfast · DOWN · ARMAGH · TYRONE · FERMANAGH · Ulster · DONEGAL

Sligo · SLIGO · LEITRIM · MAYO · ROSCOMMON · CAVAN · MONAGHAN · LONGFORD · Connacht · GALWAY · Galway · WESTMEATH · MEATH · LOUTH

IRELAND · Leinster

Dublin · DUB · Dun Laoghaire · KILDARE · OFFALY · LAOIS · WICKLOW · CARLOW

CLARE · Limerick · LIMERICK · TIPPERARY · KILKENNY · WEXFORD

Munster · KERRY · Cork · CORK · WATERFORD · Waterford

Macgillycuddy's Reeks · Carrauntoohil · 1041

Mouth of the Shannon · Golden Vale · Galty Mts. · Knockmealdown Mts. · Comeragh Mts.

Wicklow Mts. · Lugnaquilla 926

Aran Is. · Galway Bay · Cliffs of Moher · BURREN · Shannon · Lough Derg · Lough Ree · Lough Corrib · Lough Mask

North Channel · Firth of Clyde · Arran · Kintyre · Campbeltown

I R I S H   S E A

St. George's Channel · St. Brides Bay · St. David's Hd.

C E L T I C   S E A

ft m

Projection : Lambert's Conformal Conic · West from Greenwich · COPYRIGHT PHILIP'S

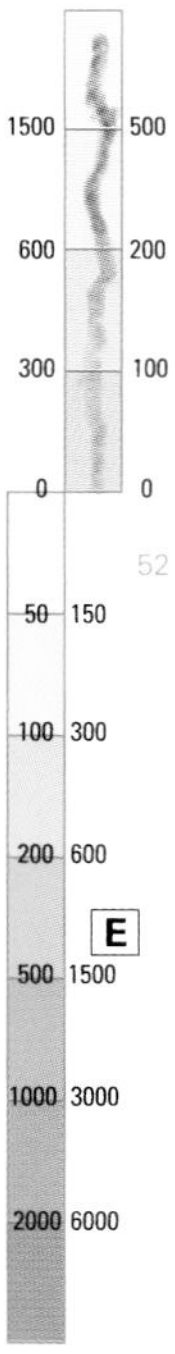

National Parks

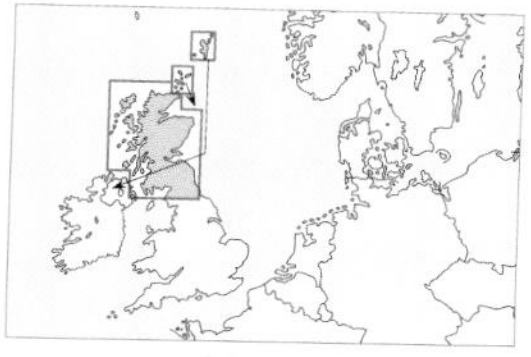

SCOTLAND 13

1:1 800 000

Key to Scottish unitary authorities on map

1 CITY OF ABERDEEN
2 DUNDEE CITY
3 WEST DUNBARTONSHIRE
4 EAST DUNBARTONSHIRE
5 CITY OF GLASGOW
6 INVERCLYDE
7 RENFREWSHIRE
8 EAST RENFREWSHIRE
9 NORTH LANARKSHIRE
10 FALKIRK
11 CLACKMANNANSHIRE
12 WEST LOTHIAN
13 CITY OF EDINBURGH
14 MIDLOTHIAN

ORKNEY IS. on same scale

SHETLAND IS. on same scale

ATLANTIC OCEAN

NORTH SEA

WESTERN ISLES

HEBRIDES

SCOTLAND

HIGHLAND

Grampian Mountains

Cairngorm Mts.

ABERDEENSHIRE

MORAY

Inverness

Aberdeen

Dundee

Perth

Stirling

Glasgow

Edinburgh

ARGYLL AND BUTE

DUMFRIES & GALLOWAY

SCOTTISH BORDERS

ENGLAND

NORTHERN IRELAND

Belfast

North Channel

Projection: Lambert's Conformal Conic

COPYRIGHT PHILIP'S

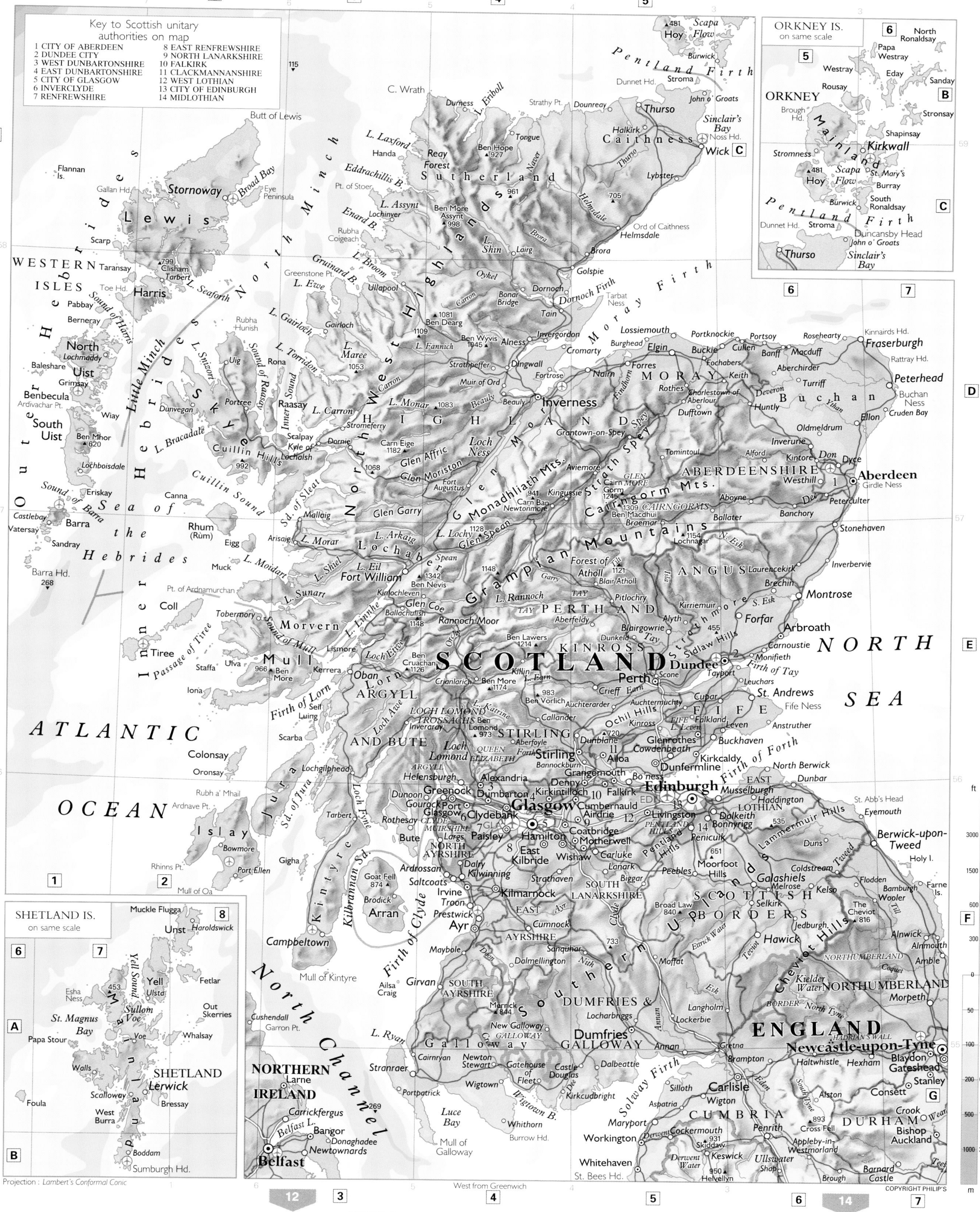

National Parks and Forest Parks in Scotland

1:1 800 000

Key to English unitary authorities on map

25 HARTLEPOOL
26 DARLINGTON
27 STOCKTON-ON-TEES
28 MIDDLESBROUGH
29 REDCAR AND CLEVELAND
30 BLACKPOOL
31 BLACKBURN WITH DARWEN
32 HALTON
33 WARRINGTON
34 KINGSTON UPON HULL
35 NORTH EAST LINCOLNSHIRE
36 STOKE-ON-TRENT
37 TELFORD AND WREKIN
38 DERBY CITY
39 CITY OF NOTTINGHAM
40 LEICESTER CITY
41 RUTLAND
42 PETERBOROUGH
43 MILTON KEYNES
44 LUTON
45 NORTH SOMERSET
46 CITY OF BRISTOL
47 BATH AND NORTH EAST SOMERSET
48 SWINDON
49 READING
50 WOKINGHAM
51 WINDSOR AND MAIDENHEAD
52 SLOUGH
53 BRACKNELL FOREST
54 THURROCK
55 SOUTHEND-ON-SEA
56 MEDWAY
57 PLYMOUTH
58 TORBAY
59 POOLE
60 BOURNEMOUTH
61 SOUTHAMPTON
62 PORTSMOUTH
63 BRIGHTON AND HOVE

Key to Welsh unitary authorities on map

15 SWANSEA
16 NEATH PORT TALBOT
17 BRIDGEND
18 RHONDDA CYNON TAFF
19 MERTHYR TYDFIL
20 CAERPHILLY
21 BLAENAU GWENT
22 TORFAEN
23 CARDIFF
24 NEWPORT

NORTH SEA

IRISH SEA

North Channel

NORTHERN IRELAND

SCOTLAND

ISLE OF MAN

Edinburgh · Glasgow · Newcastle-upon-Tyne · Sunderland · Middlesbrough · Hartlepool · Kingston upon Hull · York · Leeds · Bradford · Sheffield · Manchester · Liverpool · Chester · Stoke-on-Trent · Derby · Nottingham · Lincoln · Preston · Blackpool · Carlisle · Belfast

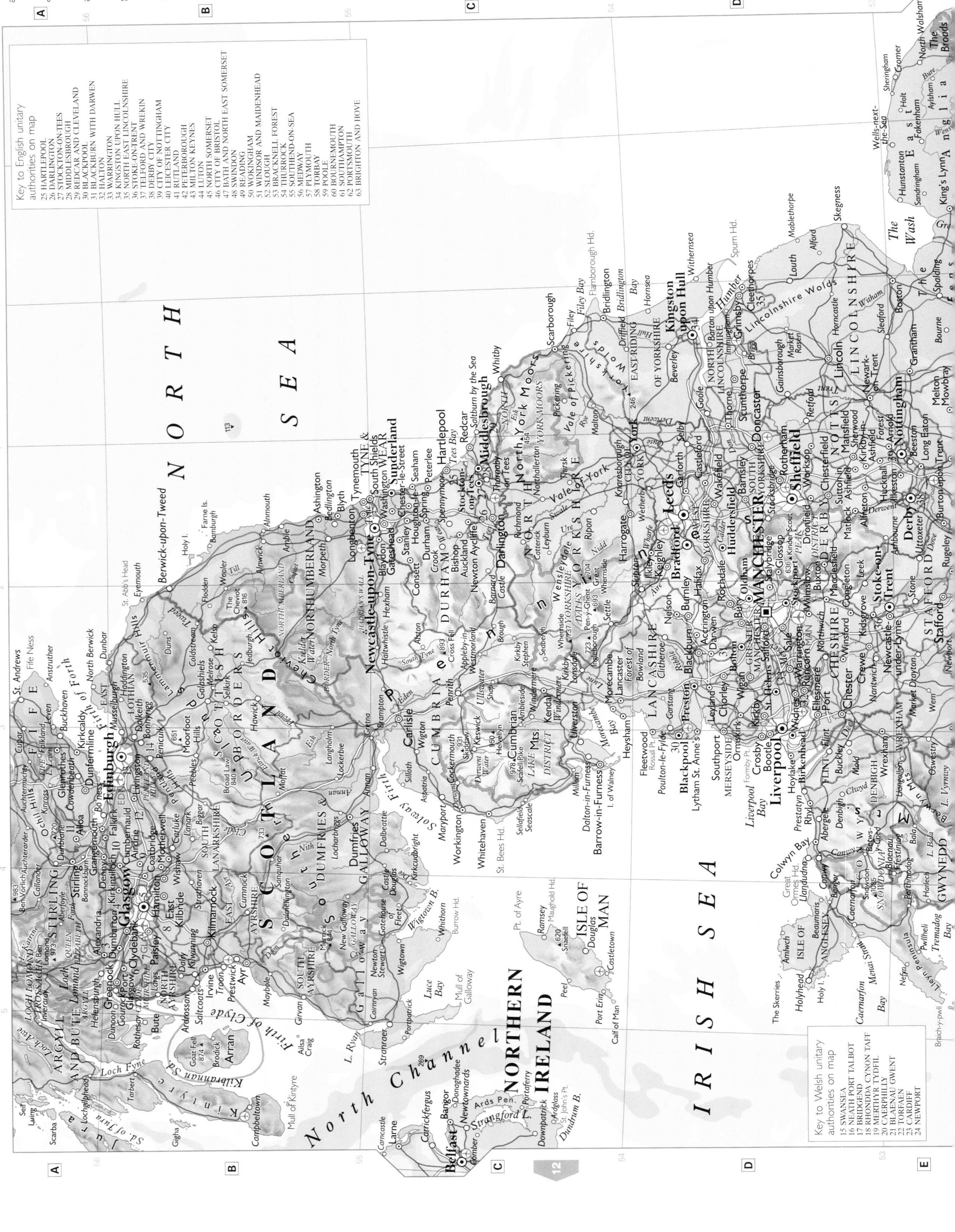

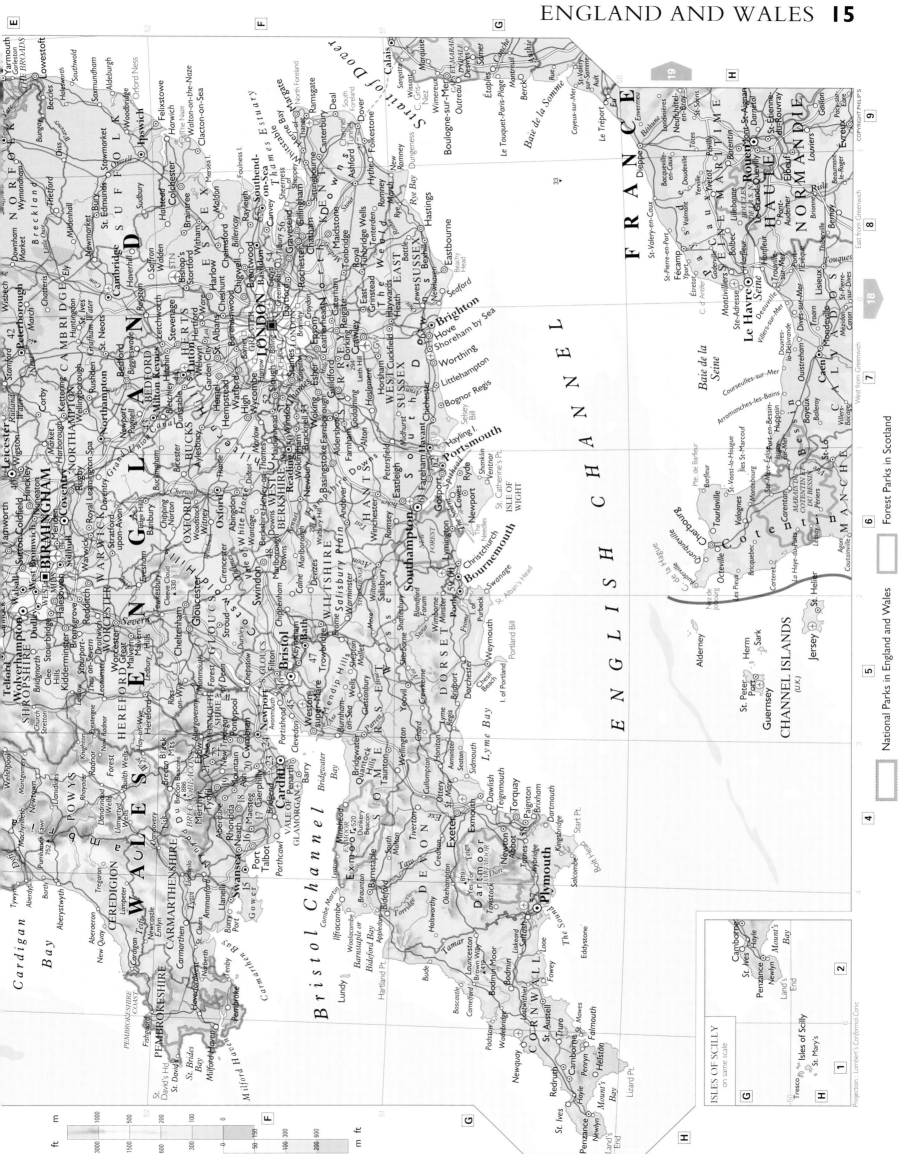

50 0 25 50 75 100 125 150 175 km
1:4 400 000
50 0 25 50 75 100 125 miles

1 2 3 4 5 6 7 8 9

ft m
3000 1000
1500 500
600 200
0 0
50 150
100 300
200 600
500 1500
1000 3000
2000 6000
m ft

Projection: Conical with two standard parallels

A T L A N T I C   O C E A N

N O R T H   S E A

C E L T I C   S E A

I R I S H   S E A

English Channel

Str. of Dover

316
1224

Shetland Is.
Yell Unst
Fetlar
Foula Mainland
Lerwick
Fair Isle

Orkney Is.
Westray Sanday
Mainland Stronsay
Kirkwall
Hoy South
Ronaldsay
C. Wrath
Pentland Firth
Thurso Wick
Helmsdale

Lewis Stornoway
North Minch
St. Kilda 789
Harris
North Uist Ullapool Lairg Golspie
Benbecula Tain Moray Firth
Portree Invergordon Buckie Banff
South Uist Dingwall Nairn Elgin Fraserburgh
Skye 1182 Inverness Spey Peterhead
Barra Mallaig Glen More Huntly Inverurie
Rhum Aviemore CAIRNGORMS Don Aberdeen
Eigg Fort William 1311 Dee Ballater Stonehaven
1342 SCOTLAND
Coll 1214 Grampian Mts.
Tiree Forfar Montrose
Mull L. LOMOND Tay Arbroath
Oban & TROSSACHS Perth Dundee
Colonsay L. Awe 973 Stirling St. Andrews
Jura L. Fyne L. Lomond Glenrothes
Islay Dumbarton Dunfermline Kirkcaldy Dunbar
Greenock Glasgow Edinburgh
Paisley Motherwell Berwick-upon-Tweed
Campbeltown East Kilbride Hamilton Galashiels
Arran Irvine 840 Jedburgh 816
Southern Uplands Cheviot Hills Alnwick
Kilmarnock Hawick NORTHUMBERLAND
Ayr Dumfries 893
Girvan Dumfries Hexham Newcastle-upon-Tyne
North Channel Kirkcudbright Annan South Shields
Malin Hd. Stranraer Carlisle Gateshead Sunderland
Buncrana Workington Penrith Durham Hartlepool
Letterkenny Coleraine Mull of Cumbrian Darlington Redcar
GLENVEAGH Ballymena Galloway Whitehaven Mts. Stockton- Middlesbrough
Donegal Londonderry Larne 978 on-Tees N. YORK MOORS
Lifford Antrim Bangor LAKE Scarborough
NORTHERN IRELAND Belfast DISTRICT Barrow- YORKSHIRE
Bundoran Omagh Lough Lisburn Douglas in-Furness Lancaster DALES Bridlington
Ballina ULSTER Neagh Lurgan I. of Man Harrogate
L. Corn Enniskillen Armagh Pennines Kingston upon Hull
Lower L. Portadown Newry Leeds York Beverley
Castlebar Erne Clones Castleblayney Blackpool Bradford Humber
Sligo Leitrim Cavan Dundalk Preston Burnley Huddersfield Scunthorpe Grimsby
Westport Roscommon Ceanannus Mor Drogheda Blackburn Halifax Barnsley Doncaster
Lough Longford Boyne Bolton Rotherham Lincoln
Mask Connemara Lough Athlone Mullingar 636 Stockport Sheffield Louth
Galway B. Corrib Ree Anglesey MANCHESTER Chesterfield Skegness
Aran Is. Ballinasloe Liffey Liverpool Warrington PEAK Mansfield The Wash
BURREN Lough Tullamore Dublin Holyhead Crewe DISTRICT Cromer
Ennis Derg Athy Dun Laoghaire Bangor Chester Stoke Derby Nottingham Grantham King's Lynn
Kilrush Nenagh Carlow Bray Colwyn Bay Wrexham on Trent Trent THE
Shannon Limerick Thurles Kilkenny Wicklow Mts. Snowdon Stafford Leicester Peterborough BROADS
953 Listowel Tipperary 926 Arklow 1085 Cambrian Mts. Shrewsbury Telford Nuneaton Norwich Great Yarmouth
Dingle Tralee Clonmel Carrick-on-Suir Wexford SNOWDONIA Welshpool ENGLAND Corby Lowestoft
Carrauntoohill Mallow Waterford Rosslare Cardigan Wolverhampton Coventry Ely Bury St. Edmunds
1041 Killarney Dungarvan Bay Aberystwyth BIRMINGHAM Rugby Northampton Cambridge Ipswich
Macgillycuddy's Reeks Blackwater Redditch Royal Milton Keynes Felixstowe
Valencia I. Bandon Youghal WALES Worcester Leamington Spa Bedford Harwich
Bantry Cork Brecon 886 Hereford Cheltenham Luton Harlow Colchester
99 Cóbh St. George's Channel Carmarthen BRECON Gloucester Oxford Hemel Chelmsford
C. Clear Kinsale Fishguard Merthyr Tydfil BEACONS Cwmbran Cirencester Hempstead Southend-on-Sea
Haverfordwest Neath Cotswold Hills Swindon High Wycombe Watford LONDON
Milford Haven Llanelli Newport Newbury Slough Thames Chatham Margate
PEMBROKESHIRE Pembroke Swansea Cardiff Bristol Bath Reading Guildford Maidstone Canterbury
COAST Port Talbot Barry Basingstoke Reigate Dover
Bristol Channel Weston-super- Winchester Crawley Ashford Folkestone
EXMOOR Mare Salisbury Fareham Hastings
Barnstaple Exmoor Taunton Yeovil Southampton Bournemouth Eastbourne Brighton Worthing
Bude 618 Exmouth New Poole Newport Portsmouth
Newquay DARTMOOR Torquay FOREST Weymouth Isle of Wight
Truro Dartmoor Exeter Plymouth
St. Austell Falmouth
Land's End Penzance
Isles of Scilly

UNITED KINGDOM
ENGLAND
IRELAND
WALES
SCOTLAND

East from Greenwich
West from Greenwich

Askøyna
Bergen
Osøyro
Stord
Bømlo Leirvik
NORWAY
Haugesund Kopervik Boknafjo
Åkrahamn
Stavanger
Sandnes
Bryne
Nærbø

Texel
Den Helder
Alkmaar
Haarlem
NETHERLANDS
's-Gravenhage
(Den Haag)
Hoek van Holland
ROTTERDAM
Dordrecht

Vlissingen
Zeebrugge
Oostende Brugge Antwerpen
Gent Mechelen
BELGIUM
Dunkerque Flandre Brussel
Calais Tourcoing (Bruxelles)
St-Omer Lille Tournai
Béthune Villeneuve-d'Ascq
Gris Bruay-la- Lens Valenciennes
Nez Buissière
Boulogne Cambrai
sur-Mer Artois St-Quentin
Le Touquet- Picardie
Paris-Plage Abbeville
33 Amiens Laon
Le Tréport
Fécamp Dieppe Pays de
C. de la Pte. de Caux FRANCE
Hague Barfleur Rouen
Alderney Bolbec
Cherbourg Le Havre Trouville-sur-Mer Seine
Guernsey Valognes Elbeuf
St. Peter Cotentin Bayeux Lisieux
Port Sark Caen
Channel Is. St. Helier
(U.K.) Jersey

COPYRIGHT PHILIP'S

1:2 200 000

NORTH SEA

UNITED KINGDOM

NETHERLANDS

BELGIUM

GERMANY

FRANCE

LUXEMBOURG

Major cities and places:

AMSTERDAM, Rotterdam, 's-Gravenhage (Den Haag), Utrecht, Haarlem, Groningen, Zwolle, Arnhem, Nijmegen, Eindhoven, Breda, Tilburg, Leeuwarden, Assen, Enschede, Apeldoorn, Amersfoort, Deventer, Den Helder, Alkmaar, Hoorn, Zaanstad, Delft, Dordrecht, Middelburg, Vlissingen, Bergen op Zoom, Roosendaal, 's-Hertogenbosch (Den Bosch), Venlo, Roermond, Maastricht, Heerlen, Sittard

Brussel (Bruxelles), Antwerpen, Gent (Gand), Brugge, Liège, Namur, Charleroi, Mons, Hasselt, Leuven, Mechelen, Oostende, Kortrijk, Tournai, Aalst, Genk, Tongeren, Verviers

LUXEMBOURG, Luxembourg, Arlon, Esch-sur-Alzette, Diekirch, Ettelbruck, Wiltz, Clervaux

Paris, Lille, Calais, Dunkerque, Boulogne-sur-Mer, Amiens, Reims, Charleville-Mézières, Valenciennes, Lens, Douai, Arras, Cambrai, St-Quentin, Laon, Soissons, Compiègne, Beauvais, Sedan, Verdun, Metz, Thionville, Nancy, Saarbrücken, Strasbourg, Châlons-en-Champagne

Köln, Düsseldorf, Dortmund, Essen, Duisburg, Bochum, Bonn, Aachen, Münster, Osnabrück, Oldenburg, Bremerhaven, Wilhelmshaven, Emden, Wiesbaden, Mainz, Koblenz, Trier, Kaiserslautern, Saarbrücken

NORDRHEIN-WESTFALEN, RHEINLAND-PFALZ, SAARLAND, NIEDERSÄCHSISCHES WATTENMEER, OSTFRIESLAND, WESTFALEN

FRIESLAND, GRONINGEN, DRENTHE, OVERIJSSEL, FLEVOLAND, NOORD-HOLLAND, ZUID-HOLLAND, ZEELAND, NOORD-BRABANT, LIMBURG, GELDERLAND, UTRECHT

VLAANDEREN, BRABANT, HAINAUT, NAMUR, LIÈGE, LUXEMBOURG

NORD-PAS-DE-CALAIS, PICARDIE, PLAINE DE FLANDRE, ARDENNES, SOMME, AISNE, OISE, MARNE, LORRAINE, VOSGES, SEINE ET MARNE

Waddeneilanden, Ostfriesische Inseln, Texel, Vlieland, Terschelling, Ameland, Schiermonnikoog, Borkum, Norderney, Juist, Helgoland

National Parks

Underlined towns give their name to the administrative area in which they stand.

COPYRIGHT PHILIP'S

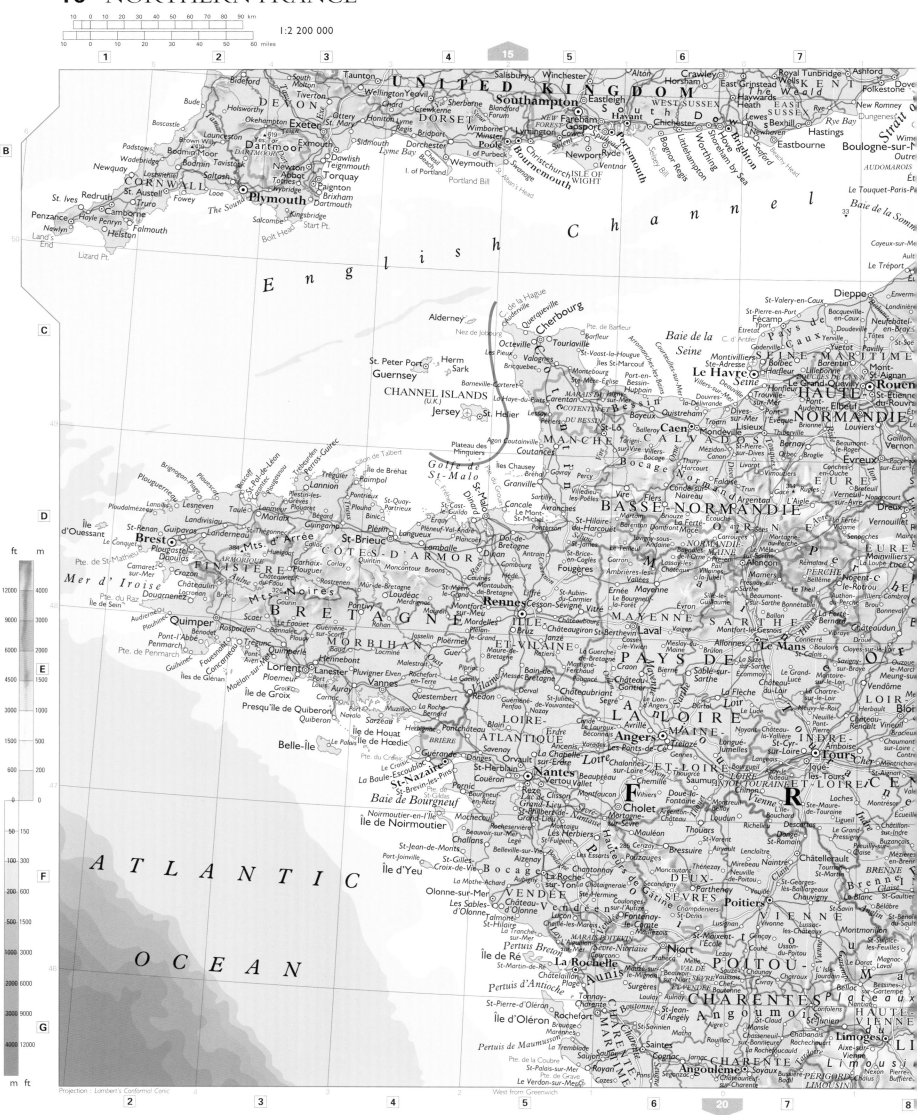

Underlined towns give their name to the
administrative area in which they stand.

National Parks and Regional Nature Parks in France

COPYRIGHT PHILIP'S

National Parks and Regional Nature Parks in France

1:4 400 000

50   0   25   50   75   100   125   150   175 km
50   0   25   50   75   100   125 miles

Projection: Conical with two standard parallels

N O R T H   S E A

B A L T I C   S E A

DENMARK

Sylt
Westerland
Föhr
Flensburg
Schleswig
Rendsburg
Holstein
Helgoland
Deutsche Bucht
Ost-friesische Inseln
Norderney
Wangerooge
Borkum
Cuxhaven
Aabenraa
Sønderborg
Kieler Bucht
Kiel
Neumünster
Itzehoe
Mecklenburger Bucht
Fehmarn
Lolland
Nakskov
Falster
Nykøbing
Møn
Gedser
Travemünde
Lübeck
Wismar
Güstrow
Rostock
Stralsund
Greifswald
Rügen
Sassnitz
Darłowo
Kołobrzeg
Usedom
Wolin
Świnoujście
WOLIŃSKI
Szczecin
Stettiner Haff
Police
Goleniów
Stargard Szczeciński
Białogard
Koszalin
POJEZIERZE

UNITED KINGDOM
Cromer
Norwich
THE BROADS
Great Yarmouth
Lowestoft
Ipswich
Felixstowe
Harwich
Margate
Dover
Calais
Boulogne-sur-Mer

Nordfriesische Inseln
Schiermonnikoog
Terschelling
Ameland
Texel
Den Helder
Leeuwarden
Groningen
Assen
Emmen
Meppel
Zwolle

HAMBURG
Norderstedt
Buxtehude
Stade
Bremerhaven
Bremen
Lüneburg
Lüneburger
Oldenburg
Delmenhorst
Leer
Emden
Aurich
Wilhelmshaven

NETHERLANDS
's-Gravenhage (Den Haag)
AMSTERDAM
Haarlem
Alkmaar
Hoorn
Kampen
Apeldoorn
Deventer
Almelo
Enschede
Hengelo
Leiden
Gouda
Hilversum
Utrecht
Arnhem
Nijmegen
ROTTERDAM
Dordrecht
Breda
Tilburg
's-Hertogenbosch
Eindhoven
Vlissingen
Zeebrugge
Oostende

BELGIUM
Brussel (Bruxelles)
Antwerpen
Gent
Brugge
Mechelen
Leuven
Turnhout
Roeselare
Kortrijk
Tournai
Mons
Charleroi
Namur
Liège
Verviers
Maastricht
Heerlen
Aachen
Dunkerque
St-Omer
Lille
Roubaix
Tourcoing
Douai
Valenciennes
Maubeuge
Arras
Béthune
Lens
Cambrai
Amiens
Abbeville
St-Quentin
Charleville-Mézières
Sedan
Dinant
Bastogne
Arlon

GERMANY
Osnabrück
Münster
Gütersloh
Bielefeld
Herford
Minden
Hameln
Hannover
Hildesheim
Salzgitter
Braunschweig
Wolfsburg
Celle
Nienburg
Verden
Stendal
Magdeburg
Dessau
Brandenburg
Potsdam
BERLIN
Fürstenwalde
Frankfurt
Cottbus
Wittenberg
Halle
Leipzig
Dresden
Görlitz
Chemnitz
Zwickau
Gera
Jena
Weimar
Erfurt
Gotha
Eisenach
Kassel
Göttingen
Nordhausen
Mühlhausen
Paderborn
Detmold
Höxter
Dortmund
Bochum
Essen
Duisburg
Oberhausen
Gelsenkirchen
Krefeld
Mönchengladbach
Düsseldorf
Wuppertal
Solingen
Köln (Cologne)
Bonn
Siegen
Marburg
Giessen
Wetzlar
Limburg
Koblenz
Wiesbaden
Frankfurt
Mainz
Offenbach
Hanau
Darmstadt
Mannheim
Ludwigshafen
Worms
Speyer
Heidelberg
Heilbronn
Karlsruhe
Pforzheim
Ludwigsburg
Stuttgart
Esslingen
Tübingen
Reutlingen
Baden-Baden
Offenburg
Freiburg
Villingen-Schwenningen
Rottweil
Ulm
Aalen
Göppingen
Crailsheim
Ansbach
Nürnberg
Fürth
Erlangen
Bamberg
Schweinfurt
Würzburg
Aschaffenburg
Bad Kissingen
Fulda
Coburg
Hof
Bayreuth
Weiden
Amberg
Regensburg
Ingolstadt
Donauwörth
Augsburg
München (Munich)
Freising
Dachau
Landshut
Straubing
Deggendorf
Passau
Rosenheim
Kempten
Memmingen
Biberach
Ravensburg
Friedrichshafen
Konstanz
Kaufbeuren
Garmisch-Partenkirchen
Zugspitze
Saarbrücken
Saarlouis
Neunkirchen
Kaiserslautern
Pirmasens
Trier
Idar-Oberstein
Bad Kreuznach
Bitburg
Prüm
Wittlich

Niedersachsen
Mecklenburg
Brandenburg
Sachsen-Anhalt
Anhalt
Sachsen
Thüringer Wald
Harz
Hochharz
Rhön
Vogelsberg
Taunus
Westerwald
Sauerland
Eifel
Pfalz
Rheinland
Hunsrück
Schwäbische Alb
Bayern
Württemberg
Schwarzwald

POLAND
Gorzów Wielkopolski
Zielona Góra
Nowa Sól
Żagań
Głogów
Legnica
Lubin
Bolesławiec
Zgorzelec
Wałbrzych
Jelenia Góra
Kłodzko
Nowy Tomyśl
Międzychód
Świebodzin
Forst

CZECH
PRAHA (Prague)
Ústí nad Labem
Děčín
Liberec
Jablonec nad Nisou
Teplice
Most
Chomutov
Karlovy Vary
Cheb
Plzeň
Klatovy
Příbram
Beroun
Kolín
Kutná Hora
Kladno
Pardubice
Hradec Králové
Trutnov
Mladá Boleslav
Tábor
České Budějovice
Jindřichův Hradec
Jihlava
Třebíč
Znojmo
Havlíčkův Brod
Pisek
Strakonice
Českomoravská Vrchovina
Šumava
Böhmerwald
Erzgebirge
Krkonoše

FRANCE
PARIS
Créteil
St-Denis
Meaux
Senlis
Compiègne
Beauvais
Noyon
Laon
Soissons
Reims
Épernay
Châlons-en-Champagne
Bar-le-Duc
Verdun
Metz
Nancy
Lunéville
Toul
St-Dizier
Troyes
Sens
Auxerre
Chaumont
Épinal
Thionville
Hagondange
Sarreguemines
Haguenau
Strasbourg
Colmar
Mulhouse
Belfort
Montbéliard
Besançon
Dijon
Beaune
Chalon-sur-Saône
Dole
Lons-le-Saunier
Mâcon
Bourg-en-Bresse
Villefranche-sur-Saône
Roanne
Thiers
LYON
St-Étienne
Vienne
Annecy
Aix-les-Bains
Chambéry
Grenoble
Valence
Montélimar
Privas
Nîmes
Avignon
Arles
Salon-de-Provence
Aix-en-Provence
MARSEILLE
Toulon
La Seyne-sur-Mer
Hyères
Fréjus
St-Tropez
Cannes
Antibes
Nice
MONACO
Monte-Carlo
Menton
San Remo
Imperia
Aubagne
Martigues
Aigues-Mortes
Camargue
Carpentras
Orange
Troyes

Île-de-France
Picardie
Champagne
Lorraine
Bourgogne
Nivernais
Morvan
Jura
Franche-Comté
Massif Central
Cévennes
Dauphiné
Provence
Alpes Maritimes
Alpes de Provence
Massif du Pelvoux
Vanoise

LUXEMBOURG
Esch-sur-Alzette

SWITZERLAND
Bern
Thun
Interlaken
Fribourg
Lausanne
Montreux
Genève
Sion
Brig
Neuchâtel
Biel
Solothurn
Aarau
Luzern
Zug
Zürich
Winterthur
Sankt Gallen
Schaffhausen
Chur
Davos
Sankt Moritz
Schwyz
Basel
Matterhorn
Jungfrau
Piz Bernina
Engadin

LIECHTENSTEIN
Vaduz
Feldkirch

AUSTRIA
Bregenz
Innsbruck
Arlberg
Landeck
Kufstein
Salzburg
Bad Ischl
Gmunden
Wels
Linz
Steyr
Amstetten
Melk
Krems
Sankt Pölten
Wiener Neustadt
Baden
Eisenstadt
Kapfenberg
Leoben
Bruck an der Mur
Graz
Wolfsberg
Klagenfurt
Villach
Spittal
Lienz
Badgastein
Grossglockner
Tirol
Steiermark
Kärnten
Hohe Tauern
Karnische Alpen

ITALY
MILANO
Torino (Turin)
Novara
Vercelli
Biella
Ivrea
Aosta
Mont Blanc
Gran Paradiso
Monte Rosa
Domodossola
Verbania
Varese
Como
Lecco
Bergamo
Brescia
Monza
Vigévano
Pavia
Lodi
Cremona
Mantova
Piacenza
Parma
Reggio nell'Emilia
Modena
Bologna
Ferrara
Rovigo
Pádova (Padua)
Vicenza
Verona
Treviso
Venézia (Venice)
Golfo di Venézia
Trieste
Conegliano
Pordenone
Udine
Gorizia
Belluno
Vittorio Véneto
Bassano del Grappa
Trento
Rovereto
Bolzano
Merano
Bressanone
Dolomiti
Mte. Marmolada
Ortles
Adamello
Stelvio
Piemonte
Lombardia
Liguria
Génova
Golfo di Génova
Savona
Imperia
Rapallo
Riviera di Levante
Riviera di Ponente
La Spézia
Carrara
Massa
Viaréggio
Lucca
Pistoia
Prato
Firenze (Florence)
Scandicci
Pisa
Arno
Empoli
Livorno
Cesena
Forlì
Ravenna
Faenza
Imola
Lugo
Comácchio
Rimini
Pésaro
Fano
SAN MARINO
Appennino
Monte Cimone
Cuneo
Mondovì
Fossano
Alba
Asti
Alessandria
Acqui
Novi Ligure
Tortona
Voghera
Pinerolo
Saluzzo
Mte. Viso
Col di Tenda
Alpi Marittime

SLOVENIA
Ljubljana
Maribor
Celje
Kranj
Koper
Postojna
Kamnik
Triglav
Karawanken
Kobarid

CROATIA
ZAGREB
Rijeka
Karlovac
Pula
Rt Kamenjak
Cres
Krk
Lošinj
Rab
Pag
Zadar
Dugi Otok
Velika Kapela
Velebit
Plitvička Jezera
Bihać

A D R I A T I C   S E A

ft   m
12000   4000
9000   3000
6000   2000
4500   1500
3000   1000
1500   500
600   200
300   150
150   50
0
50   150
200   600
500   1500
1000   3000
2000   6000
m   ft

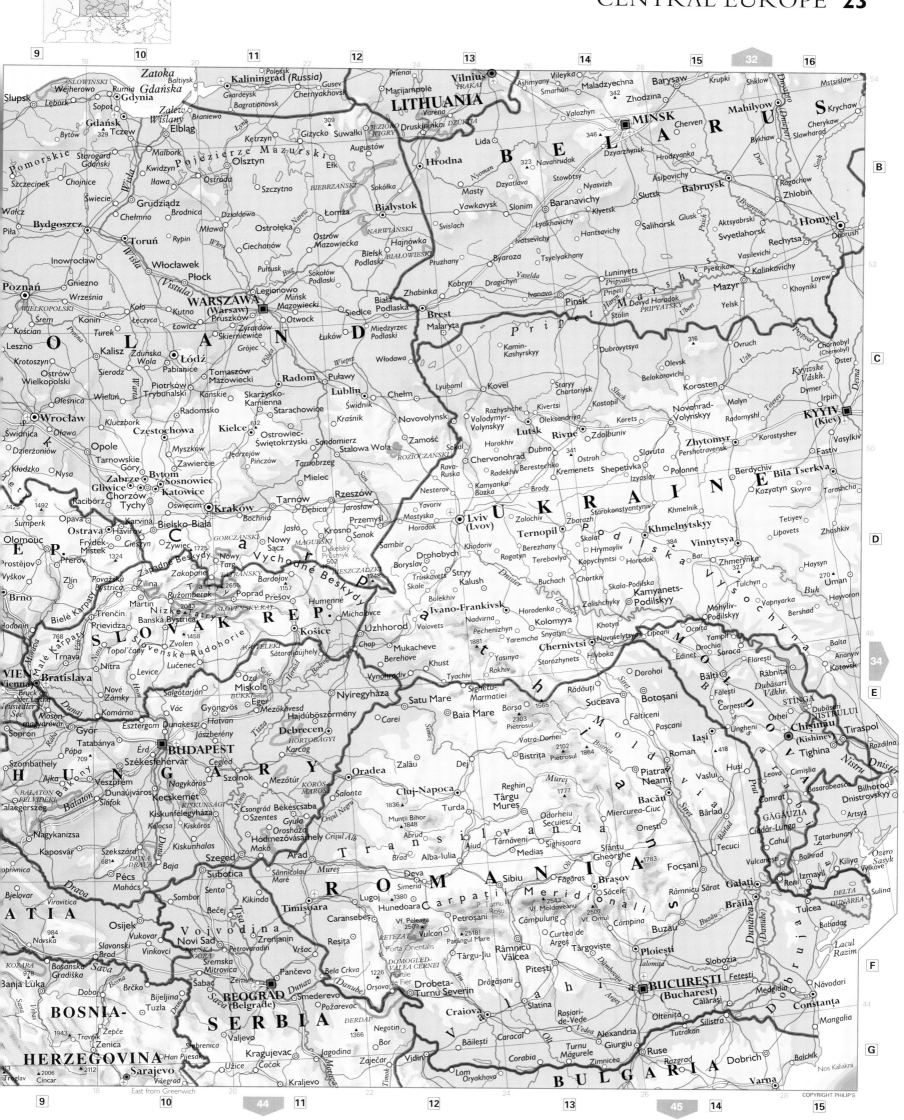

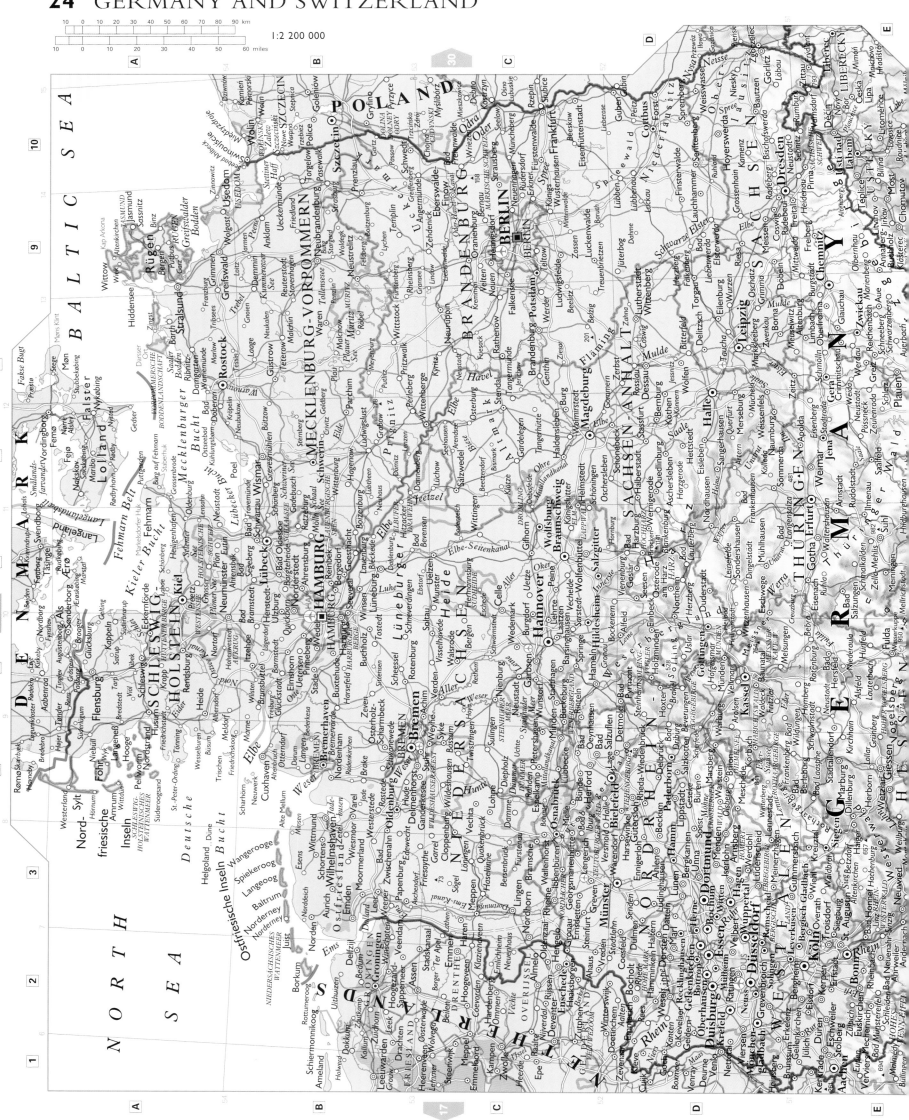

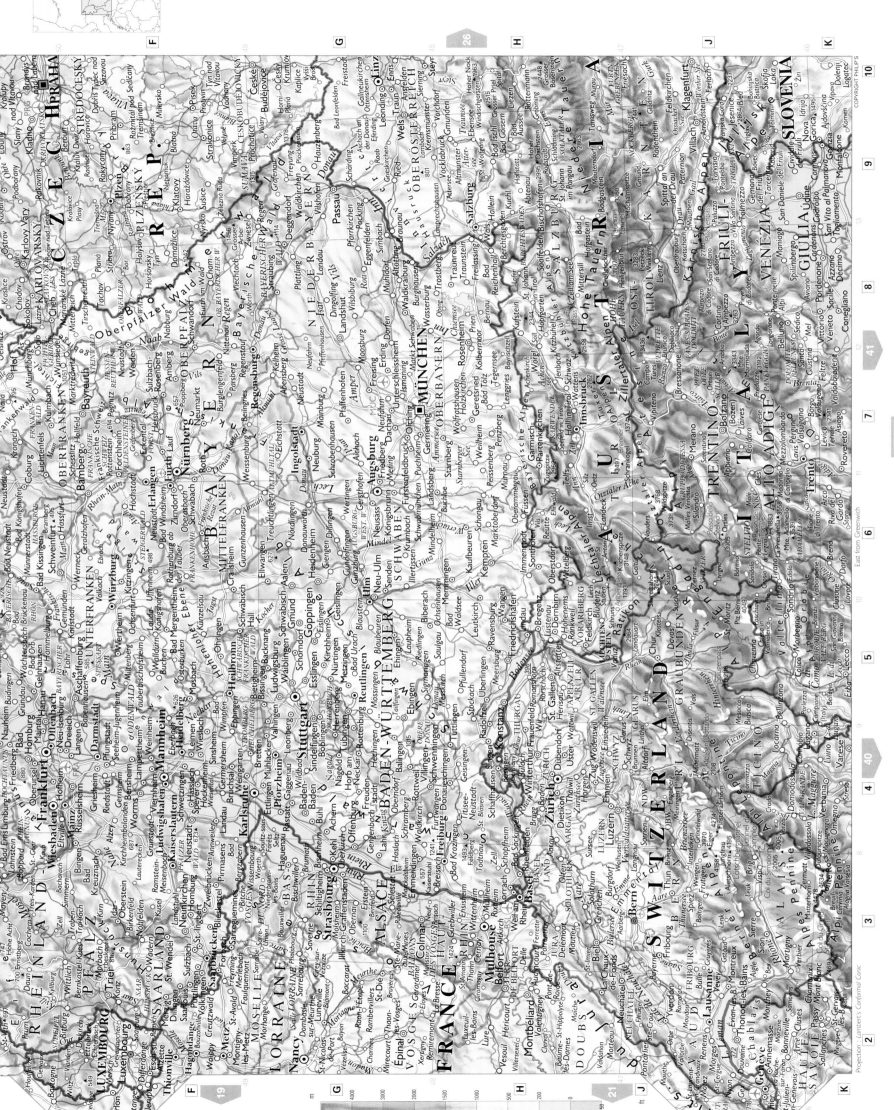

National Parks and Nature Parks in Germany

Underlined towns give their name to the administrative area in which they stand.

National Parks

Underlined towns give their name to the
administrative area in which they stand.

1:2 200 000

Projection: Lambert's Conformal Conic

East from Greenwich

Administrative divisions in Croatia:
1 Brodsko-Posavska   5 Osječko-Baranjska   9 Vukovarsko-Srijemska
2 Koprivničko-Križevačka   6 Požeško-Slavonska
4 Medimurska   8 Virovitičko-Podravska

Inter-entity boundaries as agreed
- - - - - at the 1995 Dayton Peace Agreement

National Parks

Underlined towns give their name to the
administrative area in which they stand.

COPYRIGHT PHILIP'S

1:2 200 000

10 0 10 20 30 40 50 60 70 80 90 km
10 0 10 20 30 40 50 60 miles

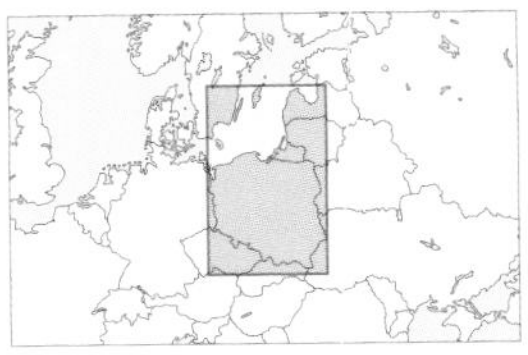

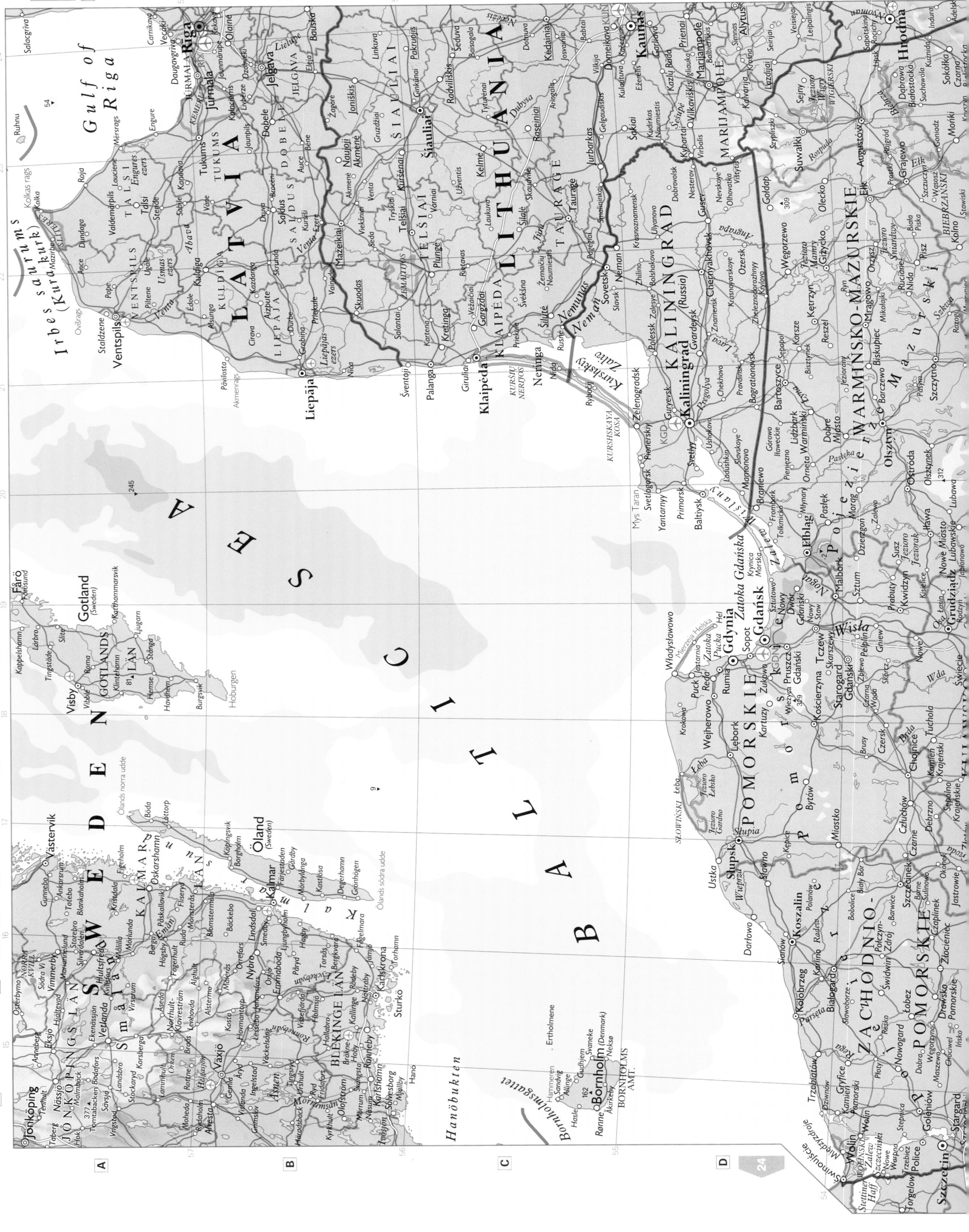

32

Gulf of Riga

Salacgrīva
Ruhnu
Kolkas rags
Irbes saurums (Kura kurk)

Jūrmala
Riga
Jelgava
JELGAVA

LATVIA

Ventspils
VENTSPILS
TUKUMS
TALSI
KULDĪGA
SALDUS
DOBELE

Liepāja
LIEPĀJA

LITHUANIA
ŠIAULIAI
Šiauliai
Telšiai
TELŠIAI
ŽEMAITIJA
Plungė
TAURAGĖ
Tauragė
KLAIPĖDA
Klaipėda
Palanga
Kretinga
Gargždai
NERINGA
Neringa
Nida

Nemunas
Neman

Sovetsk
Neman
Šilutė

KALININGRAD (Russia)
Kaliningrad
KGD
Zelenogradsk
Svetlogorsk
Baltiysk
Primorsk
Yantarnyy
Mys Taran
Chernyakhovsk
Gusev
KURSHSKAYA KOSA

Kaunas
Kaunas
Marijampolė
MARIJAMPOLĖ
Alytus

Suwałki
Augustów
WARMIŃSKO-MAZURSKIE
Olsztyn
Ostróda
Elbląg
Malbork
Elk
Giżycko
Mrągowo
Szczytno

B A L T I C   S E A

SWEDEN
Gotland (Sweden)
Visby
GOTLANDS LÄN
Öland (Sweden)
Kalmar
KALMAR LÄN
Hanöbukten
JÖNKÖPING
Jönköping
JÖNKÖPINGS LÄN
SMÅLAND
Växjö
BLEKINGE LÄN
Karlskrona
Karlshamn
BLEKINGE
Bornholm (Denmark)
BORNHOLMS AMT
Bornholmsgattet
Rønne

POMORSKIE
Gdańsk
GDAŃSK
Gdynia
Sopot
Zatoka Gdańska
Hel
Zalew Wiślany
Wisła
Tczew
Starogard Gdański
Słupsk
Lębork
Wejherowo
Kartuzy
Bytów
Chojnice

ZACHODNIO-POMORSKIE
Koszalin
Kołobrzeg
Białogard
Szczecin
Świnoujście
Wolin
Darłowo
Ustka

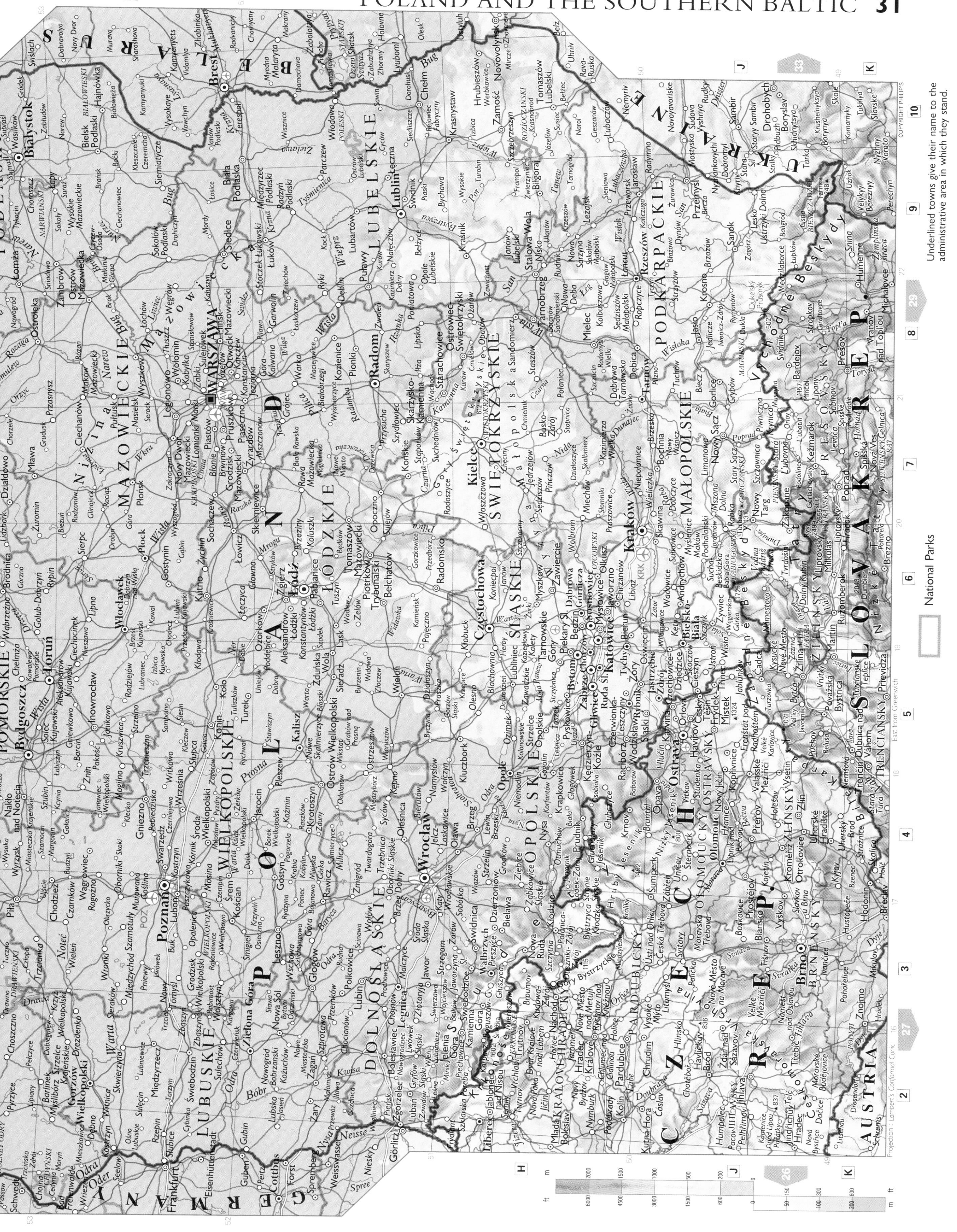

Underlined towns give their name to the administrative area in which they stand.
National Parks
Projection : Lambert's Conformal Conic
East from Greenwich
COPYRIGHT PHILIP'S
POLAND
WARSZAWA
Łódź
Kraków
Wrocław
Poznań
Gdańsk
Bydgoszcz
Toruń
Lublin
Białystok
Kielce
Radom
Częstochowa
Katowice
Rzeszów
Ostrava
Brno
Olomouc
Brest
PODLASKIE
MAZOWIECKIE
LUBELSKIE
ŁÓDZKIE
WIELKOPOLSKIE
KUJAWSKO-POMORSKIE
LUBUSKIE
DOLNOŚLĄSKIE
OPOLSKIE
ŚLĄSKIE
MAŁOPOLSKIE
PODKARPACKIE
ŚWIĘTOKRZYSKIE
CZECH REP.
SLOVAK REP.
AUSTRIA
GERMANY
BELARUS
UKRAINE

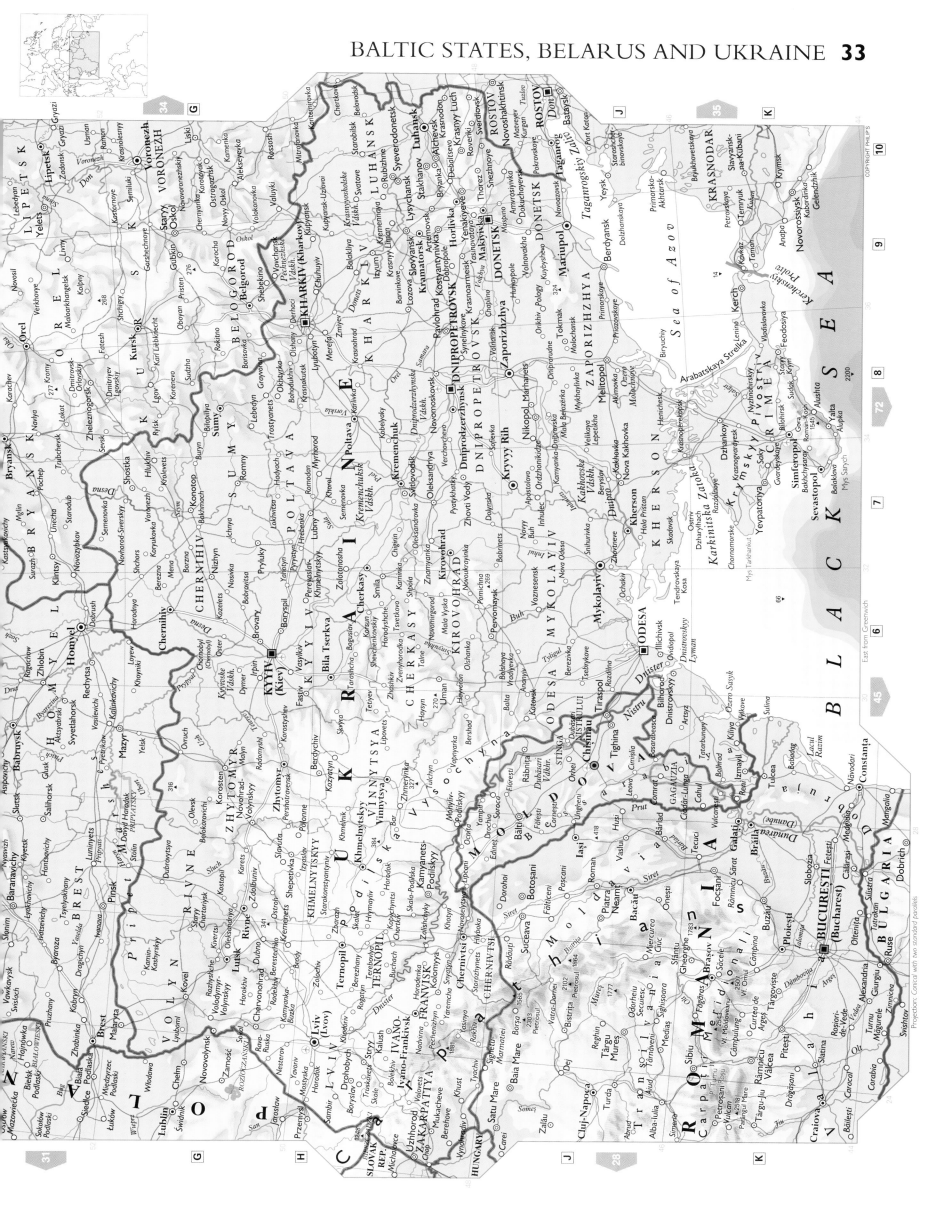

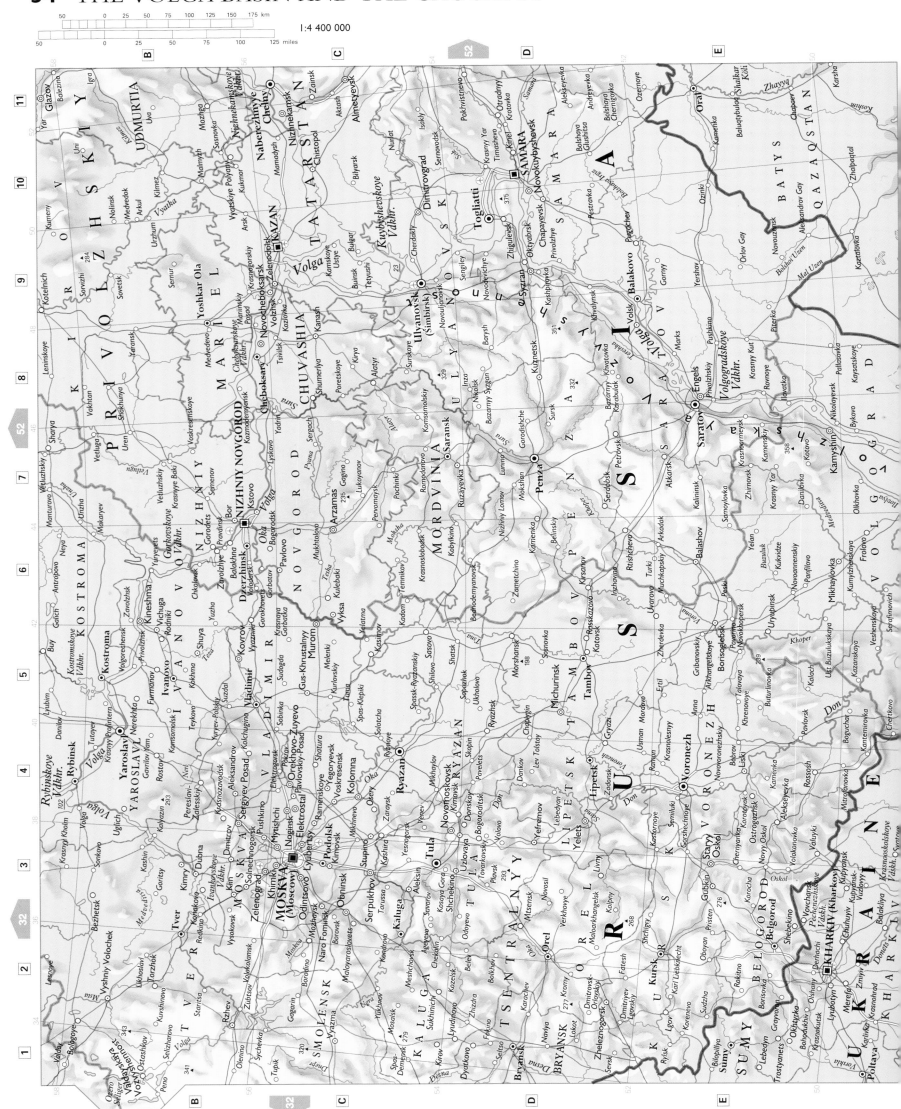

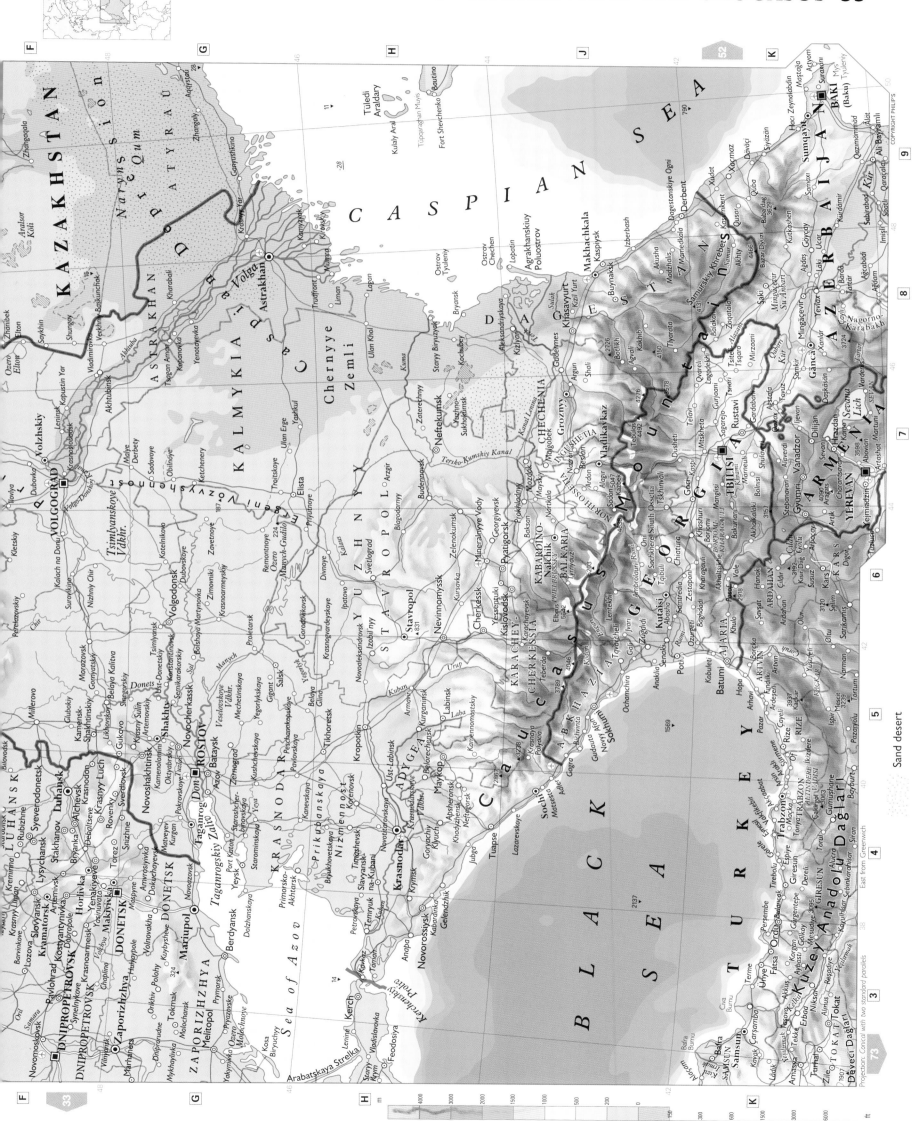

1:2 200 000

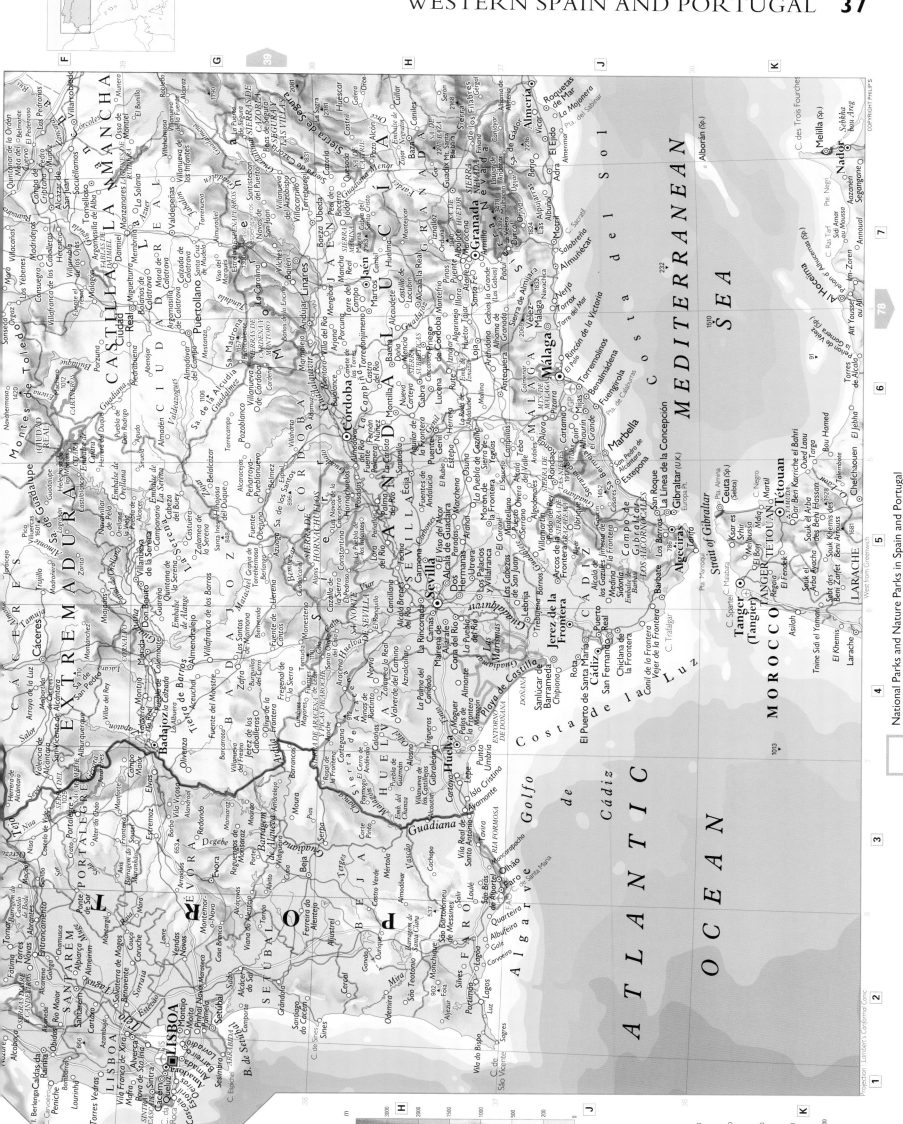

National Parks and Nature Parks in Spain and Portugal

National Parks and Nature Parks in Spain

Intermittent lakes

1:2 200 000

East from Greenwich

Underlined towns give their name to the
administrative area in which they stand.

Administrative divisions in Croatia:
Brodsko-Posavska
Koprivničko-Križevačka
Krapinsko-Zagorska

4 Medimurska
6 Požeško-Slavonska
7 Varaždinska

8 Virovitičko-Podravska
10 Zagreba čka

National Parks and Nature Parks in Italy

Inter-entity boundaries as agreed at the 1995 Dayton Peace Agreement

COPYRIGHT PHILIP'S

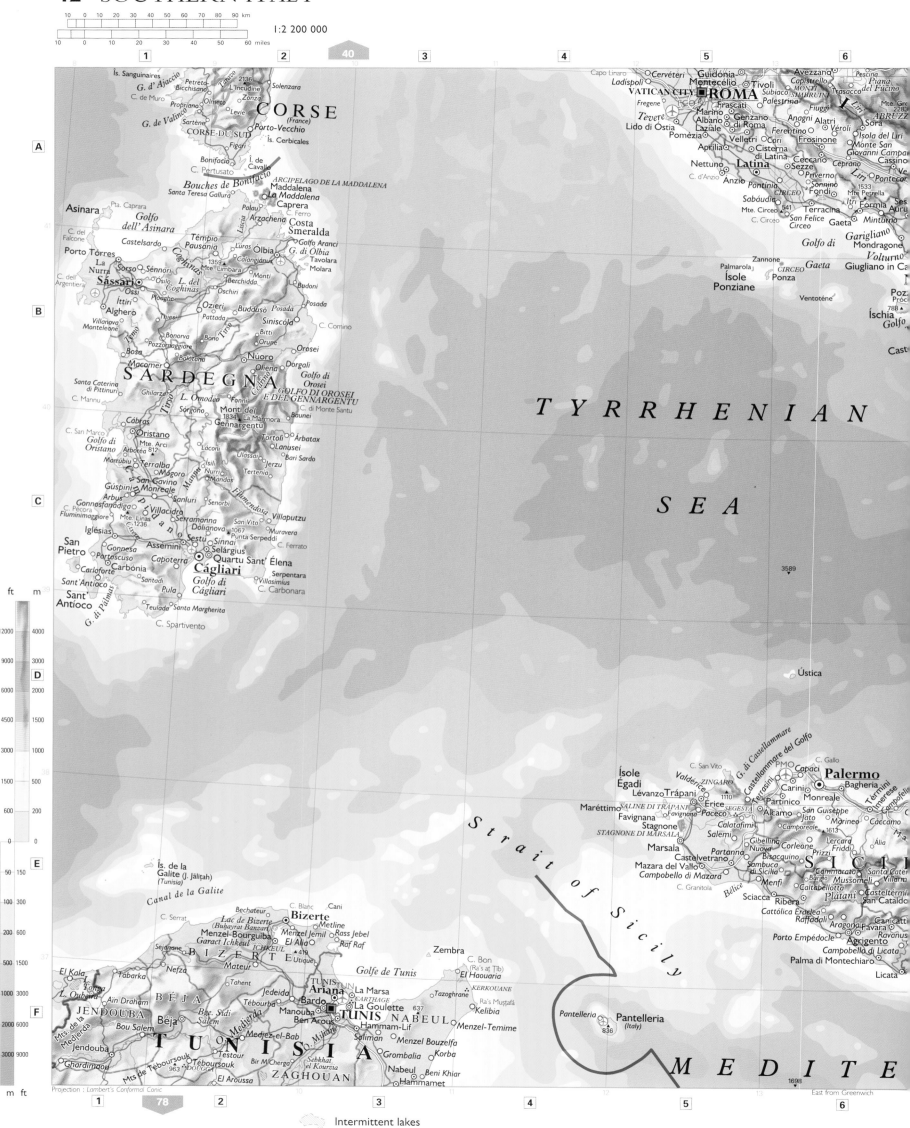

1:2 200 000

Intermittent lakes

ft   m

12000 4000

9000   3000

6000   2000

4500   1500

3000   1000

1500   500

600   200

0   0

50   150
100   300
200   600
500   1500
1000   3000
2000   6000
3000   9000

m ft

Projection : Lambert's Conformal Conic

National Parks and Nature Parks in Italy

Underlined towns give their name to the administrative area in which they stand.

1:2 200 000

Projection : Lambert's Conformal Conic

East from Greenwich

Inter-entity boundaries as agreed
at the 1995 Dayton Peace Agreement

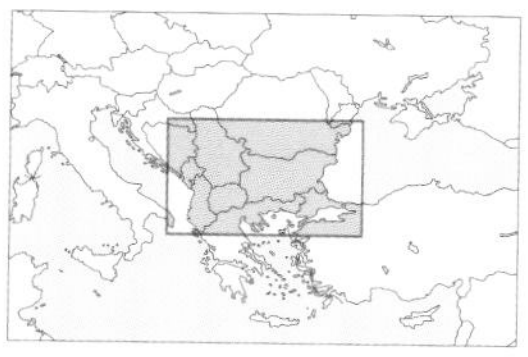

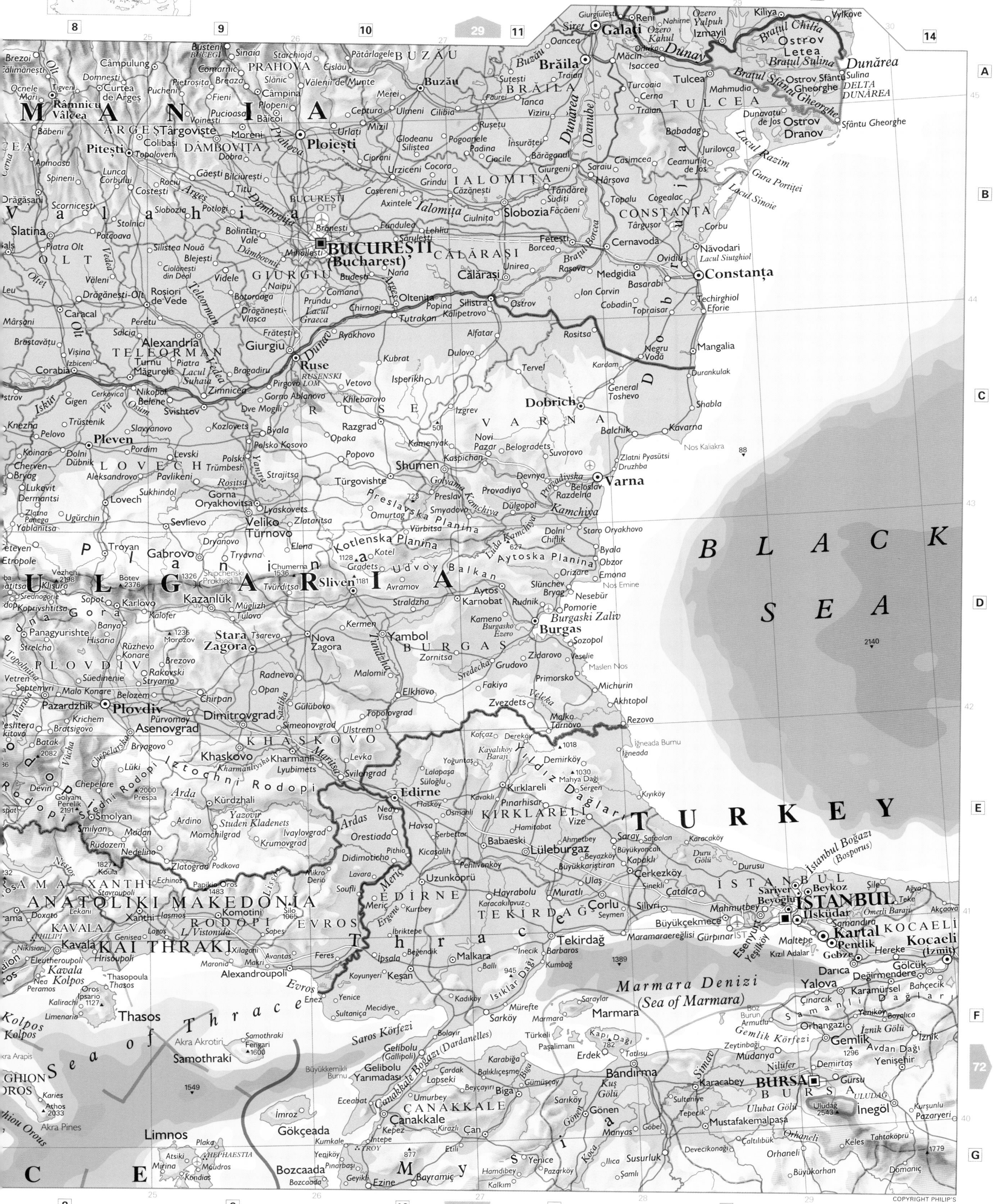

BLACK SEA

TURKEY

BULGARIA

Marmara Denizi
(Sea of Marmara)

Sea of Thrace

National Parks

Underlined towns give their name to the
administrative area in which they stand.

1:2 200 000

Projection : Lambert's Conformal Conic

East from Greenwich

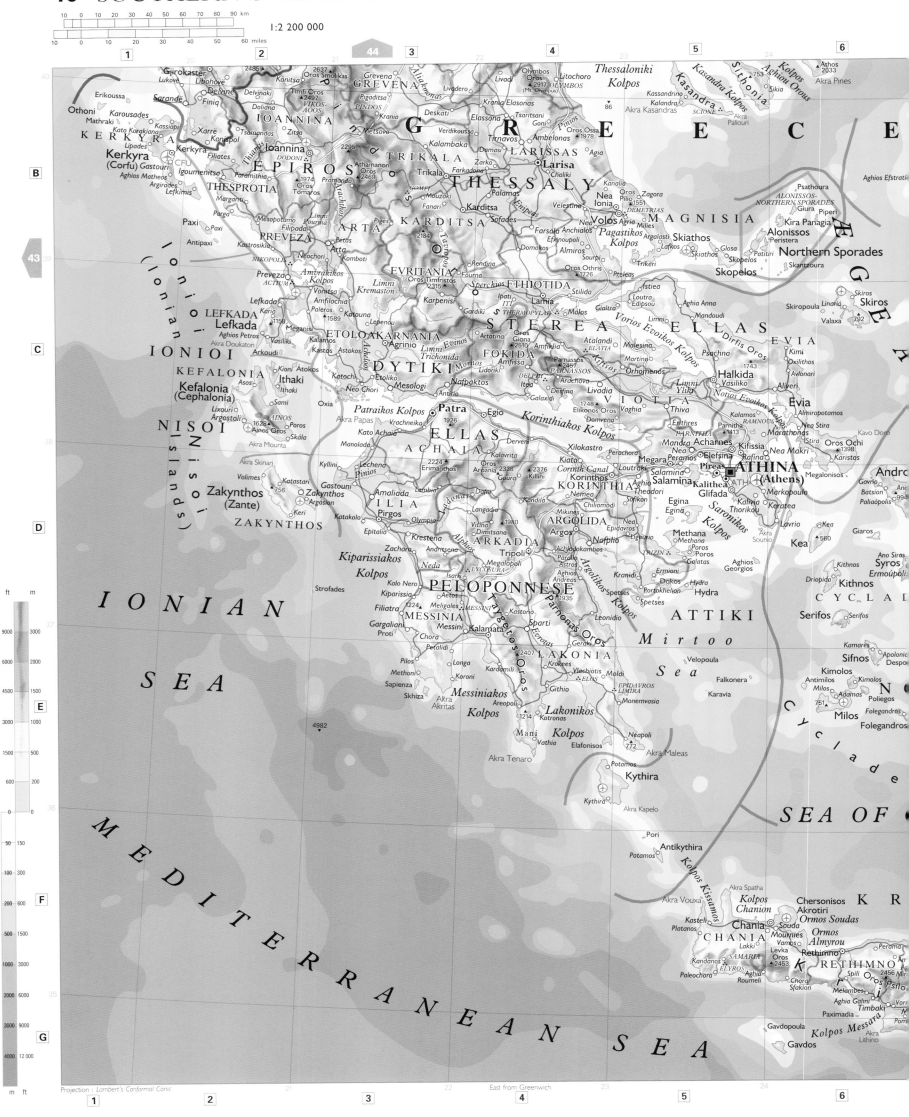

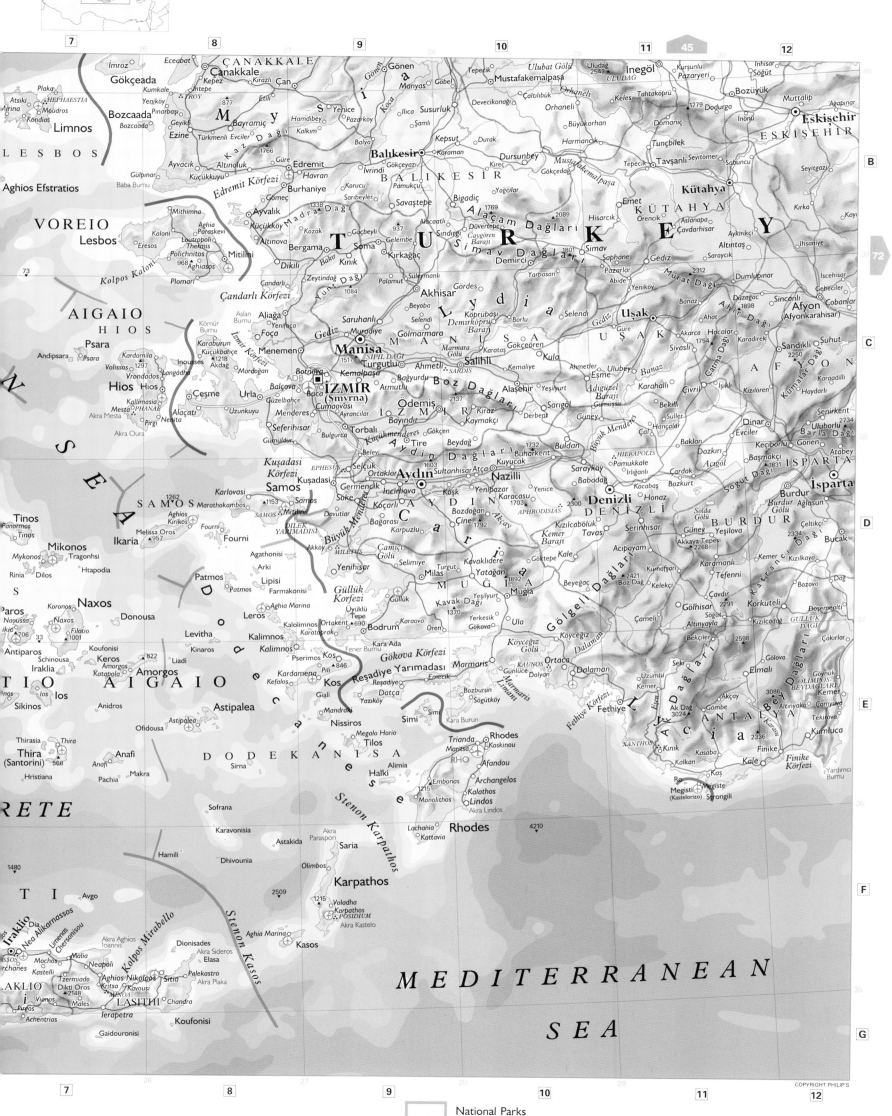

National Parks

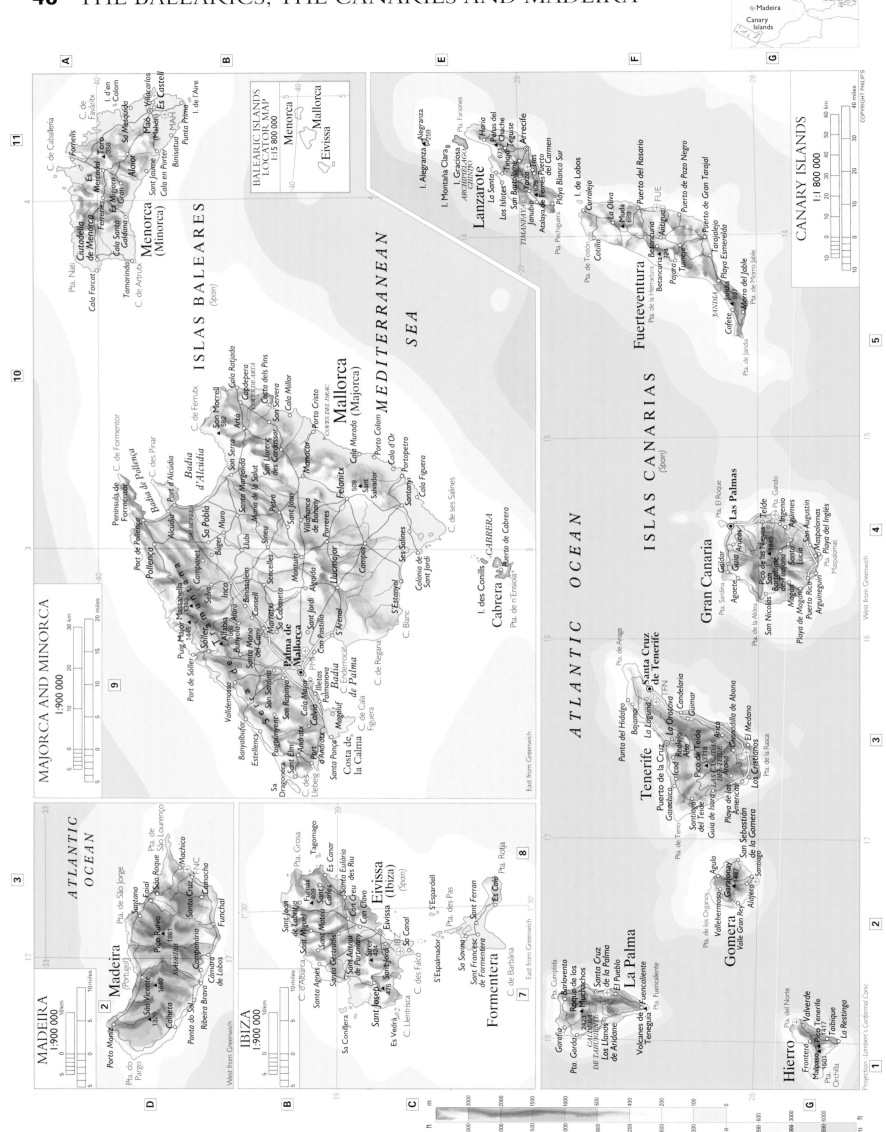

MEDITERRANEAN SEA

ATLANTIC OCEAN

Menorca (Minorca)

ISLAS BALEARES (Spain)

Mallorca (Majorca)

Cabrera

Eivissa (Ibiza) (Spain)

IBIZA
1:900 000

Formentera

MADEIRA
1:900 000

Madeira (Portugal)

MAJORCA AND MINORCA
1:900 000

BALEARIC ISLANDS LOCATOR MAP
1:15 800 000

Menorca
Mallorca
Eivissa

Lanzarote

Fuerteventura

ISLAS CANARIAS (Spain)

Gran Canaria
Las Palmas

Tenerife
Santa Cruz de Tenerife

Gomera

La Palma

Hierro

CANARY ISLANDS
1:1 800 000

COPYRIGHT PHILIP'S

Projection: Lambert's Conformal Conic

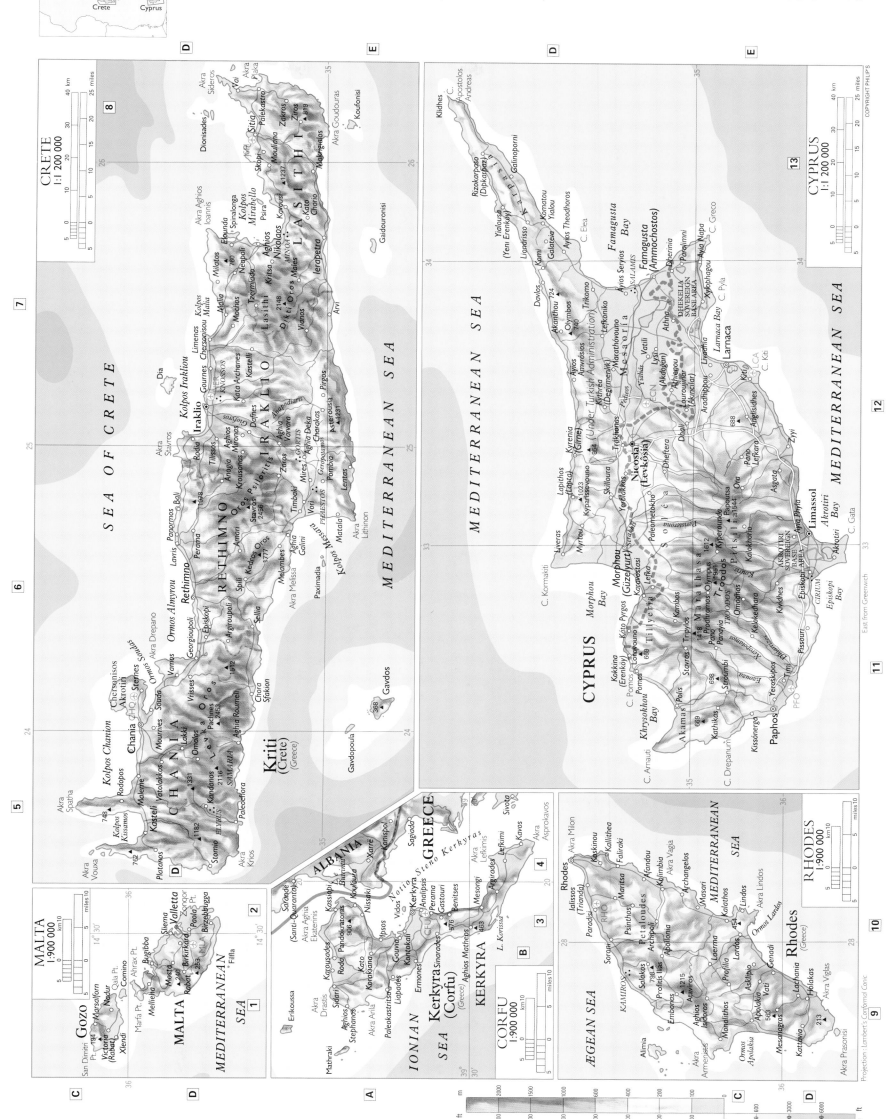

CRETE 1:1 200 000

CYPRUS 1:1 200 000

MALTA 1:900 000

CORFU 1:900 000

RHODES 1:900 000

East from Greenwich

Projection: Lambert's Conformal Conic

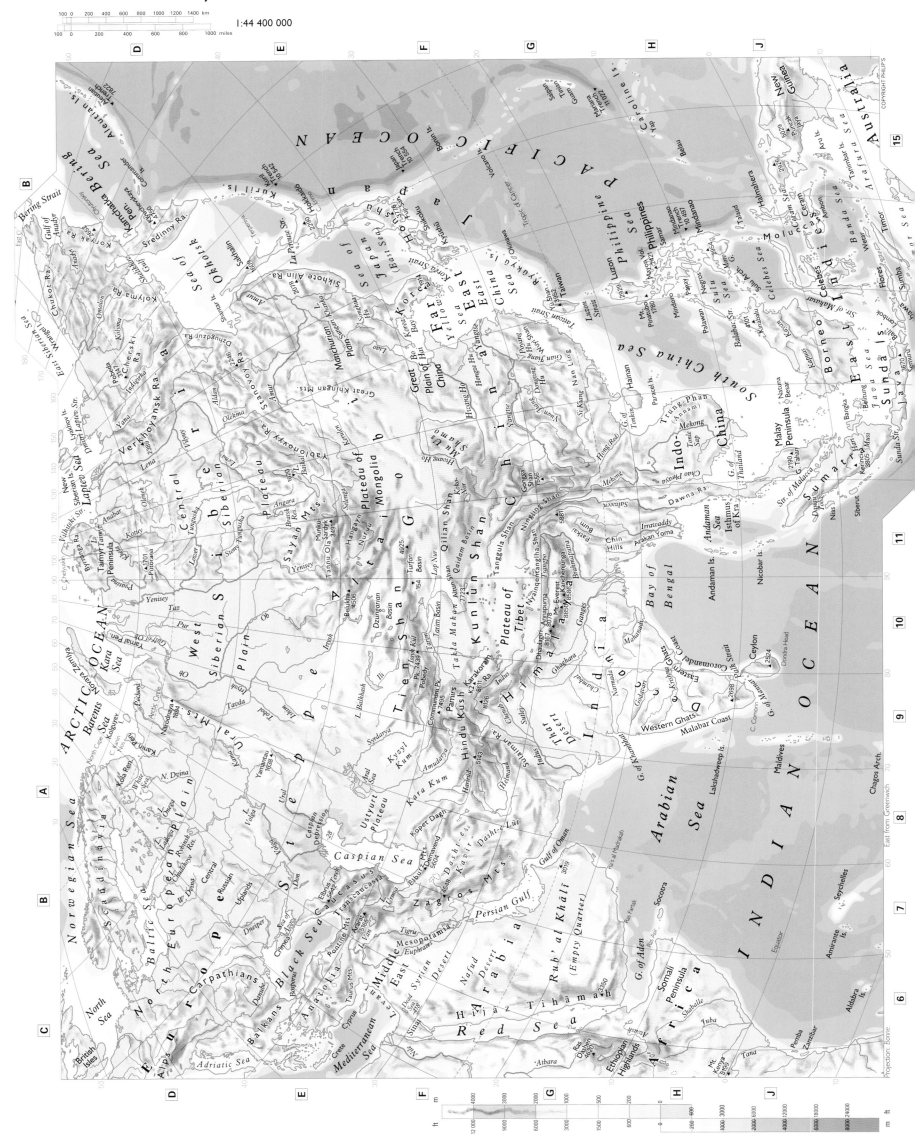

1:44 400 000

COPYRIGHT PHILIP'S

Projection: Bonne

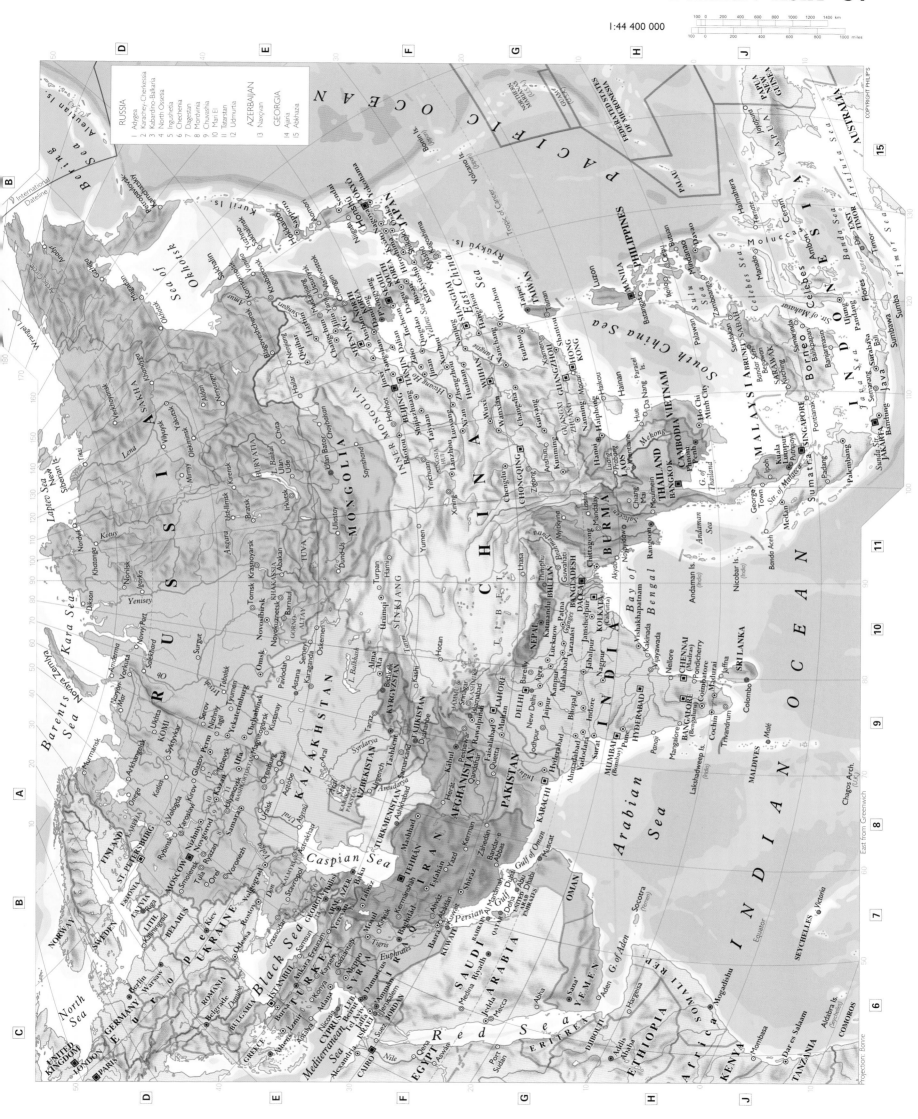

1:44 400 000

1:17 800 000

ARCTIC OCEAN

Laptev Sea

East Siberian Sea

Chukchi Sea

Bering Sea

Bering Str.

Mys Dezhneva (East C.)
Mys Navarin
International Date Line
St. Lawrence I. (U.S.A.)

Severnaya Zemlya
Ostrov Shmidta
Mys Arkticheskiy
Ostrov Komsomolets
Ostrov Ushakova
Ostrov Pioner
Ostrov Oktyabrskoy Revolyutsii
Ostrov Bolshevik
Ostrov Malyy Taymyr
Proliv Vilkitskogo
Mys Chelyuskin
Ostrova Petra

Novosibirskiye Ostrova
Ostrova Delonga
Ostrov Bennetta
Ostrov Genryetty
Ostrov Zhannetty
Ostrov Zhokhova
Ostrov Faddeyevskiy
Ostrov Novaya Sibir
Ostrov Belkovskiy
Ostrov Kotelnyy
Ostrov Malyy Lyakhovskiy
Ostrov Bolshoy Lyakhovskiy
Lyakhovskiye
Ostrov Stolbovoy
Pralив Dmitriya Lapteva

Ostrov Vrangelya
Ostrov Medvezhii
Proliv Longa

Poluostrov Gory Byrranga
Taymyr
Oz. Taymyr
Nordvik
Ostrov Bolshoy Begichev

Severnaya Zemlya

Ostrov Sergeya Kirova
Ostrov Isachenko

Pyasina
Volochanka
Khatanga
Kheta
Novorybnoye
Khatanga
Zhilinda

Ust Olenek
Tit-Ary
Tiksi
Ust Kuyga
Kazachye
Mys Buorkhaya

Olenek
Kyusyur
Bulun
Deputatskiy
Druzhina
Srednekolymsk
Nizhne Kolymsk
Ambarchik
Cherskiy
Bilibino
Pevek
Ust Chaun
Chaunskaya Guba

Dudinka
Norilsk
Talnakh
Gory Putorana
Noginsk
Nizhnyaya Tunguska
Tura
Yessey
Yukta
Kuyumba
Mutoray
Vanavara
Yerbogachen
Podkamennaya Tunguska

Turukhansk
Yartsevo
Severo-Yeniseyskiy
Yeniseysk
Lesosibirsk
Achinsk
Zelenogorsk
Ilanskiy
Kansk
KRASNOYARSK
Artemovsk
Chernogorsk
Minusinsk
Abakan
Sayanogorsk
Zapadnyy Sayan
Vostochnyy Sayan

Angara
Bratsk
Ust-Ilimsk
Kodinsk
Boguchany
Kondratyevo
Zheleznogorsk
Ust-Kut
Magistralnyy
Severobaykalsk
Bodaybo
Mama
Korshunovo
Makarovo
Kirensk
Taksimo
Karalon
Chara
Ust-Nyukzha

Yakutsk
Lena
Vilyuysk
Verkhnevilyuysk
Nyurba
Suntar
Mirnyy
Chernyshevskiy
Lensk
Olekminsk
Vitim

Sangar
Namtsy
Nizhniy Bestyakh
Pokrovsk
Sinsk

Verkhoyansk
Batagay
Batamay
Borogontsy
Ytyk-Kyuyel
Khandyga
Okhotskiy Perevoz
Ust-Maya
Aldan
Tommot
Neryungri
Nagornyy

Verkhoyanskiy Khrebet
Khrebet Cherskogo
Oymyakon
Susuman
Ust-Nera
Artyk
Ust-Omchug
Magadan
Palatka
Ola
Yagodnoye
Atka

SAKHA

DALNEVOSTOCHNYY

Kolymskoye Nagorye
Koryakskoye Nagorye
Sredninny Khrebet

Anadyr
Markovo
Beringovskiy
Ust-Belaya
Egvekinot
Uelkal
Kamenskoye
Penzhino
Manily
Tilichiki
Palana
Ust-Kamchatsk
Klyuchi
Milkovo
PETROPAVLOVSK-Kamchatskiy
Yelizovo
Vilyuchinsk

Poluostrov Kamchatka

Sea of Okhotsk

Okhotsk
Ayan
Chumikan
Nelkan
Udskaya Guba
Nikolayevsk-na-Amur
Sakhalinskiy Zaliv

Sakhalin
Okha
Nogliki
Neftegorsk
Aleksandrovsk-Sakhalinskiy
Tymovskoye
Poronaysk
Uglegorsk
Shakhtersk
Kholmsk
YUZHNO-SAKHALINSK
Korsakov
Dolinsk
Nevelsk
La Perouse Str.

Kurilskiye Ostrova
Ostrov Paramushir
Ostrov Onekotan
Ostrov Simushir
Ostrov Urup
Ostrov Iturup
Ostrov Kunashir
Ostrov Shikotan

Tatarskiy Proliv
Khrebet Sikhote Alin

Komsomolsk-na-Amur
Amursk
Khabarovsk
Bikin
Lesozavodsk
Dalnerechensk
Spassk-Dalniy
Ussuriysk
Artem
Partizansk
Nakhodka
VLADIVOSTOK

Stanovoy Khrebet
Tynda
Zeya
Skovorodino
Magdagachi
Norsk
Shimanovsk
Svobodnyy
Belogorsk
Chegdomyn
Zavitinsk
Obluchye
Birobidzhan
Raychikhinsk
BLAGOVESHCHENSK
Heihe

Yablonovyy Khrebet
Stanovoy Khrebet
Mogocha
Dzhalinda
Gulian
Amur

Chita
Shilka
Nerchinsk
Sretensk
Zabaykalsk
Borzya
Olovyannaya
Aginskoye
Karymskoye
Petrovsk-Zabaykalskiy
Ulan Ude
Gusinoozersk
Kyakhta
Zakamensk
Darhan

L. Baikal
Severobaykalsk
Slyudyanka
Irkutsk
Angarsk
Usolye Sibirskoye
Cheremkhovo
Zima
Zalari
Tulun
Nizhneudinsk
Alzamay
Tayshet

RUSSIA

BURYAT

Ordos
Dong (Manchuria)
Da Hinggan Ling
Hailar
Manzhouli
Zalantun
Baicheng
QIQIHAR
DAQING
Suihua
HARBIN
Mudanjiang
Jiamusi
Jixi
Hegang
Yichun
Jilin
CHANGCHUN
Siping
Taonan
FUYU
Songhua Hu
Fushun
SHENYANG
ANSHAN
Dandong
Jinxi
CHIFENG
Chengde
BEIJING
TANGSHAN
DALIAN
Yingkou

MONGOLIA
(Aerhtai Shan)
Altay
Bayanhongor
Arvayheer
Mandalgovi
Buyant-Uhaa
Dalandzadgad
ULAANBAATAR
Ondorhaan
Baruun-Urt
Choybalsan
Tamsagbulag
Choyr
Erenhot
Xilinhot

Hangayn Nuruu
Hentiyn Nuruu
Uliastay
Tsetserleg
Moron
Hovsgol Nuur
Hyargas Nuur
Uvs Nuur
Kyzyl
Samagaltay
Erzin
TUVA
Tannu Ola

Gobi

Gaxun Nur

CHINA

Hohhot
BAOTOU
Zhangjiakou

NORTH KOREA
PYONGYANG
Namp'o
Wonsan
Hamhung
Ch'ongjin
Kimch'aek

SOUTH KOREA
SEOUL
INCHEON
DAEJEON
DAEGU
BUSAN
GWANGJU
Ulleungdo

JAPAN
Sea of Japan (East Sea)
SAPPORO
HOKKAIDO
Hakodate
Aomori
Akita
Niigata
Toyama
Kanazawa
Sado
HONSHU
KYOTO
OSAKA
KOBE

1:4 400 000

SEA OF OKHOTSK

Sakhalin *(Russia)*

La Perouse Strait
(Sōya-Kaikyō)

HOKKAIDŌ

SAPPORO

Ostrov Moneron *(Russia)*

SEA OF JAPAN (EAST SEA)

Yamato Rise

RUSSIA

PRIMORSKY KRAY

CHINA

HEILONGJIANG

JILIN

Manchuria

Lake Khanka

Vladivostok

Ussuriysk

Nakhodka

Zaliv Petra Velikogo

NORTH KOREA

TOHOKU

AOMORI

AKITA

YAMAGATA

SENDAI

Honshū

CHŪBU

Hakodate

Muroran

Sado

Niigata

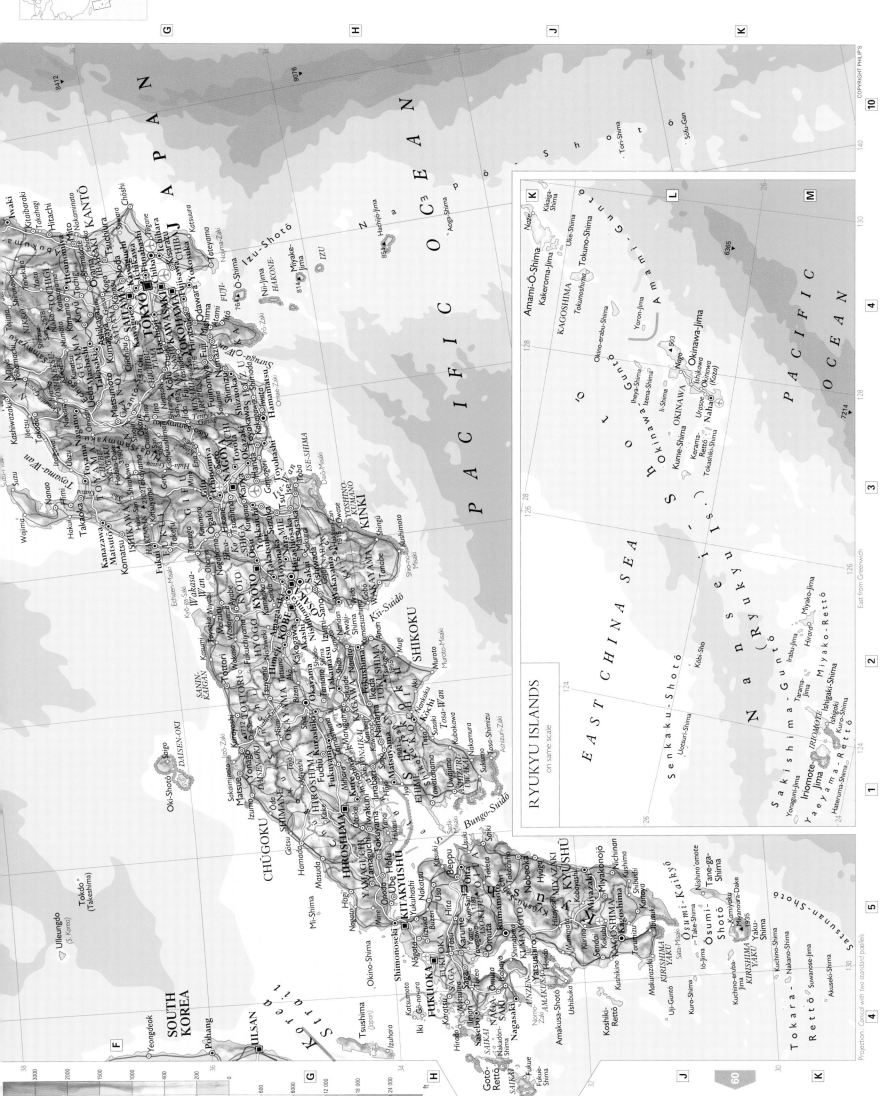

RYUKYU ISLANDS
on same scale

1:5 300 000

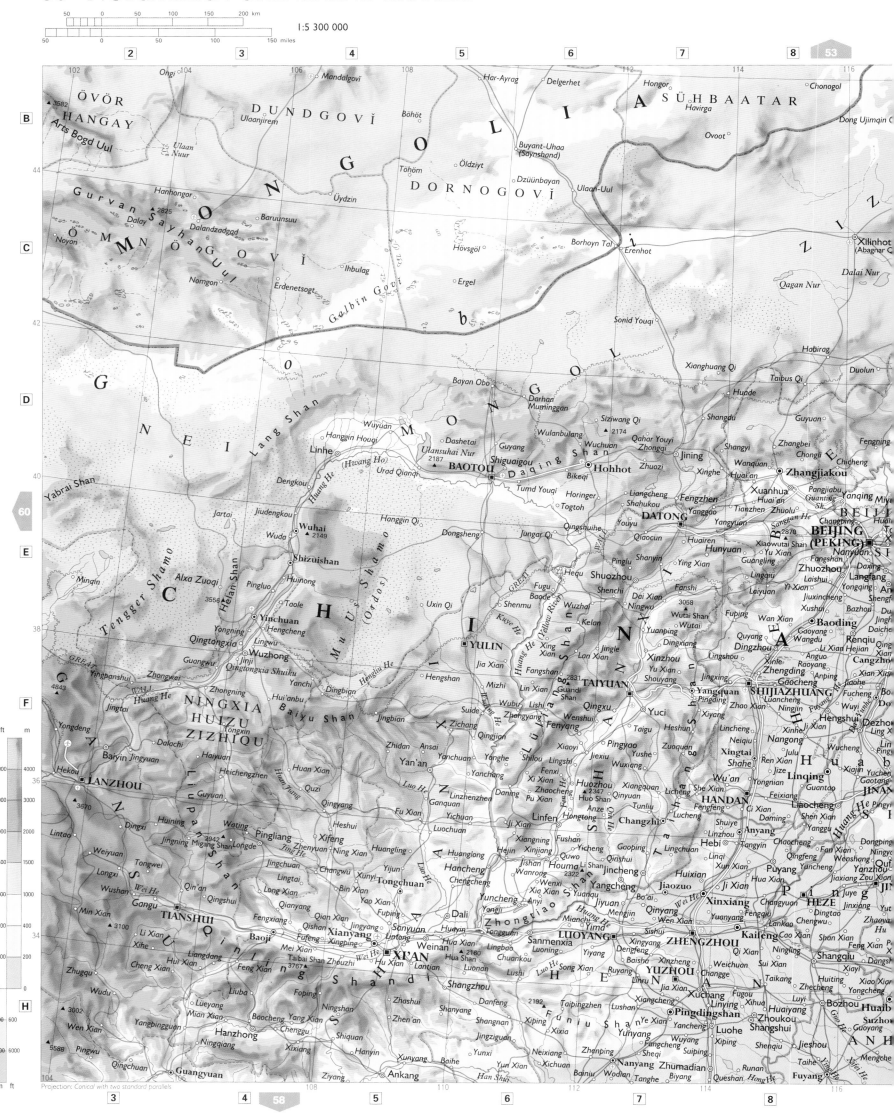

MONGOLIA

ÖVÖR HANGAY
▲3582
Arts Bogd Uul
Ongi
Mandalgoví
DUNDGOVÍ
Ulaanjirem
Böhöt
Har-Ayrag
Delgerhet
Hongor
Chonogol
SÜHBAATAR
Havirga
Dong Ujimqin Qi

Gurvan Sayhan Uul
Hanhongor
Ulaan Nuur
Üydzin
Töhöm
Buyant-Uhaa
(Saynshand)
Ovoot
Ovoot

ÖMNÖGOVÍ
Dalay
▲2825
Dalandzadgad
Baruunsuu
DORNOGOVÍ
Öldziyt
Dzüünbayan
Ulaan-Uul

Noyon
Ihbulag
Hövsgöl
Ergel
Borhoyn Tal
Erenhot
Xilinhot
(Abagnar)

Nomgon
Erdenetsogt
Galbïn Govi
b
Sonid Youqi
Qagan Nur
Dalai Nur

GOBI
o
Xianghuang Qi
Taibus Qi
Duolun

NEI
Bayan Obo
Darhan Muminggan
Siziwang Qi
▲2174
Qahar Youyi Zhongqi
Huade
Shangdu
Guyuan
Fengning

Lang Shan
Wuyuan
Dashetai
Guyang
Wulanbulang
Wuchuan
Shangyi
Zhangbei
Chongli
Chicheng

Linhe
Hanggin Houqi
(Hwang Ho)
Ulansuhai Nur
▲2187
BAOTOU
Daqing Shan
Bikeqi
Shiguaigou
Hohhot
Zhuozi
Jining
Xinghe
Wanquan
Huai'an
Zhangjiakou
Xuanhua
Pangjiabu
Yanqing

MONGOL
Dengkou
Huang He
Hanggin Qi
Tumd Youqi
Horinger
Togtoh
Qingshuihe
Liangcheng
Shahukou
Yanggao
Tianzhen
Zhuolu
Changping
BEIJING
(PEKING)

Wuhai
▲2149
Wuda
Dongsheng
Jungar Qi
Youyu
Qiaocun
Hunyuan
DATONG
Yangyuan
Guangling
Fangshan
Zhuozhou
Daxing
Langfang

Shizuishan
MU US SHAMO
(Ordos)
Uxin Qi
Heqü
Pinglu
Shanyin
Shuozhou
Ying Xian
Lingqiu
Laishui
Yongqing

Minqin
Alxa Zuoqi
Helan Shan
Pingluo
Huinong
Fugu
Baode
Shenmu
Wuzhai
Ningwu
Dai Xian
Fanshi
▲3058
Wutai Shan
Wutai
Fuping
Quyang
Baoding
Daiche

Tengger Shamo
ALXA
HELAN
▲3556
Taole
Kuye He
Kelan
Lan Xian
Jingle
Dingxiang
Xinzhou
Lingshou
Zhengding
Xinle
Raoyang
Anguo
Cangzhou

Yinchuan
Yongning
Hengcheng
YULIN
Jia Xian
Huang He
Xing Xian
Fangshan
▲2831
Guandi Shan
TAIYUAN
Yuanping
Shouyang
Yuci
Jingxing
Gaocheng
SHIJIAZHUANG
Anping
Xian

Qingtongxia
Lingwu
Wuzhong
Hengshan
Mizhi
Lishi
Zhongyang
Fenyang
Wenshui
Taigu
Pingyao
Yushe
Lincheng
Hengshui
Dezhou

NINGXIA HUIZU ZIZHIQU
Guangwu
Jinji
Qingtongxia Shuiku
Yanchi
Dingbian
Suide
Zichang
Qingjian
Wubu
Jiexiu
Wuxiang
Zuoquan
Xingtai
Shahe
Julu
Linqing
Guantao
Gaotang

GREAT WALL
Zhongwei
Zhongning
Baixu Shan
Jingbian
Zhidan
Ansai
Yanchuan
Yonghe
Shilou
Lingshi
Fenxi
She Xian
Wu'an
Yongnian
Ren Xian
Jize
Shen Xian
Daming
Linzhou
Anyang

▲4843
Yingpanshui
Hui'anbu
Tongxin
Haiyuan
Huan Xian
Heichengzhen
Quzi
Yan'an
Luo He
Linzhenzhen
Ganquan
Daning
Pu Xian
Xi Xian
Huozhou
▲2347
Huo Shan
Qinyuan
Tunliu
Changzhi
Lucheng
Feixiang
Qiu Xian
HANDAN
Fengfeng
Shuiye
Tangyin
Hebi
Chaocheng
Fan Xian
Dongbai

Lanzhou
Baiyin
Jingyuan
Dalachi
Guyuan
Huining
Dingxi
Heshui
Linzhenzhen
Yichuan
Luochuan
Ji Xian
Hongtong
Linfen
Xiangfen
Qinshui
Gaoping
Jincheng
Jiaozuo
Huixian
Ji Xian
Puyang
Qingfeng
Nanle

Lintao
Weiyuan
Tongwei
Qin'an
▲4942
Migang Shan
Jingning
Longde
Pingliang
Xifeng
Ning Xian
Huangling
Fushan
Quwo
Yicheng
Houma
Li Shan
Jishan
Wanrong
Yuncheng
Yangcheng
Bo'ai
Xinxiang
Yuanyang
Wen Xian
HEZE
Juye
Jinxiang

Longxi
Wushan
Gangu
Wei He
Jing He
Zhenyuan
Jingchuan
Changwu
Bin Xian
Yao Xian
Fuping
Hancheng
Hejin
Xinjiang
Xia Xian
Anyi
Yongji
Mianchi
Yima
Yiyang
LUOYANG
Dengfeng
ZHENGZHOU
Xinzheng
Changge
Yuzhou
Kaifeng
Cao Xian
Shangqiu

Min Xian
▲3100
Li Xian
TIANSHUI
Qin Xian
Lingtai
Long Xian
Qianyang
Qishan
Mei Xian
Fengxiang
Jingyang
Sanyuan
Xingping
XIANYANG
Lintong
Huayin
Tongguan
Sanmenxia
Luoning
Ruyang
Linru
Jia Xian
Xuchang
Linying
Xihua
Taikang
Zhecheng

Xihe
Zhugou
Baoji
Liangdang
Hui Xian
Cheng Xian
Taibai Shan
▲3767
Feng Xian
Zhouzhi
Weinan
XI'AN
Hua Xian
▲2160
Lingbao
Chuankou
Lushi
Shangzhou
Song Xian
Ruyang
Pingdingshan
Xiangcheng
Yanling
Zhoukou
Shangshui
Luyi

Wudu
Liuba
Fengxian
Lantian
Luonan
Danfeng
Shanyang
Xiping
Runan
Queshan

▲3002
Mian Xian
Baocheng
Yang Xian
Ningshan
Zhashui
Shanyang
Shangnan
Funiu Shan
▲2192
Taipingzhen
Lushan
Xiangcheng
Yichun
Wuyang
Shenqiu
Jieshou

▲5588
Pingwu
Qingchuan
Guangyuan
Hanzhong
Chenggu
Shiquan
Hanyin
Zhen'an
Xiang
Xixiang
Zhenping
Yunxi
Xichuan
Neixiang
Fangcheng
Tanghe
Biyang
Zhumadian
Taihe

Wen Xian
Ningqiang
Xixiang
Hanyin
Xunyang
Baihe
Yun Xian
Nanyang
Zhumadian
Fuyang

Ziyang
Ankang
Han Shui
Danjiang
Wodian
Hong He

ANHUI

Projection: Conical with two standard parallels

Sand deserts

SEA OF JAPAN
(EAST SEA)

YELLOW SEA
(Huang Hai)

NORTH KOREA

P'YŎNGYANG

SOUTH KOREA

SEOUL

JAPAN

HARBIN

CHANGCHUN

SHENYANG

Bo Hai

Korea Bay

Korea Strait

East from Greenwich

COPYRIGHT PHILIP'S

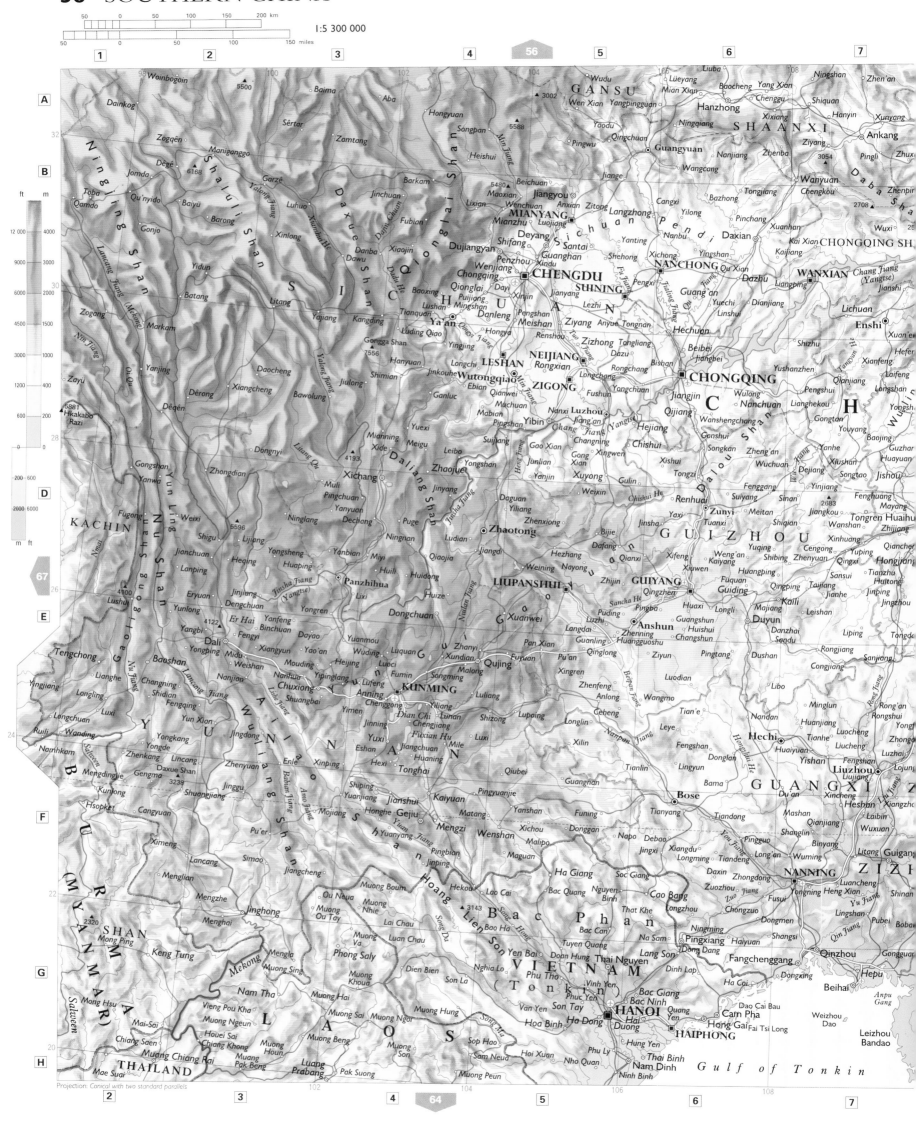

1:5 300 000

Projection: Conical with two standard parallels

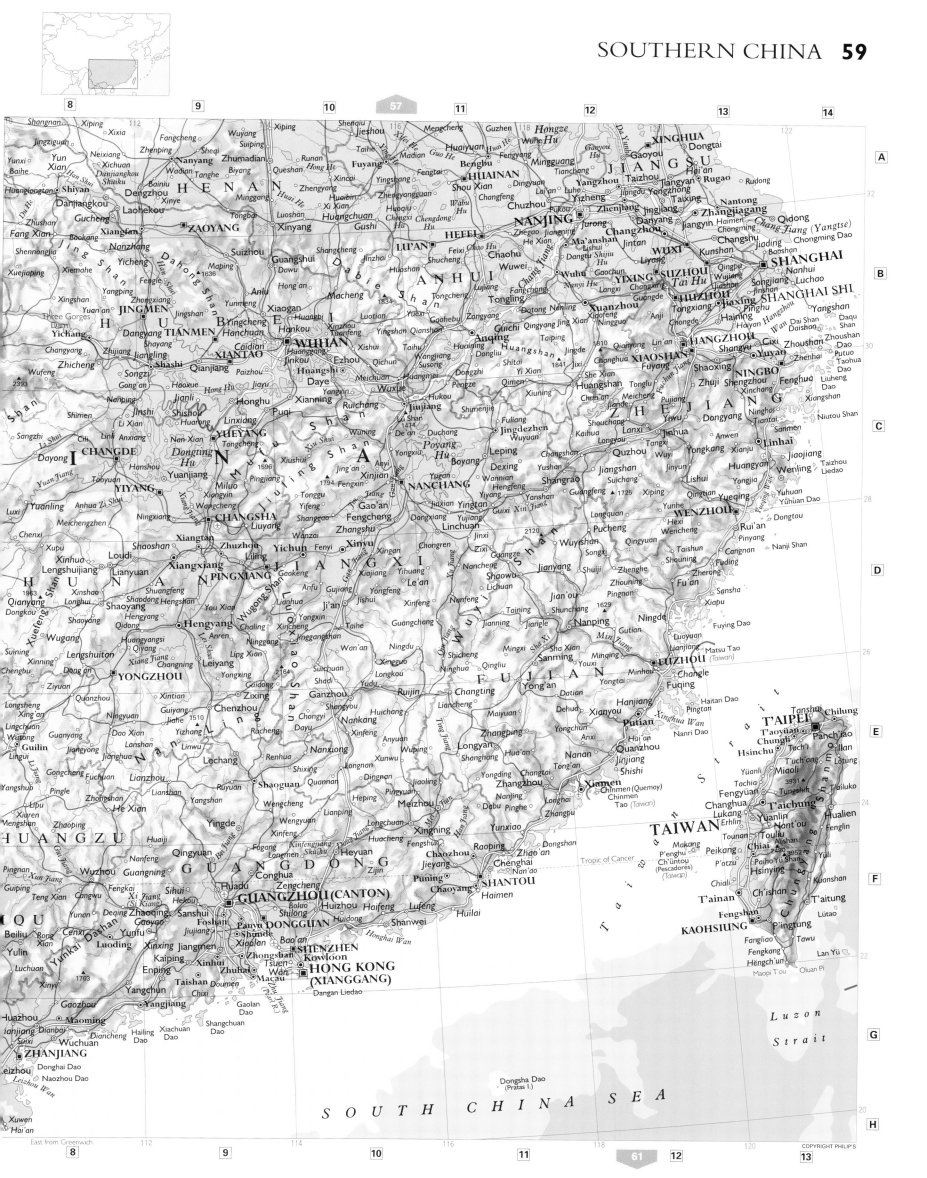

Shangnan Xiping Xixia Wuyang Suiping Xiping Shenqiu Jieshou Mengcheng Guzhen Hongze Hu XINGHUA Dongtai
Jingziguan Zhenping Fangcheng Suiping Runan Hong He Madian Guo He Wuhe Hu Gaoyou JIANGSU Gaoyou
Yunxi Yun Neixiang Nanyang Zhumadian Biyang Queshan Fuyang Huaiyuan Huai He Fengyang Mingguang Yangzhou Taizhou Jiangyan Rugao Rudong
Baihe Xian Xichuan Wadian Tanghe Bengbu Minguang Yizheng Jiangdu Yangzhong Taixing Nantong
Huanglongtan Shiyan Danjiangkou Nanzhang Biyang HUAIAN Dingyuan Tianchang Zhenjiang Jingjiang Zhangjiagang Qidong
Zhushan Danjiangkou Shuiku Baini HENAN Huaibin Xi Xian Shou Xian Dangyang Chuzhou Pukou Yizheng Jiangdu Jiangyin Haimen Chongming Chang Jiang (Yangtse)
Fang Xian Laohekou Minggang Luoshan Huangchuan Gushi Chengxi Hu NANJING Jurong Changzhou Danyang Jiangyin Chongming Dao
ZAOYANG Xinyang Tongbai HEFEI Zhegao Jiangning Jintan Liyang WUXI Changshu Jiading Chongming Dao
Xiangfan LU'AN Feixi Chao Hu Chaohu Ma'anshan Dangtu Shijiu Liyang SUZHOU Kunshan SHANGHAI
Shennongjia Yicheng Jing Shan Maping Shangcheng Dawu Shucheng Wuwei Hu Gaochun YIXING Changxing Tai Hu Qingpu Nanhui
Xuejiaping Xiemahe Fengle Huoshan Hong'an Tongcheng Lujiang Fangchang HUZHOU Jiashan SHANGHAI SHI
Yangping Zhongxiang JINGMEN YINGCHENG Xiaogan Huangpi Luotian Yuexi Gaohebu Zongyang Tongling Datong Nanling Xuanzhou Gongde TONGXIANG HAINING Haiyan Dai Shan Daishan Daqu
Xingshan Yuan'an Hanchuan Huangpi Xinzhou Yingshan Qianshan Guichi Qingyang Jing Xian Anji Chongde JIAXING Pinghu Haiyan Hangzhou Bay Putuo Taohua
HUBEI Jingshan Anlu WUHAN Hankou Macheng Yuexi Huaining Dongliu Huangshan Jingde Ningguo Lin'an Qiandaohu HANGZHOU Shangyu Zhenhai Shan
Three Gorges TIANMEN XIANTAO Huangshi Ezhou Qichun Susong Dongzhi Shitai Jixi Qianyang XIAOSHAN Shaoxing Cixi Yuyao Zhoushan
Dam Dangyang Shashi Qianjiang Huangshi Daye Meichuan Huangmei Pengze Qimen Yi Xian Huangshan Tonglu Fuyang Shangyu Zhuji Shengzhou Fenghua Zhoushan Liuheng
Yichang Changyang Zhijiang Jiangling Honghu Jiayu Wuxue Hukou Shimenjie Xiuning Chun'an Meicheng Pujiang Ningbo Ninghai Xiangshan Niutou Shan
Wufeng Zhicheng Songzi Gong'an Hong Hu Xianning Jiujiang Lu Shan De'an Fuliang Jingdezhen Kaihua Lanxi Jinhua Yiwu Dongyang ZHEJIANG Tiantai Sanmen
Nanping Jianli Puqi Wuning Duchang Leping Wuyuan Changshan Quzhou Wuyi Yongkang Xianju Linhai
Shan Jinshi Shishou Huarong Linxiang Xiu Shui Poyang Boyang Dexing Shangrao Jiangshan Suichang Guangfeng Jinyun Lishui Huangyan Taizhou
Sangzhi Li Shui YUEYANG Tongcheng Jing'an Xinjian Yugan Yanshan Hengfeng Yushan Lishui Yongjia Liedao
Cili Linli Anxiang Nan Xian Mufu Shan Anyi NANCHANG Jixian Yiyang Yingtan Guixi Xin Jiang Qingtian Yueqing
Dayong CHANGDE Dongting Yuanjiang Pingjiang Xiushui Fengxin Dongxiang Yujiang Linchuan Jinxi Longquan Yunhe Wenzhou
Yuanling Taoyuan Hu Hanshou Miluo 1596 1794 Gao'an Fengcheng Dongxiang Guangfeng Pucheng Qingyuan Taishun Cangnan WENZHOU
Yuan Jiang Anhua Zi Shui Ningxiang Wangcheng Shanggao Zhangshu Linchuan Jinxi Wuyishan Shuangxi Zherong Fuding Rui'an Dongtou
Luxi Meichengzhen Xiangjiang JIANGXI Yifeng Nancheng Wuyi Shan Songxi Hexi Pinyang Nanji Shan
Chenxi Xupu Xinhua CHANGSHA Liuyang Yichun Fenyi Xinyu Xingan Chongren Zixi Guangze Jianyang Shuiji Zhenghe Fu'an Shouning
Xiangtan Zhuzhou Liling Gaokeng Xiajiang Yihuang Shaowu Lichuan Jian'ou Pingnan Sansha
Loudi HUNAN PINGXIANG Anfu Gujiang Xinfeng Nanfeng Taining Jian'ou 1629 Ningde Xiapu
Lengshuijiang Lianyuan Xiangxiang Shaodong Hengshan You Xian Lianhua Jishui Taihe Jian'ou Shunchang Jianning Ningde Fuying Dao
Qianyang Longhui Shaofeng Qidong Chaling Yongxin Xingcheng Jinggangshan Wan'an Ningdu Jianyang Shaxian Nanping Gutian Luoyuan
Dongkou Shaoyang Hengyang Huangyangsi Qiyang Anren Ninggang Ji'an Jingdong Qingliu Minxi Sha Xi Min Jiang Lianjiang Matsu Tao
Xinning Wugang Xiang Jiang Changning Leiyang Ling Xian 2164 Suichuan Shadi Longnan Shicheng Qinghua Sanming Minqing FUZHOU (Taiwan)
Suining Chengbu Lengshuitan Dong'an YONGZHOU Yongxing Gaidong Yudu Longkou Ninghua FUJIAN Youxi Minhou Changle
Ziyuan Quanzhou Xintian Zixing Chenzhou Shangyou Ruijin Changting Liancheng Yong'an Datian Yongtai Fuqing
Longsheng Xing'an Guiyang Jiahe 1510 Huichang Maiyuan Dehua Xianyou Haitan Dao
Lingchuan Guanyang Jianghua Jionghua Renhua Dayu Xunwu Chongyi Anyuan Wuping Longyan Nanan Quanzhou Pingtan
Wutong Dao Xian Lanshan Linwu Nanxiong Changtai Tong'an Jinjiang Shishi
GUILIN Lingui Jiangyong Lechang Shixing Longnan Dingnan Jiaoling Yongding Zhangping Shanghang Nan'an Xiamen
Yangshuo Gongcheng Fuchuan Lianzhou Yangshan Wengcheng Pingyuan Meizhou Yongding Zhangzhou Longhai Quanzhou Chinmen (Quemoy)
Lipu Zhongshan Ruyuan Shaoguan Quannan Xinfeng Huacheng Meixian Hua'an Chinmen Tao (Taiwan)
Xiuren Zhaoping Yingde Heping Lianping Longchuan Meizhou Zhangpu TAIWAN
Mengshan HUANGZU GUANGDONG Qingyuan Xinfeng Heyuan Xingning Huaibei Fengshun Dongshan T'AINAN KAOHSIUNG

SOUTH CHINA SEA

Luzon Strait

Dongsha Dao (Pratas I.)

Tropic of Cancer

Taiwan Strait

T'AIPEI Tanshui Chilung
T'aoyüan Chungli Panch'iao
Hsinchu Tach'i Ilan
T'uch'ang Tungshih Lotung
Yüanli Tachia Miaoli 3931
Changhua T'aichung Hualien
Lukang Yüanlin Nant'ou Fenglin
Chiai Alishan 3952
Hsinying Paiho Yü Shan
Chiali T'ainan Ch'ishan Kuanshan
Fengshan P'ingtung T'aitung Lütao
KAOHSIUNG Fangliao Tungshih Tawu
Fengkang Hengch'un Lan Yü
Maopi T'ou Oluan Pi

ZHANJIANG Donghai Dao Naozhou Dao

1:17 800 000

Projection: Bonne

East from Greenwich

1:6 700 000

50   0   100   150   200   250   300 km
50   0   50   100   150   200 miles

1 2 3 4 **59** 5 6 7 8

A

Dongsha Dao
(Pratas I.)

Luzon Strait Itbayat I. Batanes Is. Batan I.

P A C I F I C

20

Balintang Channel

B

Calayan I. Babuyan I.

O C E A N

Dalupiri I. Babuyan Islands Camiguin I.
Fuga I.
Mayraira Pt. *Babuyan Channel*
Bangui Claveria
Bacarra Aparri Santa Ana
San Nicolas Laoag Kabugao Gonzaga
Batac Gattaran

18

Cabugao Bangued Tuao Tuguegarao
Vigan Mt. Cresta ▲1685
Santa Lubuagan Mt. Cresta
C Candon Maria Roxas Ilagan Santiago *Palanan Pt.*
Tagudin Bontoc San Mateo Palanan
Balaoan Cordillera Central Cordon
San Fernando MT. DATA Santiago Cosiguran
Lingayen Baguio Mt. Pulog ▲2928 Solano
Bolinao HUNDRED ISLANDS Bayombong Mt. Anacuao ▲1852
Alaminos Rosario *Luzon* C. San Ildefonso
Lingayen Gulf Dagupan

16

San Carlos San Manuel *Baler Bay*
Santa Cruz Bayambang San Jose Baler
D Masinloc Moncada Cuyapo *PHILIPPINE*
Iba ▲2037 Camiling Victoria Dingalan *SEA*
Concepcion ▲Tarlac La Paz Gapan Cabanatuan
Mt. Pinatubo ▲1780 Angeles *Polillo Str.*
San Antonio San Fernando Polillo Is.
Olongapo Oroni **Malabon** Patnanongan I.
BATAAN **Caloocan** Jomalig I.
Subic B. *Manila* **Quezon City**
Bataan Bay ■**MANILA** *Lamon Bay*
Dasmariñas **Pasay** Santa Cruz
Cavite L. de Bay Lucban Paracale
PHILIPPINES

14

Nasugbu Togtay San Alabat I. Daet
Balayan Lemery **Pablo** Atimonan *BICOL* Pandan Viga Catanduanes
Batangas **Lipa** Lucena Calauag Calabanga San Andres
Lobo Tayabas Bay Catanauan Naga Mt. Isarog ▲1976 Virac
Lubang Is. Verde I. Pass Boac Nabua Iriga Tabaco Lagonoy Gulf
5245 C. Calavite Lopez Marin- Ligao Mayon Vol. ▲2421 Rapu Rapu I.
duque Legazpi Donsol Sorsogon
Calapan Victoria *Tablas* Burias I. Magallanes Gubat
E Mamburao LAKE NAUJAN Mt. Baco ▲2487 Str. Bulan San Bernardino Str.
Mindoro Pinamalayan *SIBUYAN* Ticao I. Irosin
Sablayan Bongabong Romblon
APO REEF MARINE Roxas Tablas I. Sibuyan I. Allen Laoang
Busuanga I. San Jose Odiongan Masbate Aroroy Mondragon Catarman Gamay
Culion I. Ilin I. Mandaon Milagros Oras
Calamian Semirara Is. *SEA* **Masbate** Taft

12

Linapacan Str. Pandan Placer Catbalogan Paranas **Samar**
Linapacan I. Kalibo Roxas *VISAYAN* Bilinan I. Caibiran Borongan Santa
Taytay Pilar Ajuy Sara *SEA* Calubian Rita Basey Llorente
Cuyo West Pass Cuyo Is. Tibiao ▲2117 Bantayan I. Carigara Basey General MacArthur
F Cuyo Bugasong **Panay** Passi Palompon **Leyte** Tacloban Guiuan
Cuyo East Pass Pototan Cadiz Bogo Ormoc Dulag Leyte Gulf
Palawan San Jose **Iloilo** Silay Sagay Tuburan Camotes Abuyog Homonhon I.
ST. PAUL Jordan Victorias Danao Is. Baybay
▲1593 Guimaras San Carlos CENTRAL CEBU Sogod
Irahuan Hinigaran La ▲2450 **Mandaue** Bato San Dinagat I. 10 497
Honda Bay Binalbagan Carlota **Cebu** Maasin Juan *Mindanao Trench*

10

Puerto Princesa Himamaylan *SEA* Surigao Siargao I.
Kabankalan Carcar RATAH Dinagat
Mt. Mantalingajan Cayagan Is. Sipalay Argao Bohol I. Panaon I. SIKATUNA Placer
G ▲2085 Bais Oslob Tagbilaran Bucas Grande I.
1727 **Negros** Hinoba-an Tanjay *BOHOL* ▲2012 Carrascal
C. Buliluyan Bugsuk I. Bayawan Dumaguete Camiguin I. Cabadbaran Nasipit Lanuza
5576 Siaton Siquijor Cabadbaran **Butuan** Tandag
Zamboanguita Talisayan Gingoog Bayugan Marihatag
SULU *SEA* Balingasag Lianga
Dipolog Dapitan Alubijid Esperanza Hinatuan
TUBBATAHA Manukan Iligan Opol Talacogan Bislig
REEFS Oroquieta Bay **Cagayan de Oro**

8

Sindangan Ozamiz **Iligan** ▲2938 Malaybalay
Labason Tubod Marawi City Bunawan
SEA Siocon Kabasalan Pagadian L. Lanao Valencia Cateel
Balabac I. Malabang ▲2815 Panabo Baganga
Balabac Strait Midsayap Tagum
Balambangan Banggi Sibuco Sibugay Parang Pikit Pantukan Manay
Bay Cotabato MT. MALINDANG Mt. Apo ▲2954 **Davao**
H Kudat Cagayan Sulu I. *Moro Gulf* Datu Piang Kidapawan Digos Davao San Isidro
Langkon Senaja Jambongan Talayan Koronadal Gulf
Zamboanga Kalamansig Malita
Kota Turtle Is. Pilas Lebak C. San Agustin
Belud Group Isabela Palimbang 2083 **General**
Tg. Labian Basilan Str. ▲ **Santos**
G. Kinabalu Pangutaran Basilan I. Lamitan Kiamba Sarangani Bay
▲4101 Group Tinaca Pt.

6

Kota Kinabalu Jolo Jolo Samales 5824 ▼ Sarangani Is.
Papar Group Group
Keningau Parang Talipao *CELEBES*
SABAH **Sandakan** Siasi Tapul
J Melalap Kuamat Parang Pata I. Group *SEA*
Tawi-tawi Sulu Archipelago
MALAYSIA Teluk Darvel Group *INDONESIA* Kep. Talaud
Borneo Sibutu Passage Sibutu Group

Projection: Lambert's Conformal Conic East from Greenwich COPYRIGHT PHILIP'S

116 118 120 122 124 126 128

National Parks

ft m
9000 3000
6000 2000
4500 1500
3000 1000
1200 400
600 200
0 0
200 600
4000 12 000
8000 24 000
m ft

1:11 100 000

Projection: Mercator

East from Greenwich

JAVA AND MADURA
1:6 700 000

50 0 50 100 150 200 250 300 km
50 0 50 100 150 200 miles

BALI
1:1 800 000

10 0 10 20 30 km
10 0 10 20 miles

Philippines / Luzon area

Claveria, Babuyan Chan., C. Engaño, Bacarat, Laoag, Aparri, Tuao, 2048, Bangued, Vigan, Bontoc, Solano, Palanan, Palanan Pt., San Fernando, Lingayen, Baguio, 1759, Bolinao, Bayombong, Casiguran, Dagupan, Tarlac, Cabanatuan, Baler, Angeles, Luzon, Olongapo, Mt. Pinatubo, Malolos, Quezon City, Bataan, San Fernando, Polillo Is., Manila B., MANILA, Cavite, Santa Cruz, Lamon Bay, Lubang Is., Lipa, Calauag, Daet, Catanduanes, Batangas, 2188, Lucena, Naga, Virac, Mamburao, Calapan, Marinduque, Legazpi, Mayon Volcano, 2462, Sorsogon, Mindoro, Halcon 2586, Burias, San Bernardino Str., Sablayan, Romblon, Sibuyan, Masbate, Loaong, Tablas, Masbate, Oras, Taft, 5245, San Jose, Semirara, Pandan, Panay, 2117, Roxas, Sea, Samar, General MacArthur, Cuyo, Cuyo, Iloilo, San Jose de Buenavista, Cadiz, San Carlos, Ormoc, Catbalogan, Borongan, Guiuan, Culion, Guimaras, Panay G., 2465, Talibon, Leyte, Baybay, Puerto Princesa, Negros, Bacolod, Mandaue, Cebu, Maasin, Dinagat, 10 497, Tanjay, Binalbagan, Bohol, Surigao, Siargao, Mindanao Trench, Dumaguete, 5576, Siquijor, Sea, Tagbilaran, Camiguin, Tandag, Dipolog, Butuan, L. Mainit, 2012, Sindangan, Cagayan, 2425, Iligan, de Oro, Lianga, Liloy, Ozamiz, Malaybalay, Cateel, Bislig, Kabasalan, Mindanao, 2938, Parang, Tagum, Baganga, Siocon, Pagadian, Cotabato, 2954, Mt. Apo, Mati, Zamboanga, Isabela, Moro G., Datu Piang, Talayan, Koronadal, Digos, DAVAO, Basilan, Balimbing, Kiamba, 2083, C. San Agustin, Jolo, Samales Group, General Santos, Malita, Tawi-Tawi, Tapul Group, Sarangani B., 5824, Sarangani Is., Tinaca Pt.

Kepulauan Nanusa, Karakelong, Kawio, Beo, Kepulauan Talaud, Salibabu, Kaburuang, Tahuna, Pulau Sangihe, Kepulauan Sangihe, Siau, Tahulandang, Biaro, Bunaken, Bangka, 2022, Manado, Kema, Amurang, Tondano, GORONTALO, Kuandang, Kotamobagu, UTARA, Malino 2490, Tilamuta, Gorontalo, Tanjung Flesko, Tomini, Teluk Tomini

Bali / Lombok area

3332 Gunung Raung, Ketapang, Tanjung Batugondang, Singaraja, Kubutambahan, BALI SEA, Banyuwangi, Gilimanuk, Tanjung Menjangan, Gerokgak, Lovina, Seririt, Bayun, Tejakula, Glagah, Cekik, 1385 Gunung Merbuk, Kintamani, Batur, 1717, Songan, Tianyar, Kubu, Jambewangi, Kabat, Melaya, BALI, Busungbiu, Gunung Batukau 2276, Bedugul, Danau Batur, Penelokan, Gunung Agung 3142, Culik, Beluki, Rogojampi, Negara, Mendoyo, Bituriti, Jatiluwih, Rendang, Amed, Tirtagangga, Genteng, Srono, Muncar, Perancak, Pekutan, Pasar, Yehbuah, Belimbing, Tegallalang, Saren, Karangasem (Amlapura), Tegalsari, Tjiluring, Bajatrejo, Bajera, Sembung, Bangli, Manggis, Candi Dasa, Grajagan, Bali, Tabanan, Blahkiuh, Ubud, Klungkung, Lombok, Jawa, Semenanjung Blambangan, Sukawati, Gianyar, Kusamba, Montongbuwoh, Tanjung Purwo, Denpasar, Danginpuri, Sanur, Selat Badung, Sampalan, Ampenan, Mataram, Uluwatu, Jimbaran, Kuta, Toyapakeh, 530, Suwana, Lembuak, Teluk Terang, Tanjung Mebulu, Bukit Badung, Nusa Dua, Nusa Penida, Tanjung Abah, Lembar, Gerung, Blongas, Tanjung Bebera, Tanjung Pangga, Tanjung Tampa

17 INDIAN OCEAN 18

115

Java and Madura insets

Selat Sunda, Pulau Rakata, Panaitan, Anyer, Merak, Serang, Tangerang, JAKARTA, Bekasi, Karawang, Pamanukan, Kandanghaur, Indramayu, Kepulauan Karimunjawa, Bawean, Sangkapura, Pandeglang, Rangkasbitung, BANTEN, Bogor, BARAT, Purwakarta, Subang, Majalengka, Cirebon, Brebes, Tegal, Pekalongan, Kendal, Demak, Pati, Muria 1602, Rembang, Tuban, Tg. Bugel, Tanjung Pangkah, Madura, Pelabuhanratu, Tanjung Guhakolak, Sukabumi, Cianjur, BANDUNG, Garut, Sumedang, Ciamis, Kuningan, Slamet 3428, Banyumas, Purwokerto, Wonosobo, Boyolali, Semarang, Salatiga, Ngawi, Mojokerto, Bangkalan, Sampang, Tambuk 471, Sumenep, Pamekasan, Genteng, Pengalengan, Sindangbarang, Cijulang, Cilacap, Nusa Kambangan, Kebumen, Kayangan, Yogyakarta, Merapi 2911, Surakarta 3265, Madiun, Arjuna, Sidoarjo, Pasuruan, SURABAYA, Selat Madura, Ponorogo, Kediri, 2563 Liman, Probolinggo, Situbondo, Trenggalek, Pacitan, Bantul, Wates, YOGYKTA, Tulungagung, Blitar, Malang, 3676, Bromo, 3089, Banyuwangi, Wlingi, Semeru, Lumajang, Jember, 3332, Rambipuji, Pasirian, Nusa Barung, Bali, Selat Bali

Sulawesi / Celebes area

CELEBES SEA, Maratua, Tanjung Mangkalihat, Tolitoli, Buol, Paleleh, Sumalata, Moutong, Donggala, Toboli, Kepulauan Togian, Palu, SULAWESI, Pangi, Poso, 2355, Danau Poso, Tojo, Tokala 2630, Poh, Luwuk, Peleng, Banggai, Kepulauan Banggai, Taliabu, Mangole, Sanana, Kepulauan Sula, Makale, Rantemario 3440, Parang, Singkang, Kendari, Monse, Wowoni, TENGGARA, Kolaka, Pampanua, Watampone, Buton, Buapinang, Muna, Raha, Lawele, Wangiwangi, Baubau, Kepulauan Tukangbesi, Binongko, Salayar, Kepulauan Bonerate, Batuata, Tanahjampea, Kalao, Kalaotoa, Bonerate, FLORES SEA, BANDA SEA

Maluku / Papua area

PACIFIC OCEAN, Merir (Palau), 5798, Tobi (Palau), Helen Atoll (Palau), Sopi, Berebere, Morotai, Doi, Galela, Biaro, Ibu 1325, Tobelo, Akelamo, Jailolo, Halmahera, UTARA, Ternate, Tidore, Teluk Buli, Patani, Kepulauan Asia, Kepulauan Ayu, Kepulauan Mapia, Waigeo, Makian, Weda, Teluk Weda, Kayoa, Umera, Selpele, Saonek, Waibeem, Dampier, Kairoi, Manokwari, Supiori, Biak, Kasiruta, Kepulauan Bacan, Mandioli, Gani, Obilatu, Labuha, 2411, Batanta, Salawati, Kofiau, Sailolof, Segot, Kwoka 2452, Klamono, Nabire, Numfoor, Warsa, Bosnik, Kepulauan Padaido, Tanjung D'Urville, Kepulauan Kumamba, Obi, Misool, Teminabuan, Jazirah Doberai, Wasian, 2926, Ransiki, Wariap, Yapen, Selat Yapen, 1496, Serui, Bonoi, Sarmi, Saberania, Ansudu, IRIAN JAYA, Inawatan, BARAT, Bintuni, Teluk Berau, Fakfak, Kokas, Wenut, Wasior, Cenderawasih, Nubodi, 2272, Genyem, Jayapura, Sentani, Krau, PAPUA, Pegunungan Van Rees, Tariku, Bula, Seram, Weri, Ibonma, Kaimana, Karufa, Waghete, Enarotali, Pegunungan Maoke, 5029 Jaya, Puncak Sudirman, 4730, Wamena, PAPUA NEW GUINEA, Amamapare, Uta, Tembagapura, Puncak Trikora, Jayawijaya 4702, Oksibil, Mandala 4700, Kepulauan Aru, Tanahmerah, Pirimapun, Trangan, Kepulauan Tanimbar, Larat, Yamdena, Saumlaki, Selaru, Bade, Muting, Pulau Dolak, Kimaam, Kepi, Merauke, Pulau Komoran

ARAFURA SEA

Lesser Sunda / Timor

Sunda Is., 5123, Ruteng, Lombok, Aimere, Ende, NUSA TENGGARA TIMUR, Sumbawa, 2850, Sumba, Membora, Bima, Raba, Flores, Labuhanbajo, Maumere, Larantuka, Adonara, Lomblen, Pantar, Alor, Atauro, Dili, EAST TIMOR, Kupang, Waingapu, Sawu, Baing, Raijua, Dana, Sawu Sea, Roti, Ombai, Kalabahi, Solor, Baucau, Tutuala, Viqueque, 2963, Atapupu, Kefamenanu, Nikiniki

COPYRIGHT PHILIP'S

94

1:5 300 000

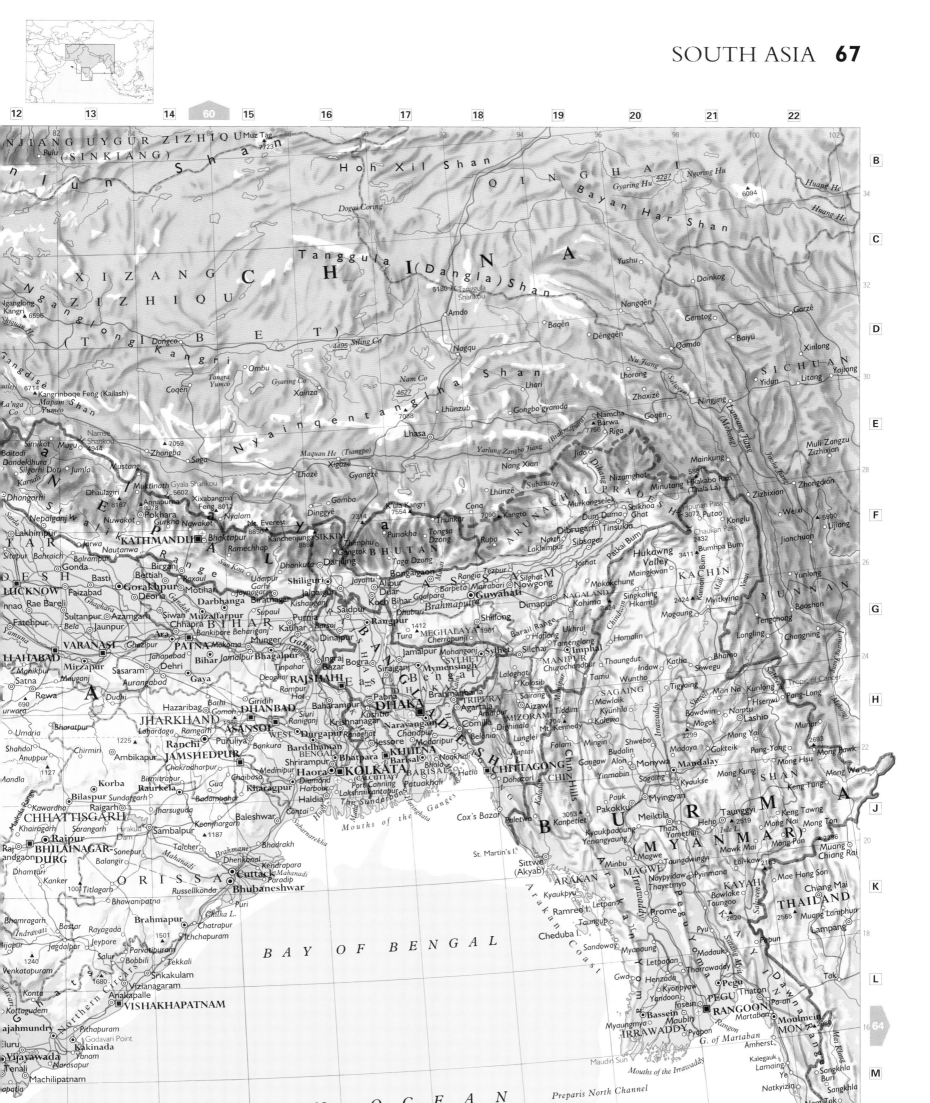

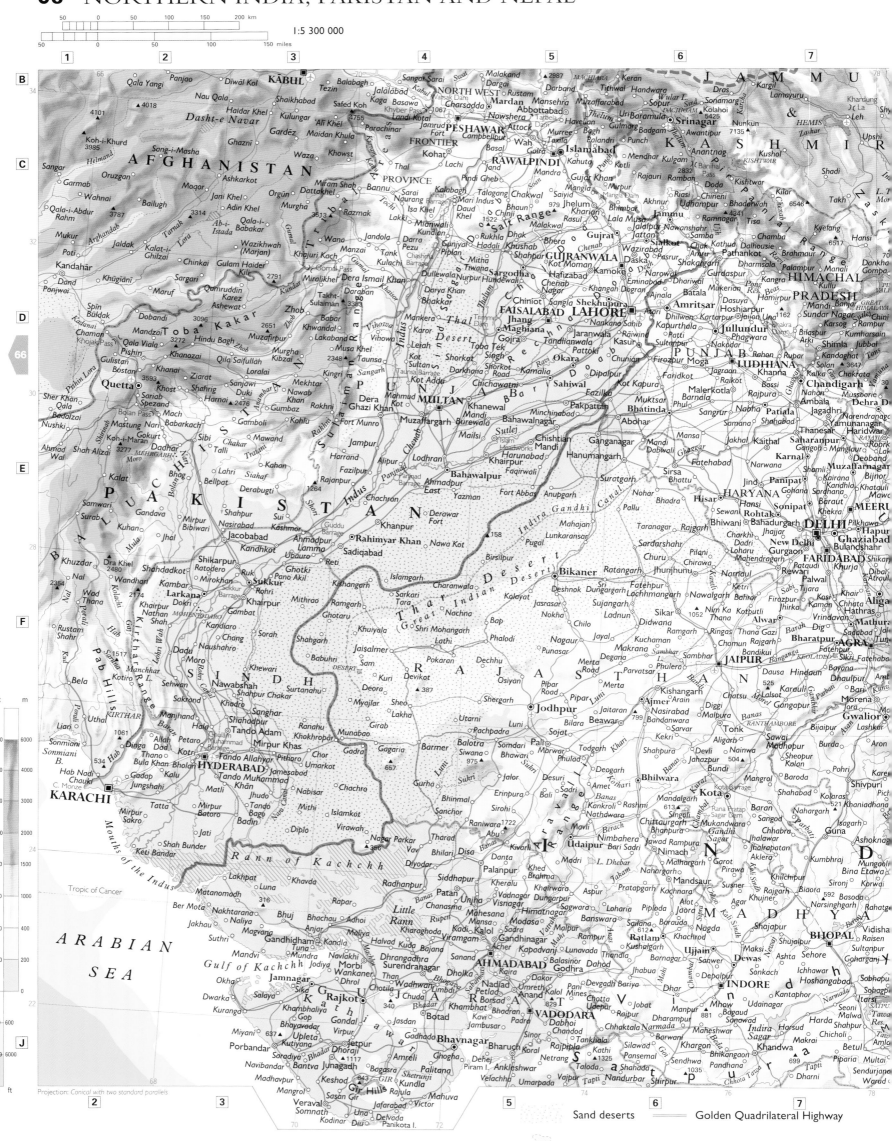

Sand deserts — Golden Quadrilateral Highway

Intermittent lakes

Projection: Conical with two standard parallels

1:6 200 000

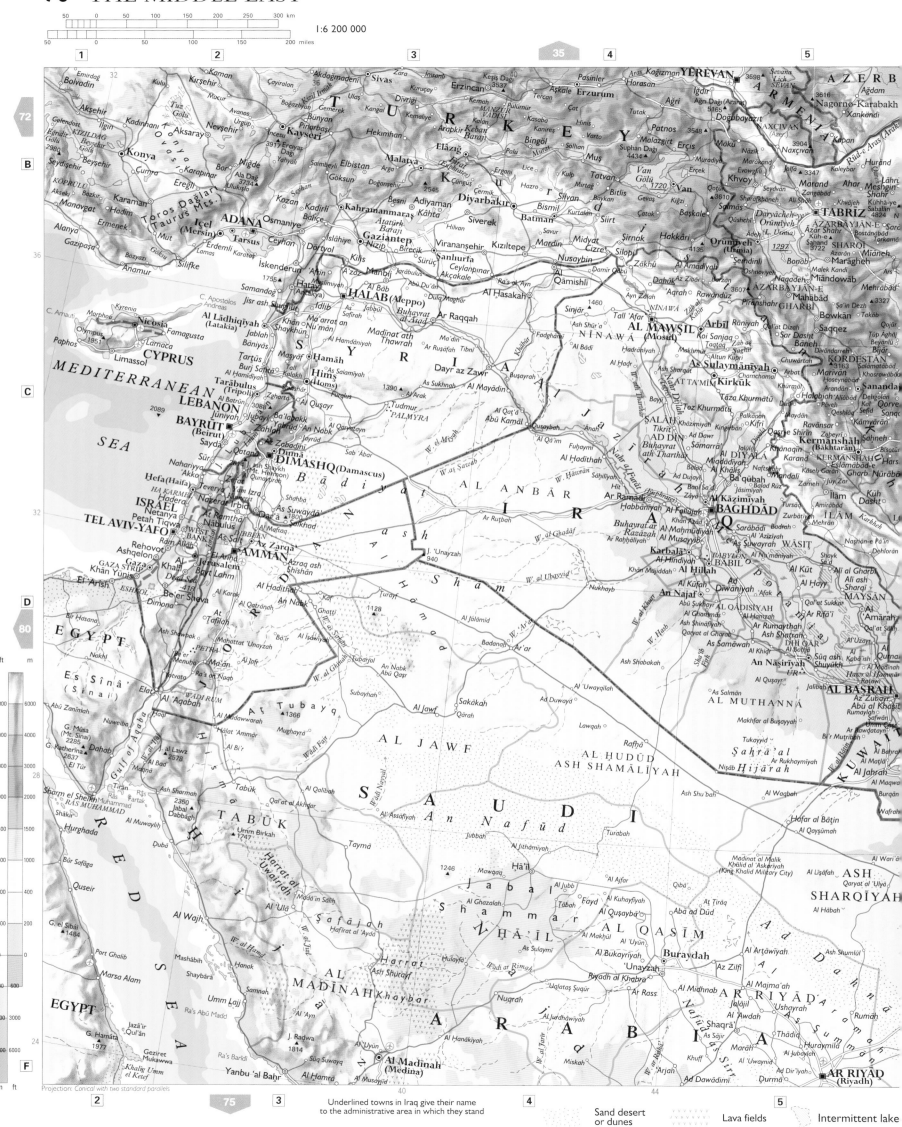

Projection: Conical with two standard parallels

Underlined towns in Iraq give their name
to the administrative area in which they stand

Sand desert
or dunes

Lava fields

Intermittent lake

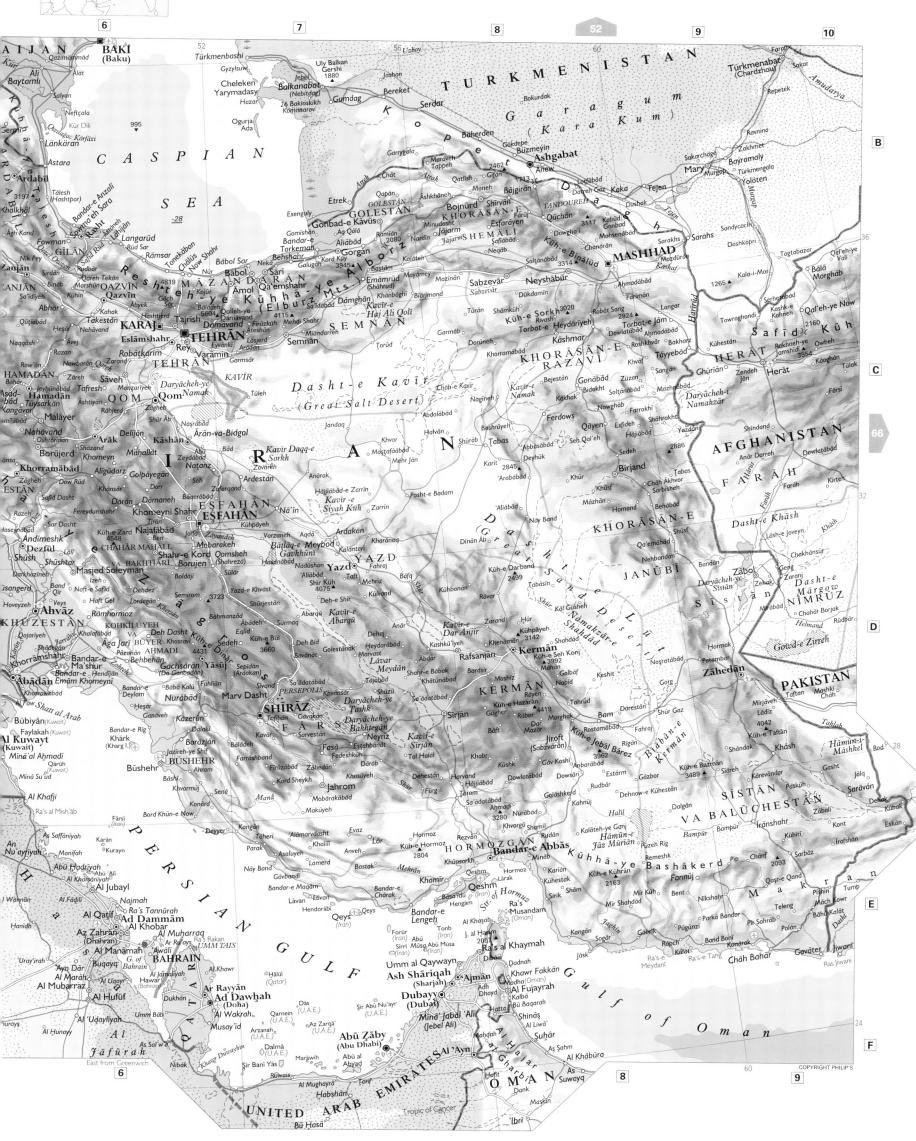

1: 4 400 000

50   0   25   50   75   100   125   150   175 km
50   0   25   50   75   100   125 miles

1 **2** **3** **4** **33** **5** **6** **7**

B L A C K   S E A

BULGARIA

A

Stara Zagora
Yambol
Aytos
Burgas
Nos Emine
Michurin
1830
2206
Ince Burun
Keremp Burnu
Sinop
Erfelek
Çatalzeytin
Ayancık
Gerze
Bafra Burnu
SAMSUN
Samsun
Terme
Ünye
Fatsa
Ordu
Perşembe

B

Edirne
Kırklareli
1018
Pınarhisar
İğneada
İğneada Burnu
Demirköy
Kilimli
Zonguldak
Çatalağzı
Çaycuma
Ereğli
Devrek
Karabük
Safranbolu
Araç
Kastamonu
Taşköprü
Durağan
Boyabat
Kürtün
SİNOP
Amasra
Cide
İnebolu
Abana
Küre
Küre Dağları
Bartın
Daday

Kırklareli
Uzunköprü
Hayrabolu
Muratlı
Çorlu
Çatalca
Çerkezköy
İSTANBUL
Kartal
Kocaeli
Sakarya (İzmit) (Adapazarı)
Düzce
Bolu
Gerede
Çerkeş
Kurşunlu
Tosya
İskilip
Osmancık
Gümüşhacıköy
Merzifon
Havza
Vezirköprü
Kavak
Çarşamba

İstanbul Boğazı (Bosporus)
Gebze
Darıca
Gölcük
Hendek
Cumaova
Akyazı
Mudurnu
Seben
Göynük
BOLU
2378
Kızılcahamam
Çubuk
Çankırı
Sungurlu
Corum
Mecitözü
Turhal
Zile
Amasya
Niksar
Reşadiye

Keşan
Enez
Tekirdağ
Malkara
Şarköy
Marmara
Marmara Denizi
Büyükçekmece
Şile
Kandıra
Karasu
Sapanca
Geyve
İznik Gölü
Mihalıççık
Nallıhan
Beypazarı
Ayaş
Sincan
Elmadağ
Kalecik
Boğazkale
Sorgun
TOKAT
Tokat
Deveci Dağları
Artova
Çırçır

C

Tekirdağ
Malkara
Gelibolu
Lâpseki
Erdek
Bandırma
Gönen
Biga
Çan
Mustafakemalpaşa
Bursa
İnegöl
Bozüyük
Eskişehir
Sivrihisar
G a l a t i a
Polatlı
Gölbaşı
ANKARA
Bala
Kırıkkale
Keskin
Yerköy
ANKARA
Çiçekdağı
Kozaklı
Sarıkaya
Çayıralan
2235
Ak Dağ
Şarkışla
Gemerek
Kangal
2802
Sivas
SİVAS
Hafik
Teçer Dağı

Çanakkale
TROY
Ezine
Bayramıç
1768
Edremit
Balya
Susurluk
Balıkesir
BALIKESİR
Uludağ
2543
ULUDAĞ
Orhaneli
Domaniç
Tavşanlı
Kütahya
KÜTAHYA
Seyitgazi
Kırka
Çifteler
Haymana
Yenice
Kuly
Tuz Gölü
Hirfanlı Barajı
Mucur
Hacıbektaş
NEVŞEHİR
Nevşehir
Kayseri
KAYSERİ
Bünyan
Sarıoğlan
Gürün
Darende
Akçadağ
MAL

Bozcaada
Baba Burnu
M y s i a
Yenice
Demirci
Simav
Gediz
Emet
Altıntaş
Banaz
Murat Dağı
Afyon (Afyonkarahisar)
AFYON
Bolvadin
Çay
Akşehir Gölü
Yunak
Sülüklü
Şereflikoçhisar
Ortaköy
Gülşehir
Avanos
GÖREME 3370
Ürgüp
İncesu
Talas
Pınarbaşı
Tomarza
Sarız
Afşin
Elbistan
Doğanşehir

D

Lesbos
968
Hios
Foça
Karaburun
Gediz
Menemen
Manisa
MANİSA
Soma
Akhisar
Kırkağaç
Salihli
Alaşehir
Eşme
Uşak
UŞAK
Sandıklı
2610
Dinar
Sultan Dağları
Eğridir Gölü
İlgın
Kadınhanı
Cihanbeyli
AKSARAY
Aksaray
Derinkuyu
Yeşilhisar
Develi
3370
Bakırdağı
KAHRAMAN-MARAŞ

Hios
1297
İzmir
İZMİR (Smyrna)
Çeşme
Urla
Menderes
SARDIS
Torbalı
Selçuk
EPHESUS
Kuşadası
Aydın
AYDIN
Nazilli
Büyük Menderes
Karacasu
Denizli
DENİZLİ
Sarayköy
Çardak
Acıgöl
Burdur Gölü
Uluborlu
Senirkent
Şuhut
Yalvaç
Akşehir
Beyşehir Gölü
Ilgın
Konya
KONYA
Obruk
Karapınar
Ereğli
Bor
NİGDE
Niğde
3734
Çamardı
Ulukışla
Pozantı
ADANA
Feke
Saimbeyli
Tufanbeyli
Göksün

Samos
1153
Ikaria
Samos
DILEK YARIMADASI
MILETUS
Söke
İncirliova
Çine
Bozdoğan
Tavas
Kızılhisar
Honaz Dağı
2528
2224
Burdur
Bucak
Isparta
ISPARTA
Eğridir
974
Gelendost
Beyşehir
Beyşehir
2980
1116
Konya
Çumra
İçeri çumra
Karaman
KARAMAN
Ayrancı
3436
Karaisalı
İmamoğlu
Kadirli
Kozan
Ceyhan
Osmaniye
İslâhiye
Gaziantep
GAZİANTEP
Nizip
Oğuzeli

E

GREECE
Fourni
Patmos
MUĞLA
Milas
Yatağan
Muğla
Ula
Köyceğiz
Gökova Körfezi
Marmaris
Ortaca
Dalaman
Köprüçay
2421
Boz Dağ
Tefenni
Söğütçüler
Ağlasun
KOVADA
Sütçüler
Seydişehir
P i s i d i a
KÖPRÜLÜ KANYON
2339
Suğla Gölü
Bozkır
2464
Hadim
Taşkent
Ermenek
Göksu
1610
Mut
İÇEL
Tarsus
İçel (Mersin)
Erdemli
Silifke
ADANA
Dörtyol
Yumurtalık
İskenderun
İskenderun Körfezi
HATAY
Kırıkhan
Kilis
A'zâz
Afrin
Manbij

Kalymnos
Kos
Astipalea
Tilos
Simi
Datça
Bozburun
Reşadiye
Fethiye
3024
Ak Dağ
3070
Elmalı
2598
Korkuteli
Serik
ASPENDOS
Manavgat
Alanya
Gazipaşa
Anamur
Anamur Burnu
Bozyazı
İncekum Burnu
Karataş
Karataş Burnu
Uluçınar
Akıncı Burnu
1755
Belen
Hatay (Antakya)
Harbiye
Reyhanlı
İdlib
HALAB
HALAB (Aleppo)
As Safirah

Dodecanese
Rhodes (Rhodes)
1215
Lindos
4210
Karpathos
1215
Kasos
Megista
Kaş
Kale
Finike
Yardımcı Burnu
Kemer
BEYDAĞLARI OLIMPOS
XANTHOS
L y c i a
Bey Dağları
P a m p h y l i a
Antalya
Antalya Körfezi
Kumluca
Demre
C i l i c i a
Gülnar
Samandağ
Yayladağı
Jisr ash Shughūr
Al Lādhiqīyah (Latakia)
Jablah
'Āşī
Ma'arrat an Nu'mān
IDLIB
Khān Shaykhūn
1385
Hamāh
Bāniyās
S Y
HAMĀH

F

M E D I T E R R A N E A N
S E A

Rizokarpaso
C. Apostolos Andreas
Kyrenia
Morphou
Nicosia
Famagusta
Polis
Olympus 1951
Troodos
Larnaca
Paphos
Episkopi
Akrotiri
Limassol
CYPRUS
2775

Ḥamāh
As Salamiyah
Maşyaf
Tall Kalakh
Shinshār
Furqlus
Al Qaryatayn
ḤIMŞ
Ḥimş (Homs)
Tarābulus (Tripoli)
Al Batrūn
3088
Zgharta
Bsharri
Al Quşayr
Ba'labak
An Nabk
LEBANON
Jubayl
Jūniyah
BAYRŪT (Beirut)
Yabrūd
Jayrūd
Sab 'Ābar
Zahlah
Az Zabdānī
Şaydā
Dūmā
DIMASHQ (Damascus)
Jaramānah
2814
Qaţanā
B ā

G

ISRAEL
TEL AVIV-YAFO
Netanya
Hadera
Hefa (Haifa)
HA KARMEL
Nazerat
Teverya
Yam Kinneret
Qiryat Shemona
Nahariyya
'Akko
Zefat
1800
AS SUWAYDĀ'
Shaba
As Suwaydā'
Qiryat Shemona
Şūr
Sayda
Qiryat
Al Qunayţirah
Izra
Dar'ā
Nābulus
WEST BANK
Dibeen
1247
Irbid
Al Mafraq
Busra ash Shām
Salkhad
Az Zarqā
JORDA
Rehovot
Ashdod
Ramla
El 'Arīḥa
As Salt
'AMMĀN
Ashqelon
Jerusalem

80 **3** **4** **5** **74** **7**

Projection: Conical with two standard parallels

Division between Greeks and Turks
in Cyprus; Turks to the North.

6

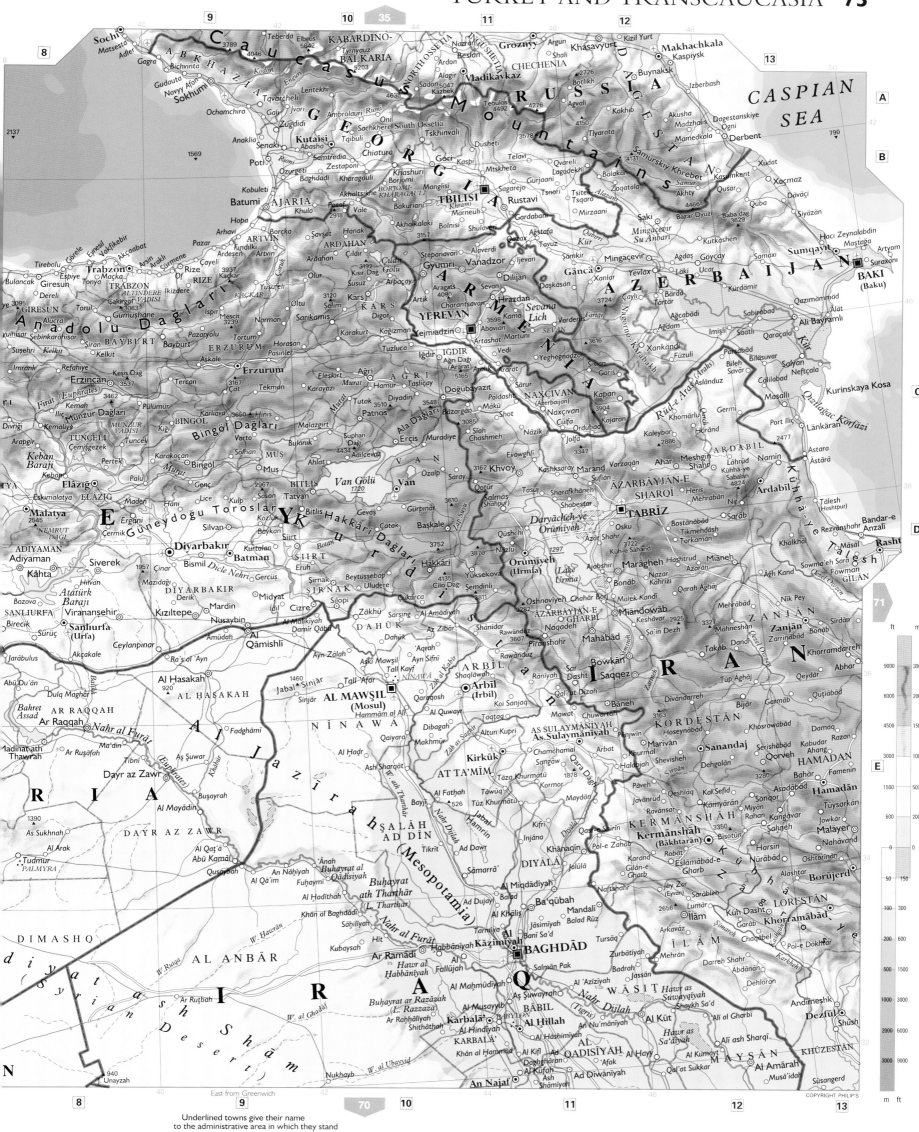

Underlined towns give their name
to the administrative area in which they stand

1:2 200 000

10 0 10 20 30 40 50 60 70 80 100 km
10 0 10 20 30 40 50 60 miles

72

CYPRUS
Paphos · Episkopi · Kividhes · Zyyi
Limassol · Akrotiri Bay
Episkopi Bay · C. Gata

M E D I T E R R A N E A N
S E A

2775
2089

LEBANON
Tarābulus (Tripoli)
Al Minā · Zgharta · Qurnat as Sawdā' 3088 · Bsharri
Al Batrūn
Jubayl · Qartabā · Ibrāhīm
Jūniyah
BAYRŪT (Beirut)
Bikfayyā · 2628 J. Sannīn
Ash Shuwayfāt · Alayh
Ad Dāmūr · JABAL LUBNĀN · Zahlah
Saydā (Sidon) · 1942 J. al Bārūk · Ḥawsh Mūssá
Jazzīn · J. ash Shaykh (Mt. Hermon) 2814
An Nabaṭīyah at Taḥta
Sūr (Tyre) · AL JANŪB · Qiryat Shemona
Marj 'Uyūn · Al Khiyām · Masʻada · 1197 · Al Qunayṭirah

HIMS
Hims (Homs)
Shinshār · Furqlus
Al Hamīdīyah
Tall Kalakh · Halbā · Al Quṣayr
ASH SHAMĀL · Al Ḥirmil
Al Burayj
2464 · Al Qaryatayn
Al Labwah
Baʻlabakk · 2616 · Yabrūd · Bi'r Ghadīr
An Nabk
SYRIA
Sirghāyā · Az Zabadānī · Dumayr · Khān Abū Shāmat
Qaṭanā · DIMASHQ (Damascus)
Dārayyā · Jaramānah · Al Ḥājānah · Jayrūd
A'rwaj · Al Kiswah · Burāq
Aş Şanamayn · As Suwaydā'
DARʻĀ · Shahbā
Izra · As Suwaydā · Salah 1800
Shaykh Miskīn · Ṣaham al Jawlān
Darʻā · Būṣrá ash Shām · AD DARŪZ · Salkhad · Malaḥ
Yarmūk · IRBID · At Ramthā · Umm al Qiṭṭayn
AL MAFRAQ

ISRAEL
Nahariyya · Me'ona · HaGalil 1208 (Galilee)
'Akko (Acre) · Zefat · Yam Kinneret (Sea of Galilee)
Mifraz Hefa · Qiryat Karmi'el · Teverya (Tiberias) -210
Hefa (Haifa) · Qiryat Ata · Nazerat (Nazareth)
Dāliyat el Karmel · HEFA KARMEL · ILA · Afula · Ṭabūk
Umm el Fahm · TEL MEGIDDO · Jenin · Bet She'an
CAESAREA · SHOMRŌN · AJLŪN · 'Ajlūn · Al Mafraq
Hadera · Hanna-Karkur · SAMARIA · DIBBĒN 1247 · Jarash
Netanya · Tulkarm · Ṭūbās · JARASH · Umm al Qittīn
HAMÉRKAZ · Nabulus · N. az Zarqā
Ra'anana · Kefar Sava
Herzliyya · Petah Tiqwa · SHILO · AL BALQA
Benē Beraq · Rosh HaʻAyin · As Salt · Az Zarqā
TEL AVIV-YAFO · Ramat Gan · Wadi as Sir · AMMAN
Bat Yam · Holon · Karama
Rishon le Ziyyon · Lod · Rām Allāh · El Arīḥā (Jericho) · Na'ūr
Yavne · Ramla · WEST BANK
Rehovot · Bet Shemesh · Jerusalem (Yerushalayim) (Al Quds) · Ma'dabā · AMM
Ashdod · Bayt Laḥm (Bethlehem) · MAʻDABĀ
Qiryat Mal'akhi · Qiryat Gat · Al Khalīl (Hebron) · 'AMMĀN
Ashqelon · TEL LAKHISH · W. al Haydān · Dhībān
N. Shiqma · Az Zāhiriyah · Dead Sea · AZ ZARQĀ
GAZA STRIP · Gaza · Sederot · Arad · 'En Gedi · W. al Mawjib
Khān Yūnis · ESHKOL · N. Ḥevron · MASADA
Rafah · Be'er Sheva (Beersheba) · En Boqeq · Al Karak · Al Qatrānah
El Daheir · Bor Mashash · Sedom · 1305 AL KARAK · Al Mazār
Dimona · -333 · W. al Hasa

JORDAN
At Ṭafīlah · J. ash Shawmari 1072
AT ṬAFĪLAH · Dana · Bā'ir
W. Bā'ir
MA'AN
Nijil · Mahattat 'Unayzah
PETRA · Wādī Mūsá · Ma'ān
Rujm Tal'at al Jamā'ah 1736
Al Jafr · Qa'el Jafr

EGYPT
Bûr Sa'îd (Port Said) · Bûr Fu'ad · BŪR SA'ÎD
Rās Burûn · Sabkhet el Bardawîl
Români · Bîr el Abd · Khalig el Tîna
El 'Arîsh
Qantâra · El Qantara · Bîr el Garârât · Bîr el Lahfân
Bîr Qaṭia · Bîr el Duweidar · Bîr Kaseiba
El Qantara · Wâhid · Bîr el Jafir
Bîr Madkûr
SHAMĀL SÎNÎ · 'Arîsh
Abu Aweigila · El Quşeima
Muweilih · Birein
Ismâ'iliya · Qezi'ot · Sedé Boqér
ISMA'ÎLÎYA · Talâta · Bîr el Mâlhi · Mizpe Ramon
Khamsa · El Buheirat el Murrat el Kubra (Great Bitter L.) · Bîr Hasana
Gineifa · G. Yi 'Allaq 1094 · Bîr Beida
El Agrûd · Hanegev (Negev Desert)
El Suweis (Suez) · Bûr Taufîq · N. Paran
Adabiya · Uyûn Mûsa · Bîr el Thamâda · El Kuntilla
Ain Sudr · Nakhl · S Î N Â (Sinai) · Yotvata · Ra's an Naqb
Rās Sudr · 948 G. el Kabrît · El Thamad · Mahattat ash Shidīyah
Ghubbet el Bûs · Gebel el Tîh · 'En Avrona
1272 · W. Abu Ga'da · W. Abel Giin · J A N Û B S Î N Î · Bîr Abu Muhammad
Bîr Abu Şandûq · Rās Matarma · Bîr el Biarât · 1592 · 1754 · Bîr al Butayyihât
Bîr el Heisi · Bîr Tâba · Elat · Al 'Aqabah · Ra's an Naqb 1435 · Bi'r al Qaṭṭār
1165 · Gulf of Aqaba · Al 'Aqabah · WADI RUM · Rum
Haql · W. an Nitwaḥ · Baṭn al Ghūl · Al Mudawwarah
AL 'AQABAH

SAUDI ARABIA
At Ṭubayq

EL SUWEIS

80

ft m
9000 3000
6000 2000
4500 1500
3000 1000
1200 400
600 200
0 0
100 300
200 600
500 1500
1000 3000
2000 6000
m ft

Projection: Polyconic
East from Greenwich
COPYRIGHT PHILIP'S

▬ ▬ ▬ 1974 Cease Fire Lines

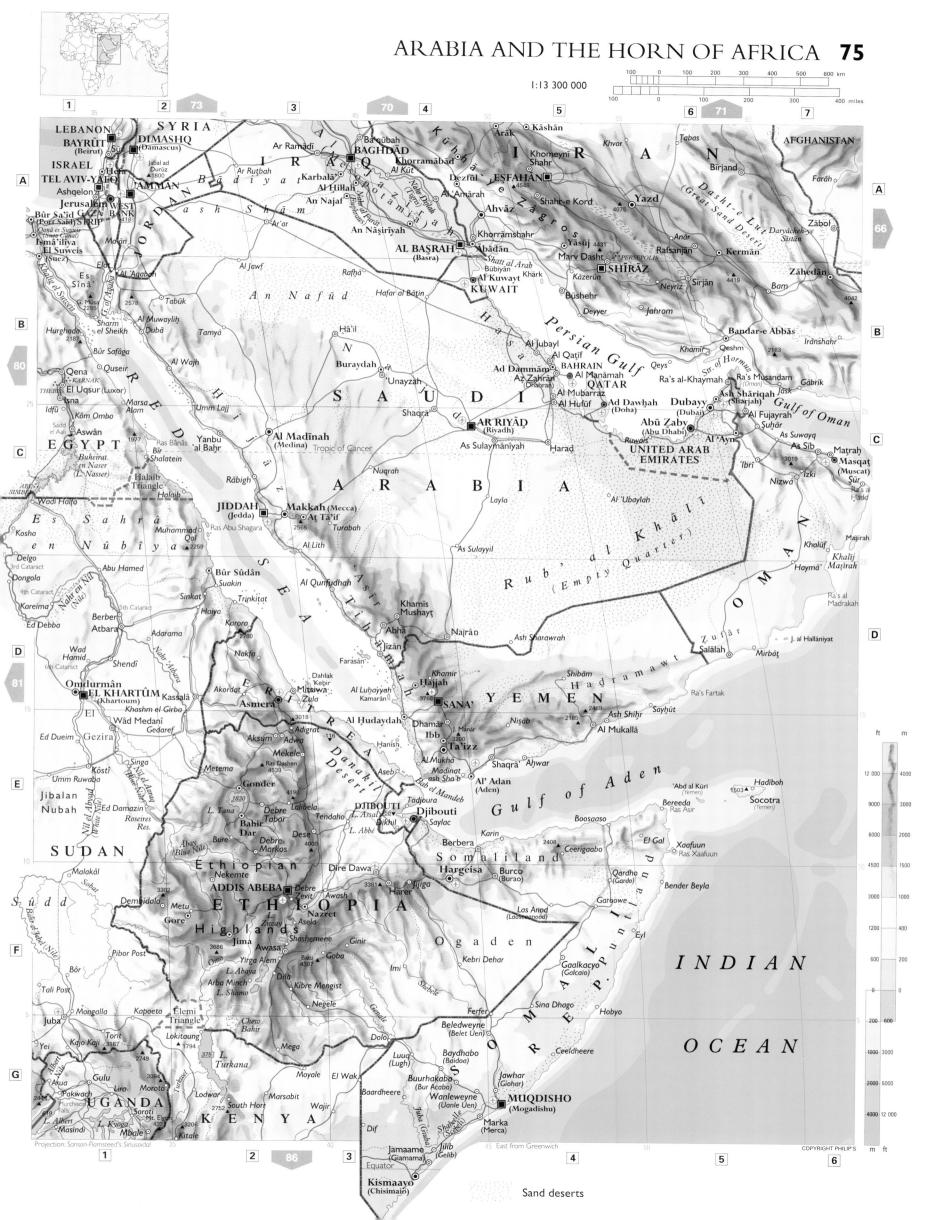

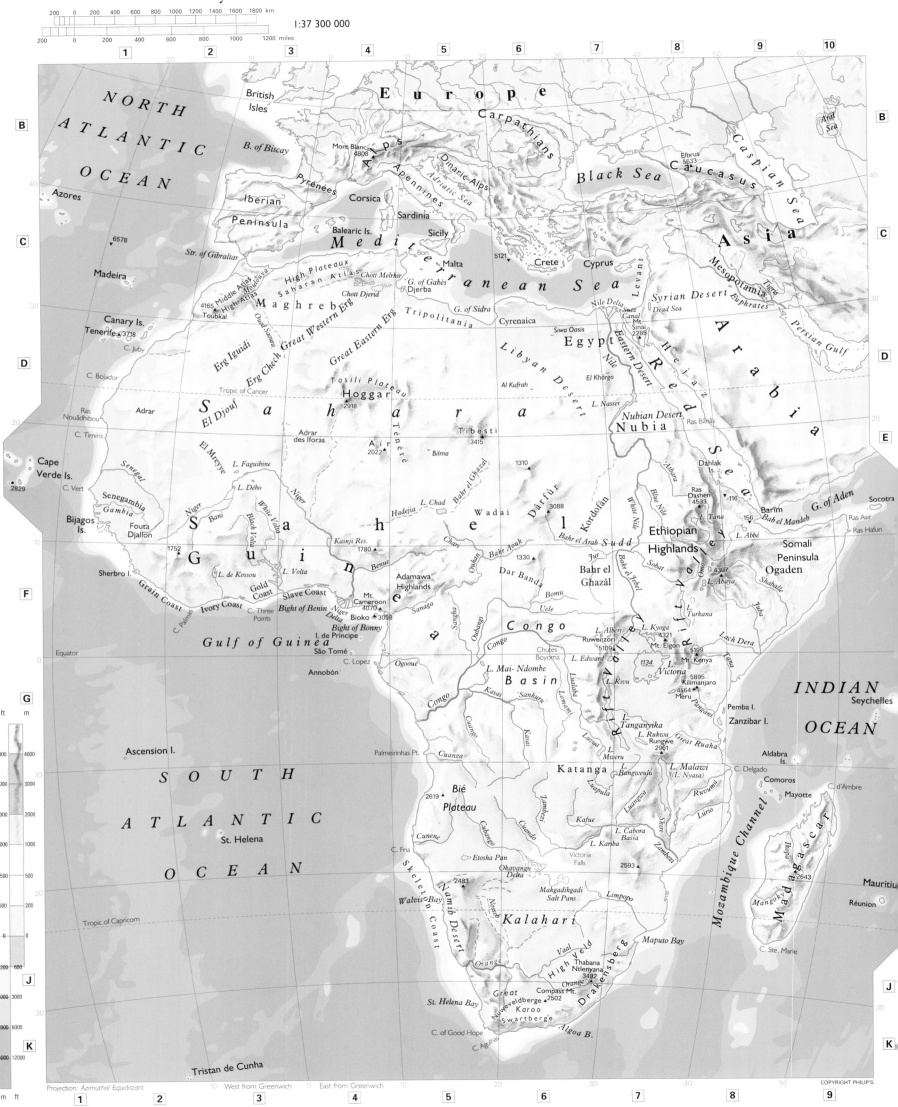

1:37 300 000

NORTH
ATLANTIC
OCEAN

SOUTH
ATLANTIC
OCEAN

Azores

Madeira

Canary Is.
Tenerife ▲3718
C. Juby

Cape
Verde Is.
C. Vert
▲2829

Bijagos
Is.

Sherbro I.

Ascension I.

St. Helena

Tristan de Cunha

British
Isles

B. of Biscay

Iberian
Peninsula

Str. of Gibraltar

▼6578

Balearic Is.

Corsica

Sardinia

Pyrénées

Mont Blanc
4808

Alps

Apennines

Dinaric Alps

Adriatic Sea

Europe

Carpathians

Black Sea

Caspian Sea

Aral
Sea

Elbrus
5633

Caucasus

Asia

Mediterranean Sea

Sicily

Malta

Crete

Cyprus

5121

Bon

Middle Atlas
High Atlas
Toubkal
4165

High Plateaux
Saharan Atlas
'Mouloúya'

Chott Melrhir

Chott Djerid

G. of Gabès
Djerba

G. of Sidra

Tripolitania

Cyrenaica

Siwa Oasis

Nile Delta
Suez
Canal

Levant

Mesopotamia

Tigris

Euphrates

Syrian Desert

Dead Sea

Hejaz

Persian Gulf

Arabia

Maghreb

Erg Iguidi

Oued Saoura

Erg Chech

Great Western Erg

Great Eastern Erg

Tasili Plateau

Hoggar
2918

Libyan Desert

Egypt

Al Kufrah

El Khārga

Nile

Mt
Sinai
2285

Eastern Desert

El Djouf

Sahara

Adrar

Ras
Nouâdhibou

C. Timiris

C. Bojador

Tropic of Cancer

Adrar
des Iforas

Aïr
2022

Ténéré

Bilma

Tibesti
3415

1310

Nubian Desert
Nubia

Ras Banâs

Red Sea

Dahlak Is.

Athbara

Ras
Dashen
4533

-116

Barim
Bab el Mandeb
-156

G. of Aden

Socotra

Ras Asir

Ras Hafun

El Mreyye

L. Faguibine

L. Débo

Senegal

Niger

Bani

Senegambia
Gambia

Fouta
Djallon

Black Volta

White Volta

Niger

Kainji Res.

1752

Sudan

Guinea

Hadejia

L. Chad

Chari

Bahr el Ghazal

Wadai

Darfûr

3088

Kordofân

White Nile

Blue Nile

L. Tana

L. Abbé

Ethiopian
Highlands

4307

L. Abuya

Somali
Peninsula
Ogaden

Juba

Shabelle

Grain Coast

C. Palmas

Ivory Coast

Gold
Coast

Slave Coast

C. Three
Points

Bight of Benin

L. de Kossou

L. Volta

Benue

Bioko ▲3008

Mt.
Cameroon
4070

Niger
Delta

Bight of Bonny

I. de Principe

São Tomé

C. Lopez

Annobón

Adamawa
Highlands

Sanaga

Sangha

Ubangi

Ouham

Bahr Aouk

1330

Bomu

Uele

Dar Banda

Jur

Bahr el
Ghazâl

Sobat

Bahr el Jebel

Sudd

White Nile

Omo

Rift Valley

Tana

Lach Dera

Equator

Ogooué

Congo

Kasai

Congo

Congo

Kasai

Cuango

L. Mai-
Ndombe

Lulonga

Lomami

Basin

Lualaba

Chutes
Boyoma

L. Edward

L. Albert
Ruwenzori
5109

1134

L. Kivu

L. Kyoga
4321

Mt. Elgon
5199

L. Victoria

Mt. Kenya
5895

Kilimanjaro
Meru
4564

Pemba I.

Zanzibar I.

Great Ruaha

Pangani

INDIAN

OCEAN

Seychelles

Palmeirinhas Pt.

Cuanza

Cunene

C. Fria

Skeleton Coast

Walvis Bay

Namib Desert

2619

Bié
Plateau

Kasai

Cubango

Cuando

L. Tanganyika

L. Rukwa
Rungwe
2961

Katanga

Luapula

Kafue

L. Mweru

L. Bangweulu

Lacua

Luangwa

Zambezi

L. Cabora
Bassa

Shire

Zambezi

L. Malawi
(L. Nyasa)

Ruvuma

Lúrio

Aldabra
Is.

Comoros

Mayotte

C. Delgado

C. d'Ambre

Mozambique Channel

Madagascar

Tsiroanomandidy

2643

Mauritius

Réunion

Etosha Pan

Okavango
Delta

Makgadikgadi
Salt Pans

Victoria
Falls

2593

Limpopo

Maputo Bay

C. Ste. Marie

Tropic of Capricorn

2483

Kalahari

Noseb

High Veld

Vaal

Orange

Orange

Great
Nuweveldberge
Swartberge

St. Helena Bay

Karoo

Thabana
Ntlenyana
3482

Compass Mt.
2502

Drakensberg

Algoa B.

C. of Good Hope

C. Agulhas

West from Greenwich

East from Greenwich

COPYRIGHT PHILIP'S

ft   m
12000 4000
9000   3000
6000   2000
3000   1000
1500   500
600   200
0   0
200   600
1000   3000
2000   6000
4000   12000
m   ft

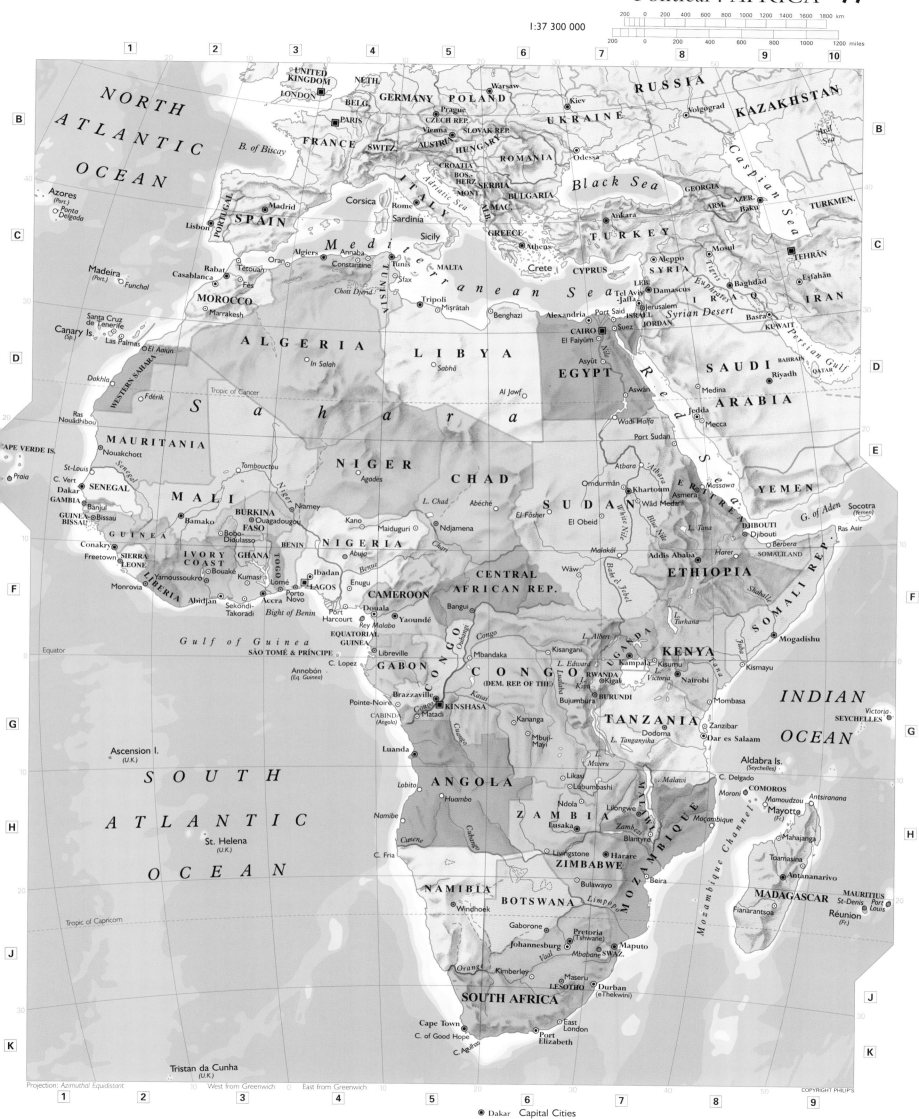

1:37 300 000

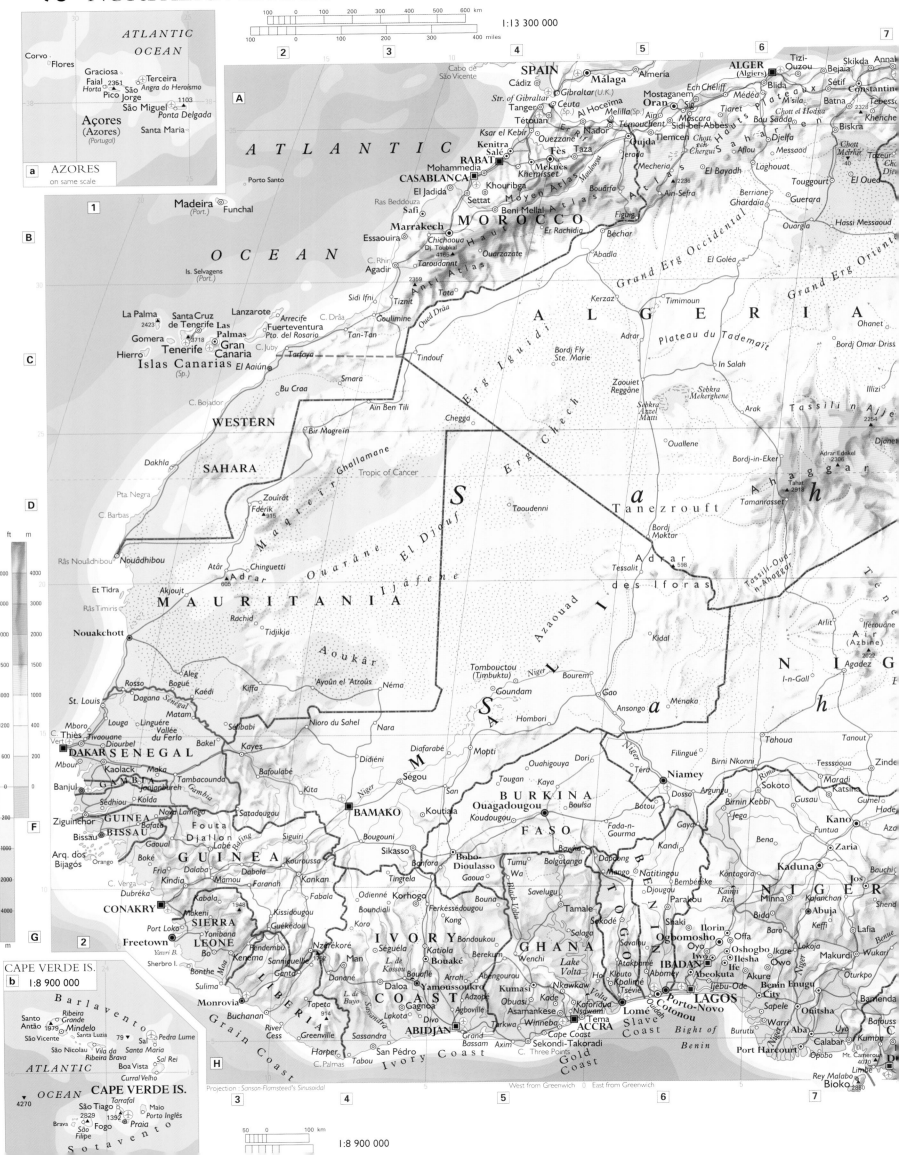

a AZORES
on same scale

b CAPE VERDE IS.
1:8 900 000

1:13 300 000

100 0 100 200 300 400 500 600 km
100 0 100 200 300 400 miles

Projection : Sanson-Flamsteed's Sinusoidal

West from Greenwich 0 East from Greenwich

1:8 900 000

50 0 100 km

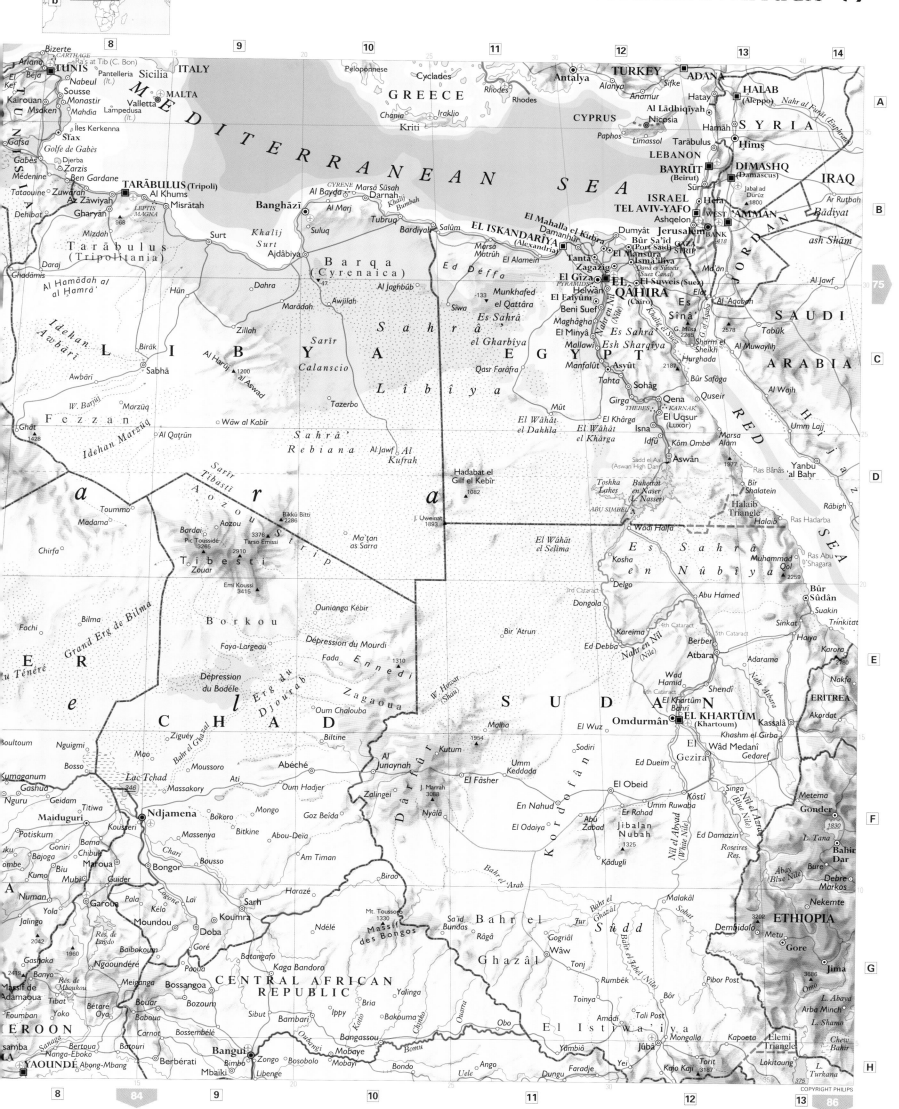

1:7 100 000

THE NILE DELTA
1:3 600 000

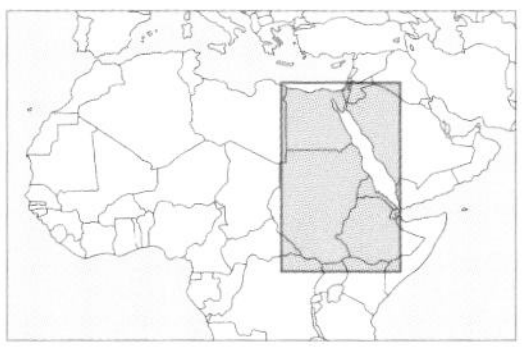

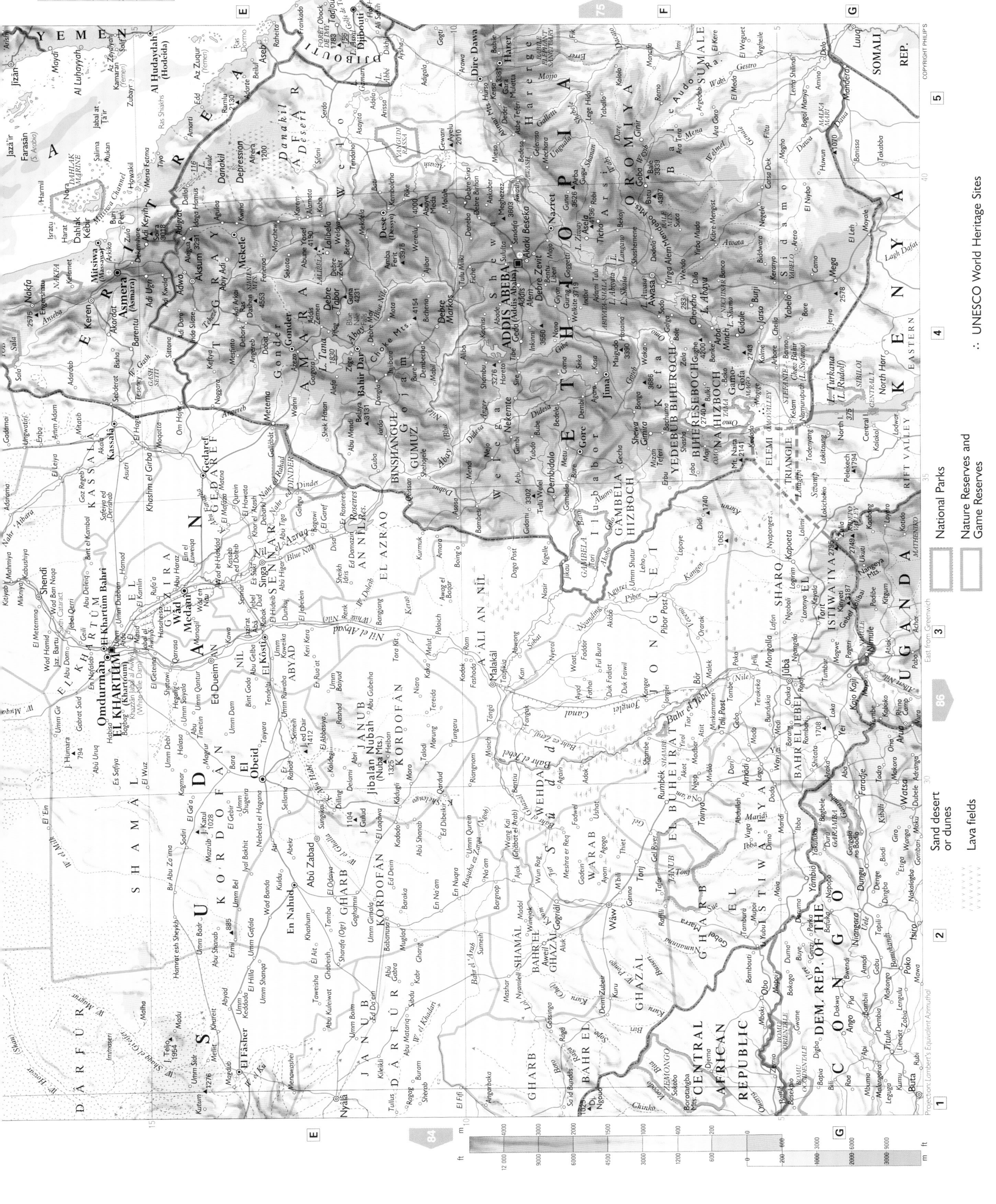

∴ UNESCO World Heritage Sites

National Parks

Nature Reserves and
Game Reserves

Sand desert
or dunes

Lava fields

East from Greenwich

COPYRIGHT PHILIP'S

Projection: Lambert's Equivalent Azimuthal

1:7 100 000

78

Projection : Lambert's Equivalent Azimuthal

West from Greenwich

Underlined towns give their name to the
administrative area in which they stand.

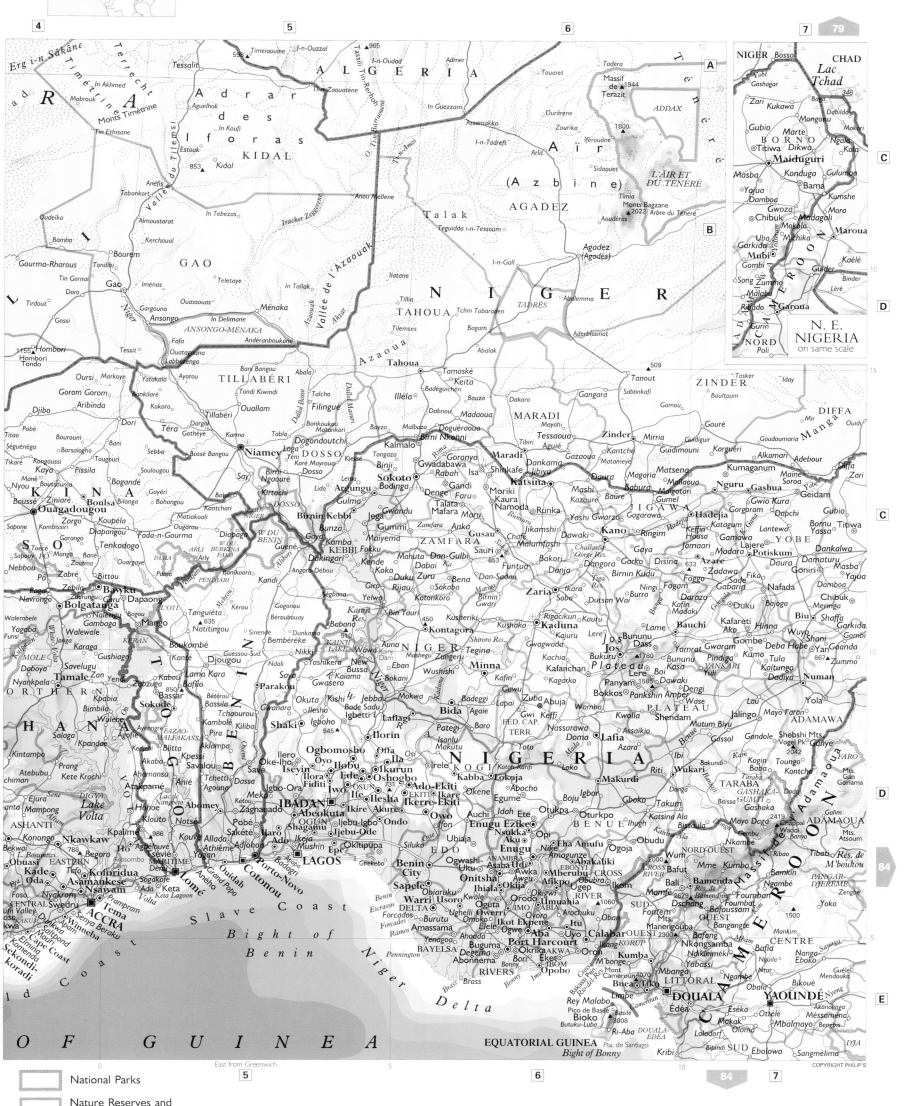

N. E.
NIGERIA
on same scale

National Parks

Nature Reserves and
Game Reserves

∴ UNESCO World Heritage Sites

East from Greenwich

COPYRIGHT PHILIP'S

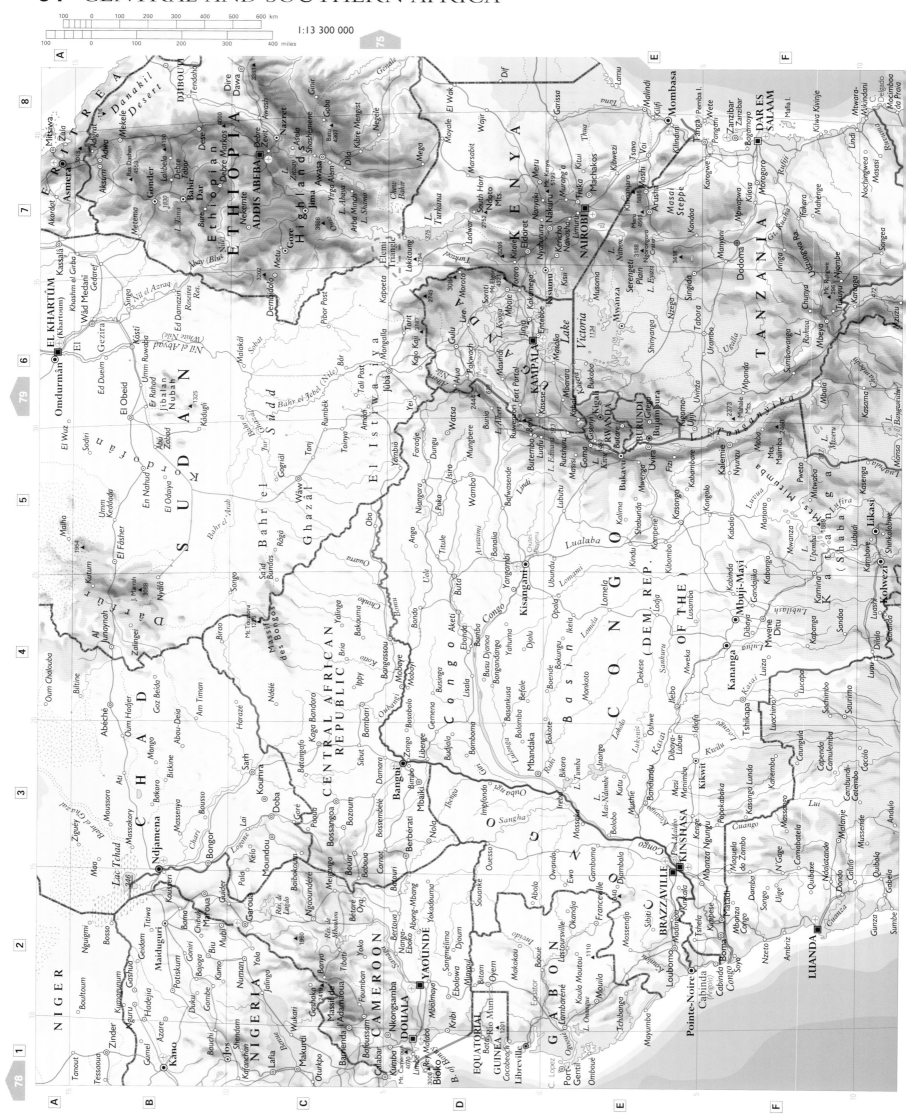

1:13 300 000

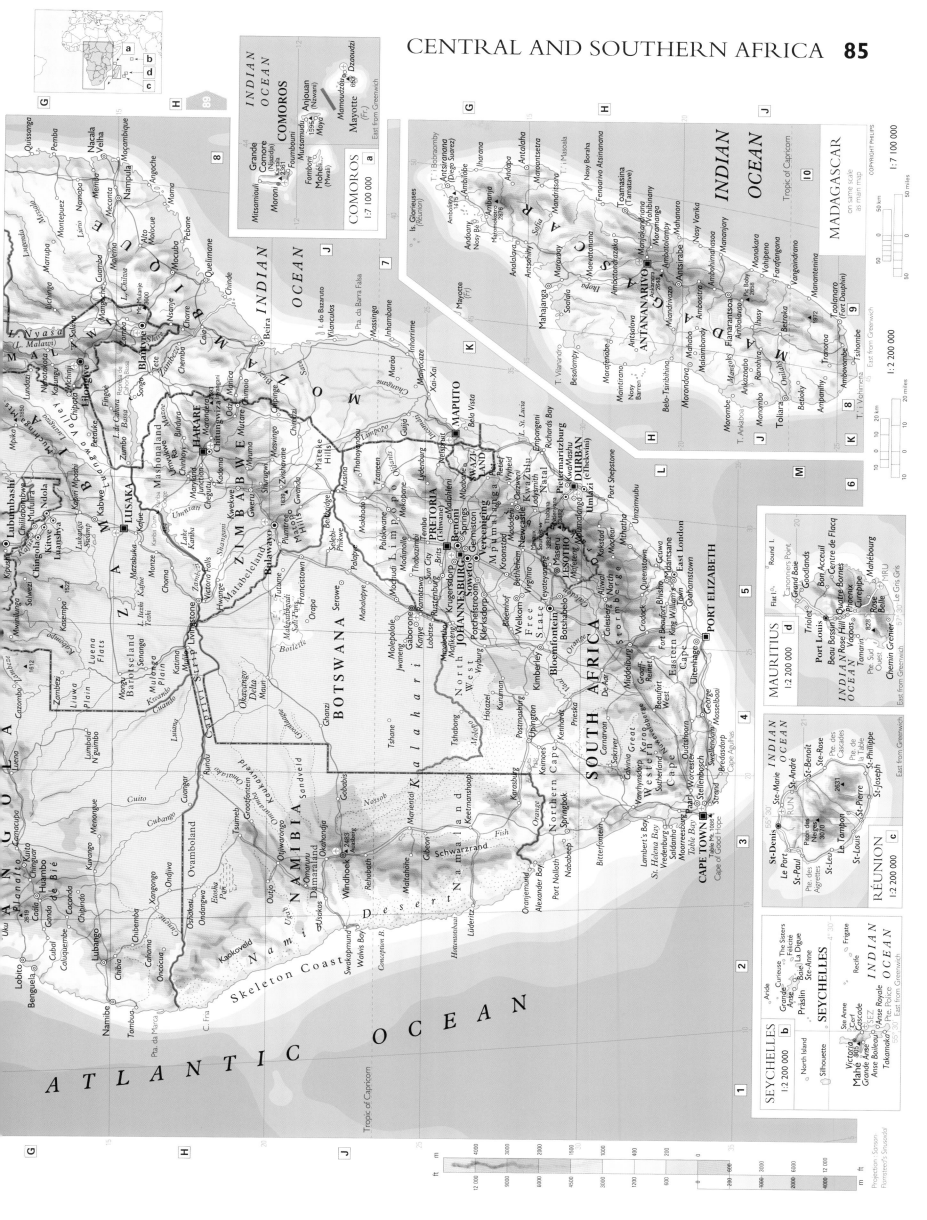

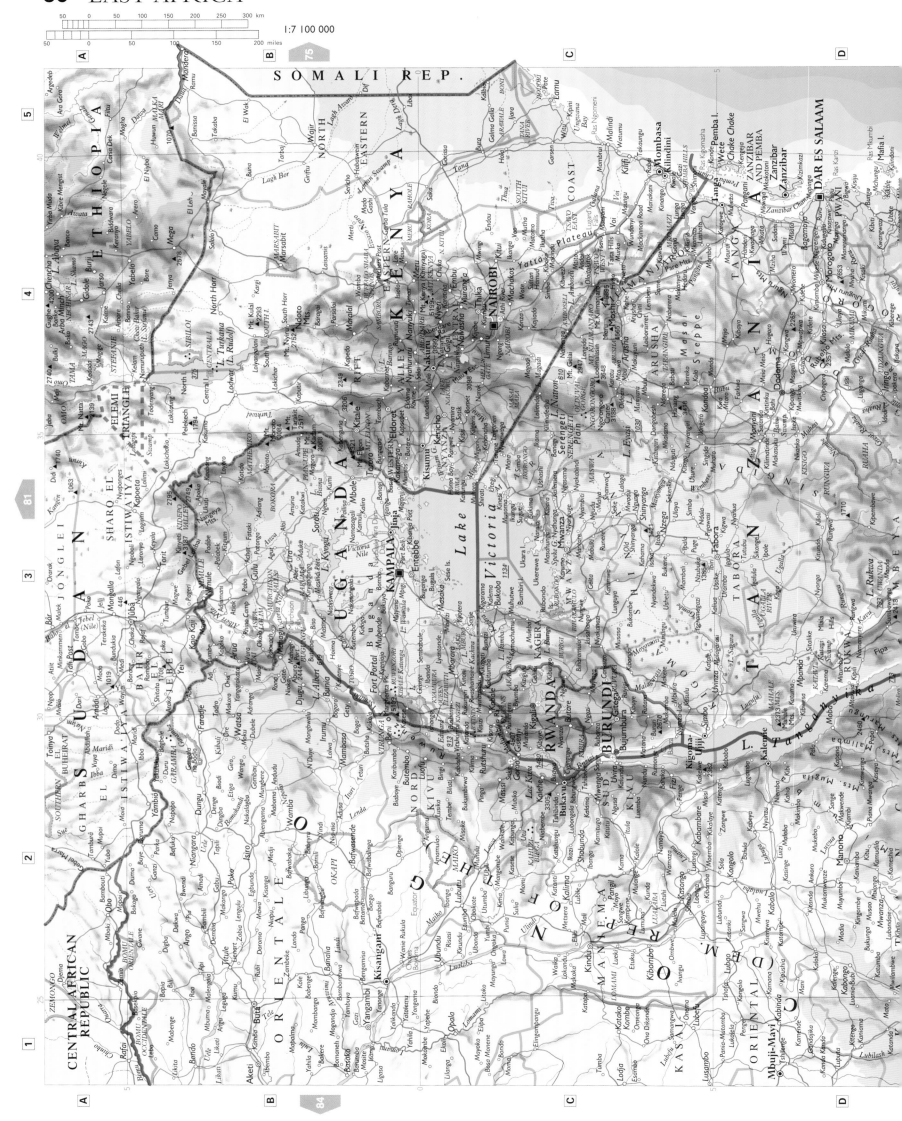

National Parks

Nature Reserves and
Game Reserves

∴ UNESCO World Heritage Sites

Projection: Lambert's Equivalent Azimuthal

East from Greenwich

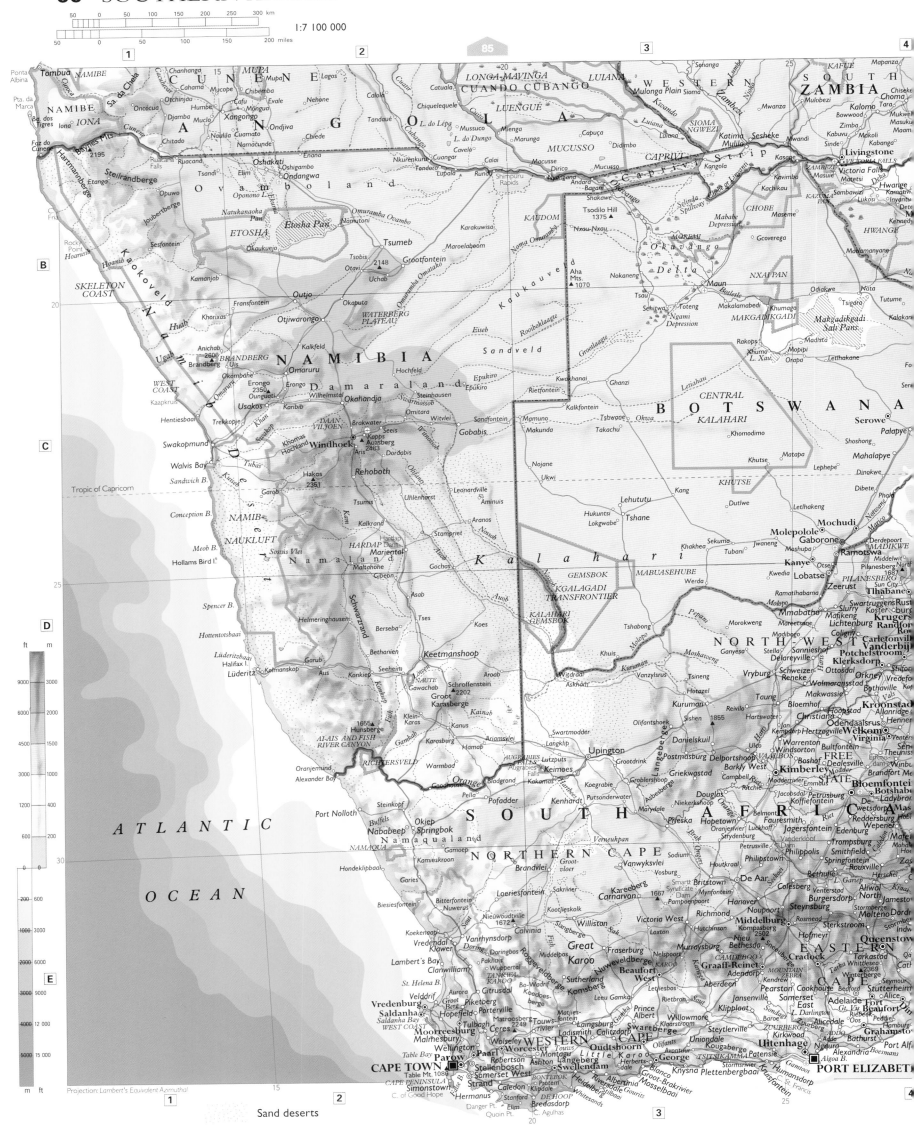

1:7 100 000

Projection: Lambert's Equivalent Azimuthal

Sand deserts

National Parks

Nature Reserves and
Game Reserves

⁂ UNESCO World Heritage Sites

MADAGASCAR
1:7 100 000

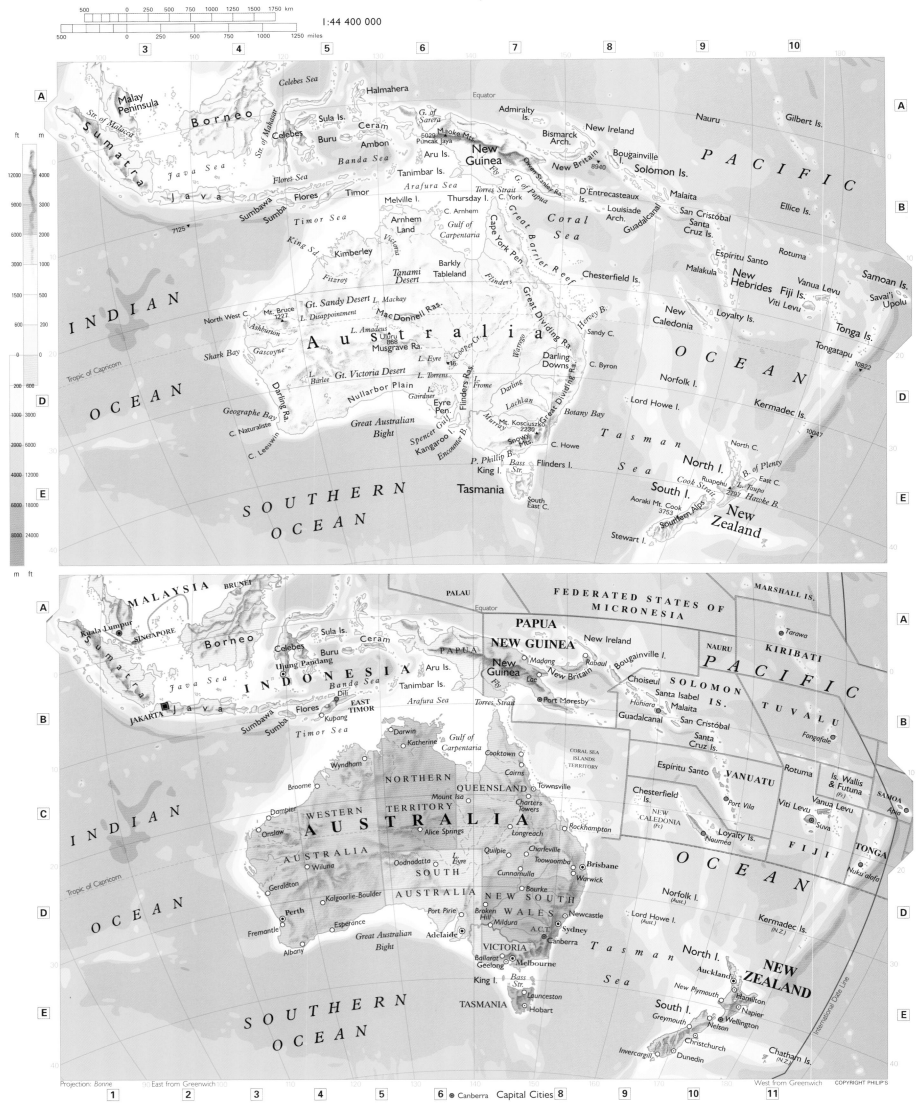

1:44 400 000

Physical map (top):

PACIFIC OCEAN

Celebes Sea
Borneo
Halmahera
Equator
Admiralty Is.
Nauru
Gilbert Is.
Malay Peninsula
Str. of Malacca
Celebes
Sula Is.
Ceram
New Ireland
Bismarck Arch.
New Guinea
Sumatra
Str. of Makassar
Buru
Ambon
G. of Sarera
Maoke Mts.
Puncak Jaya 5029
New Britain 8940
Bougainville I.
Solomon Is.
Java Sea
Banda Sea
Aru Is.
Fly
Owen Stanley Ra.
Malaita
San Cristóbal
Espíritu Santo
Rotuma
Java
Flores Sea
Tanimbar Is.
Arafura Sea
Torres Strait
C. York
G. of Papua
D'Entrecasteaux Is.
Louisiade Arch.
Guadalcanal
Santa Cruz Is.
Ellice Is.
7125
Sumbawa
Flores
Timor
Melville I.
Thursday I.
C. Arnhem
Coral Sea
Chesterfield Is.
New Hebrides
Malakula
Vanua Levu
Samoan Is.
Savai'i
Sumba
Timor Sea
Arnhem Land
Gulf of Carpentaria
Cape York Pen.
Great Barrier Reef
Fiji Is.
Viti Levu
Upolu
King Sd.
Kimberley
Victoria
Barkly Tableland
Flinders
Great Dividing Ra.
Hervey B.
New Caledonia
Loyalty Is.
Tonga Is.
Fitzroy
Tanami Desert
Sandy C.
INDIAN OCEAN
North West C.
Mt. Bruce 1227
Gt. Sandy Desert
L. Mackay
MacDonnell Ras.
Warrego
Darling Downs Ra.
C. Byron
OCEAN
Tongatapu 10822
Ashburton
L. Disappointment
L. Amadeus
Uluru 868
Musgrave Ra.
Australia
Cooper Cr.
Darling
Norfolk I.
Shark Bay
Gascoyne
L. Eyre 16
Great Dividing Ra.
Lord Howe I.
Kermadec Is.
10047
Tropic of Capricorn
L. Barlee
Gt. Victoria Desert
L. Torrens
L. Frome
Lachlan
Botany Bay
Geographe Bay
Nullarbor Plain
L. Gairdner
Eyre Pen.
Flinders Ras.
Murray
Mt. Kosciuszko 2230
C. Naturaliste
Great Australian Bight
Spencer Gulf
Kangaroo I.
Snowy Mts.
C. Howe
Tasman Sea
North C.
C. Leeuwin
Encounter B.
P. Phillip B.
Bass Str.
Flinders I.
North I.
B. of Plenty
East C.
King I.
Ruapehu
L. Taupo 2797
Hawke B.
SOUTHERN OCEAN
Tasmania
South East C.
South I.
Aoraki Mt. Cook 3753
Southern Alps
New Zealand
Stewart I.

Political map (bottom):

MALAYSIA
BRUNEI
PALAU
FEDERATED STATES OF MICRONESIA
MARSHALL IS.
Kuala Lumpur
SINGAPORE
Borneo
Sula Is.
Ceram
PAPUA
New Ireland
NAURU
Tarawa
KIRIBATI
Sumatra
Celebes
Buru
PAPUA NEW GUINEA
Madang
Rabaul
Bougainville I.
PACIFIC
Ujung Pandang
INDONESIA
Java Sea
Banda Sea
Aru Is.
New Guinea
Lae
New Britain
Choiseul
SOLOMON IS.
Santa Isabel
TUVALU
Jakarta
Dili
Java
EAST TIMOR
Tanimbar Is.
Fly
Port Moresby
Honiara
Malaita
Guadalcanal
San Cristóbal
Fongafale
Kupang
Flores
Arafura Sea
Torres Strait
Santa Cruz Is.
Sumbawa
Sumba
Timor Sea
Darwin
Katherine
Gulf of Carpentaria
CORAL SEA ISLANDS TERRITORY
Espíritu Santo
VANUATU
Rotuma
Is. Wallis & Futuna (Fr.)
SAMOA
Wyndham
NORTHERN TERRITORY
Cooktown
Cairns
Chesterfield Is.
Port Vila
Viti Levu
Vanua Levu
Apia
INDIAN
Broome
QUEENSLAND
Townsville
NEW CALEDONIA (Fr.)
Suva
Dampier
WESTERN
Mount Isa
Charters Towers
Loyalty Is.
FIJI
Onslow
AUSTRALIA
Alice Springs
Longreach
Rockhampton
Nouméa
TONGA
OCEAN
AUSTRALIA
L. Eyre
Quilpie
Charleville
OCEAN
Nuku'alofa
Wiluna
Oodnadatta
SOUTH
Toowoomba
Brisbane
Geraldton
AUSTRALIA
Cunnamulla
Warwick
Norfolk I. (Aust.)
Tropic of Capricorn
Kalgoorlie-Boulder
Bourke
NEW SOUTH WALES
Lord Howe I. (Aust.)
Kermadec Is. (N.Z.)
Perth
Port Pirie
Broken Hill
Newcastle
Fremantle
Esperance
Mildura
A.C.T.
Sydney
North I.
NEW ZEALAND
Albany
Great Australian Bight
Adelaide
VICTORIA
Canberra
Tasman Sea
Auckland
Ballarat
Geelong
Melbourne
New Plymouth
Hamilton
King I.
Bass Str.
South I.
Napier
SOUTHERN
TASMANIA
Launceston
Greymouth
Nelson
Wellington
OCEAN
Hobart
Invercargill
Christchurch
Dunedin
Chatham Is. (N.Z.)

Projection: Bonne
East from Greenwich
West from Greenwich
COPYRIGHT PHILIP'S
Canberra Capital Cities

1:5 300 000

50 0 50 100 150 200 km
50 0 50 100 150 miles

4 96 5 6 7

FIJI a
on same scale

PACIFIC OCEAN

178 E 180 Udu Pt.
Great Sea Reef Kia Ringgold Is.
Yaqaqa Labasa Rabi
Yasawa Group Bua Savusavu Bay Qamea
Nacula Nabouwalu Somosomo Str. Taveuni
Vanua Levu Batiki BOUMA Naitaba Vanua Balavu
1031 Nairai Namuka Passage
Naviti Namenalala Vatu Vara Northern Lau Group
Waya Vomo Lautoka Tavua Tomanivi Lawaki Makogai Vacata Lomaloma Tuvuca
1323 KOROYANITU Levuka Korovou Nasau Koro Cicia
Vatulele Nadi Keiyasi Viti Levu Vunidawa Ovalau Nairai Mago Lakeba
Sigatoka Korolevu Navua Unudawa Nayau Lakeba Passage Tubou
Yanuca Beqa Oneata Moce
Kadavu Passage KORO SEA Moala Fulaga Ogea Levu
Tavuki Vunisea Ono Totoya Kabara Namuka-i-Lau Yagasa Cluster Ogea Driki
Kadavu Matuku
178 E East from Greenwich 180 West from Greenwich

SAMOA
SAMOAN ISLANDS b
on same scale

PACIFIC OCEAN

14 S
Asau Safune
Falelima Safata Bay Pu'apu'a
Savai'i Satapa itea Salelologa AMERICAN SAMOA (U.S.A.)
Taga Matautu Apia Falefa Ofu Olosega Ta'u
Falelatai Sauniatu Amaile Luma Manu'a Is.
OLE PUPU PUE Safata Bay Tutuila Pago Pago Vaitogi
Leone 'Upolu
172 W West from Greenwich

TONGA c
on same scale

PACIFIC OCEAN

18 S
Fonualei Toku
Late Vava'u Neiafu Vava'u Group
Home Reef
Disney Reef
Tofua Kao Ofolanga Ha'ano Foa Ha'apai Group
Kotu Group Lifuka Uiha
20 S Fonuafo'ou Nomuka Group Oto Tolu Group
Hunga Ha'apai Mango Tonumea

TONGA
Nuku'alofa Tongatapu
Tongatapu Group 'Eua
West from Greenwich

1

---

34 174 176 178

C. Reinga North C.
C. Maria van Diemen
Houhora Heads Rangaunu B. Doubtless B.
Ahipara B. Mangonui Whangaroa Harb.
Tauroa Pt. Kaitaia Waitangi B. of Islands
Hokianga Harbour Rawene Okaihau C. Brett Opua
Waipoua Forest Kaikohe Hikurangi
Dargaville Whangarei
Whangarei Harb.
Bream Hd. Little Barrier I.
Waipu Bream B.
Kaipara Harbour Warkworth Great Barrier I.
C. Rodney
Helensville C. Colville Cuvier I.
Hauraki Gulf Coromandel
Takapuna Whitianga
Manukau AUCKLAND Carpandel
Papakura Thames Whangamata
Waiuku Pukekohe Mayor I. Mount Maunganui
Mercer Paeroa Waihi
Waikato Te Aroha Whakatane Bay of Plenty
Huntly Morrinsville Tauranga Te Puke Whakaari (White I.)
Hamilton Cambridge Whakatane Runaway
Raglan Te Awamutu Rotorua Kawerau East C.
Kawhia Kihikihi Opotiki
Kawhia Harbour Otorohanga Putaruru Rotorua Raukumara Ra. Hikurangi 1763
Waitomo Tokoroa L. Rotorua Te Karaka Waipiro
Caves Te Kuiti Mangakino Murupara UREWERA
Mokai Wairakei Motu Tolaga Bay
Mokau Waikaremoana Ormond
North Taranaki Bight Taumarunui L. Taupo Waikaremoana Gisborne
New Plymouth Turangi Poverty Bay
Inglewood Ruapehu 2797 Waikokopu
Mt. Taranaki or Mt. Egmont TONGARIRO Kaimanawa Mts. Wairoa
C. Egmont 2518 Ohakune Bay View
Opunake Stratford EGMONT Waiouru Ruahine Ra. Napier
Eltham Raetihi Hawke Bay
Hawera WHANGANUI Taihape Hastings
South Taranaki Bight Patea Mangaweka Waipawa
Waverley Marton Waipukurau
Wanganui Bulls Halcombe Dannevirke
Feilding Woodville
Palmerston North Pahiatua
Foxton Shannon Levin C. Turnagain
Paraparaumu Otaki Masterton
Upper Hutt Carterton Greytown
Lower Hutt Petone Featherston Martinborough Wairarapa
Wellington Eastbourne
Cook Strait

North Island

South Island

C. Farewell
Collingwood Golden B. D'Urville I.
KAHURANGI Takaka ABEL TASMAN Tasman B.
Karamea Tasman Mts. Motueka
Karamea Bight Nelson Havelock Pelorus Sd. Kapiti I.
Seddonville Richmond Picton
Granity Wakefield NELSON LAKES Blenheim
Westport Tadmor L. Rotoiti Seddon
Lyell Matiri Ra. Wairau Ward
Inangahua Murchison Mt. Travers 2337
PAPAROA Reefton Spenser Mts. 2885 Tapuae-o-Uenuku
Punakaiki Lewis Pass Hanmer Springs Clarence Kaikoura
Blackball Grey L. Springs
Runanga Hokitika Culverden Waiau
Greymouth Stillwater Waipara
Kumara L. Brunner Waikari Hurunui
Hokitika Jacksons ARTHUR'S PASS Oxford Amberley
Ross Arthur's Pass Waimakariri New Brighton
L. Coleridge Springfield Kaiapoi Christchurch
Abut Hd. Whitecliffs Riccarton Lyttelton
WESTLAND Methven Staveley Lincoln Banks Pen.
Aoraki/Mt. Cook 3753 Rakaia Southbridge Little River
Mount Cook Canterbury Plains L. Ellesmere Akaroa
MOUNT ASPIRING Tekapo Fairlie Ashburton
Mt. Aspiring 3033 L. Pukaki Temuka
Earnslaw 2819 Twizel Pleasant Pt. Timaru
Milford Sd. Milford Sound Ohau St. Andrews
Sutherland Falls Wanaka Tarras Waimate
Bligh Sound George Sound Arrowtown Cromwell Kurow Canterbury Bight
Queenstown Wanaka Ngapara
Secretary I. FIORDLAND L. Wakatipu Clyde Naseby Oamaru
Doubtful Sd. Te Anau Alexandra Maheno
Breaksea Sd. L. Te Anau Kingston Roxburgh Hampden
Resolution I. Manapouri Garvie Mts. Waikouaiti
Dusky Sd. Mossburn Umbrella Mts. Palmerston
Lumsden Edievale Port Chalmers
Chalky Inlet Nightcaps Kelso Otago Harbour
Preservation Inlet Te Waewae B. Ohai Mataura Milton Dunedin
Orepuki Winton Gore Clinton Mosgiel
Riverton Clifden Wyndham Balclutha C. Saunders
Tuatapere Invercargill Kaitangata
Solander I. Bluff Invercargill Owaka
Foveaux Str. Nugget Pt.
Halfmoon Bay Ruapuke I.
Stewart I. (Rakiura) RAKIURA
South West C. Port Pegasus

Southern Alps (Tiritiri o te Moana)

Westland Bight

TASMAN SEA

PACIFIC OCEAN

Projection: Conical with two standard parallels
166 East from Greenwich 168 170 172

1 2 3 4

TAHITI & MOOREA
1:900 000

B. de Matavai Pte. Aroa Pte. Vénus
Papetoai Paopao Mahina
Pao Pao Arué Popenoo
Mooreo (France) Papeete Pirae Tiarei
Mt. Tohiea 1207 Faaa Pueu
Haapiti Afareaitu Pte. Nuupere Papenoo Hitiaa
Mt. Aorai 2060 Mt. Orohena 2241 Faaone
Punaauia Mt. Terufera 1799 Lac Vaihiria Tahiti (France)
Paea Isthme de Taravao
PACIFIC OCEAN Maraa Papara Afaahiti
Atimaono Papara Taravao Pte. Tatatua
Mataiea Vairao Pueu
Mt. Roouu 1332 Tautira
Teahupoo
Presqu'île de Taiarapu

17°30'S 17°45'S
149°45'W 149°30'W 149°15'W West from Greenwich
COPYRIGHT PHILIP'S

1:900 000
10 0 10 km
10 0 10 miles

ft m
9000 3000
6000 2000
3000 1000
1200 400
600 200
0
200 600
2000 6000
4000 12 000
6000 18 000
m ft

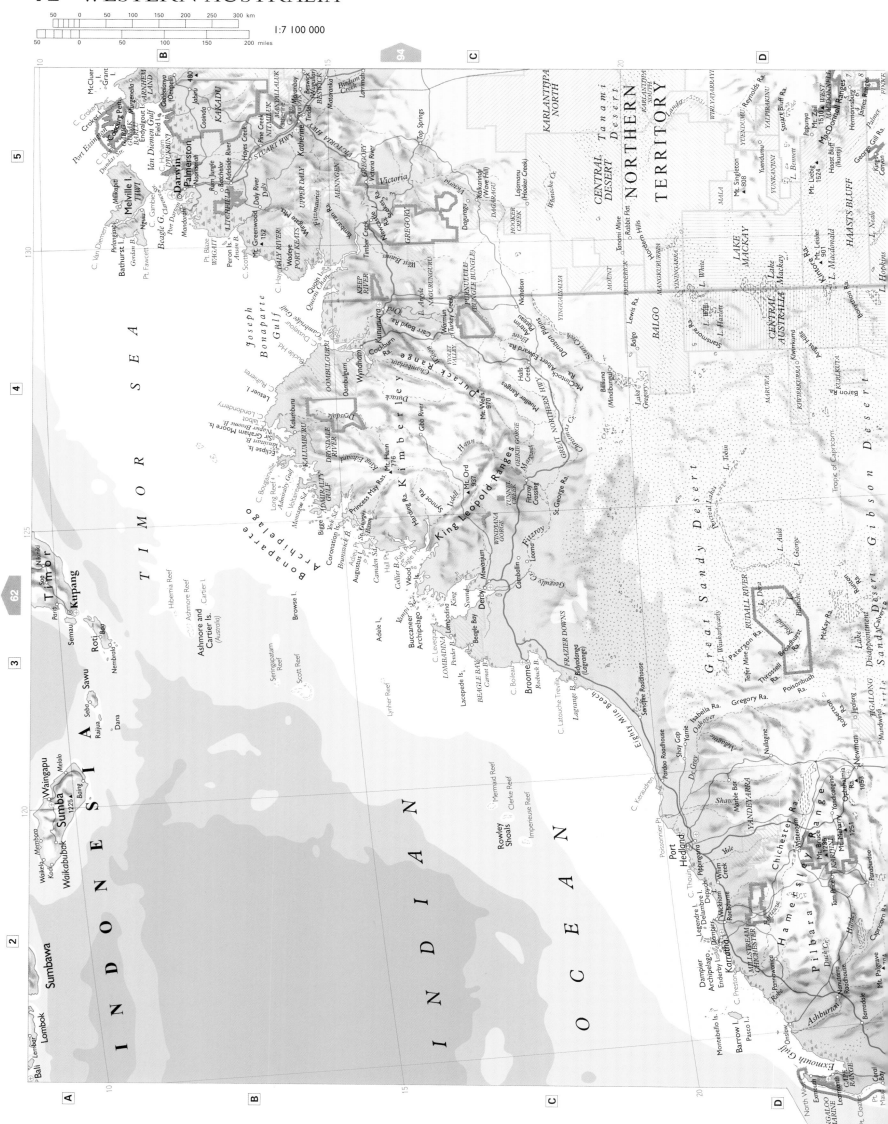

1:7 100 000

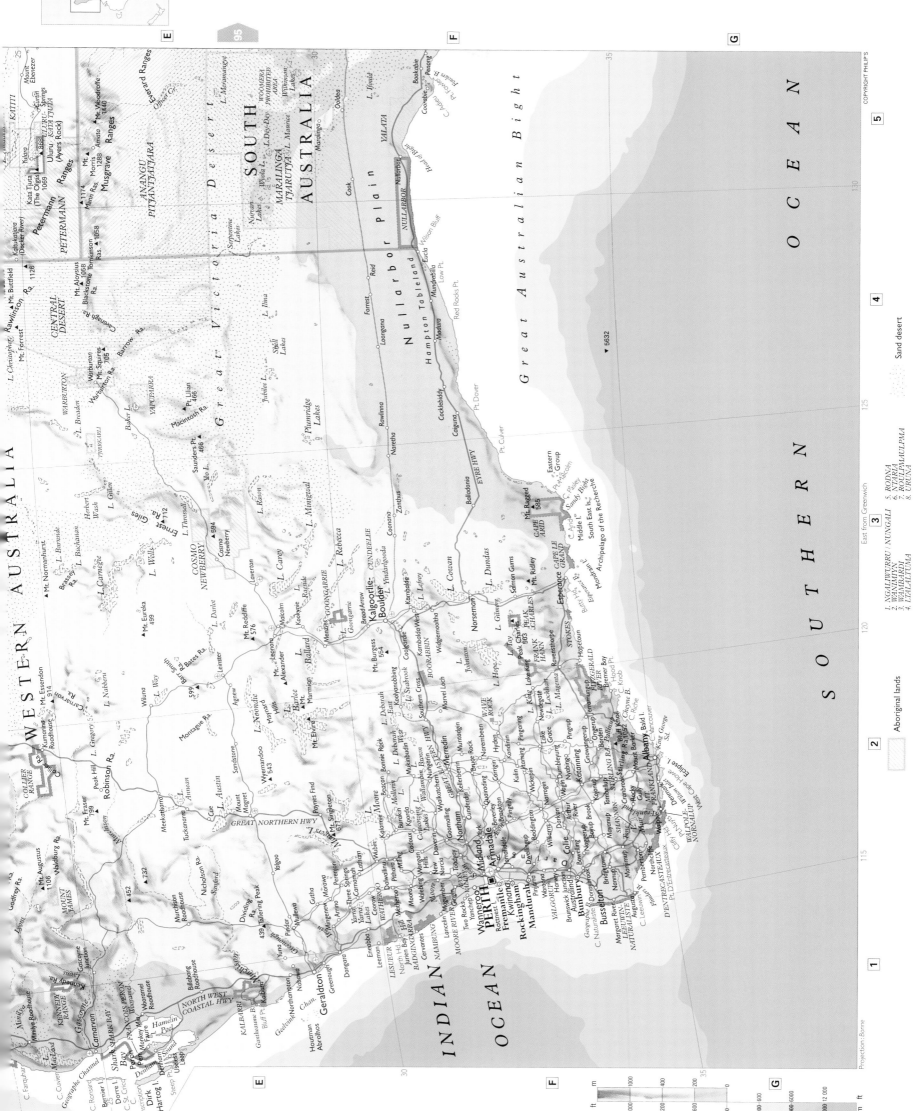

Aboriginal lands

Sand desert

1. NGALIYURRU / NUNGALI
2. WANMIYN
3. WAMBARDI
4. LIALALTUMA

5. RODNA
6. NTARIA
7. ROULPMAULTMA
8. URUNA

East from Greenwich

COPYRIGHT PHILIP'S

Projection: Bonne

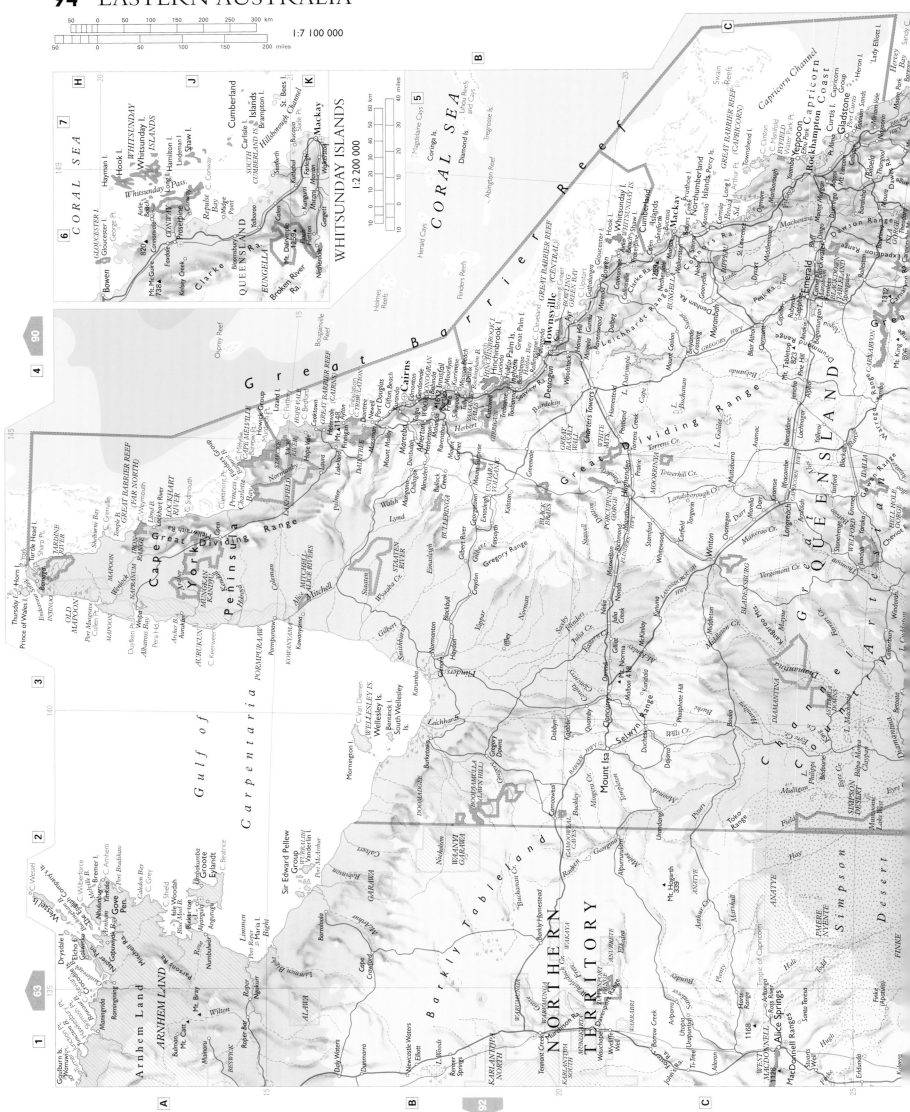

1:7 100 000

WHITSUNDAY ISLANDS

1:2 200 000

Equatorial Scale 1:48 000 000

RUSSIA
Yekaterinburg
Moskva
Tomsk
Novosibirsk
Ob
Lena
Irkutsk
Chita
Oz. Baykal
KAZAKHSTAN
Astana (Aqmola)
Semey
Aral Sea
Balqash Köl
Altai
MONGOLIA
Ulaanbaatar
Amur
Blagoveshchensk
Khabarovsk
Sea of Okhotsk
Okhotsk
Poluostrov Kamchatka
Petropavlovsk-Kamchatskiy
Shirshov Ridge
Aleutian Basin
Near Is. (U.S.A.)
Andreanof Is. (U.S.A.)
Bering Sea
Sakhalin
Kurilskiye Ostrova (Russia)
Kuril-Kamchatka Trench
10,542
Aleutian
Aleutian Trench
Komandorskiye Ostrova (Russia)
La Perouse Str.
Emperor Trough
Emperor Seamount Chain
Chinook Trough
Harbin
Changchun
Shenyang
Vladivostok
Sea of Japan
Hakodate
Sapporo
Northwest
7822
Almaty
Ürümqi
KYRGYZSTAN
TAJIKISTAN
Toshkent
AFGHANISTAN
Kabul
Srinagar
PAKISTAN
Lahore
Delhi
Kanpur
CHINA
Kunlun Shan
XIZANG
Himalaya
NEPAL
Everest 8850
Lhasa
Brahmaputra
Ganga
INDIA
Hyderabad
Chennai (Madras)
SRI LANKA
Colombo
Lanzhou
Xi'an
Chongqing
Chang J.
Kunming
Guangzhou
BURMA
Mandalay
Rangoon
Bay of Bengal
Andaman Is. (India)
Nicobar Is. (India)
THAILAND
Bangkok
CAMBODIA
Phnom Penh
G. of Thailand
Beijing
Tianjin
Taiyuan
Huang He
Dalian
Qingdao
Nanjing
Wuhan
Changsha
Hangzhou
Shanghai
East China Sea
Fuzhou
Taipei
TAIWAN
Hong Kong
Macau
Hainan
Hanoi
LAOS
Thanh Pho Ho Chi Minh
South China Sea
NORTH KOREA
SOUTH KOREA
Seoul
Kyōto
Osaka
Kitakyūshū
Yellow Sea
3776
Nagoya
Tōkyō
Yokohama
JAPAN
Shikoku
Kyūshū
Okinawa
Ryukyu-retto (Japan)
10,554
Japan Trench
Sendai
Shatsky Rise
Pacific
Midway Is. (U.S.A.)
Basin
Lisianski I. (U.S.A.)
Howla
Kyushu-Palau Ridge
Sitito-Ozima-Ridge
Iwo-Jima (Japan)
Ogasawara Gunto (Japan)
Kazan-Rettō (Japan)
Minami-Tori-Shima (Japan)
Wake I. (U.S.A.)
International Date Line
Mid-Pacific Mount
PA
PHILIPPINES
Luzon
Manila
Paracel Is.
Mindoro
Palawan
Samar
C. Engano
Philippine Sea
West Mariana Basin
NORTHERN MARIANAS (U.S.A.)
Tinian
Saipan
East Mariana Basin
MARSHALL IS.
Bikini Atoll
Enewetak Atoll
Kwajalein
Majuro
Jaluit I.
Ralik Chain
Ratak Chain
GUAM (U.S.A.)
Challenger Deep 11,022
Mariana Trench
Yap
Caroline Is.
Micronesia
Chuuk
Pohnpei
Palikir
FED. STATES OF MICRONESIA
Koror
PALAU
West Caroline Basin
Eauripik Rise
East Caroline Basin
Solomon Rise
Melanesian Basin
Melanesia
Butaritari
Tarawa
Gilbert Is.
Howland I. (U.S.)
Baker I. (U.S.)
Banaba
Nauru
NAURU
Phoenix Is.
Abariringa
Enderbury
Central
Pacific
KI
O
MALAYSIA
Kuala Lumpur
PEN. MALAYSIA
Singapore
Sumatera
Palembang
Sunda Islands
Selat Sunda
INDONESIA
Jakarta
Jawa
Surabaya
Java Sea
Bali
Borneo
SARAWAK
BRUNEI
SABAH
Sulu Sea
Sulawesi
Ujung Pandang
Celebes Sea
Halmahera
Buru
Seram
Maluku
Banda Sea
Flores Sea
Flores
Sumbawa
Sumba
Dili
EAST TIMOR
Timor
Mindanao
Davao
4101
Mindanao Trench
PAPUA
Puncak Jaya 5029
7440
New Guinea
Arafura Sea
Torres Strait
PAPUA NEW GUINEA
Admiralty Is.
Bismarck Arch.
New Ireland
Rabaul 8940
Bougainville
New Britain
Lae
Port Moresby
Louisiade Arch.
SOLOMON IS.
Honiara
Guadalcanal
Santa Cruz I. 9165
TUVALU
Fongafale
Tokelau Is. (N.Z.)
Rotuma
Is. Wallis & Futuna (Fr.)
SAMOA
Apia
INDIAN
Cocos Is. (Austral.)
Christmas I. (Austral.)
North Australian Basin
C. Arnhem
Darwin
Gulf of Carpentaria
C. York
Cairns
Mount Isa
AUSTRALIA
Alice Springs
L. Eyre
Exmouth Plateau
Broome
North West C.
Wharton Basin
Naturaliste Plateau
Geraldton
Perth
Perth Basin
Broken Ridge
Great Australian Bight
Albany
Adelaide
Coral Sea Basin
Coral Sea
Townsville
Great Barrier Reef
Great Dividing Ra.
Rockhampton
Brisbane
Darling
Murray
Sydney
Canberra
Mt. Kosciuszko 2230
Melbourne
Bass Str.
Tasmania
Hobart
Î. Chesterfield
VANUATU
Espiritu Santo
Port Vila
NEW CALEDONIA (Fr.)
Nouméa
Île Loyauté
West Fiji Basin
Vanua Levu
Viti Levu
Suva
FIJI
7570
Nuku'alofa
TONG
South Fiji Basin
Lord Howe Rise
Middleton Basin
Norfolk I. (Austral.)
Lord Howe I. (Austral.)
New Caledonia Trough
Norfolk Ridge
Kermadec Is. (N.Z.)
Kermadec Trench 10,047
NEW ZEALAND
Auckland
Wellington
Christchurch
Chatham I. (N.Z.)
Chatham Is. (N.Z.)
Dunedin
Invercargill
Bounty Trough
Bounty Is. (N.Z.)
Tasman Sea
East Tasman Plateau
South Tasman Rise
Tasman Basin
Aoraki Mt. Cook 3753
Cook Strait
Antipodes Is. (N.Z.)
Campbell Plateau
Auckland Is. (N.Z.)
Campbell I. (N.Z.)
Macquarie Is. (N.Z.)
10,822
Tonga Trench
INDIAN
OCEAN
Ninety East Ridge
Nouvelle Amsterdam (Fr.)
I. St. Paul (Fr.)
Is. Crozet (Fr.)
Kerguelen (Fr.)
Mid-Indian Ridge
SOUTHERN
OCEAN
Heard I. (Austral.)

ft / m scale
12 000 / 4000
9000 / 3000
6000 / 2000
3000 / 1000
1500 / 500
600 / 200
0 / 0
200 / 600
1000 / 3000
2000 / 6000
4000 / 12 000
6000 / 18 000
8000 / 24 000
m ft

Projection: Mollweide's Homolographic
East from Greenwich

11 12 13 14

Arctic Circle

15

ALASKA
(U.S.A.)
Anchorage
5959

Juneau

16 17 18 19 20

Bristol Bay
Gulf of Alaska

Is. (U.S.A.)

Prince of Wales I.
(U.S.A.) Prince Rupert
Queen Charlotte Is.
(Canada)

Tufts
Abyssal
Plain

R O C K Y

C A N A D A

Edmonton

Calgary

L. Winnipeg

Winnipeg

Regina

St. Lawrence

Newfoundland

Québec

St. John's

N O R T H

B

Vancouver
Vancouver I. Victoria
Seattle

Portland

Boise

Minneapolis

L. Superior

Montréal

Toronto Ottawa
L. Huron L. Michigan

Detroit Buffalo

Boston

C

Northeast

Mendocino Fracture Zone C. Mendocino

Salt Lake
City

Denver

Chicago

Missouri

L. Ontario
L. Erie

Pittsburgh

New York
Philadelphia
Baltimore
Washington D.C.

A T L A N T I C

Sacramento
San Francisco

6741

Murray Fracture Zone

4418

Kansas City

St. Louis

Cincinnati

Appalachian Mts.

D

Colorado

UNITED STATES

Oklahoma City

Memphis

Atlanta

C. Hatteras

Pacific

Los Angeles

San Diego

Phoenix

Dallas

Houston

Mississippi

New
Orleans

Atlanta

Bermuda
(U.K.)

Jacksonville

S a r g a s s o   S e a

Guadalupe
(Mex.)

Molokai Fracture Zone

Baja California

Ciudad
Juárez

San Antonio

Tampa

Tropic of Cancer

C. San Lucas

Gulfo de California

Monterrey

Gulf of Mexico

Miami

Florida Str.

BAHAMAS

O C E A N

E

Basin

Honolulu

Kauai Oahu Maui
HAWAIIAN IS.
(U.S.A.)
4205 Hilo
Hawaii

Clarion Fracture Zone Is. Revilla Gigedo
(Mex.)

Guadalajara

Mexico
5610
Puebla

Acapulco

M E X I C O

Mérida

Canal de Yucatan

CUBA

La Habana

West Indies

9200

7680

HAITI

JAMAICA
Kingston

DOMINICAN REP.

Leeward
Is.

F

Johnston I.
(U.S.A.)

C I F I C

GUATEMALA
6662
Guatemala
San Salvador
EL SALVADOR

Middle America Trench

BELIZE

HONDURAS

NICARAGUA
Managua

PUERTO
RICO
(U.S.A.)

Caribbean Sea

BARBADOS
Windward Is.

North West Christmas

I. Clipperton
(Fr.)

Clipperton Fracture Zone

Guatemala
Basin

San José

COSTA
RICA

Barranquilla

Colón Panamá
PANAMA

Maracaibo

Caracas

Palmyra Is.
(U.S.A.)

Ridge

Cooper Ridge

Coco Ridge

I. del Coco
(Costa Rica)

Panama
Basin

Medellín

Orinoco

VENEZUELA

G

Basin

Teraina
Tabuaeran
Kiritimati

Equator

I. de Malpelo
(Colombia)

Cali
COLOMBIA

Bogotá

Galápagos Fracture Zone

Galápagos
(Ecuador)

Carnegie Ridge

Quito
ECUADOR

C Y

Jarvis I.
(U.S.A.)

Malden I.

Starbuck I.

Line Islands

Guayaquil

C. Palinas

Iquitos

Amazonas

H

O C E A N

K I R I B A T I

Penrhyn
(Tongareva)

Manihiki
Pukapuka

Swains I.
AMER.
SAMOA
(U.S.A.)

Manihiki

Plateau

Suwarrow Is.

Vostok I.

Flint I.

Caroline I.
(Millennium I.)

Nuku Hiva

Îs. Marquises
Hiva Oa

Marquesas Fracture Zone

Yupanqui
Basin

Mendaña

Fracture Zone

Galapagos

6369

Trujillo

PERU

Lima

BRAZIL

6550

J

East Pacific Rise

Îs. de la Société
Bora Bora
Huahine Raiatea Tahiti
Papeete

Rangiroa

Îs. Tuamotu

Peru Basin

Cuzco
L. Titicaca

Arequipa

6866

Nevado Ancohuma
6550

Nnve

Peru-

Arica

La Paz
BOLIVIA

Niue
(N.Z.)

Cook Is.
(N.Z.)
Aitutaki

Atiu

FRENCH POLYNESIA

Îs. Gambier

Nazca Ridge

Iquique
Chile

Rarotonga

Mangaia

Îs. Tubuai

Mururoa

Tropic of Capricorn

Antofagasta

PARAGUAY

Asunción

K

Oeno I.

Henderson I.

Pitcairn I. Ducie I.
(U.K.)

Rapa

Easter Fracture Zone

Sala-y-Gómez
(Chile)

I. de Pascua
(Chile)

Sala y Gómez Ridge

San Felix
(Chile)

San Ambrosio
(Chile)

8050
Trench

San Miguel
de Tucumán

Pôrto
Alegre

Córdoba

URUGUAY

Roggeveen
Basin

Arch. de
Juan Fernández
(Chile)

Aconcagua
6962

Valparaíso

Santiago

Rosario

Buenos
Aires

Montevideo
Rio de la Plata

L

Southwest

Chile Rise

Concepción

ARGENTINA

Challenger Fracture Zone

Pacific

Menard Fracture Zone

SOUTH

M

Basin

6212

ATLANTIC

OCEAN

Pacific-Antarctic Ridge

Falkland Is.
(U.K.)

Southeast
Pacific Basin

Punta Arenas
C. de Hornos
Tierra del Fuego

Est. de Magallanes

Drake Passage

South Georgia
(U.K.)

N

West from Greenwich

1:31 100 000

Projection: Bonne

West from Greenwich

COPYRIGHT PHILIP'S

1:31 100 000

1:13 300 000

Projection: Bonne

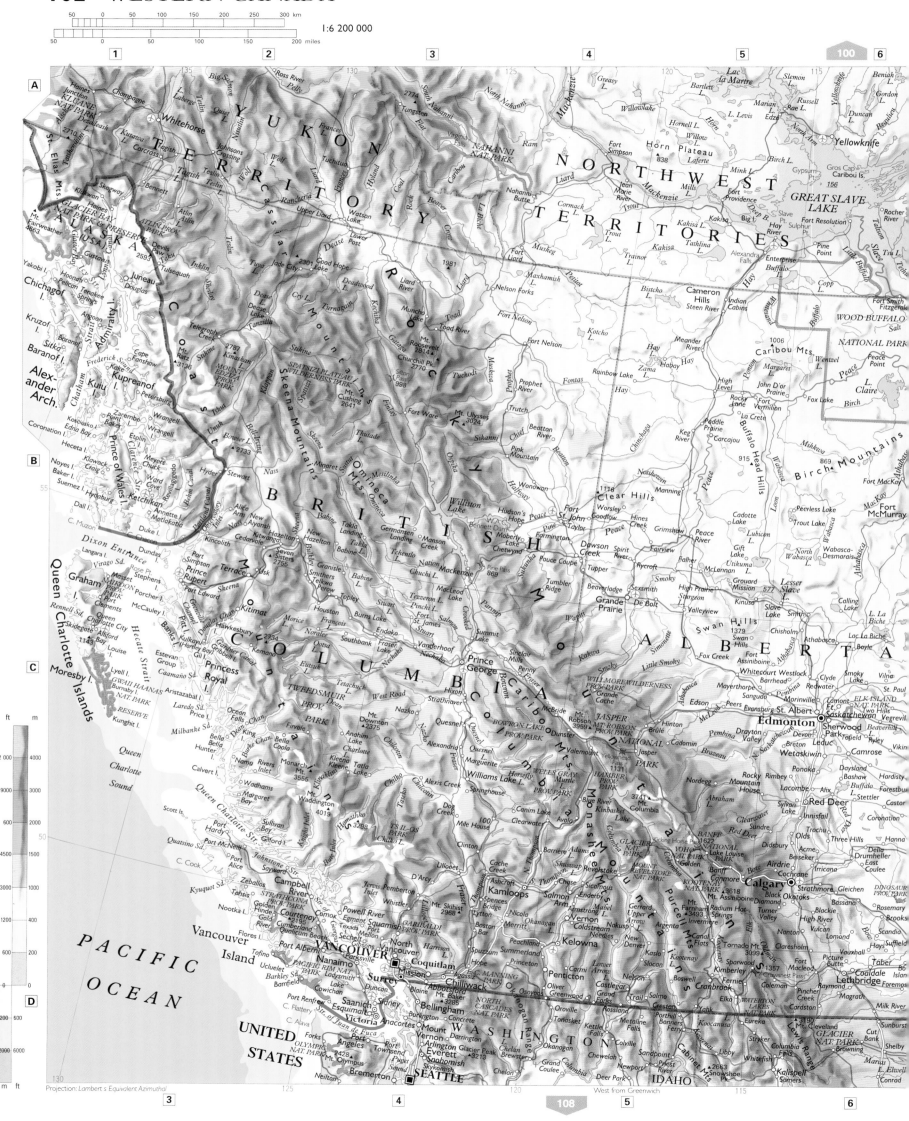

1:6 200 000

Projection: Lambert's Equivalent Azimuthal

West from Greenwich

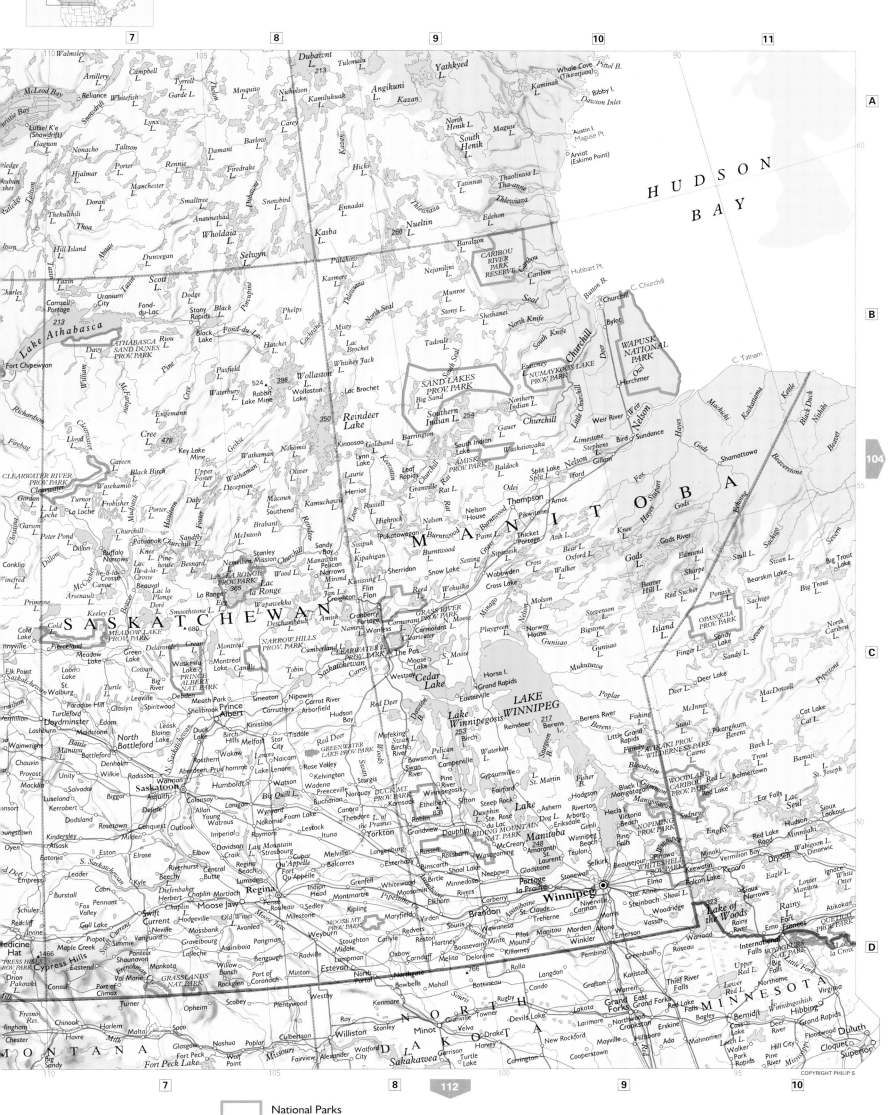

National Parks

6   101   7   8   9

A

L A B R A D O R

S E A

du Gut
Châteauguay
L. Le Moyne
L. Nachicapu
George
Fraser
South Aulatsivik I.
Paul I.
Nain
B
L. de la Hutte Sauvage
Kogaluc
Voisey B.
Tũnungayualok I.
Big Bay
Davis Inlet
L. Caniapiscau
L. Chakonipau
L. Otelnuk
Mistastin
Hopedale
Nunaksaluk I.
L. Néret
Champdoré
610
L. Tudor
L. Mistinibi
Holton
L. aux Goélands
Harp L.
Postville
Kajpokok B.
Aillik
Makkovik
Adlavik Is.
C. Harrison
Indian Harbour
Groswater B.

L. Sérigny
L. Wakuach
Attikamagen
Kanairiktok
Naskaupi
Seal L.
Nipishish
Kaipokok B.
North River
Cartwright
Table B.
Black Tickle
Island of Ponds

Schefferville
Petitsikapau
Menihek
Smallwood Reservoir
L. Melville
1128
Mealy Mts.
NEWFOUNDLAND &
Paradise River
Charlottetown
Alexis
Square Islands
Williams Harbour

L. Brisay
L. Bermen
L. Nichicun
Esker Siding
Twin Falls
Churchill Falls
Ossokmanuan L.
North West River
Goose
Happy Valley-Goose Bay
Churchill
Eagle
Port Hope Simpson
St. Lewis
Mary's
Lodge Bay
Battle Harbour
Belle Isle

Labrador

U É B E C

L. Dalmas
Nitchequon
L. Naococane
Opiscotéo
Labrador City
Fermont
Wabush
Emeril
Joseph
Shabogamo L.
Winokapau L.
Atikonak L.
Minipi L.
St-Lewis
Harbour
Lourdes-de-Blanc-Sablon
Forteau
L'Anse au Loup
Str. of Belle Isle
Cooks Harbour
L'Anse aux Meadows
St. Anthony

Mts. Otish
1128
L. Monchalagane
Petit Lac Manicouagan
Gagnon
L. Brûlé
Natashquan
L. Mécatina
St-Augustin
Rivière St-Paul
Roddickton
St. Barbe
Hare B.
Bell I. Is.
Grey
LABRADOR
Groais Is.

U
L. Plétipi
Rés. Manicouagan
L. Brûlé
1049
Romaine
Olomane
Petit-Mécatina
Port au Choix
Harbour Deep
Englee
Horse Is.
C

iscamie
L. Manouane
L. Péribonka
1049
L. Magpie
St-Jean
Aguanish
Natashquan
Musquaro
L. du Petit-Mécatina
Harrington Harbour
Hawke's Bay
White B.
La Scie
Baie Verte
Notre Dame
B.
Fogo
Fogo I.
Funk I.

Mistissini
Betsiamites
1049
L. Manitou
Sheldrake
Mingan
Havre-St-Pierre
Natashquan
Kegaska
La Romaine
GROS MORNE NAT. PARK
Rocky Harbour
Norris Point
Trout River
Daniel's Harbour
Jackson's Arm
Springdale
South Brook
Botwood
Lewisporte
Twillingate
Musgrave Harbour
C. Freels

L. Péribonka
L. Walker
Moisie
Clarke City
R.S. DE PARC. NAT. DE L'ARCHIPEL-DE-MINGAN
Pte. de l'Ouest
Port-Menier
Île d'Anticosti
320
Pte. Heath
B. of Islands
Pasadena
Deer Lake
Badger
Bishop's Falls
Glenwood
Gambo
Bonavista B.
C. Bonavista
Bonavista

t
Rés. Pipmuacan
Ste-Anne
Sept-Îles
Port-Cartier
Rivière-Pentecôte
Dét. de Jacques-Cartier
Corner Brook
Port au Port B.
Stephenville
Grand Falls
Windsor
Buchans
Red Indian L.
TERRA NOVA NAT. PARK
376
Glovertown
Gander
Catalina
Old Perlican

L. Péribonka
Godbout
Baie-Comeau
Baie-Trinité
Mont-Louis
Grande-Vallée
Pte. Sud-Ouest
Dét. d'Honguedo
Pte. du Sud
GULF OF
572
Cape St. George
C. St. George
St. George's B.
Victoria L.
Long Range Mts.
L. Maelpaeg
Jeddore
Port Blandford
Clarenville
Hearts Content
Carbonear
Conception B.

Mistassini
Forestville
Chute-aux-Outardes
Cap-Chat
Ste-Anne
Mont-Joli
Mts. Chic-Chocs
1268
Mt. Jacques-Cartier
Gaspé
Grande-Rivière
ST. LAWRENCE
St. David's
South Branch
St. George
Granite L.
St. Alban's
Terrenceville
Belleoram
Heart's
Content
Bay Roberts
St. John's
Mt Pearl

berval
Alma
Chicoutimi
Les
Escoumins
PARC DE LA GASPÉSIE
Pén. de la Gaspésie
Chandler
Î. Brion
Great Codroy
St. Andrew's
François
Fortune
Gander
Argentia
Placentia
Holyrood
Witless

nbord
Jonquière
La Baie
Saguenay
St-Siméon
La Malbaie
Tadoussac
Matane
Sayabec
Amqui
New Richmond
Bonaventure
Paspébiac
Miscou I.
Îs. de la Madeleine
(Québec)
Grande-Entrée
Cap-aux-Meules
C. Ray
Isle aux Morts
Rose Blanche
St. Pierre
C. St. Mary's
C. Race

L.-Bouchette
Rimouski
Trois-Pistoles
Matapédia
Dalhousie
Chaleur Bay
Caraquet
Shippagan
Channel-Port aux Basques
Burgeo
Marystown
Placentia B.
St. Lawrence
C. Freels

Lac
ouard
Rivière-du-Loup
Athollville
Campbellton
Tracadie
Havre-Aubert
St. Paul I.
Cape North
Cabot Strait
Miquelon
Fortune
ST-PIERRE-ET-MIQUELON
(France)

Parc des
GRANDS-JARDINS
Cabano
Dégelis
Bathurst
Newcastle
Miramichi B.
Pleasant Bay
Ingonish
St. Ann's B.
Avalon
Placentia
Peninsula
Ferryland
Trepassey

ARC PROV. DE LA JACQUES-CARTIER
1166
St-Pascal
Edmundston
Mt. Carleton
NEW
North Cape
Tignish
Alberton
CAPE BRETON HIGHLANDS NAT. PARK
532
Chéticamp

Beaupré
Î. d'Orléans
La Pocatière
Fort Kent
St-Léonard
820
Grand Falls
Plaster Rock
Rogersville
KOUCHIBOUGUAC NAT. PARK
Richibucto
PRINCE EDWARD
ISLAND
St. Peters
Souris
East Pt.
N. Sydney
Sydney Mines
New Waterford
Glace Bay

onnacona
Québec
Lévis
Montmagny
St-Pamphile
Van Buren
Caribou
Perth-Andover
BRUNSWICK
Summerside
Kensington
Montague
Georgetown
Port Hood
Bras d'Or
Sydney
Cape Breton

Portneuf
Charny
Eagle Lake
Presque Isle
Ashland
Hartland
Doaktown
Shediac
Charlottetown
Inverness
Louisbourg
Island

Deschaillons
Ste-Marie-de-la-Madeleine
Beauceville
St-Georges
Chamberlain
Houlton
Woodstock
Minto
Chipman
Bouctouche
St-Antoine
Cape Tormentine
Murray Hr.
Antigonish
Hawkesbury
Mulgrave
St. Peters

Plessisville
Thetford Mines
Chesuncook L.
1605
Patten
Millinocket
St. John
Grand L.
Oromocto
Petitcodiac
Sackville
Amherst
Pictou
New Glasgow
Stellarton
Chedabucto B.
Î. Madame
Canso

ictoriaville
Lac Mégantic
Moosehead L.
Jackman
Fredericton
Fredericton Junction
Sussex
FUNDY NAT. PARK
Springhill
Parrsboro
Minas Basin
Truro
NOVA
Upper Musquodoboit
Sherbrooke

inthe
East Angus
Asbestos
Greenville
Lincoln
St. Stephen
St. George
Hampton
Rothesay
Chignecto B.
Stewiacke
SCOTIA
Sheet Harbour

Sherbrooke
Magog
Coaticook
Bingham
Moosehead
Blacks Harbour
Saint John
Bay of Fundy
Windsor
Middleton
Enfield
Musquodoboit Harbour

ansville
Newport
Island Pond
Berlin
Mooselookmeguntic L.
Bangor
Brewer
Skowhegan
Old Town
Machias
Eastport
Grand Manan I.
Digby
Annapolis Royal
Bridgetown
Kentville
Dartmouth
Halifax
A T L A N T I C

MAINE
Rumford
Waterville
Belfast
Ellsworth
Bar Harbor
St. Marys Bay
Weymouth
Milton
KEJIMKUJIK NAT. PARK
Mahone Bay
Lunenburg
Bridgewater
Sable I.
(Nova Scotia)

NEW HAMPSHIRE
Augusta
Norway
Auburn
Lewiston
Camden
Rockland
Mount Desert I.
Rossignol
Liverpool
Shelburne

Johnsbury
Conway
Laconia
Sanford
Saco
Biddeford
Yarmouth
Wedgeport
Clark's Harbour
C. Sable
Lockeport
O C E A N
D

Hanover
Rochester
Dover
Portland
U N I T E D

Keene
Nashua
Manchester
Haverhill
Lawrence
Portsmouth
S T A T E S

tchburg
Lowell
Lynn
enfield
Newton
BOSTON
MASS
Worcester
Quincy
Brockton
Woonsocket
Cod

COPYRIGHT PHILIP'S

70   65   60   55

Tallahassee ✳   U.S. state capitals

COPYRIGHT PHILIP'S

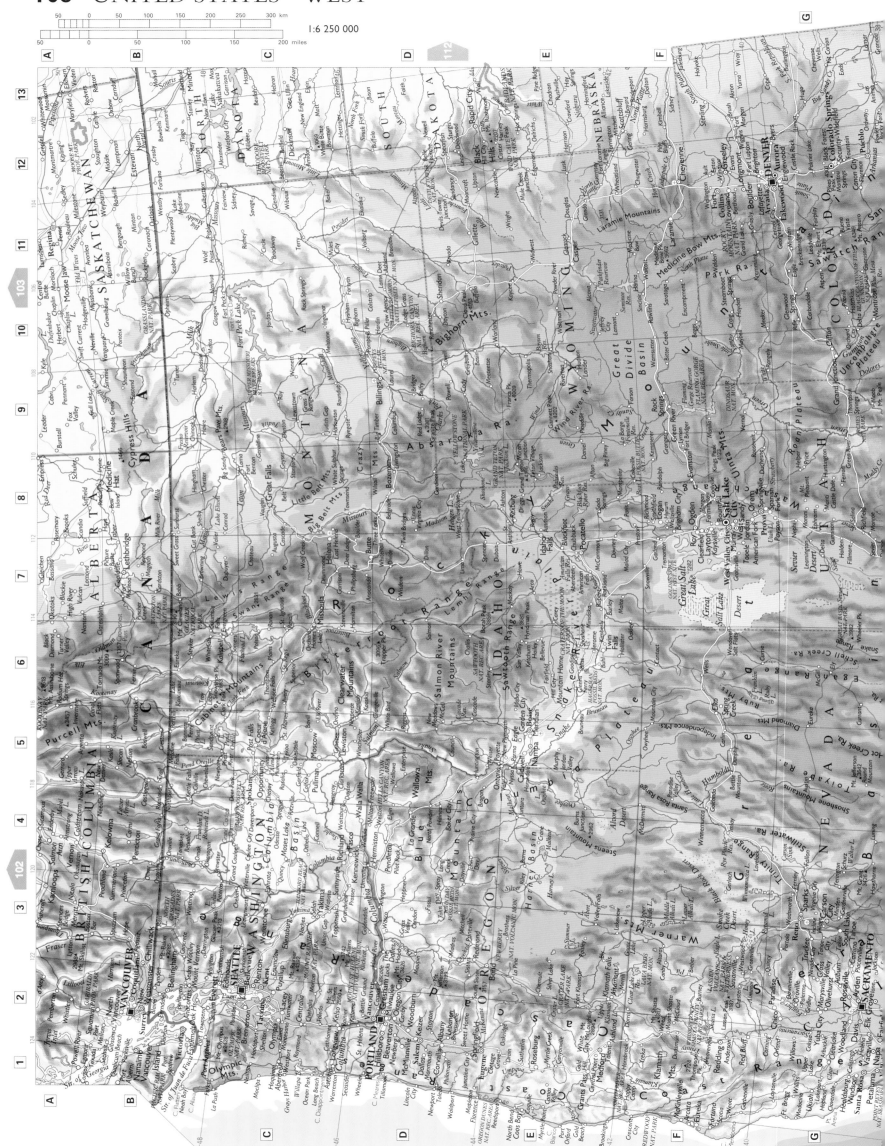

1:6 250 000

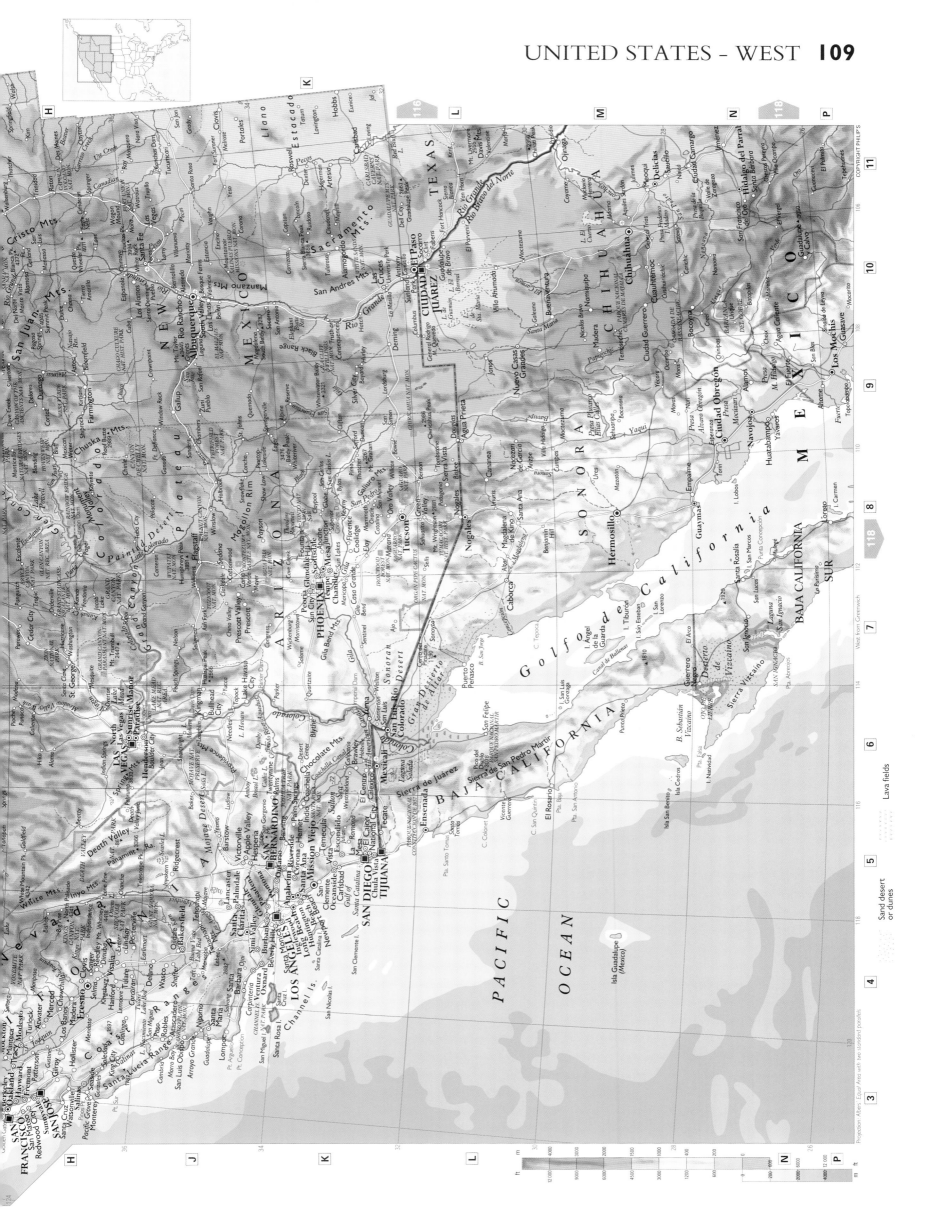

1:2 200 000

10 0 10 20 30 40 50 60 70 80 90 km
10 0 10 20 30 40 50 60 miles

WESTERN WASHINGTON REGION *on same scale*

PACIFIC OCEAN

BRITISH COLUMBIA
CANADA

Strait of Georgia

Vancouver Island

Strait of Juan de Fuca

OLYMPIC Mountains NATIONAL PARK

Mt Olympus

OLYMPIC NAT. PARK

PACIFIC RIM NATIONAL PARK RESERVE

WASHINGTON

VANCOUVER
New Westminster
Victoria
Saanich
SEATTLE
Bellevue
Everett
Bellingham
Tacoma
Olympia
Aberdeen
Centralia

MT. RAINIER NAT. PARK 4392 Mt Rainier

MT. ST. HELENS NAT. VOLCANIC MONUMENT Mt. St. Helens 2550

Mt. Adams 3742

OREGON

PORTLAND
Vancouver
Gresham
Beaverton
Hillsboro

Columbia

Pahute Mesa

Inyo Mts.

White Mts.

Owens

SIERRA NEVADA

Reno
Sparks
Carson City
Lake Tahoe 1899
South Lake Tahoe

YOSEMITE NATIONAL PARK

KINGS CANYON NATIONAL PARK

SEQUOIA NATIONAL PARK

Mt. Whitney 4418

Mt. Brewer 4136

DEVILS POSTPILE NAT. MONUMENT

Mono Lake 1949

CALIFORNIA

SACRAMENTO
Sacramento Valley
Davis
Woodland
Yuba City
Chico
Oroville

Stockton
Modesto
Turlock
Merced
Fresno
Clovis
Visalia
Tulare
Hanford

San Joaquin Valley

SAN FRANCISCO
Oakland
Berkeley
San Rafael
Novato
Napa
Vallejo
Fairfield
Vacaville
Concord
Walnut Creek
Livermore
Pleasanton
Hayward
Fremont
SAN JOSE
Santa Clara
Sunnyvale
Palo Alto
Mountain View
Cupertino
Santa Rosa
Petaluma
San Mateo
Redwood City
Daly City
Pacifica

Santa Clara Valley

Salinas Valley
Salinas
Monterey
Santa Cruz
Watsonville
Hollister

Santa Lucia Range

Paso Robles

PINNACLES NAT. MONUMENT

PONT REYES NATIONAL SEASHORE

DEATH VALLEY

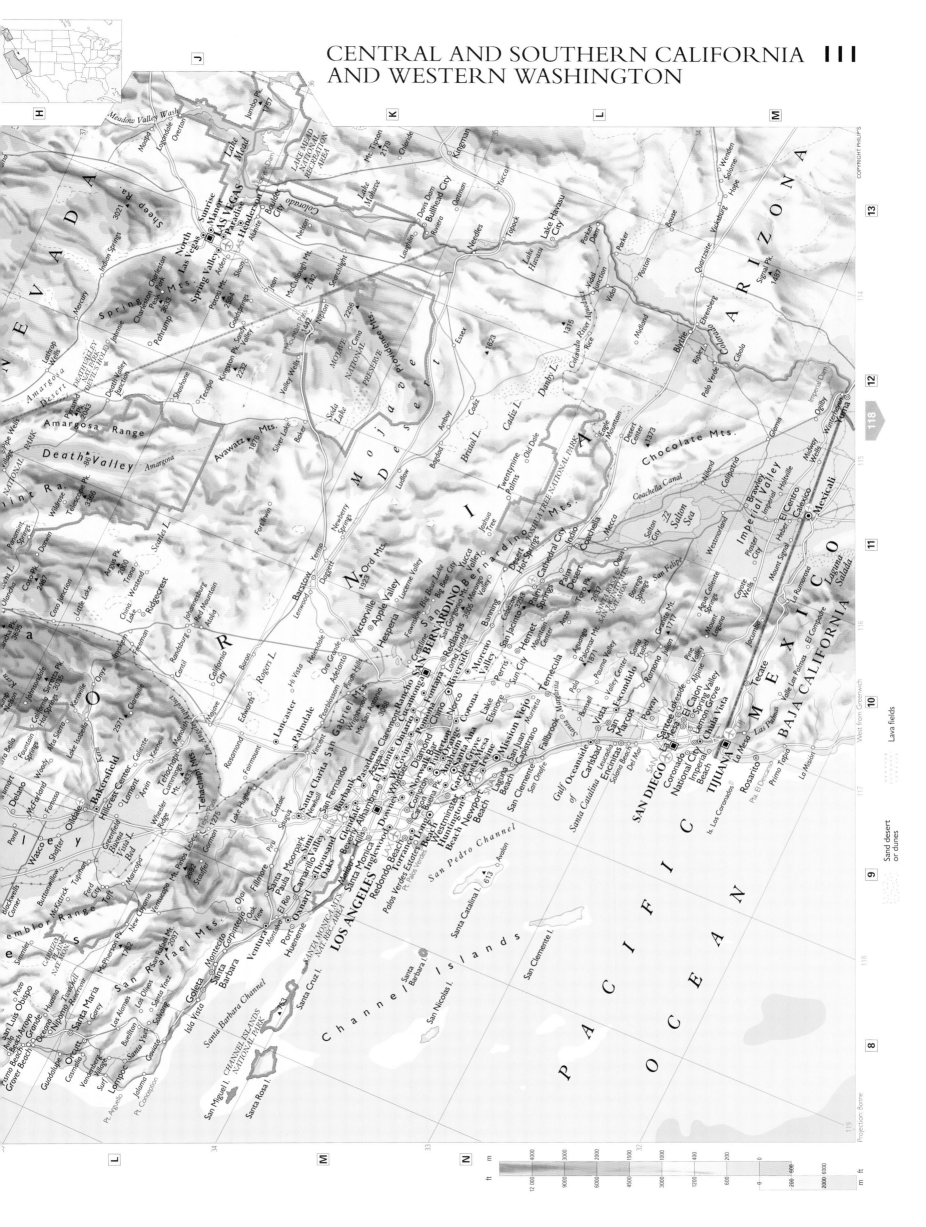

COPYRIGHT PHILIP'S

West from Greenwich

Projection: Bonne

Sand desert or dunes Lava fields

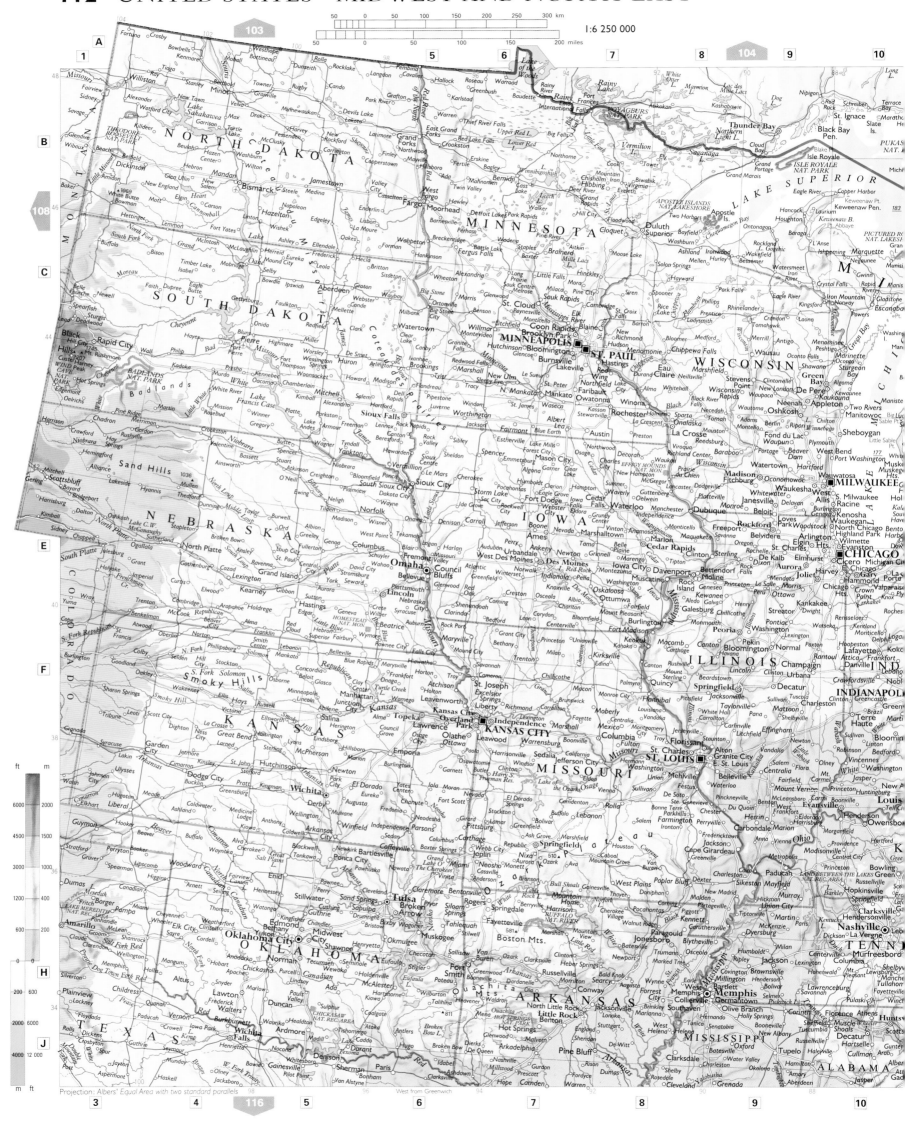

Projection: Albers' Equal Area with two standard parallels   West from Greenwich

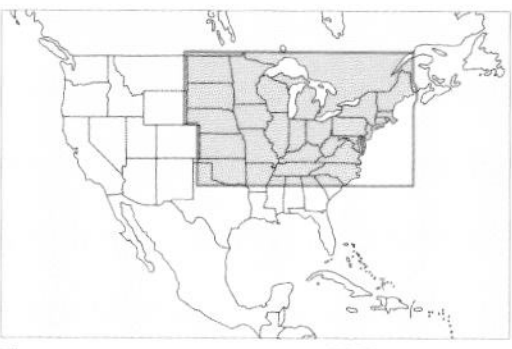

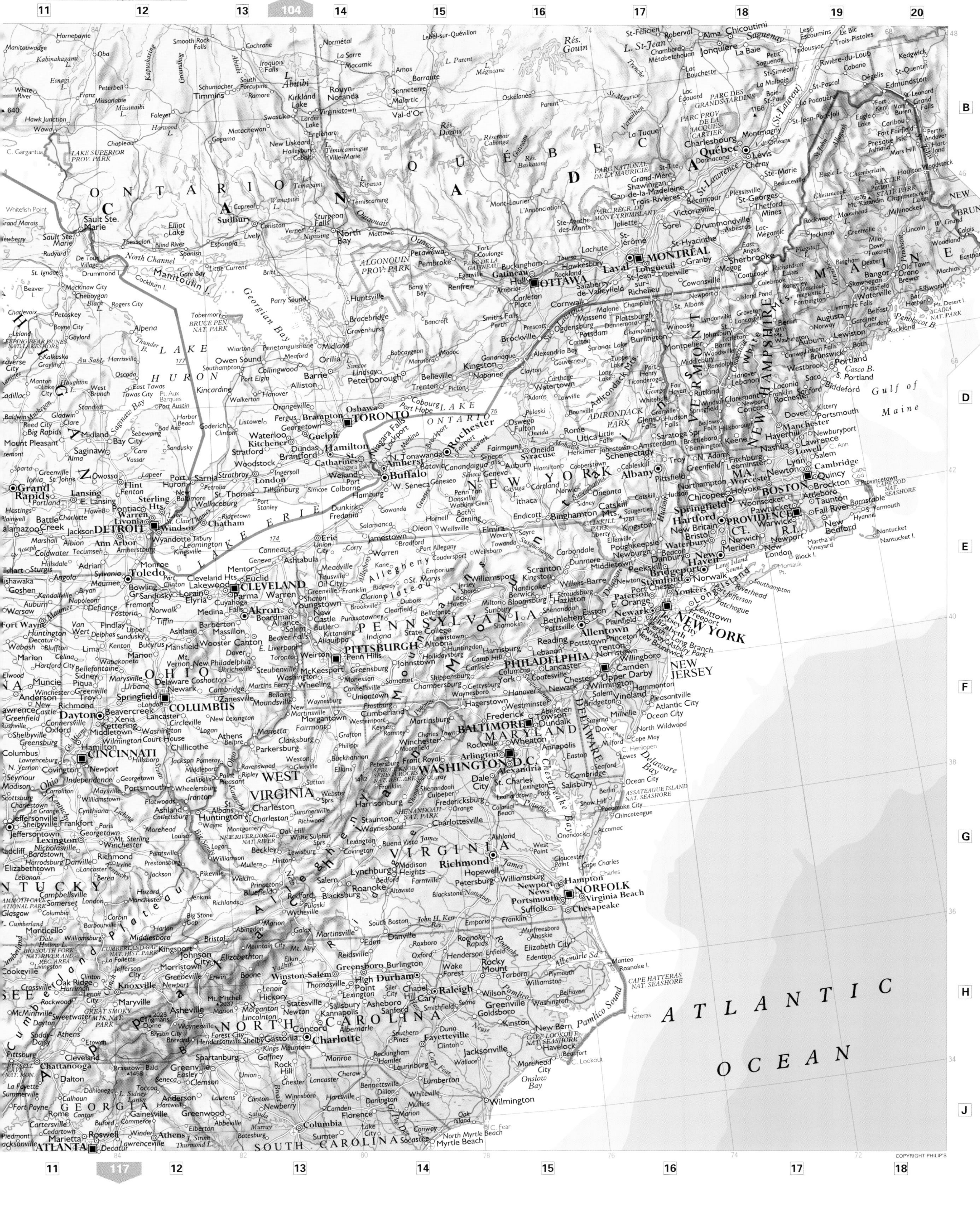

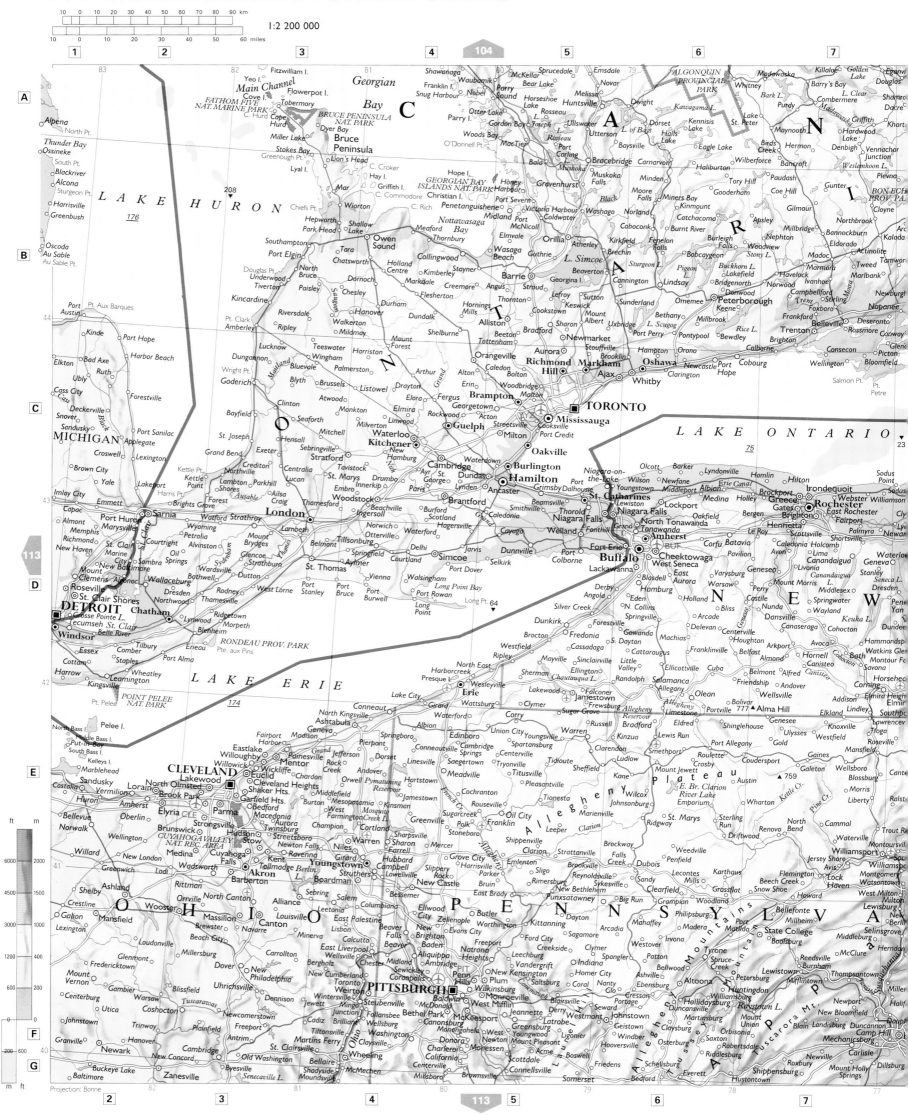

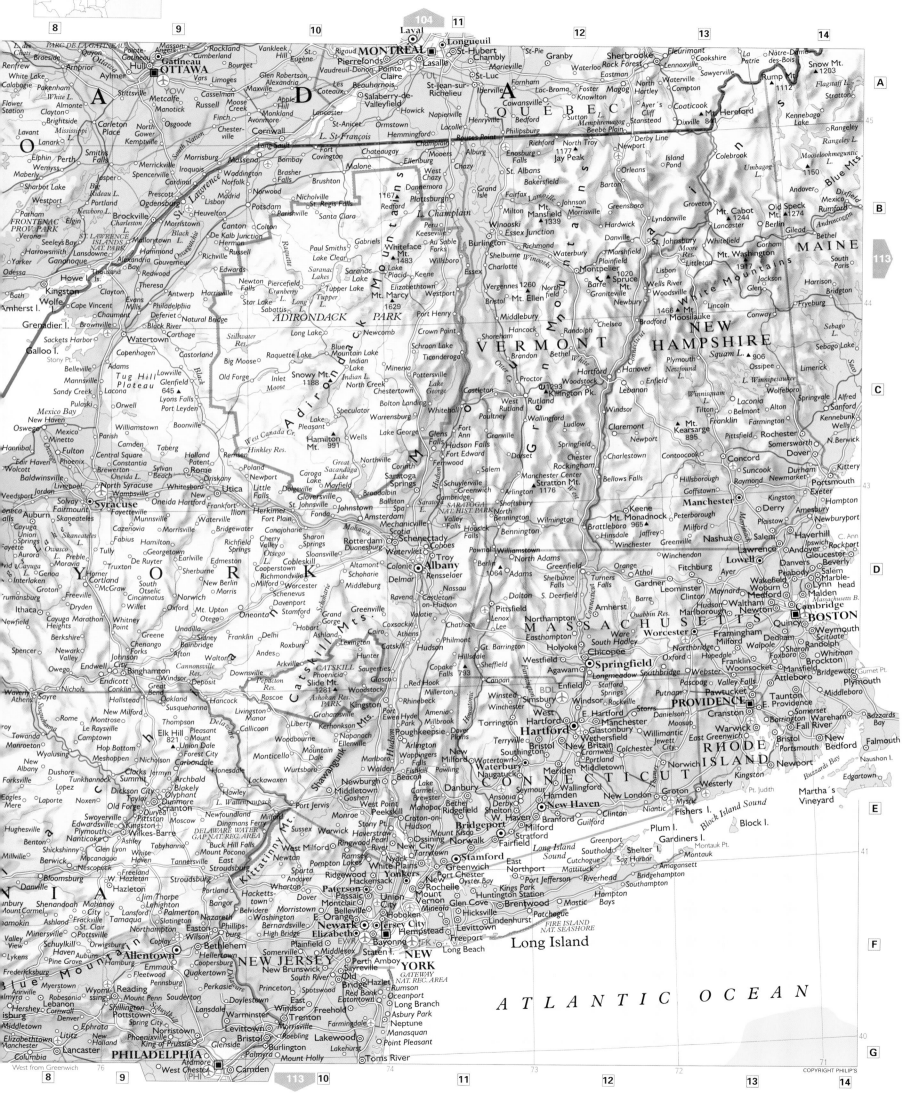

50 0 50 100 150 200 250 300 km
1:7 100 000
50 0 50 100 150 200 miles

Projection: Bi-polar oblique Conical Orthomorphic

West from Greenwich

State names in Central Mexico

1 DISTRITO FEDERAL   5 MÉXICO
2 AGUASCALIENTES   6 MORELOS
3 GUANAJUATO   7 QUERÉTARO
4 HIDALGO   8 TLAXCALA

Sand deserts

ATLANTIC OCEAN

PUERTO RICO 1:2 700 000 | d

10 0 10 20 30 40 50 km
10 0 10 20 30 miles

Pta. Agujereada
Isabela
Aguadilla · Arecibo · Manati · Vega · Barceloneta · Rio Grande
San Sebastian · Utuado · Baja · Bayamón · Carolina · Fajardo · Dewey
Mayagüez · Adjuntas · Cordillera Central · Caguas · Humacoa · Naguabo · Culebra
San German · Yauco · 1338 Cerro de Punta · Cayey · Coamp · Yabucoa · Vieques · Esperanza
Pta. Aguila · Guanica · Ponce · Guayama
I. Caja de Muertos
SAN JUAN · SJU
Ms. de Uroyan
Sierra de Luquillo
Pta. Puerca

VIRGIN ISLANDS 1:1 800 000 | e

10 0 10 20 30 km
10 0 10 20 miles

Rufling Pt. · The Settlement
Anegada · East Pt.
Virgin Islands (U.K.)
Jost Van Dyke I. · Guana I. · Great Camanoe
Hans Lollik I. · Beef · Virgin Gorda
Virgin Is. (U.S.A.) · Cruz Bay · Tortola · Road Town · Spanish Town
Charlotte Amalie · St. John I. · Peter I.
St. Thomas I. · VIRGIN IS.

ST. LUCIA 1:890 000 | f

5 0 10 km
5 0 10 miles

Cap Point · Pte. Hardy · Esperance Bay
Gros Islet
Gros Islet
Castries · Marquis
Girard
Anse la Raye · Dennery
Canaries · Millet
Soufrière · Mt. Gimie 950
Soufrière Bay · 750 Petit Piton · Trou Gras Pt.
Gros Piton Pt. · 796 · Micoud
Gros Piton · Vierge Pt.
Choiseul
Laborie · **ST. LUCIA**
Vieux Fort
C. Moule à Chique

BARBADOS 1:890 000 | g

5 0 10 km
5 0 10 miles

Crab Hill · North Point
Fustic · Spring Hall · Boscobelle
Portland · 245 · Belleplaine
Speightstown · **BARBADOS**
Westmoreland · Bathsheba · Hillcrest
Alleynes Bay · 340 Mt. Hillaby · Martin's Bay
Holetown · Massiah · Street · Ragged Pt.
Jackson · Bridgefield · Six Cross Roads
Black Rock · Ellerton · The Crane
Ivy · Edey · St. Martins
Bridgetown · Oistins
BGI · Worthing · Oistins Bay · Chancery Lane
Carlisle Bay · South Point

MAS (BAHAMAS)

ATLANTIC OCEAN

hur's Town · New Bight · Cat I.
San Salvador I. · Conception I. · Rum Cay
Long I. · Tropic of Cancer
Clarence Town · Samana Cay
Crooked I. Passage · Plana Cays
Albert Town · Snug Corner · Acklins I.
Mira por vos Cay · Cay Verde
Hogsty Reef · Turks & Caicos Is. (U.K.)
Little Inagua I. · Caicos Is. · Cockburn Town
Lake Rose · Turks Island Passage · Turks Is.
Great Inagua I. · Silver Bank Passage
Matthew Town · Mouchoir Bank · Silver Bank
INAGUA · Navidad Bank
Caicos Passage

Baracoa · Pta. de Maisi · Monte Cristi · LA ISABELA · Puerto Rico Trench
Guantánamo · Cap-Haïtien · Puerto Plata · Santiago de los Caballeros · Milwaukee Deep 9200
GUANTANAMO BAY (U.S.A.) · Jean Rabel · Port-de-Paix · La Vega · San Francisco de Macoris
Paso de los Vientos (Windward Passage) · Fort Liberté · Nagua · Samana
Gonaïves · Hinche · Pico Duarte · HAITISES · Sánchez · Sabana de la Mar
St-Marc · **HAITI** · **DOMINICAN REP.** · Hato Mayor · C. Engaño
Jérémie · Î. de la Gonâve · **PORT-AU-PRINCE** · San Pedro de Macoris · Higuey · Aguadilla · Arecibo · Bayamón · **SAN JUAN**
Massif de la Hotte · Petit Goâve · 2680 · SIERRA DE BAHORUCO · SANTO DOMINGO · La Romana · ESTE · B. de Yuma · Ponce · Carolina · Fajardo
Les Cayes · Aquin · Jacmel · Azua · San Cristóbal · I. Saona · Mayagüez · Mona Passage · Guayama
Pointe-à-Gravois · Barahona · Compostela · I. Beata · Mona Passage · **PUERTO RICO (U.S.A.)**
Pedernales · C. Beata · Isla Mona (U.S.A.)
Hispaniola · L. Enriquillo

Antilles · Virgin Gorda · Anegada Virgin Is. (U.K.)
Tortola (U.K.) · Road Town · Sombrero (U.K.)
St. Thomas · Charlotte Amalie · Virgin Is. (U.S.A.) · Anguilla (U.K.)
Christiansted · St. Maarten (Neth.) · St-Martin (Fr.) · St-Barthélemy (Fr.)
Frederiksted · St. Croix (U.S.A.) · St. Eustatius (Neth.) · Saba (Neth.) · Barbuda
1156 · **ST. KITTS & NEVIS** · Antigua · **ANTIGUA & BARBUDA**
Basseterre · St. John's
Nevis · Redonda
Montserrat (U.K.) · 914 · Soufrière Hills · Guadeloupe Passage
Ste-Rose · Le Moule · La Désirade
GUADELOUPE (Fr.) · 1467 · Pointe-à-Pitre · Marie-Galante (Fr.)
Basse-Terre · Grand-Bourg
I. des Saintes (Fr.) · Dominica Passage
Portsmouth · 1447 · Morne Diablotin · **DOMINICA**
Roseau · MORNE TROIS PITONS
Martinique Passage
Mt. Pelée · Ste-Marie
1397 · Le François
Fort-de-France · Rivière-Pilote · **MARTINIQUE (Fr.)**
St. Lucia Channel
Castries · **ST. LUCIA**
Soufrière
St. Vincent Passage
Soufrière 1234 · St. Vincent · Speightstown · 340
Kingstown · Bridgetown · **BARBADOS**
Bequia · **ST. VINCENT & THE GRENADINES**
Canouan · The Grenadines
Carriacou
840 · GRENADA
St. George's

Leeward Islands
Windward Islands
Lesser Antilles

CARIBBEAN SEA

Venezuelan Basin
Colombian Basin
Beata Ridge
I. de Aves (Venezuela)
Aves Ridge

ABC Lesser Antilles Islands
Pta. Gallinas
Oranjestad · Aruba (Neth.) · Curaçao · Bonaire
San Román · Willemstad · **NETH. ANTILLES**
Pen. de Paraguaná · ARC. LOS ROQUES
Punto Fijo · Is. Las Aves (Ven.) · Is. Los Roques (Ven.) · I. Orchila (Ven.)
I. Blanquilla (Ven.)
Is. Los Hermanos (Ven.)
NUEVA ESPARTA · Is. Los Testigos (Ven.)
I. La Tortuga (Ven.) · I. de Margarita
Tobago · Scarborough
Dragon's Mouths · Galera Point · 940
Port of Spain · **TRINIDAD**
Arima · Rio Claro
TRINIDAD & TOBAGO
San Fernando
Serpent's Mouth

COLOMBIA

BARRANQUILLA · Santa Marta · Riohacha · Uribia · GUAJIRA
Baranoa · Soledad · TAYRONA · SA. NEVADA DE STA. MARTA
ATLANTICO · Ciénaga · Santa Marta 5775 · San Rafael
Sabanalarga · ISLA DE SALAMANCA · Valledupar · Puerto Cardón · Coro · La Vela
Calamar · Fundación · Agustin Codazzi · MACURIA · Punta Espada
Galerazamba · Zambrano · Villa del Rosario · **FALCÓN** · La Concepción · Mene de Mauroa · CUEVA DE LA QUEBRADA DEL TORO
Magangué · MAGDALENA Plato · CÉSAR · Machiques · Ciudad Ojeda · Mene Grande · **LARA** · Tucacas · Puerto Cabello · Maiquetía · La Guaira
Carmen · Mompós · El Banco · ZULIA · Cabimas · Carora · **VALENCIA** · Toctuyo · **CARACAS** · **VARGAS**
Sincé · PERIJA · **MARACAIBO** · Santa Rita · Barquisimeto · YARACUY · **MARACAY** · Los Teques
Corozal · Sahagún · El Barco · Lago de Maracaibo · Trujillo · Acarigua · Villa de Cura · San Juan de los Morros · Río Chico · Caribe
Ayapel · Majagual · San Carlos del Zulia · Valera · Betijoque · **PORTUGUESA** · Yaritagua · **COJEDES** · El Sombrero · Ocumare del Tuy · Higuerote · Puerto La Cruz
Magangué · Simití · Ocaña · CATATUMBO-BARI · El Guache · San Carlos · Calabozo · Valle de la Pascua · Barcelona · Caripito
BOLÍVAR · Caucasia · Encontrados · SA. DE SAN LUIS · San Cristóbal · El Baúl · **GUARICO** · Cumaná · **SUCRE** · Maturín
Zaragoza · Cúcuta · PARAMO DE BATALLON · Barinas · Santa María de Ipire · Anaco · Cantaura · **MONAGAS**
NORTE DE SANTANDER · CORD. MERIDA · **BÁRINAS** · San Fernando de Apure · El Tigre · **ANZOÁTEGUI** · **DELTA AMACURO**
Mérida · Libertad · Ciudad Bolivia · Ciudad Guayana · Tucupita
OBA · Chita · Ciudad de Nutrias · El Pao · Sierra Imataca
VENEZUELA · Bruzual · Achaguas · Apure · Mapire · Orinoco · **Ciudad Bolívar** · Upata
Caicara · Embalse de Guri · Guasipati · Tumeremo · El Callao

Tropic of Cancer

Depth/Elevation scale (ft/m):
4000 3000 2000 1500 1000 400 200 0 · 600 6000 12 000 18 000 24 000 ft
12 000 9000 6000 4500 3000 1200 600 0 · 200 2000 4000 6000 8000 m

100 0 200 400 600 800 1000 1200 1400 km

1:31 100 000

100 0 200 400 600 800 1000 miles

Projection: Lambert's Azimuthal Equal Area

COPYRIGHT PHILIP'S

1:31 100 000

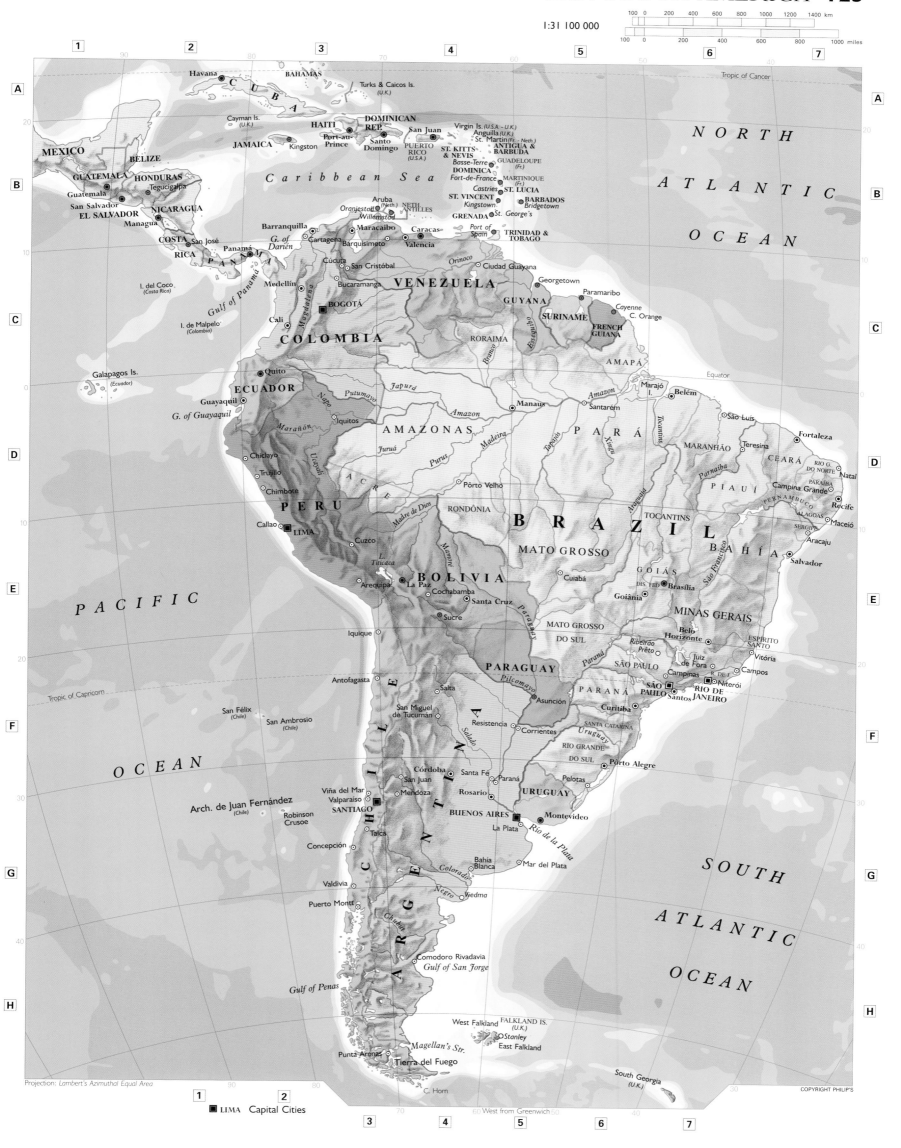

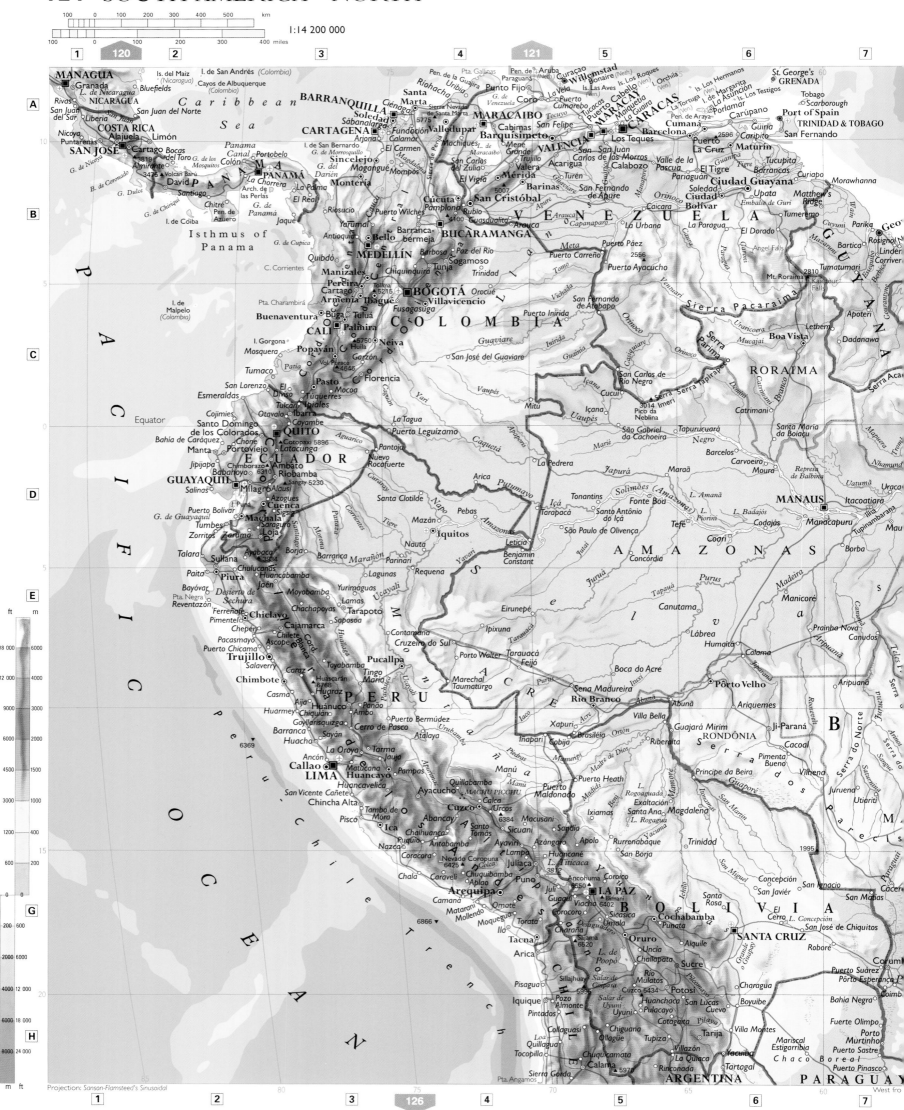

1:14 200 000

Projection: Sanson-Flamsteed's Sinusoidal

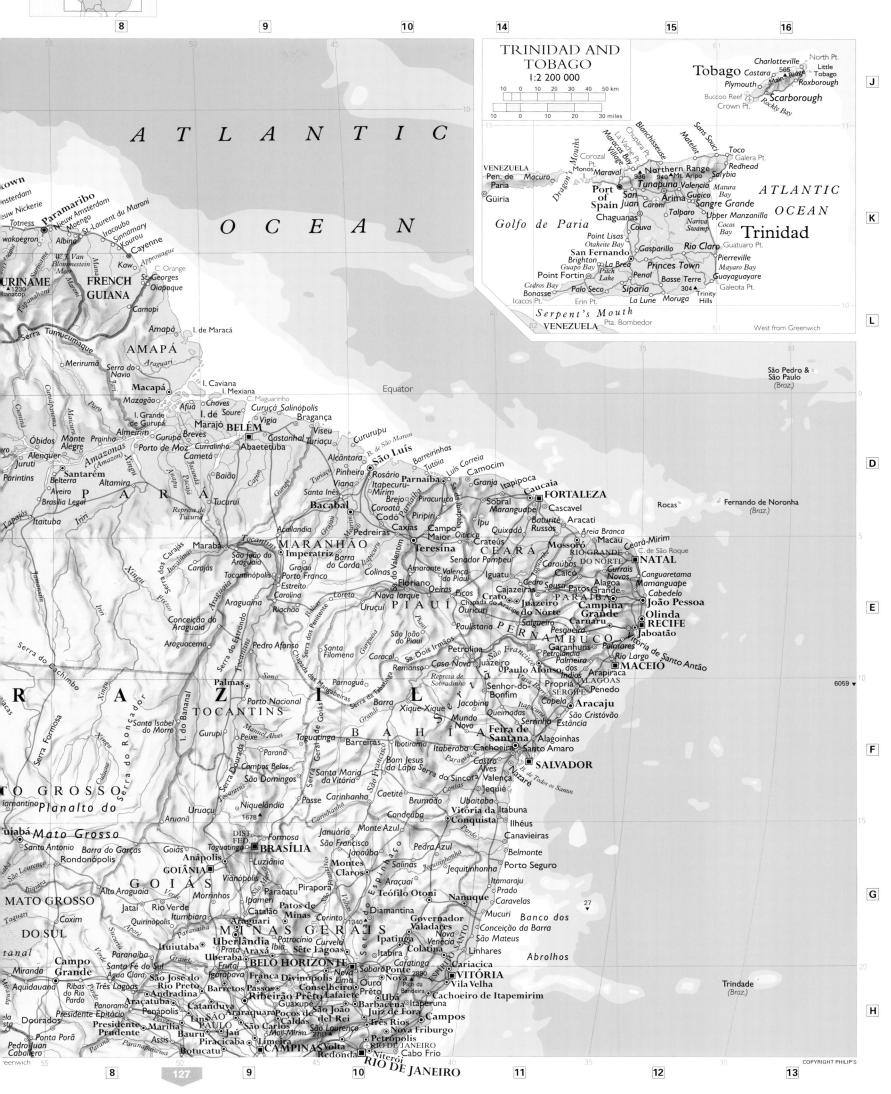

TRINIDAD AND TOBAGO
1:2 200 000

ATLANTIC OCEAN

SURINAME

FRENCH GUIANA

AMAPÁ

P A R Á

MARANHÃO

CEARÁ

RIO GRANDE DO NORTE

PIAUÍ

PARAÍBA

PERNAMBUCO

B R A Z I L

TOCANTINS

ALAGOAS

SERGIPE

B A H I A

MATO GROSSO

GOIÁS

MATO GROSSO DO SUL

MINAS GERAIS

Planalto do Mato Grosso

DIST. FED.

BRASÍLIA

SÃO PAULO

RIO DE JANEIRO

COPYRIGHT PHILIP'S

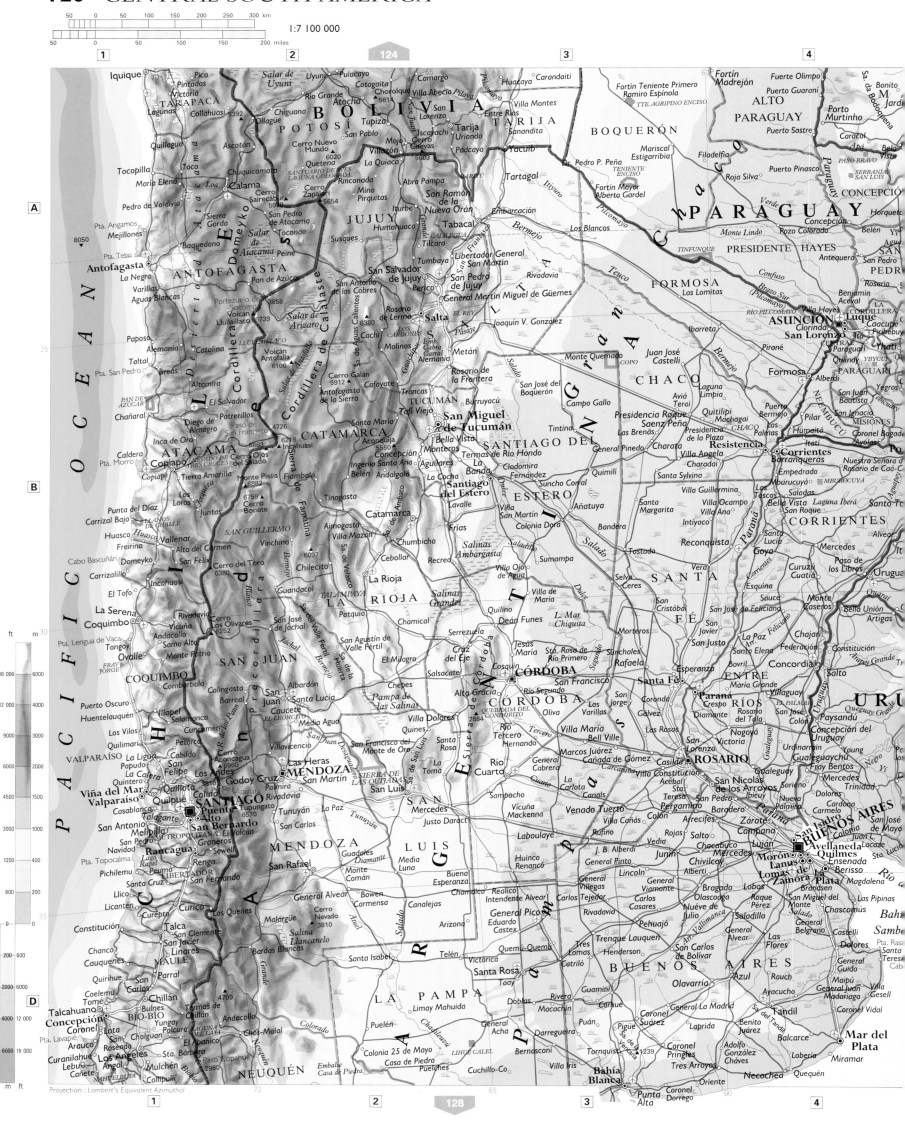

1:7 100 000

Projection : Lambert's Equivalent Azimuthal

BELO
HORIZONTE
Betim Contagem Itabirito
Congonhas
Conselheiro
Lafaiete Ouro
Campo Belo Prêto VITÓRIA
Vila
Velha
Guarapari

MATO GROSSO
DO SUL
BRAZIL
SÃO PAULO
RIO DE JANEIRO

Sidrolândia
Nioaque
Maracaju
Guia Lopes
da Laguna
Dourados
Ponta Porã
Pedro Juan Caballero

Três Lagoas
Andradina
Xavantina Mirandópolis
Nova Alvorada
do Sul
Presidente
Epitácio
Adamantina
Presidente
Prudente
Martinópolis
Rancharia
Marília
Assis
Londrina
Maringá
Cianorte
Apucarana
Mandaguari
Campo
Mourão
Cascavel
Foz do Iguaçu
Guarapuava
Ponta
Grossa
CURITIBA
Paranaguá
Joinville
São Francisco do Sul
Blumenau
Itajaí
Brusque
SANTA CATARINA
São José
Ilha de Santa Catarina
Florianópolis
Lages
Criciúma
Araranguá
Torres
Osório
PORTO ALEGRE
Viamão
RIO GRANDE
DO SUL
Santa Maria
Pelotas
Rio Grande
São José do Norte

URUGUAY

MONTEVIDEO

Andradina
Araçatuba Catanduva
Birigüi
Lins
Bauru
Jaú Rio Claro
Limeira
Piracicaba
CAMPINAS
Americana
Sumaré
Jundiaí
Osasco
SÃO PAULO
Santo André
Santos
Guarujá

RIO DE JANEIRO
Niterói
Duque de Caxias

Tropic of Capricorn

A T L A N T I C

O C E A N

COPYRIGHT PHILIP'S

West from Greenwich
55 50 45 40
5 6 7

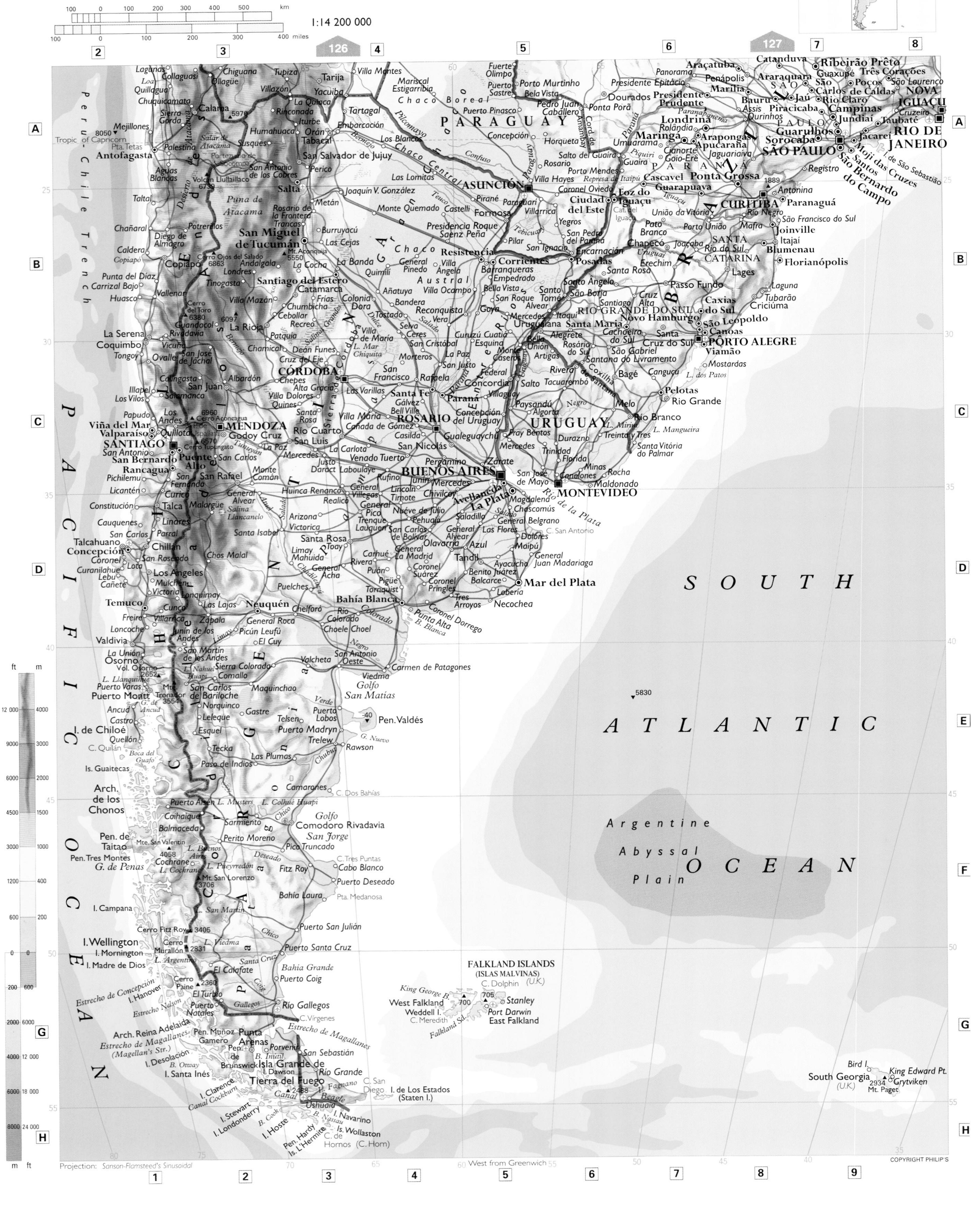

1:14 200 000

km
miles

SOUTH ATLANTIC OCEAN

Argentine Abyssal Plain

PACIFIC OCEAN

PARAGUAY

ASUNCIÓN

URUGUAY

MONTEVIDEO

BUENOS AIRES

CÓRDOBA

ROSARIO

MENDOZA

SANTIAGO

Valparaíso
Viña del Mar

SÃO PAULO

RIO DE JANEIRO

CURITIBA

PÔRTO ALEGRE

RIO GRANDE DO SUL

SANTA CATARINA

PARANÁ

NOVA IGUAÇU

FALKLAND ISLANDS
(ISLAS MALVINAS)
(U.K.)

West Falkland
East Falkland
Stanley
Port Darwin

South Georgia
(U.K.)
King Edward Pt.
Grytviken
Mt. Paget 2934
Bird I.

Tropic of Capricorn

Antofagasta

Salta

San Miguel de Tucumán

La Serena

Bahía Blanca

Mar del Plata

Neuquén

Temuco

Valdivia

Puerto Montt

I. de Chiloé

Arch. de los Chonos

Comodoro Rivadavia

Golfo San Jorge

Golfo San Matías

Pen. Valdés

PATAGONIA

Punta Arenas

Río Gallegos

Estrecho de Magallanes
(Magellan's Str.)

Isla Grande de Tierra del Fuego

Ushuaia

C. de Hornos (C. Horn)

Beagle Channel

West from Greenwich

Projection: Sanson-Flamsteed's Sinusoidal

COPYRIGHT PHILIP'S

INDEX TO WORLD MAPS

How to use the index

The index contains the names of all the principal places and features shown on the World Maps. Each name is followed by an additional entry in italics giving the country or region within which it is located. The alphabetical order of names composed of two or more words is governed primarily by the first word and then by the second. This is an example of the rule:

> Miquelon *St-P. & M.* **105** C8
> Mir *Niger* **83** C7
> Mīr Kūh *Iran* **71** E8
> Mīr Shahdād *Iran* **71** E8
> Mira *Italy* **41** C9

Physical features composed of a proper name (Erie) and a description (Lake) are positioned alphabetically by the proper name. The description is positioned after the proper name and is usually abbreviated:

> Erie, L. *N. Amer.* **114** D4

Where a description forms part of a settlement or administrative name however, it is always written in full and put in its true alphabetic position:

> Mount Morris *U.S.A.* **114** D7

Names beginning with M' and Mc are indexed as if they were spelled Mac. Names beginning St. are alphabetised under Saint, but Sankt, Sint, Sant', Santa and San are all spelt in full and are alphabetised accordingly. If the same place name occurs two or more times in the index and all are in the same country, each is followed by the name of the administrative subdivision in which it is located. For example:

> Jackson *Ky., U.S.A.* **113** G12
> Jackson *Mich., U.S.A.* **113** D11
> Jackson *Minn., U.S.A.* **112** D6

The number in bold type which follows each name in the index refers to the number of the map page where that feature or place will be found. This is usually the largest scale at which the place or feature appears.

The letter and figure which are in bold type immediately after the page number give the grid square on the map page, within which the feature is situated. The letter represents the latitude and the figure the longitude. A lower case letter immediately after the page number refers to an inset map on that page.

In some cases the feature itself may fall within the specified square, while the name is outside. This is usually the case only with features which are larger than a grid square.

Rivers are indexed to their mouths or confluences, and carry the symbol ➜ after their names. The following symbols are also used in the index: ■ country, ☑ overseas territory or dependency, ☐ first order administrative area, △ national park, ⌒ other park (provincial park, nature reserve or game reserve), ✈ (LHR) principal airport (and location identifier).

How to pronounce place names

English-speaking people usually have no difficulty in reading and pronouncing correctly English place names. However, foreign place name pronunciations may present many problems. Such problems can be minimised by following some simple rules. However, these rules cannot be applied to all situations, and there will be many exceptions.

1. In general, stress each syllable equally, unless your experience suggests otherwise.
2. Pronounce the letter 'a' as a broad 'a' as in 'arm'.
3. Pronounce the letter 'e' as a short 'e' as in 'elm'.
4. Pronounce the letter 'i' as a cross between a short 'i' and long 'e', as the two 'i's in 'California'.
5. Pronounce the letter 'o' as an intermediate 'o' as in 'soft'.
6. Pronounce the letter 'u' as an intermediate 'u' as in 'sure'.
7. Pronounce consonants hard, except in the Romance-language areas where 'g's are likely to be pronounced softly like 'j' in 'jam'; 'j' itself may be pronounced as 'y'; and 'x's may be pronounced as 'h'.
8. For names in mainland China, pronounce 'q' like the 'ch' in 'chin', 'x' like the 'sh' in 'she', 'zh' like the 'j' in 'jam', and 'z' as if it were spelled 'dz'. In general pronounce 'a' as in 'father', 'e' as in 'but', 'i' as in 'keep', 'o' as in 'or', and 'u' as in 'rule'.

Moreover, English has no diacritical marks (accent and pronunciation signs), although some languages do. The following is a brief and general guide to the pronunciation of those most frequently used in the principal Western European languages.

		Pronunciation as in
French	é	day and shows that the e is to be pronounced; e.g. Orléans.
	è	mare
	î	used over any vowel and does not affect pronunciation; shows contraction of the name, usually omission of 's' following a vowel.
	ç	's' before 'a', 'o' and 'u'.
	ë, ï, ü	over 'e', 'i' and 'u' when they are used with another vowel and shows that each is to be pronounced.
German	ä	fate
	ö	fur
	ü	no English equivalent; like French 'tu'
Italian	à, é	over vowels and indicates stress.
Portuguese	ã, õ	vowels pronounced nasally.
	ç	boss
	á	shows stress
	ô	shows that a vowel has an 'i' or 'u' sound combined with it.
Spanish	ñ	canyon
	ü	pronounced as w and separately from adjoining vowels.
	á	usually indicates that this is a stressed vowel.

Abbreviations

A.C.T. – Australian Capital Territory
A.R. – Autonomous Region
Afghan. – Afghanistan
Afr. – Africa
Ala. – Alabama
Alta. – Alberta
Amer. – America(n)
Arch. – Archipelago
Ariz. – Arizona
Ark. – Arkansas
Atl. Oc. – Atlantic Ocean
B. – Baie, Bahía, Bay, Bucht, Bugt
B.C. – British Columbia
Bangla. – Bangladesh
Barr. – Barrage
Bos.-H. – Bosnia-Herzegovina
C. – Cabo, Cap, Cape, Coast
C.A.R. – Central African Republic
C. Prov. – Cape Province
Calif. – California
Cat. – Catarata
Cent. – Central
Chan. – Channel
Colo. – Colorado
Conn. – Connecticut
Cord. – Cordillera
Cr. – Creek
Czech. – Czech Republic
D.C. – District of Columbia
Del. – Delaware
Dem. – Democratic
Dep. – Dependency
Des. – Desert
Dét. – Détroit
Dist. – District
Dj. – Djebel
Domin. – Dominica
Dom. Rep. – Dominican Republic
E. – East

E. Salv. – El Salvador
Eq. Guin. – Equatorial Guinea
Est. – Estrecho
Falk. Is. – Falkland Is.
Fd. – Fjord
Fla. – Florida
Fr. – French
G. – Golfe, Golfo, Gulf, Guba, Gebel
Ga. – Georgia
Gt. – Great, Greater
Guinea-Biss. – Guinea-Bissau
H.K. – Hong Kong
H.P. – Himachal Pradesh
Hants. – Hampshire
Harb. – Harbor, Harbour
Hd. – Head
Hts. – Heights
I.(s). – Île, Ilha, Insel, Isla, Island, Isle
Ill. – Illinois
Ind. – Indiana
Ind. Oc. – Indian Ocean
Ivory C. – Ivory Coast
J. – Jabal, Jebel
Jaz. – Jazīrah
Junc. – Junction
K. – Kap, Kapp
Kans. – Kansas
Kep. – Kepulauan
Ky. – Kentucky
L. – Lac, Lacul, Lago, Lagoa, Lake, Limni, Loch, Lough
La. – Louisiana
Ld. – Land
Liech. – Liechtenstein
Lux. – Luxembourg
Mad. P. – Madhya Pradesh
Madag. – Madagascar
Man. – Manitoba

Mass. – Massachusetts
Md. – Maryland
Me. – Maine
Medit. S. – Mediterranean Sea
Mich. – Michigan
Minn. – Minnesota
Miss. – Mississippi
Mo. – Missouri
Mont. – Montana
Mozam. – Mozambique
Mt.(s) – Mont, Montaña, Mountain
Mte. – Monte
Mti. – Monti
N. – Nord, Norte, North, Northern, Nouveau
N.B. – New Brunswick
N.C. – North Carolina
N. Cal. – New Caledonia
N. Dak. – North Dakota
N.H. – New Hampshire
N.I. – North Island
N.J. – New Jersey
N. Mex. – New Mexico
N.S. – Nova Scotia
N.S.W. – New South Wales
N.W.T. – North West Territory
N.Y. – New York
N.Z. – New Zealand
Nac. – Nacional
Nat. – National
Nebr. – Nebraska
Neths. – Netherlands
Nev. – Nevada
Nfld. & L. – Newfoundland and Labrador
Nic. – Nicaragua
O. – Oued, Ouadi
Occ. – Occidentale
Okla. – Oklahoma

Ont. – Ontario
Or. – Orientale
Oreg. – Oregon
Os. – Ostrov
Oz. – Ozero
P. – Pass, Passo, Pasul, Pulau
P.E.I. – Prince Edward Island
Pa. – Pennsylvania
Pac. Oc. – Pacific Ocean
Papua N.G. – Papua New Guinea
Pass. – Passage
Peg. – Pegunungan
Pen. – Peninsula, Péninsule
Phil. – Philippines
Pk. – Peak
Plat. – Plateau
Prov. – Province, Provincial
Pt. – Point
Pta. – Ponta, Punta
Pte. – Pointe
Qué. – Québec
Queens. – Queensland
R. – Rio, River
R.I. – Rhode Island
Ra. – Range
Raj. – Rajasthan
Recr. – Recreational, Récréatif
Reg. – Region
Rep. – Republic
Res. – Reserve, Reservoir
Rhld-Pfz. – Rheinland-Pfalz
S. – South, Southern, Sur
Si. Arabia – Saudi Arabia
S.C. – South Carolina
S. Dak. – South Dakota
S.I. – South Island
S. Leone – Sierra Leone
Sa. – Serra, Sierra
Sask. – Saskatchewan

Scot. – Scotland
Sd. – Sound
Sev. – Severnaya
Sib. – Siberia
Sprs. – Springs
St. – Saint
Sta. – Santa
Ste. – Sainte
Sto. – Santo
Str. – Strait, Stretto
Switz. – Switzerland
Tas. – Tasmania
Tenn. – Tennessee
Terr. – Territory, Territoire
Tex. – Texas
Tg. – Tanjung
Trin. & Tob. – Trinidad & Tobago
U.A.E. – United Arab Emirates
U.K. – United Kingdom
U.S.A. – United States of America
Ut. P. – Uttar Pradesh
Va. – Virginia
Vdkhr. – Vodokhranilishche
Vdskh. – Vodoskhovyshche
Vf. – Vírful
Vic. – Victoria
Vol. – Volcano
Vt. – Vermont
W. – Wadi, West
W. Va. – West Virginia
Wall. & F. Is. – Wallis and Futuna Is.
Wash. – Washington
Wis. – Wisconsin
Wlkp. – Wielkopolski
Wyo. – Wyoming
Yorks. – Yorkshire

Babadağ Turkey 47 D10
Babaeski Turkey 45 E11
Babahoyo Ecuador 124 D3
Babai = Sarju → India 69 F9
Babana Nigeria 83 C5
Babanusa Sudan 81 E2
Babar Indonesia 63 F7
Babar Pakistan 68 D3
Babarkach Pakistan 68 E3
Babayevo Russia 32 C8
Babb U.S.A. 108 B7
Babenhausen Germany 25 F4
Băbeni Romania 29 F9
Baberu India 69 G9
Babi Besar, Pulau Malaysia 65 L4
Babia Gora Europe 31 J6
Babian Jiang → China 58 F3
Bābil □ Iraq 70 C5
Babile Ethiopia 81 F5
Babimost Poland 31 F2
Babinda Australia 94 B4
Babine Canada 102 B3
Babine → Canada 102 B3
Babine L. Canada 102 C3
Babiogórski △ Poland 31 J6
Babo Indonesia 63 E8
Babócsa Hungary 28 D2
Bābol Iran 71 B7
Bābol Sar Iran 71 B7
Baborów Poland 31 H5
Baboua C.A.R. 84 C2
Babruysk Belarus 23 B15
Babuhri India 68 F3
Babuna Macedonia 44 E5
Babura Nigeria 83 C6
Babusar Pass Pakistan 69 B5
Babušnica Serbia 44 C6
Babuyan Chan. Phil. 61 B4
Babylon Iraq 73 F11
Bač Serbia 28 E4
Bâc → Moldova 29 D14
Bac Can Vietnam 58 F5
Bac Giang Vietnam 58 G6
Bac Lieu Vietnam 65 H5
Bac Ninh Vietnam 58 G6
Bac Phan Vietnam 58 G5
Bac Quang Vietnam 58 F5
Bacabal Brazil 125 D10
Bacalar Mexico 119 D7
Bacan, Kepulauan Indonesia 63 E7
Bacarra Phil. 61 B4
Bacău Romania 29 D11
Bacău □ Romania 29 D11
Baccarat France 19 D13
Bacerac Mexico 118 A3
Băceşti Romania 29 D12
Bach Long Vi, Dao Vietnam 64 B6
Bach Ma △ Vietnam 64 D6
Bacharach Germany 25 E3
Bachhwara India 69 G11
Bachuma Ethiopia 81 F4
Bačina Serbia 44 C5
Back → Canada 100 C9
Bačka Palanka Serbia 28 E4
Bačka Topola Serbia 28 E4
Bäckebo Sweden 11 H10
Bäckefors Sweden 11 F6
Bäckhammar Sweden 10 E8
Bački Petrovac Serbia 28 E4
Backnang Germany 25 G5
Baco, Mt. Phil. 61 E4
Bacolod Phil. 61 F5
Bacqueville-en-Caux France 18 C8
Bács-Kiskun □ Hungary 28 D4
Bácsalmás Hungary 28 D4
Bacuag = Placer Phil. 61 G6
Bacuk Malaysia 65 J4
Bácum Mexico 118 B2
Bād Iran 71 C7
Bad → U.S.A. 112 C3
Bad Aussee Austria 26 D6
Bad Axe U.S.A. 114 C2
Bad Bergzabern Germany 25 F3
Bad Berleburg Germany 24 D4
Bad Bevensen Germany 24 B6
Bad Bramstedt Germany 24 B5
Bad Brückenau Germany 25 E5
Bad Doberan Germany 24 A7
Bad Driburg Germany 24 D5
Bad Ems Germany 25 E3
Bad Frankenhausen Germany 24 D7
Bad Freienwalde Germany 24 C10
Bad Goisern Austria 26 D6
Bad Harzburg Germany 24 D6
Bad Hersfeld Germany 24 E5
Bad Hofgastein Austria 26 D6
Bad Homburg Germany 25 E4
Bad Honnef Germany 24 E3
Bad Iburg Germany 24 C4
Bad Ischl Austria 26 D6
Bad Kissingen Germany 25 E6
Bad Königshofen Germany 25 E6
Bad Kreuznach Germany 25 F3
Bad Krozingen Germany 25 H3
Bad Laasphe Germany 24 E4
Bad Langensalza Germany 24 D6
Bad Lauterberg Germany 24 D6
Bad Leonfelden Austria 26 C7
Bad Liebenwerda Germany 24 D9
Bad Mergentheim Germany 25 F5
Bad Münstereifel Germany 24 E2
Bad Nauheim Germany 25 E4
Bad Neuenahr-Ahrweiler Germany 24 E3
Bad Neustadt Germany 25 E6
Bad Oeynhausen Germany 24 C4
Bad Oldesloe Germany 24 B6
Bad Orb Germany 25 E5
Bad Pyrmont Germany 24 D5
Bad Reichenhall Germany 25 H8
Bad Säckingen Germany 25 H3
Bad St. Leonhard Austria 26 E7
Bad Salzuflen Germany 24 C4
Bad Salzungen Germany 24 E6
Bad Schwartau Germany 24 B6
Bad Segeberg Germany 24 B6
Bad Tölz Germany 25 H7
Bad Urach Germany 25 G5
Bad Vöslau Austria 27 D9
Bad Waldsee Germany 25 H5
Bad Wildungen Germany 24 D5
Bad Wimpfen Germany 25 F5
Bad Windsheim Germany 25 F6
Bad Zwischenahn Germany 24 B4
Bada Barabil India 69 H11
Badagara India 66 P9
Badagri Nigeria 83 D5
Badajós, L. Brazil 124 D6
Badajoz Spain 37 G4
Badajoz □ Spain 37 G4
Badakhshān □ Afghan. 66 A7
Badalona Spain 38 D7
Badalzai Afghan. 68 E1
Badampahar India 67 H15
Badanah Si. Arabia 70 D4
Badarinath India 69 D8
Badas, Kepulauan Indonesia 62 D3
Baddo → Pakistan 66 F4
Bade Indonesia 63 F9
Badeggi Nigeria 83 D6
Badéguichéri Niger 83 C6
Baden Austria 27 C9
Baden Switz. 25 H4
Baden U.S.A. 114 F4
Baden-Baden Germany 25 G4
Baden-Württemberg □ Germany 25 G4
Badgam India 69 B6
Badgastein Austria 26 D6
Badger Canada 105 C8
Badger U.S.A. 110 J7
Bādghīs □ Afghan. 66 B3
Badgingarra △ Australia 93 F2
Badia Polésine Italy 41 C8
Badiar △ Guinea 82 C2
Badin Pakistan 68 G3
Badinka ⌓ Mali 82 C3
Badlands U.S.A. 112 D2
Badlands △ U.S.A. 112 D2
Badogo Mali 82 C3
Badoumbé Mali 82 C2
Badrah Iraq 73 F11
Badrinath India 69 D8
Badulla Sri Lanka 66 R12
Badung, Selat Indonesia 63 K18
Baena Spain 37 H6
Baengnyeongdo S. Korea 57 F13
Baeza Spain 37 H7
Bafang Cameroon 83 D7
Bafatá Guinea-Biss. 82 C2
Baffin B. N. Amer. 101 B13
Baffin I. Canada 101 C12
Bafia Cameroon 83 E7
Bafilo Togo 83 D5
Bafing → Mali 82 C2
Bafing △ Mali 82 C2
Bafliyūn Syria 70 B3
Bafoulabé Mali 82 C2
Bafoussam Cameroon 83 D7
Bāfq Iran 71 D7
Bafra Turkey 72 B6
Bafra Burnu Turkey 72 B7
Bāft Iran 71 D8
Bafut Cameroon 83 D7
Bafwasende Dem. Rep. of the Congo 86 B2
Bagaha India 69 F11
Bagam Niger 83 B6
Bagamoyo Tanzania 86 D4
Bagan Datoh Malaysia 65 L3
Bagan Serai Malaysia 65 K3
Baganga Phil. 61 H7
Bagani Namibia 88 B3
Bagansiapiapi Indonesia 62 D2
Bagasra India 68 J4
Bagaud India 68 H6
Bagawi Sudan 81 E3
Bagbag Sudan 81 D3
Bagdad U.S.A. 111 L11
Bagdarin Russia 53 D12
Bagé Brazil 127 C5
Bagenalstown = Muine Bheag Ireland 12 D5
Baggs U.S.A. 108 F10
Bagh Pakistan 69 C5
Baghain → India 69 G9
Baghdād Iraq 73 F11
Baghdadi Georgia 73 A10
Bagheria Italy 42 D6
Baghlān Afghan. 66 A6
Baghlān □ Afghan. 66 B6
Bagley U.S.A. 112 B6
Bagnara Cálabra Italy 43 D8
Bagnasco Italy 40 D5
Bagnères-de-Bigorre France 20 E4
Bagnères-de-Luchon France 20 F4
Bagni di Lucca Italy 40 D7
Bagno di Romagna Italy 41 E8
Bagnoles-de-l'Orne France 18 D6
Bagnols-sur-Cèze France 21 D8
Bagnorégio Italy 41 F9
Bago = Pegu Burma 67 L20
Bagodar India 69 G11
Bagrationovsk Russia 30 D7
Bagrdan Serbia 44 B5
Baguio Phil. 61 C4
Bağyurdu Turkey 47 C9
Bagzane, Monts Niger 83 B6
Bah India 69 F8
Bahabón de Esgueva Spain 36 D7
Bahadurganj India 69 F12
Bahadurgarh India 68 E7
Bahama, Canal Viejo de W. Indies 120 B4
Bahamas ■ N. Amer. 121 B5
Bahār Iran 71 C6
Bahār Iran 73 E13
Baharampur India 69 G13
Baharîya, El Wâhât al Egypt 80 B2
Baharu Pandan = Pandan Malaysia 65 d
Bahawalnagar Pakistan 68 E5
Bahawalpur Pakistan 68 E4
Bahçe Turkey 72 D7
Bahçecik Turkey 45 F13
Bäherden Turkmenistan 71 B8
Baheri India 69 E8
Bahgul → India 69 F8
Bahi Tanzania 86 D4
Bahi Swamp Tanzania 86 D4
Bahía = Salvador Brazil 125 F11
Bahía □ Brazil 125 F10
Bahía, Is. de la Honduras 120 C2
Bahía Blanca Argentina 126 D3
Bahía de Caráquez Ecuador 124 D2
Bahía Kino Mexico 118 B2
Bahía Laura Argentina 128 F3
Bahía Negra Paraguay 124 H7
Bahir Dar Ethiopia 81 E4
Bahmanzād Iran 71 D6
Bahr el Ahmar □ Sudan 80 D4
Bahr el Jabal □ Sudan 81 G3
Bahraich India 69 F9
Bahrain ■ Asia 71 E6
Bahror India 68 F7
Bāhū Kalāt Iran 71 E9
Bai Mali 82 C4
Bai Bung, Mui = Ca Mau, Mui Vietnam 65 H5
Bai Duc Vietnam 64 C5
Bai Thuong Vietnam 64 C5
Baia de Aramă Romania 28 E7
Baia Mare Romania 29 C8
Baia-Sprie Romania 29 C8
Baião Brazil 125 D9
Baïbokoum Chad 79 G9
Baicheng China 57 B12
Băicoi Romania 29 E10
Baidoa = Baydhabo Somali Rep. 75 G3
Baie-Comeau Canada 105 C6
Baie-St-Paul Canada 105 C5
Baie Ste-Anne Seychelles 85 b
Baie-Trinité Canada 105 C6
Baie Verte Canada 105 C8
Baignes-Ste-Radegonde France 20 C3
Baigneux-les-Juifs France 19 E11
Baihar India 69 H9
Baihe China 56 H6
Ba'ījī Iraq 73 E10
Baijnath India 69 E8
Baikal, L. = Baykal, Oz. Russia 53 D11
Baikonur = Bayqongyr Kazakhstan 52 E7
Baikunthpur India 69 H10
Baile Atha Cliath = Dublin Ireland 12 C5
Băile Govora Romania 29 E9
Băile Herculane Romania 28 F7
Băile Olăneşti Romania 29 E9
Băile Tuşnad Romania 29 D10
Bailén Spain 37 G7
Băileşti Romania 29 F8
Baima China 58 A3
Bain-de-Bretagne France 18 E5
Bainbridge Ga., U.S.A. 117 F12
Bainbridge N.Y., U.S.A. 115 D9
Bainbridge Island U.S.A. 110 C4
Baing Indonesia 63 F6
Bainiu China 56 H7
Baiona Spain 36 C2
Bā'ir Jordan 74 E5
Bairiki = Tarawa Kiribati 96 G9
Bairin Youqi China 57 C10
Bairin Zuoqi China 57 C10
Bairnsdale Australia 95 F4
Bais Phil. 61 G5
Baisha China 56 G7
Baissa Nigeria 83 D7
Baitadi Nepal 69 E9
Baixa Limia-Sierra do Xurés ⌓ Spain 36 D2
Baiyin China 56 F3
Baiyü China 58 B2
Baiyu Shan China 56 F4
Baiyuda Sudan 80 D3
Baj Baj India 69 H13
Baja Hungary 28 D3
Baja, Pta. Mexico 118 B1
Baja California Mexico 118 A1
Baja California □ Mexico 118 B2
Baja California Sur □ Mexico 118 B2
Bajag India 69 H9
Bajamar Canary Is. 48 F3
Bajana India 68 H4
Bajatrejo Indonesia 63 J17
Bajera Indonesia 63 J18
Bājgīrān Iran 71 B8
Bajimba, Mt. Australia 95 D5
Bajina Bašta Serbia 44 C3
Bajmok Serbia 28 E4
Bajo Boquete Panama 120 E3
Bajo Nuevo Caribbean 120 C4
Bajoga Nigeria 83 C7
Bajool Australia 94 C5
Bak Hungary 28 D1
Bakar Croatia 41 C11
Bakassi Pen. Cameroon 83 E6
Bakel Senegal 82 C2
Baker Calif., U.S.A. 111 K10
Baker Mont., U.S.A. 108 C11
Baker, L. Canada 100 C10
Baker, Mt. U.S.A. 108 B3
Baker City U.S.A. 108 D5
Baker I. Pac. Oc. 96 G10
Baker I. U.S.A. 102 B2
Baker L. Australia 93 E4
Baker Lake Canada 100 C10
Bakers Creek Australia 94 C4
Bakers Dozen Is. Canada 104 A4
Bakersfield Calif., U.S.A. 111 K8
Bakersfield Vt., U.S.A. 115 B12
Bakharden = Bäherden Turkmenistan 71 B8
Bakhchysaray Ukraine 33 K7
Bakhmach Ukraine 33 G7
Bākhtarān = Kermānshāh Iran 73 E12
Bākhtarān = Kermānshāh □ Iran 70 C5
Bakı Azerbaijan 35 K9
Bakır → Turkey 47 C9
Bakırdağı Turkey 72 C6
Bakkafjörður Iceland 8 C6
Baklan Turkey 47 C11
Bako Ethiopia 81 F4
Bako Ivory C. 82 D3
Bakony Hungary 28 C2
Bakony Forest = Bakony Hungary 28 C2
Bakori Nigeria 83 C6
Bakouma C.A.R. 84 C4
Baksan Russia 35 J6
Bakswaho India 69 G8
Baku = Bakı Azerbaijan 35 K9
Bakundi Nigeria 83 D7
Bakuriani Georgia 73 B10
Bakutis Coast Antarctica 5 D15
Baky = Bakı Azerbaijan 35 K9
Bala Canada 114 A5
Bala Senegal 82 C2
Balâ Turkey 72 C5
Bala U.K. 14 E4
Bala, L. U.K. 14 E4
Balabac I. Phil. 62 C5
Balabac Str. E. Indies 62 C5
Balabagh Afghan. 68 B4
Ba'labakk Lebanon 74 B5
Balabalangan, Kepulauan Indonesia 62 E5
Bălăciţa Romania 29 F8
Balad Iraq 73 F11
Balad Rūz Iraq 73 F11
Bālādeh Fārs, Iran 71 D6
Bālādeh Māzandaran, Iran 71 B6
Balaghat India 66 J12
Balaghat Ra. India 66 K10
Balaguer Spain 38 D5
Balakän Azerbaijan 73 B12
Balakhna Russia 34 B6
Balaklava Ukraine 33 K7
Balakliya Ukraine 33 H9
Balakovo Russia 34 D8
Balamau India 69 F9
Bălan Romania 29 D10
Balancán Mexico 119 D6
Balanivka Ukraine 29 B14
Balashov Russia 34 E6
Balasinor India 68 H5
Balasore = Baleshwar India 67 J15
Balassagyarmat Hungary 28 B4
Balât Egypt 80 B2
Balaton Hungary 28 D2
Balaton-Felvidéki △ Hungary 28 D2
Balatonboglár Hungary 28 D2
Balatonfüred Hungary 28 D2
Balatonszentgyörgy Hungary 28 D2
Balayan Phil. 61 E4
Balazote Spain 39 G2
Balbieriškis Lithuania 30 D10
Balbigny France 21 C8
Balbina, Represa de Brazil 124 D7
Balboa Panama 120 E4
Balbriggan Ireland 12 C5
Balcarce Argentina 126 D4
Balcarres Canada 103 C8
Bălceşti Romania 29 F8
Balchik Bulgaria 45 C12
Balclutha N.Z. 91 G2
Balcones Escarpment U.S.A. 116 G5
Balçova Turkey 47 C9
Bald I. Australia 93 F2
Bald Knob U.S.A. 116 D9
Baldock L. Canada 103 B9
Baldwin Mich., U.S.A. 113 D11
Baldwin Pa., U.S.A. 114 F5
Baldwinsville U.S.A. 115 C8
Baldy Peak U.S.A. 109 K9
Bale Croatia 41 C10
Bale Oromiya, Ethiopia 81 F5
Bale Oromiya, Ethiopia 81 F5
Bale Mts. △ Ethiopia 81 F4
Baleares, Is. Spain 48 B10
Balearic Is. = Baleares, Is. Spain 48 B10
Baleine = Whale → Canada 105 A6
Baleine, Petite R. de la → Canada 104 A4
Băleni Romania 29 E12
Baler Phil. 61 D4
Baler Bay Phil. 61 D4
Baleshare U.K. 13 D1
Baleshwar India 67 J15
Baley Russia 53 D12
Balezino Russia 34 B11
Balfate Honduras 120 C2
Balgo Australia 92 D4
Bali Cameroon 83 D7
Bali Greece 49 D6
Bali India 68 G5
Bali Indonesia 63 J18
Bali □ Indonesia 63 J18
Bali, Selat Indonesia 63 J17
Bali Sea Indonesia 63 J17
Balia S. Leone 82 D2
Baliapal India 69 J12
Balige Indonesia 65 L2
Baligród Poland 31 J9
Balik Pulau Malaysia 65 c
Balikeşir Turkey 47 B9
Balıkesir □ Turkey 47 B9
Balīkh → Syria 73 E8
Balıkçeşme Turkey 45 F11
Balikpapan Indonesia 62 E5
Balimbing Phil. 63 C5
Baling Malaysia 65 K3
Balingen Germany 25 G4
Balinţ Romania 28 E6
Balintang Channel Phil. 61 B4
Balkan Mts. = Stara Planina Bulgaria 44 C7
Balkanabat Turkmenistan 71 B7
Balkhash = Balqash Kazakhstan 52 E8
Balkhash, Ozero = Balqash Köli Kazakhstan 52 E8
Ballachulish U.K. 13 E3
Balladonia Australia 93 F3
Ballaghaderreen Ireland 12 C3
Ballarat Australia 95 F3
Ballard, L. Australia 93 E3
Ballater U.K. 13 D5
Ballé Mali 82 B3
Ballenas, Canal de Mexico 118 B2
Balleny Is. Antarctica 5 C11
Balleroy France 18 C6
Ballerup Denmark 11 J6
Ballı Turkey 45 F11
Ballia India 69 G11
Ballina Australia 95 D5
Ballina Ireland 12 B2
Ballinasloe Ireland 12 C3
Ballinger U.S.A. 116 F5
Ballinrobe Ireland 12 C2
Ballinskelligs B. Ireland 12 E1
Ballon France 18 D7
Ballons des Vosges ⌓ France 19 E14
Ballsh Albania 44 F3
Ballston Spa U.S.A. 115 D11
Ballyboghil Ireland 12 C5
Ballybunion Ireland 12 D2
Ballycanew Ireland 12 D5
Ballycastle U.K. 12 A5
Ballyclare U.K. 12 B5
Ballydehob Ireland 12 E2
Ballygawley U.K. 12 B4
Ballyhaunis Ireland 12 C3
Ballyheige Ireland 12 D2
Ballymena U.K. 12 B5
Ballymoney U.K. 12 A5
Ballymote Ireland 12 B3
Ballynahinch U.K. 12 B6
Ballyquintin Pt. U.K. 12 B6
Ballyshannon Ireland 12 B3
Balmaceda Chile 128 F2
Balmaseda Spain 38 B1
Balmazújváros Hungary 28 C6
Balmertown Canada 103 C10
Balmoral Australia 95 F3
Balmorhea U.S.A. 116 F3
Balochistan = Baluchistan □ Pakistan 66 F4
Balonne → Australia 95 D4
Balotra India 68 G5
Balqash Kazakhstan 52 E8
Balqash Köli Kazakhstan 52 E8
Balrampur India 69 F10
Balranald Australia 95 E3
Balş Romania 29 F9
Balsas → Brazil 125 E9
Balsas → Mexico 118 D4
Balsas del Norte Mexico 119 D5
Bålsta Sweden 10 E11
Balta Romania 28 F7
Balta Ukraine 29 B14
Baltanás Spain 36 D6
Bălţi Moldova 29 C12
Baltic Sea Europe 9 H18
Baltîm Egypt 80 H7
Baltimore Ireland 12 E2
Baltimore Md., U.S.A. 113 F15
Baltimore Ohio, U.S.A. 114 G2
Baltinglass Ireland 12 D5
Baltit Pakistan 69 A6
Baltiysk Russia 30 D6
Baltrum Germany 24 B3
Baluchistan □ Pakistan 66 F4
Baluqtybulaq Kazakhstan 34 E10
Balurghat India 69 G13
Balvi Latvia 32 D4
Balya Turkey 47 B9
Bam Iran 71 D8
Bama China 58 E6
Bama Nigeria 83 C7
Bamaga Australia 94 A3
Bamaji L. Canada 104 B1
Bamako Mali 82 C3
Bamba Mali 83 B4
Bambara Maoundé Mali 82 B4
Bambari C.A.R. 84 C4
Bambaroo Australia 94 B4
Bambaya Guinea 82 D2
Bamberg Germany 25 F6
Bamberg U.S.A. 117 E14
Bambesi Ethiopia 81 F3
Bambey Senegal 82 C1
Bambili Dem. Rep. of the Congo 86 B2
Bamboi Ghana 82 D4
Bamburgh U.K. 14 B6
Bamenda Cameroon 83 D7
Bamendjing, Rés. de Cameroon 83 D7
Bamfield Canada 102 D3
Bāmīān □ Afghan. 66 B5
Bamiancheng China 57 C13
Bamkin Cameroon 83 D7
Bampūr Iran 71 E9
Bampūr → Iran 71 E8
Ban Burkina Faso 82 C4
Ban Ao Tu Khun Thailand 65 a
Ban Ban Laos 64 C4
Ban Bang Hin Thailand 65 H2
Ban Bang Khu Thailand 65 a
Ban Bang Rong Thailand 65 a
Ban Bo Phut Thailand 65 b
Ban Chaweng Thailand 65 b
Ban Chiang Klang Thailand 64 C3
Ban Choho Thailand 64 E4
Ban Dan Lan Hoi Thailand 64 D2
Ban Don = Surat Thani Thailand 65 H2
Ban Don Vietnam 64 F6
Ban Don, Ao → Thailand 65 H2
Ban Dong Thailand 64 C3
Ban Hong Thailand 64 C2
Ban Hua Thanon Thailand 65 b
Ban Kantang Thailand 65 J2
Ban Karon Thailand 65 a
Ban Kata Thailand 65 a
Ban Keun Laos 64 C4
Ban Khai Thailand 64 F3
Ban Kheun Laos 64 B3
Ban Khlong Khian Thailand 65 a
Ban Khlong Kua Thailand 65 J3
Ban Khuan Thailand 65 a
Ban Khuan Mao Thailand 65 J2
Ban Ko Yai Chim Thailand 65 G2
Ban Laem Thailand 64 F2
Ban Lamai Thailand 65 b
Ban Lao Ngam Laos 64 E6